FREEDOM AND CRISIS

An American History

VOLUME TWO—since 1860

W9-CMO-617

Second Edition

FREEDOM AND CRISIS

An American History

VOLUME TWO—since 1860

ALLEN WEINSTEIN
SMITH COLLEGE

R. JACKSON WILSON
SMITH COLLEGE

Generously Donated to

The Frederick Douglass Institute

By Professor Jesse Moore

Fall 2000

 RANDOM HOUSE

To Andrew and David with love
Allen Weinstein

To Ann and Mary Corley, and all their generations
R. Jackson Wilson

Second Edition
9876543
Copyright © 1974, 1978 by Random House, Inc.

All rights reserved under International and Pan-American Copyright Conventions. No part of this book may be reproduced in any form or by any means, electronic or mechanical, including photocopying, without permission in writing from the publisher. All inquiries should be addressed to Random House, Inc., 201 East 50th Street, New York, N.Y. 10022. Published in the United States by Random House, Inc., and simultaneously in Canada by Random House of Canada Limited, Toronto.

Library of Congress Cataloging in Publication Data

Weinstein, Allen.
  Freedom and crisis.

  Includes bibliographies and index.
  CONTENTS: v. 1. To 1877.—v. 2. Since 1860.
  1. United States—History. I. Wilson, Raymond
Jackson, joint author. II. Title.
  E178.1.W395 1978   973   77–17298
  ISBN 0–394–31223–6 (v. 2)

Cover photos: Beatrice and Jules Pinsley
  Electric light photo taken at EDISON NATIONAL HISTORIC SITE, NEW JERSEY (administered by The National Park Service, U.S. Dept. of the Interior.)
  Schematic drawing of Wright Bros. 1903 plane made by the Smithsonian Institution.
  Portion of front page of May 29, 1908 New York Times © by The New York Times Company. Reprinted by permission.

Text design: William Frost, Dimensions

Manufactured in the United States of America

Grateful acknowledgment is extended to the following for permission to reprint previously published material:
Joan Daves:—From "I Have a Dream" by Martin Luther King, Jr. Copyright © 1963 by Martin Luther King, Jr.
Doubleday & Co., Inc.:—From *Six Crises* by Richard Nixon. Copyright © 1962 by Richard M. Nixon.
Alfred A. Knopf, Inc.:—From *In the Court of Public Opinion* by Alger Hiss. Copyright © 1957 by Alger Hiss.
Random House, Inc.:—From *Witness* by Whittaker Chambers. Copyright 1952 by Whittaker Chambers.
Charles Scribner's Sons:—From *The Spirit of St. Louis* by Charles A. Lindbergh. Copyright 1953 by Charles Scribner's Sons.

CONTENTS

UNIT SEVEN

MODERN AMERICA 708

UNIT EIGHT

CONTEMPORARY AMERICA 816

MAPS AND CHARTS

NOTES ON SOURCES

Quotations by these foreign observers appear in the four Pictorial Essays. Minor adaptations have been made in some quoted material, chiefly to simplify selections. In the essays, the writer's name is followed by a date or dates. These represent the years in which the observations were made, if known. If the exact period is not known, the date represents the year in which the account was published.

Beauvoir, Simone de *(Essays 8, 9)* The noted French writer and philosopher made a nationwide tour of the United States between January and May 1947. *America Day by Day* (1953), based on her travels, shows her as an intelligent and sensitive reporter of the American scene.

Bremer, Fredrika *(Essay 6)* A Swedish novelist well known in her day, who traveled in America from 1849 to 1851. Her impressions, in the form of letters to her sister, appeared in *Homes of the New World* (1853).

Broughton, Morris *(Essay 9)* A South African journalist and editor of *The Cape Argus*, he came to the United States in 1956 as a guest of the State Department. By his estimation, he traveled over 10,000 miles and visited over thirty states during his three-month stay here.

Carpenter, Harry *(Essay 8)* An English sports expert, Carpenter was boxing and general sports columnist for *The London Daily Mail* from 1954 to 1962, as well as a full-time correspondent for the BBC. In his *Masters of Boxing* (1964) he spoke of Joe Louis as the "headmaster" of boxing.

Chesterton, G. K. *(Essay 6)* The English poet and novelist visited the United States on a lecture tour in 1921. His book, *What I Saw in America,* was published in London in 1922.

Colum, Padraic *(Essay 7)* This Irish man of letters made his home in the United States after 1914. He was a friend of many writers, including Robert Frost.

Cooke, Alistair *(Essay 9)* Of Anglo-Irish birth, this popular journalist and broadcaster has lived primarily in the United States since the 1930s, and became an American citizen in 1941. He is the author of many books on American culture. This selection comes from *Talk About America* (1968).

Corresca, Rocco *(Essay 6)* An Italian immigrant, he typified the penniless hopefuls who flocked to America to make their fortune. His "Biography of a Bootblack" appeared in a magazine, *The Independent,* in December 1902.

Dubos, René—See Ward, Barbara

Erkelenz, Anton *(Essay 7)* A member of the German parliament, he wrote a book called *America Today* (1927), in which he expressed an optimistic belief that the United States would some day create a culture uniquely its own.

Freymond, Jacques *(Essay 8)* On his first trip to the United States (1949–1950), Freymond, a Swiss historian, studied at Yale University and made an extended auto tour of the country. He returned for a two-month trip in 1955.

Galsworthy, John *(Essay 7)* The noted English writer gave a series of speeches in the United States that were published in a volume called *Addresses in America* (1919).

Graham, Stephen *(Essay 6)* A British traveler and journalist who visited the United States in 1913. These quotations are from his work *With Poor Immigrants to America* (1914).

Griesinger, Karl Theodor *(Essay 6)* This German historian spent five years in the United States, although he did not find the American form of democracy to his liking. His *Living Pictures from America*, published in 1858, is characterized by a cutting and ironical humor.

Hartog, Jan de *(Essay 9)* A Dutch author and playwright who made a leisurely voyage in 1958–61 from Houston to Nantucket, largely by inland waterways. He gives a charming account of his adventures in *Waters of the Western World*, published in 1961.

Hauptmann, Gerhart *(Essay 7)* In 1932 this German playwright, a Nobel prize winner, visited the United States. He remarked on leaving that the high points of his trip had been meeting O'Neill and attending *Mourning Becomes Electra*. The critique quoted here is from an interview the same year with an American correspondent.

Hawkes, Jacquetta—See Priestley, J. B.

Hilbersheimer, Ludwig and Udo Rukser *(Essay 7)* These German architects praised the innovations of American architecture and especially the work of Frank Lloyd Wright. Their article appeared in a 1920 issue of the German journal, *Art and Artist*.

Jarlson, Axel *(Essay 6)* The story of this Swedish farmer's immigration to America illustrates how the members of a single family helped each other to settle in the United States. Jarlson's narrative was published in the January 8, 1903 issue of *The Independent*.

Kipling, Rudyard *(Essay 7)* Between March and September 1889, the famous English writer (then only twenty-four) sent thirty-seven letters back to an Indian newspaper, as he traveled from India to England via the Far East and the United States. The last of his letters is titled "An Interview with Mark Twain." All this correspondence was published in *From Sea to Sea* (1890).

Kossenko, Zinaida—See Mikhailov, Nikolai

Labarca H., Amanda *(Essay 9)* A distinguished Chilean educator, feminist, and public servant, she visited the United States ten times between 1911 and 1952. She represented Chile in the first General Assembly of the United Nations in 1946.

Laski, Harold *(Essay 7)* A noted British socialist, he taught history at Harvard University from 1916 to 1920. After returning to England, he devoted himself to teaching, writing, and journalism. His *American Democracy* was published in 1948.

Leacock, Stephen *(Essay 8)* The Canadian humorist and man of letters was also a distinguished political scientist and professor at McGill University. This quotation is from *Stephen Leacock's Laugh Parade*, published in 1940.

Le Corbusier (Charles Edouard Jeanneret) *(Essays 8, 9)* This Swiss-born French architect has been called "the voice and conscience of modern architecture." He visited the United States several times during his lifetime. His book *When the Cathedrals Were White* (1947) was devoted mostly to his impressions of America.

Marias, Julian *(Essays 8, 9)* A Spanish philosopher, he helped found Madrid's Institute of Humanities. In 1951–52 Marias was a visiting professor at Wellesley College.

Maurois, André *(Essay 8)* The noted French critic and novelist was a frequent visitor to the United States, where he was a popular lecturer. In 1939 he published *Thirty-Nine States, Journal of a Voyage to America*, from which this quote is taken.

Mehdevi, Mohamed *(Essay 9)* An Iranian journalist and diplomat, he first became acquainted with the United States as a foreign student in Florida. *Something Human* (1962) was the result of his adventures hitchhiking from Florida to the West Coast.

Mikhailov, Nikolai and Zinaida Kossenko *(Essay 9)* This Russian geographer and his wife, a psychiatrist, made a tour of America in 1960. Their account first appeared in a Moscow publication the same year and was later published in the United States as *Those Americans, a Travelogue* (1962).

Münsterberg, Hugo *(Essay 7)* This German philosopher and professor at Harvard University wrote *The Americans* (1904) in order to dispel German prejudice against Americans.

Myers, Robert *(Essay 6)* A Jewish immigrant from Rumania, Myers came to the United States in 1913 and later became active in the labor movement. His recollections, *Stimmer* ["stutterer"]: *The Boy Who Couldn't Talk*, were published in 1959.

Newman, Ernest *(Essay 7)* From 1910 to 1940 he was the major British music critic. His review of Isadora Duncan quoted here was written in April

1921. Several years later, he moved to New York City, where he wrote music reviews for the *New York Evening Post*. The November 17, 1924, edition carried his appreciation of Gershwin's *Rhapsody in Blue*.

Priestley, J. B. *(Essays 8, 9)* The English novelist and critic lived in the United States in 1935–36; *Midnight on the Desert* (1937) grew out of this experience. In 1954 he and his wife Jacquetta Hawkes (an author and anthropologist) traveled in the American Southwest. Their wry and amusing collaboration, *Journey Down a Rainbow,* for which each wrote alternating chapters, was published in 1955.

Pupin, Michael Idvorsky *(Essay 6)* Born in Yugoslavia, the brilliant physicist sold all his belongings in order to come to America. In 1924 he won a Pulitzer Prize for *From Immigrant to Inventor* (1923), the story of his life.

Rivera, Diego *(Essay 7)* In 1942 the celebrated Mexican artist spoke of his contemporary, John Sloan, to American art critic Walter Pach. Rivera himself had visited the United States in the 1930s, where he painted frescoes in Detroit, San Francisco, and New York. He was much impressed with American technology.

Rukser, Udo—See Hilbersheimer, Ludwig

Russell of Killowen, Lord *(Essay 6)* Born in Ireland, this lawyer first visited America in 1883 and wrote a *Diary of a Visit to the United States of America* (published in 1910). He served as lord chief justice of England from 1894 until his death in 1900.

Sarc, Omer Celâl *(Essay 8)* This Turkish economist has spent much time in the United States. In 1950 he visited universities across the country as a guest of the State Department. He also taught at Columbia University and worked for the United Nations.

Sheridan, Claire *(Essay 7)* A celebrated British sculptress, known for her busts of Lenin, Trotsky, and Gandhi. She met Sinclair Lewis in Washington, D.C., in April 1921. A vivid account of their meeting appeared in her book *My American Diary,* published the following year.

Stevenson, Robert Louis *(Essay 6)* The Scottish writer crossed the United States in 1879 to visit an American woman he had met in Europe (and whom he eventually married). *Across the Plains* was published in 1892.

Tyrmand, Leopold *(Essay 9)* A journalist born in Warsaw, Poland, he moved to the United States in the 1960s. Portions of his writings, dealing with his experiences as a European in America, appeared in *The New Yorker*. They were collected in *Notebooks of a Dilettante* (1967).

Vay de Vaya und Luskod, Count *(Essays 6, 7)* A Hungarian nobleman, he traveled widely as a diplomat for the Roman Catholic Church. Visiting the United States several times between 1903 and 1906, he described his travels in *The Inner Life of the United States* (1908).

Von Borch, Herbert *(Essays 8, 9)* This German writer's book *The Unfinished Society* (1960) was based on notes he made while working in the United States as a newspaper correspondent.

Ward, Barbara and René Dubos *(Essay 9)* Barbara Ward, an English social scientist, lectured frequently in the United States in the period after World War II. *Only One Earth* (1972) was written with the Pulitzer-prize winning microbiologist, René Dubos, who was born in France but moved to the United States in 1924.

Wells, H. G. *(Essay 6)* The famous English novelist visited Ellis Island during his first trip to the United States in 1905. He wrote of his impressions in *The Future of America* (1906).

West, Rebecca *(Essay 7)* Born in Ireland, she became known for her writings on history and politics. Her essay on Willa Cather was originally published by the *New York Herald Tribune* in September 1927, and was reprinted in *The Strange Necessity* (1928).

White, T. H. *(Essay 9)* Best known for his books on King Arthur, this English author kept a journal while on a lecture tour in the United States. It was later published as *America at Last, the American Journal of T. H. White* (1965).

Wolff, Albert *(Essay 7)* A French art critic, he wrote for the noted French newspaper, *Le Figaro*. This selection is quoted from his 1881 review of the Impressionists' sixth group exhibition.

AUTHORS' INTRODUCTION

Freedom and Crisis is a book of discovery about the American past. The reader will quickly recognize, by glancing at the table of contents or by flipping through the pages, that this book is different from the ordinary "text." The difference is embodied in the way that *Freedom and Crisis* organizes the American experience.

Units are arranged in pairs of chapters. Every pair opens with a dramatic narrative of a significant episode in the American past. Each episode was chosen not only because it conveys an exciting story but also because it introduces many aspects of American life during the period under investigation. The chapter that follows then locates the episode within its appropriate historical context, interpreting the major forces that shaped the actions described in the episode.

This remains the book's basic format: a narrative chapter on a single episode, based on fresh documentary research, followed by an explanatory chapter linking historical fact and interpretation to the episode itself. The account of Bacon's Rebellion in Chapter 3, for example, is followed by a chapter on seventeenth-century plantation colonies. Similarly, Charles Lindbergh's exciting trans-Atlantic flight serves as the basis for a chapter on technological changes in twentieth-century America.

We have employed this novel approach to an introductory book on American history for one very good reason. Our primary concern from the start has been to write a book that would hold the interest of today's students, perhaps the most inquisitive but skeptical generation of students ever. To do this, we felt that a book had to be readable and realistic. *Freedom and Crisis* is both. The book dramatizes critical moments in the American democratic experience and deals candidly with both the extension and the denial of liberty at those times.

Freedom and Crisis is not a traditional book on United States history, then. Often such traditional books are written in the belief that there exists a certain body of data (election results, dates and outcomes of wars, treaties, major laws, and so forth) that comprises American history. We accept this idea only to the extent that most of the data of conventional texts can be found somewhere in this book. Sometimes, however, the information is located in maps, charts, and special features rather than in the text itself.

Frequently overlooked by students (and even by some teachers) is the point that this central body of data, the "facts," emerges only after a certain selection on the part of historians. There exists, after all, an almost infinite number of facts that could be chosen to represent the history of the human experience. In writing this book, we simply carried the usual selection process a step farther. Half the book is devoted to selected dramatic episodes. When linked to the accompanying chapters, the episodes form our bedrock of factual material. Using this foundation, students can then inquire into the fundamental questions of American history.

Most episodes can be read simply as absorbing stories. Thus readers will discover much about the country's past merely by studying such vivid incidents as the Boston Massacre, the Aaron Burr conspiracy, the Nat Turner revolt, the Wounded Knee Massacre, the Triangle fire, the Philippines revolt, the Bonus March, the attack on Pearl Harbor, and Watergate. But by using the interpretative chapter accompanying each episode, students will develop the ability to extract greater meaning from the facts in these dramas and, at the same time, acquire an understanding of related historical events.

Freedom and Crisis moves chronologically through the American experience, but certain themes recur and receive particular attention. The book devotes several episodes, for example, to patterns of race and ethnic relations, especially the treatment of blacks, Indians, immigrants, and other oppressed minorities. The struggle for political liberties and economic betterment, class conflicts, territorial expansion, technological change, and basic ideological and cultural disputes are also treated.

The constant interplay of factual drama and careful interpretation is the book's distinctive feature. Facts and concepts cross paths on each page, thereby avoiding the usual unhappy classroom extremes of concentrating either on what happened or on why it happened. *Freedom and Crisis* has no room for empty historical abstractions that leave students without a factual anchor. Nor does an uncontrolled flood of rampaging facts lacking solid conceptual boundaries spill endlessly off the printed pages. The paired chapter format, we believe, avoids both these extremes.

The episode-explanatory chapter pairs present a concise but comprehensive introduction to the history of the United States. Yet although the book covers the American experience, we wrote with less direct concern for coverage than for concreteness, drama, and interpretive depth. Almost every detail included in the narrative episodes has a larger meaning, so that students and instructors must work outward in this text from concrete detail to generalized understanding.

We make no apologies for this approach to studying and learning history, since professional historians use it daily. History as an act of inquiry involves putting great questions to small data, discovering general significance in particular events. *Freedom and Crisis* evolved from our belief that students are both willing and able to engage in the same process of inquiry as professional historians. In this manner each incident in the American odyssey, from the earliest European discoveries to our generation's exploration of the moon, can become a personal act of discovery for the reader, risky but rewarding.

The chapters that follow chart our personal roadmap through the American experience. The book will achieve its purpose only if it stirs the reader into beginning his or her own private journey through the past.

CIVIL WAR AMERICA

The formative period of modern America, from 1860 to 1900, began in civil war and ended in imperial conquest. The long, grueling war for national unity fought during this period freed the South's slaves only to abandon them, once freedmen, to still another form of bondage. At the same time, the country constructed the urban industrial society that forms the context of modern America's achievements and crises.

The terrible conflict that ushered in the era changed the character of both Southern and Northern life, as Chapter 24 makes clear. The problem of reconstructing the Union once the fabric of national politics had been torn apart emerged during the war itself and continued to disturb the nation for over a decade. What place should the freed Negro have in the American scene? What price should the South be expected to pay for losing its bid for independence? What new responsibilities did military victory impose upon the North? These basic issues and others emerge dramatically both in Chapter 23, the story of General Sherman's famous march and its aftermath, and in Chapter 24, which deals with the impact of Civil War and Reconstruction upon a transformed country.

23 SHERMAN'S MARCH TO THE SEA

A.W.

Early on the morning of November 16, 1864, the Union columns headed out of Atlanta, Georgia, bound southeast for the coastal city of Savannah. Northern troops, over 60,000 strong, with their horses, mules, and wagons, clogged the road. As they reached a hilltop, the soldiers turned to look back toward the town. Their commander, General William Tecumseh Sherman, recalled:

> Behind us lay Atlanta, smoldering and in ruins, the black smoke rising high in the air and hanging like a pall over the ruined city. Away off in the distance, on the McDonough road, was the rear of Howard's column, the gun-barrels glistening in the sun, the white-topped wagons stretching away to the south; and right before us the Fourteenth Corps, marching steadily and rapidly, with a cheery look and a swinging pace, that made light of the thousand miles that lay between us and Richmond. Some band, by accident, struck up the anthem of "John Brown's Body." The men caught up the strain, and never before have I heard the chorus of "Glory, glory, hallelujah!" done with more spirit, or in better harmony of time and place.

On that beautiful day of brilliant sunshine and clean, crisp air, the Civil War, already three and a half years old, seemed exhilarating, if not remote. Sherman later recalled experiencing a "feeling of something to come, vague and undefined, still full of venture and intense interest. Even the common soldiers caught the inspiration, and many a group called out to me—Uncle Billy, I guess Grant is waiting for us at Richmond!"

Although Richmond and victory for the Union were still five months away, Sherman had already made his mark in Georgia. The pall of smoke he and his troops saw above Atlanta came from the fires they had set in the town's railroad depot and machine shops. Flames soon swept into residential areas, destroying hundreds of dwellings. The general's reputation for toughness—"brutality" in the minds of most Southerners—took shape at Atlanta and on the subsequent campaign, his famous march to the sea. "We are not only fighting hostile armies," Sherman believed, "but a hostile people. We must make old and young, rich and poor, feel the hand of war."

Sherman, the tough-talking soldier, knew the South well. Born in Ohio in 1820, he attended West Point and, after graduation, spent most of his time on duty in military posts in the South. He resigned from the army in 1853. After working unsuccessfully as a bank manager in California and as a lawyer in Kansas, he tried to get back into the army. Rejected, he had to settle for the job of superintendent of a military academy in Louisiana. The school opened in 1859.

As the sectional crisis deepened, Sherman made it clear that, if Louisiana should secede from the Union, he would resign his post and do all he could to aid the national government. He kept his word when he heard of the Southern attack on Fort Sumter in April 1861. Secession, he thought, was "folly, madness, a crime against civilization." He immediately sought, and gained, reinstatement in the army. It was now more receptive to such applications, since so many regular officers had joined the Confederacy.

Sherman started as a colonel and rose rapidly in the Union high command. He served in the west as one of Grant's most trusted officers. By mid-1864, as a major general, he was assigned the mission of striking from Tennessee into Georgia and seizing Atlanta. The town, though relatively small, was an important railroad center. Confederate troops under General Joseph E. Johnston and, later, General John B. Hood fought hard to hold Sherman back. They were defeated in July at two crucial battles, those of Peachtree Creek and Atlanta. After a siege of several weeks, Atlanta fell.

Sherman's troops entered the city on September 2. Although Hood at first moved south toward safety, he later wheeled northwest

Union invasion of the South devastated the Confederate terrain as well as its morale. Marching through Georgia in 1864, General Sherman's troops occupied Atlanta and demolished much of the city—ripping up railroad tracks, destroying the depot, burning down homes, and evacuating the remainder of the residents. The fire-swept shambles behind them, Sherman's men moved on to Savannah.

toward Tennessee, hoping to harass Sherman's communications so badly that his forces would have to retreat. Inadvertently, Hood's actions may have influenced Sherman in his later decision to move to the sea without regard for communications or established supply lines.

For the time being, however, Sherman wanted to rest his troops and observe Hood's movements. He decided that Hood could be kept at bay by some detachments of his own army, plus Union troops in Tennessee.

Sherman meanwhile undertook some indirect negotiations with the governor of Georgia, Joseph E. Brown. His aim was to separate the state from the Confederacy. There was reason to hope that Georgia might pull out of the war. Brown had already withdrawn his state's militia from the rebel army. And, like many Southern politicians, he had come to detest Jefferson Davis, president of the Confederacy. Davis had stirred bitter reactions because of his insistent demands for troops and supplies from the hard-pressed Southern states. Nothing came of the negotiations; but they may have impressed on Sherman the need for bringing the hardships of war home to the Southern civilian population.

Tall, sharp-eyed, and red-haired, Sherman gained a reputation as a ruthless commander because of his march through the Confederacy.

When the war started, Atlanta—not then the state capital—had only 12,000 inhabitants. Many of them had fled as the Union troops approached. Others followed when Hood abandoned the town. When Sherman entered, he ordered the rest of the civilians to leave, since he did not want them clogging the town and interfering with his lines of communication. He and Hood agreed to a 10-day truce so that these civilians could move out.

By late October, Sherman had decided to march to the sea. On November 2 Grant wired: "I do not really see that you can withdraw from where you are to follow Hood without giving up all we have gained in territory. I say, then, go as you propose."

Sherman's bold plan called for his army of 62,000 men (5,000 of them cavalry) to move the 300 miles to Savannah without supply lines and without communications until they reached the Atlantic coast. There the Union navy could provide cover and supplies. Sherman's troops carried enough provisions for twenty or thirty days, but those were considered emergency rations. Food on the march would be "provided" by the farms and plantations along the way—not, of course, on a voluntary basis. As a result, Georgia would be made to "howl."

Sherman's Special Field Order #120 detailed the procedure he hoped to establish. Brigade commanders were responsible for organizing foraging parties. Every morning, these would move out from the four main columns under the direction of one or two "discreet officers." Foragers—or "bummers," as they soon came to be called (even by the Yankees themselves)—could seize available livestock and food supplies. They were not supposed to enter houses. Only corps commanders had the authority to order destruction of buildings, and then only in areas of resistance. Foragers for artillery units could take all the animals and wagons they needed.

If possible, foragers were to seize provisions from the rich planters rather than poor farmers. The wealthy were presumed to be more in favor of the rebellion than their humbler fellow Southerners. (This assumption fitted Northern views of secession as a conspiracy of the elite. It did not square with the facts of Southern political life.)

Sherman's field order directed his men to "forage liberally." They obeyed with a will. Men would go out in the morning on foot, seize a wagon, and then load it with everything valuable and movable they could find. One of Sherman's aides, Major Henry Hitchcock, described a foraging expedition in his diary:

> Plenty of forage along road: corn, fodder, finest sweet potatoes, pigs, chickens, etc. Passed troops all day, some on march, some destroying railroad thoroughly. Two cotton gins on roadside burned, and pile of cotton with one, also burned. Houses in Conyers look comfortable for Georgia village, and sundry good ones along road. Soldiers foraging all along, but only for *forage* — no violence so far as I saw or heard. Laughable to see pigs in feed troughs behind wagons, chickens swinging in knapsacks. Saw some few men — Whites look sullen — darkies pleased.

Stories of Union brutality, supposedly encouraged by Sherman himself, began to circulate. (They continued to circulate for generations.) But his march to the sea, devastating as it was, did not degenerate into an orgy of murder, rape, and arson. Sherman later acknowledged "acts of pillage, robbery, and violence" undoubtedly committed by some of his men. But, he argued, "these acts were exceptional and incidental. I have never heard of any cases of murder or rape; and no army could have carried along sufficient food and forage for a march of three hundred miles; so that foraging in some shape was necessary."

To Sherman, the march became just what he had ordered — harsh

A "bummer" goes his way, so loaded with booty that he cannot even hold the reins in his hands. For many of Sherman's men, the march through Georgia vindicated their months or even years of difficult military life.

but, in the main, well-disciplined. The destruction of his "scorched-earth" policy centered on three main targets: railroads, the few factories on the route, and public buildings that could serve as temporary headquarters for military units.

Sherman marveled at the skill of his men in carrying out his order to "forage liberally." One fact among many proves how proficient they were: Sherman's army started the march driving 5,000 head of cattle; they ended it with over 10,000

Where were the Confederate forces during these agonizing weeks? Some small cavalry units of the Confederate army did appear from time to time to raid foraging parties. But they had little overall effect. Hood's army had marched northwest to Tennessee and defeat. Since most Georgians of fighting age were serving with the Southern forces, the state militia had been reduced to several thousand old men and young boys. They tried to make a stand at the state capital, Milledgeville, but the Union forces swept them aside. After viewing the casualties, a Northern officer wrote: "I was never so affected at the sight of dead and wounded before. I hope we will never have to shoot at such men again. They know nothing at all about fighting and I think their officers know as little."

Milledgeville fell on November 23. Georgia state officials had fled a short time before. The invading Yankee officers decided to mock the "sovereign state of Georgia." They pretended to hold a session of the state legislature, complete with resolutions and fire-eating oratory. Then they decided to repeal the ordinance of secession. When Sherman heard about these antics, he laughed. Meanwhile, his Milledgeville "legislators" ordered the burning of public buildings in the town.

Sherman's soldiers sliced a path forty to sixty miles wide through central Georgia. Every white family along the way underwent its own particular ordeal and emerged with its own sorrowful story. Tales of the devastation became commonplace: houses broken into and sacked, food and valuables hidden only to be found by the recurrent searches of intruding "bummers," treasured family possessions tossed into the flames, cotton gins and public buildings put to the torch. "Everything had been swept as with a storm of fire," wrote one Macon newspaper. "The whole country around is one wide waste of destruction."

Contrary to Sherman's conception of his foraging troops as skilled, most Southerners in their path regarded them as greedy marauders. The experiences of two Georgia women, a mother and daughter, typified the ordeal. Mary Jones, the widow of a Presbyterian minister, owned three plantations in Liberty County, not far from Savannah. At the time of Sherman's march she and her daughter, Mary Jones Mallard, were living at the plantation known as Montevideo. Their letters and journals vividly portray the impact of war.

Mary Mallard's husband was captured on December 13 by Union cavalry near Montevideo. (Mrs. Mallard was then pregnant and expecting to give birth within days.) The first groups of "bummers" reached the

Jones-Mallard household on December 15. They searched the house and made off with a number of family keepsakes. During the next two weeks, Union raiding parties — sometimes large detachments, sometimes only a few stragglers — arrived almost daily at the home. Each group searched the premises, insulted the two women, and took what food, supplies, or family items remained to be carted away.

Mary Mallard confided unhappily to her journal on December 17.

> The Yankees made the Negroes bring up the oxen and carts, and took off all the chickens and turkeys they could find. They carried off all the syrup from the smokehouse. We had one small pig, which was all the meat we had left; they took the whole of it. Mother saw everything like food stripped from her premises, without the power of uttering one word. Finally they rolled out the carriage and took that to carry off a load of chickens. They took everything they possibly could.

"Everything" included seven of the Jones family's slaves, who — like hundreds of blacks elsewhere along the army's line of march — were pressed into service as porters, laborers, or mule drivers. "So they were all carried off," Mary Mallard grieved, "carriages, wagons, carts, horses and mules and servants, with food and provisions of every kind — and, so far as they were concerned, leaving us to starvation."

Occasionally an officer would apologize for the behavior of his men. One friendly Union soldier, a Missourian, offered to show Mrs. Jones where to hide her things. Mary Mallard noted: "He said he had enlisted to fight for the *Constitution;* but since then the war had been turned into another thing, and he did not approve this abolitionism, for his wife's people all owned slaves." A few days later, a Virginian told Mrs. Jones that "there was great dissatisfaction in the army on account of the present object of the war, which now was to free the Negroes."

More often than not, however, the raiders stalked through the houses indifferent to its inhabitants. Never knowing whether soldiers coming to the door would behave politely or insolently, the two women lived in constant fear. Several times, "bummers" threatened to return and burn down their house. Yet on other occasions, Union commanders offered them protection and safe-conduct passes to Savannah, which was still in Confederate hands. The women declined to leave, partly because of Mary Mallard's pregnancy. On January 4, 1865, she gave birth to a daughter. Her mother noted in her journal:

> During these hours of agony the yard was filled with Yankees. They were all around the house; my poor child, calm and collected amid her agony of body, could hear their conversation and wild halloos and cursing beneath her windows. After a while they left, screaming and yelling in a most fiendish way as they rode from the house.

Mary Jones's journal makes it clear that Sherman had achieved his major purpose in marching through Georgia — to demoralize beyond repair what remained of the Deep South's fighting spirit. She wrote in January 1865:

Mary Jones was one of the Southerners who felt the brunt of Sherman's attack. She wrote: "The foundations of society are broken up; what hereafter is to be our social and civil status we cannot see."

A Confederate soldier returns to find his home a shambles in the midst of a devastated land. The artist who drew this scene was A. J. Volck, a German-born dentist who lived in Baltimore. He was the best-known satirist to interpret the Civil War from the Southern point of view.

As I stand and look at the desolating changes wrought by the hand of an inhuman foe in a few days, I can enter into the feelings of Job. All our pleasant things are laid low. We are prisoners in our own home. To obtain a mouthful of food we have been obliged to cook in what was formerly our drawing room; and I have to rise every morning by candlelight, before the dawn of day, that we may have it before the enemy arrives to take it from us. . . . For one month our homes and all we possess have been given up to lawless pillage. Officers and men have alike engaged in this work of degradation. I scarcely know how we have stood up under it. God alone has enabled us to "speak with the enemy in the gates," and calmly, without a tear, to see my house broken open, entered with false keys, threatened to be burned to ashes, refused food and ordered to be starved to death, told that I had no right even to wood or water, that I should be "humbled in the very dust I walked upon," a pistol and carbine presented to my breast, cursed and reviled as a rebel, a hypocrite, a devil.

Troubling Mrs. Jones almost as much as the behavior of Sherman's soldiers was the reaction of her slaves. During the first days of Union occupation, most of them stayed on the plantation, perhaps out of fear, perhaps out of loyalty. But when it became clear that the Northern army firmly controlled the area, a number of slaves left to join the Union columns marching on Savannah. "Many servants have proven faithful," Mrs. Jones wrote in January 1865, "others false and rebellious against all authority or restraint."

Sherman himself pursued an ambiguous policy toward the ex-slaves, who were known as "contraband." He did not want them as soldiers, despite the good record of black regiments in battle when they were allowed to fight. He rejected the suggestion of General Ulysses S. Grant (by now in charge of all Union forces) that blacks be armed. He felt that his troops would object. And he had another reason. "My aim then," he later wrote, "was to whip the rebels, to humble their pride and make them fear and dread us. I did not want them to cast in our teeth that we had to call on *their* slaves to help us to subdue them."

Nevertheless, Sherman did order the formation of black "pioneer battalions"—construction units—for each army corps. "Negroes who are able-bodied and can be of service to the several columns may be taken along," Sherman instructed, "but each army commander will bear in mind that the question of supplies is a very important one, and that his first duty is to see to those who bear arms." In other words, the army was to keep blacks at a distance, using labor as needed but refraining from becoming a relief organization for ex-slaves who had left their plantations.

Sherman's prejudice against blacks was a crucial factor in his military policy. His brother John was an important antislavery Republican politician from Ohio, but William did not share his views. When still in Louisiana, he had assured Southerners that slavery was best for blacks. "All the congresses on earth," he said, "can't make the Negro anything else than what he is"—namely a slave, or a second-class noncitizen. In a letter he stated:

> I would not if I could abolish or modify slavery. I don't know that I would materially change the actual political relation of master and slave. Negroes in the great numbers that exist here must of necessity be slaves. Theoretical notions of humanity and religion cannot shake the commercial fact that their labor is of great value and cannot be dispensed with.

Whatever Sherman's own attitudes, it was clear that, from the moment his troops left Atlanta, they sparked the imagination of Georgia's slaves. As Sherman rode through the town of Covington, a day's march from Atlanta, he found that "the Negroes were simply frantic with joy." He later recalled that "Whenever they heard my name, they clustered about my horse, shouted and prayed in their peculiar style, which had a natural eloquence that would have moved a stone."

During the following weeks, as Northern troops foraged their way across Georgia, Sherman witnessed "hundreds, if not thousands, of such scenes." He wrote later that he could still see "a poor girl, in the very ecstasy of the Methodist 'shout,' hugging the banner of one of the regiments."

Thousands of slaves did more than simply greet the liberating Northern army. They joined it, striding alongside or in back of the troop columns. Wrote Mary Jones: "Negroes in large numbers are flocking to them. Nearly all the house servants have left their homes; and from most of the plantations they have gone in a body." The ranks of contraband included strong young men and women in the prime of life, mothers carrying children, and the white-haired elderly.

More than 30,000 blacks joined Sherman's army at one time or another during its four-week march. Yet only 10,000 remained with its ranks as it entered Savannah. Many were actively discouraged from remaining with the soldiers. Neither Sherman nor most of his officers and

"Negroes leaving the plough" is the title given this drawing by Northern artist Alfred R. Waud, who reported the war for an illustrated journal.

men wished to add the task of foraging to feed a huge contraband population from the food collected each day.

Sherman later remembered personally telling an old black man at one plantation that:

> we wanted the slaves to remain where they were, and not to load us down with useless mouths. We could receive a few of their young, hearty men as pioneers. But if they followed us in swarms of old and young, feeble and helpless, it would simply load us down and cripple us in our great task. I believe that old man spread this message to the slaves, which was carried from mouth to mouth, to the very end of our journey, and that it in part saved us from the great danger we incurred of swelling our numbers so that famine would have attended our progress.

In any case, the thousands of slaves who remained with Sherman's forces did not all passively trudge along waiting to be fed and taken care of. Many played active roles. They carried supplies as porters and mule drivers. Some searched out food, animals, and equipment hidden by Confederates along the way. Others built roads or repaired bridges so that Sherman's men, equipment, and supply wagons could keep to their 10-mile-a-day pace across the swampy stretches of central Georgia. Still others helped the soldiers to destroy railroads and other

Black people followed Sherman's army on foot, on horseback, and in any kind of wheeled conveyance that could be found. No one in authority was well prepared to deal with the contraband situation, and many former slaves lacked adequate shelter, food, and clothing.

strategic targets. (A favorite trick was to heat the heavy iron rails and twist them into "Sherman's neckties.")

Local blacks also served as reliable guides behind Confederate lines. One of Sherman's officers, General Oliver O. Howard, ordered one of his men to reach the Union fleet anchored off Savannah. After safely rowing a canoe past enemy posts along the Ogeechee River, the officer and his patrol:

> found some Negroes, who befriended him and his men and kept pretty well under cover until evening. Then they went ashore to get a Negro guide and some provisions [after which they passed through Confederate lines]. Soon after this they came to quite a sizable Negro house, went in, and were well treated and refreshed with provisions. When they were eating they were startled by hearing a party of Confederate cavalry riding toward the house. Of course they expected to be instantly captured, but the Negroes, coming quickly to their rescue, concealed them under the floor. The coolness and smartness of the Negroes surprised even Captain Duncan, though he had believed and trusted them. The cavalry stopped but remained only a short time, and the Negroes guided our men back to their boats.

Although few blacks aided the Union side quite so daringly during Sherman's march, the general himself acknowledged that the "large number employed as servants, teamsters and pioneers rendered admirable service."

Sherman's army marched into Savannah on December 21, along with the 10,000 black contraband. The general sent a playful telegram to "His Excellency," President Lincoln: "I beg to present you as a Christmas gift the city of Savannah, with one hundred and fifty heavy guns and plenty of ammunition, also about twenty-five thousand bales of cotton."

The message was quickly published throughout the North. Northerners had considered Sherman's army "lost" when the general had broken communication after leaving Atlanta. Sherman and his men instantly became popular heroes. "Our joy was irrepressible," said one high Washington official, "not only because of their safety, but because it was an assurance that the days of the Confederacy were numbered." Even to many Southerners, Savannah's capture seemed to foreshadow final defeat. Given the suffering that Confederate soldiers and civilians had undergone by then, the prospect seemed almost welcome.

Sherman did not order the city's residents to leave, as he had done at Atlanta. With Union ships in the harbor and his troops in control of the surrounding countryside, he felt no useful military purpose would be served by evacuating or burning the city. In fact, Sherman decided to govern Savannah's 20,000 inhabitants mildly—much to their amazement and that of other Georgians. He gave people the choice of remaining or leaving for other cities still under Confederate control.

Sherman placed one of his generals in overall command of Savannah, but the Confederate mayor and city council handled most day-to-day matters. Relations between Northerners and Southerners were polite, almost cordial. Only a few hundred citizens left the city. Most people calmly went about their business. Relief ships organized by private citizens in the North arrived regularly in January 1865, bringing much-needed food and clothing. Supplies were distributed to freed blacks and needy whites. Local markets selling meat, wood, and other necessities reopened under military supervision.

"No city was ever occupied with less disorder or more system than Savannah," Sherman wrote on December 31. "Though an army of 60,000 men lay camped around it, women and children of an hostile people walk its streets with as much security as they do in Philadelphia." Confederate newspapers raged about the alleged "barbarities" of Sherman's forces on their march from Atlanta, exaggerating the amount of property burned, and the numbers murdered or raped. Meantime the "barbarians" occupied Savannah with little friction.

In Savannah, as on the march from Atlanta, Sherman became a hero to the liberated blacks. He wrote to his wife on Christmas Day: "They flock to me, young and old. They pray and shout and mix up my name with that of Moses and Simon and other scriptural ones as well as 'Abram Linkom'." Hundreds of blacks hurried to see the general, wrote an aide. "There was a constant stream of them, old and young, men, women and children, black, yellow, and cream-colored, uncouth and well-bred, bashful and talkative—but always respectful and behaved—all day long."

It would have come as a great shock to the blacks of Savannah to learn that their hero was at that very moment being attacked in the North for his policy toward ex-slaves. Late in December General Henry W. Halleck wrote Sherman to congratulate him on the march through Georgia and his capture of Savannah. He also warned him that powerful individuals close to the President spoke critically of him, alleging that he "manifested an almost *criminal* dislike" to the Negro. "They say," added Halleck,

> that you are not willing to carry out the wishes of the government in regard to him, but repulse him with contempt! They say you might have brought with you to Savannah more than fifty thousand, thus stripping Georgia of that number of laborers, and opening a road by which as many more could have escaped from their masters; but that, instead of this, you drove them from your ranks, prevented their following you by cutting the bridges in your rear, and thus caused the massacre of large numbers by Wheeler's cavalry.

Sherman defended his decision to discourage slave runaways from joining the march on the grounds that their presence would have overburdened his army and hindered its military success. In responding to Halleck, however, he acknowledged that his sympathy for freed blacks was limited:

> Thank God I am not running for an office and am not concerned because the rising generation will believe that I burned 500 niggers[1] at one pop in Atlanta, or any such nonsense. The South deserves all she has got for her injustice to the Negro, but that is no reason why we should go to the other extreme.

It was no surprise to Sherman when Secretary of War Edwin M. Stanton arrived in Savannah on January 9, aboard the Union ship *Nevada*. Stanton was supposedly traveling on a vacation cruise and to supervise the disposition of captured Confederate cotton supplies. Actually he came to check on Sherman's handling of matters involving blacks. Stanton strongly supported Sherman's military strategy in Georgia. But he disapproved of the general's rumored hostility toward the ex-slave population, and of his refusal to use blacks as soldiers.

Sherman denied that any of his officers or troops had been hostile to slaves on their march from Atlanta. But Stanton wanted to hear about Sherman's behavior from the blacks themselves. At his request, therefore, Sherman invited "the most intelligent of the Negroes" in Savannah to come to his rooms to meet the secretary of war. Twenty black men attended the meeting with Sherman and Stanton on January 12, 1865.

Never before had any major American government official met with black leaders to ask what *they* wished for their people. Each man present began by introducing himself with a brief account of his life. The average age was fifty. Fifteen of the men were ministers—mainly Baptist and Methodist—and the other five were church officials of one kind or

---

[1]This term was considered only mildly discourteous in the 1860s. It was commonly used, even by anti-slavery Northerners.

another. Five of the leaders had been born free. Of the others, three had bought their freedom; most of the rest had been liberated by Sherman's army.

Secretary of War Stanton sat at a table facing the black visitors, making extensive notes on their remarks. Sherman, restless and uneasy over the interview, stood with two of his aides apart from the seated group. He watched the proceedings warily, pacing across the room from time to time during the exchange. The blacks had selected as their spokesman sixty-seven-year-old Garrison Frazier, a Baptist minister. He responded firmly to each of Stanton's questions.

Stanton asked first whether the men were aware of Lincoln's Emancipation Proclamation. Frazier replied that they were.

> STANTON: State what you understand by slavery, and the freedom that was to be given by the President's Proclamation.
> FRAZIER: Slavery is receiving by irresistible power the work of another man, and not by his consent. The freedom, as I understand it, promised by the Proclamation, is taking us from under the yoke of bondage, and placing us where we could reap the fruit of our own labor, and take care of ourselves, and assist the Government in maintaining our freedom.

Stanton then asked how black people could best maintain their new freedom. Frazier suggested that young men should be able to enlist in the army, and that other blacks ought to receive land to farm: "We want to be placed on land until we are able to buy it, and make it our own."

The secretary of war then asked whether the men believed that freed blacks "would rather live scattered among the whites, or in colonies by yourselves?" Frazier answered: "I would prefer to live by ourselves, for there is a prejudice against us in the South that will take years to get over; but I do not know that I can answer for my brethren."

Frazier and his black associates may have considered Stanton's next question offensive. The Secretary asked whether the ex-slaves of the South were intelligent enough to sustain their freedom while maintaining good relations with Southern whites. "I think there is sufficient intelligence among us to do so," Frazier replied simply.

The black minister was then asked what he believed were the causes and objectives of the Civil War, and whether blacks generally supported one or other side. He responded shrewdly and at length. Frazier told Stanton that blacks wished only to help the Union subdue the rebellious Confederacy. He acknowledged that the North's first war aim involved bringing the South back into the Union, that Lincoln had issued the Emancipation Proclamation mainly as a means toward achieving this end. Only the South's not freeing the slaves "has now made the freedom of the slaves a part of the war." Frazier pointed out that the thousands of runaways who had followed the Union armies, "leaving their homes and undergoing suffering," spoke clearly for the pro-Union sentiments of blacks.

Stanton then indicated that he wanted to ask a question about Sherman. The general—silently furious—left the room. In Sherman's absence, Stanton inquired about "the feeling of the colored people in regard to General Sherman" and whether Negroes regarded "his sentiments and actions as friendly to their rights and interests." Frazier's answer probably surprised Stanton, considering the rumors current in Washington:

> We looked upon General Sherman, prior to his arrival, as a man in the providence of God, specially set apart to accomplish this work, and we unanimously felt inexpressible gratitude to him. Some of us called upon him immediately upon his arrival [in Savannah], and it is probable he did not meet the Secretary with more courtesy than he met us. His conduct and deportment toward us characterized him as a friend and a gentleman. We have confidence in General Sherman, and think that what concerns us could not be under better hands.

The meeting soon ended, after Stanton had thanked his black visitors for their advice.

Stanton and Sherman spent the next three days discussing problems of policy toward the freedmen. They agreed that Sherman would issue a field order on January 16, the day after Stanton's departure from Savannah.

Special Field Order #15 set aside confiscated or abandoned land along rivers emptying into the Atlantic and on the Sea Islands—nearby islands that lie along the coast from Charleston, South Carolina, to Jacksonville, Florida. These lands were to be used exclusively for settlement by freed blacks. A freedman and his family taking up such land were to be given a "possessory title" to "not more than forty acres of tillable land" until Congress should regulate the title.

Sherman clearly viewed this scheme as a temporary one, in order to provide for freedmen and their families in the area during the rest of the war, or until Congress acted. "Mr. Stanton has been here," he confidently wrote his wife on the day of Stanton's departure, "and is cured of that Negro nonsense." By now Sherman was impatient to begin his march northward. He appointed General Rufus Saxton as Inspector of Settlements and Plantations for the entire area covered by his field order. On January 21 Sherman's army left Savannah, marching into South Carolina, the symbol of Confederate resistance.

Saxton energetically arranged to transport homeless blacks in Savannah to coastal farms. He wrote urgent letters to Northern sympathizers asking for food and supplies to help sustain the new agricultural settlements. By midsummer of 1865—with the war now over—Saxton and his aides had managed to settle more than 40,000 black people on lands covered in Sherman's order.

The people faced numerous hardships—neglected soil, old equipment (and little of it), poor seed, and shortage of supplies. But the hardworking freedmen, especially those on the Sea Islands of Georgia and South Carolina, successfully grew crops of cotton and various foodstuffs. They received support not only from Saxton and the military but also from Northern white teachers and missionaries, a number of whom traveled into the area to found schools.

Most of the planning and hard work, however, came from the freedmen themselves. Many started out with little more than the clothes on their backs. One party was led by Ulysses Houston, a minister who had been present at the interview with Stanton. Before leaving for Skidaway Island, he wrote a Northern reporter: "We shall build our cabins, and organize our town government for the maintenance of order and the settlement of all difficulties." The reporter later gave this account:

> He and his fellow-colonists selected their lots, laid out a village, numbered their lots, put the numbers in a hat, and drew them out. It was Plymouth colony repeating itself. They agreed if any others came to join them, they should have equal privileges. So blooms the Mayflower on the South Atlantic coast.

The impressive success of this resettlement led many Northerners to urge that Congress enact a general land distribution policy to help all freedmen. Landless ex-slaves also came to expect that, since 40,000 Deep South blacks had quickly and effectively settled new lands, others too would receive their forty acres in the near future. Such hopes were soon dashed.

Andrew Johnson became President after Lincoln was assassinated in April 1865. Many had believed that Johnson would be sympathetic to a generous land distribution policy once in the White House, since he had been sympathetic to black rights earlier as governor of Tennessee. But a proclamation of his in May 1865 completely shattered this belief. Johnson pardoned all former Confederates except those whose taxable property exceeded $20,000 and those who had held high military or civil positions. (Even these groups could apply for special presidential pardon.)

For the great majority of white Southerners. Johnson's proclamation not only restored civil and political rights. It also restored their property—except for slaves—even if previously confiscated as a result of temporary wartime orders such as Sherman's. Not only did the new President say nothing about the freedmen in his proclamation. He clearly intended them to resume their second-class economic status in the South, although no longer as slaves. Johnson made it plain that he intended landowning blacks such as those under Saxton's jurisdiction to surrender their newly acquired lands and return to their previous owners.

Saxton now administered the freedmen's new settlements in Georgia, South Carolina, and Florida as assistant director of the Freedmen's Bureau. This agency had been recently established by Congress to coordinate federal relief assistance to ex-slaves. Heading the bureau was Sherman's former subordinate, General Oliver O. Howard. He shared President Johnson's wish to conciliate the South. Unlike the President, though, he did not want to do so at the expense of the freedmen.

Both Saxton and Howard tried to resist and delay the restoration of black-occupied lands to their former white owners. They were support-

A Northern teacher reads to two of her pupils at a school on St. Helena, one of the Sea Islands off the coast of South Carolina. These former slaves were among those resettled by Sherman's Order #15.

ed by Stanton, who attempted various maneuvers to stave off the move. But Johnson was determined. Sherman's field order was revoked in June 1865. Saxton even traveled to Washington, but without success.

In September the former landholders of Edisto Island, then under Freedmen's Bureau control, petitioned Johnson for the return of their lands. The President directed Howard to visit the island and convince the freedmen to arrange a "mutually satisfactory solution." The President left little doubt that he wanted the blacks to pack up and leave.

Howard unhappily went to Edisto in late October. Trapped between his duty and his sympathies, he met with freed blacks in a local church. They crowded in, furious at the course of events. They refused to quiet down until a woman began the spiritual "Nobody Knows the Trouble I Seen."

The blacks then listened to Howard as he urged them to surrender their farms and return to work for the island's former white landholders. Angry shouts of "no, no" punctuated Howard's talk. One man in the gallery cried out: "Why, General Howard, why do you take away our lands? You take them from us who have always been true, always true to the government! You give them to our all-time enemies! That is not right!"

Howard patiently explained to his audience that their "possessory titles" to the land were not "absolute" or "legal." At his insistence, a committee was formed consisting of three freedmen, three white planters, and three Freedmen's Bureau representatives. It had authority to decide on the island's land ownership. (This practice was also adopted elsewhere on the Sea Islands.)

Howard still hoped to delay restoration of the property until Congress convened late in 1865. But the process of removing blacks from their assigned lands gathered momentum after he left the area to return North.

Saxton was still refusing to dispossess black landholders from the territories under his supervision, so Johnson removed him in January 1866. He was replaced by Davis Tillson, a Freedmen's Bureau official more sympathetic to presidential policy. Tillson issued an order allowing white owners to return to their former Sea Island farms and plantations. Tillson went so far as to charter a boat and accompany the first group, explaining personally to the blacks in residence that they would have to surrender their lands.

Blacks who were willing to sign contracts to work for white owners were allowed to remain. Others were driven from the islands either by Union troops or by white vigilante groups that began to terrorize black landholders throughout the Deep South during this period. One sympathetic New England schoolteacher later wrote of seeing all the freedmen on one Sea Island plantation leaving their newly acquired land with their hoes over their shoulders. "They told us that the guard had ordered them to leave the plantation if they would not work for the owners. We could only tell them to obey orders. After this many of the Sherman Negroes left the island."

For the moment, Howard's policy of delaying restoration had clearly failed. Yet shortly after Congress met in December 1865, the legislators debated the provisions of a new, postwar Freedmen's Bureau Bill designed to protect the rights of ex-slaves in peacetime. The final version of that bill was enacted by Congress over the President's veto in July 1866. It allowed freedmen deprived of their land by Johnson's restoration policy to lease twenty acres of government-owned land on the Sea Islands with an option to buy cheaply within six years. By then, however, almost all of the "Sherman Negroes" had lost their lands.

By this time, too, Congress and Johnson were struggling bitterly for the control of postwar policy toward the South. The outcome of that struggle would determine the nation's response to its millions of newly liberated blacks. Many of them probably shared the anguish of one Sea Island freedman who grieved shortly after his eviction: "They will make freedom a curse to us, for we have no home, no land, no oath, no vote, and consequently no country."

24
CIVIL WAR AND RECONSTRUCTION

A.W.

On February 23, 1861 (at a time when Sherman had just left his post at the Louisiana military academy), Abraham Lincoln slipped secretly into Washington after an all-night train ride. His aides had planned the night trip, fearing an assassination attempt at a previously scheduled stop in pro-Confederate Baltimore. On his special train the President-elect tried to sleep. But a drunken passenger kept singing the bouncy Southern melody "Dixie" over and over. Lincoln finally muttered to a companion, "No doubt there will be a great time in Dixie by and by." His concern over the impending showdown with the secessionist South was shared by most Northerners.

A thousand miles to the south, the Confederacy's president-elect took a different type of journey to his own inaugural. Lincoln had arrived in the nation's capital, according to one diplomat, "like a thief in the night." Jefferson Davis had traveled from his Mississippi plantation to Montgomery, Alabama—first capital of the rebellious states—like a conquering hero.

Davis was a moderate Southerner. Like others, he had opposed secession until after Lincoln's election. Now this group had taken charge of the South's new government, replacing many of the zealous fire-eaters who had spread the gospel of disunion during the 1850s. Southern moderates had selected Davis as their president largely because he had declared himself in favor of a peaceful settlement with the North. A West Point graduate, Davis had fought ably in the Mexican War, represented Mississippi in both the House and

the Senate, and served as President Pierce's secretary of war.

FIRST STEPS

While Davis pondered his cabinet, the Montgomery convention that had chosen him president wrote a Confederate constitution. For the most part the document copied the provisions of the federal Constitution. It included a bill of rights, and it even prohibited the slave trade. Slavery was pronounced legal throughout the Confederacy, of course. In a significant speech at Savannah, the vice president-elect, Alexander Stephens of Georgia, spoke candidly of the new government: "Its foundations are laid, its cornerstone rests, upon the great truth that the Negro is not equal to the white man; that slavery, subordination to the superior race, is his natural and normal condition."

The new Confederate congress began its work by legalizing for the South all Union laws that did not conflict with its new constitution. For two months after Davis's selection as president, the Confederate government waited for some sign of how Lincoln intended to deal with the secession crisis. Then came Sumter—and war.

A "Brothers' War" When the Civil War began on April 12, 1861, Americans gave it various names. For secessionists it was a "War for Southern Independence" or "the War Between the States." Northerners, on the other hand, considered it "the War of the Rebellion" or simply "the War for the Union." Both sides agreed that, whatever else, it was a "brothers' war," severing links among families, personal friends, and public figures according to their sectional loyalties.

This deeply painful division reached even into Abraham Lincoln's family. A Kentucky officer named Ben Hardin Helm was the husband of Mary Todd Lincoln's sister. He spent several days at the White House talking to old West Point friends. Some of them were already preparing to head south and join the Confederate army. As Helm—still uncertain—concluded his visit, Lincoln gave him an envelope containing a major's commission in the Union army. The two men grasped hands warmly and exchanged good-byes. A few days later came the news that Helm had chosen the Confederacy.

But another Kentuckian, Fort Sumter's Robert Anderson, accepted Lincoln's promotion to brigadier general that same month. He then left for the Middle West to help keep his native state in the Union.

A third officer, a fervent Unionist, turned down Lincoln's offer to be commander of all Northern troops. Instead, he accepted command of the Confederacy's eastern force, the Army of Northern Virginia. "If Virginia stands by the old Union, so will I," Robert E. Lee declared. "But if she secedes (though I do not believe in secession as a constitutional right, nor that there is sufficient cause for revolution) then I will follow my native state with my sword and, if need be, with my life." When Virginia finally broke with the Union, Lee followed.

In many ways the Confederate struggle for independence resembled the American revolt against British rule two generations earlier. Some revolutions are a struggle for colonial independence from a ruling country. Such a revolution occurred in North America in the 1770s. Other revolutions result when one section of a country tries to break away from the whole, leading to an internal war between the nation and the breakaway section. This type of separatist revolt may occur when the people of a particular region feel that their interests and values are directly threatened by those who control the national government. Such was the case in the South after Lincoln's election.[1]

National uprisings, such as the American Revolution, and separatist revolts, such as the Civil War, usually take place only after great soul-searching among those rebelling. The American people do not shift their loyalties easily. Washington, Franklin, and other Revolutionary leaders had served the British Empire faithfully for de-

Abraham Lincoln, wrote George Templeton Strong, was "a most sensible, straightforward, honest old codger; the best President we have had since Jackson's time."

Jefferson Davis suffered from poor health throughout the war. Though he was strong-willed and irritable, his devotion to the South was unquestioned.

[1]More recently, separatist revolts have taken place in Nigeria (where the Ibo province of Biafra revolted unsuccessfully) and in Pakistan (where the Bengali area formerly known as East Pakistan won its independence and became the new country of Bangladesh).

cades in war and peace. Lee, Davis, and other key Confederate leaders had served the American government before the South seceded. They finally revolted because they believed the Southern way of life—a culture based upon slavery—was directly threatened by Republican control of the central government.

Mobilization In the early months of the Civil War most Americans seemed to expect the conflict to be bloody but brief. Few realized what lay ahead. "No casualties yet, no real mourning, nobody hurt," wrote Mary Boykin Chesnut, the wife of a high Confederate officer, in June 1861. "It is all parade, fuss, and fine feathers."

A few leaders believed the situation was more serious. Among them were Lincoln and his generals and their counterparts behind the Southern lines. Mrs. Chesnut noted what Jefferson Davis had told her one evening: "Either way, he thinks it will be a long war, that before the end came we would have many a bitter experience. He said only fools doubted the courage of the Yankees, or their willingness to fight when they saw fit."

Nor did most Southerners underestimate the extent of Northern resources. In almost every respect—population, capital, and raw materials—the Union had the advantage over the Confederacy. Most important, the North could produce endless supplies of guns, ammunition, ships, and other war equipment. The South, on the other

hand, had increasing difficulty in keeping its soldiers supplied.

Neither side began with much of an army. There were only 18,000 men in the regular army in 1860, with about 1,100 officers. Only a small number of these had significant combat experience, and most of them resigned to join the Confederate Army, so that the South's officer corps was initially better trained than the North's. These officers, Northern and Southern, prepared to fight a conflict far different, in strategy and tactics, from those for which they had been trained.

Both North and South started the war using a system of volunteer enlistments. At first they recruited men for only a few months, since both sides believed that the war would be short.

On April 15, the day after the surrender of Sumter, Lincoln issued a proclamation calling up "the militia of the several States of the Union, to the . . . number of seventy-five thousand, in order to supress [the rebellion] and to cause the laws to be duly executed." The initial news of Sumter's capture outraged Northerners of almost every political persuasion—Douglas Democrats, Constitutional Unionists, Whigs, and Republicans alike. Such unity would proved short-lived. But while it lasted, people as dissimilar as abolitionist ex-pacifists and formerly pro-Southern businessmen all hailed the President's call for troops. Patriotic meetings were held in towns and cities throughout the Union, demanding swift action against the rebellious states. Eager volunteers

RESOURCES OF THE UNION AND THE CONFEDERACY, 1861

	UNION	CONFEDERACY
Population	23,000,000	8,700,000*
Real and personal property	$11,000,000,000	$5,370,000,000
Banking capital	$330,000,000	$27,000,000
Capital investment	$850,000,000	$95,000,000
Manufacturing establishments	110,000	18,000
Value of production (annual)	$1,500,000,000	$155,000,000
Industrial workers	1,300,000	110,000
Locomotives	451,000	19,000
Railroad mileage	22,000	9,000

*Including 3,500,000 slaves

rushed to join military units in almost every Northern community.

"Before God it is the duty of every American citizen to rally around the flag of the country," shouted an ailing Stephen A. Douglas at a Chicago mass meeting. Douglas, still Lincoln's most influential Northern Democratic opponent, had gone to the White House immediately after Sumter's fall to pledge to Lincoln his complete support in restoring the Union.

As the fighting dragged on, however, it became apparent to both sides that volunteers would not provide enough manpower. Even the cash bounties offered to those who enlisted would not bring in enough volunteers. Casualties mounted in 1862. First the undermanned Confederacy and then the Union turned to drafting soldiers by lottery. Wealthy or influential young men, North and South, could, and often did, avoid going to war. They could provide a paid substitute, who might cost as much as $600. Or they could claim exemption on grounds that their civilian work was essential. (Slaveholders who grew cotton, for example, could avoid service this way.) By the end of the war, the South's troop shortage had become extreme. The Confederacy had by then begun drafting and training thousands of slaves.

FIGHTING THE CIVIL WAR

Late in May 1861 the Confederate government moved its capital to Richmond. This was done partly because the large Virginia city could accommodate the growing Confederate bureaucracy more easily than Montgomery could. The move also dramatized the Confederacy's promise to defend the Upper South. Besides, Richmond was an important rail and road center. With Northern and Southern capitals and armies now only a hundred miles apart, the area of Virginia and Maryland became, for obvious reasons, the war's pivotal theater of operations.

A thick layer of gloom spread over Washington as Lincoln and his generals prepared for a Southern attack. There was talk that, for the second time in half a century, an American President might be forced to flee the White House, pursued by an invading army.

Southern Strategy   Although a number of important battles were fought during the war, the Confederates generally used an overall guerrilla strategy that resembled Washington's in the American Revolution. A friend wrote Jefferson Davis

Lee was a vigorous fifty-five when the Civil War began. Like Washington, he fought against difficult odds and was much admired by his troops.

complaining of the Confederacy's "purely defensive" strategy and of its reluctance to launch a full-scale attack on the North. Davis replied: "Without military stores, without the workshops to create them, without the power to import them, necessity, not choice, has compelled us to occupy strong positions and everywhere—selecting the time and place of attack—to confront the enemy without reserves." In other words, the South chose to conduct an "offensive defense." It tried to select the time and place for major battles carefully. At other times Southerners harassed Northern armies with cavalry raids led by such intrepid commanders as "Stonewall" Jackson, J. E. B. Stuart, Nathan B. Forrest, and John S. Mosby.

Confederate army commanders realized that it was impossible to prevent Union invasions of the South. They knew too that they had neither the manpower nor the resources to mount a full-scale invasion of the North. So the Confederates worked instead to maintain their armies in the field while fighting back the Union troops thrown against them. They hoped that a war-weary Northern public would finally force Lincoln's government to negotiate a peaceful settlement. Lee and Davis recognized, as Washington did during the 1770s, that a revolutionary army wins by not losing —that is, by displaying the capacity to endure.

Northern Strategy Recognizing the Southern strategy, Lincoln and his generals committed Northern armies from the beginning to a policy of total war against the South. They were dedicated to the complete destruction of Confederate military power and civil authority by every necessary means. George Templeton Strong wrote in his diary in November 1861:

> Were I dictator at this time, my military policy would be: (1) to defend and hold Washington, Western Virginia, Kentucky, Missouri; (2) to support Unionists in North Carolina and in eastern Tennessee; (3) to recover and hold (or destroy with sunken ships) every port and inlet from Hatteras to Galveston.

Strong's proposals resembled the North's actual strategy during the war, which was three-fold: (1) to encircle the South in an ever-tightening military net by blockading its ports; (2) to divide the Confederacy in half by seizing control of the Mississippi and Tennessee rivers; (3) to capture Richmond and destroy the main Confederate armies in Virginia, where most Southern troops were concentrated. Strong believed, as did Lincoln and his officers, that if "the rebels of the South can be locked up and left to suffer and starve," victory would follow.

Grubby-looking but brilliant, Grant was modest and reticent about his feelings. Of him Lincoln said, "I can't spare this man—he fights."

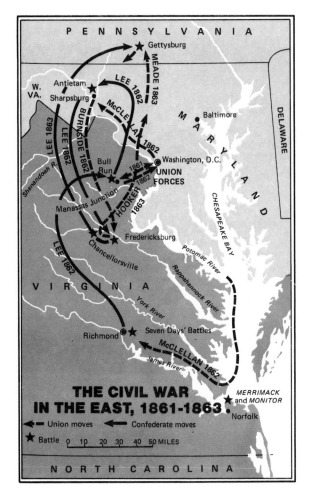

THE CIVIL WAR IN THE EAST, 1861-1863

Union moves — Confederate moves

★ Battle   0 10 20 30 40 50 MILES

Fighting broke out on April 12, **1861**, when Confederate batteries opened fire on Fort Sumter in Charleston harbor. The Union quickly began a naval blockade of Confederate shipping. The first major engagement occurred on July 21, at Manassas Junction, Virginia. There an advancing Union army under Irvin McDowell was defeated in the first Battle of Bull Run and driven back to Washington, D.C.

The year **1862** witnessed the first naval battle between ironclads—the Union ship *Monitor* and the Confederate ship *Virginia* (formerly the *Merrimack*)—on March 9 near Norfolk, Virginia. The Union offensives of that year began in March with McClellan's Peninsula Campaign, an attempt to take Richmond from the southeast. He advanced slowly to within a few miles of the city. Confederate forces inflicted heavy casualties on his troops at the end of May. During the subsequent Seven Days' Battle (June 26-July 2) Lee and Jackson forced McClellan to retreat and abandon the campaign. The Confederate army moved northward to win the second Battle of Bull Run (August 29-30). From there Lee and Jackson advanced into Maryland. Near Sharpsburg, McClellan engaged the Confederates in the Battle of Antietam (September 17). Although militarily the battle was a draw, Lee withdrew to Virginia. McClellan was replaced as Union commander by Burnside, whose overwhelming force was shattered at Fredericksburg (December 13).

In **1863** Hooker took command of the Union army, only to be defeated at Chancellorsville (May 2-4). However, Confederate losses there included "Stonewall" Jackson. Lee marched into Pennsylvania and was defeated at Gettysburg by a Union army under Meade (July 1-3). Lee retreated to Virginia, his second offensive into Union territory a failure.

Superior to the South in its navy, the North was able to impose a blockade of Southern harbors. The Confederates counteracted with fast blockade runners, joined by a number of private merchantmen. In the early years of the war they managed to slip past Union vessels in five out of every six attempts. But the Union blockade became increasingly effective. By 1865 it had choked off Southern cotton exports to Europe, as well as imports of arms and supplies.

War in the East The outcome of the Civil War was decided not by naval encounters but by land battles. Northern armies began poorly but improved their performance every year. Confederate forces scored impressive victories at the first and

second battles of Bull Run in July 1861 and August 1862. At Fredericksburg, Virginia, in December 1862, the North suffered a crushing defeat, with over 12,000 casualties.

In May 1863, at Chancellorsville, Maryland, outnumbered Southerners won another victory, though it cost them one of their best generals, "Stonewall" Jackson. They imposed a stalemate on the Virginia front and, several times, threatened to capture Washington itself.

Lincoln searched desperately for Union commanders capable of breaking the stalemate and executing major offensive operations. In the process he appointed a succession of commanding generals—George McClellan, John Pope, McClellan again, Ambrose Burnside, Joseph Hooker, and George Meade. One time, after McClellan had failed to pursue a retreating Confederate force, he received this letter: "My dear McClellan: If you don't want to use the Army of the Potomac, I should like to borrow it for a while. Yours respectfully, A. Lincoln."

The turning point of the Civil War in the East came in July 1863. Confederate troops under Lee marched into southern Pennsylvania, where they encountered a Union force near Gettysburg. After three days of costly fighting, Lee's invasion was repulsed decisively on July 3.

Each side had over 75,000 troops involved, and the South suffered almost 25,000 casualties. "The results of this victory are priceless," rejoiced the normally pessimistic Strong. "Philadelphia, Baltimore, and Washington are safe. The rebels are hunted out of the North, their best army is routed, and the charm of Robert Lee's invincibility broken."

War in the West The South's strategy of tying down and wearing out Union forces worked reasonably well in the East. Elsewhere, however, better-equipped and better-led Union troops won a series of important victories.

In February 1862 federal troops and a gunboat flotilla led by Ulysses S. Grant captured Fort Henry, on the Tennessee River, and Fort Donelson, on the Cumberland River. These moves forced Southern General Albert S. Johnston to abandon Kentucky and parts of Tennessee to the Union.

Admiral Farragut's capture of New Orleans in April 1862 and a series of Northern victories farther up the Mississippi—capped by defeat of the Confederate fleet at Memphis in June—brought most of the river under Union control. Arkansas, Louisiana, and Texas were thus isolated from the rest of the Confederacy.

In the West the decisive point was reached the day after Lee's defeat at Gettysburg. On July 4, 1863, Vicksburg fell. This key Confederate port surrendered after a six-week siege by Union troops. A final Confederate stronghold on the Mississippi—Port Hudson, Louisiana—fell later that same month.

Grant's remarkable success in this western

campaign led to his appointment as Lincoln's seventh and last commanding general. Grant appealed to Lincoln for many of the same reasons he

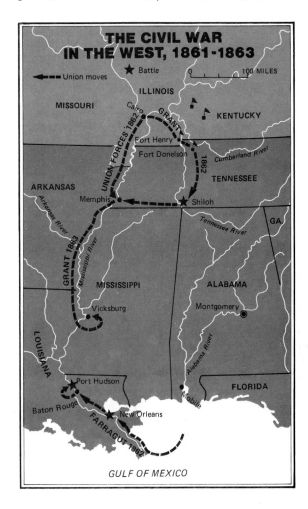

THE CIVIL WAR IN THE WEST, 1861-1863

Meanwhile, in the west, the Union won a series of important victories in **1862**. In February Grant captured Fort Henry on the Tennessee River and Fort Donelson on the Cumberland. Moving southward in Tennessee, he was attacked at Shiloh (April 6-7), but Union reinforcements forced the Confederates to withdraw into Mississippi. Union forces also made progress in their drive to gain control of the Mississippi River. Farragut bombarded and captured New Orleans in late April and proceeded up the river to Baton Rouge. To the north, a combined naval and land expedition defeated the Confederate fleet at Memphis on June 6 and captured the city.

In **1863** the Union continued its campaign to secure mastery of the Mississippi. Grant began attacking the Confederate stronghold of Vicksburg in May, and the city surrendered on July 4. With the fall of Port Hudson on July 9, the entire Mississippi was in Union hands and the Confederacy split in two.

did to most Northerners. Wrote one admirer of Grant: "He talks like an earnest businessman, prompt, clearheaded, and decisive, and utters no bosh."

Final Campaigns Grant took command of the Union forces in the spring of 1864. In May, he and Meade led a Northern force of 100,000 men against Lee's army, which had regrouped in Virginia after its Gettysburg defeat the previous year. It was in the same month that Union troops led by Sherman began their push to Atlanta.

For the remainder of the war Grant and Sherman pursued the same strategy of wearing down the enemy that Davis and Lee had hoped earlier would win for the Confederacy. No longer did Union forces concentrate on capturing Richmond or other Southern territory for its own sake. Instead, they struck directly at the remaining Confederate armies and resources—as Sherman did in Georgia. They aimed to inflict so heavy a price in casualties and physical devastation, that a war-weary South would be forced to surrender.

Beginning in June 1864, Grant's army tied down most of Lee's forces near Petersburg, Virginia. That fall Sherman led his famous march to the sea from Atlanta to Savannah. From Savannah, Sherman's forces turned north and extended their scorched-earth tactics into South Carolina and North Carolina.

Grant's troops, meanwhile, left their Petersburg trenches for frequent assaults on Lee's thinly manned lines. By early April 1865, Grant had blocked Lee's effort to retreat southward. Lee's army had by then been reduced by death and desertions from 54,000 to 30,000 men. Lee believed that further fighting was useless and that Confederate defeat was inevitable. He surrendered to Grant at Appomattox, Virginia, on April 9, 1865.

Despite pleas from Jefferson Davis for continued resistance, even if only by guerrilla bands in the Southern hills and forests, the rest of the Confederate armies still in the field surrendered by the end of May. Union troops had finally occupied Richmond after Davis and other Confederate officials had fled. For all practical purposes Southern resistance had ended by the time Jefferson Davis was captured on May 10.

A Summing Up The Civil War has been described as the "first modern war." A number of weapons and tactics associated with later military struggles were first used in its major campaigns. The basic weapon for the infantry, both Union and Confederate, was the single-shot, rifled musket, which had a range and accuracy two or three times greater than earlier, smoothbore guns. Troops could now engage in deadly fire from distances of a quarter to a half mile. Trench warfare, which later dominated much of World War I, came into being, and close-range or hand-to-hand combat was no longer inevitable.

This increased firepower of the infantry threatened both artillery and cavalry. A bank of cannon could no longer offer a solid defense; and the dash of a cavalry charge became mere vainglory when riders could easily be picked off, one by one, from a distance.

The American genius for creating new technology, shown earlier with such peaceful innovations as the cotton gin, was amply demonstrated during the Civil War, when Gatling guns (machine guns), repeating rifles, ironclad ships, and even submarines made their appearance (the latter were, for the most part, failures).

Civil War mortar

Railroads and telegraph lines revolutionized military communications, particularly for the Northern armies, who sent an estimated 6 million telegrams over 15,000 miles of wire set up by the Signal Corps. The most spectacular railroad supply system was that maintained for Sherman during the siege of Atlanta: 1,600 tons of supplies arrived daily in 16 trains from Union depots northwest of the city. European military observers flocked to the United States to study the lessons the New World's "internal war" had to offer the Old World's future struggles.

The Civil War was a modern war in the important sense that it required a break with traditional military thinking in order to achieve victory. Most Civil War generals on both sides regarded cities and territories—not enemy armies—as their objectives. They hoped to win by maneuvering rather than by fighting. By contrast, Lincoln's overall strategy was to move on all fronts simultaneously in order to crush the enemy's forces and gain control of his resources. This warfare of annihilation was a plan that tradition-bound generals scorned. Only in Grant and Sherman did Lincoln find generals who would employ his strategy successfully. They were willing to break the rules to play, and win, a new and deadly game.

Casualties on both sides in the four years of "internal war" totaled almost 40 percent of the armies; several hundred thousand soldiers gave their lives to battle. The South lost its separatist revolt for lack of manpower and equipment. "They are too many for us," Mary Boykin Chesnut despaired two days before Lee's surrender. "Nine tenths of our army are under ground!" she anguished in her diary. "Where is another to come from? Will they wait until we grow one?" Time had run out for the Confederacy, and its will to endure had been crushed.

LIFE ON THE HOME FRONTS

In the long run it would have been far cheaper to purchase the abolition of slavery, although such a course was unthinkable to both sides in 1861. Estimates of the war's total cost ran as high as $3 billion for the South and $5 billion for the North. This was three to four times the total estimated value of every slave in the Confederacy. Both the Union and the Confederacy had great difficulty in paying their enormous bills for war equipment, soldiers' salaries, and operating expenses. Both sides resorted to such financial measures as raising taxes, issuing various types of bonds, and printing vast quantities of paper money unsupported by gold or silver reserves.

Crisis in the South The overriding desire for victory led to sweeping measures in the South. Some affected the master-slave relationship. Southern slaveholders had defended their right to absolute control over their bondsmen in antebellum days. When war came, they watched helplessly as the Confederate government and Southern state governments transferred hundreds of thousands of slaves from private plantations to more urgent labor in the war effort. Slaves even became Confederate soldiers shortly before Appomattox. And throughout the war Southerners relaxed their close supervision of slave movements and activities.

Normal political life also came to a halt in the South during the war. There was no two-party system (as in the North). There was only one all-inclusive ruling, but unruly, "government party." Within the Confederacy there were people who opposed Davis's conduct of the war. They spoke their minds freely. Yet the demands of fighting a separatist revolt prevented any change in government.

CIVIL WAR MANPOWER

	UNION	CONFEDERACY
Total serving in armed forces	1,556,678	1,082,119
Killed in battle or died from wounds	110,070	94,000
Died from illness	249,458	164,000
Wounded	275,175	100,000

Many a Civil War battle exacted enormous tolls in men. Above, Confederate dead lie in a shallow trench at Chancellorsville. Union forces, below, attack on the third day of the combat at Gettysburg. Watching a similarly dramatic panorama earlier in the war, Lee had remarked: "It is well that war is so terrible—we would grow too fond of it."

The major military actions of the fall of **1863** occurred in the west. On September 9 Union forces maneuvered the Confederates out of Chattanooga, Tennessee, without a battle. Moving south into Georgia, the Union army was stopped at Chickamauga (September 19-20) and driven back into Chattanooga. In October Grant was given command of all the Union's western armies. At the Battle of Chattanooga (November 23-25) he defeated the Confederates in engagements on Lookout Mountain and Missionary Ridge.

In **1864** Grant, now in supreme command of the Union armies, took charge of the Virginia front. He began a campaign to destroy Lee's army and take Richmond. Grant struck again and again: at the Battle of the Wilderness (May 5-6), at Spotsylvania (May 8-12), and at Cold Harbor (June 1-3). Lee parried Grant's blows, inflicting heavy casualties on his opponent. In this one-month period the Union army lost approximately 60,000 men, a number equal to Lee's total strength at the beginning of the campaign. But the North could provide reinforcements of men and supplies; the South lacked reserves of both. Grant pressed on, moving south to Petersburg. He failed to capture it in a bloody four-day battle (June 15-18). However, his subsequent nine-month seige of the town cut Richmond off from the Deep South.

THE CIVIL WAR, 1863-1865

← Union moves   ⬅ Confederate moves

0   100   200   300 MILES

★ Battle

In the west, Union forces under Sherman moved out of Chattanooga in May 1864 to begin their invasion of Georgia. The opposing Confederate general, Joseph E. Johnston, fought a series of defensive actions but continued falling back toward Atlanta. John B. Hood, who replaced Johnston in July, suffered heavy losses in two pitched battles near Atlanta. It was occupied by Union forces on September 2. After the fall of Atlanta, Hood moved northwest to threaten Tennessee and the Union army's long lines of communication. Sherman sent part of his army to counter Hood's forces. He led the rest of his troops in a virtually unopposed march to the sea from Atlanta to Savannah, which fell on December 22. Meanwhile, Union forces shattered Hood's army at Nashville, Tennessee (December 15–16).

In 1865 Sherman continued his scorched-earth policy as he moved north from Savannah into North Carolina, where Johnston, restored to command, slowed his advance somewhat. In Virginia the Confederates, outnumbered more than two to one by Grant's reinforced army, were unable to lift the siege of Petersburg. On April 1, Lee's last attack (at Five Forks) was repulsed, and on April 2 he evacuated Petersburg and Richmond, moving westward. A Union army under Philip H. Sheridan, which had marched south through the Shenandoah Valley, blocked his path. Virtually surrounded by an overwhelming force, Lee surrendered to Grant at Appomattox on April 9. On April 18, Johnston surrendered to Sherman at Durham Station, North Carolina. Final Confederate capitulations occurred in Alabama (May 4) and Louisiana (May 26).

The war not only changed master-slave relations and Southern politics. It also altered the Southern economy. The cherished doctrine of states' rights received rough treatment at the hands of Confederate leaders. These men were determined to assume every power they needed to wage war. Davis centralized and nationalized the economy to a remarkable degree. If occasion demanded, he interfered freely with the rights of capitalists. The Confederacy did more than seize slaves for war work. It closely regulated foreign commerce. It confiscated food and equipment for the army from private farms. It created government-run industries to produce military equipment. And it tightly controlled what was left of private enterprise.

The Confederacy even created a Cotton Bureau, which took over planters' cotton supplies. The Cotton Bureau paid a set price for the entire crop. By running the Northern blockade, the government acted as the sole Southern salesman in Europe. Government supplies of cotton were used as security for the Confederacy's foreign loans. But the blockade grew daily more effective, and Confederate revenues from European cotton sales—its one important source of revenue—dwindled correspondingly during the war's final years.

In spite of truly heroic effort and sacrifice, the South was destitute by the end of the war. "We have no money, even for taxes, or for their confiscation," wrote Mrs. Chesnut in April 1865. "Our poverty is made a matter of laughing." Millions came close to starving. Confederate officials recommended the nutritional values of such fare as squirrels and rats to make up for the dire shortage of food. At the time of its surrender, Lee's army had enough ammunition to provide each man seventy-five rounds—but no food.

Southern economic devastation by 1865 could be measured in many ways. Compared to 1860, there were 32 percent fewer horses, 30 percent fewer mules, 35 percent fewer cattle, and 42 percent fewer pigs. Cotton crops were destroyed or rotted unpicked in the fields. Few factories remained in operation. There was almost no trade. Only a handful of banks were left, and they were nearly empty.

Prosperity in the North "We hear they have all grown rich," Mrs. Chesnut complained about Northerners in 1865. "Genuine Yankees can make a fortune trading jackknives!" Industrial growth in the North began before the Civil War, of course. But it was vastly accelerated by wartime demands to equip and supply the army. The number of Northern factories increased from fewer than 140,000 in 1860 to over 250,000 by 1870. Railroad mileage doubled during this decade. Growth in the North was aided not only by government contracts for arms and military supplies. It was helped also by wartime currency inflation, huge federal subsidies to railroads, and protective tariffs for industry.

The result was enormous inflation—high prices but also tremendous profits. There was rapid expansion in industries ranging from wool production to mining, from petroleum to iron manufacturing. Farmers prospered, too, because of the increased demand for every staple crop. Most merchants and shippers shared in the boom. Banking facilities were enlarged greatly after Congress passed several new banking acts. Senator John Sherman wrote his brother General William Sherman about the impact of the war on Northern capitalists: "They talk as confidently of millions as they formerly did of thousands." Aristocratic George Templeton Strong complained wistfully that the more sedate prewar culture of New York City was being "diluted and swamped by a great flood-tide of material wealth."

A shortage of manpower on Northern farms and in factories stimulated immigration from Europe. In 1865 alone, 180,000 new immigrants arrived on Union soil. In 1866 and 1867 the number spurted to 300,000 yearly.

Perhaps most important in the North, as in the Confederacy, was the role played by the government in stimulating economic growth. Southern Democrats had dominated Congress and the executive branch until the 1850s. They had blocked such measures as the protective tariff, a national banking system, and railroad subsidies. Now the Republicans were in control. They favored industrialization and economic growth. To further their aims, they adopted the Morrill Tariff of 1861, which raised duties. They passed the Na-

WALT WHITMAN

The poet who was best able to bring together the vitality and idealism of his generation was Walt Whitman. He was born in 1819 in Huntington, Long Island, the son of a carpenter-farmer father with leanings toward Quaker thought, and a sympathetic and understanding mother with very little education. He grew up in a family of nine children of whom both the oldest and the youngest were mentally retarded. Walter, as he was known in the family, left school early in his eleventh year and started a process of self-education that included moving from job to job—as printer's devil, compositor, carpenter, schoolteacher, newspaper writer, and editor.

Whitman's ideas were generated by his childhood in the farming and fishing community on Long Island—his associations with the haymakers and eel fishers, the baymen and pilots—and by the stimulating life of the city in which he worked. He roamed the streets, rode the ferries, and went regularly to the theater and the opera. Early in his life, books had become important to him. He read the Bible, Shakespeare, Ossian, the Greek tragic poets, the ancient Hindu poets, the Nibelungenlied, and the poems of Dante as well as Scott.

Politics were soon a consuming interest. The adult Whitman became an ardent Jacksonian and supporter of the Democratic party. Most of his newspaper jobs were with Democratic journals. The *Democratic Review* was one of the fine literary journals of the time and, through Whitman's work there, he met such literary figures as Hawthorne, Poe, Bryant, Longfellow, Thoreau, and others.

Whitman was especially imbued with the fire of Emerson's transcendentalist ideas. When *Leaves of Grass* appeared, Emerson wrote: "I am not blind to the worth of the wonderful gift of *Leaves of Grass*. I find it the most extraordinary piece of wit and wisdom that America has yet contributed. . . . I greet you at the beginning of a great career." But *Leaves of Grass*, in its first two printings in 1855 and 1856, was not a success. Some readers found it incomprehensible while others found the sexual implications shocking. With the mellowing of the author's language, finally in 1860–1861, the volume began to sell.

The Civil War became a critical influence in Whitman's life. Several of his articles at this time dealt with Broadway Hospital where he spent time helping the wounded. Then, in December 1862, he visited his wounded brother, George, a Union soldier, and suddenly realized that he had himself become a part of the war effort. With a part-time job for support, he spent the next three years serving the wounded in hospitals around the city of Washington and sometimes on the battlefields.

In 1865 Whitman published *Drum Taps*, the poems he had written during the war. Some poems are martial outbursts, describing the mobilization of the army. Others are quieter, describing a field hospital or his own lonely vigils with the dying and the dead.

Drum Taps was being printed when the news of Lincoln's assassination reached Whitman. He was inspired to write the dirge that many critics consider his masterpiece. The poem stresses that peace and beauty triumph in death, for death brings a joining of man and nature. It begins:

When lilacs last in the door-yard bloom'd
And the great star early droop'd
   in the western sky in the night,
I mourn'd — and yet shall mourn
   with ever-returning spring.
O ever-returning spring!
   trinity sure to me you bring;
Lilac blooming perennial
   and drooping star in the west,
And thought of him I love.

Richmond in April 1865. Only the shells of burned buildings surround the canal basin. Lee prepared to abandon the city on April 2, and mobs of its inhabitants set fire to the town on the eve of his evacuation.

tional Banking Acts of 1863 and 1864, which aided national banks at the expense of state banks. In addition, Congress awarded land-grant subsidies to transcontinental railroads and stimulated western settlement with the 1862 Homestead Act, which offered land to settlers for nominal sums.

The Republicans changed not only the economic habits of the North but its political life as well. Lincoln found it no easier than Davis did to govern a country at war. Throughout the conflict the President was attacked from all sides of his wartime government coalition, which was known as the Union party. Abolitionist Republicans (known as Radical Republicans) denounced him for moving slowly on the question of emancipation, while War Democrats denounced him for moving at all on the problem. Moderate Republicans criticized the slow military progress of the Northern armies.

Compared to the Confederacy, the North had a poor wartime record in the field of civil rights. In spite of Union victories, many Northerners opposed the war. Lincoln authorized a number of arbitrary military arrests of such civilians, especially Peace Democrats—called "Copperheads" by their enemies. He suspended the privi-

lege of habeas corpus[2] to keep pro-Confederate Northerners in jail once arrested.

In both sections, North and South, the war interfered with civil liberties, but in different ways. Northerners were more likely to be thrown in jail for opposing the war. Southerners were more likely to be punished for resisting government confiscation of their property. These interferences involved of course the civil rights of *white* people. Neither government troubled itself much about the rights of blacks, free or slave.

FREEDOM FOR BLACK PEOPLE

As soon as the war broke out, Northern black men tried to enlist in the Union army. They were not allowed to do so, however, until the fall of 1862. Eventually, over 186,000 blacks served as Union soldiers—almost 15 percent of all Northern troops.

[2]This privilege, guaranteed by the Constitution, provides that an arrested person can demand that legal authorities show why he or she has been imprisoned. A writ of habeas corpus (Latin words meaning "you have the body") thus protects a person against being held in jail without cause.

They were usually led by white officers and they were paid less than white troops. Union commanders were divided in their attitudes toward using black soldiers. Some welcomed them. Others, like Sherman, did not.

The Emancipation Proclamation Northern policy toward slavery changed during the war. Many Republicans in the government believed sincerely in emancipation. Lincoln, though, had always regarded it as secondary compared to the overriding importance of winning the war and reuniting the nation.

Like most Americans at the time, Lincoln believed that blacks were inferior. He never felt certain that 4 million ex-slaves could reach full equality with whites in the United States. Throughout the Civil War he tried unsuccessfully to link his moves toward emancipation with efforts to colonize freed blacks. None of these efforts worked out.

Lincoln had been elected on a platform that pledged to restrict slavery but not abolish it. He moved cautiously toward emancipation, mainly because of his military and political problems in conducting the war. Radical Republicans in Congress kept pressuring him for swift abolition. Even many moderate Northerners became fervent converts to emancipation as war casualties mounted, if only to punish the Confederacy. Such Unionists did not change their attitudes toward *black people* (and their supposed inferiority). They only changed their minds about *slavery*.

The situation was complicated by the fact that thousands of runaway slaves took refuge with the Union army. There, they were often treated — as with Sherman's army — as both a help and a hindrance. Thousands of blacks, however, did join Union army ranks. Lincoln, along with most Northerners, grew more sympathetic to emancipation.

Congress took the first step by abolishing slavery in the federal territories in June 1862. Then, in September 1862, Lincoln issued a preliminary proclamation. In it he stated that he would issue a final document on January 1, 1863, freeing the slaves in all states then in rebellion. This final document was the Emancipation Proclamation.

The Emancipation Proclamation actually freed very few people when it was issued. It did not apply to slaves in the border states fighting on the Union side. Nor did it affect slaves in Southern areas already under Union control. Naturally, the states in rebellion did not act on Lincoln's order. But the proclamation did show Americans, and the rest of the world, that the Civil War was now being fought to end slavery.

For all practical purposes the 3 1/2 million black slaves in the South found themselves free within days after Lee's surrender. It was only with final ratification of the Thirteenth Amendment, however, in December 1865, that slavery was ended completely throughout the United States.

Treatment in the North Though the Union — eventually, at least — fought to free black people, those who lived in the North faced many difficulties. In 1860 free Northern blacks numbered 225,000. Most of them were restricted to menial jobs. A rigid pattern of segregation in schools, hospitals, transportation, and other public facilities kept blacks and whites separated. Roughly 93 percent of Northern black people lived in states where they could not vote. (Only five New England states allowed blacks to cast ballots in 1865.)

Blacks were the victims of race riots throughout the North during the war. The most destructive took place in New York City in the summer of 1863. There, anger among the city's Irish working class at a new federal draft law exploded into violence during four days and nights of rioting. The new law allowed wealthy citizens to avoid the draft by buying the services of substitute soldiers — something poor laborers clearly could not afford.

Mobs of Irish workers rampaged over Manhattan Island from July 13 to July 16. They burned, looted, and killed. The rioters' main targets were free blacks and, to a lesser extent, white abolitionists and wealthy citizens. The city's outnumbered police force, also composed largely of Irishmen, fought the rioters with great bravery and discipline, finally putting down the rioting with the help of federal troops. By that time, some 1,200 persons, mostly black, had been killed.

Many thousands were injured. Property worth millions was damaged or destroyed. Other Northern cities, especially in the Middle West, experienced similar draft riots.

After the War The Thirteenth Amendment did not settle the basic questions about the future status of black Americans, especially in the postwar South. Former slaves were now free. But free to *do* what? Free to *be* what? What did freedom mean to someone raised in slavery?

Many ex-slaves simply stayed on their plantations, working for the same masters. Their old habits altered little at first, although now the whites were often as poor as their former bondsmen. "The Negroes seem unchanged," Mrs. Chesnut wrote, referring to her one-time slaves. Other former slaves left their old homes, usually for an uncertain future.

Whatever the fate of individual freed slaves, one characteristic of Southern emancipation was its peaceful nature. Despite the fears of

After General Lee surrendered the Army of Northern Virginia to General Grant at Appomatox on April 9, 1865, Confederate armies capitulated in North Carolina, Alabama, and Louisiana. Throughout the South, Confederate troops disbanded to return home, their ranks depleted by death and injury. In the days ahead, the returning veterans were to confront the desolation of a war-ravaged region: neglected fields, burned-out cities, and a worthless currency.

antebellum white Southerners, there were no bloodbaths, no vengeful attacks by ex-slaves on their former masters. Black people responded to their new freedom with dignity and grace.

Early in the twentieth century Benjamin Botkin and other folklorists traveled through the United States, recording the recollections of aged ex-slaves. One elderly man recalled:

> The end of the war, it come just like that—like you snap your fingers. Soldiers, all of a sudden, was everywhere—coming in bunches. Everyone was a-singing. We was all walking on golden clouds. Hallelujah! Everybody went wild! we was free. Just like that, we was free. It didn't seem to make the whites mad, either. They went right on giving us food just the same. Nobody took our homes away, but right off colored folks started on the move. They seemed to want to get closer to freedom, so they'd know what it was—like it was a place or a city.

The experience was exciting yet frightening for blacks, people like those who had joined Sherman's army on its march to Savannah. Many of them had never gone beyond the borders of their own farms. One ex-slave commented to Botkin:

> We knowed freedom was on us, but we didn't know what was to come with it. We thought we was going to be richer than the white folks, 'cause we was stronger and knowed how to work, and the whites didn't, and they didn't have us to work for them any more. But it didn't turn out that way. We soon found out that freedom could make folks proud, but it didn't make 'em rich.

As soon as the war was over, blacks began to organize and work for their own advancement. Historians sometimes overlook the fact that, even in 1860, there were 261,000 free blacks in the South. Tens of thousands of them were literate. These men and women—like the leaders who met with Stanton and Sherman—formed an important black leadership base at the end of the war. Many took part in black conventions held in a number of Southern cities in 1865 and 1866. They petitioned the federal government to assist freedom by granting them the franchise, protecting their civil rights, and providing land and other economic help.

The basic dilemma of Reconstruction for all those who lived through it, black and white, Southerner and Northerner alike, was its revolutionary nature. Like the Civil War itself, the postwar period had no examples on which to model itself, no constitutional provisions by which policymakers might be guided.

Compared with reconstruction periods that have followed more recent civil wars in Russia, Spain, and China, the American experience was notably mild. Confederate leaders were neither shot nor driven into exile. Indeed, many resumed their careers in American politics. Only a few, such as Jefferson Davis, were imprisoned, and these only for a brief period. No Confederate property was confiscated. Nor was there any forced redistribution of wealth imposed on the defeated South by the victorious North.

Lincoln's Approach In Lincoln's Second Inaugural Address, delivered a month before his death, he called for a generous settlement with the defeated South: "With malice toward none, with charity for all . . . let us strive on to finish the work we are in, to bind up the nation's wounds."

As early as 1862 Lincoln had indicated his desire to restore a defeated Confederacy quickly and without revenge against either its leaders or its people. Lincoln suggested a basis for Reconstruction in December 1863. He called for amnesty[3] (except in the case of key leaders) for Southerners who pledged loyalty to the Union. Southern states in which 10 percent of the 1860 electorate took such a loyalty oath and accepted emancipation would be restored immediately to the Union.

Governments in Arkansas, Louisiana, and Tennessee met Lincoln's provisions in 1864. But Congress refused to seat their representatives.

---

[3]Amnesty is a form of pardon for offenses against the government—especially to a group of persons.

The problem was complicated by the fact that Lincoln believed that the executive branch should control Reconstruction, whereas Congress wanted this power for itself. Congressional attitudes were partly a reaction to the vast expansion of presidential authority under Lincoln during the Civil War.

Republicans in Congress were led by Radicals Thaddeus Stevens of Pennsylvania in the House and Charles Sumner of Massachusetts in the Senate. They were afraid that the Democratic party, led by Southern ex-Confederates, would quickly return to national power. So they offered a much tougher Reconstruction plan in a measure known as the Wade-Davis Bill. It provided that a majority of voters in each Southern state take an "ironclad oath" swearing to their *past* as well as to their *future* loyalty. Obviously, if the electorate were composed only of whites, no ex-Confederate state could honestly meet this provision. The bill also required that the Southern states abolish slavery in their constitutions, repudiate the Confederate war debt, and disfranchise Confederate leaders. Congress passed the Wade-Davis Bill on July 4, 1864. Lincoln killed the measure with a pocket veto. Then Congress passed the nonbinding Wade-Davis Manifesto, reasserting the provisions of the earlier bill.

Therefore, by mid-1864, the stage was set for a postwar confrontation between the President and Congress on Reconstruction policy. Was the

In September of 1862, President Lincoln visited with General McClellan and his officers at Antietam, where, as the Confederates advanced into Maryland, the Army of the Potomac had caught up with General Lee. After preliminary skirmishes, on September 17, McClellan defeated the Confederates in the bloodiest battle of the war. Lee retreated across the Potomac, where, to Lincoln's dismay, McClellan was reluctant to pursue him. Angered by his General's inability to exploit the Union victory, Lincoln removed McClellan from command.

South to be restored quickly, its new state governments falling into the hands of ex-Confederate whites with a minimum of federal interference? (This is what Lincoln wanted, though he did urge Southern whites to allow at least educated blacks to vote.) Or should the Southern states undergo fundamental political changes before they could rejoin the Union? Should they, for instance, allow blacks to vote and hold office, while disbarring ex-Confederate leaders and perhaps confiscating their land?

Assassination With the war almost over, Lincoln's thoughts had turned increasingly to the problem of reconstructing the South. After a trip to Richmond early in April 1865, he spent several days working out various programs.

On the night of April 14, Good Friday evening, President and Mrs. Lincoln went to Ford's Theater in Washington to see a popular play, *Our American Cousin*. Shortly after 10 P.M. a half-crazed Southern sympathizer named John Wilkes Booth shot Lincoln as he watched the play. Booth then stabbed another member of the President's party, leaped onto the stage, rushed from the theater, and rode away. (He was shot down on April 26 by Union troops that had pursued him into Virginia.)

The wounded Lincoln was taken from Ford's theater to a nearby house. There family, friends, and government officials kept an all-night vigil. The President remained unconscious until his death at 7:22 the following morning. "Now he belongs to the ages," said Secretary of War Stanton, one of those at his bedside.

Word of Lincoln's assassination spread quickly via the telegraph. The first reaction to the event, shared by most Northerners and even many Southerners, was one of profound shock: "I am stunned," wrote George Templeton Strong, "as by a fearful personal calamity."

For Lincoln was highly popular in the North at the time of his death, a result of Union military victories beginning in 1863 and culminating in Lee's surrender. During the war itself, Southerners—as one might expect—had little affection for "Uncle Abraham." Many Northerners felt the same way, especially in the early years.

One such person was Strong, an aristocrat and avowed snob. He never liked Lincoln's lack of polish and fondness for telling jokes. Yet these very qualities endeared the President to most other Americans. And even Strong, like other Unionists, responded to Lincoln's firm leadership and genuine anguish at the war's increasing toll in human suffering: "It must be referred to the Attorney General," Lincoln once told Strong about a request to pardon a criminal. "But I guess it will be all right, for me, and the Attorney General's very chicken-hearted."

By the war's end, most Northerners probably agreed with Strong's high estimate of Lincoln's wartime achievement. The President's "weaknesses are on the surface," Strong wrote on April 11, 1865. "His name will be of high account fifty years hence, and for many generations thereafter."

Johnson's Plan Lincoln's death placed the burden of reconstructing the South on the shoulders of his former Vice President, Andrew Johnson. Johnson was a War Democrat from Tennessee and a one-time Radical on the Reconstruction issue. Once in the White House, however, he soon adopted Lincoln's basic proposals. Unfortunately, Johnson completely lacked Lincoln's basic sympathy for the problems of freed blacks. Also, he was a dogmatic man. He showed almost none of Lincoln's tact in dealing with political opponents.

Johnson, like Lincoln, believed that Reconstruction was a matter to be handled by the President. His position was strengthened by the fact that Congress was not in session for several months after he took office. Johnson readmitted the states of Arkansas, Louisiana, and Tennessee. In May 1865 he issued his own Reconstruction plan. It provided that whites in each Southern state who pledged their future loyalty to the Union could elect delegates to a state convention. This convention had to revoke the ordinance of secession, abolish slavery, and repudiate the Confederate war debt. Then the state would be restored to the Union. Johnson granted amnesty to almost all Confederates who took the oath of allegiance. The exceptions were wealthy people and

Johnson was an honest but tactless man forced to cope with uniquely difficult circumstances. Born poor, he was a self-made man and touchy about it. Jefferson Davis said he had "the pride of having no pride."

high officials. Even they could apply for a presidential pardon. By late 1865 all the Southern states except Texas had complied with these provisions. (Texas did so early in 1866.)

Southern Regulation of Blacks Congress believed that the government had a duty to assist freedmen after the war. So in March 1865 it created the Freedmen's Bureau, a temporary federal assistance agency headed by Oliver O. Howard. The bureau distributed food and medicine to poor blacks (and whites), opened schools, supervised land distribution to freedmen, and tried to defend the civil rights of Southern blacks. (It exercised these functions in helping "Sherman's Negroes" in the resettlement program.)

The Freedmen's Bureau, however, could not protect the physical security of black Southerners without the help of Union troops. This problem was clearly a most urgent one. Brutal riots against blacks occurred in Memphis and New Orleans in 1866.

After Appomattox, Union troops were mustered out of the army at a rapid rate. By the end of 1865 only 150,000 soldiers remained of the million serving six months earlier. Many of these were stationed on isolated western posts fighting Indians.

Under these conditions it was impossible for Union troops to offer the 4 million Southern blacks, most of them recently freed, any real protection. Most white Southerners had been raised to believe that blacks had no civil rights that whites were bound to respect. Killings, beatings, burnings, and other forms of physical terror directed against blacks — mostly to keep them out of politics — began soon after the war's end. Violence against blacks was often carried out by white secret societies. Several were formed after the war, primarily to keep blacks from voting. The most famous, the Ku Klux Klan, was founded in 1866. The turmoil increased during the 1870s.

Many whites in the South adopted other means to reduce black people to a state of virtual enslavement. In every Southern state new governments were elected by voters according to the provisions of Johnson's Reconstruction plan. But the Johnson state governments, as they were called, allowed no blacks to vote. They adopted so-called Black Codes to regulate the actions and behavior of freedmen. Southern whites claimed that such codes were necessary because of the threat of social disorder as a result of emancipation. There had been no major instance, however, of blacks rioting against whites anywhere in the region.

The Black Codes had some provisions to protect blacks. They legalized marriages between blacks, for instance. They also gave blacks the right to sue and testify in court. But the codes consisted mainly of restrictions. They supervised the movements of blacks, prevented them from carrying weapons, and forbade intermarriage between blacks and whites. Contracts, sometimes for life, forced black people to remain at their jobs. In some states, blacks could not own land or work at

Stern, intense, and militant, Thaddeus Stevens attacked Lincoln throughout the war for not punishing the South harshly enough.

Charles Sumner, once admonished during an argument, "But you forget the other side," thundered in reply: "There is no other side!"

any job other than farming without a special license. Black children were forced into certain job apprenticeships.

Reaction in the North Northern Republicans, both Radicals and moderates, attacked the Johnson state governments. They denounced the Black Codes and called for their immediate repeal. Most Radicals believed that the defeated Southern states should be treated, in Thaddeus Stevens's phrase, like "conquered provinces," until more repentant leaders emerged.

When Congress reconvened in December 1865, representatives and senators elected under the Johnson state governments applied for admission. Republicans in Congress refused to admit them. These Southerners who now claimed loyalty to the Union included fifty-eight former Confederate congressmen, six of Jefferson Davis's cabinet members, and four Southern generals. Most amazing of all was the presence of Alexander Stephens of Georgia, who eight months earlier had been vice president of the Confederacy!

The 1866 riots in Memphis and New Orleans gave Northerners additional evidence that the white South remained unrepentant. Thus it seemed inevitable that there would be a power struggle between Johnson and congressional

Republicans over who would control the Reconstruction process. Who was sovereign in the federal government, the President or Congress? Who could decide?

RADICAL RECONSTRUCTION

Congress answered these questions to its own satisfaction by taking the initiative completely out of Johnson's hands. By 1867 the legislature had won control. It dominated the government for the next ten years.

The Republicans who controlled Congress developed their strategy mainly through the Joint Committee on Reconstruction, which was dominated by the Radicals. This group asserted that Southern states could be readmitted only after meeting congressional requirements. The Joint Committee moved a series of measures through Congress between 1865 and 1867. Most of the bills were vetoed by the hapless Johnson, then repassed by a two-thirds majority.

First, in February 1866, came the new Freedmen's Bureau bill. It expanded the bureau's authority to protect Southern blacks, giving it the right to try in military courts persons accused of violating the civil rights of freedmen.

A Civil Rights Act of April 1866 granted to blacks the same civil rights as those enjoyed by whites. The measure also asserted the right of the federal government to interfere in state affairs to protect a citizen's civil rights.

In order to fortify their position, congressional Republicans in June 1866 adopted and sent to the states the Fourteenth Amendment. In effect, it gave blacks full citizenship. If a state denied the vote to blacks, its representation in the House would be reduced. The amendment also forbade ex-Confederate officials from holding federal or state office again without receiving congressional pardon. The Joint Committee declared that any Southern state wishing readmission would have to ratify the Fourteenth Amendment. The Johnson state governments in the South voted against ratification. (The amendment was eventually ratified in 1868.)

President Johnson hoped his Republican opponents would be defeated in the 1866 congressional election, and he campaigned personally against them. After a wild and bitterly fought campaign, however, anti-Johnson Republicans swept the election. They carried every Union state but three.

A Harsh Program When Congress met after the election, Republicans enacted their program into law. They began with the First Reconstruction Act of March 1867. Significantly, the bill's final form came from a moderate, Republican John Sherman. By this time the moderates agreed with Radicals on most key issues of Reconstruction. This law abolished the existing Johnson state governments. It provided for universal male suffrage — that is, for black as well as white voting.

The First Reconstruction Act also authorized temporary military rule of the South. Ten former Confederate states were still outside the Union. (Tennessee had ratified the Fourteenth Amendment and had been readmitted.) These states were divided into five military districts. To rejoin the Union, a state had to call a constitutional convention elected by universal male suffrage. This body, in turn, had to create a new state government that would ratify the Fourteenth Amendment and guarantee black suffrage. Three subsequent congressional acts strengthened the powers of federal army commanders in the South.

The final act in the congressional drama of Radical Reconstruction involved the effort in 1868 to remove the President through impeachment. Congress had good reason to believe that Johnson would do everything in his power to sabotage the Reconstruction acts. From 1865 to 1868, he had worked to impede every major step Congress had taken to assist Southern blacks or to enforce a harsh settlement upon the white South. In the process, Johnson had systematically interfered with congressional statutes, practically crippling effective operation (for one thing) of the Freedmen's Bureau throughout the South (as in his interference with Sherman's land program) by presidential directives.

Johnson, moreover, had appointed as federal officials in the region (including even provision-

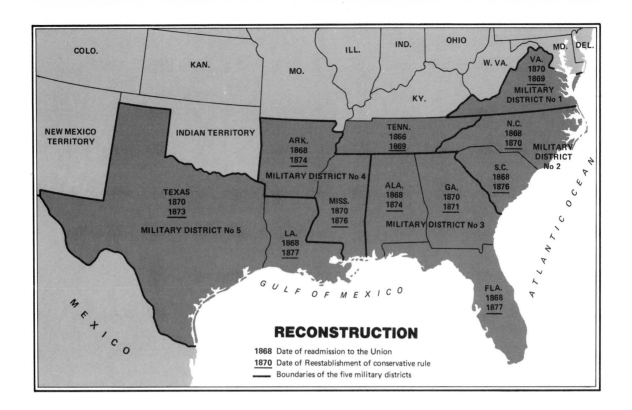

RECONSTRUCTION

1868 Date of readmission to the Union
<u>1870</u> Date of Reestablishment of conservative rule
——— Boundaries of the five military districts

al governors) ex-Confederates who had not yet even taken the oath of allegiance to the Union. He used his presidential appointment powers ruthlessly to subvert congressional aims on Reconstruction, claiming for himself absolute direction of the process even after Congress had rejected his early effort to form state governments without first securing their approval. Johnson's view of presidential authority was a broad, almost modern one (as Lincoln's had been—but during the wartime emergency). At all times, Johnson lacked his predecessor's tact in dealing with those who disagreed with him—especially in Congress.

Johnson's recurrent efforts to undermine the program of congressional Reconstruction through issuing conflicting orders to federal officials (both military and civil) in the South provoked Republican moderates and radicals to combine in self-defense. An unprecedented special session was called which passed two measures on March 2, 1867.

One of the measures virtually deprived Johnson of command of the American army by requiring him to issue all military orders through the General of the Army, Ulysses S. Grant. The second was the Tenure of Office Act. It prohibited the President from removing those officials whose appointments had been made with Senate consent, without again securing Senate approval. This law meant that Johnson could not, for example, arbitrarily fire Secretary of War Stanton. This leading Radical was the man who—along with Saxton and Howard—had tried to block presidential interference with Sherman's land distribution policy. Johnson disregarded the measure and dismissed Stanton. Then the House passed a resolution impeaching Johnson on eleven charges, including alleged violations of the two March 2 bills.

After a Senate trial, the President was acquitted, although even some of his supporters acknowledged that they were less concerned with retaining Johnson—considering him an inept and insensitive chief executive—than they were with upholding the office of the presidency. If Johnson were successfully removed by impeachment, they felt, the process would rupture violently the normal relations between the three coordinate branches of national government. Both sides in the struggle argued from reasonable positions, and the entire impeachment process indicated the underlying strength of the constitutional mechanisms, even when tested in the midst of dire political crisis.

A two-thirds majority is needed to convict the President on an impeachment charge. Thirty-five senators voted for his conviction, while nineteen (including seven Republicans) voted for acquittal. Thus Johnson was saved by a one-vote margin.

After his acquittal, Johnson grudgingly complied with the tacit promises made by his supporters to secure the votes of borderline senators. No longer did he interfere actively—for the brief remainder of his presidency—with enforcement of duly passed congressional statutes on Southern Reconstruction or with those officials charged with enforcing these laws. For the moment, Congress controlled the Reconstruction process.

The effort to unseat Johnson was the most daring episode in the Radicals' Reconstruction plans. A few Radicals such as Stevens tried to push through bills confiscating 394 million acres of land owned by the 70,000 chief leaders of the Confederacy. (Charles Sumner called the antebellum plantations "nurseries of the Rebellion.") But such measures found little support among the party's moderate majority, and therefore they did not pass.

Most aims of the Radicals were fairly limited. They worked chiefly for Republican political control of the national government. They also hoped that coalitions of black voters and friendly whites would dominate Southern politics, thereby preventing national revival of the Democratic party.

But Republicans did not have any direct social or economic goals. Only a small number of Radicals were committed to complete equality for black Americans. There was no large-scale program to provide landless freedmen with an economic base. Many blacks had been promised "forty acres and a mule." But the thousands resettled on abandoned lands—such as "Sherman's Negroes" of the Deep South—were soon dispossessed.

After the attempt to impeach Johnson, Radicals left the problems of Reconstruction in the hands of federal commanders and new state governments in the South. The quarrel between legislative and executive branches over Southern policy ended in 1868, when Republican Ulysses S. Grant was elected President. By then the central drama of Reconstruction had shifted from Washington to the South itself.

The New Radical Governments Beginning in 1867, so-called Radical state governments were set up according to congressional regulations. New black voters made up a majority of the Radical electorate in five states—Alabama, Florida, Louisiana, Mississippi, and South Carolina. Elsewhere in the South, white Radical majorities were supported by black voters. By 1870 more than 700,000 blacks and 627,000 whites were registered as voters under the Radical state constitutions.[4]

Congress readmitted Louisiana and six other states to the Union under Radical rule in June 1868. By the end of 1870 all ten ex-Confederate states had been readmitted to the Union.

Throughout the South blacks filled public offices for the first time. These were not usually the highest offices, however. Nor did blacks hold office in proportion to their percentage of voters. Only one state legislature, that of South Carolina, ever had a black majority. No black ever became a Reconstruction Southern governor. (Some states, though, had black lieutenant governors.) There were two black United States senators and fifteen congressmen during the entire period of Radical rule.

_____

[4]The Fifteenth Amendment, adopted in 1870, forbade any state from preventing citizens from voting because of race, color, or "previous condition of servitude." This was a clear effort to eliminate the hypocrisy of some Northern states that demanded suffrage for blacks in the South while continuing to deny it at home.

Congressional Reconstruction not only disfranchised many former Confederates but ensured the suffrage to black men throughout the South, who went to the polls for the first time. By 1867, black voters constituted a majority in half of the former Confederate states. Although during the course of Reconstruction blacks were elected to many public offices, at no time did they control the Governors' offices, state legislatures, or Reconstruction politics.

Many black political leaders were educated men. Some were among the most distinguished figures in the entire South. Francis L. Cardozo, for example, South Carolina's state treasurer, held degrees from the universities of London and Glasgow, making him perhaps the best-educated politician in the South of either race.

Who were the Radicals in the South? They included many different groups. Some were Southerners, most of whom had been prewar Whigs or secret Union sympathizers during the war. Many Southern businessmen and even a few planters joined the Radicals. They hoped that the new governments would have enough help from Northern capitalists and Republican politicians to rebuild the South's shattered economy. Radicals

also included nonslaveholding farmers, who, while they disliked blacks, hated ex-Confederates even more for having led them into what they considered (at least after its loss) "a rich man's war and a poor man's fight." These Southern-born Radicals were called scalawags (an often undeserved term) by former Confederates.

Other Radicals were Northerners. Tens of thousands of them went south after the war for a variety of reasons. Hostile whites referred to them bitterly as carpetbaggers, whose only aim was to fill their luggage with ill-gotten Southern wealth. Yet many were teachers—their carpetbags stuffed only with McGuffey's Readers. Like the people who went to the Sea Islands, their aim was to set up schools for the freedmen. Northern soldiers returned to the South seeking good land; 5,000 went to Louisiana alone. Businessmen sought opportunities to invest capital and to profit from the region's economic reconstruction. A number of politically ambitious people did arrive to take part in the Radical governments. But they were by no means all opportunists.

Charges of Corruption   It has often been said that Radical state governments were corrupt. There is some truth to this charge. Legislators in South Carolina, for example, paid $200,000 for $18,000 worth of furniture for the state capitol. Louisiana's Radical governor H. C. Warmouth left the state with a personal fortune of half a million dollars, most of it acquired illegally. Similar fortunes were made throughout the South.

Several points should be noted in favor of the Radical governments, however. At this time scandals tainted the Grant administration and many Northern state and local governments. The historian John Hope Franklin has termed public dishonesty after the Civil War "bisectional, bipartisan, and biracial." (Actually, the blacks in Congress were not implicated in the Grant scandals, although many of their white colleagues were.) State governments everywhere ran up enormous debts. Postwar fortunes in the South were made by Radicals and ex-Confederates, Republicans and Democrats, alike. Given the level of immorality in American politics, North and South, during Reconstruction, it seems fair to say that the Radicals were no more corrupt than other politicians at the time.

In fact, most Radical state funds were spent rebuilding a ruined economy. Somehow, the Radicals managed to begin reconstructing Southern highways, railroads, hospitals, and orphanages. They also began building schools; many Southern states had had no public school system before the war. The rebuilding had to be done for an additional 3 1/2 million people. These were the ex-slaves, who were now citizens and entitled to the use of public facilities.

An Evaluation   Historians have long debated whether Radical state governments in the South ruled poorly or well. Opinions on this question depend in part on attitudes about whether (or when) blacks should have been allowed the franchise and a role in governing. We tend to forget how short a time Radical governments actually ruled. Tennessee never underwent this type of control. Virginia, North Carolina, and Georgia had returned to conservative hands by 1871. Arkansas, Alabama, and Texas had done so by 1874. And it was all over by 1877.

Some provisions of the Radical state constitutions found approval even among ex-Confederates. The documents ended imprisonment for debt, for example, and did away with property qualifications for voting. Basically, ex-Confederate whites objected less to the corruption of Radical state governments than to their very existence — especially to the presence of blacks on the political slate. Radical rule did not end because of its failure to meet the economic and social problems of the South. Radicals were driven from power because of their insistence on meeting these problems through biracial political cooperation.

THE END OF RADICAL RULE

Two trends put an end to Radical Reconstruction. One was the increasing hostility of white Southerners. The other was the growing indifference of its Northern Republican sponsors.

Southern hostility not only increased, but it grew more violent. Thousands of blacks and white Radicals lost their lives to armed bands of whites such as the Ku Klux Klan and local "rifle clubs" that roamed the South during the 1870s. Federal troops and black state militia could suppress only a small number of these groups. Congress passed several Force Bills, making it a national offense to interfere with any citizen's civil rights (including his right to vote). But they had little effect, since only a few thousand federal troops remained in the South to enforce the laws against guerrilla groups like the Klan. To compound the Radicals' problem, Congress repealed its ironclad oath in 1871. No longer did Southerners have to swear

Louisiana was one of five Southern states to have a majority of black voters. Between 1868 and 1896 the state had 133 black legislators—38 senators and 95 representatives. They were never numerous or strong enough to control political life in Louisiana, though Oscar Dunn (center) did lead a struggle against corruption and extravagance.

Reconstructionist efforts to ensure black civil and political rights were undercut economically by the rapid emergence of sharecropping. Devoid of financial resources to buy their own land, many freedmen began to work the farms of landowners, who, also short of cash, paid them for their labor with a "share" of the crop. Soon indebted to landowners for such costs as rent, provisions, and tools, sharecroppers often became tied down by debt, as securely as they had been held by slavery.

that they had always been loyal to the Union. In 1872 a general amnesty restored civil rights (including the right to hold office) to all but about 600 high Confederate officials.

As white terrorists harassed the remaining Radical state governments, Northerners became indifferent. Republicans in Washington grew increasingly weary of the struggle to protect black civil rights. "The whole public," complained President Grant, "is tired of these outbreaks in the South."

The death or retirement of such Radical leaders as Stevens and Sumner helped restore control of Congress to more conservative, business-minded Republicans. A combination of Democrats and reform-minded "Liberal Republicans" nearly won the presidency in 1872 on a platform pledging an end to federal support for Radical regimes in the South. In 1874 the Democrats regained control of the House for the first time since before the war.

Public attention strayed even further away from the South after 1873, when a major depression swept the country. The business slump threw hundreds of thousands out of work and shifted political attention from postwar Reconstruction to the problem of economic recovery.

The Compromise of 1877   In 1876 both presidential candidates, Republican Rutherford B. Hayes and Democrat Samuel B. Tilden, promised even before the election to restore "home rule" to the South. Both pledged to remove federal support for the three remaining Radical state governments—those of Louisiana, South Carolina, and Florida. They implied that Southern whites could now

The violence of new vigilante groups, such as the Knights of the Ku Klux Klan, contributed to the overthrow of Republican rule and the demise of Reconstruction. A secret, terrorist society, the Klan formed in 1867 to restore white supremacy by harassing Reconstructionists, intimidating black voters, forcing black officials into resignation, and depriving freedmen of their rights. The tactics of the Klan ranged from pressure, ostracism, and bribery, to arson, beatings, and murder.

handle all problems connected with blacks, including political rights.

The election ended in a unique stalemate. Two sets of returns arrived from the three states yet in Radical hands. The Radicals claimed that Hayes had won, while Democrats insisted on a Tilden majority. The nineteen doubtful electoral votes (including one disputed Oregon elector) meant the difference between a one-vote Hayes margin and a clear Tilden sweep. Congress finally accepted the recommendation of a specially appointed commission to award all the disputed votes to Hayes, thereby making him President. The South, in turn, received a pledge from Hayes that all remaining federal troops would be removed from the three Radical states, that federal subsidies would be provided for a Southern transcontinental railroad then under construction, and

that a Southerner would be appointed to the cabinet.

All these promises were met, and Radical rule promptly collapsed in the three remaining states. This so-called Compromise of 1877 marked the final surrender of the North's promise to defend black political and civil rights against the former white Confederates.

During the decades that followed, conservative governments defeated black efforts to participate in Southern politics. In every subsequent election fewer blacks voted.

Violence toward black people increased for the rest of the century. The great majority of Southern blacks farmed other people's lands as tenants or sharecroppers. They were forced into a subordinate place in Southern life, being neither slaves nor completely free men.

SUGGESTED READINGS–CHAPTERS 23-24

Sherman's March

T. H. Williams, *McClellan, Sherman, and Grant* (1962); K. P. Williams, *Lincoln Finds a General: A Military History of the Civil War* (4 vols., 1949–1956); Lloyd Lewis, *Sherman, Fighting Prophet* (1932).

The Civil War

Mark M. Boatner, III, *The Civil War Dictionary* (1959); Bruce Catton, *Centennial History of the Civil War* (3 vols., 1961–1963); David Donald, ed., *Why the North Won the Civil War* (1960); Clement Eaton, *A History of the Southern Confederacy* (1954); Shelby Foote, *The Civil War* (3 vols., 1958–1974); George Frederickson, *The Inner Civil War* (1965); Paul W. Gates, *Agriculture and the Civil War* (1965); David T. Gilchrust and W. David Lewis, eds., *Economic Change in the Civil War Era* (1965); Harold M. Hyman, *A More Perfect Union: The Impact of the Civil War and Reconstruction on the Constitution* (1973); Mary E. Massey, *Bonnet Brigades: American Women and the Civil War* (1966); James M. McPherson, *The Negro's Civil War* (1965) and *The Struggle for Equality: Abolitionists and the Negro in the Civil War and Reconstruction* (1964); Allan Nevins, *The War for the Union* (4 vols., 1959–1971); Peter J. Parish, *The American Civil War* (1975); J. G. Randall and Richard Current, *Lincoln the President* (4 vols., 1945–1955); J. G. Randall and David Donald, *The Civil War and Reconstruction* (2nd ed., 1961); Benjamin P. Thomas, *Abraham Lincoln* (1952); Emory Thomas, *The Confederacy as a Revolutionary Experience* (1971); Frank Vandiver, *Their Tattered Flags* (1970); Kenneth P. Williams, *Lincoln Finds a General* (5 vols., 1949–1959).

Reconstruction

W. R. Brock, *An American Crisis* (1963); Robert Cruden, *The Negro in Reconstruction* (1969); John Hope Franklin, *Reconstruction After the Civil War* (1962); Rembert W. Patrick, *The Reconstruction of the Nation* (1964); Kenneth M. Stampp, *The Era of Reconstruction, 1865–1877* (1965); Hans L. Trefousse, *Impeachment of a President* (1975); C. Vann Woodward, *Reunion and Reaction: The Compromise of 1877 and the End of Reconstruction* (1951).

UNIT FIVE

INDUSTRIAL AMERICA

Americans thought about their Civil War in many different ways. But most of them agreed, North and South, that it was somehow a conservative war. Each side thought of itself as the conserving protector of an inherited social and political order. It was difficult for Americans to understand that what lay ahead was not a restoration of stability but a surprising burst of activity and change. The United States was transformed into a modern industrial nation in the last third of the nineteenth century. That transformation is the subject of Unit Five.

The examination, in Chapter 25, of the career of President James A. Garfield and of his assassination in 1881 by a crazed, disappointed office-seeker introduces the climate of political tensions. Chapter 26 then traces the conditions that made political careers such as Garfield's possible.

In an odd way, the people who could best have understood the revolutionary transformations of American society were those who had been most completely defeated by it: the American Indians. From the time of Jamestown, they had watched white society grow in size and power. Now, the forces of expansion increased dramatically. Railroads, miners, cattle ranchers, and farmers spilled out over the Great Plains to the Pacific Coast with fresh speed and energy.

One of the tribes that felt the forces of westward expansion most directly was the Sioux. By the close of the century, this determined people had been reduced from proud independence to reservation captivity. The destruction of their way of life reached a symbolic climax in 1890 in the battle involving Indians and United States soldiers in American American history—Wounded Knee. The defeat of the Sioux is the subject of Chapter 27. The following chapter dis-

cusses the larger process of white expansion that made their final conquest inevitable.

At the same time that postwar America was expanding geographically, a new economic landscape took shape. New inventions and manufacturing processes changed the ways that Americans earned their livings and made their goods. Giant factories in enormous cities with great immigrant and working-class populations arose. With them came the inevitable conflicts between rich and poor, employers and workers, immigrants and native Americans.

One of the most important examples of conflict was a series of events in Chicago in 1885 and 1886. It began with a labor strike at the McCormick Harvester Company, led to a famous bombing incident at Haymarket Square, and ended in the trial and execution of several immigrant German Americans.

Chapter 29 tells this story and Chapter 30 explores the background of industrialization that made the conflict possible.

Social and economic change created strains on political parties and governmental institutions, which resulted in a curious blend of politics. On the one hand the politics of the 1890s was intense in nature and characterized by close electoral contests, while on the other it was extraordinarily flat and lacking in any real economic or social significance. The emergence and failure of Populism is discussed in Chapters 31 and 32.

What comes through, then, from the late nineteenth century is a mixed picture of incredible industrial growth and geographical expansion alongside moments of crisis and bloodshed—with political leaders looking on as almost helpless and often confused spectators.

25
THE ASSASSINATION
OF GARFIELD

A.W.

On the morning of July 2, 1881, the President of the United States, James Abram Garfield, was strolling toward a waiting train in a railroad depot in Washington. The train, scheduled to depart at 9:30 A.M., was to take him on the first leg of a trip to Williams College, his alma mater. There he was to address a class reunion and enroll his two sons. Walking alongside the President and chatting with him was the secretary of state, James G. Blaine, a close political associate and friend. Already inside the train were Garfield's two sons and other members of his cabinet.

The President and the secretary of state walked toward the train platform. Neither noticed a thin, bearded figure dressed in shabby and unpressed clothing, staring at them from a few feet away. The two men broke off their conversation for a moment and prepared to step aboard the train.

Suddenly the man who had been watching them drew a pistol from his pocket. He pointed it at the President and fired twice. Garfield fell to the ground, crying out only "My God!" before he fainted. Blood spurted onto his gray traveling suit.

At the sound of the shots, Blaine had lunged toward the assassin. But when he saw the President lying on the ground, he quickly returned to his side. Along with others who had reached the scene, Blaine raised the wounded man's head. Garfield regained consciousness almost immediately.

Garfield's two sons and the cabinet members rushed from the train to join the crowd of onlookers. Some railroad workers gently lifted the heavy-set man and placed him on a ragged mattress, brought hastily from a nearby room. The first physician to arrive was Dr. Smith Townsend, the District of Columbia health officer. The doctor assumed from Garfield's appearance that the chief executive was dying. Townsend

New York Herald facsimile:

SCENE OF THE ASSASSINATION.

Map of Washington Showing Location of the Baltimore and Potomac Railroad Depot.

SHOT DOWN.

President Garfield Dangerously Wounded.

AN ASSASSIN'S WORK.

Fired at Entering the Railroad Depot at Washington.

THE SERIOUS HIP WOUND.

Carried in an Ambulance to the White House.

CHEERFUL IN THE FACE OF DEATH.

Grave Symptoms Succeeded by a More Hopeful Condition.

A STRONG MAN'S STRUGGLE

Arrest and Imprisonment of the Criminal.

CHARLES JULES GUITEAU.

An Erratic Creature of Low Antecedents—His Strange History.

MRS. GARFIELD'S SORROW

She Reaches Washington and Meets Her Husband.

After less than six months in office President Garfield was shot by a disgruntled office seeker, Charles Guiteau, as Secretary of State James G. Blaine looked on. Though the President was in a public place, he had no Secret Service protection.

gave the injured man aromatic spirits of ammonia and some brandy to ease his pain. Then he inspected the more serious of the two wounds Garfield had received—the one on the lower right side of his back. Garfield winced. The doctor's touch had reopened the wound. Townsend's face and manner remained grim but, somewhat mechanically, he assured Garfield that his back wound was not serious. "I thank you, doctor," replied Garfield in evident pain, "but I am a dead man."

After firing the shots, the assassin calmly returned the pistol to his pocket. Then, as anxious and curious spectators surrounded the bleeding President, he rushed toward a railway station exit. Just as he reached it, the exit's massive door burst open. The man who had shot the President found himself face to face with Patrick Kearney, a District of Columbia patrolman. Kearney had been running toward the sound of the shots. In an attempt to flee past the policeman, the slender, dark-complexioned figure mumbled in an excited voice, "I have a letter to send to General Sherman."[1]

Kearney, sensing that the agitated man was somehow connected with the earlier pistol cracks and the crowd now gathering on the platform, held onto him. Several railroad employees raced to the exit and reported that the President had been shot. The policeman then rushed his prisoner away from the scene. As they left the station, the man finally spoke, saying: "I did it. I will go to jail for it; [Vice President] Arthur is President."

When Kearney reached the police station, his fellow officers would not believe that Garfield had been shot. It took a few minutes before they accepted the patrolman's story. Kearney himself, still excited over having captured the man who had tried to kill the President, did not even take possession of the prisoner's gun until they had reached the stationhouse. For that matter, only then did the patrolman think to ask the assassin his name. The prisoner reached into his pocket, withdrew a small printed calling card, and handed it to Kearney, who stared at the name and address: Charles Guiteau, Chicago, Ill.

The President, meanwhile, had been carried to a police ambulance, which rushed him back to the White House. There he was placed in a second-floor bedroom. Dozens of physicians, family members, government officials, and well-wishers scurried about the sickroom for the remainder of the day. A horde of newspapermen also managed to reach the sickroom door. They pestered each visitor to the President's bedside for fresh news of his condition.

The physicians all agreed that Garfield's back wound was too serious to allow immediate removal of the bullet. They felt they could do nothing but give the President large doses of morphine to dull his pain. Their frequent bulletins to the waiting reporters seldom varied in con-

---

[1]William Tecumseh Sherman was then commanding general of the American army.

tent: "The President's wounds are grave. He remains pale, weak, and cold. Although he is not bleeding profusely *externally*, there is every chance of massive *internal* hemorrhaging."

To doctors and reporters alike, this meant only one thing: the President was dying. Several members of Garfield's cabinet joined his family and physicians in the sickroom. Together they waited for further developments throughout the long night. At one point the secretary of war walked out into the corridor for a breath of air. He turned to a reporter and said: "How many hours of sorrow I have passed in this town." With this remark, Robert Todd Lincoln, Abraham Lincoln's son, reentered the sickroom.

Garfield's spirits, and his condition, improved greatly once his wife reached his bedside. She had been recuperating in New Jersey, following a malarial infection, but hurried to rejoin her husband on receiving word of the shooting. A special train brought her to Washington. Arriving at the White House in the early evening, she spent a few minutes alone with Garfield. Then she stationed herself outside his sickroom, praying and waiting for news. The President, after being told that she had gone to bed, fell asleep himself.

An hour later Garfield awoke. He turned to the attending physician, D. W. Bliss, who had taken charge of his treatment, and asked about

The public's view of Garfield as a homespun, simple man was reinforced by the fact that he was "the last of the log cabin Presidents." This painting of his birthplace in Orange, Ohio, gives us a nostalgic view of the pure and pastoral life of Garfield's youth.

his chances for recovery. He told the physician, as Dr. Bliss later remembered, "that he desired a frank and full statement, that he was prepared to die and feared not to learn the worst." Dr. Bliss, somewhat less than frank, replied: "Mr. President, your injury is formidable [but] in my judgment you have a chance for recovery." Garfield smiled and, placing his hand upon the doctor's arm, answered simply: "Well, doctor, we will take that chance." The warmth, good humor, and optimism that had characterized James Abram Garfield throughout his rise to the presidency did not desert him during this final struggle for life.

Garfield's rise to the presidency parallels the success story of several other nineteenth-century American Presidents. He was a man of humble origins and, like President Lincoln before him, had the good sense to be born in a log cabin. The log cabin had become the American symbol of homespun integrity and was therefore very useful to budding politicians.

Garfield, who was born in Ohio in 1831, was a seventh-generation American. His ancestors came to Massachusetts Bay with John Winthrop. His father was a pioneer Ohio farmer who died when Garfield was two. His mother, Eliza, raised the future President and three other children in bitter rural poverty.

As a boy, Garfield worked at a variety of jobs, helping to support his mother while striving to earn an education. After graduating from a neighboring school called Western Reserve Eclectic Institute (later changed to Hiram Institute), Garfield worked his way through Williams College in Massachusetts. He graduated from there in 1856. Returning to Ohio, Garfield served first as a teacher and then—though still in his twenties—as principal of Hiram Institute. In 1858 he married Lucretia Rudolph, his childhood sweetheart.

Throughout the 1850s Garfield exhibited the talents that were later to win him high political office. In 1859 he ran for, and won, the Republican seat in the Ohio senate. He made friends easily, worked furiously, displayed great tact and an ability to compromise, took few extreme positions, and—above all—sought to please. When the Civil War began, the young state legislator organized a volunteer infantry regiment composed largely of his former students. Although he had no previous military experience, he mastered the appropriate army training manuals quickly and well.

Colonel Garfield's regiment was assigned to the Union army command in Kentucky. There it defeated a much larger force of Confederate soldiers at the Battle of Middle Creek in January 1862. This victory earned Garfield the rank of brigadier general. After fighting at the Battle of Shiloh, he had to leave the field because of poor health. When he returned to active duty in 1863, he served with distinction during the important Battle of Chickamauga. Garfield left the army in December of 1863 with the rank of major general. He had been elected to the House of Representatives that fall.

Garfield was then thirty-two and extremely popular in Ohio's

Western Reserve district. This area returned him to Congress seven more times. His skill as a legislative leader and orator quickly made him a leading Republican in the House. So great was his personal popularity that Ohio voters reelected him despite the fact that they did not agree with him on many issues.

Garfield, like all successful officeholders, quickly learned the skill of political survival: when to speak out on an important question, when to blur an issue, and when to remain silent. During Hayes's administration Garfield's talent for bringing together different viewpoints within the Republican party led to his selection as House minority leader. Early in 1880 he was elected by the Ohio legislature to a six-year Senate term. But he never filled this seat.

It was in that year that the Republicans held their convention to nominate a presidential candidate. They were bitterly divided among three leading contenders—former President Ulysses S. Grant, Senator John Sherman of Ohio, and Senator James G. Blaine of Maine. There was a three-way deadlock on thirty-four ballots. On the thirty-fifth a break occurred. Garfield's name was put forward as a compromise candidate. On the thirty-sixth, Garfield, who had gone to the convention as Sherman's campaign manager, emerged with his party's nomination for President.

Blaine quickly became a close political ally. Sherman remained cordial, if untrusting. Grant's managers (particularly the influential New York Senator Roscoe Conkling) never forgave Garfield, despite the fact that Chester A. Arthur, Conkling's colleague from New York, was chosen to be Garfield's running mate. Garfield and Conkling did eventually smooth over their differences, and the Republicans carried a close election with a popular plurality of only 10,000 votes. James Garfield, a mild-mannered and unforceful politician, became President of the United States.

During his years in Congress, Garfield and his family had lived modestly. When Congress was in session, they stayed in Washington. At other times they made their home in Mentor, Ohio, a small agricultural town on Lake Erie, twenty-five miles from Cleveland. They had a farm there, which they called Lawnfield. Garfield enjoyed the farm work and rural way of life. He left Mentor for the last time in 1881, for Washington and his inauguration. The letters he wrote during his few months as Chief Executive show that he often yearned to return to the peaceful isolation of Lawnfield.

Although Garfield had been a professional politican for more than twenty years, by the time he entered the White House, he retained an avid interest in cultural matters. This interest, no doubt, was a carry-over from his days as a student, teacher, and college principal. Throughout his adult life he corresponded with some of the country's leading men of letters and reformers.

But Garfield himself was not a reformer. Throughout his legislative career he allied himself with railroad, industrial, and other estab-

The Republicans' compromise candidate of 1880, dark-horse nominee James A. Garfield (shown here as a young man).

lished interests. He expressed skepticism about reforms dealing with woman suffrage, contempt for proposals to assist the Indians, and indifference toward efforts to aid blacks. Above all, Garfield was a party "regular"—a politician whose primary concern was advancing his own fortunes and those of his party.

Garfield did not know that one of the proposals he ignored would eventually mark him for an assassin's bullet. The issue was civil-service reform, which advocated filling government posts by qualifying tests rather than by political appointment. Some minor steps toward such reform were taken by Garfield's predecessor in the White House, Rutherford B. Hayes. But Garfield let the matter drop when he became President.

Instead, he put up with the hundreds who came weekly to the Executive Mansion in search of government jobs. True, they annoyed him. Daily he was besieged by a "band of disciplined office hunters who drew papers on me as highwaymen draw pistols."[2] One of these constant job-seeking visitors to the White House who "drew papers," on the President was a forty-year-old Chicago lawyer, bill collector, and itinerant preacher named Charles Julius Guiteau.

Charles Julius Guiteau's life was an interesting contrast to that of James Abram Garfield. Garfield had married happily and raised a family. His efforts as student, educator, soldier, and politican were all rewarded. The President remained secure in his early religious beliefs. He numbered among his friends and admirers not only the most powerful people in America but also many of its intellectuals. The road from log cabin to White House had been, by and large, a smooth one that he traveled with outer serenity and inner contentment. Garfield represented, for many of his generation, living proof of the continued American formula for achievement: personal integrity plus hard work plus trained intelligence yield success and happiness.

Both the personal life and public career of Charles Guiteau had been marked by frustration and failure. He was born the fourth of six children on September 8, 1841, in Freeport, Illinois. Jane Howe Guiteau, his mother, died when he was seven. The boy was raised by his father, Luther Wilson Guiteau, a Freeport bank official and religious disciple of John Humphrey Noyes.[3] Charles was usually cared for by his older sister, Frances, who maintained an interest in the boy's welfare even after her marriage to George Scoville, a Chicago lawyer.

Guiteau, like Garfield, worked extremely hard as a young man, helping his father at the bank and tending to family chores. Both young men were enthusiastic Republicans; both were physical- and mental-fitness buffs; and both dreamed of eventual success. But the quarrels between the young Guiteau and his domineering father were frequent

---

[2]White House security measures were not as strict then as they are now. Visitors were free to come and go, so that they might well run into the President as he was walking elsewhere in the Executive Mansion.

[3]John Humphrey Noyes was the founder of the Oneida Community, an experimental communal colony in upstate New York.

and stormy. In 1859, the same year that Garfield became principal of Hiram Institute, Guiteau decided to leave Freeport to seek his fortune.

The first goal he set for himself was that of obtaining a college education. Guiteau went to the university college at Ann Arbor, Michigan, where he attempted to register. But the teachers there asked that he first train for university work by enrolling at a Michigan preparatory school. Lonely, lacking funds, and keenly feeling his lack of academic preparation, Guiteau turned to religion for solace. Not surprisingly, he became interested in his zealous father's faith, the teachings of John Humphrey Noyes. In June of 1860, Guiteau left Ann Arbor to join the Oneida Community.

The Oneida Community, like other utopian settlements in mid-nineteenth-century America, was based upon religious fellowship and the principle that both work and worldly goods would be shared. Guiteau was no happier at Oneida than he had been in Ann Arbor. He was unpopular among other members of the community. Neither then, nor at any other point in Charles Guiteau's life, did he manage to keep a single close friend. A bad-tempered, solitary, and nervous figure, he often came under attack for selfishness and conceit at the community's important mutual-criticism sessions. In 1865 Guiteau left the community.

For the next fifteen years Guiteau's life consisted mainly of a series of career failures. He constantly borrowed from family members, was always in debt, and often ran away to escape arrest. He flitted back and forth between New York City and Chicago (where his sister lived). Hoping and expecting some great new career—which would be achieved instantly—Guiteau generally found himself teetering on the edge of despair.

Guiteau tried a succession of enterprises. After leaving the Oneida Community, he tried to found a religious newspaper. But he failed. He spent a short time in 1867 as a subscription and ad salesman for the Reverend Henry Ward Beecher's influential weekly paper, the *Independent*. He soon gave up the post. Then he spent a year threatening a lawsuit against Noyes and his other former brethren at the the Oneida Community. He tried to blackmail them into paying him $9,000. Otherwise, he threatened to publicize the colony's controversial sexual practices.[4] Guiteau's own father denounced his son publicly for this betrayal of Oneida. Guiteau finally stopped his abusive letters to Noyes after the latter threatened to prosecute him.

Guiteau next moved to Chicago, where he apprenticed in a law office. He was admitted to the Illinois bar in 1868. He made only one appearance as a trial lawyer. Inevitably, he lost the case. After this, his legal practice consisted almost entirely of bill collecting, a trade he followed with little success until 1875.

In 1869 Guiteau had married an eighteen-year-old girl, Anne Bunn. The union lasted five turbulent years, during which he often beat

---

[4]The community held that traditional marriage and family patterns bred selfishness and, thereby, many evils in society. Therefore, monogamy was banned, and children were cared for by the entire community.

his wife severely and sometimes even locked her in a closet overnight. In 1874 his wife divorced him.

By then, Guiteau had acquired a reputation as a sleazy and dishonest bill collector. He served a brief jail sentence in 1875 for petty fraud and abruptly, that same year, shifted his career plans once more. The penniless lawyer now announced plans to raise $200,000 in order to purchase a Chicago newspaper. Attempts to borrow the money failed miserably. Guiteau retreated to his family again. During a visit to his sister Frances, he threatened her with an ax. A physician who examined Guiteau after this incident recommended that he be placed in an insane asylum. Guiteau fled.

Now Guiteau adopted yet another vocation. He became an itinerant preacher and wandered across the country, selling religious pamphlets and preaching a version of John Humphrey Noyes's theology. Apparently Guiteau earned almost no money between 1875 and 1881. Yet somehow he managed to survive on the misplaced trust of creditors.

Charles Guiteau truly believed that Garfield's death was a necessity that would unite the Republican party and save the Republic. He claimed that the idea had come to him under "divine pressure."

In 1880 a new vision of success appeared to Guiteau. This time it was a political one. He wrote an incoherent pro-Garfield essay and had it privately printed. Then he attached himself to the Republicans' New York City campaign headquarters. There he became one of the many unwanted and unused hangers-on. Though he did nothing to bring it about, Guiteau viewed Garfield's election as a personal triumph. He immediately began making plans to apply for a high post in the diplomatic corps.

Guiteau wrote several letters to Garfield and other important Republican leaders, in pursuance of his plan. In them he asserted his importance in the party's New York victory and requested assignment to various foreign ministries. Eventually, he decided on the Paris consulship. He moved to Washington—one jump ahead of his creditors—to press this claim.

During the early months of Garfield's presidency, from March to June 1881, Guiteau became a familiar face at the White House and in the State Department corridors. He pestered Garfield and Blaine about the Paris post at every chance, by letter and even in person (when he managed to push his way through). "Never bother me again about the Paris consulship so long as you live," Blaine shouted at the pesky figure after one such May encounter. By then, Guiteau had decided that Blaine was a "wicked man." He demanded Blaine's dismissal in notes to Garfield that became increasingly intimate in tone. A new scheme for glory now began to hatch in Guiteau's crazed mind: a plan to murder the President.

Guiteau was not familiar with firearms. As his obsession grew more vivid, he purchased a revolver and practiced shooting on the banks of the Potomac. He took to following the President and observing his daily routine. On several occasions prior to the fateful day he came close to executing his scheme, only to back down at the last minute. By shooting Garfield, his odd reasoning ran, not only would his political friends be raised to power but he too would share in it.

Finally, on July 2, 1881, Charles Julius Guiteau, a man whose life had epitomized failure, managed to carry out the last of his innumerable schemes. He shot the President. Guiteau later acknowledged:

> I have had an idea [since my youth] that I should be President, and it has never left me. When I left Boston for New York, in June 1880 [to campaign for Garfield], I felt that I was on my way to the White House. My idea is that I shall be nominated and elected as Lincoln and Garfield were—that is, by the act of God.

Many blamed Garfield's opponents among the Republican party's Stalwart wing[5] (somewhat unfairly) for having allowed the assassin even a minor place within their ranks in New York during the 1880 campaign. Some even blamed Vice President Arthur. Until Garfield selected him as a running mate, Arthur had been a loyal associate of the country's leading Stalwart, Senator Roscoe Conkling of New York. Arthur remained loyal to Conkling despite his new responsibilities as Vice President.

In May 1881, Garfield insisted on appointing an anti-Conkling Republican to an important patronage post—Customs Collector for the Port of New York. Conkling and his New York Stalwart colleague, Thomas C. Platt, both resigned from the Senate. Arthur supported their decision. Conkling and Platt hoped, by resigning, to put pressure on their Senate colleagues to reject the President's nominee on the grounds of "senatorial courtesy." They planned to win Senate reelection from the New York state legislature and then to return to Washington with added power. This was the dispute between Garfield and the Stalwarts that Guiteau claimed had triggered his decision to kill the President.

In the end, Conkling and Platt lost the struggle—and their power. The two were brought down in July 1881 by Conkling's personal arrogance and an ill-timed peek over an Albany hotel transom by a political opponent, who found Platt in the company of a prostitute. Platt withdrew from the contest the same day that Garfield was shot, in order not to hurt Conkling's chances. It was no use. Neither man gained reelection. Thus, ironically, Garfield had begun to win his struggle against Conkling for control of the Republican party at the very moment he was cut down by a maddened office seeker claiming to be a Stalwart.

Garfield himself never blamed his political opponents for the shooting. Garfield also forgave his Vice President for supporting Conkling's reelection bid. During Garfield's struggle to recover from the shooting, Arthur remained at his New York City home, grief stricken and withdrawn from public notice. Garfield turned the daily management of government over to his cabinet. The rumors of a Stalwart conspiracy guiding Guiteau's hand quickly died away.

The wounded President lingered between life and death for seventy-nine days. He remained in his second-floor sickroom, only rarely

Roscoe Conkling, head of the Stalwarts, was a political boss who believed that "parties were not built by deportment or gush." He ruined his political career in an attempt to thwart Garfield's policies.

Senator Thomas C. Platt, a faithful political crony of Roscoe Conkling, followed his lead in resigning from the Senate. Promptly dubbed "Me Too" Platt, his loyalty cost him his Senate seat.

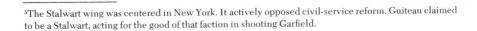

---

[5]The Stalwart wing was centered in New York. It actively opposed civil-service reform. Guiteau claimed to be a Stalwart, acting for the good of that faction in shooting Garfield.

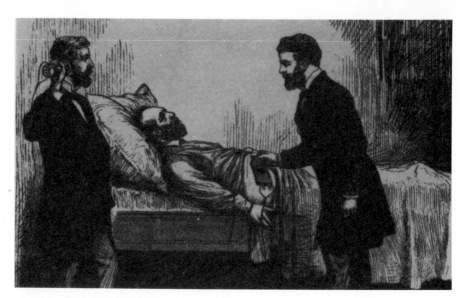

A reproduction of a contemporary sketch shows two doctors attempting to discover the location of the bullet in Garfield's body through the use of a strange telegraphlike apparatus. They never succeeded in removing the bullet.

writing official dispatches or dealing with government business. Doctors, medical consultants, and free advice poured into the White House to assist in the President's treatment. But the bullet remained lodged in his back while physicians continued their painful probing. Nothing seemed to help.

At first the President's condition improved. But a mid-July rally turned into a late-July decline. In Washington's sweltering summer heat, Garfield ran a fever that only occasionally broke. His normally robust 200-pound frame had shrunk to 120 pounds by late August. When early September brought a record heat wave, the doctors decided to move Garfield to the cooler temperatures of his oceanside summer house at Elberon, New Jersey. He was carried there by special train on September 6, but his condition continued to deteriorate. Still, almost at the end, his spirits remained good. He even tried to cheer those around him.

On the night of September 19, with only an old friend, Captain D. G. Swain, and one servant attending him, Garfield's final agony began. He awoke suddenly, clutched his heart, and cried out, "How it hurts here!" Swain handed the President a glass of water, but it failed to help. The President cried: "Swain, can't you stop this?" Then Garfield fell into a coma. Within moments Dr. Bliss and Mrs. Garfield entered the room. Mrs. Garfield sat down calmly and held her husband's hand. But the strain was too much, and she had to leave the room. Dr. Bliss remained with his patient for a few minutes, then walked quietly to a nearby study and wrote in his medical log: "Applying my ear over the heart, I detected an indistinct fluttering that continued until 10:35 when he expired. The brave and heroic sufferer, the nation's patient, has passed away."

The waiting had ended; the grieving began. Garfield's seventy-nine days of suffering before death, borne with stoic dignity, made the slain President a hero in the eyes of his countrymen. His body was brought back to Washington on September 21 to lie in state in the Capitol rotunda. Thousands — Southerners and Northerners, Democrats and Republicans alike — filed past to pay their last respects. The world's rulers also mourned. The President's widow received condolence messages from Queen Victoria of England; the emperors of China, Russia, and Japan; the kings of Belgium, Italy, and Spain; the Pope; and the sultan of Turkey.

American advocates of civil-service reform found an obvious moral in Garfield's assassination by a disappointed office seeker. Throughout his long death agony, reformers organized countless meetings protesting the spoils system and demanding government appointments based on merit alone. "Garfield dead," one historian later wrote, "proved more valuable to reformers than Garfield alive."

The great majority of Americans, however, mourned Garfield's passing more sincerely. On September 23 a special train carried the President's casket from Washington to Cleveland for burial. Crowds lined the entire route to honor the dead President, just as sixteen years earlier throngs had wept as Lincoln's funeral train followed a similar route from the East back to Illinois. Some 250,000 people from throughout the Midwest jammed Cleveland's streets for Garfield's funeral ceremony. Thousands of tributes — sermons, memorial leaflets, and letters — reached his widow at their Mentor home. The nation's grief seemed remarkably intense, considering the fact that Garfield, unlike Lincoln, had not been a war leader. Moreover he had held the highest office in the nation for only a few months.

In New York, Walt Whitman heard of the President's death. In his journal he wrote some lines that expressed the genuine sorrow of most of his less eloquent countrymen:

The sobbing of the bells, the sudden death-news everywhere,
The slumberers rouse, the rapport of the People,
(Full well they know that message in the darkness,
Full well return, respond within their breasts, their brains, the sad
     reverberations,)
The passionate toll and clang — city to city, joining, sounding, passing,
Those heart-beats of a Nation in the night.

Another New Yorker also recoiled at the awful news that evening. At Chester Alan Arthur's house the bell rang at midnight. A reporter informed the servant who answered the door that Garfield had died. "Oh, no, it cannot be true," cried Arthur, who overheard the news. "It cannot be. I have heard nothing." His face was pale, and he was crying. When the reporter persisted, Arthur could say only "I hope — My God, I do hope it is a mistake."

The man who had just become President turned and walked back to his study, where a small group of silent friends now waited. The bell rang again, and a messenger handed Arthur a telegram sent by a number of Garfield's cabinet members. It confirmed the President's death and advised Arthur to take the oath of office immediately. Arthur's friends rushed out to find a judge who could administer the oath. Someone checked it for the exact wording. Within minutes a state supreme court justice, roused from his bed, administered the oath of office to the Vice President. The next morning President Chester A. Arthur left for Washington.

On September 20, two days after Garfield's death, his assassin sent a letter to Chester Arthur. He wrote, "My inspiration is a godsend to you, and I presume you appreciate it. It raises you from $8,000 to $50,000 a year. It raises you from a political cipher to President of the United States with all its power and honors. For the Cabinet I would suggest as follows. . . ." President Arthur never answered the letter. Instead, he ordered Guiteau tried promptly. He personally helped select the prosecuting attorneys.

Guiteau, however, still seemed convinced that the Stalwarts would somehow rescue and reward him. His confidence waned, though, as the trial date neared. He continued to deny responsibility for the killing. He insisted that divine inspiration made him pull the trigger. "I am here as God's man, and don't you forget it." No independent lawyer would touch the case, despite a newspaper appeal for such assistance. When the trial began on November 14, 1881, Guiteau's brother-in-law, George Scoville, served as defense counsel.

Lines between the defense and prosecution arguments were drawn clearly from the start. Scoville argued that his client was an insane

This caricature of Garfield's assassin shows some of his crazed intensity of purpose. We can easily believe that he wrote: "I presume the President was a Christian and that he will be happier in Paradise than here."

religious fanatic and therefore could not be held legally responsible for his actions. Furthermore, the defense insisted that Garfield's wounds were not necessarily mortal. The President had died, Scoville claimed, only because of incompetent medical treatment after the shooting.

Both defense arguments had merit, although the prosecution, of course, denied them. It insisted that Guiteau, although morally evil, had killed the President while in complete possession of his faculties. He had done so for calculated political motives — namely, as a malicious and disappointed job seeker.

The case against Guiteau, then, centered on the question of his sanity. Both prosecution and defense attorneys presented "expert" medical testimony to prove their respective contentions. A majority of the doctors who had examined Guiteau found the prisoner sane within the prevailing legal definitions of sanity, which were far broader than those of today. Guiteau demonstrated his unbalanced mental state by frequently interrupting the trial to shout abusive statements at everyone, including his own lawyer. He continued to claim divine inspiration.

The prosecution argued that such outbursts were merely a cynical act by Guiteau, who was trying to portray himself as mad. Apparently the jury also believed this. It took only a half-hour on January 25, 1882, to find Guiteau guilty of murder. The prisoner vented his anger by shrieking: "My blood will be upon the heads of [this] jury. God will avenge this outrage." One doctor who had observed the trial daily, George M. Beard, a noted psychologist, disagreed strongly with the jury's decision. Beard later wrote:

> The physicians called in to make a diagnosis mistook the symptoms of insanity for the symptoms of wickedness. [This] error is quite as natural for nonexperts in insanity in our time as that of the village physician of Salem, Dr. Griggs, in witchcraft times, in attributing insanity to possession by the devil.

Nevertheless, on February 3, Judge Walter Cox sentenced Guiteau to hang.

Before sentencing, Guiteau addressed the court a final time. He insisted again that Garfield's killing had been "God's act, not mine." He compared his fate to Christ's and threatened bloody divine vengeance on the United States if he hung. In the months before his execution the condemned man continued to believe that President Arthur would issue a last-minute reprieve or pardon.

Finally, Guiteau recognized the reality ahead of him. Four days before his death, while in his cell, he scrawled a "Scene between the Almighty and my murderers." In this imaginary scene God confronts Guiteau's persecutors, including President Arthur, and condemns them along with the entire American nation. A few days later, on June 30, 1882, Charles Guiteau was hung. He went to the scaffold, fighting back tears and singing a childlike hymn he had written especially for the occasion. Then he gave a final shout: "Glory hallelujah! I am with the Lord. Glory, ready, go!"

26 POLITICS IN TRANSITION

A.W.

The economic and social landscape of the United States in the nineteenth century underwent dramatic change. The period might best be termed a transitional one. It was characterized by the emergence of a new, industrial society. In the decades after the Civil War the preindustrial issues that dominated the antebellum era were overridden in importance by the realities of a rapidly maturing industrial society. New economic and social factors, some of them grim, were changing life. They included: transcontinental railroads, a truly national market for goods, a growing monopoly in oil, the factory system, and new technology in steel and other industries. In addition, there were deplorable urban living conditions, millions of new, non-English-speaking immigrants, rising labor violence, growing discontent among farmers, and brutal poverty among workers and farmers.

These factors were clearly visible. But both Republican and Democratic politicians managed to avoid confronting them. Not until a paralyzing business depression in the 1890s and the rise of a new third party, committed to reform, did politicians finally start to deal with the problems brought about by industrial development. Before then, in the 1870s and 1880s, political leaders were more concerned with traditional issues, particularly the currency and tariffs. They argued, for example, over whether the amount of currency in circulation should be expanded or reduced. And they debated whether the United States would benefit more from raised or from lowered tariffs.

Why did politicians avoid considering the problems of the new industrial society? Basically,

they (and voters too) were unable to shift their attention from the intense issues arising out of the Civil War and Reconstruction. With the ending of war and the termination of Radical rule in the South, the old issues had disappeared. But this transitional generation of politicians, raised in the antislavery battles of the 1850s, was simply unprepared to face the new problems of an industrial nation.

Some steps were taken during this period to deal with elements in the changed economy, but these proved to be less than effective. Politicians of the era were themselves too deeply involved in the development of American industries to take an active role in helping to regulate them. Only in the face of the new political forces and new conditions of the 1890s did politicians begin to bring the unregulated corporate system under some measure of public supervision. It took more than two decades for them to realize that they could no longer ignore the urgent economic and social problems created by post-Civil War industrial growth.

A GENERATION OF ORDINARY MEN

Through the 1870s and 1880s, politics continued along at an unhurried pace. Leaders tried to avoid difficult issues. In large part the people who entered politics during this period were ordinary men, like Garfield, who displayed little achievement beyond their ability to win votes.

In *The American Commonwealth* (1888) James Bryce, an English historian, noted that in a country where all careers are open to those having talent and where "political life is unusually keen and political ambition widely diffused," the highest positions in the land are seldom "won by men of brilliant gifts."

Why did eminent figures usually not choose to run for political office in this period? First, for talented people American politics did not seem interesting or important. In European countries, officeholders in national governments generally held much more power over people's lives. First-rate men were attracted to vocations in which they felt they could make a significant impact. Politics in America was not one such vocation.

A second reason for the lack of brilliant people in politics was that success generally required a slow rise through the party ranks. The long apprenticeship in party loyalty necessary to achieve office discouraged ambitious people who wished to move quickly into positions of prominence. Also American voters, then as today, were distrustful of anyone who seemed overly eager for political power, however capable.

Finally, persons of outstanding ability may not have entered politics simply because the era seemed a quiet one, at least compared with the age preceding it. Profound ideological questions no longer separated the parties. The problems of slavery, sectional divisions, and civil war were settled. Few issues were significant enough to attract talented people into politics.

Small-Town Background   Given the lure of other fields, the slowness of the process of reaching the top, and the relative quietness of the times, the

President Garfield's home in Mentor, Ohio, was the kind of country setting most national politicians of this era preferred. Their living patterns represented a nostalgia for an older, simpler way of life in an increasingly complex industrial society.

quality of those who held high public office is hardly surprising. Nor is it surprising to find that those who did make politics their career shared very similar patterns of life. In fact, most successful figures in late nineteenth-century national politics, including the great majority of congressmen and senators, had backgrounds similar to that of Garfield. They came from small towns and cities like Garfield's Mentor, Ohio, rather than from large cities or predominantly rural areas. Furthermore, most began their careers in such professions as law, business, the ministry, or teaching.

During the 1860s and 1870s the number of politicians having business interests increased. But most politicians were nonetheless provincial in their values and outlook on life. They remained aloof and sheltered from the habits and problems of urban-industrial society. They brought to national affairs a viewpoint similar to that of their pre-Civil War counterparts. Most national elected officials, in fact, had little direct personal contact with the major new realities of a changed America—cities, industries, and immigrants.

As with most of the national politicians of this period, the Republican presidential candidates were men with roots in small cities and towns. And in 1884 all the Republican candidates but James G. Blaine came from the Midwest. Thus, even if Charles Guiteau had managed to build a successful career for himself in a city like New York, his urban and Eastern ties would probably have blocked his road to the White House.

Guiteau might have been more successful as a Democrat, however. The Democrats generally nominated presidential candidates from big cities during these years: Horatio Seymour (1868), Horace Greeley (1872), Samuel Tilden (1876), and Grover Cleveland (1884, 1888, 1892). But of this group only Cleveland succeeded in becoming President. Thus, while they controlled the big cities and even had respectable showings in congressional elections, the Democrats largely failed to take the biggest prize of all—the presidency.

Civil War Experience   As important as a small-town background seemed to be in achieving political success, there was another factor at least as important in advancing a politician's career—his

Civil War record. This was true at all levels in American politics but particularly in regard to seeking the presidency. Indeed, another reason why Guiteau could never have become President was that he had not served in the Union Army.

For many Northern voters, Republicanism was practically a family religion, sanctified by wartime sacrifices. (Most Northerners had lost at least one family member in the fighting.)

The Republican presidential candidates were usually Civil War generals. General Hayes succeeded General Grant in the presidency. He, in turn, was succeeded by General Garfield. As death and old age thinned out the number of high-ranking officers, Colonel Benjamin Harrison, and, finally, Major William McKinley entered the White House.

The Democrats, for their part, failed to choose nominees having a military background, at least on the national level. The single Democratic candidate who was a Union military man was General Winfield Scott Hancock. He lost to Garfield in 1880. It is understandable that Union officers were not nominated. The Democrats depended, for the most part, on Southern support for victory. In local and regional elections, of course, where Southern support was irrelevant, Democrats could play on old Civil War loyalties to win elections. But the presidential prize eluded them.

Codes of Personal Conduct The victorious politicians of this period, besides sharing a small-town background and Civil War experience, were also strong believers in the strictest of moral codes. They usually presented themselves to the public as family men who lived their private lives according to the rigid ethical precepts of American middle-class culture. We do not know, of course, whether this was fact or sheer image building. The author of Garfield's semiofficial campaign biography wrote, for example: "No profane word, no unseemly jest is ever heard at Lawnfield [his home]. No wines sparkle on its table. The moral atmosphere is sweet, pure, and healthgiving to heart and soul. It is a Christian family—a Christian home."

Prior to the Civil War a politician's personal habits and morality had rarely influenced the suc-

James G. Blaine had been recently involved in an allegedly crooked railroad deal. He defended himself against the charge of corruption by reading selected portions of correspondence that was to prove his innocence. Many people were unconvinced. The so-called Mulligan letters hurt his chances for the presidency in 1876.

cess of his political career. Neither Andrew Jackson's background of frequent duels nor Henry Clay's inveterate gambling prevented these men from seeking the highest prize in American politics. During the middle of the nineteenth century, however, the American family adopted a stern moral code on such questions as sexual behavior, drinking, and gambling. Voters began to apply these standards to vote seekers as well.

Perhaps the only national politician of the era to overcome hostility toward "loose" morality successfully was Grover Cleveland. He won the presidency in 1884 despite the fact—brought out in the campaign—that in his youth he had fathered an illegitimate child. Ironically, voters that year were offered a choice between repudiating either Cleveland's single offense against private morality or James G. Blaine's questionable public morality. While a senator during the 1870s, Blaine had allegedly accepted money and stocks from railroad companies in return for political favors. When the returns were in, the electorate had registered its preference for a candidate with a single confessed private lapse to one probably tainted with several instances of political corruption.

ELECTING A PRESIDENT

National politics during the 1870s and 1880s was not oriented toward issues, although some of the older issues did play a part in the elections. Basically, politicians were concerned with party affiliation and moral, ethnic, and religious differences among the electorate. Three basic factors shaped presidential elections of the late nineteenth century: a close balance in voting strength between the two major parties, high voter turnout, and a stress on party loyalty.

The Closeness of Contests The statistics for every presidential election of the era show clearly that the parties were evenly matched. In the disputed 1876 election, Republican Rutherford B. Hayes was elected by one electoral vote, although he had received almost 250,000 fewer votes than his Democratic opponent, Samuel J. Tilden. In 1880 Garfield defeated the Democratic candidate, Winfield Scott Hancock, by a comfortable electoral majority. But his nationwide popular margin was a mere 7,368 votes. Actually, Garfield received only a plurality of the votes—48 percent; a third-party candidate, James B. Weaver of the Greenback-Labor party, cut into the major parties' totals.

Democrat Grover Cleveland's presidential election history is an interesting one, for he crossed and recrossed the narrow line between victory and defeat. In 1884 Cleveland won with less than 49 percent of the popular vote. His margin in the popular vote was only 63,000. When he was defeated by Republican Benjamin Harrison in the 1888 election, Harrison received the majority of electoral votes despite receiving 96,000 fewer popular votes. Cleveland again became President in 1892 when he received 360,000 more votes than

Election night, 1892, in New York City is typical of voter enthusiasm in this era. Despite political corruption and the lack of great issues, excitement over politics ran high.

Harrison. In this race a new third party, the Populists, received over one million votes. Thus a presidential candidate once more won with only a plurality, not a majority, of the popular vote.

The closeness of these presidential contests helps to explain the efforts usually made by both Republicans and Democrats to blur their basic differences over issues at the national level. Although the Republicans supported high protective tariffs, for example, there were many in the party, including Garfield, who favored much lower rates. Similarly, the Democrats were a low-tariff party. But Cleveland's decision to press the tariff-reduction issue during his first term cost the party support from many high-tariff Democrats and independents who might otherwise have voted for him when he ran again. In order to make its position seem close to that of the other party, and hoping thereby to gain votes, each party had to muffle its internal conflicts and contradictions on such issues as the tariff.

Because of the narrow margins of victory in each presidential election, both Republicans and Democrats were essentially in competition for the support of a small group of swing voters in a few doubtful states. These voters shifted back and forth between the major parties throughout this period. Business help was often invaluable in swinging the key votes and deciding the outcome of the election. Garfield's election in 1880 owed much to the fact that John D. Rockefeller instructed his thousands of salesmen in various states in the Midwest to work actively for the Republican ticket. Similarly, in 1888, Harrison's victory was due in part to corporate money that helped finance intensive drives for votes in a few key states.

Turnout of Voters   Another basic factor in presidential elections in the late nineteenth century was a surprisingly high voter turnout. This phenomenon is somewhat more difficult to explain. There were no dramatic public issues bitterly dividing the two parties as there had been earlier — and would be in the near future. Part of the explanation, however, can be found in the popular view of elections as spectacles.

Both parties waged furious campaigns. Republicans "waved the bloody shirt" — that is,

they reminded the voters of Southern Democratic disloyalty during the Civil War. Democrats, in turn, pointed to the corrupting influence of business on the Republican party.

Political campaigns were often the greatest show in town. Huge numbers of voters marched in torchlight parades. They listened for hours to familiar but rousing partisan oratory. As participants in and spectators of such grand displays, voters reaffirmed their strong allegiance to and identification with their party.

Importance of Party Loyalty   Political loyalties among politicians and voters were clear and strong during this period. However blurred the political issues might be, this kind of loyalty strengthened the parties as an institution in American life.

Among politicians, party loyalty, or regularity, was extremely important at the national level. Presidential power, which had reached a high point with Lincoln's wartime authority, declined after the crisis of civil war ended. Presidents were largely at the mercy of Congress to achieve their programs. The President's political task was twofold: (1) to "carry" enough congressmen of his own party into office when he was elected and (2) to hold their loyalty once he was President.

Concerning the former, Presidents were not too successful. No President during this entire era governed for his entire term with a majority of his own party in control of Congress. The Democrats, for example, won control of the House in 1874, lost it in 1880, regained it in 1882, lost it in 1888, and won it back in 1890. Although Republicans controlled the Senate throughout this period, except for the 1879–1881 session, for all but two years they held no more than a slim three-vote Senate majority. There was considerable turnover in congressional membership during the 1870s and 1880s, particularly in the House.

It was even more difficult for a President to hold the party loyalty of congressmen after election. There were numerous factions in both parties. Various means of keeping the party together seemed to work, however. By the end of the era, congressional caucuses were a device used in both parties. They generally decided the legislative policies that all members were expected to, and usually did, abide by. A congressman who did not support the party could be disciplined in a number of ways. Leaders might deny him important committee assignments. They might refuse to help him in the passage of the numerous private bills that every congressman introduces yearly on behalf of his constituents. If necessary they would oppose his renomination. In these circumstances, most congressmen, of course, obeyed the dictates of their party's leaders.

Party loyalty among American voters was more easily assured. American voters adhered as firmly to their party allegiance as they did to their religious faith. If one was raised as a Democrat (or Republican), one usually remained a Democrat (or Republican) for life.

Recent studies point to the importance of ethnic backgrounds and religion as factors in the political behavior of most Americans in the period following the Civil War. A voter's ethnic, cultural, and religious ties shaped his party loyalty as much as it did his attitudes on specific economic or political issues. For example, in order to help capture the votes of the immigrants, who badly needed employment, civil-service reformers in each party complained about the use of the spoils system by urban political machines in the other party. Although jobs were dispensed through political patronage under the spoils system, and recent immigrants were thus unlikely to get them, few of these immigrants favored introducing a merit system. This, they felt, might result in jobs being awarded mainly to native-born Americans who had had greater opportunity to receive education and training.

Religious beliefs were also a factor in determining political affiliation. Recent voting studies have shown that during this period the more an individual's religion stressed correct behavior rather than strict adherence to doctrine alone, the more likely he was to vote Republican. Some Protestant religious denominations viewed politics as a moral battleground, in which state power should be used to regulate ethical behavior. For example, they supported laws prohibiting the sale of alcohol. Members of these denominations tended to support Republicans for office, whether in the 1850s or the 1890s. Certainly, Republican opposition at the state level to using public funds for parochial schools (schools particularly important for many new immigrant families) and the party's support for prohibition (viewed as an assault on Democratic-voting Catholic immigrant "drinkers") attracted large numbers of native-born Episcopalian, Congregationalist, Presbyterian, and other similar voters.

This does not mean that immigrant groups and church members voted in blocs for a single party. Nonetheless, ethnic and cultural ties did indeed influence political loyalties in the period of the 1870s and 1880s.

THE REPUBLICANS IN POWER

For three decades, from 1861 to 1892, the Republicans (except for Democrat Cleveland's 1885–1889 term) governed nationally, despite the close political balance between the parties. During this period, as already stated, the President was extremely dependent on Congress. In fact, more often than not, Congress—not the President—determined party policies and the legislation that emerged from Washington.

Americans did not seem to want strong Presidents during this period. Certainly they did not appear to need them, because of the relative quietness of the times. So, none of the Republican Presidents—Grant, Hayes, Garfield, Arthur, or Harrison—managed to wrest control of Republican policies from the Senate and House leaders.

Men like Blaine and Conkling remained the party's most influential national spokesmen throughout the period. They largely shaped national legislation during the era. Since they were Republicans, they believed in an effective and energetic national economic policy. In general, the purpose of this policy was to encourage industrial expansion. For this they were often criticized by Democratic politicians who retained their party's traditional faith—that government should not meddle actively in the economic lives of Americans.

But the Republican party, founded in an era when the national government had to expand its powers to preserve the Union, saw nothing wrong with continuing this trend at the war's end. To encourage economic development, party leaders aided business in every possible way. In accomplishing this purpose, they forged an informal alliance between the national government and the great majority of businessmen—bankers, industrialists, and merchants in foreign trade. While this alliance did further economic growth, it had other less fortunate consequences as well. It gave the era a reputation for corruption unparalleled in American history until then.

Corruption under Grant It is ironic that people who lived by strict small-town moral codes in their private lives found it difficult to maintain the same kind of integrity in public affairs. Political corruption was widespread in this period. The Grant years in particular saw some of the worst offenses against honest government in the nation's history.

A series of cabinet scandals during Grant's administration involved many people close to the President himself. His secretary of the navy sold work to contractors rather than taking honest bids. His secretary of war sold extremely profitable traderships on Indian reservations. Department of the Interior officials worked hand in hand with dishonest land speculators.

Some of the worst scandals involved the Department of the Treasury. Grant's secretary of the Treasury farmed out the collection of unpaid taxes to a private contractor who kept half of the money collected. The President's own private secretary protected a Whiskey Ring of corrupt Treasury inspectors. These officials received millions of dollars in bribes from liquor distillers to avoid payment of federal taxes. Through Grant's personal bungling, the Department of the Treasury cooperated with two New York stock speculators, James Fisk and Jay Gould, to manipulate the government selling of bullion. The two men cornered the gold market briefly in September 1869, forcing anyone else who needed gold to pay an exorbitant price for it. Although they caused a panic in the money market, Fisk and Gould made a fortune on the deal. Once they were exposed, Grant did little to punish the guilty parties in his administration.

The opportunities for politicians to profit through corrupt practices increased vastly as a result of the economic boom of the 1860s and 1870s. Many national leaders like Garfield had carefully watched their money while young, to further their education and careers. Suddenly they were responsible for handling millions of dollars in government funds. Politicians found themselves able to reap tidy sums (and benefit the country) simply by helping businessmen with government funds or favorable legislation.

The railroads were notorious seekers after these government favors. Railroad owners paid millions in bribes to public officials each year to secure cash subsidies, gifts of government land, and favorable legislation. Both Garfield and Blaine were linked to such transactions, although no specific criminal charges were ever made against either of them.

During Grant's administration, Garfield apparently profited, along with numerous other public officials, from a shady company known as the Crédit Mobilier. This was a purchasing and construction corporation organized by a few stockholders of the Union Pacific Railroad in the late 1860s. The Union Pacific stockholders retained control the Crédit Mobilier, to which they awarded huge and fraudulent contracts connected with building the railroad. Congressmen of both parties, including Garfield, were bribed with money and stocks in the Crédit Mobilier to avoid congressional inquiry into these transactions. Before the affair was exposed in 1873, the Crédit Mobilier (despite the Union Pacific's virtual bankruptcy) had paid yearly dividends to stockholders that often exceeded 300 percent of the original investment. Moreover, sometimes these excessive profits went to congressmen who had paid nothing for the stock in the first place!

Although the Grant administration provides the most famous instances of scandal, governmental corruption was not limited to the national level or to Republicans alone. In fact, some of the worst instances of corruption took place at the city level, where Democrats were more likely to be in con-

WILLIAM MARCY TWEED

From one perspective, William Marcy Tweed was three hundred pounds of grand larceny. From another, he was a major figure in the development of American city government. He was appropriately named after the New York Democratic politician, William Marcy, who had openly boasted that victors were entitled to spoils. As the boss of post-Civil War New York City, Tweed devised a method of dealing with an altered city. Most "respectable" New Yorkers wanted no part of it. If Tweed made himself a substantial profit, he could say, "I seen my opportunities and I took 'em."

By 1870, nearly a million people were crowded into the southern half of Manhattan Island, almost half of them immigrants. The city's startling growth had put enormous strains on its housing, public transportation, sanitation, and health facilities. The financial and social leaders of the city regarded the new residents with a mixture of disdain, foreboding, and bewilderment.

Tammany Hall, New York City's Democratic organization, had been working with immigrants, especially the Irish Catholics, for nearly seven decades before Tweed took over in the mid-1860s. Tweed and other leaders now increased their efforts to meet (and profit from) the incoming flood. Tammany Hall members greeted newcomers from Europe at the docks, helped them get settled, and assisted them in becoming voting American citizens.

With such support, the Tweed Ring controlled city politics. Close associates of Tweed held office as mayor and controller. The Boss himself served the public as chairman of the General Committee of Tammany Hall, president of the Board of Supervisors, deputy street commissioner, and state senator. He was grooming his close ally, Governor John T. Hoffman, for the Democratic nomination for the presidency of the United States.

The Ring, however, was interested in public office less for its own sake than as a lever on the door to the public treasury. During five years of almost uncontested power, the Tweed Ring stole between $30 and $200 million. By one estimate, only 15 cents of every tax dollar went for legitimate purposes. The Ring's classic achievement was a courthouse that cost $12 million to build, when $3 million would have been enough. Its costs included $179,729.60 for three tables and forty chairs.

Graft on such a scale could not and did not go unnoticed. Yet Tweed, sure of his power, responded to all charges with a sneering, "Well, what are you going to do about it?" Tammany's immigrant voters remained loyal, and Tweed even survived an investigation. But when, in 1871, two high-level Ring members began turning over evidence to the New York *Times,* the end came with startling swiftness. Tweed, in a desperate move, offered the *Times* $500,000 to abandon its probe, and a similar sum to *Harper's Weekly* cartoonist Thomas Nast, suggesting that he might like to study art in Europe. Neither accepted the bribes, and soon the Tweed Ring was shattered both at the polls and in the courts. Tweed was in and out of prison for the next five years; he died in jail at age fifty-five.

Twice voted into office, in 1868 and 1872, Ulysses S. Grant was the first professional soldier to become President since Zachary Taylor and the last until 1952. A West Point graduate, Grant had a lacklustre career until his rise to fame as General of the U.S. Army under Lincoln. As President, he was hampered by a lack of political sophistication, inept appointments, and opposition within his own party. His troubles were compounded by the scandals that pervaded his administration, most notably the Credit Mobilier of 1874.

trol. New York City, for instance, was run by a Democratic political organization, or "machine," known as the Tweed Ring (see page 473). Its political leader, "Boss" William Marcy Tweed, and members of his machine stole over $100 million in public revenues ($14 million in one profitable day).

Civil-Service Reform An important source of Tweed's money was from kickbacks forced from people who wanted city jobs. Once in office, the machine politicians had the power to distribute jobs. Many reformers of the era thought that this spoils system for filling political posts should be eliminated and replaced with a merit system. This, they thought, would do away with much of the corruption that had plagued the country at all levels.

Grant's successor, Rutherford B. Hayes, ordered that officeholders not be asked to make political contributions or be required to do political campaigning. But these orders were largely ignored. Garfield, as noted in the previous chapter, backed away from Hayes's civil-service commitment. With Garfield's death, public attention focused on Guiteau not merely as his assassin but as a symbol of the various evils that Americans identified with the spoils system of selecting officeholders.

Although the most blatant instances of national corruption had taken place a decade or more earlier, in 1883 Congress responded to the public outcry by passing the Pendleton Act. President Arthur, himself a one-time spoilsman, had lobbied hard for the bill. The act established a bipartisan Civil Service Commission, appointed by the President. Its purpose was to conduct competitive examinations to choose officeholders on the basis of merit. Arthur appointed three solid reformers as civil-service commissioners.

The original measure did not solve the entire problem, however, for the merit system affected only about one of every ten federal jobs. The others were to be filled as political appointments. Nonetheless, the Pendleton Act gave the President the authority to expand the number of positions classified as merit jobs. By 1900 over 40 percent of federal posts had been brought under the civil-service heading. This percentage has expanded in every decade since.

CONTINUING BUSINESS INFLUENCE

The assault on the spoils system did not have much effect on business influence within the national government. Businessmen tried less often to buy favors from individual politicians. Instead, increasing numbers of them began either running for office themselves or supporting politicians committed to business policies, through legal campaign contributions. Industrialists and bankers poured millions into Republican campaign treasuries.

Thomas Nast's cartoons exposed the unsavory Tweed Ring.

Even more important than business involvement in presidential contests, however, was the growing importance of senators who represented large corporate interests. By 1900 such businessmen, most of them Republicans, comprised a third of the Senate. Fifteen senators were involved in railroads; fifteen in extractive industries—minerals, oil, and lumber; nine in banking and finance; six in commerce; and three in manufacturing. Wealthy members of the House or Senate were not captives or "puppets" of the business interests with which they held close ties. But, on issues affecting the national economic life, their policies tended to favor businessmen and monied interests rather than farmers, laborers, and the poor. And they made only token efforts to regulate American industry or finance.

Currency Expansion Favoritism toward business interests is shown clearly in the monetary programs enacted by Congress in the era. The debate involved the amount of currency in circulation. Farmers and most other debtors favored an increase in the amount of money issued by the government. Businesses, on the other hand, especially banking interests, wanted the opposite.

To understand the farmers' demands, it is important to keep in mind that this group was experiencing especially hard times during this period. The mechanization of agriculture was a mixed blessing to farmers. It greatly added to their efficiency; but it helped create vast surpluses and consequent falling prices. Wheat, for example, which had sold for $2.50 a bushel in 1868 dropped to an average of 78 cents a bushel in the late 1880s.

While prices continued dropping, the cost of running farms remained high. Many farmers, for instance, were at the mercy of railroads that held a monopoly on transportation in their areas. These railroads often charged excessively high rates for carrying agricultural products to markets. Besides the cost of transportation, the cost of land, machinery, and tools was also quite high.

Faced with high costs and declining prices for their own products, farmers usually went into debt by mortgaging their land and goods. In the 1880s the number of mortgages soared. Of the total number of farms in the country, over 40 percent

This pro-Greenback cartoon portrays a gold-nosed government octopus linking itself to big business with its tentacles while strangling labor, farmers, and small business.

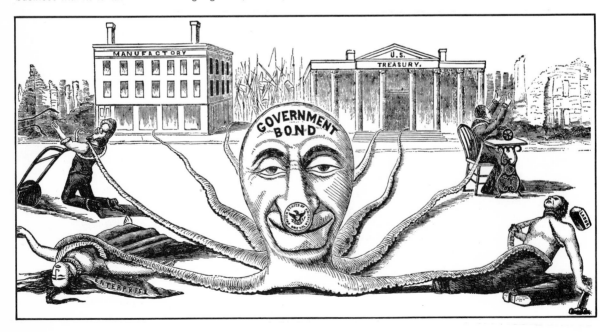

were mortgaged. In some areas, like Kansas, the figure was closer to 60 percent. Interest rates on these mortgages were high—6 to 15 percent on land and 10 to 18 percent on goods.

Farmers felt that government could relieve their distress by pumping more money into the economy. The government had increased the amount of paper money—greenbacks—in circulation during the Civil War in order to finance the war effort. After the war the government began to withdraw these greenbacks from circulation. This cutback in currency was hitting the indebted farmer particularly hard because he had borrowed when money was "cheap" or plentiful. Now he had to pay his debts in currency worth much more than its original value.

From the bankers' point of view, of course, the situation was ideal. They had a stake in seeing that money became scarcer. They would profit more on the repayment of loans, since the value of a dollar increases as its supply decreases. The government agreed with this viewpoint.

During the Hayes administration, the Specie Resumption Act of 1875 was passed, committing the United States to returning to a gold standard by 1879. The Treasury Department, to help ensure the successful "resumption of specie payments" (as it was called) in 1879, began to reduce the number of greenbacks in circulation. This policy (and the Treasury's refusal to print additional issues of greenbacks) combined with an increase in overall productive output during the 1875–1879 period to cause a total decline in the money stock. This was a direct slap at debtor interests, particularly farmers, coming as it did during the worst depression in American history up to that point.

The financial community benefited greatly, not only from the 1875 Resumption Act but from an earlier statute, in 1869, which provided that bonds issued during the Civil War should be paid off in gold. The banking community, of course, held most of these bonds. The provision meant that war bonds that had been bought with greenbacks worth less than 40 cents to the dollar could now be turned in for currency worth 100 cents to the dollar.

The resumption of specie payments (payment in gold alone) so enraged some farmers that they banded together to form a third party. They were joined by many recruits from labor and became the Greenback-Labor party in 1878. In the short run the movement was unsuccessful, since it failed to win many votes or to change the government's policy in currency. In the long run, however, it was significant in laying the basis for a far more powerful agrarian movement during the 1890s.

Agitation for expanding the currency did not stop after the initial failure of the Greenback movement. In fact, a new strategy was tried—a demand that silver be coined into dollars. In 1873 the government had stopped coining silver and put the country back on the gold standard—that is, backed money with gold alone. But in the 1870s the supply of silver increased tremendously because of the discovery of new silver deposits in the West. Many charged that silver had been demonetized illegally. By the 1880s farmers and other debtor groups saw in the "remonetizing" of silver a way of getting cheaper money. This in turn would raise crop prices and secure them relief from their debts.

Those who agitated for silver were partially successful during the 1870s. The Bland-Allison Act of 1878 required the Department of the Treasury to buy not less than $2 million and not more than $4 million worth of silver each month to back the dollar. Unfortunately, the government continuously bought the lesser amount. Though the silver interests were placated, farmers did not get much relief.

The Tariff Issue Another government policy that tended to favor business interests at the expense of other segments of society involved the tariff. The tariff debate, as old as the country itself, took on new importance with the coming of the industrial age. The original justification for a tax on imports was to protect infant industries from the competition of foreign manufacturers. But long after competition from abroad ceased to be a threat, the tariff still remained high on most goods. And it was going higher.

Again those particularly hurt by the tariff were the farmers. They complained that they had to sell their goods competitively on an open world

An antitariff cartoon of the 1880s shows the spiraling bad effects of a high tariff. The tariff wall results in a glut of products on the home market, consequent cuts in production, and then widespread unemployment, at least in this hostile cartoon.

market. But they had to purchase tariff-protected manufactured and processed goods such as farm machinery and oil. In fact, consumers in general suffered from the imposition of high tariffs. Without the competition of cheaper imported goods, they paid whatever prices domestic manufacturers set—prices that were often determined by monopolistic practices.

Republicans were by no means the only supporters of high protective tariffs. Factions in both parties backed business interests (or farmer interests) on this matter. But it was not until a

Democrat, Grover Cleveland, took office that there was a serious challenge to high tariffs. Cleveland's advocacy of a lowered tariff provided the leading issue in his reelection bid in 1888. He was defeated, as was noted earlier, partly because he had alienated the pro-tariff faction in his own party. But his downfall came mostly because businessmen poured millions of dollars into the campaign of the Republican candidate, Benjamin Harrison.

Harrison repaid his business backers by supporting the highest tariff in the nation's history. The McKinley Tariff of 1890—named after its sponsor, William McKinley—aimed not just at discouraging competition but at eliminating it altogether. It raised rates from an average of 38 percent to an average of almost 50 percent. It clearly marked a triumph for American industrialists.

Token Reform Although business influence was at its height, the government could not afford to ignore the public altogether. Some steps were taken in this period to deal with elements in the changed economy. But these proved to be less than effective. Congressmen from both parties joined in passing two basically mild bills to regulate the new giant industries.

The Interstate Commerce Act in 1887 set up a federal commission (the ICC) to oversee "reasonable and just" rates on the nation's railroads. Congress did not provide the commission with any strong enforcement powers, however. Its only avenue was the courts, and these generally consisted of pro-business conservatives. Moreover, the persons who were appointed as commissioners during the 1890s were sympathetic to the railroads. This, of course, further prevented the ICC from making any serious efforts to regulate the lines in order to ensure fair and equal treatment for all shippers.

A second law, the Sherman Antitrust Act of 1890, was also supposed to curb big business. Anticipating public reaction to the high McKinley Tariff, congressmen hoped that the Sherman Act would quiet agitation. Unfortunately, the act provided only mild and ineffective penalties against companies that formed combinations in restraint of trade. Furthermore, it was rarely applied during the 1890s. Only five years after the law was passed, the Supreme Court handed down a decision in *U.S. v. Knight* that exempted most industries from its provision. A monopoly, according to the Court, was not itself illegal. It became so only when it served to restrain interstate trade.

The immediate effect of such token efforts was to prevent a massive public outcry. In the long run, though, they only added further grievances to the growing list of problems confronting the country. The nation had lived through more than two decades of conservative rule resulting from the informal alliance of business and government. The public was ready for reform, and pressure was mounting in various parts of society to bring that about.

SUGGESTED READINGS— CHAPTERS 25-26

Garfield

Charles E. Rosenberg, *The Trial of the Assassin Guiteau* (1968); Robert G. Caldwell, *James A. Garfield: Party Chieftain* (1931); Theodore C. Smith, *Life and Letters of James Abram Garfield,* 2 vols. (1925); David M. Jordan, *Roscoe Conkling* (1971); Thomas C. Reeves, *Gentleman Boss: Chester A. Arthur* (1975).

Politics in Transition

Irwin Unger, *The Greenback Era* (1964); Allen Weinstein, *Prelude to Populism* (1970); John G. Sproat, *"The Best Men": Liberal Reformers in the Gilded Age* (1968); H. Wayne Morgan, *From Hayes to McKinley* (1969); Ari A. Hoogenboom, *Outlawing the Spoils* (1961); John A. Garraty, *The New Commonwealth, 1877–1890* (1968); Robert D. Marcus, *Grand Old Party: Political Structure in the Gilded Age* (1971); David J. Rothman, *Politics and Power: The U.S. Senate, 1869–1901* (1966); Matthew Josephson, *The Politicos, 1865–1896* (1938); Daniel J. Elazar, *The American Partnership* (1962).

Republican Politics

C. Vann Woodward, *Origins of the New South* (1951); Robert H. Wiebe, *The Search for Order: 1877–1920* (1968); Leonard D. White, *The Republican Era, 1869–1901* (1958); Stanley P. Hirshon, *Farewell to the Bloody Shirt: Northern Republicans and the Southern Negro, 1877–1893* (1962); Vincent P. DeSantis, *Republicans Face the Southern Question* (1959).

Cleveland and the Democrats

Horace Samuel Merrill, *Bourbon Democracy of the Middle West, 1865–1896* (1969) and *Bourbon Leader: Grover Cleveland and the Democratic Party* (1957).

The Tweed Ring

Alexander B. Callow, Jr., *The Tweed Ring* (1966); Seymour Mandelbaum, *Boss Tweed's New York* (1965).

27 MASSACRE AT WOUNDED KNEE

R.J.W.

There was a confusion about names — there almost always was when Indians were involved. Most whites called the tribe the Sioux. But this name was just a French abbreviation of what some of the tribe's enemies had called them. They called themselves Dakota.

There was more than one Indian name for what the whites called Wounded Knee Creek, on the Pine Ridge Reservation in South Dakota. Also, whereas some people called what had happened at Wounded Knee Creek a battle, others called it a massacre. Even the man who rode out from reservation headquarters to Wounded Knee had two names. One was an Indian name, Ohiyesa. One was a white man's name, Charles Eastman. He was a Sioux, but he had been educated in white schools in New England. In fact, he was a doctor of medicine.

But there was no confusion about what Charles Eastman saw on that bright New Year's Day morning in 1891:

> On the day following the Wounded Knee massacre, there was a blizzard. On the third day it cleared, and the ground was covered with fresh snow. We had feared that some of the wounded Indians had been left on the field, and a number of us volunteered to go and see.
>
> Fully three miles from the scene of the massacre, we found the body of a woman completely covered with a blanket of snow, and from this point on we found them scattered along as they had been hunted down and slaughtered. When we reached the spot where the Indian camp had stood, among the fragments of burned tents and other belongings, we saw the frozen bodies lying close together or piled one upon another. I counted eighty bodies of men, who were almost as helpless as the women and babes when the deadly [gun] fire began, for nearly all their guns had been taken from them.
>
> Although they had been lying in the snow and cold for two days and nights, a number had survived. Among them I found a baby of about a year old, warmly wrapped and entirely unhurt. Under a wagon, I discovered an old woman, totally blind and helpless.

Big Foot, seventy-year-old chief of the Sioux, was one of 146 Indians killed by the U. S. Seventh Cavalry at Wounded Knee. He was found dead three days later, frozen grotesquely where he had fallen.

Eastman began to load the few survivors into wagons to return to the agency (reservation headquarters), where he had set up a small hospital. Two groups of white men stayed behind at Wounded Knee. One was a troop of the U.S. Seventh Cavalry. The other was a group of about thirty white civilians who had agreed to bury the dead, at a charge of two dollars a body. They found the body of the chief of the Indians, an old man named Big Foot, frozen half sitting, half lying down. Ill with pneumonia, he had been lying on a blanket on the winter ground when the shooting started.

It took until the next day to dig a big, open grave. Then the bodies were gathered. Under an unusually strong January sun, the grave diggers sweated; many worked in their shirtsleeves. They stacked 146 dead Indians — 128 men and women and 18 children — in the pit. Then, while the cavalrymen stayed out of sight, the civilians gathered in a half-circle around the grave to have their photograph taken. For the photographer, they held their rifles, not shovels. Then they shoveled dirt in over the bodies. When the diggers and the cavalry rode away, nothing was left at Wounded Knee but the fresh dirt of the grave and the charred poles of the Indian tepees that had been put up only a few days before. The battle, or massacre (it was really some of both), was over.

Wounded Knee was the last and most tragic moment in a long, difficult, and often ugly process: the conquest of the Sioux Indians. The conquerors were the white citizens and blue-coated soldiers of the United States. The process began before the Civil War. At that time the Sioux were a powerful tribe, probably numbering well over 20,000. They hunted on millions of square miles of the plains west of the Missouri River.

The Sioux resisted the invasion of white miners, farmers, and ranchers. They fought often, and they usually won. In the summer of 1876 they won two astonishing victories. At Rosebud Creek, in what is now Montana, they attacked a large column of cavalry and infantry and forced the soldiers into a retreat. Then, just a few days later, the Seventh Cavalry, with General George A. Custer commanding, attacked a large Sioux camp on the Little Bighorn River, just a few miles from Rosebud Creek. Custer divided his force, and the Indians killed Custer as well as most of the Seventh, one of the most experienced cavalry units operating in the West.

But there were too many other soldiers. Though the Sioux were never defeated, their surrender was inevitable. In 1877, just a year after "Custer's last stand," the great war chief Crazy Horse led many of his followers onto a reservation that had been recently set aside for the Sioux. Crazy Horse was murdered a short time later. Some of his people fled to Canada to join the other outstanding Sioux leader, Sitting Bull. About 2,500 Sioux then tried to survive in Canada. But hunger and cold—and the fact that white people had slain most of the buffalo—finally drove them back to the reservation. In 1881 Sitting Bull surrendered—"came in," as it was said. This was the end of a golden age for the Sioux, one that had lasted more than a century.

Originally, before white Europeans had come to North America, the Sioux had lived very much like the Indians of the eastern seaboard. Their territory was not the open plains of the Dakotas, but the woods and lakes of Minnesota and Wisconsin. There, they had built permanent bark

The Sioux moved onto reservations such as this one at Pine Ridge, South Dakota, in 1877. This traditional form of tribal encampment in tepees was one of the Sioux practices that disturbed the whites. Reservation policy encouraged separate and permanent houses for each Sioux family.

houses, used canoes, and hunted only small game. They had also farmed. This life was disturbed by indirect contact with white civilization. The Sioux were driven out of their woodlands and onto the Great Plains by another tribe, the Chippewas. The Chippewas had come into contact with the French in Canada and had obtained guns in trade for furs. The guns gave the Chippewas an overwhelming advantage, and the Sioux had had to retreat to the west and south, out onto the great Plains.

But what began as a painful retreat soon turned into a triumphant new life. Gradually, the Sioux themselves obtained guns. They also discovered another European "import," the horses descended from the mounts the Spanish had brought into Mexico and the southwest. Together, these European tools—the horse and the rifle—transformed Sioux culture. For the first time, they could hunt buffalo. The plains were transformed from a barren, hostile environment into a hunting paradise. The buffalo herds became a source of meat, clothing, and shelter. The old bark houses gave way to hide-covered tepees that could be moved from one hunting area to another. This nomadic life brought the Sioux into contact (and conflict) with other Plains tribes. Hunting and warfare became the central focus of the Sioux economy and culture. For men, status in the tribe became dependent on skill and bravery in hunts and skirmishes. To a Sioux man, the tools of the hunt—his ponies, his rifle, his bow and arrows—were everything. The rituals of hunting and warfare gave meaning to his life. Any work that was not part of hunting, like preparing hides or drying meat or gathering berries, belonged to women. By the early part of the nineteenth century, the new society the Sioux had built on the plains was confident, prosperous, and expanding. They hunted all the way from the Missouri River to the valleys of the Little Big Horn Mountains on the eastern edge of the Rockies.

But, almost as soon as this civilization was established, it was challenged. The whites, with their cannon, their railroads, their plows, and their reservations, eventually destroyed the Sioux way of life. The whites slaughtered buffalo by the thousands, until practically none were left. Then the whites insisted that the Sioux live again in permanent houses. Government rations of beef, flour, and beans substituted for the hunt. It did not help much if a kindly agent sometimes allowed the men to "hunt" their twice-monthly ration of cattle. Games like this could not replace the old life. The authority of warriors and chiefs had depended on their skill in violent and dangerous activities. Reservation life was, above all, peaceful. The white agents even forbade the most holy annual ritual of the Sioux, the Sun Dance. And they insisted, too, that the men of the tribe could have only one wife.

What was happening was simple, and, from the Sioux point of view, tragic. They had been defeated by a much more powerful and complex society. Some of them—the "nonprogressives"—might resist in a few ways. They could reject the cotton shirts and trousers of the white man and continue to wear Indian clothing. They could insist on wearing their hair in the traditional long braid. But resistance could not revive the old life. They had long ago accepted some of the white man's ways

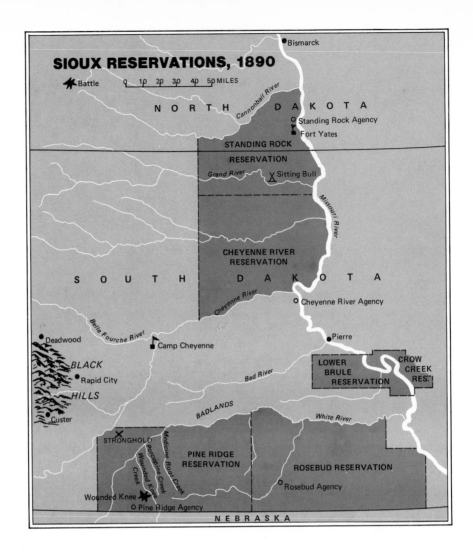

SIOUX RESERVATIONS, 1890

and tools. The horse and the rifle had been useful in the old life. But the government, with the "Great Father" President at its head, had plans for the Sioux that were utterly at odds with the old ways.

American policy was aimed at one long-range goal—to make each Indian family into a self-supporting, farming unit. In the old life, the tribal band, not the family, had been the basic social unit. The band moved, hunted, ate, and worshipped together, and families tended to merge imperceptibly with the common life of the band. The white vision saw each family gathered in its own log house, wearing white men's clothes, gathered around its own, private fire in a white man's stove, and, preferably, worshipping the white man's God instead of the old Sioux god, Wakan Tanka. To well-intentioned reformers in the East, this meant "raising the Indian to civilization." To whites in the West, it meant a final end to the Indian as a barrier to westward expansion.

For the Sioux, all of this meant a divided world. Even those who wanted to cooperate most, the so-called "progressives," lived a double life. A man might put on white clothes; he might plow and harvest, have only one wife, and send his children to white men's schools. But still there was the old life, alive in memory but dead in fact. George Sword, for example, was a progressive. He was even a member of the Indian police force the agents used to help keep order. But George Sword's description of his religious beliefs captures the painful division of loyalty that existed in the minds of even the most "civilized" Sioux:

> When I believed that Wakan Tanka was right, I served him with all my powers. In war with the white people, I found their Wakan Tanka superior. I then took the name of Sword, and have served their Wakan Tanka according to the white people's manner.
> I became chief of the United States Indian police, and held the office until there was no trouble between the Sioux and the white people. I joined the church and am a deacon in it and shall be until I die.

But all this Christianity and "progress" has not erased the old ways in George Sword. He was still a member of the Oglala band of the Dakota tribe, and his spirit might find itself in the Sioux's heaven, not the white man's:

> I still have my Wasicun [ceremonial pouch] and I am afraid to offend it, because the spirit of an Oglala may go to the spirit land of the Dakota.

This divided consciousness, unable to choose finally between the old and the new, the Indian and the white, touched every area of life for the reservation Indians. To the whites who watched them, the Indians seemed almost like children in their confusion. In fact, the Sioux men, especially, had been deprived of their adult roles in the hunt and battle. So their maturity *was* at stake.

One of the whites' main hopes for destroying the old Sioux culture was to educate a new generation in white schools. They took numbers of Sioux children away from their parents and put them in distant boarding schools. The Sioux reaction was mixed. They could hope that this process would make their childrens' lives better. But there was the inevitable resentment, too, the feeling that their children had been, in effect, kidnapped by the whites.

Even when the white schools were close to home, the Sioux sent their children to them reluctantly. When a new school was opened at Pine Ridge, Sioux parents brought their children in on the first day, but stayed outside the building, milling about, curious and frightened. Their fears were increased when the white teachers pulled down the shades, so no one could see what was happening inside. Suddenly, a gust of wind blew one of the blinds aside for a moment. The Indians got a glimpse of something that filled them with horror. A white woman was holding one Sioux boy while another woman cut his hair. The whole meaning of the reservation experience came quickly into the focus. In the old life, a Sioux male's long braids were a symbol of his manhood.

Here were white women scissoring away, symbolically, the tribal badge of masculinity. The Sioux parents, alarmed and outraged, charged into the school and took their children out.

Only at odd moments and in ineffective ways did the Sioux resist the relentless white pressure on their old ways. The whites controlled the Indians' sources of food, blankets, fuel, housing. The whites even controlled the ownership of an Indian's individual plot of land. The Sioux, like other American Indians, did not have a clearly defined concept of private property—especially private property in land. But they could see plainly that their survival depended on the white man's mysterious concept of land ownership. To lose the land would be to lose everything. Finally, the whites had one ultimate threat: the cavalry that was still stationed in forts scattered all around the Great Plains.

The deep conflict between Indian and white ways came to the surface in 1883, when a Senate investigating committee visited the Sioux. Sitting Bull, who had been one of the Sioux leaders at the Battle of the Little Bighorn, came to testify. But the chairman would not recognize Sitting Bull as chief. Sitting Bull got up and left. All the Indians followed him. But several of the progressive Indians returned to plead with the committee to use its influence with the Great Father to get better treatment for the Indians. Soon even Sitting Bull swallowed his hurt pride and returned to apologize.

Then Sitting Bull gave a remarkable account of what defeat had meant to the Sioux. They had been wealthy in their own terms, with land, ponies, and buffalo aplenty. In one lifetime the white man had reduced them to poverty.

> Whatever you wanted of me I have obeyed. The Great Father sent me word that whatever he had against me in the past had been forgiven and thrown aside, and I accepted his promises and came in. And he told me not to step aside from the white man's path, and I am doing my best to travel in that path. I sit here and look around me now, and I see my people starving. We want cattle to butcher. That is the way you live, and we want to live the same way. When the Great Father told me to live like his people, I told him to send me six teams of mules, because that is the way the white people make a living. I asked for a horse and buggy for my children; I was advised to follow the ways of the white man, and that is why I asked for those things.

Sitting Bull's ideas were a little confused, at least by white standards. But he summed up neatly the dilemma of the Sioux. He was still proud of himself and his tribal ways. He resented the whites' failure to understand this pride. But another side of him recognized defeat and was prepared to plead with the whites not for less civilization but for more. In Sitting Bull, and in almost all the other reservation Indians, pride, resentment, hunger, and begging were so intermixed that a meaningful pattern of life was almost impossible.

The situation was the same among all the Sioux. During the 1880s the Indians were gradually becoming "civilized." But the hunger and anger were just below the surface. Some crucial event or idea was all that was needed to bring the conflict with the whites back into the open, tip the scales one way or the other, and offer the Indians a clear choice between the old life and the new.

A new idea did come, and from an unpredictable direction. In the summer of 1889—about a dozen years after Crazy Horse had surrendered his band of hostiles—the Sioux began to hear rumors of an Indian messiah (or savior) who had come to earth in the West. They had learned enough of Christianity on the reservation to understand the alien notion of a messiah. If it were true that a messiah had come to save the Indians from the whites, surely it was worth investigating, they thought.

The Messiah was said to be at the Paiute reservation at Walker Lake, Nevada. Three of the six Sioux reservations[1] selected important men to make the trip west. It was about a thousand miles away—farther than almost any of the Sioux had ever traveled. Pine Ridge Reservation sent eight men, including Kicking Bear, who was to become the most effective disciple of the new Messiah. One of the men from Rosebud was Short Bull. The Cheyenne River Reservation, with a smaller population than either Pine Ridge or Rosebud, sent one man.

The eleven Sioux started west by train. Railroads had by then penetrated all the major western areas, and Indians hopped freight cars with little or no opposition from the white railroad men. When the Sioux reached Wyoming, they found that other tribes—Cheyennes, Arapahoes, Bannocks, and Shoshonis—had also sent wise men to seek the Messiah. The whole group then traveled south to Walker Lake. There the Paiutes gave them wagons to complete the pilgrimage. Soon they were in the presence of the Messiah.

His Indian name was Wovoka, his white name Jackson Wilson. He was about thirty-five years old. He was Paiute, but he had grown up close to a white ranching family named Wilson. (They gave him his English name.) The Wilsons were a religious family. From them Wovoka had learned in some detail how Jesus had controlled the wind and the seas, how he had promised eternal life to his followers, and how other whites had crucified him. Wovoka was apparently the son of a Paiute shaman, or medicine man.[2] One day in 1889, when he was ill (and perhaps delirious) with a high fever, there was an eclipse of the sun. This led him to believe that he had been taken up to heaven. After talking with God, he had been returned to earth to bring salvation to the Indians.

Wovoka's doctrines were a fairly straightforward Indian version of some of the basic teachings of the New Testament. In a sermon to some visiting Cheyennes he summarized his new faith:

Wovoka, the Messiah, claimed to be sent by God to save his people. He preached nonviolence and brotherly love. He demanded of his followers only that they dance the Ghost Dance and await the resurrection of their dead.

[1]One so-called Great Sioux Reservation had been created in 1868. It consisted of about 43,000 square miles in what is now South Dakota, and it was administered from several agencies on or near the land. In 1889 the Sioux territory, much reduced in size, was broken up into six separate reservations—Pine Ridge, Rosebud, Lower Brule, Crow Creek, Cheyenne River, and Standing Rock.
[2]Almost all American Indians relied on shamans, men or women who were thought to have supernatural powers such as being able to foretell the future or cure the sick.

You must not hurt anybody, or do harm to anyone. You must not fight. Do right always.

     Do not tell the white people about this. Jesus is now upon the earth. The dead are all alive again. I do not know when they will be here; maybe this fall or in the spring. When the time comes there will be no more sickness and everyone will be young again.

In a simplified way Wovoka was telling his disciples that the dead would be resurrected soon. The earth would tremble; a new earth would cover the old. But true believers need not be afraid, because they would soon enjoy perfect life, youth, and health. In the meantime, the Indians should live in peace with the whites.

    Do not refuse to work for the whites, and do not make any trouble with them until you leave them. When the earth shakes, do not be afraid, it will not hurt you. That is all. You will receive good words from me again some time. Do not tell lies.

Ghost shirts, emblazoned with brightly colored thunderbirds and buffaloes, were supposed to protect Indians from the white man's weapons in battle.

Wovoka gave the visiting Cheyennes some clay for making the sacred red paint of the Paiutes. Symbols drawn with it were signs of their salvation. Then he advised them: "When you get home, you must make a dance to continue five days. You must all do it in the same way."

This was the famous Ghost Dance from which Wovoka's new religion soon took its name. During the five days it lasted, men and women sang certain songs and went into hypnotic trances. It was during the dance that Indians were supposed to be able to visit their departed relatives in heaven.

When Short Bull returned to South Dakota, he gave his version of the Ghost Dance religion to his excited Sioux audience. The tone was much more militant than Wovoka's. Short Bull promised punishment for those who refused to be converted—just as the Christian missionaries promised damnation for those who rejected their Messiah. He also promised victory over the hated and feared soldiers for those who wore holy shirts into battle. The shirts were supposed to protect wearers from the bullets of the whites.

    If the soldiers surround you, three of you, on whom I have put holy shirts, will sing a song around them, then some of them will drop dead. Then the rest will start to run, but their horses will sink into the earth. The riders will jump from their horses, but they will sink into the earth also. Then you can do as you desire with them. Now, you must know this, that all the soldiers and that race will be dead. There will be only five thousand of them left living on the earth. The guns are the only things we are afraid of, but they belong to our father in heaven. He will see that they do no harm.

It was not only Short Bull who brought back this interpretation from the visit to Wovoka. A similar version of the Ghost Dance faith emerged on all the Sioux reservations during the summer of 1890. The Sioux were offered a new ritual, the Ghost Dance, and a new faith, which held that the whites would soon be buried in the earth and the Indians would once again own the plains. There is no way of knowing how sincere Short Bull was. Nor is there any way of knowing whether Sitting Bull—who soon became a disciple of the Ghost Dance—really be-

During the Ghost Dance, which went on for five days, the Sioux worked themselves into a trance. Believers thought they could visit their dead while in this state.

lieved in the coming resurrection. Most of the Sioux probably rejected the Ghost Dance and decided to continue along the white man's path. For many, though, the religion of Wovoka offered great hope for the return of the old life and the end of their humiliating captivity. There can be no doubt that large groups of Sioux did accept the Ghost Dance.

Agents on all the reservations tried to stop the dances, using Indian police. But, time and again, the dancing Sioux refused to be cowed. They threatened their own police with rifles, insulted the agents, and began to behave like the Sioux of the 1870s. The agents reacted in various ways. When the police failed to make the Sioux obey, some of the agents refused to issue rations to those Indians who were active Ghost Dancers. At least two of the agents asked for federal troops. One, a new agent at Pine Ridge, was so incompetent that the Indians named him Young-Man-Afraid-of-Indians. White newspapermen, always hungry for a sensational news story, began to write about "hostile" Sioux. And white settlers in the Dakotas began to demand protection from the government.

Finally, after a tug of war between the Department of the Interior and the Department of War in Washington, the government authorized the army to send infantry and cavalry onto the reservations. This move brought about the first real confrontation since 1876 between the Sioux and the dreaded bluecoats. On November 20, 1890, cavalry and infantry units occupied Pine Ridge and Rosebud. A few days later the entire Seventh Cavalry arrived at Pine Ridge. This was Custer's unit, and it included many veterans of the Little Bighorn.

The effect on the Sioux of the appearance of the troops was overpowering. Instead of retreating to the outer edges of the reservations,

Kicking Bear spread the doctrines of the Messiah to Sitting Bull and the Standing Rock Reservation. But he gave the new faith a militant interpretation that caused a white reaction.

most of the Indians at Pine Ridge and Rosebud immediately left their cabins and camps and gathered around the agency buildings. They pitched their tepees in rambling confusion and hoped that they would not be suspected of any wrongdoing. It was as though the only way to safe from the rifles and cannon of the army was to be right under the noses of the officers and agents.

Thus the arrival of the army segregated the Indians. Those who wanted peace with the whites—those who had the good sense to be afraid—had gathered at the agencies. Only the most militant of the Ghost Dancers, led by Kicking Bear and Short Bull, decided to hold out. They were gathered along the creeks not far from the Pine Ridge Agency— at Medicine Root, Porcupine, and Wounded Knee.

About a week after the cavalry's arrival, several hundred of the militant Indians broke for open country. They plundered the farms of the peaceful Indians who had fled to the agencies, and they raided the agency cattle herds for beef. Then about 600 warriors and their families struck out for a low plateau at the northwest corner of Pine Ridge. This area was known as the Stronghold. Here the Indians had grass, water, cattle, ponies in large numbers, and plenty of guns and ammunition. They announced that they intended to stay all winter, dancing, and then see what the spring brought.

Fortunately, the officer in command at Pine Ridge decided to be cautious. He sent one messenger after another to the Stronghold, promising that there would be no punishment if the Indians surrendered and returned to the agency. In turn the Indians had to agree to give up the Ghost Dance and return the cattle and other things they had taken. The messengers were badly treated, but some of the men at the Stronghold wanted to surrender. It seemed clear that sooner or later the Indians would disagree among themselves and the threat of uprising would be broken. The situation at Pine Ridge settled into a stalemate, with neither side ready to force a confrontation.

Now the scene of the action shifted north to Standing Rock Reservation, where Sitting Bull kept his camp. The nonprogressive Indians regarded Sitting Bull almost reverently. He was probably not as great a war chief as Crazy Horse had been. But Sitting Bull had held out against the whites longer than any other Sioux leader. And his people believed that he had extraordinary powers as a medicine man.

The agent at Standing Rock was James McLaughlin, a tough, fair, and experienced agent. For years he had struggled to gain moral leadership of the Indians, and for years Sitting Bull had stood in his way. McLaughlin had been looking for a way to break Sitting Bull's hold over the nonprogressive Indians at Standing Rock. When Sitting Bull took up the forbidden Ghost Dance, McLaughlin decided that arresting him would be the best course. McLaughlin wanted to delay the arrest until winter, when the Indians stayed indoors to avoid the bitter cold and to rest. The agent also believed that the arrest should be made by the Sioux Indian police, not by the cavalry units stationed near the agency at Fort Yates.

When the Sioux faced the white men's cameras, they either dressed in their most formal clothing and struck stiff poses or they presented themselves the way Sitting Bull and some of his family did in this photograph—modest, uncertain, and huddled together. Most whites faced the new experience of being photographed in exactly the same two ways, of course.

In November 1890, McLaughlin began to enlarge his Indian police force. He ordered them to keep a close watch on Sitting Bull's camp and make certain that the old chief did not leave.

In mid-December McLaughlin learned that Sitting Bull had been invited to the Stronghold, where he would join the Pine Ridge and Rosebud Sioux under Short Bull and Kicking Bear. The agent was determined to stop Sitting Bull from taking his group to Pine Ridge. He knew that a stalemate had developed there, and he felt that Sitting Bull's presence might be enough to tip the scales toward open warfare between the Sioux and the cavalry. So McLaughlin ordered Sitting Bull's arrest. He commanded the Indian police, who were led by an experienced lieutenant, Bull Head, to sneak into Sitting Bull's camp at dawn on December 15. They were to arrest the chief and bring him into the agency.

Bull Head and the police met the command with mixed feelings. Most of them were progressives. They prayed to the white man's God before starting their mission. But the thought of Sitting Bull still brought back memories of the great days of the Sioux. One of the police, He Alone, whose white name was John Lone Man, later remembered the way he felt when the orders were read and translated to the police. (The English here is the work of an educated relative of his.)

I'm simply expressing my viewpoint as one who had reformed from all the heathenish ways, formerly one of the loyal followers of Chief Sitting Bull. But ever since I was about ten years of age, I had participated in a good many buffalo hunts and fought under Sitting Bull. But the most important fight I took part in was the Custer fight. After this fight I still went with Sitting Bull's band to Canada. Even after Sitting Bull was returned to Standing Rock Reservation, I remained in his camp, where I tamed down somewhat. We all felt sad.

The police gathered in the early evening of December 14 and passed the night telling war stories. Then, just before dawn, Bull Head ordered He Alone and the thirty or so other police to get ready.

Sitting Bull's camp stood on the north bank of the Grand River. The police, circling from the east, crossed the river to cut off any possible excape southward toward Pine Ridge. Soon they could see Sitting Bull's log cabin. In front of it stood the very tall tepee that was the headquarters for the Ghost Dance. Sitting Bull's two wives, his son Crow Foot, and several other children and relatives lived in the cabin. Other tepees were scattered around it. The police paused for a moment, then crossed the river again. He Alone recalled:

> We rode up as if we attacked the camp. We quickly dismounted, and while our officers went inside we all scattered around the cabin. It was still dark, and everybody was asleep, and only dogs greeted us.
>
> Bull Head knocked at the door, and the Chief answered, *"How, timahel hiyu you."* [All right, come in.]
>
> Bull Head said, "I come to arrest you. You are under arrest."
>
> Sitting Bull said, "How. Let me put on my clothes and go with you."
>
> When Sitting Bull started to go with the police, one of Sitting Bull's wives burst into a loud cry which drew attention. No sooner had this started, when several leaders were rapidly making their way toward Sitting Bull's cabin. Bear That Catches, particularly, came up close saying, "Now, here are the metal breasts[3] just as we had expected. You think you are going to take him. You shall not do it."

By now the entire camp was up and angry. The police might still have been able to arrest the sleepy Sitting Bull if Crow Foot, his seventeen-year-old son, had not intervened. Sitting Bull had been grooming Crow Foot to be a chief, filling his youthful head with tales of courage in battle. As He Alone described it, Crow Foot upset the delicate balance of fear and anger:

> Just about this time, Crow Foot got up, moved by the wailing of his mother and the remarks of Bear That Catches, and said to Sitting Bull, "Well, you always called yourself a brave chief. Now you are allowing yourself to be taken by the metal breasts."
>
> Sitting Bull then changed his mind, and said, *"Ho ca mni kte sni yelo."* [Then I will not go.]
>
> Lieutenant Bull Head said to the chief, "Come now, do not listen to any one."
>
> I said to Sitting Bull, "Uncle,[4] nobody is going to harm you. Please do not let others lead you into any trouble.
>
> But the chief's mind was made up not to go, so the three head officers laid their hands on him, pulling him outside. By this time, the whole camp was in commotion. Bear That Catches pulled out a gun from under his blanket and fired into Lieutenant Bull Head, wounding him. I ran up toward where they were holding the chief, when Bear That Catches raised his gun. He pointed and fired at me, but it snapped [misfired]. I jerked the gun away from his hands and laid him out. It was about this moment that Lieutenant Bull Head fired into Sitting Bull while still holding him, and Red Tomahawk followed with another shot which finished the chief.

---

[3]"Metal breasts" was a reference to the policemen's badges.
[4]Indians often used words like "Uncle" and "Father" as terms of respect.

There was more shooting, and soon the Ghost Dancers ran for a line of trees. After a time the police took shelter in Sitting Bull's cabin. The inner walls of the cabin were unfinished but hung with strips of brightly colored sheeting, sewn together and tacked to the walls. Suddenly, one of the policemen noticed a movement in a corner, behind the sheeting. He Alone raised the curtain:

> There stood Crow Foot, and as soon as he was exposed to view, he cried out, "My uncles, do not kill me. I do not wish to die." Lieutenant Bull Head said, "Do what you like with him. He is the one that has caused this trouble." I do not remember who fired the shot that killed Crow Foot—several fired at once.

Just after Crow Foot was killed, the cavalry units from Fort Yates arrived. The remaining members of Sitting Bull's band scattered toward the south.

He Alone and the rest of the Indian police went home filled with the confusion that was so much a part of reservation life. He Alone performed a Sioux ritual. He built a small shelter and dropped hot stones into water to create a steam bath "that I might cleanse myself for participating in a bloody fight with my fellow men." Then he burned all the clothes he had worn to Sitting Bull's camp. Next, He Alone set out to perform a white man's ritual:

> The next day, I took my family into the agency. I reported to Major McLaughlin. He laid his hand on my shoulders, and said, 'He Alone is a man. I feel very proud of you for the way you have carried out your part in the fight with the Ghost Dancers.' I was not very brave right at that moment. His comment nearly set me a-crying.

Four Indian policemen died at Sitting Bull's camp. Two more (including Lieutenant Bull Head) would soon be dead of their wounds. One of them, Shave Head, asked McLaughlin, "Did I do well, father?" McLaughlin nodded. Shave Head went on:

> Then I will die in the faith of the white man, to which my five children already belong. Send for my wife, that we may be married by the Black Gown [priest] before I die.

Shave Head's wife came, but too late. The next day, the six dead Indian police were buried. A squad of bluecoats fired honorary volleys over the graves, and taps were blown.

At least eight of Sitting Bull's followers had died. Their bodies were left where they had fallen. Only Sitting Bull was buried. A few moments after completion of the ceremonies for the Indian police, Sitting Bull's body, in a plain coffin, was lowered into a grave in the Fort Yates cemetery. The only people who watched were three officers, serving as official witnesses, and the four guardhouse gravediggers.

None of Sitting Bull's followers was present at his burial. Most of them—about 400—had fled south and west from the Grand River camp. The authorities at Standing Rock had a number of nightmarish ideas about what might happen next. The Standing Rock Ghost Dancers might join Chief Big Foot on the Cheyenne River, where the dance had been in full swing for weeks. On the other hand, the frightened Sitting Bull group might strike out for the Stronghold, where Short Bull and Kicking Bear still held out. Or they might set Big Foot in motion toward the Stronghold too, with terrible results. News of the death of Sitting Bull, likely to spread like prairie fire, could ignite the entire Sioux reservation system.

Agent McLaughlin immediately sent friendly scouts to find Sitting Bull's band. Upon finding them, the scouts were able to persuade over half to return to the Standing Rock Reservation. Some of those who simply scattered sooner or later also went back to their homes around Grand River. The rest—fewer than a hundred—headed south to join Big Foot.

They reached a camp that was already nervous and confused. Big Foot had been a great chief. But he was old now, in his seventies, and his control over his band was slipping. The band's medicine man, Yellow Bird, was a fanatical Ghost Dancer. Many of the young braves were ready to bring about their hoped-for victory over the whites. There were about 200 in the band, and all of them were aware of mounting pressure from the white soldiers.

The War Department had ordered Big Foot's arrest, on the false theory that he was almost as large a source of potential trouble as Sitting Bull had been. An observation camp, Camp Cheyenne, had been established by the cavalry just a few miles up the Cheyenne River. Infantry units from the east were trying to cross the Missouri River, which was partially ice-covered.

For several days Big Foot wavered among various alternatives. At one point he was convinced by messengers from the cavalry to go to the Cheyenne River Agency. But many of his young men wanted to go to the Stronghold instead. Big Foot had also been invited by the Pine Ridge chiefs to go there to settle the troubles. He had a great reputation as a diplomat, and he was offered a hundred ponies to heal the split between the "friendly" Sioux and the Ghost Dancers at Pine Ridge. Most of the time, however, Big Foot seemed to want only to stay put at his own camp and wait.

Finally, for reasons that are difficult to guess, Big Foot made his decision. He would go to Pine Ridge, make peace, and accept the gift of ponies. What he did not realize was that leaving his reservation when the whites were so frightened of a Sioux "uprising" would make him a fugitive "hostile" in the eyes of the military. Almost immediately, new orders went out for Big Foot's arrest. His band was to be disarmed and their horses taken. Then they would be marched to the railroad and sent to Omaha—far away from their own reservation lands. Big Foot never understood that this was the army's plan. He assumed that he was going to Pine Ridge on a mission of peace.

Big Foot's band left camp on December 23, under the cover of night. As soon as the officers at Camp Cheyenne realized that the old chief had gone, a desperate series of cavalry units started patrolling the line between Big Foot's camp and the Stronghold. But the chief passed east of the patrols. The band moved very slowly, for Big Foot had caught pneumonia. He rode in a wagon without springs. Soon Big Foot was bleeding from his nose. And it was bitterly cold for the old man. At one point, in a pass through a steep wall along the Bad River, Big Foot's men had to dig out a road for the wagon. Big Foot managed to reach Porcupine Creek, only about thirty miles from the Pine Ridge Agency, without being sighted by the army. He sent men ahead to tell the Sioux he was coming.

On December 28, five days after starting south, Big Foot's band was finally "captured" by the Seventh Cavalry. When the Indians and cavalry met, there was a tense moment. The cavalry formed a skirmish line and brought up cannon. Big Foot's braves formed a battle line in front of his wagon. But then the cavalry commander came forward. He and Big Foot shook hands, and the chief accepted an "escort"—going, he thought, to Pine Ridge. Together, the cavalry and the Indians made their way to a trading post at Wounded Knee Creek.

The officer in charge had wisely not tried to disarm the Sioux, and he let them keep their horses for the trip. He even transferred Big Foot into an ambulance wagon. When the two groups reached Wounded Knee, the Indians were issued rations. The rest of the Seventh Cavalry came from Pine Ridge to join the patrol. The Indians pitched their tepees in a low hollow near a ravine that led into the creek. There were 102 men and 230 women and children. The soldiers—a total of about 500—camped on a rise just to the north. Armed sentries surrounded the Indians, but on the whole everything seemed peaceful enough.

Soon the Indians settled down and the cavalry—except for the ring of sentries around the Indian camp—went to sleep. Only a few officers, veterans of the Little Bighorn disaster, stayed up late. They celebrated over a keg of whiskey someone had brought from the agency.

The next morning Colonel James Forsyth, commander of the Seventh Cavalry, asked all the men of Big Foot's group to gather in a council between the tepees and the cavalry encampment. The sentries remained in place. The rest of the cavalry units drew up, mounted, around the Sioux men and their camp. Forsyth asked the Indians for their weapons.

Big Foot tried diplomacy. From his ambulance bed he quietly advised his men to give up the bad guns but hide the good ones. Soon Forsyth sent twenty of the Indians to the tepees to bring the guns. Meanwhile, however, the Sioux women (who understood the value of a weapon) had hidden the rifles that the Sioux had bought, stolen, or taken in battle. The Indians returned to the council with only two old, broken cavalry carbines.

Forsyth heightened his search. He placed a line of troops between the Sioux braves and their camp and sent his own men into the tepees. But this search uncovered only thirty rifles, most of them old and useless. This left one other real possibility: the Sioux were hiding their rifles under the blankets they kept draped over their shoulders against the cold.

By now the situation was very delicate. Forsyth ordered Big Foot brought out on his blanket. The medicine man, Yellow Bird, was dancing around, chanting Ghost Dance songs, urging the young braves to be firm. In the tepees women were hastily packing, ready to run.

Suddenly, one Indian, Black Coyote, pulled a rifle from his blanket and began to shout, holding the weapon over his head. He was probably deaf and, by the Indians' own testimony, a little insane. Two soldiers grabbed him and struggled for the rifle. It went off, firing overhead. In what may have been a signal, Yellow Bird threw a handful of dust into the air. Several braves pulled rifles from their blankets and aimed at the cavalry. "By God, they have broken," an officer shouted. The Indians fired, and at about the same moment came the command "Fire! Fire on them!"

No one could stop what happened next. Big Foot was quickly killed. Cavalry carbines ripped into the group of Sioux men. The bullets that did not find a Sioux body passed on across the ravine into the tepees. Women ran this way and that, followed by children. Some of the Indians broke toward the creek, where they were cut down by waiting cavalrymen. Others ran into the ravine.

Corporal Paul Weinert manned one of the Seventh Cavalry's small, rapid-fire cannon on the hill. Like the other cavalrymen, he was surprised when the firing started. But within a moment or two, he was caught up in the battle, pumping shots angrily wherever he saw moving Sioux:

> All of the Indians opened fire on us. Lieutenant Hawthorne ran toward me and was calling, when suddenly I heard him say, "Oh, my God!" and then I knew he had been hit. I said: "By God! I'll make 'em pay for that," and ran the gun into the opening of the ravine. They kept yelling for me to come back. Bullets were coming like hail from the Indians' Winchesters. I kept going in farther, and pretty soon everything was quiet at the other end of the line.

Corporal Weinert was a soldier with a sophisticated weapon. The experience of Catching Spirit Elk, a Sioux who had surrendered his rifle, was almost the opposite of Weinert's:

> Then followed firing from all sides. I threw myself on the ground. I then jumped up to run toward the Indian camp, but was then and there shot down, being hit on my right leg, and soon after was shot again on the other leg. When the general firing ceased, I heard an interpreter calling out, saying the wounded would be kindly treated. I opened my eyes and looked about and saw the dead and wounded all around me.

Some officers did what they could to prevent women and children from being shot down. But the Indians (at least those who still had weapons) were fast and accurate with their repeating rifles, and the soldiers

The Sioux who died at Wounded Knee were buried in a mass grave. With them died the last remnants of Indian resistance on the Western plains.

sometimes fired at anything that moved. When the artillery on the hill opened up on the Indians in the ravine, the shells exploded on all without regard to age or sex. Apparently, too, some of the soldiers broke ranks and chased down fleeing Indians. These were the bodies Charles Eastman found miles away from Wounded Knee.

The actual battle lasted only a few minutes and the cavalry's mopping-up only a short time longer. About 150 braves rode out from Pine Ridge, too late and too few to help their comrades. The cavalry gathered their own dead (25) and wounded (39) and returned to the Pine Ridge Agency. They took some of the wounded Sioux with them and left the rest on the field. There were at least 146 Indian dead—about half of them men. Some bodies were probably taken away during the next two days, before Eastman's party arrived to rescue the living and bury the rest. All in all, probably 200 Sioux and whites had died.

Wounded Knee was followed by a few small skirmishes. But soon Pine Ridge was pacified. The Stronghold Indians had given up while Big Foot's band was on the march. The Ghost Dance was over. Spring came and went, but the earth did not cover the white man, as the Messiah had promised. Paul Weinert, the cannoneer, received a Congressional Medal of Honor for his part in the action at the edge of the ravine.

A small white church was later built at the Sioux mass grave, on what came to be called Cemetery Hill. In 1903, with the help of missionaries, the Indians put up their own small monument, burying Wounded Knee in the past.

This monument is erected by surviving relatives and other Ogalalla and Cheyenne River Sioux Indians in memory of the Chief Big Foot Massacre, Dec. 29, 1890. Col. Forsyth in command of U.S. troops. Big Foot was a great chief of the Sioux Indians. He often said, "I will stand in peace till my last day comes." He did many good and brave deeds for the white man and the red man. Many innocent women and children who knew no wrong died here.

28
SETTLING THE LAST FRONTIER

R.J.W.

There is nothing unique about the history of the Sioux. It is true they resisted the whites longer and more ferociously than most other Indians, east or west. And they were the only tribe that, inspired by the Messiah's new religion, developed a militant resistance to reservation life. But, despite these differences, they were finally defeated in a manner typical of the way in which white Americans subdued all the Indians.

The defeat of the Sioux and the other Plains Indians was just one part of the history of continental expansion. White Americans had begun moving west in the 1830s. In decades after the Civil War, this movement increased in speed and recklessness.

THE LAST WEST

Until the 1840s, America had a clearly drawn frontier. It was possible at each census before then to draw a zigzag line from north to south showing how far settlement had advanced in each decade. But after the Mexican War this was no longer true. The drift of pioneers into Oregon, the settlement of Texas and Utah, and the discovery of gold in California created isolated pockets of white settlement thousands of miles beyond the old frontier line near the Mississippi. By the early 1850s it was evident that the Pacific Coast would be settled fairly quickly, organized into territories, and carved into states. California had already been admitted

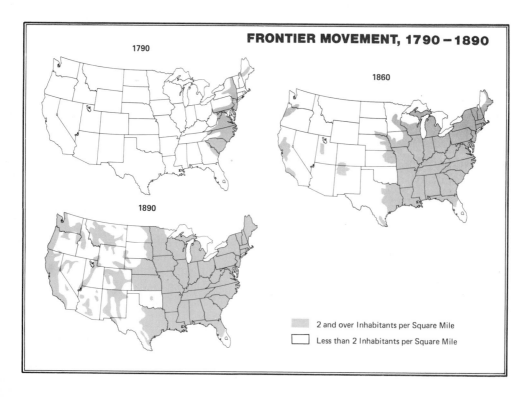

FRONTIER MOVEMENT, 1790–1890

1790

1860

1890

2 and over Inhabitants per Square Mile

Less than 2 Inhabitants per Square Mile

to statehood as part of the Compromise of 1850. Oregon entered the Union nine years later.

Between the Pacific Coast and the old frontier in eastern Kansas and Nebraska lay a vast stretch of plains and mountains. It formed an area larger than the whole territory over which Washington governed as President. This region was the last frontier, the last region to be settled by white Americans.

The Great Plains begin in the first tier of states west of the Mississippi River, and extend west to the Rockies. In 1836 the Senate Committee for Indian Affairs declared that the Great Plains were an "uninhabitable region." The Indians there "are on the outside of us, and in a place which will forever remain on the outside." In fact the plains were given an official name, "The Great American Desert." The weather there is dry. There is no water in many of the rivers during most of the year. The land is not covered with trees but with stubborn grass. Only the Indian and the buffalo seemed able to thrive. The Rocky Mountain region also seemed to offer little to encourage settlement. For many years its great peaks and high valleys were the home of only small Indian bands and a few American fur traders.

There were many reasons why this myth that the West could not be settled came to an end. Three of the earliest and most important factors were gold, railroads, and cattle. As miners, railroad men, and ranchers moved into the region, they systematically seized Indian lands. Then came the final pioneers of the last West, the farmers. In 1890 the Census Bureau announced that the frontier no longer existed.

THE MINING FRONTIER

The discovery of gold and silver had been responsible for the rapid development of California. Miners who reached the Pacific Coast too late to find gold easily soon began to drift east over the mountains, looking for new bonanzas. In 1858 prospectors found gold near Pike's Peak in Colorado. Soon people were pouring into new, ramshackle towns like Denver, Pueblo, and Boulder.

Their covered wagons proclaimed "Pike's Peak or Bust!" A year after the first strike about 100,000 people — mostly men without their families — had moved into the area. Like most other Western gold and silver strikes, the Pike's Peak boom did not last. The earliest prospectors soon raked off the surface gold. The remaining precious metal was buried deep in the mountains, where it could be mined only with expensive machinery that individual miners could not afford. Within three months in 1859 the population of the Colorado goldfields dwindled to about 50,000. But enough men stayed to create a pocket of white settlement in the mountains.

A similar process was under way farther west, in what is now Nevada. Miners from California found gold near the western border of the region in the late 1850s. In 1859 they discovered the famous Comstock Lode. One of the richest single mines in America, it produced over $200 million worth of gold and silver in the thirty years following its discovery. Thousands of men rushed over the mountains from Sacramento to build nearby Virginia City. Soon the town had five newspapers, a miniature stock exchange, and a horde of prospectors, saloonkeepers, prostitutes, and gamblers. A few men became enormously wealthy. Most of the prospectors, however, went away disappointed.

Some miners who stayed found small pockets of loose gold that could be mined with a pan or a sluice, a simple trough that runs water downhill over dirt and loose rocks, washing out the heavy gold dust. This kind of mining, called placer mining, soon washed off the free metal near the surface. The only way to make the goldfields pay off on a large scale over a long period was to invest money in machinery that could dig out hard rock below the surface. This meant that the miner's frontier quickly became a corporate frontier, exploited by mining companies owned by Eastern investors. Within a few years any successful field soon became an industrial development. And the prospectors scattered again in search of a new discovery and easy pickings elsewhere.

The California Gold Rush that had excited so many thousands of Americans in 1849 was repeated over and over again throughout the West.

Virginia City, Nevada, sprang up after the discovery of silver nearby in 1859. Mark Twain described it as "the liveliest town that America ever produced" in its early years. Schools, churches, and "respectable" businesses replaced saloons and gambling halls after the initial excitement of silver fever had died down.

Open-pit mining, utilizing expensive heavy machinery to dig through the surface of hard rock to the ores below, helped turn the miner's frontier into a corporate frontier.

In the late 1850s a small strike was made in eastern Washington, but it seen petered out. Restless miners headed farther east, up the Snake and Salmon rivers into Idaho. There they built Boise, Silver City, and other new mining towns. By 1861, the start of the Civil War, there were probably 30,000 white men in Idaho.

During the Civil War—while their countrymen were battling at Bull Run and Chickamauga—white miners moved from Idaho into Montana. There they struck gold and silver at Last Chance Gulch (which later became the city of Helena) and Alder Gulch (Virginia City). By 1863 Idaho had enough citizens to organize as a territory, and Montana followed a year later.

The last Western gold rush occurred in 1874. In the Black Hills of South Dakota, in the heart of the Great Sioux reservation, an army expedition commanded by General Custer found traces of gold. According to a treaty between the United States and the Indians, the hills belonged to the Sioux "forever." For a short time the government tried to prevent white men from entering the Black Hills. But the pressure to find gold was too great. Within two years about 7,000 whites had built Deadwood and Custer City. The Sioux lands had been decisively invaded.

TRANSPORTATION WEST

The influx of miners, together with the settlement of Oregon and California, led to demands for quick, safe, and economical land transportation between the settled East and the Far West. Every new mining town wanted to be linked to the rest of the country. People who lived on the west coast wanted an overland route as an alternate to the long sea voyage around South America.

Trail, Stage, and Pony The Oregon Trail, Santa Fe Trail, and other routes followed by pioneers in the 1840s and early 1850s were more or less protected by army posts along the way. But they were far from being real roads. Something else seemed necessary.

In 1858 the first stage road was finally cut through the countryside for the Butterfield Overland Express. Its route ran 2,000 miles, from St. Louis south through Indian Territory,[1] then across

---

[1]This region—corresponding roughly to the present state of Oklahoma—was set aside in 1834 for Indians removed from east of the Mississippi. Later, parts of it were reserved for Western Indians, too.

This 1859 sketch shows a stage near Tucson, Arizona, on the Butterfield Overland Express route. Passengers had to endure the rough ride through desert lands on springless seats.

Texas, New Mexico, and Arizona. The ride was rough and usually very hot; although it took twenty-four days, the overland trip was faster than the sea voyage. Soon other stage and freighting companies were opening additional roads across Colorado and Utah to California.

In 1860 businessmen set up a mail service known as the pony express. Small, lightweight boys, like jockeys, rode big horses (not ponies) in relays between St. Joseph, Missouri, and Sacramento, California. The young riders were able to carry a message across the country in ten days. The pony express prospered for only about a year, however. In 1861 the first telegraph line was put through to the west coast. The time for sending and receiving cross-country messages was then cut to a split second.

A Transcontinental Railroad All these ways of getting people, goods, and information across the country were only preludes to the most dramatic and successful method of all, the railroad. A transcontinental railroad had been a dream since the 1840s — to move people through the West to California. The North and the South, however, had not been able to agree on the western part of the route. The North wanted a line to run from Chicago to San Francisco. The South insisted on a route through Texas to southern California.

The Civil War ended this competition. By seceding, the South lost its right to participate in the decision making. In 1862 Congress settled on a route between Council Bluffs, Iowa, and San Francisco. The same law provided for enormous financial support from the federal government. There would be two companies. The Central Pacific would build east from San Francisco. The Union Pacfic (a patriotic name suited to wartime) would go west across Nebraska and Colorado. They were to meet somewhere in the middle.

A railroad line spanning the continent would not have been possible without the help of thousands of Chinese laborers, who did much of the work on the Central Pacific.

Each railroad would be given a right of way 400 feet wide. In addition, the government would lend the railroads up to $48,000 for each mile of track laid—less for flat country, more for mountain track. Most important, the railroads would be given 6,400 acres for every mile of track completed. In 1864 this land allowance was doubled.

The Central Pacific started building toward the east slowly. The company lacked funds, and labor was scarce. But gradually these problems were resolved. The Lincoln administration cooperated by allowing the railroad to claim flat-country miles as mountain miles, thus entitling the companies to the largest possible federal loans. The labor problem was solved by importing thousands of Chinese. In 1864 the railroad laid only about 20 miles of track, but by 1867 the pace was up to 20 miles a month.

At the other end of the proposed route the Union Pacific also built slowly, at first. But it picked up speed by bringing in thousands of Irish immigrants to lay rails. In 1868 alone the Union Pacific laid 425 miles of track.

In May 1869, after only five years of construction, the two work gangs met at Promontory Point, Utah, just east of the Great Salt Lake. The last tie put down was coated with silver; the last spike was gold. A telegraph operator cabled east and west: "Hats off—prayer is being offered." Then there was a wait of almost fifteen minutes. Again the telegraph clicked: "We have got done praying. The spike is about to be presented." Railroad officials took turns with the hammer; the first blow was a bad miss, but the work was done. The two locomotives eased forward until they touched. The nation celebrated almost as wildly as it had at the end of the Civil War. Chicago's parade was seven miles long. The nation was joined, east to west, across a desert that an earlier generation had believed would never be settled.

During the next fifteen years three more routes were opened across the Rockies. Iowa, Missouri, Kansas, and Nebraska were crisscrossed by rails. In the process the government gave the railroad companies almost 180 million acres of public land, and it lent them over $100 million. Because of complicated regulations that allowed railroads to delay choosing the land they wanted to keep along their rights of way, they were able to keep great stretches of land for years. At one point the railroads controlled—at least on paper—almost all of Iowa and Wisconsin. The Northern Pacific, whose route crossed the northern tier of states between Lake Superior and the Pacific, controlled a strip of land larger in area than many European nations. The same kind of situation developed in Arizona and New Mexico. By 1885 the railroads held land totaling almost a sixth of the entire country.

Many of the congressmen and senators who voted these huge grants to the railroads did so in the belief that most of the land in the "Great American Desert" was of little value. The motive behind the first transcontinental lines was not to build a transportation network for the Great Plains and the Rockies but to build a link to the Pacific Coast. It took a generation's experience to make clear that the intervening territory was valuable, that it would be settled and farmed. As things turned out, the railroads may have been a very efficient mechanism for disposing of the public lands, at least in some areas. The government's own land policy was confused and often corrupt, and the public interest may, on balance, have been served about as well by the railroad grants as by the government's direct land grant practices.

FROM BUFFALO TO CATTLE

In any case, the first important effects of the railroads on the Great Plains had less to do with land ownership and cultivation than with animals. The railroads created a new industry on the plains—ranching. Building the railroads not only hastened the destruction of the buffalo herds, it also made possible the systematic exploitation of another set of resources: grass and cows.

Early in the sixteenth century the Spanish had begun importing European cattle into America. Over the years the cattle had multiplied. Some had escaped and become wild, especially in southern Texas around the Nueces River. These were the famous Texas longhorns—lanky, tough, long-horned, and too dangerous to be captured or

THE LAST FRONTIER
c.1860-1890

┼┼┼ Railroads
••••• Cattle trails
⚒ Mining sites
🐂 Cattle raising areas after 1880

0   100   200   300 MILES

herded on foot. They roamed at will over the open range, a huge expanse of grass that was part of the public domain. By 1860, there were probably 5 million head of longhorns in Texas.

The Mexicans had learned to rope, brand, and even herd longhorns. In fact, it was Mexicans and not Americans who were the first cowboys. They originated almost all of the tools of the cowboy's trade, from his big hat and kerchief to his tooled leather saddle and boots. Mexico, however, had no real market for beef. The situation was different in the United States.

The Civil War sent beef prices soaring in both the North and the South. The beef herd in the Northern states was smaller at the end of the war than it had been at the beginning. At the same time, the population had grown by more than 20 percent. Thus the demand and price for beef had increased. A man could buy a longhorn steer in Texas for as little as three dollars. The same steer in Chicago was worth ten times as much.

The Long Drive By 1866 the Missouri Pacific Railroad had pushed its line west to Sedalia, Missouri, just east of Kansas City. That same year the first large group of Texans drove enormous herds north across Indian Territory to reach the rail line. The men ran into many difficulties. Part of the route passed through dense forests. The longhorns, unaccustomed to woods, panicked and refused to be driven through the trees. The Indians (whose treaty gave them control of all white travel across their land) harassed the cowboys. This early attempt showed, however, that it was possible to herd cattle safely over hundreds of miles to the railroad—and thus to Eastern markets.

Thus began the twenty-year era of the "long drive." As the years passed, the railroads extended farther west. New cattle towns replaced Sedalia. Among them were Abilene (probably the most successful), Wichita, and Dodge City. Between 1866 and 1888, Texans drove as many as 6 million head of cattle over the grasslands to Kansas.

For those who succeeded, the profits of the long drive were enormous. Cattlemen claimed that as much as 40 percent profit per year was not unusual. Like the miner's frontier, the cattleman's bonanza soon attracted thousands of eager Easterners. Each usually had a few hundred dollars and a dream of running a vast ranch. Like the prospectors, most of the would-be ranchers were disappointed. Many of them either returned home or switched to another line of work such as running a store or saloon.

The long drive, despite the romantic myth of the cowboy it fostered, was a business. It required capital if it was to succeed on a big scale. In the end only the lucky few who had been there first (like the prospectors in California or Nevada) became "cattle barons." In the long run, it was Eastern and European investors, with enough capital to buy and move large herds, who controlled most of the industry.

The long drives of cattle from the rich grasslands of the Southwest to Northern markets lasted through the 1880s. They created vast fortunes for a few fortunate cattle barons and gave the country the legend of the cowboy.

The End of the Open Range   The long drive had a brief existence. Gradually, people north of Texas realized that, as the railroads came closer, it made sense to breed and feed cattle nearby instead of driving them up from Texas. During the 1880s the long drive from Texas was replaced by an even wilder cattle bonanza in other plains territories to the north. In 1860 there were no cattle at all in the northwestern plains, and there were only a few in Kansas and Nebraska. By 1880 Montana, the Dakota Territory, Wyoming, and Colorado had great herds, totaling almost 4 million head.

But the days of the open range, when cattle wandered on public land from one spring to the next, could not last long. The cattle industry soon found itself in a situation faced earlier by tobacco and cotton growers—overproduction. Rapid expansion led to an overstocked range. The grass could not support so many cattle. The increased supply also caused prices to fall. Between 1885 and 1886 the price of a steer dropped from thirty dollars to ten dollars. The following winter on the plains was the bitterest in memory. Thousands of cattle starved and froze to death. The cattle bonanza was over.

THE DEFEAT OF THE WESTERN INDIANS

The miners, railroaders, and cattlemen brought about the final chapter in the conflict between whites and Indians. It was a conflict older than Jamestown and as dark as any aspect of American history. The whites cloaked their actions with high-sounding expressions like "civilization against savagery" or "Manifest Destiny." But the facts were very simple: the white men came and took the Indians' lands.

White people in the New World had always regarded the Indians as a "problem." For most whites—whether they were French, Spanish, or English—the Indians were seen either as a people to be exploited through trade or slavery or as a barrier to westward expansion. A few whites sympa-

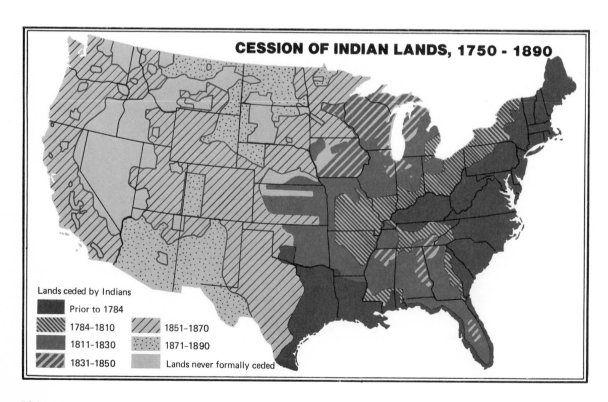

CESSION OF INDIAN LANDS, 1750 - 1890

Lands ceded by Indians

- Prior to 1784
- 1784–1810
- 1811–1830
- 1831–1850
- 1851–1870
- 1871–1890
- Lands never formally ceded

thized with the Indians and did what they could to protect them from the worst aspects of white civilization. But even to those who were sympathetic, helping meant teaching the Indians to "adjust to civilization."

The Indians might be a "problem" for the whites, but for the Indians the whites meant disaster. At stake for the whites was only the delay of continental expansion for a generation or so. The stakes for the Indians were much higher. They were in danger of losing their culture, their freedom, their identity as human beings, and, in many cases, their lives. This was true from the time Cortes invaded Mexico, through Bacon's Rebellion and the removal of the Cherokee and other tribes westward,[2] down to the final conquest of the tribes of the West.

Advantages of the Whites White people's ways were overpowering to the Indians. In the first place, the whites' methods of dealing with the environment were totally unlike those of the Indians. Some Indians farmed a little. But the whites were able to cultivate vast stretches of land, first with teams of mules or oxen, then with machinery. Some Indians, like the Navajos, made ornaments out of silver or gold. But the whites came for gold and silver in droves. Big new towns and frightening machines and explosives changed the face of the mountains and valleys of the Rockies. The Indians hunted wild animals, which seemed numerous enough to last forever. But the whites killed off the wild animals, fenced in the range, and raised great herds of cattle instead.

These were the main weapons of the whites—farming, mining, and ranching. Along with these the whites brought strange powers and "medicine" that made the Indians' situation hopeless indeed—the railroad, soldiers' machine guns and cannons, and the telegraph.

Another weapon of the whites against the Indians was something they did not use on purpose—indeed, the whites feared it themselves.

[2]In the 1830s the federal government forced the so-called Five Civilized Tribes—the Cherokees, Chickasaws, Choctaws, Creeks, and Seminoles—to move from the Southeast to Indian Territory. The Indians suffered so much on the trip west that the journey became known as the trail of tears.

These Mandan Indians survived a smallpox epidemic in 1872. Indians had no immunity to white men's diseases like smallpox and therefore died by the thousands when exposed to them.

This was disease. Smallpox, measles, and other sicknesses may have wiped out as many as half the Western Indians before any significant number of whites even arrived in their territory. The germs traveled with traders and so preceded actual white migrations by decades. The Indians had no inherited resistance or immunity to many diseases of the whites, since the germs had been "imported" from Europe. Indians died by the band and even by the tribe from sicknesses that only made most whites uncomfortable.

Finally, the whites had an advantage that probably counted more than anything else—numbers. They poured west by the thousands. In one change of seasons, between one Sun Dance and another, the whites seemed able to throw up towns like San Francisco, Denver, or Deadwood—towns with populations larger than the whole Sioux nation.

One by one, the tribes of the Great Plains, the California-Intermountain area, and the Northwest Coast were made to realize that the whites were a force they could neither understand nor control. Some groups, like the Sioux, the Kiowas, and the Apaches, fought back. They were sustained by their myths, their magic, and their hatred of the cavalry that invaded their villages, shooting men, women, and children. But, in the end, all the tribes were defeated. Only something as unusual as the Messiah's Ghost Dance could convince the Indians—and only a few at that—that there was any way to combat the enveloping white civilization.

Dealing with the Tribes From the beginning, United States policy toward the Indians had been contradictory. On the one hand, the government treated tribes as independent nations with whom it could make treaties. On the other hand, Indians were not citizens but wards of the government, subject to federal control. In addition, the American nation was growing with incredible speed. Again and again, government aims that seemed practical in one decade were obsolete ten years later.

In California and Oregon, and in the frontier regions of the Rockies, relations between whites and Indians were poorly controlled by the government. Groups of whites simply drove the Indians out, murdering many of them in the process. The Indians of California suffered especially. They had settled around Spanish missions and learned farming and various crafts. After the Spanish missions were closed down in the 1830s, the Indians were defenseless against the greedy whites. In the ten years after the Gold Rush of 1849, some 70,000 of these mission Indians died from starvation, disease, and outright murder.

On the Great Plains, whites might band together to attack Indians. But the government and its army played a much larger role in keeping the peace there than it did farther west. After 1850 the history of Indian-white relations settled down to a fairly steady rhythm of treaties, uprisings, war, and new treaties. The Indians were always the losers. Even when they won the battles, they lost in the making of the treaties.

This process began in 1851 at Fort Laramie on the Oregon Trail. To protect the trail, the government called hundreds of Indian leaders together and persuaded them to agree not to bother the wagon trains crossing their territory. Each tribe accepted boundaries to its hunting grounds. In return, the government promised to leave them in peace.

These agreements left the Indians in possession of almost all of the Great Plains. But, accepting boundaries laid out by Washington opened the door to a new government tactic—getting each tribe, by a separate treaty, to give up part of its lands. By 1865 the Indians had given up all of Kansas, most of Nebraska, the central half of Utah, and almost all of Texas.

The Sand Creek Massacre Much Indian land was surrendered peacefully, in return for promises of peace and annual shipments of government supplies, called annuities. But in 1861 in Colorado, a government attempt to move Cheyennes and Arapahoes onto a small reservation at Sand Creek resulted in the Indians waging a three-year guerrilla war. In 1864 the leader of the warring Indians, Black Kettle, tried to make peace with the whites. The army and the territorial government refused. The unyielding commander of the Colorado militia, Colonel John Chivington, told Black Kettle: "My rule for fighting white men or Indians is to fight them until they lay down their arms and surrender."

Black Kettle led his people to a camp at Sand Creek, where he hoped to be left in peace. But the Indians woke on November 29, 1864, to find 1,000 of Chivington's militia surrounding them. The militia rushed the camp, shooting at everything that moved. When the "fight" was over, 450 Indians were dead. Only about 50 had escaped the massacre. The next year the Cheyennes and Arapahoes had to sign a new treaty. It forced them to leave their Colorado plains for a barren corner of Indian Territory.

Negotiations with the Sioux The Sioux fared better, at least for a time. Their agreement at Fort Laramie in 1851 gave them one of the largest hunting areas in the West—most of the Dakota

CHIEF JOSEPH

Hinmaton-Yalaktit was his name— "thunder coming out of the water and over the land." He was a chief in the tribe the whites called Nez Percé—"pierced nose"—because of their habit of wearing nose ornaments made of shells. Joseph was his white man's name, and, like his biblical namesake, he was taken as a captive into a distant and hostile land. Before he went, however, he did two things. He fought the most brilliant and sustained military campaign against the United States Army ever waged by any American Indian leader. And he made the most poignant and famous surrender speech any American Indian ever delivered.

The surrender and the speech were the outcome of a long train of events that parallel very closely what happened to the Sioux and the other tribes of the West. In 1863, the Nez Percé ceded most of their lands to the United States and agreed to live on a small reservation in Idaho. A portion of the tribe, however, refused to recognize the treaty and became renegades. For ten years, the government did not try to enforce the treaty, and all the Nez Percé had to do was fend off the aggressive behavior of individual white squatters. This was the situation when Joseph, at age thirty-three, became chief after his father's death in 1873.

In 1876 (the year of Custer's expedition against the Sioux), the government decided to enforce the treaty and move the "renegade" Nez Percé onto the Idaho reservation. A group of Joseph's warriors, almost certainly without his blessing, went on a rampage and killed twenty or so white settlers. Reluctantly, Joseph was drawn into a situation in which he knew final victory was impossible. He decided to strike out for Canada.

The force Joseph led into the mountains was an impractical one. It contained fewer than 200 fighting men, who had to protect and care for about 600 women and children. But Joseph was able to lead this group on a superb fighting retreat that covered more than a thousand miles of difficult wilderness. He ran when he could and fought when he had to. In August 1877, he defeated the cavalry in a desperate struggle on the Big Hole River in Montana. Finally, Joseph got his people into the Bear Paw mountains, only thirty miles from Canada.

At this point, the thirty-seven-year-old chief thought he had won, and stopped to allow his dozens of wounded and helpless followers to rest. But he was overtaken by a force of cavalry, and had to decide, and quickly, whether to run, to surrender, or to fight. He chose to fight, and kept the cavalry at bay for five days. On October 5, he surrendered his beaten force: eighty-seven men, almost half of them wounded, and about 350 women and children. To this broken remnant of the Nez Percé, Joseph made his speech:

I am tired of fighting. The old men are all dead. [My brother] who led the young men is dead. It is cold, and we have no blankets. The little children are freezing to death. My people, some of them, have run away to the hills. No one knows where they are. I want to have some time to look for my children and see how many I can find. Maybe I shall find them among the dead.
Hear me, my chiefs. From where the sun now stands, I will fight no more forever.

Joseph and his people were taken first to Kansas and then to Indian Territory, where many of them died of disease. A small group was eventually returned to Idaho. But Joseph never went home. He was transferred to a reservation in Washington state, and he lived to visit a new "Great Father" in Washington, D.C., Theodore Roosevelt, in 1903. Joseph died in 1904, at the age of sixty-four. The official cause of death was entered as a broken heart.

Territory and the region around the Powder River in eastern Wyoming and southern Montana. But by 1865 miners had crowded into Montana at Bozeman, Virginia City, and Helena. These towns soon demanded a road connecting them with the Oregon Trail. This road would cross the Yellowstone River, skirt the Sioux hunting areas around the Big Horn Mountains, and cross directly over the valley of the Powder River.

In the summer of 1865 the cavalry moved into the area to construct forts and begin work on the road. A Sioux chief, Red Cloud, led his people in a two-year attack on the road and the forts. And in 1868 the government made a new treaty that seemed to give the victory to Red Cloud. The road was abandoned. But the Sioux, in return, had to agree to a reservation that included only the Dakotas west of the Missouri—the so-called Great Sioux Reservation. According to the treaty, they could still hunt in the Powder River country. For the first time, however, they had accepted a reservation to replace the large domain that their 1851 treaty had recognized.

The same commission that made the 1868 agreement with the Sioux dealt with other Plains tribes in the same way. Reservations were created in Indian Territory for the southern groups—the Kiowa, Comanche, Arapaho, Cheyenne, Osage, and Pawnee tribes. Between 1868 and 1874 the northern tribes—Crow and Blackfoot, Shoshoni and Mandan—also accepted new, restricted reservations. By 1876 the Plains Indians had given up over three-fourths of the land they had held under the Fort Laramie Treaty.

The Battle of the Little Bighorn The policy of concentrating Indians on reservations was applied once again in the Black Hills area of South Dakota. The treaty of 1868 guaranteed the Tetons complete possession of the Black Hills. But in 1874 rumors of gold led to a reconnaissance of the area by a military column of the Seventh Cavalry under Colonel George Custer. Custer's men found gold, and the resulting rush into Deadwood and other mining towns made conflict between the Sioux and the whites inevitable.

The Grant administration tried for a time to hold the prospectors back. The army even re-

moved some of them. But finally the government gave in and allowed the prospectors to enter the Black Hills "at their own risk." The next step was as cruel and illegal as any the government ever took against the Sioux. To prevent clashes between the miners and the Indians, Washington ordered all the Sioux to report to reservation agen-

A wagon train expedition, protected by Colonel George Custer's cavalry, entered the Black Hills of South Dakota in search of gold in 1874. Within three years the Sioux were forced off their lands and onto reservations.

cies. Any who remained outside would be considered automatically "hostile" and liable to attack. Many of the Sioux obeyed the order. But about 8,000 of them defied the government and gathered in the area of the Big Horn Mountains for their annual summer encampment and Sun Dance.

In June 1876 the army launched powerful forces of infantry, cavalry, and artillery against these Indians. One column, marching north from the Platte River, met Crazy Horse at Rosebud Creek on June 17. The army was beaten back in fierce fighting. Crazy Horse returned to the Sioux camp at the Little Bighorn River, where 8,000 Teton Sioux had gathered—the most powerful single force of Indians the army would ever face. Another army column advanced from the east. On June 25 the Seventh Cavalry, again under Custer's command, rode foolishly to the attack. The Sioux killed almost all of Custer's force in the most famous (and, from the white point of view, perhaps the most stupid) Indian battle in American history.

Another cycle of treaty, war, and new treaty was about to be completed. Within a year the Sioux were forced to give up their important Black Hills area. They were now forced onto a reservation covering only the central part of South Dakota, between the Missouri River and the Black Hills. But their troubles were not over. A railroad was pushing toward the reservation, and the remaining Sioux stood in its path. Farmers and ranchers were also beginning to look longingly at the land that the Sioux still held.

A Changing Indian Policy The idea of private property is so deeply rooted in white society that it is sometimes difficult to grasp the native Americans' concept of land "ownership." Most tribes looked on the land in more or less the same way that fisherman look on the sea—as a place to hunt. No Indian thought of himself as owning a piece of the land. He might own his horses, his weapons, his tepee. But the land itself was the "property" of the whole tribe, to be used communally and protected from other tribes.

When the various tribes of the plains agreed to give up their land, they did so as tribal units, not as individuals. When they accepted their "reser-vations," too, they accepted them as tribes, not as individual property owners.

Reformers, most of whom lived in the East, believed that private property was an essential feature of "civilization." To break the Indians' old, communal concept of land, the reformers proposed that the reservations be divided into lots and given to the Indians in "severalty"—that the Indians be treated as "several" or separate individuals. Westerners, anxious to exploit the Indians, agreed with this proposal. Their enthusiasm was a result of some simple arithmetic. If every Indian family was given an individual farm, a lot of reservation land would be left over. There simply were not enough Indians, in most tribes, to "fill" the reservations. The remaining land could become available to whites.

This new policy became law in 1887 in the Dawes Severalty Act. The next year, after much argument, some trickery, and probably some bribery, the whites persuaded the Sioux to accept the new plan. The one big Sioux reservation could then be broken down into five smaller ones that were, all together, less than half as large in area as the original. The same policy was applied to the other Plains Indians. One after another, the tribes settled for 160 acres per family. One after another, they realized that this meant giving up about half their tribal lands. The resulting demoralization provided a fertile ground for the new Ghost Dance religion. No matter what the intentions of the whites who wrote and supported the Dawes Severalty Act, it was a disaster for the Indians. In 1887, Indians held about 130 million acres of land in the United States; by 1930, after forty years of the Dawes Act, the total had been reduced to less than 50 million acres.

With the new policy came even stronger efforts to convert the Indians to white civilization—to make them "walk the white man's road," as Sitting Bull put it. These efforts hardened the conflict in attitudes between the progressive Indians, who accepted the new ways, and the nonprogressives, who clung to the old ones. The division was dramatized when Sitting Bull was arrested by Indian police from his own tribe. Even after the "reforms" of the 1880s, American policy toward the Indians was a calamity. They were reduced to a condition in some ways worse than that of the freed slaves in the South.

FARMING ON THE PLAINS

Mining, railroads, and cattle ranching had created a scattered pattern of settlement on the Great Plains and in the Rockies. Miners gathered in towns that were separated by hundreds of miles. Railroads created towns but only along their rights of way. And ranchers needed only a few cowhands to handle even very large herds. The actual white settlement of the plains had to await the slower migrations of farmers away from the Mississippi and onto the dry grasslands.

The Homestead Act The pace and pattern of settlement depended very much on government encouragement. In its youth, the Republican party had been the party of "free soil," which meant both agriculture without slavery and free land for any American. One of the first measures promoted by the Lincoln administration was the Homestead Act of 1862. According to this law, any citizen (or any immigrant who had taken the first step toward becoming a citizen) could claim 160 acres of public land, just by paying a fee of $26–34. If he "lived upon or cultivated" the land for five years, the land became his, free and forever. If the homesteader did not want to wait five years, he could pay for the land at $1.25 an acre and own it after six months.

The Homestead Act resulted in over half a million claims, totaling 80 million acres. But if its purpose was to award most of the public lands of the West to simple farmers, it was a failure. Much more land was given to railroads and states or sold directly to speculators than was ever acquired by small farmers.

Moreover, many of the homestead claims were phony. By law it was possible to transfer ownership at any time to any other person or corporation. So, for example, a rancher could have each of his hands claim a homestead and then (for a small bribe) transfer ownership to the ranch. Any land speculator could do the same, just by paying a bribe to a stranger passing through.

Other Land Acts Congress made the situation worse by passing several more laws that promoted corruption and the robbery of public land. First, in 1873, came the Timber Culture Act, which allowed a homesteader (or a rancher or speculator) to claim an additional 160 acres if he would plant trees on 40 of the acres. In 1877 Congress passed the Desert Land Act, which allowed an individual to claim 640 acres of land if he would begin irrigation. Under the law, ranchers took up section after section of land, especially in the Southwest, since they needed it for grazing cattle. They had their friends swear that it was irrigated (even if they had only poured a bucket of water on it in the presence of their "witnesses").

Even more corruption resulted from the Timber and Stone Act of 1878. This law applied to forest land that could not be farmed but that was highly profitable for timber. Under this law any citizen or immigrant could purchase up to 160 acres of Western forest for $2.50 an acre. Lumbermen used the same tricks that ranchers and other speculators used. They imported sailors, prospectors, and others to buy land and then sign it over to a company for a small fee. And, since one good log sold for about $2.50, every tree but the first from any acre of land was pure profit. Under these laws over 20 million more acres of potentially valuable public land fell into the hands of corporations and speculators.

Hardships and Solutions Despite the fact that many of the profits went to land speculators and big corporations, Western lands were opened to the American people. Though they might have to pay $10 an acre to a speculator instead of getting homestead land virtually free from the government, farmers moved out onto the plains anyway. The majority came from the states bordering the Mississippi. Most of the rest were immigrants. Almost no workers from Eastern cities made the trip west. But the men and women who did settle on the plains performed a monumental task. In the thirty years after 1870 they brought more land under cultivation than had been cleared and

From the 1860s through the 1880s settlers rolled across the plains in prairie schooners like these, conquering one frontier after another. Hardships endured along the way paled in comparison with those met in taming the land.

plowed by all the generations of farmers from the settlement of Jamestown to the Civil War.

These farmers confronted problems that they had not met farther east. They found that their old ways of plowing and planting would not work. For one thing, rainfall was scarce, rivers often ran dry, and the water table[3] was low. Farmers had to haul water from long distances or collect it in holes when it did rain. New well-digging machinery, invented in the 1880s and 1890s, however, enabled people to dig deeper wells. And

steel windmills made it easier to pump the water up. Plains dwellers also developed dry farming. This technique—by which a farmer covers a plowed field with a blanket of dust—conserves the moisture in the soil.

Another problem on the plains was lack of wood. Farmers living there often made their first homes from cakes of sod. For fuel they burned old hay or dried cow dung. Fencing was a special problem until the invention of barbed wire in the 1870s.

A farm family soon learned that, while sixty acres of land could support them farther east, five times as much was needed on the plains. Plowing,

_____

[3]The water table of an area is the supply of water within the ground.

Homesteaders like this Montana farmer took advantage of the government offer of cheap land in the West. Many failed, but those who mastered the harsh climate turned the Great Plains into the bread basket of America.

planting, and harvesting extensive acreage were greatly aided by the invention of mechanized farm equipment (see Chapter 30).

Nature seemed to do things on a grand scale on the plains. In summer the wind blew hot, and twice as hard as in the East. In winter blizzards howled down out of the mountains, burying homes and killing livestock. Tornadoes, dust storms, and plagues of locusts and grasshoppers were frequent.

Dry years drove thousands of farmers back east. Many of those who stayed barely survived. In the end, though, farmers turned the plains into the world's most efficient area for producing wheat, corn, and other grains. By 1880 American flour—like American beef and pork from the same area—was being exported in great quantities all over the world.

In all this the Indian was, of course, the great loser. The whites' successes on the plains did seem to prove what white Americans had always believed—that the Indians could not make "proper" use of their environment because they lived too much with it and not enough from it. White men were able to exploit even the tough plains environment, to draw from it enough food to feed not only most of the United States but part of the rest of the world, too. The Indian, in contrast, had been willing to settle for the little he needed to maintain his way of life. A full century was to pass before white Americans began to ask themselves seriously whether the Indian's way was not somehow at least as good as theirs. Only one thing was certain: in his "primitive" way the Indian had respected nature more. He had never viewed his world as an object to be owned, changed, and exploited. This, at least in part, was what the battle at Wounded Knee was all about.

SUGGESTED READINGS– CHAPTERS 27-28

Wounded Knee

Stanley Vestal, *Sitting Bull* (1957); C. M. Oehler, *The Great Sioux Uprising* (1959); Robert M. Utley, *The Last Days of the Sioux Nation* (1963); James Mooney, *The Ghost Dance Religion and the Sioux Uprising of 1890* (1965).

General

Frederick Jackson Turner, *The Frontier in American History* (1929); Walter P. Webb, *The Great Plains* (1931); Henry Nash Smith, *Virgin Land: The American West as Symbol and Myth* (1950); Thomas D. Clark, *Frontier America* (1959); R. A. Billington, *Westward Expansion* (1960).

The Plains Indians

F. G. Roe, *The Indian and the Horse* (1955); R. K. Andrist, *The Long Death: The Last Days of the Plains Indians* (1964); Dee Brown, *Bury My Heart at Wounded Knee* (1971).

Land Policy

B. J. Hibbard, *A History of the Public Land Policies* (1924); R. M. Robbins, *Our Landed Heritage* (1942).

The Mining Frontier

Mark Twain, *Roughing It* (1872); G. C. Quiett, *Pay Dirt: A Panorama of American Gold Rushes* (1936); R. W. Paul, *Mining Frontiers of the Far West* (1963).

The Cattle Frontier

E. E. Dale, *The Range Cattle Industry* (1930); J. B. Frantz and J. E. Choate, *The American Cowboy, Myth and Reality* (1955); Lewis Atherton, *The Cattle Kings* (1961).

The Farming Frontier

Everett Dick, *The Sod-House Frontier* (1937); F. A. Shannon, *The Farmer's Last Frontier* (1945); J. A. Malin, *The Grasslands Agriculture of North America* (1947); Gilbert C. Fite, *The Farmer's Frontier* (1966).

29 STRIKE AND VIOLENCE IN CHICAGO

R.J.W.

April 15, 1885

My Dear Virginia,

We have had a week of trial and anxiety on the great subject of disturbances in our main factory—the serious labor troubles we have encountered—a great "strike," and all the resulting derangement of our relations—old and pleasant as they were—with our workmen.

Trouble has come to hundreds of families in consequence; hatred and fierce passions have been aroused; and an injury has resulted to our good name.

It began with a few molders and went on, one force operating on another, until 1,200 men went out, part of them by intimidation and part of them led by ignorant and blind passion. It ended by our conceding the terms demanded.

What a sore heart I have carried these days!

Your Devoted Mother

This letter was written by a bewildered woman in her early seventies to her daughter. The writer, Nettie Fowler McCormick, was the widow of Cyrus Hall McCormick. An ambitious and ingenious Virginia farm boy, McCormick had made millions of dollars from the invention and manufacture of the reaper, a machine that harvested crops mechanically. He opened his Chicago factory, the McCormick Harvester Works, in the 1840s. It was the largest producer of harvesting machines in the world.

Nettie McCormick had always paid close attention to the family business. Now, just a year after her husband's death, a stable and profitable enterprise seemed to be falling to pieces before her eyes. At first, she remembered, her husband had known all of the original twenty-three workmen by name. He had worked alongside them in the little Chicago factory. Even when, after a few years, there were about 200 workers producing over 1,000 reapers a year, he could still name those who had been with the company for any length of time.

As the business grew, relations with the workers had become more difficult. During the Civil War, when labor had been scarce and prices had jumped every week, there had been many strikes or threats of strikes. McCormick had been forced to agree to one wage increase after another. But after the war ended, McCormick was able to cut wages in the plant five times in five years.

During the two decades after the Civil War, the McCormick company had grown rapidly. In 1884, when Cyrus McCormick died, the main factory covered dozens of acres. Its modern machinery, including two huge steam engines that supplied power for the whole factory, covered 12 acres of floor space. On these floors, about 1,300 men—100 per acre—put in six 10-hour days a week. They turned 10 million feet of lumber and thousands of tons of iron into about 50,000 reapers a year. And these machines were making possible an agricultural miracle in the United States.

For the McCormicks, the result was money and status. In 1884, the company showed a profit of 71 percent. The family lived in a great mansion staffed with servants. They had invitations to the "best" Chicago homes, counted other wealthy people among their friends, sent their sons to Princeton, traveled luxuriously, and supported carefully selected philanthropies. Nettie Fowler McCormick had ample reason to be concerned about "our good name."

She had some reason to carry a "sore heart," too. The McCormick workers had always seemed contented enough. Nine out of ten of them were Germans, Norwegians, or Swedes, and most lived in the neighborhoods just west of the factory—neighborhoods built by the McCormicks—with Swedish and German street names. All this made the strike of 1885 difficult for Nettie Fowler McCormick to understand. Perhaps her husband's death was part of the problem. But McCormick's was still a family business. Her son, Cyrus McCormick II, had taken over the presidency, and other members of the family had always held important positions in the company. What had happened, then, to the "old and pleasant" relations with the workmen?

The problem had to lie, the McCormicks believed, with some small, misguided minority within the plant. And the most likely candidates for this role were clearly the molders. Ethnically, the molders were a distinct group. Almost all of them were Irish—"fighting Irish," as one plant official called them. And they had a tight, successful craft union, Molders Local No. 233. This union had been making trouble for the McCormicks for twenty years. There were only about ninety molders,

Cyrus Hall McCormick invented the first successful reaping machine in 1834. He turned his invention into a booming business, employing new sales methods such as installment buying.

Nettie Fowler McCormick, wife of the founder of the McCormick Works, understood little of the underlying causes of worker discontent at the plant in 1885.

Prior to the mechanization of the molding floor at the McCormick Works, much of the labor was done by unskilled and semiskilled workers. Pouring the molten metal into molds was the job of the common laborer, but working the metal into shape required more skill and was more highly paid.

but their operation was crucial to the manufacture of reapers. They could bring production to a complete standstill, and they had successfully used the power of this threat several times. Every time old Cyrus McCormick had tried to cut wages, the molders had been the first to resist.

The strike of 1885 had its origins in a decision by the new young president of the company to cut wages again. In December 1884, he had announced a 10 percent pay cut throughout the work force—except for the molders, who were to be cut by 15 percent. At first, there was quiet. Even the molders appeared to accept the reduction. But they were only biding their time until production reached its annual peak in the spring. In March of 1885, the molders demanded that the wage cut be restored to them. When McCormick refused, the molders came out on strike. And, to the McCormicks' alarm, some of the other workers followed them out.

McCormick was anxious to prove himself. To break the strike, he sent telegrams to McCormick salesmen all over the Midwest, asking them to send strikebreaking molders to Chicago. He even had these workers listed on the company payroll as "scabs"—the union term of insult for nonunion workmen who replaced striking members. The newcomers were housed inside the plant in a barracks listed in the company records as "scab house."

But McCormick's efforts to break the strike did not work. The "scabs" could not be trusted. Early in April, these two revealing telegrams were sent from company headquarters to salesmen in Iowa and Illinois:

> To Tom Braden, Agent, Des Moines, Iowa: Out of the lot of men you sent us yesterday, but two of them showed up in Chicago. We find it not safe to ship these critters at our expense unless nailed up in a box car or chained.

To J. F. Utley, Agent, Sterling, Illinois: The gentleman you sent to us as a molder did not remain over an hour or two until he packed his valise and skipped. We took special pains to get him into the Works by his riding with Mr. McCormick in his buggy. If you are able to do so, try and collect back his Rail Road fare.

Just a week after Cyrus McCormick had sneaked this unreliable scab into the plant, hidden in the president's own buggy, the strike reached a climax. On April 14, with the police scattered all over the city to patrol a local election, strikers had attacked McCormick workers outside the plant. McCormick—like many other companies of the period—had hired a small private army of the Pinkerton "detective" agency to maintain peace. A wagon loaded with Pinkerton men with a case of Winchester repeating rifles tried to enter the plant gate. The strikers set upon the wagon and burned it, and the rifles disappeared into the crowd. The captain in charge of the few Chicago police still in the area did nothing. His name—O'Donnell—was as obviously Irish as that of any molder.

The violence confirmed the McCormick family's opinion of the "fighting Irish" molders. If twenty years' experience were not enough, the Pinkerton agents' secret reports confirmed what the family had long suspected: They were the victims of an ethnic conspiracy. Just after the violent episode of April 14, one Pinkerton "detective" had submitted this report.

The assault on the Pinkerton police during the strike of last week was urged by Irishmen, who are employed at McCormick's as molders and helpers. These Irishmen are nearly all members of the Ancient Order of Hibernians [an Irish social fraternity] who have a bitter enmity against the agency.

To the Pinkertons, it seemed clear that the molders were actually supported by their fellow Irishmen on the police force:

It looks somewhat strange that these men at McCormick's could have police protection. On each occasion, the police stood by during the assaults and made no effort to stop the outrage.

Once, during the strike, a group of molders had attacked a group of non-union workers outside the plant gate. The police, according to Pinkerton reports, had this time not merely stood by but had actually chased and arrested the Pinkerton men who were trying to restrain the molders:

The police made the utmost speed in calling a patrol wagon, which followed the Pinkerton men and arrested them! The men who made the arrests were treated by the strikers in saloons, and from their talk and insinuations, the police urged the mob to more violence by saying the Pinkerton men were sons of bitches, no better than scabs, there to take the bread out of women and children's mouths.

After the molders' triumphant April 14 attack on the Pinkertons, Cyrus McCormick went looking for help and advice. He appealed first to the mayor, Carter Harrison. But Harrison remembered full well that the McCormicks had consistently opposed him in local politics. He politely advised the young industrialist to give in to the molders' demands.

McCormick then turned to what he hoped would be a more sympathetic listener, old Philip Armour, head of a large meat-packing company and a veteran of many labor troubles. But even Armour told McCormick that the molders had won. There seemed to be no choice. McCormick offered to give back to the molders 5 percent out of their original 15 percent pay cut. But they refused this, and he ended by restoring the whole 15 percent.

To both Cyrus McCormick and his mother, their defeat at the hands of a few Irishmen was a painful mystery. But it was a mystery that had to be solved. Cyrus wrote to his mother as he mulled over the problem:

> The whole question of these labor troubles is vast and important and throws more new light on a department of our manufacturing interests which we have not hitherto studied with sufficient depth and understanding.

But to this twenty-five-year-old, who had only two years earlier been taken out of Princeton to run the plant, "depth and understanding" were limited to one fact and one conclusion. The fact was that a handful of disaffected molders could bring the entire McCormick enterprise to a standstill. The conclusion was that such a situation must be avoided in the future by making the skills of the molders unnecessary. He wrote his mother:

> I do not think we will have a similar trouble again because we will take measures to prevent it. I do not think we will be troubled if we take proper steps to weed out the bad element among the men.

McCormick went to work at once to "weed out" the offending Irish molders. He focused his efforts on a daring technological gamble. During the summer of 1885, the summer following the strike, the McCormick Company bought a dozen new pneumatic molding machines. They were supposed to perform mechanically most of the foundry tasks that the skilled molders had always done by hand. The machines were expensive, and they were experimental. No one knew whether they would work. McCormick hoped that they would enable the company to rid itself once and for all of the troublesome molders.

In August the McCormick foundry was closed for two months so that the machines could be installed. The closing was not unusual, since reapers were manufactured seasonally—much like automobiles are today, with a new model season every fall. August and September were always light months at the harvester works. But when the foundry reopened for full production, not one molder who had participated in the spring strike was back on the payroll.

McCormick seemed to have won a complete victory. All he had done was spend a vast sum of money on the new machinery. A few months after the machines went into operation, he wrote his mother triumphantly that the machines:

are working even beyond our expectations and everybody is very much pleased with the result. Two men with one of these machines can do an average of about three days work in one. Add to this fact that we have only nine molders in the whole foundry (the rest are all laborers), and you can see what a great gain this will be to us.

But McCormick was being more optimistic than he should have been—probably to reassure his anxious mother. Actually, there were troubles with the machines. In October the McCormick Company complained to the manufacturer that the castings turned out by the pneumatic molding device were too brittle to use. And in November Cyrus McCormick was called home from a trip to New York because of a crisis in the foundry. He wrote in his diary for Wednesday, November 11: "Telegram from mother urging come home at once about molding machines—probably failure. Critical situation."

The machines were fixed, but even when they worked they seemed to require an endless amount of labor to keep them functioning. Before the machines were installed, the total wage bill in the foundry was about $3,000 a week. After the machines had been in operation for about six months, foundry wages totaled $8,000 a week. Most of the labor was common, unskilled work. But gradually the company had to hire additional new molders to supervise the work. Economically, the machines were a complete failure.

Still, the new technology had broken the molders union at McCormick. And the union was unhappy. The leader of the molders was a veteran union man named Myles McPadden. He devised a new scheme that was much more dangerous to the McCormicks than the old union, with only ninety members. If there was to be no molders union, then McPadden would simply organize all the other workers in the plant into one union or another. The workers were discontented, so the time was ripe. By February of 1886, he had succeeded in organizing every major group of workers in the plant. The skilled workers—blacksmiths, machinists, and so on—joined the Metalworkers Union. McPadden encouraged the others to join the Knights of Labor, a general, nationwide union. Only 300 of the 1,400 McCormick workers remained nonunion. The lines of a new strike battle were shaping up clearly.

During this time McCormick, too, was busy. After his frustrated attempt to enlist Mayor Harrison's help, McCormick had gone to some lengths to make peace with the powerful political leader of the city. In every election before 1885 the McCormicks had opposed Harrison. After that year they supported him. As a result, Captain O'Donnell, the Irish police official who had been sympathetic to the workers in the spring of 1885, was replaced. The new man in charge of the area where the works were located was Police Inspector John Bonfield.

Bonfield had a reputation as a tough antilabor cop. He had once literally beaten his way through a crowd of strikers, shouting a slogan for which he became famous: "Clubs today spare bullets tomorrow." If there was going to be trouble in 1886, McCormick could count on the police in a way impossible a year before.

In mid-February 1886, a union committee representing all three unions—the Knights of Labor, the Metalworkers, and the Molders—presented McCormick with a series of demands:

> First, that all wages of laboring men be advanced from $1.25 to $1.50 a day. Second, that all vise hands[1] be advanced to $2.00 a day, and that blacksmith helpers be advanced to $1.75. Third, that time the men spend in the water closet [the toilet] not be limited as heretofore. Fourth, that, inasmuch as the molding machines are a failure, the preference should be given the old hands. The scabs in the foundry must be discharged, and a pledge given that no man would be discharged for taking part in a strike.

The company offered to meet some of the demands, but not the fourth, which must have made Cyrus McCormick furious. The unions rejected the offer and called a strike.

Before the strike was scheduled to begin, however, the company announced a complete shutdown of the plant for an indefinite period of time. Union pickets started marching near the plant, but they were kept away by 400 city policemen, now under Bonfield's command. To show its gratitude, the company served free hot meals to the police, with Cyrus McCormick sometimes personally pouring the coffee.

After two weeks the works were reopened, but only to nonunion employees. There was a loyal holdover force of only eighty-two men. The company furnished them with pistols. McCormick hoped they would lead an enthusiastic rush for jobs. But only 161 men showed up the first day. The second day was not much better. Once again the company's agents scoured the region for workers. Gradually, the company's situation improved a little. McCormick was willing to sacrifice almost half a year's production in order to settle the union question once and for all.

For the men on strike the situation was just as important. If they lost, their future at McCormick (or any other manufacturing plant in the city) was dim. As March turned into April, families got hungrier and tempers hotter. The explosion McCormick had avoided the year before by giving in to union demands now looked inevitable.

The situation at McCormick was complicated by the fact that during the spring of 1886 there were strikes all over Chicago. On May 1 all the unions in the city began a general strike for the eight-hour day. This was one of the largest and most heated labor actions in American history. The strike at McCormick merged with the more general agitation, involving thousands of skilled and unskilled workers from plants all over the city.

Then, on May 3, two days into the strike for an eight-hour day, a lumber workers union held a mass meeting to hear an address by August Spies, a radical labor agitator. The meeting took place on Black Road,

---

[1]"Vise hands" refers to workers who used a vise, a tool for holding metal being worked. They had a skill and were, therefore, to receive higher wages than the "laboring men," who were unskilled workers.

just a short distance from the McCormick factory. Some McCormick men were at the meeting, even though none was a lumber worker.

The McCormicks had been so desperate for workers that they had already granted the eight-hour day (with ten hours' pay) to their scab workers. So, at 3:30, two hours before the former 5:30 closing, the bell at the plant rang, and the strikebreaking workers streamed out of the plant. The striking union men at the meeting watched the strikebreaking workers leave the plant on their new short schedule.

The sight proved too much. Several hundred men, some of them McCormick strikers and some of them lumber workers, mobbed the scabs leaving the plant, driving them back inside the gate. The strikers began to smash windows, unleashing anger that had been building for months. About 200 policemen, under Inspector Bonfield, were there. Suddenly, they began firing their revolvers into the crowd, forgetting Bonfield's slogan about using clubs to spare bullets. When the noise died away, two workers lay dead and several others had been wounded.

August Spies, who had been addressing the meeting of lumber workers near the McCormick Works, followed the crowd and witnessed the violence that occurred. The next day, in the newspaper office where he worked, he heard that a mass meeting was scheduled at Haymarket Square to protest the shootings at McCormick. A circular announcing the meeting was being printed in both German and English when Spies arrived at the paper:

Attention Workingmen!

GREAT

MASS-MEETING

TO-NIGHT, at 7.30 o'clock,

AT THE

HAYMARKET, Randolph St., Bet. Desplaines and Halsted.

Good Speakers will be present to denounce the latest atrocious act of the police, the shooting of our fellow-workmen yesterday afternoon.

Workingmen Arm Yourselves and Appear in Full Force!

THE EXECUTIVE COMMITTEE.

Spies agreed to address the meeting, but he insisted that the final line in the circular be omitted. About 200 of the circulars had already been printed, but the line was removed from the rest. Few of the 20,000 circulars that were finally distributed on the streets of Chicago contained the threatening reference to arms.

August Spies was not, strictly speaking, a workingman. He might best be described as a radical journalist. At the time of the Chicago troubles he was thirty years old and the editor of the *Arbeiter-Zeitung*, a German-language newspaper with a radical viewpoint. He was also the business manager of an organization called the Socialistic Publishing Society, a propaganda organization of a small political party known as the Socialist Labor Party.

From time to time Spies had been in trouble with the police. Only a year before, during the McCormick strike of 1885, he had angered the police by intervening in the case of a poor German servant girl. She had been arrested by the police and held in jail for several days. When Spies and the girl's mother went to the jail, they discovered that the girl had been molested repeatedly. Rather than keep quiet, Spies swore out a warrant for the police sergeant in charge of the jail. He lost the case for lack of evidence, but he became well known to the Chicago police.

Spies was, in short, a politically active radical who did not hesitate to condemn people in positions of authority. He was also a committed

Workers gathered in Haymarket Square to protest police treatment of striking workers. The speakers' oratories were fiery and the police ordered the crowd's dispersal, leading to violence that was to set back the labor cause for some time.

socialist politician. Furthermore, he hoped that the rally at Haymarket would attract enough people to fill the square, which could hold about 20,000.

Spies reached Haymarket Square late, at about 8:30 on the night of May 4. He must have felt disappointed. No meeting was in progress, and there were only about a thousand people scattered around the square. The other main speaker, a socialist named Albert R. Parsons, was nowhere in sight. Spies climbed on a wagon, sent someone to look for Parsons, and began his talk. He was a good speaker, and soon the small crowd became enthusiastic:

> The fight is going on. Now is the chance to strike for the oppressed classes. The oppressors want us to be content. They will kill us. The day is not far distant when we will resort to hanging these men. [Applause, and shouts of "Hang them now" came from the crowd.] McCormick is the man who created the row on Monday, and he must be held responsible for the murder of our brothers! [More shouts of "Hang him!"]

Spies went on in the same vein for about an hour, trying to rouse his working-class audience to anger and a sense of solidarity against their "oppressors." Then someone announced that Albert R. Parsons had been found. Spies turned over his wagon rostrum to the second speaker.

The crowd had been waiting for Parsons, for he had a reputation as a spellbinder. Unlike Spies and many other Chicago socialists, he was a native American. Born in Alabama in 1848, Parsons came from a family whose ancestry went back to 1632 in New England. He was a self-trained printer in Texas before the Civil War. During the war he fought for the Confederacy in a Texas artillery company. After the war Parsons became converted to socialism and moved to Chicago, the center of working-class politics in the United States.

Like Spies, Parsons was not a worker at all but a political journalist. He edited a radical workingmen's paper called the *Alarm*. The Haymarket rally was just one more in a long series of political speeches for him. His speech was much like that of Spies but slightly stronger in tone:

> I am not here for the purpose of inciting anybody, but to speak out, to tell the facts as they exist, even though it shall cost me my life before morning. It behooves you, as you love your wife and children — if you don't want to see them perish with hunger, killed or cut down like dogs in the street — Americans, in the interest of your liberty and independence, to *arm*, to *arm* yourselves!

Here again there was applause from the crowd and shouts of "We'll do it! We're ready!"

What Parsons and Spies did not know was that the crowd was full of police detectives. Every few minutes one or another ran back to a nearby station house to report what the speakers were saying. Waiting in the station were almost 200 policemen, fully armed, and under the command of none other than John Bonfield.

Parsons and Spies probably did not notice Mayor Carter Harrison in the crowd, either. Only the mayor's presence had kept Bonfield from breaking up the meeting. As Parsons finished, the mayor left; it was obvious to him that everything was peaceful. It was almost ten o'clock and rain was in the air. Most of the crowd, too, began to drift off as the third speaker, Samuel Fielden, began to talk.

Suddenly, 180 policemen (a group almost as large as the crowd itself) marched into the square and up to the wagon where Fielden was speaking. One of the captains turned to the crowd and said: "In the name of the people of the State of Illinois, I command this meeting immediately and peaceably to disperse." After a moment the police captain repeated his order. The crowd was already starting to melt away (it was almost 10:30 by now). Fielden had stopped speaking and was climbing down from the wagon platform. "We are peaceable," Fielden said to Bonfield.

At that moment, without any warning, a dynamite bomb was thrown (it is not known from where or by whom) at the police. The fuse burned for a second or two after the bomb struck the ground. Then it went off with a deafening roar. Screams split the air as people ran in all directions. A number of policemen lay on the ground, one dead and the others wounded. Quickly, the police re-formed their ranks, and some of them began to fire into the crowd. Other policemen waded into the confusion swinging their clubs. The uproar lasted only a minute or two. Then suddenly the square was empty.

In addition to the dead policeman there were seventy-three wounded, six of whom died later. Four civilians were killed, and the official reports listed twelve as wounded. The twelve were those who had been too badly hurt to leave the square. Probably several times as many limped or struggled home and never became official statistics.

Like most riots, the Haymarket affair had been short. And, considering what could have happened, very few people were hurt. But the incident occurred on the heels of trouble at the McCormick plant, in the midst of the strike for an eight-hour day, with 80,000 Chicago working-

A contemporary sketch of what happened after a bomb exploded in Haymarket Square shows workers as well armed as police in battlelike poses. Pictures such as this fed the popular notion of union men as anarchists.

men off the job. Thus the Haymarket bomb touched off a near panic in the city and much of the rest of the nation. Thousands of respectable citizens convinced themselves that a dangerous conspiracy of anarchists, socialists, and communists was at work to overthrow the government and carry out a bloody revolution. One of the leading business magazines of the day, *Bradstreets'*, spoke for thousands of Americans when it said of the Haymarket incident:

> This week's happenings at Chicago go to show that the threats of the anarchists against the existing order are not idle. In a time of disturbance, desperate men have a power for evil out of proportion to their numbers. They are desperate fanatics who are opposed to all laws. There is no room for anarchy in the political system of the United States.

Also important was the fact that many people had been frightened and angered by a recent flood of immigration from Europe to America— and many of the "anarchists" were also foreigners. Not only in Chicago, but all over the nation, newspaper editorialists and public speakers demanded the immediate arrest and conviction of the alien radicals who had conspired to murder honest policemen and subvert law and order. The result was a swift and efficient series of illegal raids by the Chicago police. They searched property without warrants. They imprisoned people without charging them and threatened potential witnesses. All in all, the authorities arrested and questioned about 200 "suspects"—probably none of whom had anything at all to do with the bombing.

In this heated atmosphere, fueled by journalists who whipped up unreasonable fears of an anarchist conspiracy, a jury met to determine if indictments could be brought against anyone for the violence. It decided that, although the specific person who threw the bomb could not be determined, anyone who urged violence was a "conspirator" and as guilty of murder as the bomb thrower. On the basis of this decision another jury met and indicted thirty-one persons on counts of murder. Of the thirty-one, eight were eventually tried, all of them political radicals. Most had not even been present at the Haymarket bombing.

The effect of the Haymarket Affair had now become clear. What had begun weeks before as an ordinary strike at the McCormick Works had been transformed into a crusade against political radicalism, most of which was said to be foreign in origin. Only Parsons and Samuel Fielden were not German or of German descent. The names of the other six would have been as natural in Berlin or Hamburg as in Chicago: August Spies, Michael Schwab, Adolph Fischer, George Engel, Louis Lingg, and Oscar Neebe.

In one way or another, all the defendants had some connection with the labor movement and with political agitation for revolution. Several of them were anarchists, though their ideas about anarchism as a philosophy were vague. They might as well have called themselves socialists, as several of them did at one time or another. In general, they were intellectuals. Their jobs were connected with radical journalism in either the English- or German-language press. They did not all know one another, but by the time their trial was over, most of them were probably "comrades," a word they used more and more in the months ahead.

On the other side of the battle were all the forces of law, order, and authority. True, some agreed with Mayor Harrison that the Haymarket meeting had been peaceful, that the whole idea of a conspiracy was a false and legally incorrect notion. But most of Chicago society (including even many elements of the labor movement) favored a quick conviction and the hanging of all eight defendants. The judge who tried the case, the prosecuting attorney, most business leaders, almost all the local clergymen—almost everyone who had anything to say in Chicago— were convinced even before the trial began that the defendants were guilty. Moreover, most of Chicago's leading citizens, and their counterparts in the rest of the country, agreed that the trial was a struggle to the death between American republicanism and foreign anarchism. The entire established order of American society, with very few exceptions, was determined to make an example of the "conspirators."

The Haymarket trial began on June 21, 1886. The first three weeks of the seven-week trial were spent selecting a jury. Under Illinois law the defense had the right to reject a total of 160 jurors on peremptory challenges—that is, without having to discuss a juror's qualifications and abide by the judge's decision. As one prospective juror after another was called, it became clear that most of them were extremely prejudiced against the defendants. The defense attorneys quickly used up their 160 challenges. They then had to show cause for turning down a juror and depend on the judge, Joseph Gary, to rule fairly. Again and again, plainly biased jurors were accepted by the judge—whose own prejudice against the defendants became apparent as the process went on. The result was a jury composed of twelve citizens who obviously wished to hang the defendants.

In his opening statement, prosecuting attorney Julius Grinnell set the tone of the entire trial:

> Gentlemen, for the first time in the history of our country people are on trial for endeavoring to make anarchy the rule. I hope that while the youngest of us lives this will be the last and only time when such a trial shall take place. In the light of the 4th of May, we now know that the preachings of anarchy by these defendants, hourly and daily for years, have been sapping our institutions. Where they have cried murder, bloodshed, anarchy, and dynamite, they have meant what they said. The firing on Fort Sumter was a terrible thing to our country, but it was open warfare. I think it was nothing compared with this insidious, infamous plot to ruin our laws and our country.

It was obvious that this would not be an ordinary murder trial. The defendants would be judged by their words and beliefs. A ninth "conspirator," Rudolph Schnaubelt, had fled. The prosecution would try to prove that he had thrown the bomb. The next step would be to convict the other eight of conspiracy, which would carry the same penalty as murder itself. And they would be convicted by the fact that they had made speeches and written newspaper articles urging violent revolution. Day after day the prosecution offered evidence about the defendants' beliefs, their writings, and even pamphlets they had supposedly helped to sell.

The prosecution had weak cases against the individual defendants. They were able to prove that one of the defendants, Lingg, had actually made bombs. But Lingg was a stranger to most of the others, and he had not even been at Haymarket Square. Parsons, Spies, Fischer, and Schwab had left the square before the bomb was thrown. George Engel proved that he had been home drinking a glass of beer with his wife. In the end the prosecution's case rested on a theory of "general conspiracy to promote violence." No evidence of a single violent act was brought into court that could withstand even the mildest cross-examination by the frustrated defense attorneys.

After four weeks of testimony the jury retired. The jury members had been instructed by Judge Gary in such a way as to make conviction almost inevitable, and they needed only three hours to discuss the matter. After this short deliberation the jury filed solemnly back into the courtroom. It was ten o'clock, August 19, 1886, when the foreman read the verdict.

> We the jury find the defendants Spies, Schwab, Fielden, Parsons, Fischer, Engel, and Lingg guilty of murder in the manner and form as charged, and fix the penalty at death. We find Oscar Neebe[2] guilty of murder in the manner and form as charged, and fix the penalty at imprisonment in the penitentiary for fifteen years.

Years later Judge Gary recalled that "the verdict was received by the friends of social order with a roar of almost universal approval."

Before they were sentenced, each of the defendants made a speech to the court. Spies spoke for all of them when he said, in a German accent that he had never lost:

> There was not a syllable said about anarchism at the Haymarket meeting. But "anarchism is on trial," foams Mr. Grinnell. If that is the case, your honor, very well; you may sentence me, for I am an anarchist. I believe that the state of classes—the state where one class dominates and lives upon the labor of another class—is doomed to die, to make room for a free society, voluntary association, or universal brotherhood, if you like. You may pronounce the sentence upon me, honorable judge, but let the world know that in A.D. 1886, in the state of Illinois, eight men were sentenced to death because they believed in a better future.

There were appeals, of course, first to state courts and then to the Supreme Court of the United States. One by one the appeals failed. Then there were pleas to the governor of Illinois for mercy, and the sentences of Fielden and Schwab were commuted to life. Lingg, the bomb maker, who was probably half mad, committed suicide in jail—using dynamite set off by a fuse that he lit with his jail-cell candle. The other

---

[2]Oscar Neebe was the youngest defendant; almost no evidence had been presented against him. Most of the jury's three-hour deliberation was devoted to this case.

Albert Parsons, August Spies, George Engel, and Adolph Fischer were hanged on November 11, 1886, after one of the most unfair trials in American history.

four condemned men—Engel, Spies, Parsons, and Fischer—were hanged on November 11.

As the four stood on the scaffold, ropes around their necks and hoods over their heads, Spies broke the deep silence by shouting: "There will come a time when our silence will be more powerful than the voices you strangle today!"

At the McCormick Works the situation had returned to normal months earlier. On May 7, 1886, three days after the Haymarket bombing, Cyrus McCormick was able to write in his diary: "A good force of men at the works today, and things are resuming their former appearance." Three days later, taking full advantage of the public outrage over the "devilish plot," as McCormick called it, at Haymarket Square, the McCormick Works quietly resumed the ten-hour day. On Monday, May 10, McCormick wrote: "Things going smoothly. We returned to 5:30 closing hour today, instead of 3:30."

30
FACTORIES, CITIES, AND IMMIGRANTS

R.J.W.

This chapter examines the creation of a new social and economic setup in the United States: the industrial order. In some sense industry is as old as human society. People have always made things — tools, weapons, clothing, and so on. But, beginning in the eighteenth century, their ability to make goods began to increase rapidly. The so-called industrial revolution that resulted originated in England and spread quickly to the rest of Western Europe and to the United States. By the time of the Civil War this revolution was well under way in North America, fed by inventions like the steam engine, the cotton gin, and the reaper. After the war, industrialization drastically altered the basic patterns of life in the United States.

Everything had to be changed, since every element of this new system had to hang together. Raw materials, like coal and iron for making steel, had to be found and developed. Cheap transportation, like railroads, had to be available to bring these materials to factories and to take finished products from them. Workers had to be hired to operate the factories. And agriculture had to be improved so that fewer and fewer people would be needed to grow more and more food. More and more machines were needed to provide a livelihood for more and more factory workers, who would in turn make still more machines. Nothing could happen at all unless everything else happened — and in the proper order, too. Every factory functioned as part of a chain of invention, materials, transportation, and workers.

The McCormick Harvester Company, for example, was only one part of a complicated series of events and machines. The reapers made at the McCormick Works enabled farmers on the Great Plains to produce unheard-of quantities of grain. Some of this grain was milled into flour, for bread eaten by people like McCormick's molders. Other farm products fed cattle, which were slaughtered in big cities at factories owned by men like Philip Armour.

The new transcontinental railroads were necessary to take the reapers west and bring the flour and beef east. Since there were not enough workers to lay the new rails, Irish and Chinese were encouraged to immigrate. The McCormick plant, too, was tended by immigrants, and it was German immigrants who were the main victims of the Haymarket Riot. The city of Chicago itself was a new kind of city, built around railroads and factories, in a way that no other American city had ever been built — a great barracks for the workmen at dozens of factories like the McCormick Works.

In achieving its own industrial system, the United States was transformed. It had once been a nation in which nine out of every ten people lived on farms or in rural communities. By the end of the nineteenth century it was the world's most productive industrial nation. The landscape had been remade. The people had been changed, too. There had always been immigrants to the United States. But new industries attracted different types of immigrants in great numbers. In the end the daily lives and even the language of Americans were changed. New words like "telephone," "subway," "scab," and "millionaire" became common speech. They signaled just how deep and complete the change had been.

TECHNOLOGICAL CHANGE

Few of the men and women who made or watched the industrial revolution understood its complexity. Most of them probably regarded it as a product of technological change — the invention of new types of machines or the improvement of existing ones. Certainly one of the most obvious changes of the nineteenth century was that many things that had once been done slowly by hand were now being done rapidly by machine.

An Agricultural Revolution Agriculture was a prime example of the replacement of hand labor by machine power. The most rapid and striking introduction of new agricultural technology took place on the Great Plains. On these flat and treeless expanses, plowing, planting, and harvesting could be done on a scale that would have stunned colonial settlers and even most plantation owners of the Old South. But what happened on the plains was just an exaggerated version of what went on in all areas of American agriculture: the industrialization of the farm.

At first, the new machinery was fairly simple. McCormick's earliest reapers, built before the Civil War, were small. They were drawn by one horse and worked by one or two men. Another invention — a steel plow that could cut deeper and faster than the old iron plow — was a further small step. But gradually the new technology gained force and speed. Reapers were soon equipped with automatic binders that could fasten grain into bunches mechanically. The single steel plow was soon modified into a multiple, or gang, plow that could cut three or four furrows at one time.

Soon other new machines appeared. One could plow and plant at the same time. Another, the combine, added to the reaper a mechanical thresher, which could separate grain from stalks. A combine could move quickly through a wheatfield, gathering wheat and leaving behind only waste to be plowed under in the spring. The machine accomplished its work without a single human hand touching either the earth or the wheat plants.

During most of the nineteenth century new machinery was still driven primarily by animals. Some steam engines were used, but the final mechanization of farms had to await the gasoline-driven tractor in the twentieth century. Still, even before the tractor, the life of the American farmer had been fundamentally altered by technology.

Farming gradually came to resemble the running of factories, in which a product for sale was processed and made ready by machinery. Sooner or later, almost every step in all but a few kinds of agriculture was mechanized.

The result of the mechanical changes in agriculture was to double and redouble the volume and pace of food production. In 1840 it took more than three hours of human work time to produce a bushel of wheat. In the 1890s the time had been cut to ten minutes. In 1840 a bushel of corn required almost five hours of labor, from planting to final processing. In the 1890s the time had been cut to forty minutes.

Hand in hand with the reduction of hours was a marked decrease in the number of farmers needed to produce food. Mechanization made it possible for a tiny minority of Americans to feed the large majority. Those who left farms were then free to work for the railroads and in oil fields, iron mines, factories, and offices — thereby aiding the process of rapid industrialization.

The amount of land under cultivation doubled between the Civil War and 1900. The net result of the agricultural revolution was an enormous abundance of food.

Improving Rail Transport The agricultural revolution depended not only on new technology on the farms but also on new methods of carrying food from the farms to the cities — that is, railroads. It was railroads that brought Wyoming beef, Kansas wheat, and Louisiana rice to the table of a McCormick molder. Without the new railroad network built after the Civil War, the mechanization of agriculture would have had small effect.

Railroads, like farms, benefited from new technological developments. The principle of the steam engine remained the same. But almost every other mechanical aspect of railroading changed drastically during the generation after Appomattox.

The old railroads had used iron rails, small and dangerous wood-burning engines, and tiny, rickety coaches and freight cars. The new lines used steel rails that would last for many years without cracking or rusting. Because they could support almost twenty times as much weight as iron rails, larger engines and cars could be built. The typical pre-Civil War engine had weighed about 20 tons. By 1900 some engines weighed as much as 300 tons. The coal-burning locomotive became a giant source of power that could pull huge freights over the most difficult grades efficiently and safely. Freight cars increased in weight from 10 tons to over 100 tons.

Railroad mileage increased, too. In 1870 — even after the completion of the first transcontinental line — there were only about 60,000 miles of track in the United States. By 1900 there were over 250,000 miles. This total was greater than the entire railroad mileage of Europe, including Russia. Other inventions like the telegraph and the electric signal made it possible to control complicated traffic patterns and freight yards. The trains and tracks of 1900 were as dramatically different from those of 1850 as the jet plane is from the first wobbly aircraft of the 1920s. These new giants of the landscape transformed the process of moving food, objects, and people from one place to another.

MANUFACTURING

Taken by themselves, the technological changes in agriculture and the railroads would have meant little. They were important only in their relation to other parts of the new industrial system. In this system it was manufacturing that was crucial.

By 1900 — a little more than a century after Washington had taken the oath of office — the United States was the leading manufacturing nation in the world. Many factors made this growth possible. Americans found new beds of coal. They discovered iron ore in Michigan and Minnesota. They opened oil fields in Pennsylvania, the Ohio Valley, and the southern Great Plains. These raw materials and energy sources fed in turn the new factories of Pittsburgh, Chicago, and dozens of other cities. Mechanized agriculture made it possible for millions of people to move to cities to work in industrial plants. A high tariff kept down competition from foreign manufactured goods.

Alabama, rich in iron ore and coal, became a center of the steel industry. Steel was produced in giant blast furnaces, like these of the Tennessee Coal, Iron, and Railroad Company of Ensley, Alabama, and transported by rail to other centers.

Most important of all were the new machines and processes that enabled Americans to produce so much so quickly.

The Steel Industry   Steel was (and still is) very close to the heart of the new economy. It is stronger than iron, more resistant to rust, and easier to shape or mold. People had been making small quantities of steel for centuries, but the process was slow and difficult, since it depended on hand labor. In the 1850s an Englishman named Henry Bessemer invented a converter that could turn iron into steel by blowing a blast of hot air through the molten iron. The process was spectacular to watch, sending a brilliant shaft of sparks and smoke skyward. The economic results were just as startling. For the first time it became possible to produce steel in massive quantities.

The combination of the Bessemer converter, the demand for steel from the railroads and other industries, and the discovery of additional sources of iron ore and coal created a new industry. In 1870 the United States produced only about 77,000 tons of steel. By 1900, steel production had increased to over 11 million tons a year—an increase of almost 2,000 percent. Pittsburgh became the first (and is still the largest) of the steel towns. But eventually cities like Birmingham, Alabama, and Gary, Indiana—built almost entirely around the steel industry—sprang up in what had until then been open countryside.

Other Industries   What happened in steel was repeated in dozens of other industries. The sewing machine and other inventions made it possible to manufacture shoes and clothing on a mass scale. Steam-powered mills using steel equipment could cut lumber or grind wheat or print newspapers with a speed and efficiency no one had dreamed of earlier (see chart, page 665).

Another new industry grew up based on electricity. The foremost American in this field was the versatile Thomas A. Edison. Throughout the late nineteenth century a stream of inventions poured from his laboratories. These included the phonograph, the first practical electric light bulb, the storage battery, the dynamo, the electric voting machine, and the motion picture.

An industry also developed rapidly around the discovery of oil and new ways of refining it. It yielded kerosene to light lamps and fuel stoves. Heavier oils lubricated the motors of the new technology. Beginning around 1900, it became important as a source of gasoline for the internal combustion engine (see Chapter 38). This vast industry had simply not existed in 1800.

A revolution in communications began in 1876, on the hundredth anniversary of the Declaration of Independence. In that year a young inventor named Alexander Graham Bell exhibited the first working model of the telephone. At first the telephone was purchased only by individuals

In 1877 the telephone was the subject of a humorous song. By the turn of the century it had revolutionized communications in every major city in the United States. Just fifty years after its invention almost every middle-class American home had its own telephone.

who wanted to communicate between two specific locations, like a house and a factory or office. But soon there were enough phones in use to create the first telephone exchange. It was opened at New Haven, Connecticut, in 1878. Other cities and towns followed suit.

Soon cities began to link up with one another. The first connection linked New York and Boston in 1884. New York and Chicago were joined in 1892. By 1915, when lines connected New York and San Francisco, it was possible to place calls between any two cities in the nation.

The only way to measure the magnitude of what was happening to the United States is to use statistics. In 1869 the value of American manufactured goods was about $1.5 billion. By the end of the century the figure was more than $4.5 billion. In 1869 about 2 million workers ran American shops, mills, and factories and the market value of the average person's yearly work was only about $940. By 1900, when almost 5 million men and women worked in industry, the market value of their average yearly effort was almost doubled, to nearly $1,800.

By the 1890s the United States had more steel, more rails, more electric trolleys, more telephones, and more electric lights than any other nation in the world. To accomplish all this, Americans mined more metal, cut more lumber, dug more iron ore, and pumped more oil than any other country.

THE GROWTH OF "BIG BUSINESS"

Technology and manufacturing were crucial in making the United States an industrial nation. Equally vital were new methods of organizing industry and business.

The Factory System   At the beginning of the Civil War, the majority of Americans who worked in industry were employed in small shops and mills — a tailor shop, for example, or a blacksmith's or harnessmakers. In 1870, when the revolution in industry was already well under way, the average

industrial plant had only eight employees. A median plant (one halfway between the largest and the smallest) had thirty workers. By 1914 the average plant had twenty-eight workers, and the median 270. In 1870 no factory in America employed over 1,000 workers. By 1914 several had over 10,000 workers.

What was occurring, in other words, was a change that went beyond the technology of production and the rate of manufacturing. It was nothing less than a parallel revolution. The factory was replacing the traditional small shop.

In a traditional shop (or in the home manufacture of items like cloth or soap), work centers on the person. Power is supplied mainly through human toil. The same worker is involved in all stages of production, from spinning thread, for example, to weaving the final cloth.

The idea behind a factory (first introduced into England in the late eighteenth century) is very different. Work in a factory centers on a machine. Power is mechanical, not human. Parts are nearly identical, and so they are interchangeable. Most important is the division of labor. Each worker specializes, performing only one step in a chain. He or she may never touch or see the raw material. He or she may never look at or handle the final product. The result is mass production — manufacturing large numbers of articles in standard shapes and sizes.

Changes in Organization   Factories were inevitably larger than shops. They cost more money to build and equip with machinery. More and more capital was needed in order to enter and compete in almost any line of business. As the factory system grew; so did the size of companies.

Growth in turn demanded changes in the organization of business. Mass production required a sizable investment. This made it difficult for family firms and partnerships to be truly competitive. So, large corporations gradually replaced companies owned by one family or a few partners.

The corporation is an old idea. The Virginia Company and the Massachusetts Bay Company were both corporations. The idea is as simple as it is old. If many people invest in an enterprise by buying stock in it, the company can grow much

ANDREW CARNEGIE

One of the dominant myths of the late nineteenth century was the rags-to-riches notion. In fact, most successful businessmen of the period were not born to rags at all, but came into the world with at least modest advantages. But, regardless of the facts, the most captivating idea in American culture was the image of the "self-made man." And, of all the industrial magnates of the day, the man who best fitted the picture was Andrew Carnegie. His life contained all the right ingredients: poor but honest parents, a daring willingness to gamble on innovations, and an almost blinding financial success.

The real picture, of course, was a little more complicated. Carnegie was the son of poor Scottish immigrants, yes. But his parents were poor because the skilled trade of weaving they had practiced in Dunfermline, Scotland, was a craft already being destroyed by technological innovation when Carnegie was born in 1835.

This family of skilled craftsmen had for generations been articulate and politically active. When his parents immigrated to the United States in 1848, Carnegie already had the fair beginnings of an education in literature and politics.

Carnegie started as a bobbin boy in a cotton factory in Allegheny, Pennsylvania, where his parents settled. By the time he was thirty years old, he had made what, by the standards of the day, was already classed as a great fortune: $400,000. The fortune derived from hard work, yes; but it was helped along by a powerful patron who was president of the Pennsylvania Railroad. When this patron was appointed assistant secretary of war in the Lincoln administration, Carnegie accompanied him to Washington as an aide. There, he was in a superb position to learn the crucial role that railroads and iron and steel would play in the new, industrialized economy.

Carnegie's first fortune came from railroading, bridge building, oil, and a series of clever speculations. He had, always, a somewhat ambiguous attitude toward his own material success. In fact, he sometimes seemed to *fear* money, as though it might destroy his character. In 1868, in a remarkable memorandum to himself, he listed his assets and the income they could produce:

An income of $50,000 per annum! . . . Beyond this, make no effort to increase fortune . . . . Man must have an idol—the amassing of wealth is one of the worst species of idolatry—no idol more debasing than the worship of money . . . . To continue much longer overwhelmed by business cares and with most of my thoughts wholly upon the way to make more money in the shortest time, must degrade me beyond hope of permanent recovery.

Such thoughts had only a limited effect on Carnegie's career. Within five years, he was embarked on the creation of Carnegie Steel, which he made into a model of vertical integration and efficiency. When he finally sold his interest in the company to the new trust, United States Steel, in 1901, it was worth $250,000,000.

But Carnegie did try to rescue himself from "idolatry" in a variety of other ways. For one thing, he wrote—five volumes of books and essays, a remarkable accomplishment for a man of affairs. For another, he engaged in the systematic cultivation of literary and philosophical friends in both England and America. He also embarked on a progam of "scientific philanthropy" that eventually totaled about $350 million, dotting the landscape with what came to be called "Carnegie libraries." Carnegie was not at all typical of the entrepreneurs of the period. But his articulateness and his rhetoric of benevolence combined to make him a model for the popular cult of individual struggle, success through fair competition, and enlightened capitalism as the economic basis of American democracy.

larger than if it is funded by only a few individuals. If the company fails, each investor has lost only the value of his stock. He cannot be held responsible for any of the corporation's debts.

Just as there had been American factories before the Civil War, so had there been corporations. But their number increased greatly after the war. The corporation became the standard way of organizing business, just as the factory became the characteristic method of organizing production.

Mass production required not only corporate investment. It also demanded that each firm market its product efficiently on a broad national scale, instead of selling just locally. To remain in business, a corporation had to create effective distributing and selling divisions. It had to buy raw materials on a large scale. Ideally, in fact, it would purchase its own source of raw materials—for example, a forest for a paper company or cotton plantations for a textile mill.

In other words, mass production made it profitable for a company to invest money in all the stages of its industry, from original materials to final sales. Economists call this phenomenon vertical integration. It involves a business firm not only in manufacturing but in all the other stages and phases relating to the business. An oil company that owned wells, pipelines, and refineries and had its own sales force would be almost perfectly integrated. It would be freed from dependence on any other economic unit—except, of course, customers.

Competition and Consolidation The new industrial order brought a new kind of competition into the American economy. Before mass production, small shops and mills had catered to limited territories. They competed only where one territory bordered on another. But large corporations needed large markets to absorb their massive outputs. Thus a number of companies might find themselves competing for the same customers.

To win a big market, a corporation might advertise heavily. It might hire high-pressure salesmen and reward them with big commissions. But the most obvious way to win a market was to cut prices. A large company with efficient factories and lower production costs could force its competitors into bankruptcy simply by lowering prices beyond the point where the smaller firms could stay in business.

In one industry after another a few corporations gradually emerged as the leading firms. Each was too large and powerful to be driven out of business by the others. Each was too small to be able to control the whole market. Whenever this happened—and it happened sooner or later in most industries—the firms entered a period of cutthroat competition.

Most American businesses did not welcome such competition. In the 1880s and 1890s they tried to find ways to avoid it. The railroads led the way. Railroad owners had witnessed the havoc and ruin that could be created when one railroad waged a price war with another. By a process of trial and error the railroads worked out private agreements among themselves to control freight rates. Railroads also developed a system of grouping their customers in "pools"; each line was entitled to a certain share of the market. Gradually, too, the railroads had become consolidated into a few major lines, each one absorbing dozens of smaller companies. The Pennsylvania and New York Central railroads dominated the Northeast. The Southern Railway controlled much of the South. The Louisville and Nashville line was supreme in the Ohio Valley.

By agreements and consolidations the railroads had become the models for big business. Other industries soon copied what railroad leaders had learned and used the economic devices they had developed. Consolidation became the order of the day.

No matter what industry was involved, the process was the same. First, a few large competing firms would emerge. A period of intense and costly competition would follow. Then firms would consolidate as a way of avoiding competition. During its period of rapid growth the McCormick Harvester Company was competing with a handful of other large manufacturers of agricultural machinery. In the years after the Haymarket Affair, however, the McCormicks began to realize that competition was wasteful and unnecessary. Early in the twentieth century McCormick merged with its competition to form the huge International

Harvester Company. Since then, it has produced practically all the harvesting machinery manufactured in the United States.

A similar development occurred in the steel industry, which was dominated for almost half a century by a Scotch immigrant, Andrew Carnegie. Carnegie was a classic example of the "rags-to-riches" success story. At thirteen he came to America with his family and immediately went to work. At eighteen he was a telegraph clerk for the Pennsylvania Railroad. During the quick railroad expansion of the Civil War years, Carnegie realized that iron and steel for rails and bridges were the key to the railroads' future, and that railroads, in turn, were the key to an expanding economy. He saved every cent and invested daringly but successfully. By 1872 he was able to build his own steel plant near Pittsburgh.

Carnegie's company grew with the industry. By 1890 he was producing almost a third of a million tons of steel. By 1900 this amount had nearly tripled. At the same time, Carnegie worked to achieve vertical integration. He bought iron ore deposits, steamers to transport ore on the Great Lakes, and railroad cars to carry it overland—in fact, everything that he needed for making steel.

In the meantime the process of competition had eliminated all but a few other steel companies. In 1892 the Carnegie Company was reorganized to combine seven other corporations in which Carnegie had acquired a controlling interest. In 1901 the largest steel concerns in the nation were all merged into one great new corporation, the United States Steel Corporation. The power behind this consolidation was another dominant figure of the period, J. Pierpont Morgan, a New York banker and financier. Morgan spent nearly half a billion dollars to buy out Carnegie and set up this supercorporation. Like International Harvester, the giant company dominated its industry. It produced almost all of some forms of steel and three-fifths of the total steel made in the United States.

The Trust An even more stunning example of consolidation brought John D. Rockefeller into control of the oil industry. Rockefeller started out as a poor boy, like Carnegie. He too saved every cent (except for the 10 percent tithe he regularly gave to the Baptist Church). Starting with one refinery in Cleveland, Rockefeller by 1872 had created the giant Standard Oil Company.

Rockefeller also created a new device that made it even easier to consolidate an industry—the trust. A trust in industry is an arrangement in which several companies sell themselves to a group of trustees. The companies are paid for with shares in the new trust itself. Only paper changes hands, but the result is a group of directors who control the operations of several companies.

Through the Standard Oil Trust the Rockefeller interests acquired almost total control of the oil industry. The trust could phase out unnecessary plants. It could take full advantage of mass production and distribution techniques to provide most of the kerosene that lighted American lamps and the oil that lubricated American machines. Rockefeller himself summed up adequately the reasons for the trust:

> It has revolutionized the way of doing business all over the world. The time was ripe for it. It had to come, though all we saw at the moment was the need to save ourselves from wasteful conditions [of competition]. The day of combination is here to stay. Individualism has gone, never to return.

One by one the main American industries passed from competition to consolidation. It might occur through giant corporations created by mergers, like International Harvester or United States Steel. Or it might result from the formation of trusts—which involved everything from cottonseed oil to sugar to whiskey. By 1900 a few large concerns controlled almost all the major facilities of production and distribution in the United States.

THE NEW AMERICANS

Industry has always needed people, and the new industrial order was no exception in this respect. The growth in agriculture, railroads, and industry demanded millions of people, both as workers and as consumers.

U.S. GROWTH OF POPULATION, 1870-1910

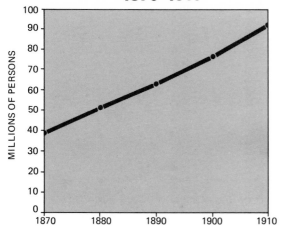

The American population kept pace with the growing industrial order. For every 100 persons living in the United States in 1870, there were 126 in 1880, 158 in 1890, 190 in 1900—and in 1910 a surprising 230! In one generation the population had more than doubled, from about 40 million in 1870 to over 90 million forty years later.

These were the millions who moved into the Great Plains and the Rockies, bringing about the final collapse of the Western Indians. These were the millions that bought McCormick's harvesters, worked in his factory, and built the railroads that carried his reapers into every flat corner of the country where grain could be planted and harvested by machine.

These millions, however, were not just more of the same kinds of Americans who had lived here in Jacksonian times. They were a new people, with different languages, different religions, and different ways of life. Andrew Jackson's common man was almost certain to be "native" American, white, Protestant, and a farmer. His parents or grandparents might have immigrated to the United States, but they would probably have come from England or Scotland. When they arrived here, they would have found the language, the way of worshiping God, and the customs familiar and comfortable.

The common man in New York in 1900 was more likely to be a Jew from Poland or a Roman Catholic from Italy. He lived in a city and proba-

bly had a job in a factory. His English might be poor, his memories of the "old country" at least as important to him as his hopes for the new. He represented a social revolution that had accompanied the revolutions in technology, industry, and business—the creation of an urban immigrant working class.

Shifting Trends in Immigration There have always been immigrants in America, at least from the time when the Indians began to cross over from Asia into Alaska. In the years since the American Revolution, the actual proportion of immigrants to the total population did not change much. Two other things happened instead: (1) the nature of the immigrant population changed; and (2) the immigrants (along with other Americans) began to congregate in urban centers. These two changes made factory cities like Chicago the gathering places for a new kind of American: the poor immigrant from a country where English was not spoken and where an Anglo-Saxon Protestant was rare.

In 1790, when the United States took its first census under the new Constitution, nine out of ten Americans (except for the black slaves in the South) had English or Scotch ancestors. This pattern changed somewhat with the "old immigration" of the 1840s and 1850s, when large numbers of Germans, Scandinavians, and Irish began to immigrate. However, most of the Germans and Scandinavians were Protestants, though their languages were strange to American ears. And though many native-born Americans resented the Catholicism of the Irish, these immigrants at least spoke English. In 1865 the United States had only about 200,000 inhabitants who had been born in Southern or Eastern Europe. They were easily absorbed by a total population of about 40 million.

By 1914 this picture had changed dramatically. A "new immigration"—mainly from Italy, Russia, and Austria-Hungary—flooded into the United States. Poverty drove many of these people from their home countries. Some men left to avoid the military draft, which discriminated against the poor. Jews wanted to escape the official anti-Semitism of Russia and Poland. Armenians fled from persecutions carried out by the

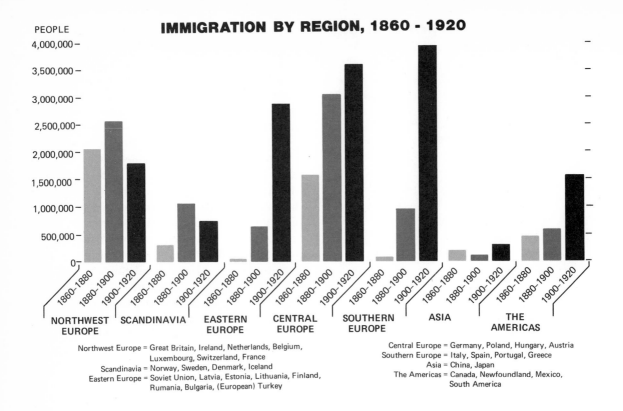

IMMIGRATION BY REGION, 1860 - 1920

PEOPLE

4,000,000
3,500,000
3,000,000
2,500,000
2,000,000
1,500,000
1,000,000
500,000
0

1860-1880 1880-1900 1900-1920 (repeated for each region)

NORTHWEST EUROPE   SCANDINAVIA   EASTERN EUROPE   CENTRAL EUROPE   SOUTHERN EUROPE   ASIA   THE AMERICAS

Northwest Europe = Great Britain, Ireland, Netherlands, Belgium, Luxembourg, Switzerland, France
Scandinavia = Norway, Sweden, Denmark, Iceland
Eastern Europe = Soviet Union, Latvia, Estonia, Lithuania, Finland, Rumania, Bulgaria, (European) Turkey

Central Europe = Germany, Poland, Hungary, Austria
Southern Europe = Italy, Spain, Portugal, Greece
Asia = China, Japan
The Americas = Canada, Newfoundland, Mexico, South America

Turkish government. The new immigrants were drawn to the United States by advertisements of cheap steamship transportation, by rumors of free land and golden opportunity, and by a massive propaganda campaign conducted by railroads anxious for workers and for customers to buy up their lands.

Immigration from Southern and Eastern Europe amounted to only a trickle in the 1860s and 1870s. But by the 1890s over half the immigrants to America were from Southern and Eastern Europe. In the next decade—the peak decade for immigration in the history of the United States—the proportion of new immigrants rose to over 75 percent. In simple terms this means that over 6 million Italians, Russian Jews, Hungarians, and other immigrants from Southern and Eastern Europe came here between 1901 and 1910.

Reactions to the Newcomers The strike at McCormick and the Haymarket Affair occurred just before the new immigration reached its peak in the United States. But prejudice had already been aroused by the entry of Irish and Germans and by the beginnings of the influx from Eastern and Southern Europe. Both the McCormick strike and the trial of the so-called Haymarket radicals occurred in an atmosphere of fear and bigotry. The Pinkerton report on the "fighting Irish" molders and the newspaper comments on foreign "anarchists" make it clear that events in Chicago would have been different had they not taken place at the time of this bewildering flood of immigration.

The new immigrants were not only different in culture, language, and religion. They also behaved in a different way from those who had preceded them. They moved into a society that was no longer predominantly agricultural and rural, but urban. So they did not fan out onto farms as most of the old immigrants had done. Instead, they followed the lead of millions of other Americans and settled in cities. Two-thirds of foreign-born residents in the United States lived in towns or cities by 1900.

Bewildered and often victimized in America, new immigrants clustered together in their own city neighborhoods, or ghettos.[1] People from a particular province or even a particular village would move into buildings on the same block, recreating much of the culture of their Old World homes. As the new immigration increased, so did antiforeign sentiment. Ghetto dwellers earned a reputation among "native" Americans for being clannish, dirty, superstitious, and generally undesirable. They were considered strange, chattering in their odd languages, and somehow suited only for city life. Actually, of course, they were no more "natural" city dwellers than were the English who had come to Virginia and Massachusetts in the seventeenth century. They were simply caught in

---

[1]The word "ghetto" dates back to the Middle Ages. It is Italian and may come from *borghetto*, meaning a small settlement outside the town. The term originally applied to the Jewish quarter of a city.

a phase of the industrial revolution—the creation of an urban society.

Becoming "American" In the era of the new immigration the goal was assimilation—taking on the traits of the new society so as to blend with it. But becoming an "American" was not an easy process for most Europeans who migrated to this country in the late nineteenth century. Foremost was the problem of language. Real assimilation meant being able to take advantage of American economic and political opportunities. And this in turn depended upon knowing the language.

Since a knowledge of English brought with it an almost immediate economic advantage over those who could not speak or write the language, most immigrant parents sacrificed the income they would have received from their children's labor to send their children to the free public schools. Workers often attended special night school class-

The new immigrants from Southern and Eastern Europe fueled the industrial machine by their labor. Forced to live in cities where the jobs were, they clustered in crowded and unsanitary ghetto areas like New York's Lower East Side.

es after their exhausting days in the factories. A Jewish immigrant, Mary Antin, recalls:

> Education was free. It was the one thing that my father was able to promise us when he sent for us; surer, safer than bread or shelter. On our second day in the country a little girl from across the alley came and offered to conduct us to school. We five children between us had a few words of English by this time. We knew the word "school." We understood. This child, who had never seen us till yesterday, who could not pronounce our names, who was not much better dressed than we were, still was able to offer us the freedom of the schools of Boston!

Countless immigrants must have felt similar emotions at the discovery that schooling — so restricted in Europe — was so readily available in the United States. In the words of Mary Antin, "No application made; no questions asked; no examinations, rulings, exclusions; no fees."

Learning English was the first step in assimilation. After that many immigrants joined some form of voluntary association that would put them in contact with native-born Americans. For city dwellers, the most available of such groups were the political parties. They provided favors, food, and jobs for poor and needly immigrants (see page 474). They also helped "Americanize" them.

"Boss" Richard Croker of Tammany Hall in New York described the function of his political machine as taking the city's newcomers, who "do not speak our language and do not know our laws, yet are the raw material with which we have to build up the state," and turning them into Americans. He asserted that a political machine like Tammany "looks after them for the sake of their vote, grafts them upon the Republic, makes citizens of them, in short; and although you may not like our motives or our methods, what other agency is there by which so long a row could have been hoed so quickly or so well?"

Another strong influence on the new immigrants was a small number of "old" immigrants — those who had arrived before the great influx.

Children old enough to work in factories did so by day and attended school at night. The goal was assimilation: shedding enough of the old folkways to enter "native" American society.

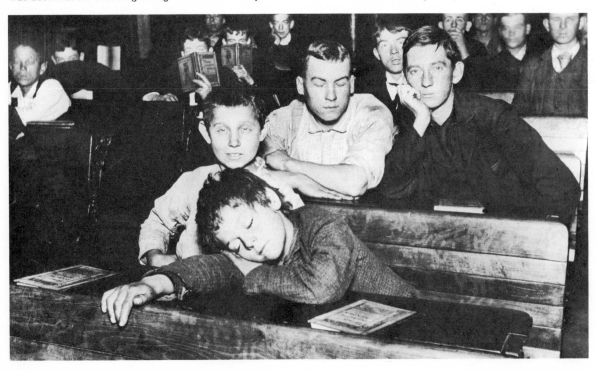

They had learned English and then helped recruit workers from Europe for factory labor in the United States. They often paid the newcomers' transportation and helped them settle in the ghettos of American cities.

Such men were sometimes called *padrones* (an Italian word meaning "patrons"). They might be paid by three different groups: (1) employers, for supplying cheap labor; (2) political machines, for delivering the votes of immigrants once they became citizens; and (3) the immigrants themselves, for favors received. Often the *padrones*—who existed among Jewish, Greek, Armenian, Polish, and other immigrant groups, as well as among the Italians—were ward leaders in political organizations. They provided a link between the concerns of the ghetto newcomers and those of the citywide machine.

URBANIZATION

In the ancient world, only two great cities—Rome and Alexandria—had populations of over half a million people. By the time George Washington was born, Rome and Alexandria had long ago declined. The only cities to have reached a comparable size since were London and Paris. At the time of the Haymarket Affair, however, Chicago had become a great city. In fact, by 1900 the United States had six cities with more than half a million inhabitants.

The process of urbanization was not confined to the United States. All the industrializing nations of Western Europe experienced it, too. The factory system demanded high concentrations of workers, and the agricultural revolution made it possible for millions of people to leave their farms—whether in Germany or in Maine—and move to towns.

The United States experienced three great migrations in the generation after the Civil War. One was from the East to the Great Plains and the Far West. Another was from Europe to America. The third was from the country to the city. Of the three, the movement from farm to city was easily the most extensive.

In 1800 only about three Americans out of every hundred lived in towns larger than 8,000. By 1900 this proportion had grown 1,000 percent; almost a third of the nation lived in cities of over 8,000. In 1800 there had been only six cities larger than 8,000; in 1900 there were over 400.

This increase was not gradual and smooth. Most of it came in the half-century after the end of the Civil War. During this period at least 15 million "native" Americans moved out of farming areas and into cities, and their number was swelled by an almost equal number of new immigrants who settled in cities instead of on farms. Statistics tell the story. Between 1870 and 1900 the population of the United States increased by about 35 million people. During the same period the urban population increased by about 24 million. The cities, which cover such a small proportion of the land, had absorbed more than two thirds of the total increase.

Technological Factors A city is not just a collection of people in a small area. Like industry, modern cities were made possible by technological change. In the centuries before the industrial revolution the size of a city had been determined mainly by the transportation available. It could not be too big, because a person had to be able to walk or travel by wagon or carriage to a marketplace or job and back home again. After about 1880, however, cities began to experience a transportation revolution. The introduction of electricity made it possible to replace slow and awkward horse-drawn transport with fast, clean trolleys, elevated trains, and subways. These improvements meant that people could live many miles from their place of work and still be part of a vast city.

Electricity also made it possible to light city streets. Cleveland, in 1879, became the first city to have electric street lighting. Similarly, the introduction of the telephone in the 1880s meant that homes, offices, and factories could be tied together in an almost instantaneous communications network.

At first, city buildings themselves were a limiting factor. Even with the thickest walls, a stone or brick building could not extend higher

A turn-of-the-century view of a typical Midwestern city, Kansas City, Missouri, shows that the pulse of American life had quickened and taken on an increasingly urban character. The city itself was being transformed—trolleys transported people as once horses had done.

than fifteen stories. To build a structure even this high, builders had to make windows smaller and smaller because glass could not support the weight. A second problem was that human legs could tolerate only so many stairs. The first problem was solved by the invention of the skyscraper in the 1880s. This development was pioneered by a Chicago architect, Louis Sullivan. Skyscraper construction—in which walls were hung on steel frames—made possible structures as tall as a hundred stories. Thus even more people could be concentrated, level upon level, on smaller parcels of land. The second problem was solved at about the same time by the invention of the electric elevator.

INDUSTRY AND CULTURE

Economically and socially, the most important facts about American society in the period following the Civil War were industrialization, urbanization, and immigration. These facts together brought about a change in the landscape that was almost brutally obvious—the crowded, dirty, smoky city, with its alien working class. But people very often do not or *will* not see and acknowledge what is most plain. In their art and architecture, their novels and magazines—in all the areas

AN INFLUX OF NEWCOMERS

All Americans are immigrants or the descendants of immigrants. Over the centuries, every year has brought its share of foreigners seeking freedom and opportunity. Their numbers reached a high point in the late nineteenth and early twentieth centuries, when hundreds of thousands poured through the "golden door."

Some observers of this influx felt that the United States could not absorb all the newcomers. Others disagreed, especially those who realized that hosts of earlier immigrants—among them the Irish, Germans, and Swedes of the earlier nineteenth century—had indeed become Americans.

[For further information on the foreign observers quoted in this essay, see "Notes on Sources."]

PICTORIAL ESSAY 6

My uncle Olaf, a seaman, used to come to us between voyages, and he was all the time talking about America; what a fine place it was to make money in. The schoolmaster told us one day about the great things that poor Swedes had done in America. A man who had lived in America once came to visit near our cottage. He said that food was cheap in America and that a man could earn nearly ten times there as in Sweden. So at last it was decided that my brother was to go to America.

[AXEL JARLSON, 1903]

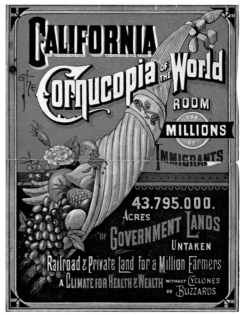

Railroad poster soliciting immigrants

The emigrants flocked into the mess-room from the four doors to twenty immense tables spread with knives and forks and toppling platters of bread. Nearly all the men came in in their hats—in black glistening ringlety sheepskin hats, in fur caps, in bowlers, in sombreros, in felt hats with high crowns, in Austrian cloth hats, in caps so green that the wearer could only be Irish. A strange gathering of seekers, despairers, wanderers, pioneers, criminals, scapegoats.

[STEPHEN GRAHAM, 1913]

Between Decks in an Emigrant Ship

We carried our luggage out at eight, and in a pushing crowd prepared to disembark. At 8:30 we were quick-marched out of the ship to the Customs Wharf and there ranged in six or seven long lines. All the officials were running and hustling, shouting out "Come on!" "Hurry!" "Move along!" and clapping their hands. Our trunks were examined and chalk-marked on the run—no delving for diamonds—and then we were quick-marched further to a waiting ferry-boat [for Ellis Island].

[STEPHEN GRAHAM, 1913]

Immigrants disembarking in New York City

A doctor examining boys at Ellis Island

I visited Ellis Island yesterday. The central hall is the key. All day long, through an intricate series of metal pens, the long procession files, step by step, bearing bundles and trunks and boxes, past this examiner and that, past the quick, alert medical officers, the tallymen and the clerks. On they go, from this pen to that, pen by pen, toward a desk at a little metal wicket— the gate of America. Ellis Island is quietly immense. It gives one a visible image of one aspect at least of this world-large process of filling and growing and synthesis which is America.

[H. G. WELLS, 1906]

Waiting for processing at Ellis Island

We were carefully examined, and when my turn came the examining officials shook their heads and seemed to find me wanting. I confessed that I had only five cents in my pocket and had no relatives here, and that I knew of nobody in this country except Franklin, Lincoln, and Harriet Beecher Stowe, whose Uncle Tom's Cabin *I had read in a translation. One of the officials, who had one leg only and walked with a crutch, with a merry twinkle in his eye said in German: "You showed good taste when you picked your American acquaintances." I learned later that he was a Swiss who had served in the Union army during the Civil War.*

[MICHAEL PUPIN, 1874]

George Bellows, *Cliff Dwellers*

Italian saw sharpener at work on the sidewalk

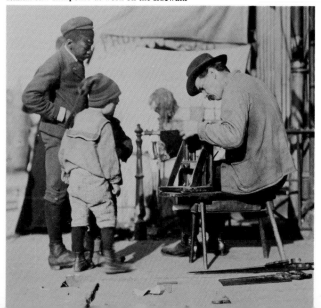

There was a bootblack named Michael on the corner. When I had time I helped him and learned the business. Francisco, too, worked for the bootblack, and we were soon able to make the best polishes. Then we thought we would go into business.

We had said that when we saved $1000 each we would go back to Italy and buy a farm, but now that the time is coming we are so busy and making so much money that we think we will stay. We meet many people and are learning new things all the time. We were very ignorant when we came here, but now we have learned much.

[ROCCO CORRESCA, 1902]

Immigrant iron workers in Pennsylvania

The work given to the new arrivals is generally of a rudimentary nature, but it teaches them to work, and the wages, although low, at least enable them to live, besides giving them the chance of joining the great labor unions of the country and taking if ever so small a part in the industrial pursuits of the people among whom they have come to live.

[COUNT VAY DE VAYA UND LUSKOD, 1908]

←*The inhabitants seem to have come from all quarters of the globe and to represent every known type. The streets, wide as they are, are yet too narrow to hold the masses of people who surge to and fro in them. Everyone is busy; everyone carries a parcel containing articles of clothing or food. Bargaining goes on in all the languages imaginable, and one hears an Italian praising his oranges as in the piazza of St. Lucia; a German discussing sausages of doubtful origin with a French urchin, who plays the part of a chef at the corner of the street; and Russian emigrants share their vodka, as a token of friendship, with Polish Jews.*

[COUNT VAY DE VAYA UND LUSKOD, 1908]

In the evening my sister and I took a walk; she went shopping and asked me to go with her. I saw a Jewish sign (in Hebrew letters) in a window reading "Kosher Butcher." I stopped and admired it very much and said to my sister, "This is the first time I see Hebrew letters in a window." In Rumania it is not allowed. Then I started to realize what anti-Semitism really meant and what an anti-Semitic country Rumania was.

[ROBERT MYERS, 1913]

Jewish hot potato vendor, New York City

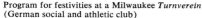

Program for festivities at a Milwaukee *Turnverein* (German social and athletic club)

German band, Cincinnati

The German in America is badly off. Where in the world can he find a wife? He has little opportunity for family life. So the young people get acquainted only in public places, in restaurants, concerts, the theater, balls. But what can they learn of each other there? Everything, except that which relates to a wife and her duties.

[KARL GRIESINGER, 1858]

Polish store, Chicago

Courtesy Chicago Historical Society

Those who are Americanized are American, and very patriotically American. Those who are not thus nationalized are not in the least internationalized. They simply continue to be themselves; the Irish are Irish; the Jews are Jewish; and all sorts of other tribes carry on the traditions of remote European valleys almost untouched. Very often these exiles bring with them not only rooted traditions, but rooted truths.

[G. K. CHESTERTON, 1921]

Returning to the log house, we spent the evening—twenty-one Swedes altogether—in games, songs, and dancing, exactly as if in Sweden. I felt myself happy in being with my countrymen, happy to find them so agreeable and so Swedish still in the midst of a foreign land.

[FREDRIKA BREMER, 1850]

Harvesting, by the Swedish American painter Olaf Krans

Irish politicians, Chicago

Courtesy Chicago Historical Society

I made the acquaintance of two local celebrities (Irish), namely Paddy Ryan and Michael McDonald. Paddy is a fighting man lately defeated in the twenty-four-foot ring by a compatriot, Sullivan. Michael McDonald runs a granite quarry. But his principal importance arises from his political position. He is supposed to direct and control what is called the rowdy element in Chicago—largely made up of our countrymen—and this gives him very great local influence. He is a rough diamond, with a decisive, masterful way about him, which clearly marks him out as a leader of men. His friends claim for him that he returned the present mayor of Chicago—the first Democratic mayor returned for Chicago for thirty years.

[LORD RUSSELL OF KILLOWEN, 1883]

PE 6–8 / *The Chinese have built a great part of the Northern Pacific from the Continental Divide to the Pacific. As we sped along, we came upon their encampments again and again in forest glades, by the shores of the rivers and lakes, on the outskirts of the cities— always a community apart. It is said to their credit that they insist, when they can, on being located near water for purposes of personal cleanliness.*

[LORD RUSSELL OF KILLOWEN, 1883]

Chinese workmen on a Western railroad

In a place so exclusively Mexican as Monterey, you saw not only Mexican saddles but true vaquero riding—men always at the gallop up hill and down dale, and round the sharpest corner, urging their horses with cries and gesticulations and cruel spurs, checking them dead with a touch, or wheeling them right-about-face in a square yard. In dress they ran to color and bright sashes. Not even the most Americanized could always resist the temptation to stick a red rose into his hatband.

[ROBERT LOUIS STEVENSON, 1879]

Mexican horseman in California

The growth of New York City depended upon improved transportation facilities like the Brooklyn Bridge. The bridge's completion in 1883 made it possible to live outside Manhattan and commute to work by steam car, by carriage, or on foot.

of their culture—native, white, middle-class Americans seemed determined to ignore the realities of their age. At both the popular and the sophisticated level, middle-class culture seemed almost serene in its lack of awareness of industrial capitalism and its social consequences. To some extent, of course, the practice of ignoring, evading, or denying "reality" is a characteristic of culture in any society. But Americans in the 1870s and 1880s were abnormally, almost absurdly consistent in their unwillingness to come to terms culturally with the actualities around them.

This characteristic of American culture was not confined to the sentimental and quaint books and essays published for a middle-class, primarily female, readership. It was evident in the most talented and sophisticated intellectuals, too. Henry James wrote great novels and stories, as great as any ever published in English. But his subject matter was the elegant and complicated lives of wealthy Americans, usually set in Europe. And even when one of James's heroes was a businessman, as in *The American* (1876), he appeared in the novel only *after* he had made his fortune and arrived in Europe in pursuit of "culture" and an aristocratic French bride.

Henry James was born to wealth, cultivated society, and European travel. Samuel Clemens was born in Missouri into a modestly well-to-do family and spent much of his life scratching for a living as a journalist. As "Mark Twain," he wrote about plain people. But his plain people were not immigrants or factory workers. And his settings were the small towns of the Mississippi, where boyish and innocent characters like Huckleberry Finn and Tom Sawyer had their "adventures." *Huckleberry Finn* (1885) was a great novel by almost any standard. But it was hardly a novel that confronted American realities. Samuel Clemens lived in Hartford, Connecticut, a modern city; he was married to the daughter of a coal baron. But the closest he came to an examination of such realities was when he fantasized about the experience a technologically inventive Yankee might have if he suddenly woke up in medieval England, as in *A Connecticut Yankee in King Arthur's Court* (1887).

What was true of Mark Twain and Henry James was equally true of lesser talents. Even when novels were about businessmen—as in William Dean Howells's *The Rise of Silas Lapham* (1884)—the real subject seemed to be not business but society and romance, and the action occurred after the fortune was acquired. One of the most popular novels of the period was, on the surface at least, about industry, technology, and the city. Edward Bellamy's *Looking Backward* (1886) was a utopian romance about Boston in the year 2000. The utopia was, in theory at least, highly industrialized, urbanized, and socialistic. And the response of middle-class readers was enthusiastic. But, beneath its appearance of relevance to nineteenth-century realities, *Looking Backward* really described a pleasant, small Boston in which the factories, the poor, and the immigrants had disappeared as though by magic.

In the 1890s, a few books did try to deal with the more sordid aspects of factory and slum life. Jacob Riis's *How the Other Half Lives* (1890) described a slum in vivid language that alarmed his primarily middle-class, native audience:

> Cherry Street. Be a little careful, please! The hall is dark and you might stumble over the children pitching pennies back there. Not that it would hurt them: kicks and cuffs are their daily diet. They have little else. Here where the hall turns and dives into utter darkness is a step, and another, another. A flight of stairs. You can feel your way, if you cannot see it. Close? Yes! What would you have? All the fresh air that ever enters these stairs comes from the hall-door that is forever slamming, and from the windows of dark bedrooms.

Stephen Crane's *Maggie: A Girl of the Streets* (1893) was a darkly realistic account of the way that slum poverty turned innocent girls to sordid lives. But such books came only after decades of industrialization. And they created almost as much scandal as if they had been about sexual perversions. For the most part, writers and other intellectuals provided no insight whatever into the lives and difficulties of the new, alien, urban working class.

On the level of popular culture, the picture was much the same. A revolution in printing technology had made inexpensive books and magazines easily available, and a flood of popular fiction poured off the new steam-driven presses. But most of the stories and books dealt with rural life or the doings of chaste and sentimental small-town girls; or they had as their heroes idealized Western cowboys, romantic sailors, or heroic figures from ancient history.

A new type of popular fiction did emerge after the Civil War, the tale of business success. The most successful promoter of the rags-to-riches formula was a Harvard-educated former clergyman, Horatio Alger. His *Ragged Dick: Or, Street Life in New York* (1867) was a sensational sales success. For the next thirty years, under titles like *Jed the Poorhouse Boy* and *Struggling Upward*, Alger sold over 200 million copies of his stories.

Superficially, at least, the Alger stories reflected important economic realities. But the reflection was indirect and distorted. Alger did not deal with the adult, business careers of his heroes. Instead, he wrote coy exercises in moralism, designed to show how Ragged Dick, or Tattered Tom, or Poorhouse Jed overcame orphanhood and poverty by saving the drowning daughter of a wealthy, sonless merchant. The books always ended just as their heroes were about to embark on adult careers in commerce. The reader was left to assume that, in their adult lives, Alger's heroes would continue to thrive through a steady application of "pluck."

The practice of turning away from economic and social realities that was so central to the literature of the 1870s and 1880s was equally characteristic of the art and architecture of those decades. The greatest American artist of the period, James McNeill Whistler, painted mostly portraits and nocturnal landscapes. When Whistler did depict a scene of contemporary social or economic activity, the subject was more likely to be European than American (as in *The Last of Old Westminster*, PE 7-2).

Most artists confined themselves to painting scenes of nature or of domestic life—as in Mary Cassatt's *The Bath* (PE 7-3); or portraits of the wealthy in which the sources of wealth were carefully ignored—as in John Singer Sargent's 1897 study of *Mr. and Mrs. Isaac Newton Phelps Stokes* (PE 7-3). Winslow Homer, who probably was the second most talented American painter of the period, used his muscular and vivid style primarily on seascapes. When he did paint men at work, they were almost always fishermen in aged boats—an ardently preindustrial subject matter.

Architecture was even more flagrantly systematic in denying the actualities of industrialism. The expanding society of the period required an enormous number of new buildings—campuses for colleges and universities, building for banks and corporations, homes and summer houses for new millionaires, railroad stations, and so on. But even the most talented architects were mired in a contest to restore ancient styles. The familiar, reliable Greek and Roman styles that had been so popular since the Revolution were pressed into service again. There was an astonishing revival of Gothic and Georgian, especially in campus architecture. And anyone could stare for days at the largest of the new railroad stations, with their Greek columns or baroque decorations, without gaining any clue as to what the function of the building actually was.

In 1893, to celebrate Columbus's "discovery" of America, the industrial city of Chicago spent two years and about $15 million to create the World's Columbian Exposition. About 700 acres of Lake Michigan shoreline were transformed into a remarkable "White City." The exposition was a climactic moment in the long attempt to disguise the realities of the industrial system, with the newest inventions of the industrial era housed in wood-and-cardboard imitations of the buildings of ancient Greece and Rome. A seductive network of broad, tree-lined walks and lagoons made the buildings look like a virginal "congregation of brides."

New sources of power like the dynamo had to compete with the most sentimental and anti-industrial kinds of displays—a solid silver statue of a woman, sent by Montana; a statue of a knight sent by California, with armor made entirely of prunes; a full-sized model of the *Santa Maria*, sent over by Spain; a replica of the great hall at Versailles, built by the French; a "hootchy-kootchy" dancer with the archaic stage name of "Little Egypt." It all lived up to the description published by the Chicago *Tribune:* "a splendid fantasy of the artist and architect." American culture, it seemed, was not yet ready to acknowledge the staggering changes wrought by the new industrial order.

SUGGESTED READINGS–
CHAPTERS 29-30

Haymarket

Henry David, *History of the Haymarket Affair* (1936).

General

T. C. Cochran and William Miller, *The Age of Enterprise* (1942); Samuel P. Hays, *The Response to Industrialism, 1885–1914* (1957); E. C. Kirkland, *Industry Comes of Age: Business, Labor and Public Policy, 1860–1897* (1961); Robert Wiebe, *The Search for Order, 1887–1920* (1968).

Industrialization

Lewis Mumford, *Technics and Civilization* (1934); Roger Burlingame, *Engines of Democracy* (1940); T. C. Cochran, *Railroad Leaders, 1845–1890* (1953); G. R. Taylor and I. D. Neu, *The American Railroad Network* (1956); Charles Singer, ed., *A History of Technology: The Late Nineteenth Century* (1958).

Business Organization and Leaders

Andrew Carnegie, *The Autobiography of Andrew Carnegie* (1920); Matthew Josephson, *The Robber Barons* (1934); Allan Nevins, *A Study in Power: Rockefeller* (1953); E. C. Kirkland, *Dream and Thought in the Business Community, 1860–1900* (1956); R. G. McCloskey, *American Conservatism in the Age of Enterprise* (1957); Alfred D. Chandler, *Strategy and Structure: Chapters in the History of the Industrial Enterprise* (1962); J. F. Wall, *Andrew Carnegie* (1971).

Immigration

Jacob Riis, *How the Other Half Lives* (1890); John Higham, *Strangers in the Land* (1955); Barbara Solomon, *Ancestors and Immigrants* (1956); Leonard Dinnerstein and F. C. Jaher, eds., *The Aliens: A History of Ethnic Minorities in America* (1970); David Ward, *Cities and Immigrants: A Geography of Change in Nineteenth-Century America* (1971).

The City

Arthur M. Schlesinger, *The Rise of the City, 1878–1898* (1933); Robert H. Bremner, *From the Depths: The Discovery of Poverty in America* (1964); Constance M. Green, *The Rise of Urban America* (1965); Stephan Thernstrom, *The Other Bostonians: Poverty and Progress in the American Metropolis, 1880–1970* (1973); Samuel B. Warner, *The Urban Wilderness: A History of the American City* (1973).

Culture

Warner Berthoff, *The Ferment of Realism, 1884–1919* (1965); Robert G. McCloskey, *American Conservatism in the Age of Enterprise* (1961); Irvin G. Wyllie, *The Self-Made Man in America* (1954); Barbara Novak, *American Painting of the Nineteenth Century* (1969).

31
THE ELECTION OF 1896

A. W.

For a week, arguments had raged through the lobby and corridors of Chicago's Palmer House hotel. Bellboys no longer looked up when a long-haired Southerner or a flat-voiced Midwestern farmer loudly debated a well-dressed Eastern delegate, or when reinforcements for both sides rushed to join the verbal melee. Only when it seemed the discussion would turn into a fistfight did hotel employees quietly suggest that the gentlemen might like to continue their chat elsewhere.

Since delegates to the Democratic National Convention had begun pouring into Chicago, these employees had heard the same argument many times. At its most basic level, it seemed dull, a technical question of economics. The United States government, in this year of 1896, promised to pay to each holder of a dollar bill one dollar in gold. Overexcited Democrats from the South and the West now demanded that the government be empowered to redeem its paper money in silver as well as gold. Equally aroused politicians from New York, Pennsylvania, and Massachusetts angrily retorted that such a policy would destroy the credit of the government.

Chicagoans grown sick of the nonstop bellowing over the currency issue in most of their downtown hotels, restaurants, and bars, could find no relief outside. Marching, shouting, prosilver convention delegates filled the sidewalks and streets, singing along with the marching bands imported by each presidential candidate to improve his chances.

If there was an eye to this emotional storm, it was probably an upstairs corridor at the Sherman House, the hotel where a small, "foreign-looking" politico held court. He would beckon to a waiting silverite, hold a short, animated conversation in which he did most of the talking, and dismiss his auditor and summon another in the same gesture. The next man would then scuttle forward to talk to John Peter Altgeld, gover-

Independent-minded John Peter Altgeld, the first Democratic Governor of Illinois in 36 years, had been a German immigrant, Civil War soldier, Chicago lawyer, and Judge, before winning the highest state office in 1893.

nor of Illinois and the closest thing at the moment to a leader of the silver forces.

Altgeld had been through controversy before. Two years earlier, when a railroad strike paralyzed Chicago, he had refused to call in federal troops, arguing that local forces were adequate to maintain order. When President Grover Cleveland, less interested in maintaining order than in breaking the strike, sent in troops anyway, Altgeld berated his party's leader. He was in turn attacked by conservatives all over the country, the Chicago *Tribune* calling him "the lying, hypocritical, demagogical, sniveling Governor of Illinois."

Earlier, Altgeld, realizing that the move might make him a "dead man politically," had pardoned the three Haymarket anarchists still in prison. He had long been troubled by charges of prejudice from the judge and jury and by the inadequacy of the evidence against the accused. This action caused the more conservative elements of the press to conclude that Altgeld was an anarchist himself.

Neither of these acts, however, bothered the silver forces who looked to him for leadership. Many of the Southern and Western farmers now thronging Chicago had risen up and in Alabama schoolhouse meetings and Kansas county conventions taken the Democratic party away from its astonished former owners.

The silver Democrats had swept state after state, and now they came to Chicago with a clear majority of the delegates. But the more perceptive among them would have traded any one of the marching bands for a strong presidential candidate. Altgeld, the most important figure in the movement, was disqualified because he was German born, although he had come to America at the age of three months. With the silver forces divided among several weak candidates, silverites feared a compromise that would allow the outnumbered gold men to name the candidate.

They feared one gold man in particular. In ability and intellect, William Collins Whitney was the only man in Chicago comparable to Altgeld. Both were farm boys who had become city lawyers—Altgeld in Chicago, Whitney in New York. But whereas Altgeld had gone into labor law and politics, Whitney had worked for the Vanderbilts, the railroad magnates, and moved on rapidly to build his own future. With the same brilliance and ruthlessness that had amassed him $40 million, he had engineered Cleveland's nomination and election in 1892 and gained a reputation as the most effective organizer in American politics.

Whitney rolled into Chicago as the brains of the "gold train," carrying the elite of the Eastern Democrats to the convention. The train, stocked with choice food and wines, carried cabinet officers, United States senators, and state party bosses. In previous years, this group had controlled the Democratic party; six of the last seven Democratic candidates for President had come from New York, and the seventh from Pennsylvania. Now they journeyed nervously, hoping that Whitney could work his magic and save them from humiliation.

Whether Whitney could do it, or whether the silver forces could agree on a candidate, remained in doubt when the convention opened.

Fifteen thousand people jammed Chicago's Coliseum, facing giant portraits of Jackson, Jefferson, and James Buchanan, with galleries rising in rows above the convention floor.

William Jennings Bryan, a thirty-six-year-old former congressman from Nebraska, owed loyalty to neither Whitney nor Altgeld. A strong silverite, he had his own ideas about who should lead the movement. On the convention's second night, before returning to his modest, two-dollar-a-day hotel room, Bryan uttered the following words to his wife and a friend: "So that you both may sleep well tonight, I am going to tell you something. I am the only man who can be nominated. I am what they call the logic of the situation."

The next day, the delegates waited expectantly as Bryan, famous as an orator but hardly considered a serious candidate, approached the stage to close the debate over the platform. Bryan began by warning that farmers were through with meekly asking the East for assistance. He reviewed the previous year's steady growth of silverite protest and challenged those Eastern gold Democrats who argued that returning to a dual monetary standard—gold *and* silver—would "disturb" the country's business interests.

The petitions of farmers had been scorned by Eastern men of wealth, Bryan shouted. Their entreaties had been disregarded, and— "when our calamity [the depression] came"—their begging had been mocked. "We beg no longer," he cried, "we entreat no more; we petition no more. We defy them!" From that moment, Bryan held most of his 15,000 listeners in his hands. Their cheers interrupted him constantly as he heaped scorn upon the Eastern gold Democrats and their arguments. The audience's enthusiasm reached its height as Bryan's speech drew to a close. Even the most hostile listener would be forced to acknowledge that Bryan had transformed the convention briefly into a sort of revival meeting.

"You shall not press upon the brow of labor this crown of thorns," cried Bryan, in one of the most famous perorations in American history. "You shall not crucify mankind upon a cross of gold!" For five seconds Bryan stood in dead silence, his arms outstretched in a Christlike pose.

Then the convention went mad. Dignified judges and legislators screamed and danced in the aisles. Silverites carried Bryan on their shoulders. State after state dipped its standard in front of Nebraska's, while silver politicians fought through the crowd to pledge Bryan their votes. One gold delegate grabbed a nearby newsman, hauled him to his feet, and bellowed, "Yell, damn you, yell!"

"I have enjoyed a great many addresses, some of which I have delivered myself," remembered Clarence Darrow, who would one day debate the Creation with Bryan in a Tennessee court, "but I never listened to one that affected and moved an audience as did that. Men and women cheered and laughed and cried. They listened with desires and hopes and finally with absolute confidence and trust. When he had finished his speech, amidst the greatest ovation I have ever witnessed, there was no longer any doubt as to the name of the nominee."

New York financier William C. Whitney, a lifelong Democrat despite his substantial wealth, had supported Grover Cleveland in 1884 and 1892, and served as Cleveland's Secretary of the Navy.

The thirty-six-year-old "boy orator," Nebraska Congressman William Jennings Bryan, was hoisted onto the shoulders of supporters, following his powerful "Cross of Gold" speech at the Democratic Convention in 1896.

Bryan's nomination on a silver platform delighted the South and the West. Two people less enthralled were the kingmakers of the convention, Whitney and Altgeld. Whitney, along with much of the stunned Eastern democracy, immediately announced that he would neither support nor vote for the ticket. Altgeld, despite the triumph of silver, was also disappointed. "It takes more than speeches to win victories," he told a friend the day after Bryan's triumph. "I have been thinking over Bryan's speech. What did he say, anyhow?"

Three weeks before, down the river in St. Louis, the Republicans had named Bryan's opponent. Their convention contrasted sharply with the hubbub and activity of the Democrats'. It was, one newspaper noted mournfully, the dullest convention anyone could remember.

Which was exactly how Marcus Alonzo Hanna wanted it. Hanna had worked for three years to lock the convention up for his friend Wil-

William Jennings Bryan's "Cross of Gold" metaphor had little appeal to his opponents in the business and industrial communities, no more than the candidate himself or his proposals for economic reform. The cartoon above, depicting Bryan as a trampler of scripture and vendor of sacrilegious souvenirs, accuses him of dragging Christian symbols into the dust.

liam McKinley of Ohio, and he wanted no disturbance that might unlock it. Although Eastern Republicans demanded a flat statement in support of gold and Republicans from Rocky Mountain silver-mining states wanted *their* metal endorsed, Hanna determined that the issue would not get out of hand.

McKinley had followed the path of the ambitious small-town Ohioan to success in Republican politics, the same trail that had led James Garfield to the White House. A former congressman and governor, McKinley had written the party's last tariff bill in 1890, a high tariff measure to "protect" American industries. If, as a friend admitted, "McKinley was no intellectual giant," he nevertheless understood politics, made friends easily, and came from the right state for a Republican candidate.

McKinley had every asset for political success except money. And while he did not possess much of that himself, he had the next best thing: an extremely wealthy friend and political backer. Mark Hanna, though he owned a shipping company, a bank, a street railway, an opera house, and much of the Cleveland area's Republican party, was more than just rich. He had been born to money, and he married much more of it, but he had then made a great deal more for himself and had thoroughly mastered all his businesses. Hanna believed in the durability of the

Mark Hanna, McKinley's campaign manager in the 1896 election, boss of the Ohio Republican machine and later of the national one, was a wealthy industrialist anxious for political power.

new industrial system. If the system could weather violent strikes, surely it could also withstand the threat of free silver. He had informed the panicky members of the Cleveland Union League Club, "There isn't going to be any revolution. You're all a lot of damned fools."

Over the years, Hanna had mastered national politics with McKinley as he had mastered his own shipping empire. With negotiating skill and with a personal expenditure of $100,000, Hanna won most of the delegates west and south of Pennsylvania for his candidate and brought him to St. Louis in possession of a clear majority of convention delegates.

Only the money question provided any interest. McKinley himself, now under pressure from both sides, had during his congressional career supported both gold and silver at different times. "McKinley isn't a gold-bug, McKinley isn't a silver-bug," mocked Speaker of the House Thomas Reed, who was his only real rival. "McKinley is a straddle-bug." Throughout the preconvention campaign, the candidate simply refused to answer letters asking his views on currency. When Easterners complained, Mark Hanna roared, "I don't give a damn what Wall Street thinks of McKinley's silence; they can go to hell down there. We are not going to nominate McKinley on a Wall Street platform."

Hanna now skillfully allowed the Eastern Republican bosses to push him into a flat declaration for gold, thus easing their resentment over McKinley's nomination. A handful of silver Republicans walked out, eventually to support Bryan. Hanna, wearing a blue shirt with white polka dots and an enormous diamond in his tie, watched happily as the convention overwhelmingly nominated his friend.

The nominee, who had fought for thirty years for the protective tariff, did not believe that currency could really decide the election. "Thirty days from now," McKinley told a friend, "you won't hear anything about silver."

William McKinley, Republican Governor of Ohio and protege of Mark Hanna, was the last Union army officer to reach the White House.

The friend disagreed. "Thirty days from now," he told McKinley, "you won't hear about anything else."

In this extraordinary election year, one more party had to meet in convention. The wave of rural anger and desperation that had rolled over the Democrats had also created an entirely new party, the Populists, also known as the People's party. Growing steadily in strength since its first appearance in 1890, the Populist party increasingly stressed silver as the answer to the farmer's problems. If the Populists now joined with the Democrats, who had declared for other reforms as well as silver, the combined ticket might sweep the country. But with two separate silver tickets, Hanna's Republicans would enjoy an easy victory.

The Populist delegates who now marched into St. Louis bore little resemblance to the Republicans who had preceded them. Populists were a ragtag collection of veterans from earlier third parties, like the Grangers and the Greenbackers, and bankrupt farmers hoping desperately for help from the movement, with a scattering of urban radicals, including some Socialists and a few labor people. It was not the usual free-spending convention crowd; many in it were poor, and some had walked to St. Louis or skipped meals to get there. To complete the bucolic atmosphere, the Populists presented awed Eastern reporters with a dazzling array of beards and whiskers, a sight rarely seen among urbane men of fashion.

On the key issue of endorsing Bryan, the Populists split along sectional lines. Midwestern and Western Populists, accustomed to cooperate with Democrats and encouraged by Democratic National Chairman James K. Jones, favored fusion with the Chicago ticket. Gaily singing, "We'll shoot the gold-bugs, every one," they were willing to join every effort to help boost the chances of silver. "I care not for party names," declared "Sockless Jerry" Simpson of Kansas. "It is the substance we are after, and we have it in William J. Bryan."

For Southern Populists, fusion with the Democrats was more distasteful. Like all political questions below the Mason-Dixon line, the Populist movement had become entangled in the race issue. Southern party members had declared racism to be a tool of the wealthy in oppressing the farmers and had welcomed blacks into the party. Hundreds of thousands of black farmers had joined the Colored Farmers' Alliance, working closely with the Southern Farmers' Alliance. In Georgia, Populist leader Tom Watson had called out dozens of white party members to stand guard over the house of a black leader who had been threatened. In North Carolina, white Democrats were stunned when a Populist legislature with black members adjourned for a day after the death of Frederick Douglass.

Because of such policies, Southern Populists had been beaten, shot at, and defrauded by the ruling Democratic machines. They would not now support a Democratic candidate. "Avoid fusion as you would the devil," wired Watson from Georgia. "Texas is here to hold a Populist

The delegates to Populist conventions, such as this one (held in a huge tent), were an amalgam of alliance leaders, politicos, visionaries, and other enthusiasts. In 1896 their ranks were divided over the presidential nomination, since free silverites and fusionists favored the Democratic candidate, young Nebraska Congressman William Jennings Bryan, who was to win the Populist nomination as well. The third party rejected the Democrats' vice presidential nominee in favor of Georgia Populist Tom Watson, a concession to those who wanted an independent Populist slate.

convention," cried one Southerner, "and we're going to do it before we go home."

Although the Populists lacked the organization of the older parties, making high-level wheeling and dealing difficult, a compromise did emerge. The party would nominate Watson for Vice-President. To assure the Southerners that the more numerous fusionists planned no betrayal, the Vice-Presidential ballot was held first. Only after Watson had been put on the ticket did the Populists name Bryan for President. The pro-fusion convention chairman did not bother to inform delegates of the telegram he had received saying that Bryan did not want the nomination without Sewall.

Now that he was the candidate of two major parties, not to mention the National Silver party, the Single-Taxers, the Christian Socialists, and a faction of the Prohibitionists, Bryan offered himself and his remedies to a stricken country. The unrest in American politics only reflected a greater instability in the American economy, as the United States entered the fourth year of the most severe depression in its history.

At its worst point, the depression of the nineties left two and a half million workers unemployed. Some Americans were reported to have starved to death. Many employers responded to depression (and the labor surplus) by cutting wages. In response, strikes exploded across the land. Half a million workers walked out, and the disputes prevented another two-thirds of a million persons from working. The Pullman strike centered in the Chicago railyards, and Altgeld had tried unsuccessfully to keep Cleveland from intervening. It was only one of a series of bitter struggles.

A single pathetic protest best reflects the desperation of the depression of the 1890s. A small businessman from Ohio, Jacob Coxey, vowed to send "a petition in boots" to Congress, asking for a $500 million public-works program to help the unemployed. "Coxey's Army," as it was derisively dubbed, never numbered more than 600, but it was reported by newspapers as if it were a vast horde come to sack the Capitol and lay waste the District of Columbia. Correspondents dogged the "army" on its slow journey through Pennsylvania, writing about the half-dozen comic-opera figures capering on elderly horses, ignoring the ragged unemployed marching with something like hope in their eyes. Only a few hundred reached Washington, where Congress ignored them and Coxey was arrested for walking on the Capitol lawn.

Despair ran even deeper on American farms throughout the Great Plains and down into the cotton fields of the South. There, the depression only intensified the crisis that began in the late 1880s. Overproduction was crushing the army of wheat, corn, and cotton growers. The more the farmer produced, the lower prices fell, forced downward by the law of supply and demand. Many gave up, and thousands of covered wagons rolled East across the Mississippi, bearing signs reading, "In God We Trusted, In Kansas We Busted."

Farmers reacted to this situation with stunned anger, believing that *they*, and not the railroad owners or the farm-machinery producers

"Coxey's Army" of unemployed, shown on their way to Washington in 1894, wanted to petition Congress for work relief. While not driven out at bayonet point (as was to be the case with the "Bonus Army" of 1932), the 500 or so of Coxey's troops who arrived at the Capitol were confronted by police and placed in custody for endangering the public health. General Coxey was arrested for walking on the grass and put in jail.

Jacob S. Coxey, on the right, upon his release from jail in Washington, D. C. in 1894, after serving 20 days. An Ohio businessman and Populist, Coxey proposed public works and federal relief to combat depression and, with his "Army" of the unemployed, marched on Washington to demand Congressional action. In the center is Carl Browne and on the left, with silk hat, Christopher Columbus Jones.

or the meat packers, formed the backbone of the country. Yet debts piled higher and higher, while middlemen profited handsomely. There was something wrong somewhere, probably a calculated conspiracy to defraud farmers of their rightful share of national wealth.

In a thousand sun-baked courthouse squares, farmers cheered orators who demanded action. "What you farmers have to do," declared Mary Lease, a fiery woman known affectionately as "Mary Yellin," "is raise less corn and more hell!" In 1890, several farm groups had organized the Populist party to do just that. The Populists had elected three senators and twenty-five congressmen that year, and in 1892 its presidential candidate had carried four states and polled over a million votes. The party also elected governors and state officials, sometimes allying with an older party on a combined ticket.

The Populist showing in 1892 startled most the country—and shocked the East. Populists demanded government ownership of railroads and telegraphs. Their platform also demanded an end to gambling in stocks, the direct election of the President and United States senators, and the secret ballot. And in a direct attempt to aid the mortgaged farmers, the Populists asked for no limit on the coinage of silver.

Requiring money to be backed only by gold, reasoned the Populists, greatly limited the amount in circulation. If the government could print money based on silver as well, and bought all silver mined in the country for that purpose, the resulting inflation would make mortgages easier to pay off and would raise farm prices. They spurned the arguments of bankers and industrialists that Europe would not accept money based on silver and that such a program would produce financial chaos. The Populists saw the issue as a battle of Eastern greed against Southern and Western sweat. "It is a struggle," explained "Sockless Jerry" Simpson, "between the robbers and the robbed."

The story of most presidential elections begins with the congressional election two years earlier. In the fall of 1894, in the midst of a depression and a farm crisis, the voters emphatically rebuked Cleveland and the Democrats. "The Democratic losses will be so great," predicted Thomas Reed, "that their dead will have to be buried in trenches labeled 'Unknown.'" The morning after the election, the trenches contained 113 of the 218 Democrats in the House. Cleveland's policies had shattered his party. Under intense pressure from their constituents, and with no reason to remain loyal to the administration, Democrats from the South and the West now rushed to embrace "free" silver.

Now the Democrats and the Populists had a candidate to go with the issue. Bryan, having captured the nomination with his stirring oration, now embarked upon a radically different kind of campaign. Presidential candidates, by tradition, remained at home, pleased and flattered by the efforts their friends were making on their behalf, but pretending to be far too modest to campaign for themselves. In the four months between convention and election, Bryan altered this pattern, traveling 18,000 miles, making 600 speeches, and addressing approximately five million persons. Republicans mocked his nickname, "the Boy Orator of the Platte," pointing out that the Platte River was six inches deep and a mile wide at the mouth; but Bryan's entranced audiences had apparently not heard the quip.

Across the nation, even in the supposedly hostile East, they yelled as the Democratic convention had yelled. After Bryan's triumphant tour of New England, a friend told him that he had never seen such a response. "You ought to come with me to Ohio, Indiana, and Kansas," smiled the confident nominee. "These people have given us a great reception in the East, but the West is on fire."

A Bryan speech in the West resembled a revival meeting more than a political rally. The crowd listened not with the skepticism usually accorded politicians, but with total trust and belief, cheering and responding at all the right moments. Before crowds so thick he sometimes could not reach the speaker's platform, Bryan painted a picture of a new America—a country whose abundant wealth would not be controlled by a small group, a country in which farmers would have their rightful place, in which the land across the Mississippi would not be an exploited colony of the East. Young and good-looking, Bryan appeared "every inch an Apollo," and farm wives as well as farmers were swept along in the spell of the new champion of the West.

Conservatives and Republicans, on the other hand, feared for their ticket. Hanna, panicked at the reception Bryan received that summer, went to McKinley, who was observing political tradition in his hometown of Canton. Hanna insisted that McKinley must campaign. The GOP candidate shook his head. "I might just as well put up a trapeze on my front lawn and compete with some professional athlete as go out speaking against Bryan," he reasoned. Hanna, reconsidering, agreed, and went off to New York to start his own campaign.

Joined by James J. Hill, railroad magnate of the Northwest, Hanna began visiting corporation offices. "I wish that Hanna would not talk so freely about money," complained one insurance company president, but the Ohio industrialist refused to play the hypocrite. He never denied that he proposed to beat Bryan by getting and spending more money than had ever been seen in an American election. Hanna extracted a quarter of a million each from John D. Rockefeller and J. P. Morgan. Four Chicago meat packers gave $100,000 apiece, and Hanna assessed banks and insurance companies one-quarter of 1 percent of their assets. The books of the Republican National Committee showed collections of $3.5 million, twice those of any previous campaign, but other estimates ranged from $10 million to $16 million being spent to beat silver. Cartoons in Democratic newspapers depicted Hanna in a suit checked with dollar signs.

With the money, Hanna sent out hundreds of speakers, preceding and following Bryan, including many converted Democrats. (He caused a furor at one luncheon by growling that some of the turncoat Democrats were not worth what it had cost to convert them.) Hanna's funds also enabled Republican headquarters to send out 250 million pieces of mail, including 120 million pamphlets, many of them in German, Swedish, Polish, Italian, Yiddish, and other languages. "He has advertised McKinley," complained the young Theodore Roosevelt, "as if he were a patent medicine!"

Bryan meanwhile had enough problems with his own party. Most major Democratic newspapers in the East refused to support the ticket. Immediately after Bryan's nomination, while gold Democrats were still stunned, Henry Watterson, editor of the influential and conservative Louisville *Courier-Journal*, wired from Europe, "Another ticket our only hope. No Compromise with Dishonor."

Taking that for their slogan, gold Democrats met in Indianapolis and nominated Senator John M. Palmer of Illinois, former Union Army general, for President, and former Confederate general Simon Bolivar Buckner of Kentucky for Vice President. The two old campaigners stumped actively, less for themselves than just to shake Democrats loose from Bryan. "Fellow Democrats," invited Palmer toward the end of the campaign, "I will not consider it any great fault if you decide to cast your vote for William McKinley." The Cleveland administration supported Palmer; when the secretary of the interior endorsed Bryan in August, Cleveland promptly fired him.

Bryan had also been unable to deal with the Populists' gift of a second running mate. Watson had accepted under the impression that the Democratic nominee, Arthur Sewall would retire, making Watson the candidate of both Democratic and Populist parties. Democratic chairman Jones, no longer the eager seeker of Populist support, replied coolly, "Mr. Sewall will, of course, remain on the ticket, and Mr. Watson can do what he likes." What Watson did was to campaign through the

West, urging Populists to vote for Bryan-Watson instead of Bryan-Sewall. (In most states, the slates combined on a single ticket of electors, with the vote to be cast for the vice-presidential candidate who led in the state's popular vote.) This policy was suicidal, since in the event of a Bryan victory neither Watson nor Sewall would share his majority and the Republican Senate would elect a Vice President. In the Democrats' idea of fusion, charged Watson, "We play Jonah while they play whale." Bryan dealt with the problem after a fashion by never formally accepting the Populist nomination.

A few Populists would never have supported Bryan anyway. "The Free Silver movement is a fake," sneered Henry Demarest Lloyd, one of the movement's few intellectuals. "Free silver is the cow-bird of the reform movement. It waited until the nest had been built by the sacrifice and labor of others, and then it laid its eggs in it, pushing out the others which it smashed on the ground." So saying, Lloyd groused off to vote Socialist Labor.

Feeling that their entire way of life was threatened, however, Republicans and conservatives intensified their attacks on Bryan. "Anarchists, Socialists, and destructives in society" supported Bryan, according to a Republican senator; *Harper's Weekly* compared Bryan and Altgeld to leaders of the French Revolution. But despite such invective, or perhaps because of it, the Republican New York *Herald* predicted in October that Bryan would get 237 electoral votes, thirteen more than needed for victory.

Hanna, however, had spotted the Nebraskan's weakness. "He's talking silver all the time," noted the Republican national chairman, "and that's where we've got him." The Chicago platform, with many planks favorable to labor, had gained Bryan the endorsement of Socialist leader Eugene V. Debs and J. K. Sovereign of the Knights of Labor, as well as the indirect support of Samuel Gompers of the American Federation of Labor. But even when speaking to workers, Bryan never stressed those planks, preferring to concentrate on currency. However attractive inflation appeared to a farmer with a heavy mortgage, it looked far different to a steelworker working twelve hours for a dollar a day. Bryan apparently saw no reason to broaden his appeal; as one observer commented, Bryan led a revolution without understanding it.

The Nebraskan would have had problems with urban workers, who were largely immigrants, anyway. He neither drank nor smoked nor gambled, and he always wore about him an aura of rural, prudish evangelism. This cultural difference could not but make segments of the urban labor force uneasy. Their apprehensions about the Boy Orator of the Platte increased when Monsignor John Ireland, a ranking Catholic leader, came out against free silver.

Both McKinley and Hanna had excellent reputations among labor groups. McKinley had signed several prolabor bills as governor of Ohio, and his refusal to send troops to break a strike had once led the Chicago *Herald* to compare him with Altgeld. Hanna had rarely suffered any labor trouble in his far-flung enterprises, and was known to have bellowed during one major strike: "Any [business] man who won't meet his men halfway is a goddamn fool!"

McKinley proved to be a formidable campaigner in his own way. Although he would not go to an audience, audiences came to him, to sit on his front lawn and listen to him speak from the porch. Seven hundred and fifty thousand people came to Canton that fall, encouraged by the special rates provided by friendly railroads. The reduced fares, a Democratic newspaper commented sourly, made it cheaper to visit McKinley than to stay home.

Many industrialists now decided to aid McKinley in their own way. "You may vote any way you wish," some factory owners were reputed to have informed their workers, "but if Bryan is elected on Tuesday the whistle will not blow on Wednesday." The idea spread rapidly, and a number of workers claimed to have received such warnings at factory gates or in their pay envelopes. "Boys," said a Bryan adviser, "I am afraid this beats us."

Possibly it did, although it was more likely that Hanna's efforts had decided the outcome. On November 3, Bryan came up half a million votes short. He carried no state north of the Mason-Dixon line nor east of the Mississippi. He still might have won, but he lost four Democratic border states as well as California, Oregon, Iowa, Minnesota, and North Dakota in the West. In several of these states the vote was close, with the Palmer Democrats holding the balance. Bryan's rural stalwarts managed to win mainly the agrarian strongholds of the South and most of the prairie states for their eloquent standard-bearer.

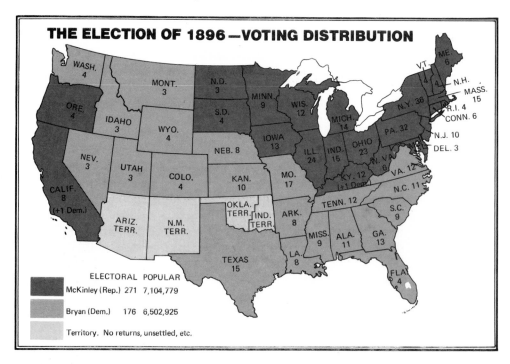

THE ELECTION OF 1896—VOTING DISTRIBUTION

ELECTORAL POPULAR

McKinley (Rep.) 271 7,104,779

Bryan (Dem.) 176 6,502,925

Territory. No returns, unsettled, etc.

Democrats charged that the Republicans had simply bought the election. The Democratic party, said Altgeld bitterly, was "confronted by all the banks, all the trusts, all the syndicates, all the corporations, all the great papers. It was confronted by everything that money could buy, that boodle could debauch, that fear of starvation could coerce."

The returns outlined the voters who decided the election. Bryan had failed to break through labor's fears, carefully fostered by Republican propaganda. He had failed to persuade dairy farmers that silver would help them, and he lost every dairy state, from Ohio to Wisconsin. Although he had repudiated the Democratic administration, the party could not escape the nation's bitterness over the depression. "I have borne the sins of Grover Cleveland," explained the candidate who most strongly opposed Cleveland's "Bourbon Democracy."

Republicans rejoiced at the election result. Hanna had saved the gold standard; the forces of "anarchism" (as conservatives fearfully viewed Bryan's Democratic and Populist supporters) had been beaten back. McKinley could be expected to offer the country a "safe" administration, by which it was understood that he would retain the gold standard, raise tariff rates still higher, and avoid reforms. Thus it was that McKinley went to the White House.

Bryan cushioned his disappointment somewhat by writing a book on the campaign. In deference to both his beliefs and his own career, he called it *The First Battle*. He was certain that during his lifetime the forces favoring reforms in America would regroup for future political campaigns. The 1896 election result, therefore, saddened him less than it did many of his agrarian supporters, about whose frustrations Vachel Lindsay wrote in an elegy to the campaign:

Election night at midnight:
Boy Bryan's defeat.
Defeat of western silver.
Defeat of the wheat.
Victory of letterfiles
And plutocrats in miles
With dollar signs upon their coats,
Diamond watchchains on their vests
And spats on their feet . . .
Victory of the neat.
Defeat of the aspen groves of Colorado valleys,
The blue bells of the Rockies,
And blue bonnets of old Texas,
By the Pittsburg alleys.
Defeat of alfalfa and the Mariposa lily.
Defeat of the Pacific and the long Mississippi.
Defeat of the young by the old and silly.
Defeat of tornadoes by the poison vats supreme.
Defeat of my boyhood, defeat of my dream.

32
THE CRISIS OF THE 1890s

A. W.

The political turbulence of the 1896 election followed a long history of farm protest against the new industrial America. Jefferson, Jackson, and other great leaders in the past had assured the small farmer, armed with the vote, that he was the backbone of America. The Populists were only the last of a series of farm organizations to reflect the farmer's growing belief that since the Civil War the balance of power and wealth had shifted to the corporations—and that the balance must be redressed.

Although the thrust of the farmer's complaints remained the same, issues varied over the last three decades of the nineteenth century. Originally, farmers had demanded stricter control of the railroads. Then, in two separate movements, currency reform seemed the root of the problem. Finally, the Populists focused on the process of government corruption and demanded a change in the selection of leaders; they wanted direct election of senators, primary elections, and secret ballots.

The Populist party achieved some significant gains in state government, but after 1896 it never posed a national threat. Some farmers would be swayed by the reformist rhetoric of Theodore Roosevelt; others, as we saw, remained with Bryan and the Democrats. A few would take a different path; when Oklahoma was admitted to the union in 1907, it contained more Socialists than any other state in the nation. But with the rise of the cities, whatever the farmers did would matter less and less politically. The failure of the farmers' movement was written not in election returns, but in census figures.

SETTLING THE WEST

Even after the passage of the Homestead Act during the Civil War, and despite subsequent government actions to make settlement of the plains attractive, Americans were reluctant to farm much past the Mississippi Valley. The notion of the Great American Desert, where nothing would grow and Indians abounded, died hard. Settlers heading west would rather go all the way to California or Oregon than stop in between in Kansas, Nebraska, or the Dakota territory.

Almost immediately after the war, heavy government subsidies helped to crisscross the plains with new railroad track. Roads like the Kansas Pacific, the Southern Pacific, and the Santa Fe now appeared out of nowhere. Only heavy settlement of the area could make these roads profitable. The railroads, along with Western newspapers and local boosters, set out to recruit the needed settlers.

There was enough land for all of them. Not only did the government provide land virtually free to settlers under the Homestead Act, but the railroads had received millions of acres of public land in subsidies. They now used this land to lure farmers, selling it as cheaply as twenty-five cents an acre, and offering easy credit terms.

As a result of this effort, a tremendous boom in Western land took place. The population of the Dakota territory soared 853 percent between 1870 and 1880, and that of Kansas and Nebraska tripled. Some settlers mortgaged their homesteads to buy more land. Eastern and European money eagerly bought up Kansas mortgages, confident that prices would continue to rise. Not only settlers, but towns and cities went deeply into debt with the expectation that the boom would last forever. Well into the 1880s, bumper crops and financial boom flourished together, and farmers deeply in debt to banks and agricultural machinery companies considered themselves rich because of the book value of their heavily mortgaged land holdings.

Between 1860 and the turn of the century, the mileage of railroad tracks increased by the thousands each decade, criss-crossing the plains. Heavily subsidized by state and federal governments, the railroad companies preceded and stimulated settlement, expanded, and overexpanded. By the 1890s, many overextended companies had fallen into bankruptcy, and others into the hands of eastern banks and financiers.

More than any other industry, the railroads were anxious to stimulate western settlement, populate the plains, and reap the profits therefrom. Through advertisements such as this one, setting forth the delights of cheap land in Kansas, the railroad company hoped to profit from the sale of its excess acreage, the transportation of migrants to it, and, eventually, from the freight rates the settlers would pay for transportation of their produce. By the end of the century, the Atchison, Topeka, and Sante Fe line, running from Kansas to California, was one of the five major transcontinental railroads.

Atchison, Topeka & Santa Fe
RAILROAD.
THREE MILLION ACRES
LANDS.

LIBERAL TERMS TO IMPROVERS.
11 YEARS CREDIT, 7 PER CENT INTEREST.
No Part of the Principal payable for Four Years.
FINE GRAIN-GROWING REGION.
Tracts of one and two thousand acres available for Neighborhood Colonies, or for Stock Farms.
Excellent Climate, with Pure Flowing Water.

"I would say, that in the course of many years, and through extensive travel, I have not seen a more inviting country, nor one which offers greater inducements, with fewer objections to settlement, than these lands of the A. T. & S. F. R. R."—*Extract Report of Henry Stewart, Agricultural Editor American Agriculturist.*

For full particulars inquire of

A. E. TOUZALIN,
Land Commissioner, Topeka, Kan.

HEARTH and HOME

Issued Weekly.

THE GRANGERS

Having come out to the West through the benevolence of the railroads, Plains settlers slowly learned how completely they had fallen into the power of the railroad barons. Only by the railroad could they send their produce to Chicago and New York, and only by the railroad could they bring out the farm machinery and barbed wire necessary to farm the plains. Towns flourished or went bankrupt depending on the route of the road.

But even as new settlers rode the Rock Island Line out to the plains, farmers further east were learning how helpless they too were against the railroad. From Ohio to Minnesota, farmers had united into the Patrons of Husbandry, also known as the Grange. The Grange was partially a social institution, but also a cooperative alliance with some political interests. By the early 1870s, it had taken over several legislatures and had passed bills regulating railroad freight and storage rates. The railroads immediately attacked the new laws in the federal courts.

In the first decision, *Munn* v. *Illinois* (1877), the Supreme Court upheld an Illinois Granger law regulating Chicago grain storage companies. But over the next ten years, as Presidents Hayes, Arthur, Cleveland, and Harrison appointed a series of corporation lawyers as Supreme Court justices,

The National Grange of the Patrons of Husbandry, founded in 1867, fostered cultural progress, agricultural improvement, and community spirit. Due to gains in membership during the 1873 depression, the Grange could soon claim 20,000 local lodges, mainly in the midwest and south. On Independence Day, 1873, proclaimed as the "Farmers' Fourth of July," the Illinois lodge shown convened at an outdoor rally to denounce the railroads, plan collective action, and read "The Farmers' Declaration of Independence," which demanded freedom from the tyranny of monopoly.

the Court slowly whittled away at *Munn v. Illinois.* By 1890, in *Chicago, Milwaukee, and St. Paul Railway Company* v. *Minnesota,* it practically prohibited the states from regulating any railroad engaged in interstate commerce. The Grangers rapidly faded from political significance.

CRISIS ON THE PLAINS

Two blows—one a sudden act of nature, the other a steady process of technical advance and hard work—broke the speculative bubble on the plains. In 1886 and 1887, the weather turned on the homesteaders. Blistering summers with little rain were followed by miserable winters. Thousands of settlers were at once wiped out financially and began the slow, painful trek back east of the Mississippi. The inflated prices of land collapsed, and investors no longer clamored for Plains mortgages.

The settlers who survived, when the rains returned and their corn again grew high, faced a worse problem. East of the Mississippi and in much of the West as well, advances in farming technology and efficient use of chemical fertilizers had tremendously increased American agricultural production. This increase sent the prices of wheat, corn, and hogs skidding downward. If, in a frantic attempt to catch up, farmers increased production, further price drops resulted. A bushel of wheat had plummeted from $1.19 in 1881 to 49 cents in 1894. The American farmer, whose productivity using indifferent soil had astounded the world, was being destroyed by his own success. Farmers now found it more profitable to burn corn for fuel than to sell it at current prices.

Farmers could blame themselves for creating part of the predicament. Many, out of greed, had dangerously overextended themselves. Before giving up entirely, farmers would mortgage virtually everything they owned. In Kansas and North Dakota, for example, the number of mortgages declared in 1890 amounted to one for every two citizens. Many farmers, having mortgaged their horses and wagons, did not even have the option of fleeing to the East. A steady deflation

since the Civil War, with less and less money in circulation, had crippled the mortgaged farmer. He had to pay back his loan in dollars that had doubled in value since he borrowed them.

Yet farmers had also worked hard, and they now felt bitterly that the rules had been changed on them. They had no difficulty in coming up with people and institutions to blame. Somewhere, the farmers knew, someone was getting rich from their labor.

Railroads stood at the top of the list of indictments. There was little competition among the roads servicing the plains. Generally, only one ran into an area, and the farmer had no choice as to how to ship crops to market. Even when two railroads were within traveling distance, they had generally agreed upon rates beforehand, and the farmer again had little or no choice. Large growers received preferential rates, a practice justified by the railroads' claim that they must turn a profit on their investment. Farmers retorted that the railroads now had far more stock outstanding than the road was worth.

Even without considering the Granger cases, farmers expected little help from their state governments. The railroads exerted great power in the governments of many states.

Farmers also denounced other businesses that they felt were exploiting them. They charged that the farm machinery companies had formed a trust to keep the prices of their equipment high. Livestock raisers attacked the Chicago meat packers for making huge profits.

The Plains farmers also stressed the need for a remonetization of silver, a cause they had adopted from the Greenbackers. Since the time of the earlier reform movement, in the late 1870s, the situation had worsened for debtors. A dollar, worth twice its 1865 value in 1877, was worth three times its 1865 value by 1895. To heavily mortgaged farmers, this meant a financial war of attrition that they were bound to lose. Behind the country's virtual abandonment of silver money— "the Crime of '73"—they saw an alliance of their enemies: railroads, grain storage companies, money lenders, Wall Street, and foreign bankers.

This bitterness was fed by the intensity of the farmers' outrage, which had roots far deeper than economics. The center of American life was shifting rapidly to the city, and the farmer felt abandoned and despised. National magazines began carrying more and more stories and articles about city life, and the farmer saw his children deserting farm areas for the more exciting cities. Worst of all, a deep and justified suspicion existed that the new urbanites laughed at farm folk and looked down on them as "hicks." The conditions of farm life, especially in the West, were not such as to foster tolerance toward critics or opponents. Existence on a plains homestead was a constant round of hard physical labor and mind-numbing chores, with little contact with the outside world.

SOUTHERN AGRICULTURAL PROBLEMS

Although the problems of the Southern farmer differed from those of the Plains homesteader, the two were partners in misery. When the plantation

Dry, dusty, deficient in rainfall and timber, the Great Plains had once been an unpleasant obstacle for westward bound pioneers. After the Civil War, both the railroads and the federal government stimulated western settlement, through favorable land acts and land sales, but the migrants to the plains still had to confront an inhospitable terrain, in which large acreage and expensive mechanized equipment was needed for success. Although many families failed, those who remained transformed the unpromising flatlands into a fertile source of grains and livestock.

system collapsed at the end of the Civil War, millions of acres became available for land-hungry poor whites and freed slaves. Few of them, however, could afford to buy the land outright, and investors eager to buy up Nebraska mortgages showed no interest in investing in Alabama cotton land.

Poor farmers in the South, therefore, were compelled to obligate themselves heavily to use the land. Most farmers, including the great majority of blacks, became sharecroppers, farming someone else's land and turning over a large portion of the crop to the owner. Generally, the southern farmer kept no more than half of the harvest. Many kept only one-third.

To support themselves while the crops were growing, farmers mortgaged themselves again, this time to local storekeepers. (And very often now, moreover, the landowner and the storekeeper tended to be the same person.) In exchange for supplies, the storekeeper received a lien on the farmer's crops. The crops, when they came in, rarely amounted to enough to wipe out the standing debt. Year by year, the debt increased, obligations to the storekeeper/landowner preventing the sharecropper from leaving the land. The result was a system of peonage. For black farmers, it was not much better than slavery, and, as the twentieth century approached, more and more white farmers became "croppers."

Further, the landowners and storekeepers demanded that the farmer grow the crop that could be most easily turned into cash—namely, cotton. This prevented Southern farmers from growing enough food crops to maintain their families, and took a heavy toll on Southern soil, which now required large doses of fertilizer. To make matters worse, the price of cotton was rapidly declining; from 1870 to 1890 it was cut almost in half.

Moreover, Southern farmers shared with the plains settlers the problems of currency appreciation and the railroads. In the South, railroads allied themselves with the Democratic rather than the Republican party, but they controlled state governments just as effectively. Southern farmers came to share their Western compatriots' interest in railroad regulation, and, being as deeply in debt, shared also a growing enthusiasm for free silver.

THE COMING OF THE FARMERS' ALLIANCE

Throughout American history, farm organizations had sprung up, scored some temporary successes, and then faded away. But in the late 1880s, a group appeared and began to spread with astounding speed. Helped along by the able leadership of several remarkable personalities, Farmers' Alliances enrolled millions of members in the South and the West. By the end of the decade, the Southern Farmers' Alliance had enrolled three million members, with another million and a quarter in the Colored Farmers' Alliance. The Northern Farmers' Alliance, comprised overwhelmingly of farmers from states west of the Mississippi River, counted about another million. No previous farm organization had been able to come close to such numbers.

Like the Grange, the Alliance was partly social in its objectives, giving farmers a chance to get together occasionally. Also, like the Grange, it distributed pamphlets seeking to educate farmers about their condition and the reasons behind it. In many states, both in the West and the South, the Alliance took an active role in politics and managed to elect legislators favorable to its aims. In some states, it established railroad commissions, only to find, as the Grange had, that such controls turned out to be inadequate. The Alliance, however, had far greater numbers than the Grange had ever claimed, as well as a more impressive geographical distribution.

Political scientists and reformers in the 1870s and 1880s frequently complained that "Gilded Age" politics lacked meaning. They professed to find little difference between the parties, and charged that elections reflected not popular choices on issues, but only a sordid struggle for government offices and power. True or not, soon after the farmers' massive entry into politics, the

THE INCREASE OF FARM TENANCY
IN THE SOUTH–1890

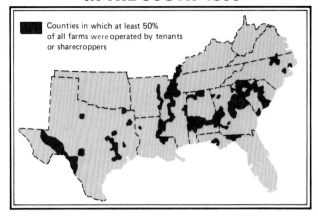

Counties in which at least 50% of all farms were operated by tenants or sharecroppers

parties indeed began to represent different ideas. This culminated in the bitter struggle of the 1896 campaign, when each side expected the destruction of the country should the other side win. It also culminated in the destruction of the balance between parties, leading to an unbroken, sixteen-year Republican rule in Washington.

While farmers gained strength, the tariff continued as the dominant surface issue in American politics. The farmers eventually came to oppose the tariff, seeing it as one more example of government aid to the rich and powerful, but they never felt as strongly about it as they did about silver and railroads. Republicans, however, saw the tariff as one of the keys to American (and their own party's) prosperity.

As Congress gathered in 1889, Republicans for the first time in fourteen years had working control of the presidency, the Senate, and the House. In 1890 they seized the opportunity, under the leadership of William McKinley, to pass the highest tariff in history. The McKinley bill flatly intended to protect as many American industries as possible from foreign competition.

The bill roused widespread opposition. Most Democrats attacked it; some were even known to send peddlers through the Midwest with items to sell at wildly inflated prices (which would be blamed on the tariff). When the votes were counted that November, Democrats had won an overwhelming victory, capturing heavy control of the House. Many senior Republican congressmen, including McKinley himself, lost their seats.

THE FOUNDING OF THE POPULIST PARTY

Alliance members in both the South and the West entered politics on a large scale in 1890. In the South, Alliance members won impressive victories within the Democratic party, running against railroads and their alliances with conservative, or "Bourbon" Democratic leaders. The Alliance elected three governors and claimed control of eight state legislatures. More than forty Southern Democratic congressmen announced that they favored the Alliance platform. The election also produced dramatic leaders for the Southern farmers, such as one-eyed "Pitchfork Ben" Tillman of South Carolina and slight but fiery Tom Watson of Georgia.

The plains farmers, however, had resolved to strike out for themselves. Angered by their lack of power within the existing party system, many farmers decided to bolt to the new party. From Minnesota to Colorado, farmers sang, "Good-bye, My Party, Good-bye," and named independent tickets. All across the plains, orators for the new party described Democrats and Republicans as nothing more than different fronts for the same railroad machine. A large number of the new agitators were women: Mary Elizabeth Lease, a lawyer with four children, became one of the most popular speakers on the Plains. Older reform protest figures joined in large numbers, and the Populists—although predominately agrarian in membership—also contained many Socialists, "Single Taxers" (followers of Henry George), "Nationalists" (disciples of Edward Bellamy), and Knights of Labor within their ranks.

From the 1890 returns, the new party seemed to make a promising start. It elected great numbers of state legislators, and two United States senators. Five Alliance congressmen were chosen from Kansas, and two more, along with a sympathetic Democrat named William Jennings Bryan, from Nebraska. Where the Alliance could not muster enough strength to win, it got the votes of enough normally Republican farmers to elect a large number of Democrats.

Both sides in the debate over a third party gained from the election. Westerners were now confident that a new party could succeed; the Southerners that they could gain control of the Democratic party. In a series of conventions over the next year, from Florida to Nebraska, they fought the issue out. Slowly the Southerners, unhappy at the conservatism of the national Democratic leadership, began to come around. At the organization of Congress, twenty Southern Democrats joined the Western Alliance men in supporting Tom Watson for Speaker of the House. Finally, in July 1892, delegates from the Northern and Southern Alliances and other organizations met in Omaha to take the final step, to nominate an independent Populist candidate for President of the United States.

Their candidate, and their platform, reflected the party more closely than convention products usually do. General James Baird Weaver, the candidate, was a veteran of the Civil War and of two decades of activism for reform and Prohibition. He had run for President as the Greenback candidate in 1880 and served three terms in Congress as a Greenback Democrat. As a new Populist and an old soldier, Weaver campaigned over the entire country.

"We meet in the midst of a nation brought to the verge of moral, political, and material ruin," warned the 1892 Populist platform. The time had come, the Populists announced, when either the railroads would own the people or the people would own the railroads. They demanded the end of national banks and the issuance of all money by the government, based on free coinage of silver. The program reflected the party's largely rural and agrarian base. Therefore, although there were planks that defended the right of unions to organize and denounced the oppression of factory workers, these were not central Populist concerns. And, although the platform also demanded a graduated federal income tax, direct election of senators, and other constitutional or political reforms, these were not central Populist concerns either.

What the new party wished, above all, was a series of reforms designed to help American farmers overcome what they felt were the unfair handicaps imposed upon agriculture in the United States by industrial growth. The most important of these demands was strict regulation or government ownership of the nation's railroads, which farmers believed discriminated against them. They also wanted an increase in the supply of money through remonetizing silver, since the Bland-Allison Act had been largely ineffective. Finally, they proposed establishing a government subtreasury warehouse system in which farmers could deposit their crops and receive loans up to 80 percent of the current market value of these crops. They would redeem the crops and sell them when open market prices had risen to acceptable levels. With this radical platform and a radical candidate, the Populists prepared to go before the nation.

THE ELECTION OF 1892

One reason for the willingness of some Southern Alliance members to leave the Democratic fold was the rapidly deteriorating condition of that party. Grover Cleveland, defeated for reelection in 1888, appeared to be the overwhelming favorite for his third nomination. Cleveland had never been much of an economic reformer. Since leaving the White House, he had practiced law in partnership with J. P. Morgan's attorney in Wall

Booker T. Washington

An ex-slave whose achievements in a thirty-five-year career spanned several important realms of national experience, Booker T. Washington may have been the single most influential American of his era in the field of race relations. His claim to greatness rests on his accomplishments as a teacher, educational pioneer, social theorist, fund raiser for philanthropic causes, advisor to Presidents, writer, politician and, most importantly, as the undeposed spokesman for black Americans.

Born on a Franklin County, Virginia plantation in 1856, Booker T. Washington lived in a slave cabin with his mother, sister, and brother until emancipation, when the family moved to West Virginia. In later years Washington credited his mother's "high ambitions for her children" as a dominant influence on his early years. He taught himself the alphabet using a Webster spelling book and, soon afterwards, he attended night school where he learned to read and write. In 1872, he entered Hampton Institute. He earned his board as a janitor while studying at Hampton, and graduated in 1875 after training as a brick-mason.

Most of Washington's adult life was spent in the South, first as a teacher in another Negro school before joining Hampton's staff in 1879 and then, two years later, becoming the head of a new Negro school being organized at Tuskegee, Alabama, which became world famous as the Tuskegee Institute.

During the 1880s, Washington addressed educational groups and public gatherings, in both the North and the South, covering such topics as race relations, the importance of education for black Americans, and the virtues of black-white harmony at almost any cost (including the temporary shelving of Negro demands for political rights and legal equality until a strong educational and economic base had been created).

Undoubtedly Washington's most famous statement of his central themes came during an 1893 speech at the Cotton States and International Exposition at Atlanta. At the Exposition, Washington called for friendship between the races while bluntly accepting the pattern of caste segregation then prevalent in every section of the country: "In all things that are purely social we can be as separate as the fingers, yet one as the hand in all things essential to mutual progress." Washington was praised by white moderates throughout the country. At the same time, many other black political leaders viewed the speech with dismay as an invitation to continued white interference with expressions of Negro militance.

Washington established rural extension programs at Tuskegee Institute designed to assist Southern farmers, helped found the National Negro Business League, and participated in many other activities intended to maximize black economic action and educational opportunity. In addition to these accomplishments, Washington wrote ten books and numerous articles. His most famous book, *Up From Slavery* (1901), further enhanced his extraordinary public reputation. Washington died while still maintaining his rigorous work schedule at the age of fifty-nine in November 1915. Even critics of his "accommodationist" philosophy have recognized that, within the pantheon of American black leaders, Booker T. Washington served as the monumental personal bridge who linked the tragic centuries of slavery with the long and continuing twentieth-century struggle of Negro Americans to achieve full equality and justice.

Street. He opposed free silver coinage even more strongly than the incumbent Republican President, Benjamin Harrison.

But even after Cleveland's nomination, the Southern Alliance split wide open over the question of leaving the Democrats. Regardless of any other issues, the Democrats were known in the South as "the white man's party." Joining the Populists meant public branding as a traitor to the white race. The South's best-known Alliance politicians were on opposite sides of the split. Tillman, governor of South Carolina and boss of the state Democratic party, refused to bolt, despite his well-known detestation of Cleveland; Watson led his Georgia followers into the Populist party and nominated a full state ticket to oppose the Democrats.

The Populists alarmed the white Southern establishment even more by openly appealing to the black vote. In many Southern states they allied closely with the Republicans, for whom blacks normally voted (when they were allowed to vote). In the campaign that followed, Southern Democrats used any weapon they could to smash the Populist-Republican-black alliance. Blacks were terrorized into staying away from the polls, or marched there by force to vote Democratic. When General Weaver campaigned in the South, Democrats broke up his rallies; Mary Lease claimed that in Georgia they made "a walking omelette" of the Populist candidate. Opponents shot at Populists, pressured them with economic threats, and if necessary stuffed the ballot boxes.

Without the race issue, Populist campaign-

Songs, revelry, and flag-waving characterized this election night crowd in 1892, as two U. S. Presidents contended for office. The Republican incumbent, Benjamin Harrison, and his Democratic challenger, former President Grover Cleveland, had few differences in policy, except on the tariff, but the Populist nominee, ex-Union General James B. Weaver, ran on a platform of economic reform that was to win him 22 electoral votes in the west.

ers faced little violence on the plains. There the Democrats, who were the minority party, established working arrangements with the Populists in most states. Democrats partially accepted the Populist platform, and Cleveland supporters, positive that they could not carry Kansas or Nebraska, planned to hurt Harrison by giving the states' votes to Weaver. The Democratic National Committee even supplied some under-the-table funds to the Populists for that purpose.

When the returns came in, Populists took a mixed view of the results. Cleveland won, but Weaver had polled a million votes (almost 10 percent) and carried five states, and the party claimed five senators and ten congressmen. Yet Populism had failed to make any serious inroads in the South, and had carried only Kansas on the plains.

The decline that had spurred the nation's farmers to take active steps for their own relief had no such effect on the rest of the country's workers. They failed to join the Populist movement. Several factors help to explain this. For one, the Populists never succeeded in breaking down the traditional political loyalties of most Americans, since party loyalty was extremely important to voters at this time. Even under the impact of economic depression, most people remained with their normal parties.

It was also true that the depression that began in 1893 occurred during a Democratic administration—Cleveland's second term. This resulted in political gains for the major opposition party even more impressive than those made by the Populists. In fact, Republicans almost doubled their number of House members in 1894—moving from 127 to 244—while the Democrats lost 113 seats. This was the most rapid major reversal of national political strength in American history, marking the first step in ending the close balance between the parties that had existed during the 1870s and 1880s.

Besides the depression working against them, there were other problems that the Populists could not overcome. The South presented the Populists with a unique set of problems that impeded their growth. There the new party attempted, for the first time since Reconstruction days, to create a biracial political coalition of black and white farmers against the business interests that still dominated most Southern state governments. For a time they made striking gains. But the political opponents of Southern Populism played upon such deeply felt racial fears and hostilities so effectively that, by the end of the decade, the new party had lost almost all its influence in the South. In that region, in fact, Populism had the ironic effect by 1900 of raising the race issue to an intensity and importance that it has maintained throughout most of the twentieth century.

Populist strength was sapped, especially in the industrial states, by internal tensions among its diverse sources of support. Such tensions between utopians and pragmatists often characterize reform movements. The Populists' agrarian leaders tended to be the movement's practical figures. Their overriding concern was for specific, immediate, and achievable goals such as free coinage of silver, the subtreasury plan, and other measures that would improve the economic bargaining position of most American farmers.

DEMOCRATS, DEPRESSION, DISASTER

Shortly after Cleveland took office for the second time, a business panic ushered in yet another of the series of depressions that had struck the nation at twenty-year intervals throughout the nineteenth century. Banks began to fail in 1893, and businesses laid off millions of workers in the cities and factory towns. By 1894, at the height of the depression, probably one out of every five workers was unemployed. Four out of five were living at subsistence level. As his first order of business, then, Cleveland would have to deal with a problem that had not figured in the campaign at all. At the same time, the price of farm products continued to decline disastrously on the world markets, while production costs skyrocketed.

Observers offered many explanations for the depression and suggested many ways to deal

Democrat Grover Cleveland, who had won the presidency in 1884 and lost it four years later, returned to challenge the Republican incumbent, Benjamin Harrison, in 1892. Cleveland also served as reform Governor of New York before becoming President.

Treasury. By early 1895, the Treasury had only a three-week gold supply left. Cleveland and his secretary of the Treasury now arranged to buy $60 million in gold from a syndicate headed by J. P. Morgan and the Rothschilds, paying an extraordinarily high rate of interest. Cleveland's action may have saved the Treasury, but it did nothing for his popularity.

MCKINLEY AND PROSPERITY

The Republicans' comfortable though hard-fought victory over Bryan in 1896 appeared to put an end to the threats of radicalism and Populist agrarianism. Aided immensely by an economic upturn during the summer and fall of 1896, especially by a significant rise in farm prices, depression gave way to recession at an accelerating pace that soon produced recovery and helped to defuse agrarian protest. Mark Hanna had advertised McKinley as the "Advance Agent of Prosperity." Hanna appeared to be right, and Bryanism appeared to be doomed.

Perhaps the most striking feature of the 1896 election, however, was the Republicans' ability to put together a national majority that cut across class lines. McKinley won the votes not only of industrialists and the middle class, but also of a majority of urban workers. Bryan failed to capture the cities and the votes of most industrial laborers, despite prolabor planks in the Democratic platform. Many urban workers clearly felt that their economic interests were better protected by a probusiness Republican President than by a Democratic candidate who spoke (in the rich twang of Midwestern rural America no less) mainly about the problems of farmers. Moreover, Bryan had failed to hold together many of the Democratic party's traditional supporters in business, the middle class, and various ethnic groups. This failure may have been the single most important factor in his defeat.

But if Bryan failed in 1896 to create that farmer – laborer – small-businessman coalition that he believed could win national power and make needed political and economic reforms, he did lay

with it. The conservative Cleveland accepted the prescription offered by big business. Confidence, he contended, had been shaken by the Sherman Silver Purchase Act, passed three years earlier by Congress as a sop to silver feeling. Cleveland claimed that the country had lost faith in its currency and noted the rush to exchange Treasury Department silver certificates for gold, a rush that was rapidly depleting the nation's gold reserves. In the midst of the depression, with sentiment for unlimited silver coinage sweeping the South and West, Cleveland called Congress into special session to repeal the law and silver coinage altogether. Using all his powers of patronage, Cleveland jammed repeal through Congress.

Worst of all, Cleveland's policies seemed to have no effect on the depression. Banks still closed their doors, workers remained unemployed, and gold continued to pour out of the

the groundwork for such reformers, not only within the Democratic party but among Republicans as well. In the process, Bryan set a precedent for active presidential campaigning that almost all subsequent major party candidates followed in the twentieth century. In the end, therefore, the struggle for change in American society gathered momentum during the late 1890s despite Bryan's defeat, despite the disappearance of Populism, and even despite the country's return to economic prosperity.

McKinley's cabinet, even more conservative than the bimetallist President, wanted no tinkering with the financial machine. For his part, McKinley, who was not a reactionary on most issues, insisted on raising the tariff even beyond the demands of most conservatives. The resulting Dingley Tariff of 1897 pushed rates upward to an average of 52 percent.

Prosperity, not political enthusiasm, provided the key to the McKinley administration's success. The economic upturn of 1896–1897 continued full force, and even the strongest argument of the silverites—the contention that reliance on gold, a metal in short supply, strangled and would continue to strangle the nation's debtors—could no longer hold up. New discoveries of gold in Australia, Alaska, and South Africa dramatically increased supplies, and a strong inflationary trend accompanied the return to agricultural and industrial prosperity. In 1900, Congress and McKinley gave the country the Gold Standard Act, a law committing the federal government to a single monetary standard: gold. Another section of the law aimed at increasing the amount of national bank notes in circulation. Within a year, the dollar total of such notes almost doubled.

Nineteen hundred was also a presidential election year. From the start, McKinley had little to worry about. Bryan, again the Democratic candidate, had little hope, and his confusion over campaign strategies revealed his dilemma. Populism was dying during the late 1890s as rapidly as it had grown in the early years of the decade. Sensing this, Bryan tried to make antiimperialism his central campaign theme. A bored or even hostile response caused him to switch in midstream, and he gave primacy to the monopoly issue. Bryan did not abandon the free-silver stand (he insisted on a silver plank in the Democratic platform), but obviously his "second battle" would be no rerun of the first, except in the election returns. McKinley again won handily, and to conservative Republicans all things seemed right.

Prosperity's "advance agent" did not live to enjoy the fruits of this happy political situation. Within six months of his second inaugural, William McKinley was dead, victim of an assassin's bullet. In September 1901, McKinley journeyed to Buffalo, New York, to open the Pan-American Exposition of that year. Waiting for him amidst an almost adoring public was a young man named Leon Czolgosz. The Detroit-born son of Polish immigrant parents, Czolgosz was twenty-eight in 1901. He had survived, barely, the economic troubles of the nineties. He espoused the ideas of radical anarchists, though he had never joined any group in the movement. In 1901, he decided to kill the President. Without difficulty, Czolgosz joined the mass of people crowding around McKinley, who was "receiving" in one of the exposition buildings, shaking hands with all comers. Two shots rang out; one of them wounded McKinley mortally. A few days later the President died, and Theodore Roosevelt, a young New York Republican who had been chosen for the vice-presidency in order to slow down his political career, became the new President. Roosevelt differed from McKinley greatly in style and slightly in principles. It would be Roosevelt's job, first, to restore domestic tranquillity, which had been jolted by the third presidential assassination in almost as many decades. Then, he would be charged with maintaining prosperity, so recently returned, while consolidating America's new and enlarged role in the world. To these tasks, Roosevelt would add one of his own: the advocacy of reform in American society, at first cautiously but with growing boldness as his presidency progressed.

SUGGESTED READINGS— CHAPTERS 31-32

Election of 1896

Robert F. Durden, *Climax of Populism: The Election of 1896* (1964); Stanley Jones, *The Presidential Election of 1896* (1964); Paul W. Glad, *McKinley, Bryan and the People* (1964).

The Gilded Age

Harold U. Faulkner, *Politics, Reform and Expansion, 1890–1900* (1959); J. Rogers Hollingsworth, *The Whirligig of Politics* (1963); H. Wayne Morgan, *William McKinley and His America* (1963); Paul W. Glad, *The Trumpet Soundeth: William Jennings Bryan* (1959); Paolo E. Coletta, *William Jennings Bryan: Political Evangelist, 1860–1898* (1964); Arnold M. Paul, *Conservative Crisis and the Rule of Law, 1887–1895* (1960); Margaret Leech, *In the Days of McKinley* (1959); Richard J. Jensen, *The Winning of the Midwest* (1971); Morgan Kousser, *The Shaping of Southern Politics* (1974); Paul Kleppner, *The Cross of Culture* (1970); Ray Ginger, *The Bending Cross: A Biography of Eugene V. Debs* (1948); Edward C. Kirkland, *Industry Comes of Age* (1961); Lazar Ziff, *The American 1890s: Life and Times of a Lost Generation* (1966).

Populism

John D. Hicks, *The Populist Revolt* (1931); Norman Pollack, *The Populist Response to Industrial America* (1962); Walter T. K. Nugent, *The Tolerant Populists: Kansas Populism & Nativism* (1963); Lawrence Goodwyn, *Democratic Promise: The Populist Movement in America* (1976); Fred A. Shannon, *The Farmers' Last Frontier: Agriculture, 1860–1897* (1945); Allan G. Bogue, *Money at Interest* (1955); C. Vann Woodward, *Tom Watson: Agrarian Rebel* (1938); Francis B. Simkins, *Pitchfork Ben Tillman* (1944). Martin Ridge, *Ignatius Donnelly* (1962).

UNIT SIX

PROGRESSIVE AMERICA

The new century brought to Americans confidence in their own ability to control the nation's destiny. It also brought concern for the unresolved problems of industrial growth, urban squalor, and immigrant poverty. The business depression of the 1890s had ended by 1898, returning the country's middle and upper classes to full prosperity. A global empire had been won almost without cost or exertion.

The chapters that follow describe the decades of confidence, concern, and change within American society from 1900 through the Depression. The first of these chapters on the Triangle Fire dramatizes the lives of southern and eastern European immigrant workers in New York City garment factories. Underpaid and impoverished, they struggled to unionize the clothing industry. Only when a flash fire killed scores of young female workers at the Triangle Com-

pany did their appeal for better working conditions receive a hearing.

Chapter 34 then opens with a discussion of the urban world within which most of these recent immigrants lived. The chapter explores the varieties of industrial reform efforts. Since the political life of progressive America (1900–1917) often concerned the struggle for change, Chapter 34 also examines the connections between reform activities and partisan politics.

Popular confidence rose during these decades partly because of the ease with which the United States assumed a leading role in world affairs. Chapter 35 portrays one of the unhappier consequences of that new role—the unsuccessful revolt by Filipino nationalists against American takeover of their islands. The Philippine Revolt serves as the context for a general discussion in Chapter

36 of American foreign policy. The chapter traces developments from the country's brief involvement in the Spanish-American War to its costlier participation in the First World War. The connections between domestic concerns in progressive America and the nation's actions as a major global power emerge clearly.

One of the most widely publicized instances of American technological superiority was Charles Lindbergh's pioneering flight across the Atlantic in 1927. His feat captured the imagination of a machine-oriented world. Lindbergh's story unfolds in Chapter 37.

In the accompanying chapter the achievements, attitudes, and patterns of the optimistic, mechanically advanced America that produced Lindbergh's flight are examined. From the vantage point of the 1970s, the

United States of the progressive era may seem, whatever its problems, a less complicated and perhaps even happier society. Certainly this country's leaders—even most of its critics—looked to the future with a measure of confidence that withstood involvement in a world war and collapsed only during the 1930s under the onslaught of the Great Depression.

The defeat of the Bonus Marchers in 1932, narrated in Chapter 39, symbolized the old order's inability to respond effectively to the vast human suffering of the times. Most of the marchers were unemployed World War I veterans who had come to Washington seeking aid. The accompanying chapter deals with the Depression and other social manifestations of the times: the "red scare," prohibition, Scopes, Sacco-Vanzetti, and the alarming popularity of the Ku Klux Klan.

33

THE TRIANGLE FIRE

A.W.

In September 1909, two hundred Jewish and Italian immigrant workers at New York City's Triangle Shirtwaist Company walked off their jobs. The previous year, Triangle's owners had organized an Employees Benevolent Association, a so-called company union, designed to head off unions organized by the workers themselves. But the tactic had not worked. Protesting miserable working conditions and poor pay, the workers at Triangle—most of them young women—sought to gain recognition of their union by their employers. They were led by officials from the recently organized International Ladies' Garment Workers' Union (ILGWU). They had also received the support of the Women's Trade Union League (WTUL).

The Triangle strikers and workers in other shirtwaist shops in the city had a number of complaints. They were forced to work in crowded, unclean factories. Fire hazards and unsanitary conditions presented a serious threat to their health. Windows and doors in the shops were often nailed shut. Rarely did the sun penetrate the factory lofts, which workers referred to as sweatshops.

Long hours and low wages added to the workers' discontent. Most employees in New York's garment factories worked a fifty-six-hour, six-day week. When a factory owner had a rush order, he could force employees to work overtime at night or on Sunday without pay. Wages in the shirtwaist industry were as low as $6 a week. Employers often deducted penalties from the workers' pay for mistakes made in sewing clothes. They charged the workers fees for "renting" the machines and using electricity. In addition, employees were subjected to a series of petty fines for talking, smoking, or singing on the job.

It was against such conditions and in the face of active opposition by the police, who were openly sympathetic to the factory owners, that the workers finally took a stand.

The Triangle Shirtwaist Company occupied the top three floors of the ten-story Asch Building in Lower Manhattan. A fire, which raged on those floors on March 25, 1911, ultimately affected the working conditions of a large segment of American laborers.

The strike dragged on into winter. Workers at nonstriking shirtwaist companies grew angrier as they watched police and hired thugs abuse the striking employees. On the evening of November 22 the city's shirtwaist workers held a mass meeting at Cooper Union to discuss the situation.

Within a few days between 10,000 and 20,000 workers, mainly young women, had walked off their jobs. The strike affected over 500 shirtwaist and dressmaking companies, including all the smaller shops and most of the big companies in the city. "The Uprising of the Twenty Thousand," as the ILGWU called the walkout, was the first industry-wide strike of immigrant workers in New York City. It was also the largest strike by women ever staged in the United States up to that time.

The shirtwaist[1] industry was a relatively recent one. The 1900 federal census described it as a "branch of the garment industry that has developed during the last decade." Before 1900 many of the garments produced in New York City and elsewhere came from workshops in ghetto slum apartments. Families were paid according to the number of garments produced. This piecework system proved inefficient. Clothing production gradually shifted to new loft buildings constructed especially for the trade.

---

[1]The shirtwaist was a tailored blouse for women usually made of sheer cotton and styled somewhat like a man's shirt.

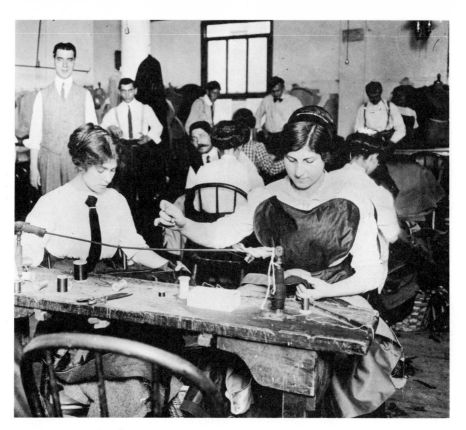

Sweatshops like the one shown here were common to the garment industry. Unskilled women laborers usually worked under skilled male machine operators in crowded, poorly ventilated, and unsafe shops.

By 1910 New York had become the national center for the garment industry. The city's 600 shirtwaist and dress factories employed over 30,000 workers. They sold more than $50 million worth of clothing annually. In the new shops skilled machine operators, usually men, supervised crews of young women who performed simple, unskilled tasks. At large factories such as Triangle, the machine operators, called contractors, were paid by the owners not only for their own work but for the labor of their crews as well. The contractors, in turn, paid weekly salaries to their female assistants. This system was often abused by dishonest contractors, who cheated young women workers out of their proper wages.

Four out of every five workers in the garment trades were women. In the Uprising of the Twenty Thousand, 75 percent of the strikers were young women between the ages of sixteen and twenty-five. Almost all had been born abroad or to recently arrived immigrant families. Most of the workers were either Jewish or Italian. Most of the factory owners were Jews.

The 1909 garment trade's strike marked the first time that many of these immigrant workers managed to set aside their mutual fears and suspicions to work for common economic interests. The strike brought Jewish and Italian women together on the picket line and in the union. Thus it set a pattern for future cooperation in the labor movement among the city's ethnic communities. Jewish union organizers learned a smattering of Italian, while Italian leaders acquired enough Yiddish to make themselves understood. Political and community leaders from each ethnic group also worked together on behalf of the strikers. Meyer London, a socialist lawyer who later became the country's first Jewish congressman, cooperated with Fiorello La Guardia, a young state legislator who later became the country's first Italian congressman. La Guardia, the son of a Jewish mother and an Italian father, symbolized the alliance then being forged by the two groups.

Black workers were frequently hired as strikebreakers, or scabs, in the garment factories. Several hundred of them joined the Uprising of the Twenty Thousand. One black shirtwaist striker—a "real born American," as she described herself—kept a diary of the events. In it she recorded her shop's reaction to the November 22 call for a general strike:

> It's a good thing, this strike is. It makes you feel like a real grown-up person. . . . I simply can't get over the way little Ray Goldousky jumped on a chair and suddenly, without a minute's notice, stopped the electricity [in the shop]. Why, we were simply stunned. Before you could say Jack Robinson, we all rose, slipped on our duds, and marched down the stairs, shouting, yelling, and giggling about our walkout, as they called it.

Similar incidents in New York's garment factories that week shocked the industry's manufacturers into taking action against the strikers. Antistrike activities ranged from encouraging police brutality against strikers to organizing company unions among the minority of workers who did not support the strike. Employers also tried using "carrot-and-stick" tactics. They offered incentives to those who remained on the job and hired hoodlums to beat up workers on the picket line. The anonymous shirtwaist striker noted in her diary that the Triangle Company promised nonstrikers "from fifteen to twenty dollars weekly, free lunch, and dancing during the noon hour." These tactics, however, failed to break the morale and unity of the shirtwaist strikers. The Uprising of the Twenty Thousand continued throughout the bitterly cold winter of 1909–1910.

Somehow the tens of thousands of strikers managed to maintain orderly picket lines at each shop. Every day the police dragged away dozens of frozen, poorly clad young women from the lines. By Christmas Day, the arrests tallied 723. Yet those who were arrested and later bailed out of jail usually returned to the picket lines the next day.

The strike was an important event not only for women garment workers but also for woman suffrage reformers, ghetto community lead-

Strikers in the shirtwaist strike of 1909–10 sold copies of the *Call,* a New York socialist daily, in order to publicize their demands and raise money for their living expenses while on strike.

ers, labor officials, and socialist politicians. All these groups donated time and money to make the strike a success. The "uptown" supporters were joined by several of the city's most active reform groups: The Women's Trade Union League, the National Women's Suffrage Association, the Political Equality Association, and the National Civic Federation.

A host of muckraking reporters,[2] academics, social workers, and other professionals also worked on behalf of the strikers. Many of these middle- and upper-class reformers were German Jews whose ancestors had come to the United States during the mid-nineteenth century. The strike gave them an opportunity to display their solidarity with poorer Jews from the Lower East Side, most of whom had recently left Eastern Europe for the United States.

Everywhere on the Lower East Side community leaders worked in support of the strike. They included union officials from the United Hebrew Trades, Socialist party orators from both the Jewish and Italian communities, sympathetic rabbis and priests, and editors of Jewish newspapers. A number of other New York newspapers supported the striking workers, as did many of the city's residents. An open meeting held on December 5 drew over 8,000 pro-strike demonstrators. Pressure mounted on the garment trade employers to resolve the dispute.

A settlement was finally reached in February 1910. The agreement came in two stages. It represented a victory for the union, though

---

[2]Muckraking reporters were writers of the late nineteenth and early twentieth centuries who exposed corrupt conditions in business and government.

not a total triumph. At first the shirtwaist workers rejected several compromise offers arranged by arbitrators who brought the two sides together. Then a number of smaller manufacturers began settling privately with the ILGWU. In these agreements, however, neither the union nor the union shop was recognized.

By February 15, 1910, only 1,100 workers, from 13 shops, were still away from their jobs. The ILGWU officially declared the strike over. More than 300 firms had accepted the union's terms completely, and 19 shops (including Triangle and other large firms) had agreed to open-shop compromises, that is, to allow employers to continue hiring *non*union as well as union employees. The garment workers had made several important gains in the settlements: reduction of the workweek to 52 hours, a two-hour limit on night work, wage increases of 12 to 15 percent, and a promise by employers to end the contractor system of payment.

Later that year, prominent Jewish citizens of New York City helped to arrange a second agreement between employers and workers. Louis Brandeis, a Boston lawyer, served as chief arbitrator between union and management. Brandeis skillfully played on the common Jewish background of garment employees and garment employers. Many of the employers themselves had begun as poor workers.

On Labor Day evening both sides agreed to a "Protocol of Peace," which became a milestone in American industrial relations. Its provisions included a privately run Joint Board of Sanitary Control – representing union, management, and the public – set up to oversee health and safety conditions in garment factories. Although the agreement eventually broke down, the Protocol represented a significant victory for the ILGWU. Its membership skyrocketed from 400 to 60,000 workers in the months following the "uprising."

At the Triangle Company, however, the union remained unrecognized. Many strikers were not rehired, and most of the strikebreakers who had worked during the walkout were kept on the payroll. Some workers complained that the major effect of the settlement was to end the phonograph music and dancing contests that had been provided for nonstriking employees. Otherwise, work returned to normal at the country's largest shirtwaist shop, at least until the afternoon of March 25, 1911.

The Triangle Shirtwaist Company occupied the top three floors of a new loft structure, the Asch Building, in lower Manhattan. The ten-story building, constructed in 1901, was located on the northwest corner of Green Street and Washington Place. It stood next to New York University and a block east of Washington Square. Since the turn of the century, over $150 million had been spent on the construction of loft factories in lower Manhattan. The new buildings, made of brick or stone, were supposed to be fireproof, but they had wooden frame interiors that could easily catch fire. Few of the buildings had adequate fire escapes or staircases.

Using such buildings, manufacturers took advantage of cheap insurance rates, low operating costs, and a concentrated labor supply. State law required employers to allow 250 cubic feet of air per worker. But the law did not specify where the air space should be. Loft buildings, with their ten-foot-high ceilings, enabled owners to crowd hundreds of employees onto a floor and still meet the space requirements. (The extra space was above the worker's heads; it was not distributed among employees.) At Triangle about 500 people jammed the Asch Building's top three floors.

The Triangle employees never had a fire drill. Even though several small fires had occurred on the premises in 1909, no improved safety measures had been taken. There were only two narrow staircases leading down from the Triangle's three floors. All but one of the doors leading to the stairways were kept closed (often bolted) to prevent employees from loitering or stealing fabric. The single fire escape in the building went down only to the second floor, so that it was difficult to reach the street in case of emergencies. The only other means of descent were two small freight elevators, each above five feet square. Huge piles of cloth, tissue paper, rags, and cuttings covered the company's tables, shelves, and floors. The floors and machines were soaked with oil, and barrels of machine oil lined the walls. All these factors made the Triangle factory highly flammable.

As the day's work drew to a close on Saturday, March 25, 500 Triangle workers finished their chores and prepared to leave the building by the one open door on the eighth floor. A company guard stationed at the exit checked the women's handbags for cloth fragments. The time was 4:30 P.M. Saturday's weather was brisk and sunny — a perfect early spring afternoon.

Hardly had the guard rung the closing bell when a young woman employee on the eighth floor ran up to Samuel Bernstein, the company's production manager, and cried: "There is a fire, Mr. Bernstein." The manager and several other men, who had battled a small fire on the floor two weeks earlier, tried to put out the blaze with pails of water. But the flames shot up even higher. One of the men later remembered: "It was like there was kerosene in the water; it just seemed to spread it." Bernstein quickly realized that it would be impossible to stop the fast-spreading flames. He shouted to an assistant: "You can't do anything here. Try to get the girls out!" Bernstein and a few others tried to lead the stunned workers out in orderly fashion. But screams of "Fire!" soon filled the eighth floor.

Panic and confusion spread with the inferno. The 225 eighth-floor workers scurried across the smoke-filled room toward the various exits. As they ran, many called out the names of relatives — sisters and brothers, fathers and mothers — who also worked for Triangle. A young bookkeeper on the floor, Diana Lipschitz, sent an urgent message by interoffice teletype to the tenth floor: "The place is on fire. Run for your lives." The bookkeeper who received the message at first thought that Diana was joking. But the flames soon spurted through the tenth-floor windows, igniting bundles of cloth. Employees on that floor spread the alarm and hurried toward the exits. Because the Asch Building was supposedly fireproof, the blaze could not damage the walls or floors. But the flames curved in a swirling mass through the eighth-floor windows and engulfed the ninth and tenth floors within minutes.

On every floor workers pressed against one another in a desperate effort to reach the exits. The intense heat from the surrounding flames seared their bodies. Those on the eighth floor who had pushed their way down the congested stairway collapsed on lower floors, where firemen later found them.

Employees on the ninth floor, meanwhile, had not received even a teletype warning of the blaze. They learned of the danger only when the fire darted through the windows, bursting into pockets of flame. Most of the women dashed frantically toward exits. Others froze in fear and remained at their machines. When they discovered that the door next to the freight elevators was locked, the women rushed toward the other stairway. Over 150 workers fought for access to the twenty-inch passageway that led to the open stairway.

On the tenth floor those who did not escape via the roof crowded into the two freight elevators. Jammed with fleeing workers, the cars began their descent to the ground floor. Then, some workers still trapped on the top floors started jumping into the elevator shafts to land on top of the descending elevators. One elevator operator, Joseph Zito, recalled that so many girls hit the top of his car that it would not work: "It was jammed by the bodies." Nineteen bodies were later found wedged into one of the elevator shafts. The other elevator broke down when its power circuit became waterlogged by the spray of the fire hoses.

By 4:45 P.M. the top three floors of the Asch Building were engulfed in flames. Escape was no longer possible.

By this time, the fire on the top floors of the Asch Building was visible in the street below. Within minutes a crowd gathered around the

The sidewalk in front of the Triangle Company was strewn with the bodies of those who had jumped to their death at the height of the blaze. The fire department's safety nets were too weak to break the victims' falls.

building to watch the blaze. One policeman watching the scene observed: "It's mighty hard work burning one of those fireproof buildings, but I guess it's lucky it's Saturday afternoon. It looks as if everyone is out of the place." Suddenly, an object that looked like a bale of dress material dropped from an eighth-floor window.

The firemen's nets caught only a few of those who jumped. More often, as Fire Captain Howard C. Ruch recalled, the bodies—which struck the ground with a force almost a thousand times their actual weight—"didn't break through the nets; they just carried them to the sidewalk. The force was so great it took the men off their feet; they turned somersaults over onto the bodies." Sometimes, a group of girls would join hands before jumping from the ledge, soothing their fears in a joint death fall.

Fifteen minutes after the firemen arrived, the fire was brought under control. In those few minutes, 46 people jumped to their deaths. The charred remains of 100 workers were later recovered from inside the building. Most of those who perished were Jewish. All but 21 of the victims were women, and a dozen were so badly burned or disfigured that they were almost unrecognizable. In fact, 7 persons were never identified.

Hundreds of workers had managed to escape the flames. Those injured, stunned, and weeping survivors soon filled the hospitals and ghetto apartments of the Lower East Side. Police officials hurriedly tried to find coffins for the dead. On East Twenty-sixth Street a huge, enclosed pier was converted into a temporary morgue. The Triangle dead were piled up on sidewalks near the Asch Building while firemen watered down the smoldering building.

Police Department "death wagons" rode throughout the evening, bringing the dead to the temporary morgue. Policemen searched through personal belongings in an effort to identify victims. Fourteen engagement rings were later found on one floor alone of the Triangle factory. These and other rings collected at the morgue testified to a particularly bitter aspect of the tragedy, namely, the marital hopes and expectations of this young and largely female contingent of workers. Some of the victims had stuffed their skimpy pay envelopes inside their clothing. Others still had their wages clutched in their hands.

Many of the Jewish families on the Lower East Side had relatives or friends working at Triangle, and the community's grief was almost unbearable. Tens of thousands rushed to the East Twenty-sixth Street pier searching for missing friends or relatives. They were joined by numerous Italian and other immigrant families. The police finally let the frantic throng file through the pier a few dozen at a time. Inside the temporary morgue the bodies of the Triangle victims had been laid out in coffins in neat rows.

Heartbreaking scenes of recognition filled the night. A mother, discovering her daughter's body, would break down into uncontrollable wailing and have to be escorted out. A young woman, finding her sister's

Thousands of mourning relatives and friends filed through the temporary morgue on the East 26th Street pier to identify the victims. Some were never identified.

charred body, would simply faint. Some women completely lost control and tried to kill themselves, either by swallowing poison or by jumping off the pier. Police and onlookers stopped at least a dozen such attempts.

In the days following the fire, the Triangle victims were buried quietly by their families. Friends and relatives from the Lower East Side attended the funerals. They poured out their grief and sorrow. Reformers and community leaders arranged a series of memorial meetings to honor the victims. A fund-raising appeal conducted by the Red Cross, Jewish community groups, and the WTUL collected over $120,000 to assist needy families. Several of the victims had been the sole supports of their families, in either New York or "the old country." Half a dozen families had lost two sisters (one sister, a widow with five children); another had lost two brothers. In one Italian family a mother and two daughters were killed in the fire.

On April 5 a symbolic mass funeral was held in lower Manhattan. Over 100,000 people—mainly women who lived and worked on the Lower East Side—marched silently in the rain for five hours to honor the Triangle dead. As they approached the Asch Building, the women who marched gave way completely to their emotions. According to one paper's report, they uttered "one long-drawn-out, heart-piercing cry, the mingling of thousands of voices, a cry that was perhaps the most impressive expression of human grief ever heard in this city."

Who was to blame for the tragedy? This question haunted New Yorkers in the weeks that followed the Triangle disaster. "That a terrible mistake was made by somebody," *The New York Times* observed, "is easier to say now than to point out just where the blame for this destruction of human life may be placed."

The city's fire department bore a share of the responsibility, despite the bravery of those who fought the blaze. The department had failed to enforce even those few mild safety laws that were on the books. Moreover, its equipment was inadequate for fighting fires in the city's new loft buildings. The tallest fire ladders reached only to the sixth floor, although half the city's factory workers—more than 300,000—worked in lofts above this floor. Some of the department's safety nets were so weak that they broke under the force of falling bodies.

The City Buildings Department, too, had to accept a measure of the blame. The Asch Building, like most of New York City's garment shops, lacked adequate safety features. Several months earlier, a factory inspector had warned the owners of the Asch Building of such violations as insufficient exits and locked stairway doors. But the department made no effort to ensure that these conditions were corrected. There were only 47 inspectors in Manhattan to check over 50,000 buildings. Of these buildings 13,600 had been listed as dangerous by the fire department the previous month. Inspectors managed to visit 2,000 buildings in March, but the Asch Building was not among them.

Nor were the fire insurance companies innocent of blame. Insurance brokers in New York suffered heavy losses from the numerous fires that occurred in the city's loft buildings. Yet the insurance industry failed to insist on safety standards that might have reduced fire hazards. Rather, they preferred to pay off after a fire and then raise a company's premium costs. Higher policy rates also meant higher commissions for insurance brokers. During the 1890s a group of insurance companies attempted to offer cheaper rates to manufacturers who installed sprinkler systems in their factories. These companies were soon driven out of business by the city's powerful insurance industry. It was simply easier and more profitable to leave the "fireproof" firetraps alone and settle afterward.

At the time of the fire the Triangle Shirtwaist Company carried insurance policies totaling $199,750. The Triangle owners eventually collected full repayment for their losses in equipment and property damage. Under the terms of these insurance policies, they were also given an extra indemnity of $64,925, or $445 for each worker killed. The company's owners defended themselves against charges of responsibility for the fire by pointing out that building inspectors had never entered a complaint against the firm and that an employee carelessly dropping a cigarette might well have started the fire.

On April 11, a week after the public funeral for the Triangle victims, the company's owners, Isaac Harris and Max Blanck, were indicted by a grand jury and charged with manslaughter. Their trial began in New York eight months later, on December 4. Crowds of women gathered outside the courtroom each day screaming "Murderers! Murderers!" A heavy police guard was called in to protect the defendants. Harris and

Not much remained of the "fireproof" Asch Building once the fire had run its course. The Triangle owners collected insurance money for losses in equipment and property damages though their building had inadequate safety features.

Blanck—"the shirtwaist kings"—engaged as their defense counsel a well-known Jewish lawyer, Max D. Steuer.

In order to simplify the case, the state decided to try the pair only for responsibility in the death of a single worker, Margaret Schwartz, who died in the fire because of the locked ninth-floor door. Most testimony centered on three questions: (1) Was the ninth-floor door kept locked regularly? (2) Was it locked at the time of the fire? (3) Most importantly, did Blanck and Harris know it was locked?

The jury took less than two hours to find the shirtwaist kings not guilty. As one jury member later told a newsman: "I believed that the [door] was locked at the time of the fire. But I could not make myself feel certain that Harris and Blanck knew that it was locked."

One interesting sidelight to the tragedy emerged during the trial. The Triangle owners kept their exit doors locked for fear that employees would steal garments or pieces of fabric. At one point the prosecutor asked Isaac Harris: "How much in all the instances would you say was the value of all the goods that you found had been taken by these employees? You would say it was not over $25, wouldn't you?" Harris turned pale before responding: "No, it would not exceed that much."

If Harris and Blanck had been convicted, the Triangle fire might have been forgotten more easily. The public might have been satisfied that justice had been done. As it turned out, the acquittal of Blanck and Harris sparked a new effort to improve the conditions under which New

York City's laborers worked. Responding to public pressure, the state legislature created the New York Factory Investigating Commission in June 1911, to study working conditions in the state.

Among the commission's most active members were two politically powerful New York City Democrats, State Assembly Majority Leader Alfred E. Smith and State Senate Majority Leader Robert F. Wagner, Sr. They helped throw the Tammany machine's full support behind the commission's many proposals for reform. Other members included Samuel Gompers of the AFL and Mary Dreier of the WTUL. Many experts on factory safety and working conditions assisted the commission. Among them were progressive reformers such as Belle and Henry Moskowitz, and young social workers such as Frances Perkins, who later became the nation's first woman cabinet member as secretary of labor.

The Triangle Commission, as it was popularly called, went far beyond an investigation of fire hazards alone. It studied almost every type of labor problem in New York. In 1911 the group held public hearings in the state's major manufacturing cities and heard 222 witnesses. Staff field inspectors visited 1,836 factories in 20 industries. Smith, Wagner, and their associates talked with factory workers who had lost limbs because of unsafe machinery. They examined the "doctored" records kept by many companies on employees' wages and hours. Commission investigators watched hundreds of women leaving factories at 5 A.M., after working ten-hour shifts. They studied the horrible conditions in the disease-ridden tenements where workers lived.

On farms in upstate New York, commission members observed migrant women working alongside their children for eighteen hours and more a day. In canneries across the state they saw children of five working full time. The conditions wore no party label; the worst offenders among New York's manufacturers included both Republicans and Democrats. In a factory belonging to a leading upstate Democratic progressive, for example, Smith and Wagner found "the vilest and most uncivilized conditions of labor in the state."

By 1900 at least 1,700,000 children under the age of sixteen were in the labor market. One result of the Triangle fire was the passage of laws limiting child labor and improving working conditions for women and children.

Between 1911 and 1915, Smith and Wagner introduced over sixty bills based on their investigations. Despite much conservative opposition in the legislature, the two Tammany Democrats managed to pass fifty-six of their proposals by fusing the votes of Democratic regulars and antimachine reformers. The bills they passed called for the creation of a Bureau of Fire Prevention and the enforcement of strict fire safety codes (including compulsory fire drills and the installation of sprinklers in factories). Two other major bills provided for an increase in the number of factory inspectors and a strengthening of the supervisory authority of the state's Department of Labor.

One of the most hard-fought proposals in the legislature was a bill calling for a 54-hour workweek for women and minors. When cannery owners objected to the measure, Smith replied sarcastically that they wished to revise the Bible to read "Remember the Sabbath to keep it holy—except in canneries." The bill passed. Other laws forbade night factory work for women, prohibited smoking in factories, and called for better ventilation and sanitary facilities. Child labor was outlawed in tenement manufacturing and canneries. Sunday work was forbidden ("one day's rest in seven"), and insurance (workmen's compensation) was provided for employees injured in accidents. Other laws forbade employment of children under fourteen (*anywhere*) and required improved working facilities, rest periods, and minimum wages for women and children.

In the Triangle Commission's four years of existence, Smith and Wagner helped to pass the most enlightened code of industrial reform in the country. Their work served as a model for legislators in other states and foreshadowed many of the federal laws enacted under the New Deal. In the following decades, both men were to become leading Democratic progressives, and their concern for the improvement of working conditions in the state stemmed in large measure from their experiences on the Triangle Commission.

This sense of what Frances Perkins called "stricken conscience" was felt by Smith, Wagner, and Perkins—as well as by many of their colleagues in the legislature. Among them was a young, unknown Democratic senator from upstate who rose before the state senate one day to speak on behalf of a bill for a 54-hour workweek. The measure previously had been defeated by only one vote. Wagner had since rounded up an additional vote for the bill, and still another supporter—Manhattan's colorful East Side Democrat, "Big Tim" Sullivan—was now racing across Albany to cast the tie-breaking ballot.

The youthful Democratic senator began "filibustering" (speaking on irrelevant subjects—mainly, in this case, on birds) to stall for time until Sullivan could reach the senate floor. When Republican leaders opposing the bill complained that the subject of birds had nothing to do with the bill, the speaker responded that he was "trying to prove that nature demands shorter hours." His filibuster continued until Sullivan arrived. Only then, confident that the bill would now pass, did Senator Franklin Delano Roosevelt return to his seat.

34
NEW WAVES
OF REFORM
A.W.

The miserable working conditions that provoked the great shirtwaist-industry strike of 1909 were typical of American manufacturing in the half-century of industrial growth that followed the Civil War. Workers in manufacturing plants toiled an average of fifty-nine hours each week. They earned less than $10 per week for their backbreaking labor.

By contrast, most of their employers—the manufacturers, bankers, and merchants who directed the course of economic development in the United States—profited handsomely from the workers' long hours and low wage rates. Between 1860 and 1900 the country rose from fourth to first place among the world's industrial nations, producing more in 1900 than Britain, France, and Germany combined.

The rewards for business success during this period were high indeed. In 1890 an estimated 200,000 people owned 70 percent of the country's wealth. A survey taken in 1892 showed that close to 4,000 people had become millionaires since the Civil War. Almost all these individuals made their fortunes in manufacturing, railroads, trade, or finance. This great concentration of wealth among America's upper classes only added to the discontent of the nation's industrial laborers.

Union organization seemed to hold the only promise of changing the working conditions of American workers. But despite the efforts of union leaders and rank-and-file organizers throughout the period, no strong, united workingman's association emerged among the industrial labor force of the United States. Instead, in this era of eco-

nomic growth, industry-wide unions came and went. The ILGWU, for example, was only the latest in a line of unions attempting to organize the garment industry, the earlier ones having failed at the task.

At the turn of the century, 10 million men and women, over a third of the entire labor force, worked in factories. Yet the union movement had succeeded in organizing less than 4 percent of America's industrial workers. What was this union tradition? Why had it failed to mobilize the country's underpaid, overworked, and poorly treated laboring masses?

THE RISE OF ORGANIZED LABOR

Those who led or took part in the Uprising of the Twenty Thousand inherited a tradition of industrial union activity more than a half-century old. In Jacksonian America, factory workers and craftsmen attempted to form their own unions. Few of these trade organizations lasted beyond the Civil War. In the half-century afterwards a number of major unions were formed. Almost all these unions employed the strike weapon, though rarely with complete success. During the 1880s, for example, over 24,000 strikes occurred in the United States, involving over 6½ million workers.

During the turbulent depression years of the 1890s, 3 million people were thrown out of work, perhaps 15 to 20 percent of the country's work force. Over 7,000 strikes were called during this period. Between 1894 and 1896 numerous small armies of the unemployed marched on Washington demanding federal relief assistance.

By the early twentieth century the infant ILGWU, which was to lead the great shirtwaist strike of 1909, had counterparts in every other industry in the country. Like the garment union, most of these organizations were small and had to struggle for existence. The experience of the 1909 garment workers' strike demonstrates many of the difficulties unions encountered in organizing.

Difficulties in Union Organization For one

thing, few unions were as successful as the ILG-WU in persuading workers from different ethnic backgrounds to put aside their fierce hatreds and work for common goals. Indeed, the 1909–1910 strike was the first time that most of New York City's Jewish and Italian workers actually banded together in one union. More often, tensions among nationality groups, differences in language, and racial hostilities within the working class hampered union organization.

Employers skillfully exploited these ethnic and national hostilities to divide workers. When Jews went on strike, Italians would work, and vice versa. When both groups went on strike, blacks were called in to scab. Furthermore, the influx of Southern and Eastern European immigrants in the late nineteenth and early twentieth centuries kept wage rates down in most industries. More often than not, the labor supply greatly exceeded demand. Employers had little difficulty filling the unskilled and semiskilled positions at their plants.

Employers resorted to a variety of tactics to defeat the efforts of union organizers. These included the use of strikebreakers (such as the hoodlums who attacked ILGWU picketers), and the hiring of scabs (another tactic employed by Harris and Blanck). Employers also used blacklisting — the denial of work to union officials by all the firms in an industry — and lockouts of striking workers. Firms like the Triangle Company sometimes enlisted the aid of sympathetic policemen and judges who harassed strikers with arrests and court action. Another important weapon of management was the yellow-dog contract, in which new workers agreed not to join a union as a condition of their employment.

Attempts at Union Organization At the national level the union movement faced a number of difficulties in the half-century after the Civil War. Several national unions rose and fell because of unsuccessful strikes, the opposition of the middle class, and the inability of unions to hold the loyalty of most workers. The National Labor Union played a prominent role briefly during the depression of the 1870s. The Knights of Labor, under the leadership of Terence V. Powderly, became a major force in the labor movement in the following decade. These unions favored improvement of the American worker's economic state and a broad program of reform within American society.

The Knights had many self-employed or salaried middle-class Americans in its membership. During the 1880s it tried unsuccessfully to organize a series of strikes and to set up cooperative factories and stores — owned by the workers themselves — as an alternative to the privately run corporations. Leaders of the Knights were blamed for the Haymarket Affair of 1886 and were attacked as "anarchists." Actually, they had played no part in the bombing. Membership in the Knights of Labor nevertheless declined from 700,000 in 1886 to 74,000 by 1893. The union played an insignificant role in the labor movement during the 1890s, joining finally with the agrarian-led Populist party. By 1900 it had lapsed into obscurity.

American socialists were also influential in the union movement during these decades. Most of the leading figures in the ILGWU at the time of the garment strike, for example, held socialist beliefs or even positions within the immigrant wing of the American socialist movement. Similarly, socialists had been important in the Knights of Labor, the Western Federation of Miners, and other groups.

The leading force within American unionization during this period was the American Federation of Labor (AFL). It was a loose confederation of independent craft unions and semi-industrial affiliates such as the ILGWU. The AFL was formed in 1881 under the leadership of Samuel Gompers. A one-time socialist, Gompers criticized earlier union organizations such as the Knights for stressing general reforms in American society.

The labor movement, Gompers believed, should concentrate exclusively on winning economic gains for the working class. It should leave the tasks of reform to others. Union leaders should devote all their time and energy to raising workers' wages, reducing hours, and improving working conditions. Gompers also believed that unions should avoid independent political action, such as the affiliation of the Knights with the Populist party in the 1890s. Instead, labor should support its political friends and oppose its enemies,

Samuel Gompers, shown here at a meeting to organize the 1909 garment workers' strike, founded the American Federation of Labor around such craft unions. Using both the strike and collective bargaining, he forged a powerful national labor organization.

regardless of party. When asked at a congressional hearing what the unions wanted, Gompers replied simply: "More!"

By the time of the New York garment-industry strike, the AFL, under Gompers's leadership, had become the country's dominant national labor organization. It was also the most powerful union politically and economically up to that time.

REFORMERS IN THE LATE NINETEENTH CENTURY

Union leaders were not the only people concerned about the conditions of American workers. Socialists, middle- and upper-class reformers, and city politicians all worked to improve conditions for American laborers. Their suggested solutions to the problems posed by industrial society, though, were as different as the backgrounds from which these reformers emerged.

The Socialist Vision In the late nineteenth century a group of socialist writers became the first generation of critics to tackle the dilemmas of ur-

ban-industrial America. They were grouped as socialists because they held in common the belief that ownership and control of industry, land, and so forth, should be shared by the community as a whole. These writers put forth a series of proposals for a complete overhaul of American institutions. In *Progress and Poverty* (1877–1879) Henry George attacked the inequities of the American economic system. Edward Bellamy's *Looking Backward* (1888) presents a vision of a socialist utopia. His book became a bestseller in the 1880s and 1890s. Henry Demarest Lloyd's *Wealth Against Commonwealth* (1894) attacked the corrupt business practices of the Standard Oil Company. Other influential critics of American industrial life included economist Richard Ely, "social gospel" minister Washington Gladden, and utopian writers Ignatius Donnelly and William Dean Howells.

Uppermost in the minds of these late nineteenth-century reformers was the notion that, if conditions in the nation's slums, factories, and farms were not improved quickly and drastically, the United States would explode into class warfare. Surely, they reasoned, abused workers would not tolerate such conditions indefinitely. They believed that a social catastrophe was close at hand. It could be prevented only by an immediate and total alteration in the nation's social and economic structure.

They offered no single remedy. Some, like Lloyd, Bellamy, and Howells, believed in a socialist commonwealth. They argued, though, over the details of Utopia and how to achieve it. Others, like George, felt that a single tax on unearned income from land would somehow provide enough money to solve the nation's problems. All these reformers were united in their belief that a single problem underlay all the social ills of the United States. Find and correct this overriding problem—"the root of our social difficulty," as George put it—and Americans could begin moving toward an era of moral and social perfection.

In this utopian vision of the United States these late nineteenth-century reformers resembled their pre-Civil War, preindustrial counterparts. Garrison, Emerson, and Fuller had also walked a thin line between social criticism and religious prophecy. However "practical" their remedies, therefore, people like George and Bellamy were basically seers. They preached a gospel of total reform, without which total catastrophe would result.

The Settlement House Movement The struggle to improve the lives of the immigrant poor, both in the factories and in the ghettos, was aided by a number of middle-class reformers and socially conscious members of the American upper classes. Women like Mrs. Belmont and other affluent leaders of the Women's Trade Union League who were active in the shirtwaist strike are representative of this trend.

During the 1880s and 1890s many college-educated women became concerned especially with the slum conditions under which immigrant workers lived. They helped to organize settlement houses in the ghettos of East Coast and Middle Western cities. There, foreign-born workers received food and shelter and learned how to speak English. They were given help in understanding and exercising their rights as Americans. In 1889 Lillian Wald founded the Henry Street Settlement in New York City. Jane Addams and Ellen Gates

Starr founded Chicago's Hull House that same year.

By 1910 over 400 settlement houses had been established in the country's slum districts. On New York's Lower East Side, settlement workers assisted the victims of the Triangle fire and their families. In the previous year they had provided money and support for the striking garment workers. As valuable instruments for Americanizing immigrant communities, the settlement houses helped immigrants to improve their working and living conditions at a time when most middle-class Americans remained indifferent or even hostile toward the foreign-born poor.

Municipal Reorganization For some reformers, however, the settlement-house movement seemed an inadequate response to the many problems of America's enlarged industrial cities. It was somewhat like putting bandages over a festering infection without treating the infection itself first. For such reformers the roots of the infection seemed clear: the inefficiency and corruption of urban political machines in alliance with equally corrupt business interests. Democratic politicians such as Al Smith and Robert Wagner, Sr., viewed New York's Tammany machine as the logical friend of the immigrants. But reformers such as Henry George and, later, Fiorello La Guardia believed that the machines merely exploited the immigrants, using their trust and votes to line the pockets of ward heelers, city officials, and local businessmen.

Reform groups such as the National Civic Federation (which later helped to organize the Triangle Fire Commission investigation) sparked a concern among voters for driving the political machines from office. These groups sought to run urban government more efficiently and less corruptly than the machines. They also tended to be dominated by wealthy citizens, leading businessmen, and other upper-middle-class or upper-class figures within their communities.

Municipal reformers, then as today, included businessmen, lawyers, ministers, and journalists—professionals concerned with the concentration of power in the hands of working-class-supported political machines and giant corpora-

JANE ADDAMS

"Even as a little child, she seemed inclined toward special work of some sort. In fact, she was anxious for a career." This is how, with some dismay, Mrs. John H. Addams described her stepdaughter Jane. After all, a girl born to a prosperous family in Cedarville, Illinois, in 1860 was not supposed to have such ambitions.

Jane's heart had been set on the newly opened Smith College for Women, but her father's wish was that she follow the path of her older sisters and enter the Rockford (Illinois) Seminary. She did as he asked and entered the seminary in 1877. Here, the foundations of her feminism were laid down, and, resisting pressure from Anna Sill, Rockford's indomitable head, to become a missionary, Jane decided to become a doctor. Accordingly, she enrolled in the Woman's Medical College of Pennsylvania. Unfortunately, never physically strong, her health broke and she was forced to withdraw.

For eight troubled years she traveled, read, and attended the social functions that suited Mrs. Addams's plans for her. It was a period of frustration, nervousness, and unhappiness. At long last, during a European tour with her friend Ellen Gates Starr, an idea began to take shape in Jane's mind. In London she witnessed a match-girls' strike and later she visited Toynbee Hall in London's East End, the University settlement that sought to alleviate the bitter human consequences of industrialization.

The two young women discussed these ideas and decided to return home to implement them. They searched for a suitable base of operations and found the decaying Hull mansion in the heart of one of the poorest districts in the city, a crowded area bursting with Greek, Italian, Russian, German, Sicilian, and other immigrants. In September of 1889, they moved in, and invited the neighbors to stop by.

Before long two things happened. First, neighbors, most of them immigrants, started coming—to attend lectures and to form clubs. Second, a number of talented men and women moved into Hull House. By 1893, Hull House was the center of some forty clubs, a day nursery, gymnasium, dispensary, and playground, cooking and sewing classes, courses in art, music, and language, a cooperative boardinghouse for working girls, and a little theater; each week 2,000 people entered its doors.

Under Jane Addams's leadership, Hull House took on another, more far-reaching task. It became a clearing house for various reform movements. The residents pressured legislators to act on such matters as child labor, factory inspection, recognition of labor unions, protection of immigrants, and industrial safety.

Jane Addams did not permit her energies to be siphoned off into the special enterprises sponsored by Hull House, but she remained the focus and center of the undertaking. She became sought after as a lecturer. Honors were bestowed upon her. She became the first woman president of the National Conference of Charities and Correction and in 1910 became the first woman to receive an honorary degree from Yale University. In 1931, sharing the award with Nicholas Murray Butler, she was given the Nobel Peace Prize.

A heart attack laid her low in 1933, and in 1935 she was stricken with cancer. She died at the age of seventy-four. She had been at Hull House for forty-six years and it stood as a monument to this remarkable woman who had devoted herself to humanitarian causes and had never swerved from what she conceived to be her duty.

tions. Many were native-born Protestants. Most had had little direct contact with foreign-born, largely Catholic and Jewish immigrants until they began a career of reform.

Quite often, these basic cultural differences between immigrants and reformers made it difficult, if not impossible, for the two groups to join successfully. Their interests were also often in direct conflict. New immigrants depended on the very political favors—jobs and other assistance from local political bosses—that the reformers wanted to eliminate. Moreover, the immigrant culture was more tolerant of gambling and drinking than the reformer's tradition of stern Protestant moralism. These differences over values certainly diluted the effect of municipal reformers in curing urban ills.

A NEW GENERATION OF REFORMERS

Many of those who had opposed unions and other reform movements prior to the 1890s gradually became convinced of the need for basic reforms in American society. They had been deeply affected by the tumultuous events of the nineties: the depression, the social unrest on farms and in factories, the deepening class conflict.

By the turn of the century many middle-class Americans saw the dangers. Conservative journalists such as William Allen White, "big business" lawyers such as Clarence Darrow and George Norris, and middle-of-the-road Republicans such as Theodore Roosevelt had all concluded that the future political and social health of the American republic depended on a variety of reforms. They sought improvements in the conditions under which the urban poor lived. They also wanted to bring giant trusts under governmental supervision in the public interest. These various reform interests came together in a movement that historians have labeled "progressivism."

The Progressive Movement However different progressive reformers were in their social and economic concerns, most shared certain fundamental beliefs. For one thing, unlike the Bellamys and Georges of the previous generation, they did not believe in imminent social catastrophe. Rather, they were highly nationalistic and optimistic about the future of the United States. Herbert Croly, one of their most influential writers, argued that this "promise of American life" consisted of "an improving popular economic condition, guaranteed by democratic political institutions, and resulting in moral and social [improvement]."

Nationalism and reform, then, went hand in hand. Both impulses were based on an idealistic faith in American potential. Most progressives believed that a decent society for all Americans could be created through gradual reform rather than through revolutionary changes. The reformers of the previous generation had not been so confident.

Progressive reformers harnessed their optimism about domestic affairs to a firm belief in the value of Christian morality. It was within this "ethical climate" that much reform legislation of the era took shape. To Frances Perkins the new climate was dominated by "the idea that poverty is preventable, that poverty is destructive, wasteful, demoralizing, and that poverty in the midst of potential plenty is morally unacceptable in a Christian and democratic society." An end to poverty, injustice, and unregulated economic power, the preservation of the nation's natural resources, a return to honest government—all this, the progressives believed, would follow from applying Christian ethics to reshaping the social environment.

Another belief shared by progressive thinkers was a confidence in the use of "experts" to manage public affairs. Professional advisers such as those who had assisted the Triangle Commission would provide rational, scientific measurement of the country's problems; they would also suggest efficient means for tackling social ills. Often this argument for "efficient" and "scientific" government cloaked the efforts of business groups and wealthier Americans to retain control of government—especially at the city and state level—and to deny power to the immigrant-supported urban political machines. In short, there was an important elitist, "antidemocratic" dimension to *certain* aspects of progressivism.

Progressive reformers called for the establishment of legislative investigating bodies at all levels of government, and the use of expert advisers — brain trusts — to help city and state governments develop programs of reform. They wanted to create regulatory agencies to supervise business practices. Progressives also favored the establishment of nonpartisan commissions or councils to eliminate machine corruption in city government. The independent commission form of city government originated in Galveston, Texas, in 1900. By 1914 it had spread to over 400 American cities, although not to most larger ones.

Finally, more reformers of the era believed strongly in the value of publicizing social problems as a first step toward solving them. As early as 1898 Congress had established a commission to study the giant business trusts. The commission eventually published nineteen volumes on American social and economic problems. In addition, many states set up investigatory groups to study business corruption. This technique of exposure was carried out most systematically under the reform governorship of Robert M. LaFollette in Wisconsin from 1901 to 1906. LaFollette's efforts to uncover business abuses and press for needed social legislation set a pattern for reform administrations in other states.

Newspapers and magazines provided a forum for investigations of social problems by muckraking journalists. Ida Tarbell wrote an explosive exposé of the Standard Oil Company. Lincoln Steffens studied corrupt city political machines. David Graham Phillips examined Senate corruption. Magazines such as *McClure's* and *Harper's Weekly* increased their circulation to the hundreds of thousands by becoming champions of reform.

New Politics for the Cities Nowhere was the belief in the need for "rational" government stronger than at the local level. Progressives were as appalled by corrupt city politics as they were by dirty tenements and unsafe factories. All three conditions came under the attack of municipal reformers. Beginning in the 1890s, reform groups won control of a number of cities and began deal-

Ida M. Tarbell's stunning exposés revealed the way giant corporations gained advantage over competitors by securing special rates (rebates) from railroads. Her landmark study of the oil industry appeared in *McClure's* magazine, which established it as the leading muckraking periodical.

Lincoln Steffens, one of the leading reformer journalists, wrote numerous articles exposing political corruption in city government. His autobiography gives an accurate account of the development of the muckraking movement.

Upton Sinclair is best remembered for his novel, *The Jungle,* which told of brutal and unsanitary conditions in Chicago's stockyards. The public revulsion it aroused resulted in the passage of the Meat Inspection Act of 1906.

ing with slum and factory conditions. In New York City, for example, after driving Tammany Hall from power in 1901, Mayor Seth Low worked closely with reformers to improve parks and playgrounds, tighten housing laws, and strengthen the city's health services to the poor. But, despite Mayor Seth's efforts, much remained to be done, as conditions in the city at the time of the Triangle fire demonstrated.

In other cities, too, the concern for social reform proved strong. During the 1890s and 1900s three remarkable Middle Western businessmen— all self-made millionaires—became pioneers in urban reform. Their cities served as models for social reformers throughout the country.

Hazen Pingree, mayor of Detroit, Michigan, from 1889 to 1896, and then governor of the state, fought corruption by politicians and local industrial groups, especially street railways and gas companies. Pingree authorized the construction of a city-owned electric lighting plant and urged public ownership of other such utilities. In Toledo, Ohio, Samuel M. "Golden Rule" Jones, mayor of the city from 1897 to 1904, established free kindergarten day-care facilities for working mothers, pressed for a minimum hourly wage and other social legislation, and supported public ownership of utilities.

Thomas Johnson, Cleveland's mayor from 1901 to 1909, became a social reformer after reading Henry George's *Progress and Poverty*. He, too, fought the private utility interests and urged public ownership. Johnson sponsored a number of social welfare projects, including the construction of municipal bathhouses (a crucial urban health measure, since many tenement houses did not have adequate bathroom facilities) and careful inspection of consumer meat and dairy products.

All three Middle Western mayors ran nonpartisan governments, dominated by professional administrators and reformers who took over the jobs that had formerly been filled by political appointees. Unfortunately, driving political machines from office did not always produce improvements in ghetto or factory conditions. Unlike Mayors Pingree, Jones, and Johnson, many municipal reformers were less interested in improving slum conditions than in eliminating the

Tom Johnson, Cleveland's reform mayor, instituted reforms, including city planning, that made that city one of America's best-governed. He had his own political machine, observing, "It all depends on whether a boss is a good one or a bad one."

power and corruption of immigrant-supported political machines. In Pittsburgh, for example, two-thirds of those involved in trying to revise the city's charter came from upper-class backgrounds and were closely tied to the city's leading banks and industries.

Changes at the State Level Many of the major reforms of this period were achieved at the state level. In a number of states progressive reformers were elected governors. Among them were Robert LaFollette in Wisconsin, Charles Evans Hughes in New York, Hoke Smith in Georgia, Hiram Johnson in California, and the Southern-born president of Princeton University, Woodrow Wilson, in New Jersey. Each state had its special problems, each its particular group of "entrenched interests." In Massachusetts, the railroads and insurance companies dominated; in California, it was the powerful and corrupt labor unions.

Almost all reform governors fought for stricter regulation of railroads, public utilities, and industries within their states. They tried to force corporations to pay a fair share of taxes and to conserve natural resources like forests and mines, which provided raw materials for industry. Finally, they fought to make state government more democratic through such reforms as the initiative, the referendum, and the recall.[1]

During the first two decades of the century, many states enacted broad programs of social legislation dealing with the wages and hours of factory workers, the employment of women and children, and safety conditions in tenements and factories. Maryland adopted the first statewide

workmen's compensation law in 1902. A year later Oregon passed a law restricting women's industrial work to ten hours per day. Illinois adopted the first measure providing public assistance to mothers with dependent children in 1911. And Massachusetts passed the first minimum wage law (applying to women and children) in 1912. All these measures were landmarks in the struggle of progressive reformers to achieve economic and social justice for all Americans.

Amending the Constitution Suffrage—the right to vote—had been a central concern of the woman's rights movement for several decades. In 1910 the American labor force included over 8 million women, many of them college-educated. During this period 36 percent of all professional jobs were held by women. Yet, prior to World War I only eleven states had granted women the right to vote.

Between 1914 and 1919 woman's rights advocates gave the suffrage issue national im-

---

[1]The initiative is a device by which a small number of citizens, sometimes as few as 5 percent, can bypass the legislature and force a vote upon measures at general elections. The referendum forces legislatures to return proposed laws to the electorate, who then approve or reject the proposals. The recall, perhaps the most controversial device, allows the electorate to remove an elected official from office. It requires a special election, called after a certain number of voters have signed a petition asking for the official's removal.

Women concentrated on making political gains in the early twentieth century. An intense campaign, and their increasing importance in the labor market, finally gained them full suffrage on a nationwide basis by constitutional amendment—the Nineteenth.

portance by conducting a massive campaign of petitions, lobbying, picketing, and nonviolent demonstrations. The campaign was sponsored by two national associations of woman suffrage advocates, led by Carrie Chapman Catt and Anna Howard Shaw. The picketing and demonstrations that had brought public sympathy for the demands of shirtwaist employees during the Triangle strike worked with similar effect for the suffragettes. The involvement of women in war work during World War I brought the movement increased public support. In June 1919 Congress responded by passing the Nineteenth Amendment, giving women the right to vote. The amendment received final state ratification in August 1920. Later that year, for the first time, American women in every state voted in a presidential election.

Another progressive interest, the temperance movement, had been a concern of reformers since before the Civil War. Municipal reformers joined the anti-alcohol drive for two major reasons. First, there was much political corruption associated with urban liquor dealers. Second, reformers felt that alcoholism was destroying the moral fiber and social well-being of many Americans.

The prohibitionists made their first gains at the local and state levels. A number of Southern and Western states voted themselves "dry." During World War I many of the same groups that later pushed the woman suffrage amendment through Congress secured passage of the Eighteenth Amendment, which forbade the sale and distribution of alcoholic beverages. Ratified by the states in January 1919, the amendment took effect the next year. It was considered the most impressive yet the most debatable triumph of progressive moralism.

In 1913 progressive reformers won two other important victories. The Sixteenth Amendment instituted a federal income tax. And the Seventeenth Amendment provided for direct election of senators instead of their election by state legislatures. An amendment prohibiting child labor passed Congress under intense reform pressure. It met strong opposition from the business community, however, and failed to win ratification by the states.

PROGRESSIVISM IN THE WHITE HOUSE

With the death of William McKinley on September 14, 1901, Theodore Roosevelt became the third man in less than forty years to succeed to the presidency because of an assassin's bullet. At forty-three, he was the nation's youngest President. Roosevelt came to the White House with a distinguished career in public service. He had served as state legislator, federal official, city police chief, army colonel, governor of New York, and Vice President. An energetic and impulsive man, Roosevelt responded candidly to McKinley's death: "It is a dreadful thing to come into the presidency this way; but it would be a far worse thing to be morbid about it."

Roosevelt's Square Deal for America Roosevelt moved cautiously during the next few years to take control of the Republican national machinery from McKinley's close friend Senator Mark Hanna of Ohio. In his first term he made few reform proposals. He did, however, publicize reform more and more, especially as his second term drew to a close. During this period no other American did as much as Theodore Roosevelt to educate his fellow citizens to the need for political and social change. He called the presidency "a bully pulpit." He often mounted its steps to criticize "malefactors of great wealth" and others—trusts, political bosses, destroyers of natural resources—who endangered his vision of a "square deal" for all Americans.

But Roosevelt did far more than simply publicize reform. Despite his strong party loyalties and keen appreciation of political patronage, he brought into government service a remarkable number of reformers. Roosevelt appointed William Howard Taft as secretary of war, conservationist Gifford Pinchot as chief of the Forest Service, James R. Garfield (the son of the former President and a dedicated conservationist) as secretary of the interior, and the great jurist Oliver Wendell Holmes, Jr., as Supreme Court justice.

Unlike his Republican predecessors in the White House, Roosevelt worked for the support of the black community. He employed Booker T. Washington, president of the Tuskegee Institute in Alabama, as his chief adviser on Southern Republican appointments. Washington's relationship to Roosevelt was perhaps the high point of the black leader's national influence during a long and distinguished public career.

Washington was born into slavery in 1856 and, after a difficult struggle for his own education, founded Tuskegee in 1881 with assistance from Northern white philanthropists. Tuskegee, under Washington's leadership, stressed vocational training, reflecting his belief that blacks in the South could advance only by concentrating on economic training and self-improvement. Washington's basic message seemed eminently reasonable to many blacks and whites in the region, especially considering the rise in violence directed toward blacks, the spread of caste segregation, and the overall white hostility toward black aspirations during the late nineteenth and early twentieth centuries in America.

Washington's reputation among Southerners, black and white, reached its apex in 1895 when he spoke in Atlanta, urging regional blacks to restrain their demands for political rights in favor of economic self-help, while pleading with whites for sympathy and assistance. Washington's speech became known as the "Atlanta Compromise," accepting as it did the "separate but equal" doctrines of the day. His views drew support also from Roosevelt and many other white progressives, who did not (for the most part) believe in a politically equal role for blacks. Washington came under increasing attack during his final years, however, from younger black leaders such as W. E. B. DuBois. The new breed—often Northern-born and well-educated professionals—demanded *immediate* action to achieve full political and civic equality for black Americans, and they condemned the Tuskegee educator for advocating patience and (or so they believed) accepting a subordinate role for blacks. Many of Washington's critics knew little, however, about his quiet, covert efforts to raise money needed to launch legal battles against segregation statutes, or of his efforts to ensure that (at least in the North) blacks were organized as an effective political voting block. It

was in this context that Washington interpreted his connection with Theodore Roosevelt as still another opportunity to secure influence and exercise patronage on behalf of his Southern black constituency and their white allies.

Underlying Roosevelt's actions and policies during his administration were certain firm beliefs shared by other progressives as well. Among them was the belief that government must begin to intervene in the economy to bring unregulated businesses under control. It was argued that such a move would reduce class tensions in American society as well. Toward this end Roosevelt lobbied actively to push several important reform measures through Congress. The Elkins Act of 1903 forbade railroads to give rebates[2] to large industrial companies. The Hepburn Act of 1906 strengthened the powers of the Interstate Commerce Commission (ICC) to regulate the nation's railroads.

Nevertheless, Roosevelt sometimes needed prodding from the public—for example, on the question of food and drug regulation. Americans were alerted to the vile conditions under which Chicago slaughterhouses and processed-meat plants operated by Upton Sinclair's 1906 novel, *The Jungle*. (Ironically, socialist Sinclair's portrayal in that same book of the horrendous living and working conditions among Chicago's immigrant community was ignored by many of its readers.) Pressure from muckrakers and from reformers such as Dr. Harvey W. Wiley of the Department of Agriculture forced passage in 1906 of both a Pure Food and Drug Act *and* a meat-inspection bill. The former banned the production or sale of fraudulently labeled or adulterated goods. Meat packers and other manufacturers managed to adulterate the measures themselves, however, so that the final versions provided, among other things, that the government and not business pay the costs of inspection. Still, the laws were milestones in their day.

---

[2]Rebates were special rates, lower than the published ones, granted secretly to users who accounted for a large share of freight traffic. Farmers felt especially cheated by these special rates, usually granted to industries.

Theodore Roosevelt surrounded himself with conservationists like John Muir who believed that the natural environment must be protected. Through Roosevelt's influence, 148,000,000 acres of forests were set aside for national parks like Yosemite, seen in the background.

In these and other regulatory measures, Roosevelt received much support from the business community. For many business leaders, federal action seemed the most rational response to the country's growing industrial problems. Thus the railroads favored tighter federal regulation to eliminate the rebate system and avoid even more rigid state regulation. Similarly, giant lumber corporations endorsed federal intervention to enforce a rational set of guidelines for the industry.

An energetic outdoorsman, Roosevelt did much to educate the American public to the need for environmental protection. The Newlands Act, passed in 1902, authorized federal funds for the construction of dams and reclamation projects in the West. In 1907 Roosevelt signed an executive order converting over 17 million acres of forest land in Western states to national reserves. He also withdrew from private sale many valuable natural resources, including coal and mineral lands, oil reserves, and water-power sites. In 1908 he summoned the nation's conservation experts to a White House National Conservation Congress. Its purpose was to plan future policies for the protection of natural resources.

Busting the Trusts In 1902 Roosevelt began a policy of "trust busting." He moved to break up many of the giant corporations that had been organized by industry mergers during the previous decade. At first Roosevelt sought only to regulate the trusts through appropriate legislative channels. He asked Congress to pass legislation authorizing the federal licensing of corporations, full disclosure of company earnings and profits, and other supervisory measures. But the conservative majority in Congress rejected these proposals. So Roosevelt took on the trusts himself, using the powers given to the President by the 1890 Sherman Antitrust Act.

The President's first target was the National Securities Company. This was a consolidation of three major railroad systems: the Northern Pacific, the Great Northern, and the Chicago, Burlington, and Quincy. New York banking houses, led by Rockefeller and J. P. Morgan, had organized the merger to put an end to damaging competition among the three lines. Roosevelt ordered his Attorney General, Philander C. Knox, to file suit against the Northern Securities Company for violating the Sherman Act. In 1903 the Supreme Court declared the merger illegal and ordered the Northern Securities Company dissolved.

Roosevelt brought similar antitrust actions against several other giant corporations. These included Standard Oil, the American Tobacco Company, and DuPont. In this policy, which proved highly popular politically, Roosevelt asserted the supremacy of federal authority over private economic interests.

In his antitrust campaign Roosevelt insisted that he opposed not large corporations as such, but corporate action against the public interest. The exact nature of that interest, Roosevelt felt, was something the President must judge. He wrote: "Our objection to a given corporation must be not that it is big, but that it behaves badly." In 1902 Roosevelt used his authority to force the settlement of a coal strike that threatened to deprive residents of the East Coast of fuel during the winter months. With the aid of Wall Street banker J. P. Morgan he forced coal company executives to accept a settlement favorable to the United Mine Workers. It was the first time that an American President had intervened in a labor dispute on behalf of the striking workers.

Roosevelt's actions toward big business were not always consistent, however. He came to private arrangements with U.S. Steel and other giant corporations to avoid invoking antitrust action. In some labor disputes he called in federal troops as strikebreakers. At heart, he believed that the federal government had to play the role of a neutral third party in resolving major disputes on industrial relations.

Roosevelt had been elected to the presidency in his own right in 1904, winning by the greatest landslide of any presidential contest since the pre-Civil War period. When he left the White House at the end of his second term in 1909, he bequeathed to his hand-picked successor, William Howard Taft, a well-formulated set of reform proposals for congressional action. These proposals included thorough governmental regulation of business, federal supervision of the stock market, a federal workmen's compensation law, and compulsory arbitration of labor disputes.

Taft and the Old Guard The new President showed little interest in carrying out Roosevelt's proposals. Not that Taft opposed reform completely. During his four years as President he supported the constitutional amendments providing for an income tax and for direct election of senators. In addition, Taft initiated twice as many antitrust actions as Roosevelt. But unlike his predecessor, he never acquired an image as a trust buster. Under Taft's administration Congress established the eight-hour day for government workers, widened the ICC's authority to include interstate communications systems, and extended a tax on corporate profits. Taft also gave genuine and vigorous support to the conservation movement.

In other areas, however, Taft remained a conservative, politically allied to the Republican Old Guard. In 1910 Taft's Interior Secretary, Richard Ballinger, made an agreement with private firms allowing them to develop valuable coal and water-power sites in Alaska. Chief Forester Gifford Pinchot objected to this decision, but Taft supported Ballinger and fired Pinchot. This move infuriated Roosevelt and marked the beginning of a political break between the two men

Taft also supported Republican conservatives in their battle for control of Congress against a coalition of reform Democrats and Republicans.

He worked actively for the defeat of leading Republican insurgents in the 1910 congressional election. Again Taft's actions angered Republican reformers, among them Senator Robert LaFollette, the party's most prominent progressive. Later that year Taft cooperated with the Republican Old Guard in helping to pass the Payne-Aldrich Tariff, a high-tariff measure beneficial to big business. The battle over the Payne bill split congressional Republicans into conservative and progressive wings. Roosevelt, usually more politcally astute than Taft, had dodged the issue. GOP reformers wished to lower the tariff, while most conservatives favored upward revision. Long before the close of his term in office, Taft had lost the support of most Republican reformers. They turned again to Teddy Roosevelt for leadership.

The Election of 1912 Roosevelt did not disappoint them. Beginning in 1910, he toured the country, supporting party insurgents against Taft and denouncing the Ballinger-Pinchot affair. He made it evident that he wished the Republican party's nomination for an unprecedented third term in the White House. Roosevelt's active campaigning helped him to capture the presidential primaries in six states. But in most states presidential nominations were made by party conventions rather than by primary elections. Taft had gained control of the party machinery during his four years in office. Thus in June 1912 the Republican national convention nominated Taft for a second term.

Republican progressives led by Roosevelt and LaFollette then split from party ranks. In August 1912 they organized the Progressive (or Bull Moose) party, which nominated Roosevelt for the presidency. The new party attracted the attention of the country's leading reformers. Its 1912 convention, held in Chicago, was attended by such figures as Jane Addams, William Allen White, and George W. Perkins—all activists in the era's various reform movements.

"We stand at Armageddon, and we battle for the Lord!"—Roosevelt shouted this rallying cry to Progressives at the Republican convention in June 1912. He was a man with a mission. He wanted to regain the presidency because

Many cartoons, such as this one, appeared during the 1912 presidential nominating conventions. Cartoonists had a field day depicting Roosevelt and the "Bull Moose" party.

he had a Progressive program, his "New Nationalism," that he wanted to see enacted into law. In his characteristic way he was ready to do battle. "I feel as fit as a bull moose," he told reporters.

When he lost the nomination, the Progressives would not accept the end of their dream. On August 5, 1912, they met as the newly formed Progressive, or "Bull Moose," party. Here in Chicago they would nominate Roosevelt as their presidential candidate.

The religious note that Roosevelt had sounded at the Republican convention seemed to find its real audience here. One historian has described the delegates as "a group of well-dressed, serious citizens with the respectability of Sunday School superintendents." The gathering seemed more like a religious revival meeting than a political convention. Speaker after speaker took the podium to deliver rousing, emotion-packed sermons on social justice. An already converted audience listened intently and often tearfully. Occasionally they would be moved to respond with hymns, feet stomping, and quotes from the Bible.

These were the men and women who for

years had sought reforms in their own communities. They were frequently isolated from the rest of society because of their beliefs. One writer described them as "men of character who had fought against local grafting politicians. College professors, social workers, businessmen of vision and independence, farmers tired of seeing agriculture on the cross—[all] were enlisting in a cause they loved for unselfish service."

On the second day of the convention Roosevelt rose to present his "Confession of Faith" in political and economic reform. Before he could speak, 15,000 people came to their feet to welcome him. They poured out all of the emotions that had been building in them since he was denied the Republican nomination.

Roosevelt did not disappoint them. His mood matched theirs. When it came time for him to accept their nomination, he launched the crusade in fervent, enthusiastic terms:

> Six weeks ago here in Chicago, I spoke to the honest representatives of a convention which was not dominated by honest men; a convention wherein sat, alas! a majority of men who, with sneering indifference to every principle of right, acted so as to bring to a shameful end a party which had been founded over half a century ago by men in whose souls burned the fire of lofty endeavor. Now to you men who, in your turn, have come together to spend and be spent in the endless crusade against wrong, to you who face the future resolute and confident, to you who strive in a spirit of brotherhood for the betterment of our nation, to you who gird yourselves for this great new fight in the never-ending warfare for the good of mankind, I say in closing what I said in that speech in closing: We stand at Armageddon and we battle for the Lord.

The Progressive party platform reflected a broad concern for major reforms in American life. It called for tighter governmental regulation of giant industries and financial companies, national presidential primaries, woman suffrage, and the initiative, referendum, and recall. Progressives also favored the prohibition of child labor, minimum wage standards for women, workmen's compensation, and a variety of banking and currency reforms.

On July 2, the Democrats nominated for the presidency a moderate reform candidate, Governor Woodrow Wilson of New Jersey. The Democratic platform favored collective bargaining for unions and revisions in the country's banking system. Unlike the Progressives, the Democrats sought the abolition of giant corporations rather than their regulation. Wilson called his program the New Freedom.

The Republicans, too, ran on a platform of moderate reform. They favored, among other legislation, tighter regulation of trusts and banking and currency changes. Thus, although Taft was more conservative than either Roosevelt or Wilson, he could hardly be considered an opponent of reform. A fourth candidate, Socialist Eugene V. Debs, ran on the most radical platform of all. Debs had led the American Railway Union during the Pullman Company strike of 1894. He served a jail term for his efforts, emerged from prison a confirmed socialist (largely the result of having read the works of other American socialists such as Edward Bellamy and Henry Demarest Lloyd). Debs ran for the presidency as the socialist candidate five times. He again served a jail sentence during Wilson's second term as President because of his opposition to American involvement in W.W. I. In this curious election of 1912, all four candidates were committed in varying degrees to reform.

In the end the Republican split sent Wilson to the White House. Roosevelt received 4,126,000 votes and Taft 3,483,000. Had these votes been combined, the Republicans could have retained control of the presidency. Wilson received 6,286,000 popular votes, less than 45 percent of the total. But he won enough state pluralities to capture a majority of electoral votes. For the first time since the depression of the 1890s, the presidency returned to Democratic hands. In the election the Democrats gained control of both houses of Congress. Thus the new President had a working majority to pass his legislative program.

Wilson and the New Freedom During his first term in office Wilson proceeded to enact his programs. Though he applied stern moral standards to the conduct of foreign relations, Wilson was a skillful realist about domestic affairs. He quickly tossed the notion of breaking up the trusts into the political ashcan. Instead, adopting Roosevelt's more moderate idea of regulating giant corporations, he helped push several bills through Congress to achieve this purpose.

The Federal Trade Commission Act of 1914 established a bipartisan body to supervise industry and prevent unfair methods of competition in interstate commerce. The Clayton Antitrust Act, passed that same year, strengthened the 1890 Sherman Act by spelling out specific business practices that violated the antitrust laws. The Clayton Act also restrained the government from using court injunctions against striking unions.[3] Though on paper the new law seemed a powerful weapon, it actually did little to regulate the behavior of giant corporations or aid organized labor.

One reason for this was that Wilson began permitting corporate leaders and their lobbyists to meet informally with administration officials and regulatory commission members in efforts to settle possible violations without penalty to industry. Businessmen quickly became adept at "co-opting" those nominally charged with overseeing them. In 1913 Wilson helped to steer through Congress the Underwood Tariff, the first downward revision in tariff rates since before the Civil War.

In December 1913 Congress passed the Federal Reserve Act, which created the present American banking system. The new law established twelve regional Federal Reserve banks, which were to serve member banks in their various geographic districts across the country. The Federal Reserve banks issued paper currency, supervised bank credit, and controlled other banking practices. The act also required existing national banks to become members of the Federal Reserve.

The financial "Panic of 1907," which severely disrupted the business community, had persuaded even many conservative bankers and businessmen of the need for greater national coordination of the banking system. The Federal Reserve System's regulatory mechanisms, it was hoped, would prevent the recurrence of such massive runs on banks by depositors demanding immediate currency payments. The 1913 act also marked the acceptance of this new quasigovernmental institution as a means of both regulating the national banks and setting overall monetary policy for the United States.

Wilson was supported in all these measures by his close associations with Southern Democrats. Some historians have called his election "the revolution of 1912" because, for the first time since the Civil War, Southerners regained a large measure of national influence. Born and raised in the South, Wilson felt most comfortable with those from his native region, many of whom became his closest advisers. He appointed a number of Southerners ambassadors and awarded others with high-level government jobs. Several of his cabinet members came from the South; others, like Wilson himself, were of Southern background ("the South in exile," as some called it).

The Senate Majority Leader, Thomas Martin of Virginia, and the House Majority Leader, Oscar Underwood of Alabama, worked closely with the new President. During Wilson's administration fifteen out of seventeen Senate committees were led by Southern chairmen. These senators helped to formulate Wilson's domestic program and steer it through Congress. The Federal Reserve Act was largely the work of three Southerners, including Wilson's Secretary of the Treasury, Carter Glass of Virginia. The Clayton Antitrust Act was sponsored by Henry Clayton of Alabama, and House Majority Leader Underwood led the fight for the tariff-revision bill.

Protest and Progress Wilson's Southern background also had less fortunate consequences, however. Segregation officially came to Washington under Wilson's regime. Governmental offices and other public facilities in the city were ordered segregated by race. In doing this, Wilson was only following a practice that had become common af-

---

[3]An injunction is a court order requiring or forbidding certain activities. Business and government have sometimes used the injunction as an antiunion weapon to prevent strikes.

ter Reconstruction. In the late nineteenth century, "Jim Crow" laws[4]—that is, laws keeping blacks and whites apart in all public places—were enacted throughout the South (with little protest from the North). In 1896, in the case of *Plessy* v. *Ferguson,* the Supreme Court ruled that "separate but equal" facilities were constitutional. The decision was based to some extent on pseudoscientific assumptions of the day shared by many middle-class progressives in both the North and South. They believed that blacks (as well as Southern and Eastern Europeans) were essentially inferior. With the approval of the court, white supremacy asserted itself, in segregated railroad cars, restaurants, schools, and other public facilities and institutions.

In the early twentieth century the problems of black Americans were brought to the nation's attention by a group of young black businessmen and professionals under the leadership of the great scholar W. E. B. DuBois. In 1905 they founded the militant Niagara Movement to press for an end to Booker T. Washington's policy of "accommodation" with whites. The leaders of the Niagara group sought a return to active agitation for complete political and civil equality of blacks with whites—the earlier goals of Radical Reconstruction.

Four years later, members of the Niagara Movement and white supporters of black civil rights formed the National Association for the Advancement of Colored People (NAACP). DuBois was appointed editor of the NAACP's journal, *The Crisis.* Active in the new organization were several reformers who would support the garment workers' strike that same year: Lillian Wald, Jane Addams, and publisher Oswald Garrison Willard (William Lloyd Garrison's grandson). The NAACP grew rapidly in the next decade. It quickly took the lead in opposing the segregationist policies of the Wilson administration.

Wilson found himself under growing pressure from other groups of reformers as his first term drew to a close. There seemed little chance that he could again slip into the White House

[4]The laws got their name from a song sung by Thomas Rice in a Negro minstrel show.

W. E. B. DuBois, the first black to receive a Ph.D. from Harvard, founded the NAACP to agitate for black political rights. When he died in 1963, his goals were beginning to be realized, though he himself, disheartened, had moved to Africa.

through a split in Republican ranks. Roosevelt had rejoined his party, and most Progressives were unhappy with Wilson's refusal to support social welfare legislation. Concerned over the political situation, Wilson began a determined campaign to win over reform-minded voters by pushing several progressive measures through Congress.

The Federal Farm Loan Act, passed in May 1916, aided domestic agriculture by expanding the credit resources of American farmers. The Adamson Act, passed the same year, provided an eight-hour day for railroad workers. The Kern-McGillicudy Act created a model workmen's compensation program for federal employees. In August of 1916 Congress attempted to deal with the problems of child labor by passing the Keating-Owen Act, which outlawed the interstate shipment of products manufactured by children under fourteen. (Two years later the law was declared unconstitutional.) Wilson nominated progressive lawyer Louis Brandeis to the Supreme Court and fought for his confirmation in Congress against conservative opposition. Brandeis became the first Jewish Supreme Court justice.

During the election of 1916 Democrats stressed Wilson's skill at maintaining American neutrality during the growing war in Europe (see Chapter 36). But it was the President's energetic sponsorship of reform measures that won him the support of the labor movement and most middle-class reformers. In a hard-fought campaign against Republican Charles Evans Hughes, Wilson won reelection by narrow popular and electoral margins. In his second term he devoted most of his attention to the problems of fighting a war and winning the peace. Domestic reform took a back seat to world affairs during Woodrow Wilson's last four years in office.

SUGGESTED READINGS-CHAPTERS 33-34

Triangle Fire

Leon Stein, *The Triangle Fire* (1962); Daniel Aaron, *Men of Good Hope: A Story of American Progessives* (1951); Irving Howe, *World of Our Fathers: The Journey of the East European Jews to America* (1976); Moses Rischin, *The Promised City: New York's Jews, 1870–1914* (1960); Charles E. Zaretz, *The Amalgamated Clothing Workers* (1934).

Synthesis and Interpretations

Samuel P. Hays, *Response to Industrialism, 1885–1914* (1957); Richard Hofstadter, *The Age of Reform* (1955); Gabriel Kolko, *The Triumph of Conservatism* (1963); Christopher Lasch, *The New Radicalism in America* (1965); Henry F. May, *Protestant Churches and Industrial America* (1949) and *The End of American Innocence* (1959); Robert H. Wiebe, *The Search for Order, 1877–1920* (1968) and *Businessmen and Reform* (1962).

States and Cities

Robert H. Bremner, *From the Depths: The Discovery of Poverty in the United States* (1956); Roy Lubove, *The Progressives and the Slums: Tenement House Reform in New York City, 1890–1917* (1962); Zane L. Miller, *Boss Cox's Cincinnati* (1968); Irwin Yellowitz, *Labor and the Progressive Movement in New York* (1965).

Roosevelt, Taft, and Wilson

George E. Mowry, *The Era of Theodore Roosevelt, 1900–1912* (1958); John Blum, *The Republican Roosevelt* (1954); William H. Harbourgh, *The Life and Times of Theodore Roosevelt* (1961); Donald F. Anderson, *William Howard Taft* (1973); Arthur S. Link, *Woodrow Wilson and the Progressive Era* (1954) and *Wilson* (5 vols., 1947–1965).

The Progressive Movement

Samuel P. Hays, *Conservation and the Gospel of Efficiency* (1959); Philip Taft, *The A. F. of L. in the Time of Gompers* (1957); Gabriel Kolko, *Railroads and Regulation, 1877–1916* (1965); Richard Lowitt, George W. Norris, *Making of a Progressive* (1963); William O'Neill, *The Progressive Years* (1975) and *Divorce in the Progressive Era* (1967); David Thelen, *Robert La Follette and the Insurgent Spirit* (1976); Blake McKelvey, *The Urbanization of America 1860–1915* (1963).

Progressive Journalism

Richard Hofstadter, *The Progressive Historians* (1968); David W. Noble, *The Paradox of Progressive Thought* (1958); Charles Forcey, *Crossroads of Liberalism* (1961); Justin Kaplan, *Lincoln Steffens* (1974); David M. Chalmers, *Social and Political Ideas of the Muckrakers* (1964).

Reform Movements

Roy Lubove, *The Professional Altruist: The Emergence of Social Work as a Career, 1880–1930* (1965); James H. Timberlake, *Prohibition and the Progressive Movement* (1963); David Kennedy, *Birth Control in America: The Career of Margaret Sanger* (1970); Lawrence Cremin, *The Transformation of the School: Progressivism in American Education* (1961); Eleanor Flexner, *Century of Struggle: The Women's Rights Movement in the United States* (1974); Jeremy P. Felt, *Hostages of Fortune: Child Labor Reform* (1965).

35
THE PHILIPPINES REVOLT

A.W.

At age thirty, Emiliano Aguinaldo was a seasoned revolutionary. The son of a prosperous farmer from the island of Luzon, he was a member of the Katipunan, the Filipino movement for independence. In August 1896, Aguinaldo joined a revolt against Spain, which had held the Philippines as a colony since the sixteenth century. Two months later the rebels proclaimed the existence of the Tagal Republic. When the first president of the republic died, Aguinaldo became president and commander in chief of the insurgent forces.

But revolutionary organization and high-sounding titles alone could not defeat the Spanish in the field. Nor could Spain's colonial power crush the rebels. In December 1897, after more than a year of seesaw guerrilla warfare, both sides recognized the stalemate and signed a treaty.

Spain, apprehensive over the threats posed to its Caribbean empire by rebellion in Cuba and political unrest in Puerto Rico, agreed to consider reforms in the Philippines. In turn, Aguinaldo and other leaders of the rebellion agreed to leave their country for three years. They went to Hong Kong, a British colony on the southern coast of China. Meanwhile, the Spanish deposited 400,000 pesetas in a Hong Kong bank in the rebels' name. If Spain enacted the promised reforms, this trust fund would be used to educate Filipinos abroad. If Spain failed, the insurgents could use the money to buy arms and resume the war.

The Filipinos soon became convinced that they had been tricked. Spanish Governor-General Miguel Primo de Rivera did not declare a general amnesty, as expected. Reforms acceptable to the rebels did not come to pass. The trust fund that rested in Hong Kong now seemed to the rebels to be no more than hush money, a bribe to silence Filipino leaders. From their headquarters in the British colony, the insurgents began planning for future campaigns.

The American destruction of the Spanish fleet in Manila Bay on May 1, 1898, brought the United States into an era of overseas expansion. Gaining the Philippines from Spain proved easier than winning the loyalties of the Filipino people, as events of the next four years would show.

During this period, rebellion in Cuba brought on a crisis in Spanish-American relations. (Americans and their government were sympathetic to freedom movements in Latin America.) As Spain and the United States moved closer to war, the Filipino rebels thought about an alliance with the United States. Then, in April 1898, Aguinaldo was told that the American consul in Singapore, W. Spencer Pratt, wanted to discuss important matters of interest to both countries. The Filipino agreed to meet with Pratt in Singapore.

The Aguinaldo-Pratt talks took place in the Raffles Hotel, legendary center of "East Asian intrigue" and British colonial power at the turn of the century. Pratt claimed that Spain had broken the terms of the truce. He urged Aguinaldo to resume the rebellion. The consul added some important news: "As of the other day, Spain and America have been at war. Now is the time for you to strike. Ally yourselves with America, and you will surely defeat the Spaniards!"

Aguinaldo was clearly interested in this proposal, but he remained cautious: "What can we expect to gain from helping America?" Pratt assured him: "America will give you much greater liberty and many more material benefits than the Spanish ever promised you." When Aguinaldo asked whether such an arrangement could be put in writing, Pratt sidestepped. He obviously had no authority to speak for Washington. Yet he continued to offer verbal assurances.

Consul Pratt also told Aguinaldo that he would try to arrange for the rebels to be transported to Manila on American ships. Pratt contacted Commodore George Dewey, commander of the United States Pacific

Commodore George Dewey created the conditions for United States involvement in protracted guerrilla warfare in the Philippines. He needed Filipino help to defeat Spain but did not reckon with Filipino nationalist feelings after the conflict.

fleet in Hong Kong. The cable to Dewey read: "Aguinaldo, insurgent leader, here. Will come Hong Kong. Arrange with Commodore for general cooperation insurgents Manila if desired." The Yankee sailor answered quickly and tersely: "Tell Aguinaldo come as soon as possible." When informed of Dewey's okay, Aguinaldo promised that if his forces obtained sufficient arms the Filipino people would rise against the Spanish. Pratt, seldom at a loss for reassuring words, told him that Dewey felt that "the United States would at least recognize the independence of the Philippines under the protection of the United States Navy."

Commodore Dewey never met with Aguinaldo before the United States Pacific squadron sailed for Manila. A few years later he denied all knowledge of a political deal. Dewey dismissed Consul Pratt as a "busybody interfering with other people's business," a man whose letters he simply filed and ignored. Toward the Filipinos, Dewey adopted a paternal and disapproving stance. "They seemed to be all very young, earnest boys," he recalled. "I did not attach much importance to what they said or to themselves."

Certainly Dewey did not believe the rebels' boasts that they already had 30,000 armed men in the Philippines, with many more available. Why then did Dewey agree to take Aguinaldo and other Filipino leaders to Manila? By his own account, to get rid of them. "They were bothering me. I was very busy getting my squadron ready for battle, and these little men were coming aboard my ship at Hong Kong and taking a good deal of my time." So he consented to transport the rebels, though in the end only one Filipino went along.

Despite his denials, Dewey did want something from the Filipinos. He needed troops to occupy Manila and other parts of the Philippines if and when he defeated the Spanish navy. Aguinaldo and his followers might help Dewey accomplish the job.

On May 1, 1898, American forces defeated the Spanish navy in Manila Bay. The spectacular victory reaffirmed the rise of American military power on the world scene. The United States squadron blew the remnants of the decaying Spanish navy out of the water. (Some of Spain's ships were hulks, rotting at dockside, with guns that would not function.) Within a few hours it was over. Spain no longer ruled the Philippines. Yet Manila remained to be captured and occupied. The Spanish army had not been routed, nor had its commander indicated a willingness to surrender.

The victory at Manila Bay reopened the question of Dewey's need for Filipino support. From his ships Dewey could do nothing. Spanish artillerymen had allowed Dewey to anchor close to Manila's shore, but the commodore was reluctant to subject the city to a prolonged bombardment. Moreover, his small Marine battalion was an insufficient landing force. The commodore felt that with 5,000 troops he could end the war in one day. But he did not have 5,000 troops. Insurgent Filipinos were the only immediately available source of military manpower.

Early in May, Dewey sent for the rebel leader. Aguinaldo and a dozen of his associates arrived from Hong Kong in Manila on a United States Navy auxiliary vessel. Within a few days Dewey and Aguinaldo met for the first time. Their versions of the encounter are as different as the men themselves.

According to Aguinaldo, the American commander repeated the familiar assurances about American disdain for acquiring colonies and its support of Filipino independence. Dewey also requested that the insurgents resume fighting. He supplied them with sixty-two rifles and some abandoned Spanish naval guns. The United States commander stressed that all promises were guaranteed "by the word of honor of Americans." Finally, Aguinaldo claimed that Dewey instructed him to have a Filipino national flag prepared. It would be hoisted as soon as Spain surrendered.

Dewey presented an equally questionable account of the events. Shortly after meeting with Aguinaldo, Dewey claimed, the secretary of the navy instructed him to avoid entangling the United States in alliances with the Filipino insurgents. Dewey complied because he was bound by obedience and because he did not like the insurgents. He had little faith in their cause. He considered the soft-spoken Aguinaldo an "unimpressive little man," though he recognized the Filipino's enormous prestige among his people.

Dewey admitted that the insurgents might be of service in clearing the shoreline from the naval base of Cavite, which the Americans had now occupied, to Manila City. Thus he allowed the rebels to enter the Cavite arsenal. But he warned that Filipinos and Americans should keep at a distance from each other. The United States commander continued to maintain that Aguinaldo had been forced on him by the barrage of pleas from the American consuls in Hong Kong and Singapore. Dewey also insisted that he never believed the Filipinos wanted independence. How could they? Aguinaldo "considered me as his liberator, as his friend."

Friend would soon become foe, and Aguinaldo himself bore some of the blame for his later disillusionment with the United States. During his months of exile in Hong Kong and his first few weeks back in the Philippines, Aguinaldo seemed to accept everything the Americans promised. His proclamations and public letters of the time praised the United States in lavish terms.

The distance that Dewey sought to create between himself and Aguinaldo was quickly established. American officers had begun complaining about the many Filipinos inside the Cavite naval base. These "natives," they argued, might be friends or foes. So Dewey told Aguinaldo that he and his men must leave the arsenal but could remain in the town of Cavite. From its headquarters in the town, the Aguinaldo movement grew. Enlistees poured in, many of them armed with captured Spanish rifles.

On May 21 Aguinaldo felt militarily strong enough to issue a proclamation outlining his ultimate aims: "Everything appears favorable for attaining independence. The hour has arrived for the Philippines to be-

Emilio Aguinaldo was evaluated differently by his enemies and his own people. To Dewey he was at first a nuisance and later an "Oriental despot." To the Filipinos, however, he symbolized their hope for independence.

long to her sons." Aguinaldo advised his men to fight a "civilized" war, warning that "if we do not conduct ourselves thus, the Americans will decide to sell us or else divide up our territory, as they will hold us incapable of governing our land." Like it or not, Aguinaldo knew, the Filipinos would have to deal with the United States.

Throughout May, Manila remained in Spanish hands. The Americans had made no commitments to the rebels, but United States troops were on the way. In June the Filipino insurgents announced the establishment of a provisional government and issued a declaration of independence.

On June 23, Aguinaldo dissolved the dictatorship and declared himself president of the revolutionary government. In an effort to win support from the United States and other nations, the Filipinos promised to work for two primary goals: independence and the establishment of a representative, republican government.

By the time Aguinaldo formally declared independence, he and his forces controlled most of Cavite province and almost surrounded Manila. From the panic-stricken city, Dewey received requests from Spanish officials to help evacuate foreign and Spanish civilians, as well as wounded soldiers. Some were placed aboard foreign ships in the harbor. Aguinaldo, mindful of the need to wage war in a manner approved by Europeans, allowed civilians and wounded soldiers to pass through his lines. His cooperative spirit reached its height in mid-July when he helped pick the spot for a landing of United States soldiers. Thanks to the insurgents' advice, admitted Dewey, "we were able to land our troops within easy striking distance of their objective," a position more than halfway between Cavite and Manila.

But American gratitude did not mean acceptance of the Filipino forces as a political entity. According to Dewey, in fighting their way up the coast and surrounding Manila, the insurgents had merely prepared "a foothold for our troops when they should arrive." American army units, under General Wesley Merritt, entered Manila on June 30. From then on, the war against Spain became an exclusively American affair.

American soldiers quickly moved to replace the Filipinos in the trenches dug near the Manila fortifications. One of General Merritt's officers tried to convince the insurgents to pull out of the line and turn their trenches over to the Americans. In return he offered to supply the rebels with cannon and other artillery. The local Filipino commander consulted Aguinaldo. Aguinaldo would comply, but only if the request and the offer were put in writing. This concession demonstrated the Filipino leader's desperate desire for legal recognition of his government's standing. Pull out first—then we will furnish the paper, answered the Americans. Aguinaldo ordered his troops out of the trenches. But they never saw the cannon, nor did their commander receive written confirmation. Once again, as in Cavite, Aguinaldo had yielded to an American request under American pressure. This decision proved extremely costly to the rebel cause.

With insurgent forces neutralized and Aguinaldo's political status in doubt, the American capture of Manila proceeded swiftly and with little bloodshed. On August 13 the city capitulated. The United States now ruled the Philippines. On August 17 a War Department dispatch said that Filipino insurgents would not form part of the occupation forces:

> The United States, in possession of Manila City, Manila Bay and harbor, must preserve the peace and protect persons and property within the territory occupied by the military and naval forces. The insurgents and all others must recognize the military occupation and authority of the United States.

What was in store for the Philippines beyond the period of military occupation? In Washington, President McKinley began the process of reconciling the facts of conquest with the arguments of territorial expansionists. At first McKinley opposed taking all of the Philippines, though he held open the possibility that the situation might change. The President favored keeping Luzon, the large island in the northern part of the archipelago, and establishing a United States naval base at Manila. McKinley wished to show Europe that "a lofty spirit" guided American actions. But he also supported the "general principle of holding on to what we get."

These statements reflect McKinley's personality and his tactical approach to political decision making. The President worked hard to create the impression that he was forced to act. He wanted to make it appear that public opinion and the pressure of events directed the outcome of the Philippine conflict. In reality, as McKinley surely realized, the decision to take Manila made full-scale American involvement in the Philippines unavoidable.

The Treaty of Paris, which ended the Spanish-American War, was signed on December 10, 1898. Spain agreed to grant Cuba independence and to cede Puerto Rico and the tiny Pacific island of Guam to the United States. The United States also received the Philippine Islands, for which it paid Spain $20 million. "A goodly estate indeed!" crowed the head of the American delegation. He wrote President McKinley: "Perhaps the treaty may be an acceptable Christmas offering to you from the American commission."

During the negotiations between the United States and Spain, Aguinaldo tried desperately to gain legal standing for his revolutionary government. On August 6, shortly before Manila capitulated, he issued a memorandum to all foreign powers. It asked recognition of the belligerent status of the insurgents, a first step toward full diplomatic recognition. It also sought support for their ultimate aim of independence. Claiming to control fifteen provinces—an assertion not far from the truth at the time—and that the 9,000 Spanish prisoners in his hands were being treated with the "same consideration observed by cultured nations," Aguinaldo declared that the Philippines had "arrived at that state in which it can and ought to govern itself." But other countries refused to recognize the rebels. Nor did the United States indicate a willingness to consider Philippine independence seriously. Filipino insurgents were not America's allies, stated a directive from Washington. They had merely cooperated with Americans "against a common enemy."

Under these circumstances, tension between Americans and Filipinos mounted. In December 1898, President McKinley sent a message to the new military commander in the Philippines, General Elwell S. Otis. The President assured Otis that the United States wished to pursue a policy of "benevolent assimilation" in the islands and bestow the "blessings of good and stable government." But he warned Otis that all obstacles to achieving these ends were to be removed. Before publishing McKinley's message, General Otis cut out several sections critical of the Filipino rebels. When a junior United States officer in the city of Iloilo mistakenly printed the entire text, Filipino resentment grew.

The insurgents' reactions in January 1899 were firm but still friendly. Aguinaldo rejected the American claim to rule his country and accused the United States of betraying a loyal ally. In the United States another Filipino leader, Felipe Agconcillo, tried to reason with the new colonial power in terms of its own declared ideals: "I cannot believe that in any possible action on the part of the American republic toward my country there is an intention to ignore, as to the ten millions of human beings I represent, the right of free government." He concluded his memo with the warning that the accidental or impetuous act of one Filipino or American soldier might trigger a full-scale war.

On February 4, 1899, just such an act occurred. An American soldier on guard duty near Manila challenged a Filipino to halt. When the Filipino disobeyed, the sentry shot and killed him. Fighting between Americans and Filipinos, confined during the previous six months to isolated incidents, broke out all along the outskirts of Manila. The war was on. And as even Dewey had to admit: "Perhaps the insurrection was bound to break out."

Inevitably, each side circulated conflicting reports about the incident. The Filipinos accused the Americans of deliberate provocation. They denied that they had initiated the attack, adding that they were unprepared and that several of their leaders were on leave. They also asserted that Aguinaldo had believed the initial exchange of shots to be accidental. The day after the incident, the rebels claimed, one of their generals proposed an immediate cease-fire to General Otis. But Otis rejected the offer, and ordered the fighting to continue "to the grim end."

McKinley responded with an equally one-sided account. First, he brushed off the cease-fire claim: "There appears to have been no such application." Second, McKinley claimed, no American officer had promised the rebels independence.

Throughout the war, American military leaders tried to downgrade the enemy. American officials viewed Aguinaldo as a bandit, who robbed his own people and lived in luxury on the proceeds of his looting. Whatever Aguinaldo's shortcomings, he remained the leading Filipino insurgent for two years, the chief symbol of resistance to colonial power and of hope for independence.

General Otis, who predicted a quick and easy suppression of the rebellion, failed at the job. Otis boasted that his 21,000 troops would crush the insurgents in a few weeks. He repeated this promise with depressing regularity for the next twelve months. The gap between his fantasies and the realities of the Philippine war can be measured by the increased number of troops the general soon demanded. Shortly after the outbreak he had asked for 35,000. A year later he had 70,000 men and wanted 30,000 more.

In the spring of 1899, the United States Army drove northward from Manila to occupy—or pacify, as the government called it—the island of Luzon, center of Tagal resistance. In April, American forces captured the insurgent capital of Malolos. Aguinaldo and his followers fled farther north. But in mid-May they had to give up their provisional capital at San Isidro. Then, instead of mounting an all-out American attack, General Otis halted the advance. The rainy season had just begun, and many of the troops were scheduled for immediate return home. So Otis, a cautious field commander, suspended military operations.

Back in the White House McKinley remained optimistic. He assured Theodore Roosevelt that "Otis had things entirely in hand and that the insurrection would be speedily put down certainly after the opening of the dry season."

THE PHILIPPINES REVOLT, 1896-1902

AGUINALDO CAPTURED MARCH 1901 — Palanan

✈ Battle

0   MILES   200

LUZON

AGUINALDO PUT ASHORE
APRIL 30, 1898

San Isidro
Malolos

SPANISH FLEET DESTROYED — MANILA TAKEN AUGUST 13, 1898
MAY 1, 1898   CAVITE
MANILA BAY   BATANGAS

PHILIPPINE
ISLANDS

SOUTH CHINA
SEA

SAMAR

PACIFIC OCEAN

PANAY
Iloilo   LEYTE   Balangiga
LEYTE GULF
CEBU
NEGROS
BOHOL

PARAGUA

MORO
TRIBE

SULU SEA   MINDANAO

SULU
ISLANDS   CELEBES SEA

In the meantime, the Schurman Commission, a mixed civilian-military commission headed by the president of Cornell University, Jacob Schurman, was formed to investigate conditions in the Philippine Islands. A preliminary report, issued in the fall of 1899, found much to praise in the Filipinos. It expressed great interest in the islands' natural resources and potential for economic growth. But the report stressed that immediate self-government was out of the question and that the American presence must continue, to ensure peace and order. The commissioners concluded: "Whatever the future of the Philippines may be, there is no course open to us now except the prosecution of the war until the insurgents are reduced to submission." The report delighted McKinley.

Most Americans agreed that Filipinos were unprepared for self-government. Some, like Republican Senator George F. Hoar of Massachusetts, protested that Filipinos should be left to govern themselves, whatever the results. But the majority felt otherwise. They predicted that an American pullout would quickly produce internal wars and anarchy. This they were sure would be followed just as quickly by the intervention of other foreign powers. Theodore Roosevelt hoped that Filipinos might be able to govern themselves at some future, undeter-

Combat in the Philippines was particularly grueling. Fought in jungle terrain against twin unseen enemies—the guerrilla insurgents and disease—the war produced over 7,000 American casualties.

mined date. But he warned that the "consent-of-the-governed doctrine must not be pushed to an extent that would restore savagery."

William Howard Taft, at the time a federal judge, later went to the Philippines as the first American governor. He expounded on the theory of Filipino inferiority. In 1902 the Senate committee investigating the war asked Taft whether Filipinos were in fact so ignorant that a few leaders could easily misguide them. Taft replied: "That is quite possible, and that is one of the chief reasons why the Filipino people are utterly unfit for self-government." Americans had to lead the way, Taft asserted, for the Filipinos lacked any knowledge of how to carry on a government. The United States could not remain "blind to their serious defects, many of which are due to the environment, social and political, which has been presented by their history of three hundred years."

General Robert P. Hughes spoke more bluntly. In referring to one of the Filipino ethnic groups, he testified: "These people do not know what independence means. They probably think it is something to eat. They have no more idea what it means than a shepherd dog."

The suspension of American offensive operations in the spring of 1899 gave Aguinaldo and his followers time to regroup—and make a key decision. The insurgents knew they could not defeat the rapidly growing United States forces in conventional warfare. From then on, Aguinaldo and his staff decided, Filipino rebels would engage in guerrilla tactics. In order to succeed, they would have to depend on their own countrymen's support, voluntary or forced, and on their ability to blend in with the civilian population.

Aguinaldo's tactical switch posed new and serious problems for the United States Army. When a later American general, Arthur MacArthur, resumed his northward advance in Luzon in October 1899, his men had trouble distinguishing friend from foe among the Filipinos. The guerrillas tried to wear down the enemy by ambushing American patrols and firing at night into towns occupied by United States troops. Along the trails between villages, Filipino rebels set booby traps—pits lined with sharpened bamboo spears and covered with foliage. General Hughes complained: "As to actual engagements, there were very few. It was very hard to get an engagement of any kind. You could get what we would call a little skirmish, and probably there would be ten or twelve killed."

Though Americans denied that the Filipino army had any legal standing, guerrilla prisoners were not automatically executed as rebels. Instead, a generous American amnesty policy for the insurgents allowed for a decent gap between the official United States position and the actual treatment of those Filipinos who wished to surrender.

Many insurgents did surrender and swear allegiance to the United States. Some even joined American troops to crush the rebels. Combat reports often mentioned the Macabebe soldiers. They were Filipinos who fought with and supported the United States throughout the war. But American officials in the Philippines rejected the idea of forming an all-Filipino regiment. "To put in command of a Filipino a thousand men with a thousand rifles would not be wise," warned Taft. Still, many Filipinos cooperated with the Americans, and, as in most wars, the majority of the population remained uninvolved. These facts bolstered the American argument that Aguinaldo and his forces actually hurt the Filipinos more than anyone else.

Filipinos who continued to resist and rejected the American offer of amnesty received rough treatment. Captured insurgent leaders were shipped to Guam, and "enlisted men" were imprisoned. For a short while, Americans even set up security camps for Filipino civilians. (This same tactic, when employed by Spain in Cuba, had enraged the American public.) In the insurrectionary province of Batangas, American officials ordered a ban on all trade, hoping that wealthy Filipinos who supported the insurgents would yield to the pressure.

In the field, United States soldiers routinely burned Filipino villages. Sergeant Leroy Hallock testified that he had participated in the burning of a village of over 3,000 people. He claimed that he had heard of other burnings, including a town of 10,000 inhabitants. Another enlisted man recalled: "If a column was marching along and was fired upon, it was the practice to burn the buildings in that neighborhood. That impressed the natives with the fact that they could not fire upon us with

War atrocities committed by Americans, such as the burning of the native district of Manila in 1899, caused divisions of popular sentiment at home. Mark Twain suggested bitterly that the field of stars on the flag be "replaced by a skull and crossbones."

impunity, although they did not often do very great damage." No specific orders had been issued authorizing such indiscriminate reprisals, but they continued.

The issue that stirred the most controversy during the Philippine war, both in the islands and in the United States, was the "water cure." This was a method of torturing prisoners by forcing them to swallow enormous quantities of water. The water cure apparently became the standard means of obtaining information from rebel prisoners and civilians suspected of aiding the enemy. Charles S. Riley, an enlisted man from Massachusetts, described repeated attempts to question the *presidente*, or mayor, of a Filipino village:

> One of the men of the Eighteenth Infantry went to his saddle and took a syringe from the saddlebag, and another man was sent for a can of water . . . holding about five gallons. Then a syringe was inserted, one end in the water and the other end in his mouth. The water was forced into his mouth from the can, through the syringe. The syringe did not seem to have the desired effect, and the [army] doctor ordered a second one, and a handful of salt was thrown into the water. The interpreter stood over him in the meantime asking for information. Finally he gave in and gave the information.

When reports of such atrocities began to leak out in the American press, officials disavowed them. But William Howard Taft added the final irony in this unsuccessful attempt by American civil and military officials to deny the facts, unpleasant but true, of widespread torture: "There never was a war conducted," insisted Taft, "whether against inferior races or not, in which there was more compassion and more restraint and more generosity than there have been in the Philippine Islands."

Early in 1900 the superior military strength of the United States forces began to make itself felt. In May, General Otis resigned rather

Filipino guerrillas were not highly regarded as soldiers by the American military. General Arthur MacArthur claimed that they "could not hit a stack of barns" with their guns. But it took 70,000 American troops three years to defeat them.

Frederick Funston reaped most of the acclaim for the capture of Aguinaldo, including a Medal of Honor. But, although the plan was his, it was the Tagals and the Macabebes who actually captured the Filipino rebel leader.

than work under the all-civilian Taft Commission, which had been sent to Manila to set up a civil government. Otis's replacement, General Arthur MacArthur, already on the scene, harried the Filipino guerrillas whenever and wherever he could find them.

But the biggest setback for the insurgents' cause came with the capture of Aguinaldo himself. During late 1900 and early 1901, Aguinaldo's whereabouts remained a mystery. Some American military men and journalists began circulating rumors of his death. MacArthur knew better. In February 1901, United States troops captured an insurgent soldier carrying dispatches from Aguinaldo to rebel officers in the field. The messages did not pinpoint the location of rebel headquarters, but they indicated that the captive knew where to find Aguinaldo. Interrogation began, and before long the courier talked: Aguinaldo could be found in the village of Palanan, in the mountains of Luzon near the northeast coast.

But how could the Americans get to Aguinaldo? Thirty-six-year-old Brigadier General Frederick Funston, head of a volunteer regiment from Kansas, had a plan. The intercepted messages called for the movement of small groups of rebel reinforcements toward Aguinaldo's headquarters. Funston decided to use eighty Macabebe scouts pretending to be rebel reinforcements. He and four other American officers would go along, supposedly as prisoners. One additional and crucial element remained: several Tagals loyal to the United States would be needed to pose as leaders of the expedition. Funston found three such men; the messenger who had been captured was to be their guide. General MacArthur gave his approval to the plan, but with misgivings. Instead of wishing Funston well, he remarked: "I fear I shall never see you again."

The march to Palanan proved more difficult than the capture itself. The expeditionary force landed by gunboat on the east coast of Luzon, about a hundred miles from its objective. In heavy rain, the men had to struggle for several days across rough terrain near the shoreline and then through dense jungle. It had been decided, for reasons Funston never made clear, that the Tagal officers and the Macabebes would enter the village about an hour before the Americans.

On March 23, 1901, the Macabebes arrived in the rebel camp. They were relieved to find only a handful of insurgent soldiers to greet them. The Tagal officers entered rebel headquarters to confer with Aguinaldo and his staff. As the conversation wore on, all but two of the insurgent officers drifted out of the room. An expedition officer leaned out of the window to give the Macabebes the signal to open fire. Aguinaldo, thinking that his own men were firing in the air to welcome the fresh troops, rushed to the window to tell them to stop wasting ammunition. At that point one of the Tagal officers seized Aguinaldo. The others opened fire on the insurgent guards. It was all over before Funston and his American companions arrived.

At the sound of the firing, Funston had rushed to the rebel headquarters. Aguinaldo now asked if the "capture" was some kind of joke.

When Funston identified himself, Aguinaldo's shoulders drooped in resignation and defeat. On March 28 the group returned to Manila. Aguinaldo was imprisoned in the governor's mansion. When General MacArthur arrived, ever skeptical, he asked Funston: "Where is Aguinaldo?" Funston was able to reply triumphantly: "Right in this house."

Aguinaldo had sworn many times that he would never be taken alive. For several weeks American officers pressured him to swear an oath of allegiance to the United States. On April 19 he agreed to take the oath. He promised to issue a proclamation calling on Filipinos to lay down their arms in order to avoid further bloodshed. Aguinaldo's declaration suddenly made him a hero in American eyes. The *New York Times*, which had once described Aguinaldo as an "enslaver" and a "criminal aggressor," now found him to be "honest and sincere," a "natural leader of men with considerable shrewdness and ability."

On July 4, 1901, Taft took over as civil governor of the Philippines. He left a revealing account of his reception in Manila: "The populace that we expected to welcome us was not there, and I cannot describe the coldness of the army officers and the army men who received us any better than by saying that it somewhat exceeded the coldness of the populace."

Still, the rebellion—the ill-fated and barely understood war of national liberation—continued. Its center shifted southward to the island of Mindanao. The inhabitants of the island were Moros. They were Moslems who opposed the American presence but had never accepted the authority of the Tagals in Manila. Fire fights and armed conflict broke out. One fire fight in northern Mindanao left ten Americans dead and forty wounded. Fighting between American troops and Moro rebels continued off and on for another twelve years.

In the meantime, the "unfriendly" island of Samar exploded. Company C of the regular Ninth United States Infantry was stationed on the island in the fishing village of Balangiga. Hundreds of Filipino workmen, supposedly loyal to the United States, fell on the Americans with

More than 20,000 Filipino insurgents died in the three-year conflict—and independence was not achieved.

knives, bolos (machetes), and bare hands. A few soldiers escaped in a boat to another island. They were the only survivors. The massacre at Balangiga would not be forgotten. For the next six months American troops called for revenge, in the same way that a previous generation of American soldiers had sought to avenge Custer's defeat at the Little Bighorn.

Major Littleton Waller of the Marines received the punitive assignment. The area commander, General Jacob ("Hell-Roaring Jake") Smith, told Waller that he wanted the Samar rebellion ended quickly. Smith ordered Waller to remove all Filipino civilians from the island's interior and place them in stockades. Those who resisted, especially those capable of bearing arms, were to be considered enemies and shot. Waller asked what the cutoff point was. Anyone more than ten years old, replied Smith. Waller and his men did as they were told.

The pacification of Batangas province followed the same script. Miguel Malvar, head of the revolutionary government there, had 5,000 men and was better organized than the rebels on Samar. The American general, J. Franklin Bell, an ambitious young man who only three years before had been a lieutenant, saw his chance and took it. He waged an intense campaign, herding thousands of civilians into security camps. In April 1902, after several months of dodging and fighting on the run, Malvar surrendered. The last sustained pocket of armed Filipino resistance had been eliminated.

The war between American troops and Filipino rebels had lasted more than three years. Countless Filipinos had lost their homes in the burning of towns and villages. Thousands of rebel soldiers had been killed or wounded in the fighting. The United States had not gained an easy victory. Almost as many Americans died in the Philippine conflict as in the war with Spain. And the rebellion had cost the United States $160 million, or eight times the "indemnity" paid to Spain for the islands.

On July 4, 1902, the United States government declared the Philippine insurrection officially over. President Roosevelt then sent a special message to the Army.

The President praised American soldiers for the rapid accomplishment of their mission, despite great hardships in more than 2,000 skirmishes and battles. Teddy Roosevelt was still mentally fighting Indians, for he went on to say: "Utilizing the lessons of the Indian wars [the army] relentlessly followed the guerrilla bands to their footholds in mountains and jungle and crushed them." With surprisingly few exceptions, the President maintained, American troops had been humane and kind to both prisoners and civilians. They had fought bravely against "a general system of guerrilla warfare conducted among a people speaking unknown tongues, from whom it was almost impossible to obtain the information necessary for successful pursuit or to guard against surprise and ambush." The army, declared Roosevelt, had added honor to the flag.

36
BECOMING A WORLD POWER

A. W.

By 1900 many Americans came to question the presence of American soldiers in the Philippines. Wasn't the war with Spain fought to liberate Cuba, an island ninety miles off the coast of Florida? Then why was the United States involved in places halfway around the globe? Whose interests were served by such overseas commitments? Answers to these questions lay tangled in the history of late nineteenth-century America and in the international power struggles of an imperialist age.

For most of the nineteenth century, Americans had been more than content to search for and use the wealth of their own country. America was their Garden of Eden. And although many of its products were sold overseas (much cotton went to Britain, for example), the United States had avoided foreign political ties. America had allied itself with a foreign power only once in its history — during the Revolutionary War, when it signed an alliance with France. Concerned with domestic problems and opportunities, Americans had concentrated on developing their own continent.

GAINING AN OVERSEAS EMPIRE

Two major factors helped to change this attitude and promote American interests overseas. First, domestic industry grew at an astounding rate dur-ing the second half of the nineteenth century. A massive and efficient transportation network was constructed across the American continent. Much of the country's agriculture was mechanized, and heavy industries were established. By 1900 the United States was the world's leading economic power, one that could play an influential role beyond its own territorial borders.

Second, the major nations of Europe had been scrambling for empire in Asia and Africa. They were carving up these two continents into colonial dependencies, much as Spain had done three centuries earlier in the New World. As the nineteenth century ended, Americans entered into the same race. American power was to expand not only into the Caribbean and the rest of Latin America but into the Far East as well.

Arguments for Empire Basically, the United States shunned overseas political involvement. But many Americans argued for commercial expansion during the late nineteenth century. Why shouldn't the United States seek additional markets for its agricultural products and manufactured goods? The periodic recessions and depressions in the decades following the Civil War reinforced the argument for commercial expansion. Many business leaders had begun to feel that domestic markets were saturated. The new industrial complex seemed to be producing more goods than Americans could buy. Substantial cuts in production were out of the question. They would only put large numbers of American workers and farmers out of work. In turn, unemployment might cause political unrest and social instability. Perhaps the surplus from American factories and farms could be channeled into enlarged and more profitable markets overseas.

Other expansionists argued for American imperialism on strategic grounds. The chief spokesman for this point of view was Alfred T. Mahan, a naval officer and instructor at the Naval War College. In 1890 Mahan advanced his theory in a series of lectures, which he later published as *The Influence of Sea Power on World History.* Mahan asserted that, through the ages, naval power had been primarily responsible for national or imperial power. He also held that no country

In this illustration Uncle Sam looks longingly over the sea and says, "The world is my market; my customers are all mankind." Industrial and agricultural growth encouraged the late nineteenth-century belief in the necessity of overseas outlets to absorb American surpluses.

could maintain commercial expansion without a strong navy and overseas ports (bases, for example, such as the Philippines and other Pacific islands).

Mahan's ideas quickly gained favor with imperialists in every major European country. More important, they also influenced several American foreign policy makers at the turn of the century. Chief among the American advocates of a strong navy were Roosevelt, McKinley's assistant secretary of the navy, and John Hay, who served as secretary of state under McKinley and later under Roosevelt himself.

Expansionism also had its defenders outside the business and military communities. Many Americans prided themselves on the myth of Anglo-Saxon racial superiority and the dominance of

U.S. FOREIGN TRADE, 1870 - 1910

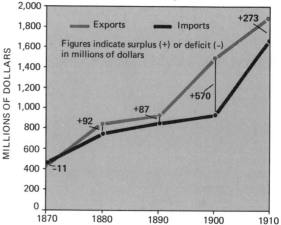

Western culture. For both selfish and humanitarian reasons, they argued that the United States had a moral duty to uplift and enlighten its less civilized neighbors. The culture and religion of the Anglo-Saxons should be exported to "heathen" lands for everyone's good. This spirit was captured in 1899 by the British poet of imperialism, Rudyard Kipling. His "White Man's Burden" was written and first published in the United States. It reflected the mood of many Americans who were then debating the virtues of keeping the Philippines.

Current theories of evolution seemed to support the claims of Anglo-Saxonists. In his book *Origin of Species* (1859) Charles Darwin argued that through the process of natural selection only the "fittest" would survive. Individual animal species might adapt and prosper while others declined and perhaps disappeared. So-called social Darwinists extended these generalizations to the domains of the social scientist, businessman, and politician. That is, individual nations and empires might attain greatness at the expense of their less fit neighbors. These ideas were powerful "scientific" supports for the missionary zeal of the expansionists.

Extending the Monroe Doctrine Although the United States moved cautiously and with uncertainty at first, it soon began to behave like a world power. Its debut on the world scene as a leading economic power provoked a great deal of controversy. But as the nineteenth century drew to a close, the prospect of increasing commercial activity abroad became highly attractive to American businessmen and politicians alike.

Even Grover Cleveland, who opposed acquiring new territories, supported commercial expansion. The severe depression that began during his second administration (1893–1897) gave the President added reason to seek foreign markets. Commercial expansion might cure some of America's economic ills. It might help the nation start its slow climb back to prosperity. But a drastic change would be needed in the pattern of America's overseas trading. Historically, farm products—not manufactured goods—had been the country's main export and source of foreign ex-

change. American business leaders began arguing for expanding the sale of industrial goods to non-industrialized countries such as China, the Philippines, and Latin American nations.

As early as 1889, Benjamin Harrison's secretary of state, James G. Blaine, had organized the first Pan American Congress, to promote American commerce in the Western Hemisphere and increase United States influence in Latin American affairs. During the 1890s a significant number of American businessmen responded to this opportunity by investing in Latin America. The United States thus began the process of replacing Britain as Latin America's major foreign investor. Both Harrison and Cleveland supported these efforts.

Cleveland's Latin American policy received a major test in 1895 when a crisis arose between Britain and Venezuela. The two nations disagreed over the boundary line between Venezuela and British Guiana. When the British threatened to use force against Venezuela, some Americans demanded that President Cleveland step in and apply the Monroe Doctrine to curb the European power. Stung by accusations of cowardice and beset by domestic problems, Cleveland decided to force a confrontation. He insisted that Britain submit to arbitration of the boundary dispute. Sensing that Cleveland was not bluffing, the British agreed.

The President's actions led to an important extension of the Monroe Doctrine: European powers could no longer resolve conflicts in the Western Hemisphere by military means. In a note to the British government, Secretary of State Richard Olney declared that the United States considered itself "practically sovereign" in this hemisphere. The will of the United States, Olney boasted, "is law." American industrial power and growing military and naval power made these phrases more than empty words.

The Problem of Cuba Another incidence of American expansionism concerned Cuba, the island ninety miles south of Florida. Americans have always been interested in Cuba. From the early decades of the republic, American politicians eyed the island with interest and greed. By the beginning of the nineteenth century, Spain had lost most of its overseas empire. The remnants of that empire—Cuba, Puerto Rico, and the Philippines—became all the more valuable to the Spanish as their power waned. During the second half of the nineteenth century, substantial American trade developed with the Spanish islands of the Caribbean. The situation appeared stable. But periodically groups of Americans called for absorbing Cuba, either by purchase or by force.

Cubans resented Spanish rule, which was repressive and corrupt. They had revolted unsuccessfully in the 1860s. By the 1890s they had had enough. At that time, the economic crisis in the United States had reduced the American sugar trade with Cuba. The Spanish island colony suffered sharply from the effects of the American depression. In 1895 a Cuban revolutionary movement called Cuba Libre ("Free Cuba") moved for independence. The Cuban rebels embarked on a new war of national liberation, a war similar to the revolution then under way against Spanish rule in the Philippines.

Neither Cuba Libre nor the Katipunan in the Philippines had sufficient strength to push out the Spanish without outside help. But Cuban rebels engaged in guerrilla warfare to wear down the Spanish soldiers. The Cubans also burned sugar plantations and anything else of value, hoping to drive out Spanish landowners. In response, Spanish officials set up reconcentrados, or "detention camps," for civilians suspected of helping the rebels. Thousands of Cubans died in the camps because of poor food, inadequate sanitation, and lack of medical attention.

The United States had been sympathetic but strictly neutral during the earlier Cuban revolution. But in the 1890s Americans gave increasing support to the Cuban rebels. A variety of factors led Americans toward direct intervention in Cuba. First, Americans had little sympathy for Spain and its culture. Many still believed in the "black legend."[1] Second, Spanish troops were committing atrocities. (Little did most Americans think that their own soldiers would shortly be act-

ing in a similar manner to suppress the Filipino revolt.) Third, many American businessmen had investments in Cuba, though these investments were small. Finally, an increasing determination among Americans to become the dominant Caribbean power made events in Cuba of vital concern to Washington.

The Cuban question soon became a leading issue in United States politics. During the 1896 presidential election year, Congress passed a resolution calling for recognition of the belligerent status of the Cuban rebels. President Cleveland, a Democrat who opposed territorial expansion, rejected the resolution. Cleveland's successor in the White House, Republican William McKinley, also opposed intervention in Cuba. McKinley was apparently less eager for expansion than most other members of his party. The Republican platform of 1896 was openly proexpansionist and favored involvement in the Caribbean. McKinley remained firm.

But events in Cuba and America's desire to impose its will in the Caribbean won over McKinley's promises. "Jingoism"—boastful patriotism—soon took hold of the nation. Two sensationalist New York City papers, William Randolph Hearst's *Journal* and Joseph Pulitzer's *World*, helped to stir up the interventionist frenzy. Both Hearst and Pulitzer ran stories, some of them deliberate lies, attacking Spanish cruelty in Cuba and praising the rebels. The stories spread to other newspapers across the country. By early 1898 it had become clear that Spain could not put down the Cuban rebellion. Nor would the United States allow the stalemate to continue much longer.

On the night of February 15, 1898, an explosion aboard the U.S.S. *Maine* in Havana harbor settled the issue of United States intervention. The battleship had been sent to Cuba to demonstrate American concern for the Cuban situation. The explosion killed 260 American sailors. Spain, which had the most to lose from American intervention in Cuba, hastily sent notes of regret to Washington. The cause of the explosion was never determined. But public opinion in the United States placed the blame squarely on the Spanish. "Remember the *Maine*" became the slogan of

[1] This was the English notion—dating back to the days of Queen Elizabeth and the defeat of the Spanish Armada—that the Spanish were a particularly cruel and treacherous people.

WALTER REED

The year 1900 had been called the year of yellow fever in Cuba. The Spanish-American War had brought thousands of American troops there. Now, with the war over, hundreds of men lay near death from the disease in Columbia Barracks in Havana. Doctors and nurses worked untiringly to try to save the victims, frustrated by lack of knowledge as to what caused the disease and how it was transmitted. Among them was a dedicated army doctor, Major Walter Reed.

On his return from Cuba, Reed strode into the office of the surgeon general of the United States Army in Washington, D.C., and requested that he be sent back to Cuba with the equipment and personnel needed to conduct a full study of the dangerous, often fatal disease known as yellow fever.

Walter Reed, a practicing doctor and a research scientist, was peculiarly suited to the task he sought. Born 1851 in Farmville, Virginia, he showed as a boy the love of knowledge, force of character, self-control, and sense of honor that marked his whole life. At sixteen he entered the University of Virginia by special permission. In nine months he graduated, third in his class. He then went to Bellevue Hospital Medical College in New York and received the degree of M.D. a year later.

After hospital experience and work as an inspector of the Board of Health in Brooklyn, Reed decided to enter the army as a surgeon in 1874. He wanted a future that would be secure, so that he could carry on scientific research. The examinations for a commission in the Army Medical Corps were notoriously difficult, but he passed them brilliantly in 1875.

He was commissioned in February 1875, married on April 25, 1876, and left immediately for his station in Arizona. Thus began several years of garrison duty at army posts in the West. In 1890 he was assigned to duty in Baltimore and this gave him the opportunity for special studies in bacteriology at Johns Hopkins University. Up to the time he began his investigations into yellow fever, his most important work had been the study of typhoid fever in army camps during the Spanish-American War. One of the conclusions of this study was that the common house fly is a typhoid carrier.

Now he urgently wanted to discover how yellow fever was transmitted. The theory then accepted was that a person caught the disease upon coming into contact with the clothing or bedding of an infected person. Dr. Reed did not agree. Several clues had been uncovered leading to the possibility that a certain kind of mosquito carried the disease and infected people with its bite.

Soon his orders came through. He was to return to Cuba to organize and direct the work of three doctors. Reed and his group set up the experimental situation. In one building, volunteers slept on bedding that had been in contact with yellow fever victims. In another, volunteers lived in uncontaminated surroundings but were exposed to the suspected mosquitoes. Those bitten by the mosquitoes did contract yellow fever. The culprit was proved to be a mosquito of the species *Aedes aegypti*.

Armed with the knowledge that the mosquito was the culprit, United States sanitary engineers launched on the Herculean task of cleaning up the filth in and around Havana in which the mosquitoes bred. They were so successful that by 1902 there was not one case of yellow fever in Cuba. It was also eradicated from the United States, where epidemics had struck periodically on the eastern seaboard. And when work began on the Panama Canal, the mosquito-control measures taken there removed the workers from the peril of yellow fever.

American interventionists. The United States government began to pressure Spain to grant Cuba independence. But Madrid would not accept the loss of its Cuban colony.

On April 11, 1898, McKinley sent a message to Congress, asking for authority to use American troops in Cuba. The President described Americans as "a Christian, peace-loving people" who still hoped to achieve a just solution through diplomacy rather than war. But Spain would not modify its position, even with the certainty of American armed intervention. By late April the two nations were at war.

War with Spain The Spanish-American War of 1898 was over within a few months. American forces dominated Spanish military and naval power. Spanish soldiers and sailors fought brave-

---

Military action in the Spanish-American War of 1898 occurred largely on two fronts, the Philippines and Cuba, although a brief and almost bloodless American invasion of Puerto Rico led to rapid surrender of the island's Spanish garrison. Hostilities commenced in the Pacific. The United States Asiatic Squadron under Commodore George Dewey sailed from Hong Kong in late April to attack the Spanish Philippines. On May 1 Dewey destroyed the Spanish naval force in Manila Bay with no loss of American lives.

In the Caribbean theater, the Spanish fleet under Admiral Pascual Cervera arrived in Santiago Harbor in May and was blockaded there by an American naval squadron. The blockade was reinforced June 1 under the command of Rear Admiral William T. Sampson. In late June, United States troops under General William R. Shafter landed in Cuba at Daiquiri and Siboney and marched on Santiago. This force included the Rough Riders, a volunteer cavalry regiment under Colonel Leonard Wood and Lieutenant Colonel Theodore Roosevelt. On July 1, the troops captured the heights north and east of Santiago in the battles of El Caney and San Juan Hill. They then began an artillery bombardment of Santiago.

On July 3, Admiral Cervera attempted to run the United States blockade and escape from Santiago harbor. But Sampson's force destroyed the entire Spanish fleet in a four-hour battle along the coast. The Spanish garrison of Santiago soon surrendered (July 17). Hostilities were ended in the Caribbean by July 25.

In the Pacific Dewey's naval squadron was reinforced in July by the arrival of American troops under General Wesley Merritt. On August 13, United States troops and Filipino guerrillas occupied the city of Manila.

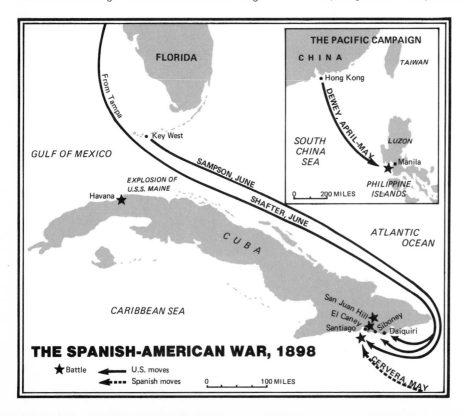

THE PACIFIC CAMPAIGN

THE SPANISH-AMERICAN WAR, 1898

★ Battle   → U.S. moves   ◄--- Spanish moves   0   100 MILES

ly, but they were hopelessly ill-equipped for war. Spain won no battles and suffered heavy losses. American casualties were light. Many more soldiers died from disease than from combat.

When the fighting ended in the summer of 1898, United States forces had won Cuba and Puerto Rico. In the Philippines, Dewey's squadron held Manila Bay while awaiting the arrival of American troops. Spanish officials reluctantly agreed to meet with American negotiators to hammer out a treaty that would end Spain's status as an imperial power.

During the short struggle, American expansionists achieved their longstanding wish of annexing Hawaii. In 1893 a revolutionary movement backed by American businessmen successfully overthrew the Hawaiian monarchy and sought annexation to the United States. But, like Texas between 1836 and 1845, Hawaii had to sit out a period of uneasy independence—five years—until United States politics entered into an expansionist phase. By mid-1898 annexationist forces had

gained a majority in the House and the Senate. Congress passed a joint resolution declaring Hawaii a territory of the United States.

When Spanish and American negotiators met in Paris to work out the terms of a peace, the fate of the Philippines had not yet been established. But all signs pointed to a continued American presence on the islands. President McKinley's stance of indecision fooled few people—least of all Emilio Aguinaldo and other Filipino leaders. The President had clearly been drawn into the expansionist camp. For several months McKinley played a waiting game while expansionist forces in the Senate gathered support for a Spanish-American treaty.

In the end, McKinley demanded what he had perhaps had in mind all along. Determined to "educate the Filipinos, and uplift and civilize and Christianize them," McKinley asked Spain to give up all of the Philippines. The Spanish had to agree. The Treaty of Paris was signed in December 1898. The United States gained control of

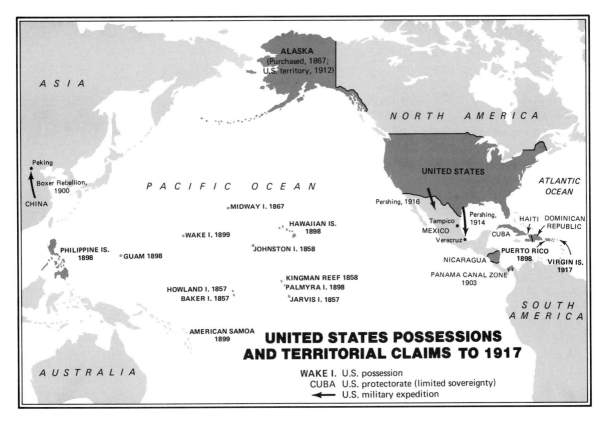

UNITED STATES POSSESSIONS
AND TERRITORIAL CLAIMS TO 1917

WAKE I. U.S. possession
CUBA U.S. protectorate (limited sovereignty)
⟵ U.S. military expedition

Cuba, the Philippine Islands, Guam, and Puerto Rico.

Most Americans had supported the war with Spain. But the Treaty of Paris, which proposed immediate acquisition of an American overseas empire, ran into stiff opposition. Many Americans feared that imperialism would tarnish American democracy at home by imposing arbitrary rule abroad upon alien peoples who were, in addition, nonwhite. (Racism, in short, played an important role in the anti-imperialist movement at the time.) Others objected to imperialism on moral grounds. Nations or cultures, they argued, should not be taken over by larger nations merely because they were too weak to resist. An anti-imperialist movement organized to fight the peace treaty. In the Senate many Democrats and a minority of Republicans opposed imperialism. William Jennings Bryan, the Democratic presidential candidate of 1896, led the antitreaty forces.

But at the last minute Bryan changed his course. The day before the vote on the treaty, fighting broke out between American troops and Filipino rebels. Americans regarded the uprising as a show of ingratitude on the part of the Filipinos. Bryan announced that the challenge had to be met firmly. He threw his support to the treaty, though he declared that he would continue to oppose imperialism. The Senate ratified the Treaty of Paris in February 1899. Bryan, who again opposed McKinley in the election of 1900, attempted to make imperialism the central issue of the campaign. Bryan and the Democrats were defeated overwhelmingly. The American people had voted for empire.

The Search for Asian Markets Early in the nineteenth century a few American businessmen had entered into a prosperous trade with China. But, even with the "opening" of Japan in the 1850s, the volume of United States trade in Asia never reached the proportions anticipated by American business leaders. By the end of the century, overproduction in America's factories generated new and powerful pressures for foreign trade. The lure of the China market made itself felt again.

But participation in the China market could not be accomplished without political involve-

ment in Asia. The European powers had already carved up China into "economic spheres of influence."[2] American businessmen believed they could compete successfully in China if they were given a fair opportunity. In September 1899, Secretary of State John Hay sent a series of diplomatic notes to Japan and the major European powers. In the notes he asked them to support a new trade policy in China. This policy became known as the Open Door. Hay recognized the existence of foreign spheres of influence in China, but he asked the European nations to grant other countries free-

---

[2]A nation often established with other nations a world area where it would hold a dominant economic position. Once other countries agreed to accept this arrangement, the area in question would be free from the competition of other nations.

This Chinese Boxer, a member of the society whose official title was the Fist of Righteous Harmony, believed that his country's survival depended upon expulsion of foreign powers threatening to divide China for economic profit. The Boxer Rebellion nearly led to the extinction of China as a national entity.

trade privileges within these spheres—thus keeping the Chinese door open to all who wanted to trade there. Hay also called on the European powers to guarantee Chinese "territorial integrity"—that is, to avoid outright political partition of the country. The European nations did not formally reject Hay's proposals, though some grumbled about American interference. Hay announced boldly that the Open Door was accepted by all, although he was too sanguine in this judgment.

While America was seeking support for its Open Door policies, a group of Chinese nationalists, called Boxers, organized to drive foreigners from their country. In 1900 they began killing foreign missionaries and diplomats. Survivors fled to Peking and the temporary safety of the British legation. There, they withstood a two-month siege until troops from their own countries relieved them. The United States participated by rushing in troops from bases in the Philippine Islands. The Boxer Rebellion was ended. Within a few months peace—and imperialism—were reestablished. In July, Hay issued a second series of diplomatic notes. In them he asked the victorious European powers to preserve Chinese territorial integrity. Hay reaffirmed America's desire to "safeguard for the world the principle of equal and impartial trade with all parts of the Chinese Empire." Not wishing to risk a major war, the imperialist powers agreed not to divide up China. They accepted instead a sum of money from the Chinese in payment for their losses.

In comparison with other powers, the United States had acted as a friend and protector of China. But did the Open Door represent an American willingness to guarantee Chinese territorial integrity? The United States had not signed a formal agreement with China, or with any other foreign nation, to enact its Open Door policy. Hay quickly admitted that his country would not go to war to enforce the Open Door—not in 1900 at any rate. European imperialistic powers had battled to a draw in China with the creation of economic spheres of influence. Hay's Open Door declarations filled the partial vacuum created by this stalemate. The Open Door would work to America's advantage only so long as no other major power embarked on an all-out push to dominate China.

INTERVENTION IN LATIN AMERICA

The growth of United States industrial and military power, combined with America's interest in the Caribbean, meant that Britain's position as the leading Caribbean power would not last long. In 1895, during the first Venezuelan crisis, the Cleveland administration had asserted America's new role in the Western Hemisphere. The events of the next decade confirmed this role.

Building a Canal to the Pacific A fifty-year-old treaty between Britain and the United States became an early casualty of America's new attitude of expansion. The 1850 treaty called for participation by both nations in the construction of any canal across Central America. In February 1900, Secretary Hay negotiated another accord with the British ambassador, Lord Pauncefote. Under the Hay-Pauncefote Treaty, Britain granted the United States exclusive rights to build a canal. But the American government was prohibited from fortify-

Roosevelt's famous boast that "I took the canal zone and let Congress debate" is caricatured here. Roosevelt is seen heaving his shovelful of Panamanian soil on Bogota, capital of Colombia, the country from which Panama was detached.

ing it. This compromise did not satisfy the United States Senate. The treaty was quickly rejected. Hay returned to the negotiating table, pulled a few teeth from the reluctant British lion, and produced a second agreement. The revised treaty placed no limitations on military fortification of the canal. The United States had only to promise that during peacetime all nations could use the canal on equal terms.

Americans next turned their attention to the question of where the Central American canal should be built. The shortest route was across the Isthmus of Panama, a province owned by Colombia. The Colombian government had sold the rights to the Panama site to a French company, headed by Ferdinand DeLesseps (builder of Egypt's Suez Canal). After several unsuccessful attempts to build a canal, the French offered to sell their rights for $109 million. Another proposed site, in Nicaragua, was a much longer route. But it was less expensive and free of foreign entanglements.

President Roosevelt and Congress argued the relative merits of both routes and initially favored the Nicaraguan site. Then, early in 1902, the French company lowered the price for sale of its rights to $40 million. Roosevelt quickly changed his mind in favor of the Panama site. Permission also had to be obtained from Colombia. In January 1903, Secretary Hay signed a treaty with Colombia agreeing to pay $10 million and an annual rent of $250,000 for a one-hundred-year lease on a canal zone in Panama.

But the Colombian senate, in a burst of patriotic pride and financial self-interest, rejected the canal treaty. President Roosevelt complained about the "bandits" of Colombia and their insistence on national honor. Roosevelt considered intervening in Panama under the terms of an 1846 treaty with Colombia. This granted the United States the right to maintain "free transit" across the isthmus. But United States troops were then busy fighting in the Philippines. Besides, the 1846 treaty required the agreement of Colombian authorities for the use of force in Panama.

In November 1903 a revolt in Panama settled the canal question. The revolt was organized by Philippe Bunau-Varilla, an agent of the French canal company. The Panamanian rebels received immediate United States aid. American ships were sent in to prevent Colombian forces from landing on the isthmus. Within a few days the new Panamanian government declared independence. Bunau-Varilla was appointed its chief representative to the United States. Bunau-Varilla and Secretary Hay quickly came to an agreement on an American-operated canal. Under the treaty the United States granted diplomatic recognition to Panama and obtained a perpetual lease on a canal zone.

Roosevelt's "big stick" diplomacy in Panama received sharp criticism from some Democrats in Congress. But the majority of Americans approved of the deeds and the bluster of their President. Some years later Roosevelt acknowledged with few apologies: "I took the canal zone and let Congress debate, and while the debate goes on, the canal does also."

In 1914 the Panama Canal opened to merchant shipping. The canal was acclaimed as a marvel of American engineering. It also put the finishing touch on a program for United States domination of the Caribbean and economic penetration of Latin America.

Policing the Caribbean   While negotiations were being carried on in Panama, a second international crisis erupted in Venezuela. The dispute involved an attempt by European powers to collect debts owed their citizens by Venezuela. In December 1902, Britain, Germany, and Italy sent warships to blockade the Venezuelan port of La Guaira. An international court decided that the three nations that had blockaded Venezuela should be given priority in collecting their debts.

Roosevelt contested this decision. America could not permit European powers to use force to settle disputes in the Western Hemisphere. When a similar financial crisis arose in 1905 in the Dominican Republic, another Caribbean country, Roosevelt moved quickly to avoid European intervention. American officials took over the government and the financial affairs of the Dominicans.

In 1904 Roosevelt announced to Congress that the United States would not tolerate "chronic wrongdoing" by any Latin American country. If political or economic developments in Latin America invited the danger of European intervention, the United States could intervene first. The President's message, which became known as the Roosevelt Corollary to the Monroe Doctrine, asserted the role of the United States as an "international police power" in the Caribbean. The statement was actually a broad departure from the earlier doctrine.

Elsewhere in the world, Roosevelt also tried to project an American presence in global affairs in a variety of ways: by mediating (at Portsmouth, New Hampshire) an end to the Russo-Japanese War; by participating along with European heads of state in the Algeciras Conference of 1906 called to negotiate conflicting Great Power claims in Morocco; by sending the American fleet ("the Great White Fleet") on a "goodwill" tour of the world that had the effect of demonstrating America's growing naval might; and by pressing Congress for modernization of the armed forces.

Dollar Diplomacy Theodore Roosevelt's successor, William Howard Taft, pursued Roosevelt's policies in Latin America. He favored economic penetration of foreign nations, a policy that became known as dollar diplomacy. Taft urged American capitalists to invest millions of dollars in overseas ventures, especially in the Caribbean. Such investments, he said, would bring Wall Street handsome profits. More important, they would serve the interests of American security. Also, American guardianship of the Western Hemisphere would benefit the people of Latin America. It would ensure them political stability and economic growth.

Nicaragua mounted the most serious challenge to the new American policy. Nicaraguan President José Zelaya, a strong opponent of the United States, tried to avoid the snares of dollar diplomacy. In 1909 he canceled special economic privileges granted to an American mining company. Zelaya's downfall came quickly. A revolutionary movement, supported by American businessmen, overthrew the Nicaraguan president. The United States granted diplomatic recognition to the new regime, took over the government's finances, and sent in the Marines to protect American interests. The pattern for implementing dollar diplomacy had been clearly established.

Idealism Versus Intervention in Mexico In 1913 Woodrow Wilson, a Democrat, moved into the White House. In his campaign Wilson had promised a more liberal internationalism. He wanted a new foreign policy to curb the growing imperialist impulse. Wilson's choice for secretary of state, the anti-imperialist William Jennings Bryan, gave some indication that Republican policies would be modified or abandoned. Wilson stated that his aim in Latin America was to support "the orderly processes of just government based upon law, and not upon arbitrary or irregular force, and to cultivate the friendship of our sister republics of Central and South America."

But idealistic aims proved no match for big-power politics. As President, Wilson used military force in Latin America even more than his Republican predecessors. Seeking to bring peace and "constitutional liberty" to the unstable governments of Latin America, he sent troops into the Caribbean to put down a rebellion in Haiti. A year later, in 1916, the President ordered United States Marines into the Dominican Republic. There a military government was established under the Department of the Navy. Troops remained in both countries throughout Wilson's administration.

Wilson played his strongest and most controversial role as a moralist when he intervened in the Mexican revolution that had begun in 1910. The President at first refused to recognize the government of General Victoriano Huerta, who had risen to power in 1913. An unsavory politician, Huerta had ordered the murder of his predecessor, Francisco Madero, Mexico's first freely elected president in decades. Wilson wanted Huerta to resign and permit free elections in Mexico. Though such goals might have been welcomed by the Mexican people, they could hardly be imposed from outside by persuasion alone.

Huerta refused to budge from the presidential palace in Mexico City. But Wilson remained determined to "teach the South American republics to elect good men." Early in 1914 the President allowed ships to supply arms to Huerta's foes. In April, Huerta's forces arrested a group of American sailors who had landed at the port of Tampico. Washington demanded formal apologies. Huerta agreed but only on the condition that the United States support his government. Wilson and Bryan refused. When the President learned that an arms shipment from Germany—intended for Huerta's forces—was nearing the Mexican port of Veracruz, he decided to act.

In the meantime, Congress had granted Wilson permission to use armed force against Huerta. A message went out to the United States naval commander in the Caribbean: "Take Veracruz at once." American forces quickly seized Veracruz. Mexican opposition rose within a few days. Fighting broke out, and both sides suffered heavy casualities. Wilson, who had not anticipated bloodshed, found himself in an embarrassing position. Americans protested the involvement—and the death of United States soldiers. Withdrawal of troops had to be arranged by a mediating commission of three South American countries.

Wilson's problems regarding Mexico were not over, however, Huerta was overthrown in July 1914 by the Constitutionalist forces of Venustiano Carranza. As the new president tried to consolidate power, civil war again broke out in Mexico. In November 1915 Wilson gave unofficial support to Carranza's government. This move angered other pretenders to the Mexican presidency, particularly "Pancho" Villa. Operating in northern Mexico, Villa decided to teach the "gringos" a lesson. Early in 1916, Villa's forces stopped a train and killed sixteen American engineering students. Villa then crossed the border to raid the New Mexico town of Columbus, an act of revenge that cost seventeen American lives. The calculating and cold-blooded Villa hoped to lead America into military intervention in Mexico. Then, as the leading opponent of the United States, he would gain support from those people who supported Carranza.

Villa guessed correctly about United States intervention. But he misjudged its political consequences. Americans were enraged by Villa's actions. General John J. Pershing—soon to gain fame and glory as commander of the United States Army in France—led a "punitive" expedition

General John J. Pershing and his hastily mobilized American troops invaded Mexico in 1916 in pursuit of "Pancho" Villa. The mission was a failure and may even have convinced Germany of America's military unpreparedness.

deep into Mexico. Villa could not be found. Instead, American troops fought a bloody skirmish with Carranza forces. The battle was unwanted by both sides. The incident threatened another Veracruz. But anti-interventionists in Congress won out over those who wanted war. Early in 1917 Pershing's forces were withdrawn from Mexico. For most Americans it had become clear that Wilson's Mexican policy meant continuous trouble. By this time, too, the American people had become far more concerned with developments in Europe, where a devastating war had been raging since 1914.

THE UNITED STATES AND WORLD WAR I

Europe had enjoyed a period of relative peace during the century after Napoleon's defeat in

1815. International rivalries did not die down, and many short but limited wars broke out. Yet Europeans managed to avoid a general war. European leaders relied on the balance of power to maintain peace and political stability. But in 1914 the assassination of Archduke Franz Ferdinand, heir to the Austro-Hungarian throne, set off a chain reaction that resulted in World War I. Two powerful blocs emerged quickly once the war began: the Central powers (Germany, Austria-Hungary, and Turkey) and the Allies (Britain, France, Italy, and Russia).

The United States tried to stay out of the war. Whatever their personal opinions or sympathies, most Americans preferred neutrality. In 1914 Wilson issued a proclamation calling on all Americans to remain impartial "in thought as well as in action." But over the next three years a combination of factors edged the United States closer

and closer to the side of the Allies and involvement in the European war.

The Road to War European powers violated America's rights as a neutral nation. American shippers tried to continue, and even expand, commerce with both sides. As in the case of the Napoleonic Wars a century before, American interests quickly clashed with those of Britain, the world's leading sea power. The British declared the North Sea a military zone. Before a neutral ship could pass through British waters, it had to enter a British port. There the ship's cargo was examined for war materials. British escorts would then lead the neutral ship through minefields to safety. Many Americans protested, and Wilson publicly condemned the British practice. But the United States clearly was not going to make the

EUROPE AT THE START OF WORLD WAR 1

Allies
Central Powers
Neutrals

0   200   400 MILES

issue a cause for war. No American lives were lost as a result of the British regulations. No American seamen were impressed into the British navy, as in the War of 1812.

The Germans knew that their navy was no match for British sea power. For the most part, German battleships and cruisers remained at anchor in home ports. Instead, the Germans turned to the submarine as a means of crippling their enemies. The British blockade of Continental Europe, launched soon after the war, threatened the German people with starvation. Germany fought back by declaring all-out submarine warfare. The Germans announced that any belligerent ships found in the waters surrounding the British Isles would be torpedoed without warning. Loss of life in such cases usually ran high.

Wilson denounced the German declaration as a violation of American neutral rights. Many Americans condemned submarine warfare as immoral. In the spring of 1915 the British passenger liner *Lusitania* was torpedoed by a German submarine off the Irish coast. Over 1,000 people died, including 128 Americans. Germany refused to accept responsibility for the incident or pay indemnities for American losses. The Germans pointed out that Americans had been publicly warned not to sail on British ships. Besides, the *Lusitania* carried arms as well as passengers. But Wilson drafted a strongly worded note to the Germans insisting that they end their surprise attacks. Secretary of State Bryan resigned rather than sign the message, which he believed was an ultimatum to Germany. When another British ship was torpedoed a few months later, Wilson threatened to cut off diplomatic relations with Germany. The Germans, fearful of drawing the United States into the war, gave in to Wilson's demands: German submarine commanders would no longer fire on British passenger liners without warning.

Economic factors also contributed to American intervention on the side of the Allies. The United States had always traded more with Britain than with Continental Europe. The onset of world war, combined with British domination of the seas, ensured an expanded trade with Britain and its allies. Americans might have to endure annoying British regulations, but at least most American ships could get through to Britain. Between 1914 and 1916 Allied purchases in America quadrupled. It soon became apparent that Britain and France would need loans in order to continue trading. Wall Street stood ready. Anti-interventionists, led by Secretary of State Bryan, argued that such loans were contraband and would inevitably drag the United States into the war. Again Wilson proclaimed strict neutrality. He did not move to prohibit credit to the Allies, however. The loans were, after all, big business, and the United States economy was booming.

Moreover, America was closely tied to Britain, both culturally and politically. Since the end of the nineteenth century, relations between Britain and the United States had improved dramatically, though the two nations had not entered into a formal alliance. Most Americans sympathized with Britain and its allies. German Americans, as well as Irish Americans who opposed Britain's policies in Ireland, were notable exceptions. One of the strongest supporters of Britain was Wilson himself. The President admired British culture and the parliamentary form of government. In contrast, Germany's image in America had suffered a complete change during recent decades. Americans had once viewed Germany as a country of poets and philosophers; they came to see it as a stark and frightening nation of militarists.

Within the context of these three factors — neutral rights, economic interdependence, and cultural ties — Wilson tried to maintain a course of neutrality. By 1916 the war had reached a stalemate. Neither side seemed capable of gathering enough strength to defeat the other. Hundreds of thousands of soldiers died in a series of brutal, inconclusive battles. Wilson attempted to use American prestige and the threat of use of American power to negotiate a European peace. His trusted adviser, Colonel Edward M. House, crossed the Atlantic several times to confer with foreign ministers and heads of state. European statesmen listened to House — America was too powerful to ignore — but they did not heed his message. They had fought too long and suffered too many losses to accept Wilson's "peace without victory." The British and French skillfully played along with Wilson and House, banking ultimately on American intervention to bring an Allied victory.

The war dragged on indecisively for three years. Early in 1917 Germany renewed unrestricted submarine warfare, cutting off food and supplies to the French and British. Germany knew that this action would bring the United States into the war. But Berlin hoped to smash the Allies before a large American force could be mobilized and sent to Europe.

Wilson acted. Early in 1917 Washington received news of a revolution in Russia and the establishment there of a constitutional government. The overthrow of the Russian czar removed many of the moral problems that Wilson faced in seeking support for American involvement on the side of the Allies. In April the President asked Congress to declare war on Germany. Wilson called upon Americans to embark on a great crusade, a "war to end all wars" and make the world safe for democracy. In his message to Congress Wilson noted: "It is a fearful thing to lead this great peaceful people into war. But the right is more precious than peace."

The Great Crusade   When the United States entered World War I, the major European powers were nearly exhausted. On both sides men previously considered too old or too young for combat were pressed into military service. But after April 1917 the Allies suddenly had a great new reservoir of manpower to draw upon—the young manhood of the United States. The regular American army was small. Close to a million soldiers had to be recruited initially (over 4 million were eventually recruited). But America prepared willingly to meet the demands of Wilson's crusade. Military conscription was accepted by most Americans with fewer objections than during the Civil War or during the war in Vietnam.

The German submarine campaign achieved startling success during the first six months of 1917. But the Allied navies soon devised an effective countermeasure: the convoy system. A single ship crossing the Atlantic had little chance against the German submarine fleet. But a large group of troop ships and freighters traveling together could

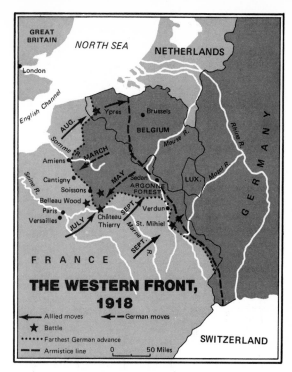

THE WESTERN FRONT, 1918

War broke out in July 1914, one month after Serbian nationalists had assassinated Archduke Franz Ferdinand of Austria. Although the United States was neutral for the first three years of the conflict, its ships were at times boarded by the British and at other times threatened by the Germans. In early 1917, after the Germans renewed unrestricted submarine warfare against all shipping, the United States broke off diplomatic relations with Germany. Provoked by continued German submarine attacks, the United States declared war on Germany in April of that year. The United States entered the war on the side of the Allies as an associated power. In June an American Expeditionary Force under General John J. Pershing arrived in France.

In March 1918, after years of trench warfare, the Germans began an offensive with the Second Battle of the Somme, intending to reach the English Channel. The Allies (including the United States) later set up a unified command for the Western Front under French General Ferdinand Foch. In May, the German armies approached to within fifty miles of Paris. The turning point of the war came in July, when the German advance was stopped at the Second Battle of the Marne. Allied advances in the second half of 1918 were marked by major offensives at Belleau Wood in June – July, Ypres in August, St. Mihiel in September, and the Meuse-Argonne Forest drive of September – November.

The Military position of the central Powers deteriorated rapidly during the summer of 1918. On November 11, an armistice was signed, putting an end to the war.

The Meuse-Argonne offensive in World War I was noted for its vastness —1,200,000 American troops—and its human costliness—over 120,000 casualties. Sergeant Alvin York, the prewar conscientious objector, became famous here for his singlehanded capture of 132 Germans.

reach Europe in relative security. The rate of sinkings by German submarines fell rapidly. Most important, nearly all American soldiers completed the passage to France safely.

The large but still untested American army—General John J. Pershing's American Expeditionary Force—went into action late in 1917. French generals, hungry for more manpower, had originally called for small-sized American units, which they wished to integrate into their own commands. Pershing worked cooperatively with the French commanders and with the Allied commander in chief, Marshal Ferdinand Foch. But he and other senior American officers insisted that the Americans operate as an independent army.

American soldiers soon were allotted their own sector of the Western front to defend. American troops also helped the Allies hold their positions. Then they joined the Allied counteroffensive in the summer and fall of 1918. By November Germany was beaten. The Kaiser fled into exile in Holland. Worn out by four years of brutal warfare and beset by unrest at home, Germany asked for peace.

At home, America had organized its wartime economy as quickly and effectively as it had mobilized its soldiers. The United States had

begun to prepare for war as early as 1916. In that year Congress created the Council of National Defense, a mixed governmental and business commission. During the war the council supervised a network of agencies that controlled every aspect of the American economy. Under Bernard Baruch the War Industries Board supervised the allocation of raw materials and set production goals. The Food Administration controlled prices, and a War Trade Board regulated imports and exports. Congress established at least half a dozen other agencies, all of which reported to the President.

Wilson used his presidential war powers to the limit in waging a battle against dissent. Most Americans supported the war. But sizable minorities did not. German Americans opposed United States support of the Allies for ethnic reasons. Socialists and radicals condemned the war as a "capitalist" venture for profit. During the first months of American participation, German Americans suffered the abuse (and sometimes the assaults) of their fellow citizens. But when it became certain that Germany would have to yield to the Allies, radicalism came to be regarded as the prime threat to Wilsonian peace. In November 1917 Communist forces in Russia overthrew the new constitutional government and withdrew their nation from the war. With the new "Red scare," radical dissenters replaced German Americans as the nation's principal outcasts.

A government propaganda machine, the Committee on Public Information, was set up to publicize war efforts and to censor information or newspaper opinions unfavorable to the Allied cause. Congress enlarged the offensive against dissent by passing strict laws against treason. By the time the war ended, almost all Americans had been enlisted in the crusade.

Wilson the Peacemaker At the war's end Wilson turned his energies and ideals to the formidable task of obtaining a fair and lasting peace. The President had outlined his proposals for peace— the Fourteen Points—even before the armistice. The Germans surrendered in November 1918, hoping that Wilson's peace program would guide Allied policy.

The American President called for a new world order. It would help to eliminate worldwide political and economic rivalries. He sought to substitute international cooperation for the unstable and dangerous balance-of-power politics that had led the world to war. Wilson also proposed national self-determination for ethnic groups in the decaying European empires. Finally, Wilson called for a "general association of nations," a league of all the countries in the world. The league's members would cooperate actively to avoid future international conflicts.

In January 1919 Allied negotiators met at the palace of Versailles, a city a few miles from Paris. The peace conference was attended by Wilson and other Allied heads of state: Premier Georges Clemenceau of France, Prime Minister David Lloyd George of Britain, and Premier Vittorio Orlando of Italy. Clemenceau's overconcern with French security, though understandable, gave Wilson the most trouble. Lloyd George sought a middle ground, though he always kept the interests of the British Empire in mind. Orlando, junior partner of the Allies, did not participate in most of the "summit" deliberations.

The treaty that emerged from Versailles was a compromise. But it still remained compatible with Wilsonian goals. The President was de-feated overwhelmingly on several issues. Despite Wilson's call for "open convenants of peace, openly arrived at," most of the treaty negotiations took shape in secret conferences among the Allied "Big Three"—Wilson, Lloyd George, and Clemenceau. Wilson compromised on national self-determination, allowing European leaders to redraw the political map of Europe. He agreed that Germany and its allies should pay staggering amounts in war damages. The Allied powers greedily divided up Germany's colonies, ignoring the wishes of the inhabitants of those areas. Nonetheless, some of the Fourteen Points were incorporated into the treaty. Perhaps most important for Wilson, the Treaty of Versailles called for the establishment of an international peacekeeping body, the League of Nations.

But dedication to ideals does not ensure success in politics, as Wilson quickly found out. Wilson brought the treaty and the League home to debate and disaster. A small group of isolationists in the Senate were opposed to any American participation in an international league. They feared that a headlong rush into internationalism would curb essential American rights and hurt American interests. Other American senators wanted to be convinced. If Wilson had confided in these senators and attempted to work out a compromise with them, the treaty and the League of Nations might have been saved.

The Fight Over the League On July 19, 1919, Woodrow Wilson submitted the Treaty of Versailles with its League of Nations covenant to the United States Senate. A poll taken earlier in the year showed that sixty-four senators—the necessary two-thirds majority—favored ratification. But time and events had reduced that figure. Everyone knew that trouble lay ahead.

One source of the trouble was Wilson himself. He had created hostility be neglecting to ask any leading Republican to accompany him on the peacemaking mission. Then, too, he was a stubborn man. Once he made a decision, he was certain that it was right. He refused to compromise.

Another source of trouble lay in the diverse reactions of the senators to the treaty and the League. Some thought the treaty dealt unfairly

Despite President Wilson's desire for "Open Diplomacy," The Treaty of Versailles, signed on June 28, 1919, was largely the work of the "Big Three." Shown here as they left the Palace of Versailles: French Premier Georges Clemenceau, to the left, hat in hand, followed by President Wilson, with British Prime Minister David Lloyd George on the right. Wilson's hopes for American approval of the Treaty, which included provisions for an international League of Nations as well as others of his 14 Points, were to be shattered by the Senate's rejection.

with various nations, but they favored the League of Nations. Others had no trouble with the treaty itself but feared that the League would take away American independence and possibly lead the United States into war again. And there were those who thought the treaty provisions were unjust and that the League would only uphold these injustices. Several Republicans objected to the League simply because they thought that members of both parties should have had a stake in its creation.

Battle lines were being drawn. There were forty-seven Democrats and forty-nine Republicans in the Senate, divided into three discernible groups. First there were those who were willing to ratify the treaty immediately—forty-three Democrats. Then there were the "reservationists" —about thirty-five Republicans and one Democrat —who wanted some of the provisions changed before they would agree to vote for ratification. Finally there were the "irreconcilables"—the remaining Republicans and three Democrats. This last group vowed never to sign the treaty under any circumstance.

At the center of this controversy was Senator Henry Cabot Lodge of Massachusetts, the new chairman of the Foreign Relations Committee.

Lodge disliked Wilson and objected to the treaty, which he thought was too easy on Germany. He was therefore, at heart, an irreconcilable. But he thought he knew a better way of defeating the treaty. As he said to one senatorial colleague, "I do not propose to beat it by direct frontal attack, but by the indirect method of reservations."

Before the treaty went to the Senate for a vote, it was stalled for two months in the unfriendly Foreign Relations Committee. When it emerged forty-nine revisions and amendments were attached to it. The disheartened Wilson was adamant. Democratic senators were not to vote for it with these "Lodge reservations." "Never! Never!" said Wilson. "I'll never consent to accept any policy with which that impossible name is so prominently identified."

He kept his word, and enough Senate Democrats stayed loyal to him to defeat the treaty with reservations. On November 19 it was all over. The Senate adjourned and the treaty that Wilson thought would be his crowning achievement would not be considered again. The United States would never join the League of Nations.

Wilson saw all Senate opposition to the treaty as betrayal of the highest trust, the cause of world peace. During the long debate, he had cracked the whip of party discipline over Democratic senators and had gone on the campaign trail seeking public support for his treaty. The trip ended tragically when Wilson suffered a stroke, which left him partially paralyzed. It was in this enfeebled state that Wilson watched the Senate reject the treaty and, with it, his dream of American leadership for world peace as a member of the League.

Wilson began looking ahead to the presidential election of 1920, which he hoped to turn into a "solemn referendum" on the League. The election became instead a referendum on Wilsonian politics. Republican Warren G. Harding, who promised Americans a retreat from internationalism and a return to "normalcy," won a landslide victory. All hope for American participation in the League of Nations vanished.

SUGGESTED READINGS—CHAPTERS 35-36

Philippines Revolt

Leon Wolff, *Little Brown Brother: America's Forgotten Bid for Empire* (1961); John M. Gates, *Schoolbooks and Krags: The U.S. Army in the Philippines, 1898–1902* (1972); Joseph L. Schott, *The Ordeal of Samar* (1964); Teodoro M. Kalaw, *The Philippine Revolution* (1969).

Becoming a World Power

William A. Williams, *The Roots of the Modern American Empire* (1969); Walter LaFeber, *The New Empire: An Interpretation of American Expansion, 1860–1898* (1963); Betty M. Unterberger, *America's Siberian Expedition* (1956); Christopher Lasch, *American Liberals and the Russian Revolution* (1962); H. Wayne Morgan, *America's Road to Empire* (1965); Robert E. Osgood, *Ideals and Self-Interest in America's Foreign Relations* (1962); Howard K. Beale, *Theodore Roosevelt and the Rise of America to World Power* (1956).

Imperialist Stirrings

Rubin F. Weston, *Racism in U.S. Imperialism* (1972); Foster R. Dulles, *The Imperial Years* (1956); Bradford Perkins, *The Great Raprochement: England and the United States, 1895–1914* (1968); Robert L. Beisner, *Twelve Against Empire: The Anti-Imperialists* (1968); David F. Healy, *The United States in Cuba, 1898–1902* (1963); Edward F. Berbusse, *The United States in Puerto Rico, 1898–1900* (1966); Thomas J. McCormick, *China Market: America's Quest for Informal Empire* (1967); Paul A.

Varg, *Missionaries, Chinese, and Diplomats* (1958); Raymond A. Esthus, *Theodore Roosevelt and Japan* (1966); Clarence C. Clendenen, *The United States and Pancho Villa* (1961); P. Edward Haley, *Revolution and Intervention: The Diplomacy of Taft and Wilson with Mexico, 1910–1917* (1970).

War With Spain

Julius W. Pratt, *Expansionists of 1898* (1936); William A. Swanberg, *Citizen Hearst* (1961); Frank Freidel, *The Splendid Little War* (1958).

Wilson and Diplomacy

Ernest R. May, *Imperial Democracy* (1961); Arthur S. Link, *Wilson the Diplomatist* (1957); Dana G. Munro, *Intervention and Dollar Diplomacy in the Caribbean, 1900–1921* (1964); Edward H. Beuhrig, *Woodrow Wilson and the Balance of Power* (1955); N. Gordon Levin, *Woodrow Wilson and World Politics* (1968).

Wilson and War

John M. Cooper, Jr., *The Vanity of Power: American Isolationism and the First World War* (1970); Seward W. Livermore, *Politics is Adjourned: Woodrow Wilson and the War Congress* (1966); Horace C. Peterson and Gilbert C. Fite, *Opponents of War, 1917–1918* (1957); Robert K. Murray, *Red Scare* (1955); Thomas A. Bailey, *Woodrow Wilson and the Lost Peace* (1944) and *Woodrow Wilson and the Great Betrayal* (1945); John A. Garraty, *Henry Cabot Lodge* (1953).

37 LINDBERGH'S FLIGHT

R. J. W.

The captain was a little man, dapper and very French. But he sought a big prize: $25,000 for the first man to fly an airplane from New York to Paris. His name might sound somewhat strange—even funny—to American ears: René Fonck. But his reputation was formidable. He had been the youngest French air ace in the Great War of 1914 (as World War I was known until World War II). Without being seriously injured himself, he had shot down at least seventy-five German planes. In a war that had turned the new aviators into overnight heroes, Fonck's reputation for skill, courage, and "dash" was probably greater than that of any other pilot. Now, in the summer of 1926, he was preparing for a flight that could make him an even greater hero, both in France and in the United States.

Compared with any of the planes Fonck had flown during the war, his new silver-colored craft was huge. Like most of the other large aircraft of the day, it had three engines and two wings—a biplane, it was called. Its large cabin was equipped for a crew of four: a pilot, a copilot, a mechanic, and a radio operator. The problem that Fonck faced was simply getting the plane off the ground with enough fuel to fly the 3,600 miles to Paris. All summer he tested the plane in New York, gradually increasing the gasoline load for each test.

At daybreak on September 21 Fonck's plane was pulled onto the east-west runway at Roosevelt Field, a small airport on Long Island. The wind was blowing from the west, as it almost always does after dawn on Long Island. So Fonck would take off from east to west. To get the plane off the ground he and his crew would have to attain a speed of eighty miles an hour. One by one, the engines were turned up to their maximum power. The blocks were pulled away from the wheels, and the plane began to move. It lurched slightly, having over 2,000 gallons of gasoline aboard, and chased its own awkward shadow down the dirt runway.

When the plane passed the halfway point on the small airstrip, it did not have the speed needed for takeoff. The small crowd of onlookers waited for Fonck to cut power. But something had gone wrong, either with the pilot or with his controls. The plane simply roared on. The runway ended. The plane took a sharp, short drop into a gully, then exploded and burst into flames. Somehow Fonck got out, and so did his navigator. But the copilot and the radio operator burned to death.

Despite the crash, the man who had offered the $25,000 prize — Raymond Orteig, a Frenchman who managed two hotels in New York — announced that his offer still stood. For a while Fonck's crash made headlines and kept alive the idea of a New York—Paris flight. Late in February 1927 others began to announce that they would make the flight. It was soon obvious that a real contest was developing. It would not be merely a battle between one airplane and the ocean but a race among several aviators and their planes. The stage was set for what the public began to sense would be the greatest thrill of the decade.

By the end of March 1927 there were four serious contenders. One was the *America*, a plane piloted by Admiral Richard E. Byrd, who had gained fame as the first man to fly to the North Pole. Byrd was backed with over $100,000 from a wealthy New York merchant. His three-engined plane, with a wingspan of over seventy feet, was huge by the standards of the day. It seemed to have the best chance.

A second entry was another trimotored craft, the *American Legion*, named after and supported by the veterans' organization. It too was backed with $100,000. Unlike Fonck's plane and Byrd's *America* the *American Legion* carried only two men. A third entry was a plane known as the *Columbia*, a single-winged, single-engined craft. The *Columbia* would soon set the world endurance record by flying for over fifty hours. Finally, there was a French entry, a single-engined biplane called the *White Bird*. Its pilot and copilot, a pair of French aces from the Great War, planned to make the flight in reverse — from Paris to New York. The *White Bird* was said to have the most powerful gasoline engine ever put into an airplane.

By mid-April the weather had warmed up enough to make flight over the North Atlantic seem possible. On April 16 Commander Byrd took his *America* up from a New Jersey airport for its first test flight. Byrd and three crewmen tested the plane for a few hours and then brought it down for its first landing. The heavy landing gear touched ground smoothly. But almost at once there was a sound of splintering wood and wrenched metal. The *America* flipped over and skidded to a halt on its back. All four men managed to escape. Byrd had a broken wrist, and two of the other crewmen were badly hurt. They would not be able to fly again for weeks.

Ten days later the *American Legion* was in Langley Field, Virginia, undergoing its last test flight. The plane had flown well in earlier attempts. But both its designers and pilot knew it was too heavy. To find out whether the plane could make the Paris flight, the pilot and copilot decided to fly it from Virginia to New York with a full load of gasoline. The takeoff was slower than usual. For a moment it seemed as if the plane would not clear a line of trees at the end of the runway. To avoid them, the pilot banked to the right a few degrees. The slight turn was too much. It upset the delicate balance of the plane. The *American Legion* slid downward into a wet marsh and turned over. The pilot and copilot were trapped inside the cabin that filled first with gasoline fumes and then with water. By the time rescuers came wading through the marsh, the two men were dead.

Four men had been killed and three others hurt, and the race over the Atlantic had not yet begun. On both sides of the ocean, in America and in France, newspapers stirred public excitement to a high pitch. Surely one of the planes would make it sooner or later. But no one knew what might happen next or who might be injured or killed. The race to Paris had the competitive excitement of a World Series or a heavyweight championship fight. And it had the danger and drama of war. In the United States the race gained as much importance in the public's mind as had the war of 1898, the sinking of the *Lusitania*, or the declaration of war in 1917. In France the excitement was heightened by the memory of Fonck's crash. Moreover, the entry into the contest of two other young ace pilots from the Great War, Charles Nungesser and Francis Coli, held great promise. Both had been wounded a total of twenty-six times in air combat. Between them they had won almost every medal that their government could award.

At dawn on May 8 Nungesser and Coli took off for New York from Le Bourget airport near Paris. A great crowd gathered to watch the two heroes and their *White Bird*. Nungesser got the wheels off the ground, but too soon. The *White Bird* dropped back down on the runway with a thud. Finally, it gathered speed and left the ground almost two-thirds of a mile down the long strip.

The next morning, American newspapers reported that the plane had been sighted over Newfoundland. Paris celebrated with an excitement that almost matched that on the day of the armistice. Nungesser and Coli had dropped their landing gear over the ocean to save weight and lessen wind resistance. New Yorkers watched the harbor where the Frenchmen hoped to land and keep afloat until they could be reached by waiting boats. But the *White Bird* was never seen again. In France the celebrations quickly came to a shocked end.

The death toll in the New York — Paris race had reached six in less than a year. The world's most experienced pilots — backed by large sums of money, flying the best airplanes that modern technology could provide, with the most powerful motors ever developed — had all failed.

The man who was finally going to win the race to Paris had been reading every newspaper report he could find on all the airplane tests, takeoffs, and crashes. When Fonck's plane burned, Charles Lindbergh was flying airmail between Chicago and St. Louis. When Byrd and the others announced that they would enter the competition, Lindbergh was in San Diego supervising the construction of a new plane for himself. When Nungesser and Coli took off from Paris, he was waiting in San Diego for the weather to clear over the Rocky Mountains and the Great Plains, so he could fly east to St. Louis. From there he would go on to New York to make his attempt.

Lindbergh had only $2,000 of his own money, carefully kept for him by his mother in Detroit. He was only twenty-five years old. He looked even younger, so that almost everyone called him a boy. Worst of all, he decided on what struck everyone as a suicidal idea: to make the flight in a single-engine plane with only himself in the cockpit. He had been able to persuade some St. Louis businessmen to back him to the extent of $15,000. But this was a small sum compared to the support that Byrd's group and the *American Legion* had. Still, late in the summer of 1926, just before Fonck's crash, Lindbergh had come to an almost religious conviction that he could make the Paris flight.

At first Lindbergh tried to negotiate with several large aircraft companies. He was turned down. No one wanted to risk a company's reputation on an insane stunt like flying from New York to Paris alone. Then Lindbergh sent a plain but daring telegram to Ryan Airlines, a small, little known factory in California:

RYAN AIRLINES, INC.   FEB. 3, 1927
SAN DIEGO, CALIFORNIA

CAN YOU CONSTRUCT WHIRLWIND ENGINE PLANE
CAPABLE FLYING NONSTOP BETWEEN NEW YORK AND
PARIS. IF SO PLEASE STATE COST AND DELIVERY DATE.

Surprisingly, the answer came quickly. The small company could build the plane, and it could do so for the amount of money Lindbergh had at his disposal. But it would take three months, the telegram said. Lindbergh answered:

RYAN AIRLINES   FEB. 5, 1927
SAN DIEGO, CALIFORNIA

COMPETITION MAKES TIME ESSENTIAL. CAN YOU
CONSTRUCT PLANE IN LESS THAN THREE MONTHS.
PLEASE WIRE GENERAL SPECIFICATIONS.

Again the company answered quickly, making as much of a guess as a calculation. It could build a plane capable of carrying 380 gallons of gasoline at a cruising speed of 100 miles per hour, with an engine rated at only 200 horsepower. (This was less than half the power of the big engine that had taken the *White Bird* out over the Atlantic. It was also much less than the power supplied by the three engines of Byrd's great

This drawing shows the plane Ryan Airlines built for Lindbergh. Although the goal of the design was simplicity, sacrificing safety for the need to carry as much gasoline as possible, the plane was quite a sophisticated piece of machinery.

America.) Most important, the company promised to have the plane ready in time.

By the last week in February, Lindbergh was in San Diego working out the details on his plane. Neither Lindbergh nor the engineer who designed the plane knew how far it was to Paris. They drove to the San Diego public library to measure off the distance on a globe with a piece of string. Lindbergh remembered it this way:

> "It's 3,600 miles." The bit of white grocery string under my fingers stretches taut along the coast of North America, bends down over a faded blue ocean, and strikes the land mass of Europe. It isn't a very scientific way of finding the exact distance between two points on the earth's surface, but the answer is accurate enough for our first calculations. The designer was making quick calculations in pencil on the back of an envelope. "Maybe we'd better put in 400 gallons of gasoline instead of 380," he concludes.

Lindbergh's project was simple, almost amateurish: hastily drafted telegrams, bits of string stretched across a public-library globe, figures on the back of an envelope, and "maybe" calculations. But with no more detailed or expert plans, he decided to go ahead.

The mechanics and carpenters at Ryan started work at once on the plane that Lindbergh would call the *Spirit of St. Louis.* They built it almost literally around the pilot. The narrow, simple cockpit was just large enough to hold Lindbergh's tall, skinny body (and then only if the overhead ribs were hollowed out a little to make room for his head). In the end the plane would be only about three feet taller than Lindbergh

The cockpit of the *Spirit of St. Louis* was a model of stripped-down efficiency. The wicker seat was probably uncomfortable but lightweight. Only side windows were thought necessary since there was not much to see in flight. Leg room was limited by the controls.

himself. Moreover, it would have a smaller engine than any of the other planes in the race. But this was the secret of Lindbergh's plane—simplicity. He would build the smallest, simplest plane possible, a machine designed with only one purpose: to carry enough gasoline for the trip. Everything else—comfort, safety, complicated navigating equipment—would be sacrificed to save weight, weight that could be turned into gallons of gasoline.

On April 26, the day the two pilots of the *American Legion* were killed in Virginia, the *Spirit of St. Louis* was finished. Two days later Lindbergh was ready for his first test flight. He squeezed himself into his seat in the cockpit. He could touch the sides of the fuselage with his elbows. To the front the cockpit was blind. Shiny metal sloped all the way up from the engine to the top of the wing. There were only two side windows and a glassed-in skylight overhead. For takeoffs and landings he had to lean out of one of the side windows. But the plane was designed for only one important takeoff and landing. The rest of the time, over the Atlantic, there would be nothing to see but ocean, clouds, sun, and stars.

Directly in front of Lindbergh's face was a small cluster of instruments—an air-speed indicator, a turn-and-bank indicator, a fuel-flow meter, a compass, and one or two others. The plane carried a pitifully small survival kit containing a rubber raft, a flashlight, a canteen of water, some matches, and string. Surrounding the cockpit were nothing but gasoline tanks. One tank rested in the nose between the pilot and the engine. Another lay behind the cockpit in the fuselage. And there were more tanks in the wings overhead. There was no radio, no heater to provide warmth at freezing altitudes, no sextant for navigational sightings, not even a parachute. The *Spirit of St. Louis* was built to carry only gasoline—over a ton of it, as it turned out, weighing more than the plane and the pilot put together.

To Lindbergh, as he walked onto the sunny runway in San Diego, the *Spirit of St. Louis* was a thing of beauty and awe:

> What a beautiful machine it is, resting there on the field in front of the hangar, trim and slender, gleaming in its silver coat! All our ideas, all our calculations, all our hopes, lie there before me, waiting to undergo the acid test of flight. For me, it seems to contain the whole future of aviation.
> "Off! Throttle closed."
> I'm in the cockpit. The chief mechanic turns the propeller over several times.
> "Contact!"
> He swings his body away from the blade as he pulls it through. The engine catches, every cylinder hitting. This is different from any other cockpit I've been in before. The big fuel tank in front of me seems doubly large, now that I'm actually to fly behind it.
> I signal the chocks [blocks in front of the wheels of the plane] away. The *Spirit of St. Louis* rolls lightly over the baked-mud surface of the field.

The *Spirit of St. Louis* moved very quickly. Its tanks were almost empty for this first test flight.

> The tires are off the ground before they roll a hundred yards. The plane climbs quickly, even though I hold its nose down. There's a huge reserve of power. I spiral cautiously upward. I straighten out and check my instruments. I circle over the factory, watching little figures run outdoors to see the machine built actually flying overhead. I rock my wings and head across the bay.

During the next week Lindbergh tested the *Spirit of St. Louis* for speed, control, and, most important, takeoff under load. More and more gasoline was filtered by hand into the tanks for each run. With a load of slightly over 300 gallons the plane took off easily. But continued landings with large loads were dangerous. Lindbergh decided to stop the tests.

The *Spirit of St. Louis* had needed a little more than 1,000 feet of runway to take off with 300 gallons. From this and other data, the Ryan designers made a theoretical calculation that, fully loaded with 400 gallons, the plane would need 2,500 feet of hard runway. Rather than tempt fate, as the crew of the *American Legion* had done by testing with a full load, Lindbergh decided to trust the plane and the designer's arithmetic. He was ready. And he knew Byrd's *America* had been repaired and was undergoing final tests. The *Columbia,* too, was ready. Both planes were poised on Long Island. Time counted more than tests.

But time seemed to work against Lindbergh. A big storm blanketed the western United States, moving with painful slowness eastward. Lindbergh had to wait several days until the rain and clouds had moved east. On the evening of May 10 he began the first leg of his trip, from San Diego to St. Louis. He flew the 1,500 miles in record time. It was the longest nonstop solo flight ever made. Then, after a night's sleep, he headed for New York.

Lindbergh arrived on Long Island on May 12. He had set another record for the fastest transcontinental flight in history. The crews of Byrd's *America* and the *Columbia* came over to shake his hand and wish him luck. There was a crowd. Newspaper photographers and reporters pushed and shoved their way to Lindbergh, shouting for pictures and answers to their questions. A crowd of people climbed to the roof of a small building next to the hangar where Lindbergh parked the plane. Their weight caused a wall to collapse. Something new and strange was happening to Lindbergh. The newspapers and the public were making him into a hero, almost a myth.

Even without Lindbergh, the New York—Paris contest had all the elements of an exciting publicity event: death, drama, and competition. But Lindbergh's entry into the race added new elements. He was going alone, thus he could become an object of hero worship in ways that the crews of the other planes could not. He was tall, thin, blue-eyed, and handsome in a boyish way. And along with his youthful good looks went other personality traits that soon endeared him to the newspapers. Above all, he was modest, shy, and simple.

All these traits combined to present a picture of an innocent young man ready to dare the impossible, alone. Lindbergh was the honest, plain-spoken, cowboy-like young man from the West. He was a modern David challenging the Eastern Goliaths, with their money, their experience, their financial backers, and their head start. In short, he was an underdog. The *Spirit of St. Louis,* too, was simple and seemingly innocent compared with the other planes in the race. It was a sentimental favorite.

Lindbergh could not leave his hotel room without being mobbed by people anxious to touch him "just for luck." And the newspapers played his story for all it was worth. They nicknamed him "Lucky," "The Flyin' Fool," or just "Lindy." (He had always been "Slim" to his friends.) All the hero worship that the Americans of the 1920s usually reserved for baseball players like Babe Ruth or movie stars like Rudolf Valentino was now showered on the twenty-five-year-old airmail pilot. The worship was made more serious by the fact that "The Flyin' Fool" was doing something real and dangerous, not merely hitting baseballs or posing for motion picture cameras.

In most ways this public personality created for the new celebrity

What attracted the public to Lindbergh, besides his boyish good looks, was the power he had of symbolizing what was best about the country: not just daring, but moral courage and independence of spirit.

was only a myth. Lindbergh may not have had Byrd's $100,000, but he had finally obtained solid backing from St. Louis businessmen. And even if the *Spirit of St. Louis* was smaller than the other planes, it was still a sophisticated piece of machinery, created by advanced technology. It was a little silly for newspapers to write of Lindbergh and his plane as though they were a cowboy hero and his beloved horse.

Nor was Lindbergh's background as simple as the newspapers tried to make it appear. He came from a well-to-do, educated family. His father had been a congressman. Lindbergh had been to college for a time and held a commission as captain in the Army Air Service Reserve and the Missouri National Guard. He had been chief pilot for the airmail company in St. Louis. He was, despite his youth, an experienced professional pilot, flying an advanced aircraft.

But there was just enough truth to the mythical picture to make it stick. It probably infected Lindbergh somewhat, too. He had always been a bit wild, even though he was shy. Cars, motorcycles, ice boats— anything that involved speed—had always fascinated him. When he was just twenty he dropped out of college to learn to fly. He bought his first craft, a war-surplus plane, even before he had made a solo flight, and he almost crashed it on his first takeoff.

Lindbergh had barnstormed all over the West, crashing regularly and surviving only with luck. He had walked on airplane wings while in flight and done dangerous parachute jumps for one aerial circus after another. Four times he had been forced to parachute for his life from planes that had collided, run out of gas, or gotten lost at night.

All this—combined with Lindbergh's shyness and boyishness, his faith in himself and his plane—did smack of something supernatural and mythical. So the hero worship that began almost as soon as he reached Long Island was probably inevitable. At times the publicity and the public attention irritated Lindbergh. Reporters went so far as to burst into his hotel room without knocking to discover what kind of pajamas, if any, he wore to bed. But the irritation could not overcome the excitement. Lindbergh was becoming, even before takeoff, a national hero.

The *Columbia* was scheduled to take off on May 13, the day after Lindbergh reached Long Island. But the weather was closed in over New York and the North Atlantic. The same storm that had delayed Lindbergh in San Diego was making its slow progress north and east. So the *Columbia* had to wait. Lindbergh was able to test and tune his engine, to check and recheck every instrument. A noisy crowd that sometimes numbered over a thousand gathered around the hangar to watch him. By May 16 he was ready. As far as he could tell, Byrd was ready too. In the *Columbia* organization there was a legal quarrel over who would be the pilot. One of the men who had trained for the flight had secured a court order preventing the plane from taking off without him. But the court order could be lifted at any minute. So there seemed to be a real chance that two or possibly even three planes would take off from Roosevelt Field on the same morning.

The storm persisted for three more days. Then, on the evening of May 19, the forecast called for clearing skies. Though it was not clearing rapidly, Lindbergh made his decision. He would fly, even if it meant taking off into a rainy sky from a muddy field. He bought five sandwiches "to go." A few hours later the *Spirit of St. Louis* was towed to the west end of the Roosevelt Field runway. Lindbergh had decided to take off before dawn, while the wind was east to west. This was the opposite direction from the one Fonck had taken the preceding autumn. Not far behind the *Spirit of St. Louis* was the scorched area, marked by a bent propeller stuck into the ground as a tribute, where Fonck's plane had burned.

Slowly, carefully, mechanics strained five-gallon cans of gasoline into Lindbergh's plane. The tanks were oversized. They had a capacity of 450 gallons instead of the 400 that the designers had planned earlier. Lindbergh decided to fill them to the brim, even though it meant a dangerous overload for the takeoff. In the hangars of the *America* and the *Columbia*, there was only darkness and silence. No one else was going to fly.

As he looked over the situation, Lindbergh wondered whether he should go. He was overloaded with gasoline. The field was muddy. The wheels of the *Spirit of St. Louis* sank into the earth as though warning him that flight was out of the question. The wet weather affected the engine, which turned about thirty revolutions per minute slower than it should have at full power. Worst of all, the process of getting ready took so long that Lindbergh lost the night wind. By the time he was ready to fly, the breeze had shifted to his back, creating a tailwind of five or six miles per hour. This meant he would need even more speed on takeoff.

Lindbergh's only guidelines were the San Diego tests. They had demonstrated theoretically that he should be able to take off in 2,500 feet on a hard runway with no wind and with full engine power. At the end of the Roosevelt Field runway were a ditch, a tractor, some telephone wires and then a hill with a line of trees. He had to clear them all. He considered towing the *Spirit of St. Louis* through the misty rain and mud to the other end of the runway to get the help of the wind. He thought about postponing the flight altogether. But he decided to go.

Lindbergh looked around at the crowd that had gathered to watch. Nearby there were the mechanics, the engineers, several policemen, all looking into the dark cockpit at his pale face.

> Their eyes are intently on mine. They've seen the planes crash before. I lean against the side of the cockpit and look ahead, through the idling blades of the propeller, over the runway's glistening surface. I study the telephone wires and the shallow pools of water through which my wheels must pass. A curtain of mist shuts off all trace of the horizon. Sitting in the cockpit, in seconds, minutes long, the conviction surges through me that the wheels *will* leave the ground, that the wings *will* rise above the wires, that it *is* time to start the flight.
>
> I buckle my safety belt, pull goggles down over my eyes, turn to the men at the blocks, and nod. Frozen figures leap to action. I brace myself against the left side of the cockpit and ease the throttle wide open.

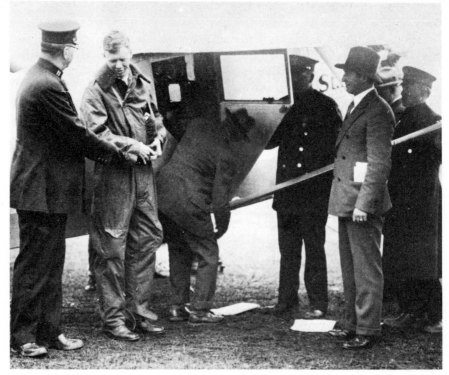

Moments before the takeoff: Lindbergh readies himself for the flight, while policemen guard and his backers inspect the plane that will carry him to Paris.

The *Spirit of St. Louis* feels more like an overloaded truck than an airplane. The tires rut through mud as though they really were on truck wheels. Even the breath of wind is pressing me down. The engine's snarl sounds inadequate and weak.

A hundred yards of runway passes. How long can the landing gear stand such strain? I keep my eyes fixed on the runway's edge. I *must* hold the plane straight. Pace quickens—the tail skid lifts off ground—I feel the load shifting from wheels to wings. The halfway mark is just ahead, and I have nothing like flying speed.

The halfway mark streaks past. Seconds now to decide. I pull the stick back firmly, and—*the wheels leave the ground!* The wheels touch again. I ease the stick forward. Almost flying speed and nearly 2,000 feet ahead. The entire plane trembles. Off again—right wing low—pull it up—ease back onto the runway. Another pool, water drumming on the fabric [covering the fuselage]. The next hop's longer. I could probably stay in the air, but I let the wheels touch once more.

The *Spirit of St. Louis* takes herself off next time. Full flying speed. The controls taut, alive, straining—and still a thousand feet to the telephone wires. If the engine can hold out one more minute. Five feet, twenty, forty. Wires flash by underneath. Twenty feet to spare!

Green grass below—a golf links. People looking up. A low, tree-covered hill ahead. The *Spirit of St. Louis* seems balanced on a pinpoint, as though the slightest movement of controls would cause it to topple over and fall. Five thousand pounds suspended from those little wings. Five thousand pounds on a blast of air.

Now I'm high enough to steal glances at the instrument board. The earth inductor compass needle leans steeply to the right. I bank cautiously northward until it rises to the center line—65 degrees—the compass heading for the first 100-mile segment of my great-circle route to France and Paris. It's 7:54 A.M. Eastern daylight time.

Back in San Diego, when Lindbergh and the designer of the *Spirit of St. Louis* had measured the distance of the flight across a library globe, the string had made a straight line between New York and Paris. But on a flat map, where the lines of latitude are straightened out into parallels, the route had to bend into an arc known as a great circle. The route Lindbergh would take curved north and east from New York, up the east coast over Cape Cod, then out over the ocean to Nova Scotia. Lindbergh planned to change his course every hundred miles (about one hour's flying time in the *Spirit of St. Louis*). He would head a few degrees farther south and east across the southern coast of Newfoundland and then out over the North Atlantic.

As Lindbergh flew up the coast on this route, people waited on streets and housetops to watch him pass. Despite the fact that his navigating equipment was primitive, he managed to reach the Nova Scotia coast only a few miles off course. Every hour excited messages were telephoned to New York giving details of his progress. In the twelfth hour of his flight, Lindbergh passed over St. John's, Newfoundland, then out over the ocean:

> I come upon it suddenly—the little city of St. John's, after skimming over the top of a granite summit. Farther ahead, the entrance to the harbor is a narrow gap with sides running up to the crest of a low coastal range. Twilight deepens as I plunge down into the valley. It takes only a moment, stick forward, engine throttled, to dive down over the wharves (men stop their after-supper chores to look upward) and out through the gap. North America and its islands are behind. Ireland is 2,000 miles ahead.

Throughout the flight Lindbergh faced the ever-present dangers of engine failure, storms, and the possibility of a structural weakness in the *Spirit of St. Louis* itself. But between Newfoundland and Ireland there were two additional dangers. The first was sleep. Lindbergh had not slept all the night before his takeoff. During the next night and the day after, as he flew over the ocean, he fought back the terrible temptation to close his eyes for just a few seconds of rest. Despite its virtues, the *Spirit of St. Louis* was not a very stable plane. Lindbergh knew that if he relaxed his hold on it for more than a moment, he might crash. He had to hold his eyes open with his hands. Once he even had to hit himself full force in the face to keep awake.

The second danger was ice. This hazard hit Lindbergh suddenly after he had climbed over 10,000 feet, trying to clear a bank of clouds about 200 miles east of Newfoundland. He was suddenly aware of being cold himself. (He had left the glass out of the side windows of the *Spirit of St. Louis*, hoping that the fresh air and engine noise would keep him alert.) Cold? He jerked himself wide awake. If *he* was cold, what about his plane?

> Good Lord! There are things to be considered outside the cockpit! How could I forget! I jerk off a leather mitten and thrust my arm out the window. My palm is covered with stinging pinpricks. I pull the flashlight from my pocket and throw its beam on a strut. The entering edge is irregular and shiny! *Ice*!
>
> I've got to turn around, get back to clear air—quickly!

Lindbergh fought the urge to turn quickly. He knew that if he did, the ice on the wings might cause the plane to go out of control. Instead, he eased the *Spirit of St. Louis* around in a long, slow curve back toward Newfoundland.

> I throw my flashlight [beam] onto the wing strut. Ice is thicker! Steady the plane. Everything depends on the turn indicator working till I get outside the cloud. Just two or three more minutes.
>
> My eyes sense a change in the blackness of my cockpit. I look out through the window. How bright! What safety have I reached! I was in the thunderhead for ten minutes at most, but it's one of those incidents that can't be measured by minutes. Such periods stand out like islands in a sea of time.

After this brief but dangerous encounter with the night sky, Lindbergh picked his way cautiously toward Ireland and dawn. (Since he was flying west to east, into the sunrise, he was experiencing the shortest night of any man before him in history.) He sipped cautiously at the quart canteen of water. For the rest of the time he just flew his plane, waiting for moonrise, then sunrise, then landfall. He later recalled the twenty-eighth hour of his flight.

> I keep scanning the horizon through breaks between squalls. Is that a cloud on the northeastern horizon, or a strip of low fog – or – *can it possibly be land?* It looks like land, but I don't intend to be tricked by another mirage. I'm only sixteen hours out of Newfoundland. I allowed eighteen and one-half hours to strike the Irish coast.
>
> But my mind is clear. I'm no longer half asleep. The temptation is too great. I can't hold my course any longer. The *Spirit of St. Louis* banks over toward the nearest point of land.
>
> I stare at it intently, not daring to believe my eyes, watching the shades and contours unfold into a coastline. Now I'm flying above the foam-lined coast, searching for prominent features to fit the chart on my knee. I've climbed to 2,000 feet so I can see the contours of the country better. Yes, there's a place on the chart where it all fits — Valentia and Dingle Bay, *on the southwestern coast of Ireland!* I can hardly believe it's true. I'm almost exactly on my route, closer than I hoped to come in my wildest dreams back in San Diego. What happened to all those detours of the night around the thunderheads? Where has the swinging compass error gone?
>
> Intuition must have been more accurate than reasoned navigation.
>
> The southern tip of Ireland! On course, over two hours ahead of schedule; the sun still well up in the sky, the weather clearing!

Now it was easy. So easy that Lindbergh himself fell into the temptation of making a myth out of his own achievement:

> I'm angling slowly back onto my great-circle route. I must have been within three miles of it when I sighted Ireland. An error of fifty miles would have been good dead reckoning under the most perfect conditions. Three miles was — well, what was it? Before I made this flight, I would have said carelessly that it was luck. Now, luck seems far too trival a word, a term to be used only by those who've never seen the curtain drawn or looked on life from far away.

After Ireland the landmarks appeared rapidly — a lighthouse, the coast of England and the coast of France, "like an outstretched hand to

As the clock struck 10 P.M. the *Spirit of St. Louis* came to rest on the runway at Le Bourget airport. To the French, who had gathered by the thousands to celebrate the "Flyin' Fool's" success, Lindbergh was the epitome of "a real American."

meet me." For the first time Lindbergh felt hungry. He ate one of the sandwiches, stale and dry now, that he had bought in New York. He picked up a series of beacon lights marking the route between London and Paris. Then the city arose before him. He circled the brightly lit Eiffel Tower and then turned northeast to look for Le Bourget. "You can't miss it," he had been told. He was like a tourist.

It was almost ten o'clock at night in Paris. Lindbergh was confused by an incredible number of lights around the dark spot where the airport ought to be. A factory, he thought. He did not know that he had suddenly become the most famous man in the world. Thousands of Parisians had rushed out to the airport to greet the American flyer. The roads leading to Le Bourget were jammed with cars with headlights blazing.

Finally, Lindbergh was able to pick out floodlights showing the edge of a runway. He dragged the field once, flying low over it to check for obstructions—a tractor or maybe some sheep let out to crop the grass, he thought. He brought the plane in as carefully as possible, as though he were teaching a student to fly. The plane felt sluggish. By his own guess he still carried a lot of gasoline. His own reflexes seemed slow. Lindbergh had never landed the *Spirit of St. Louis* at night. He glided in at an angle so he could peer out of his side window.

It's only a hundred yards to the hangars now. I'm too high, too fast. Drop wing. Left rudder. Careful. Still too high. I push the stick over. Below the hangar roofs now. Straighten out. A short burst of the engine. Over the lighted areas. Sod coming up to meet me. Careful. Easy to bounce when you're tired. Still too fast. Tail too high. Hold off. Hold off. But the lights are far behind. Ahead, there's nothing but night. Give her the gun and climb for another try?

The wheels touch gently. Off again. No, I'll keep contact. Ease the stick forward. Back on the ground. Off. Back, the tail skid too. Not a bad landing, but I'm beyond the light. Can't see anything ahead. The field *must* be clear. Uncomfortable, though, jolting into blackness. Wish I had a wing light, but too heavy on the takeoff. Slower now, slow enough to ground-loop safely. Left rudder. Reverse it. The *Spirit of St. Louis* swings around and stops rolling, resting on the solidness of earth, in the center of Le Bourget.

I start to taxi back to the floodlights and hangars. But the entire field ahead is covered with running figures!

The American public was intoxicated by Lindbergh's adventure, a solo flight across the Atlantic. He was honored as a national hero in cities throughout the country —here in a parade in New York City.

38
A "NEW ERA"

R. J. W.

When Lindbergh completed his ground loop at Le Bourget, and turned to taxi back to the lighted area around the hangars, all he could see was a running crowd. About 100,000 Frenchmen had broken through police lines to rush onto the field, almost hysterical over this new hero. All day, the transatlantic cables, the newspapers, and radios had been full of news of the flight. And for hours before Lindbergh landed, Parisians had been fighting heavy traffic to drive out to Le Bourget to greet this "Flyin' Fool."

As soon as the *Spirit of Saint Louis* touched down, the crowd rushed the plane. Lindbergh was afraid (as he was to be for months, whenever he made announced landings anywhere in the world) that the people would lose their heads and run into his spinning propeller. When he tried to climb out of his cramped cockpit, the crowd grabbed him. For a long time, he could not even set foot on French soil, but was passed through the crowd, from shoulder to shoulder. In the din, he shouted for a mechanic, someone to protect the plane; but no one could hear or understand him.

In the log he kept of the flight, Lindbergh made this brief, slightly bitter entry: "May 20, Roosevelt Field, Long Island, New York, to Le Bourget Aerodrome, Paris, France. 33 hours. 20 min. Fuselage fabric badly torn by souvenir hunters." The first part of the entry, the flight, was what was significant to Lindbergh. But the second part, the half-crazed hero worship of the crowd, is just as important to understanding the full significance of what Lindbergh had done and become. In Paris, but even more in New York and dozens of other American cities, Lindbergh was adored.

From the time he landed at Le Bourget, his life was not his own. People crowded around wherever he went. They stole his hats in restaurants. He could not keep shirts, or even underwear, because laundry employees swiped them for souvenirs.

More than any other man of his generation, Lindbergh captured the imagination of his contemporaries. Newspapers printed more stories about him and his flight than they had about the death of President Wilson. More people — 4 million the police said — turned out to see him in a New York parade than had ever come out to look at any President. Something about Lindbergh and his feat touched a deep and responsive chord in the America of the 1920s.

On the face of it, there was no overwhelming reason for Lindbergh's fantastic fame. As a matter of cold fact, his flight had proven nothing — except that a superb pilot, blessed by some luck, could fly a specially built airplane 3,600 miles. The *Spirit of Saint Louis* could carry no passengers and no cargo. In fact, Lindbergh had refused to carry even one pound of mail, though he was offered $1,000 to do so. Lindbergh was not even the first man to fly the Atlantic. Eight years earlier, in 1919, a British dirigible had done it *twice*. That year, too, an American seaplane had crossed from New York to England, landing several times on the ocean. And in the same year, two pilots had made it nonstop from Newfoundland to Ireland, to win a prize of $50,000 — double Lindbergh's prize. For a variety of reasons, when Lindbergh made his flight in 1927, almost no one seemed to remember these earlier feats, while "Lucky Lindy" quickly became a household word.

The causes of Lindbergh's incredible celebrity have to be found outside his actual accomplishment. They lie in deep changes that had occurred in American society. Americans were excited about Lindbergh for reasons that had more to do with them than with him. They projected more significance into the event than it really had. When masses of people experience such excitement, they tend to see historical actors as demons or heroes. They oversimplify the world, and thus make some new kind of sense out of their own lives. This process often has very little to do with reality. Lindbergh became a symbol. His contemporaries saw in him what they wanted to see, making him into a sort of mirror for the technological and social changes that had transformed American society in the twentieth century.

REACHING A MASS AUDIENCE

One of the reasons for Lindbergh's rapid rise to fame was the publicity he received from the press and the radio. Since the 1890s the newspapers of the United States had been increasing in number and circulation. They competed fiercely for the attention of the public. This expansion of newspapers was only part of an important revolution in communications that began in the nineteenth century and still continues today.

One by one, new inventions brought people's lives closer together. These included the telegraph, the telephone, the phonograph, the camera, the radio, and the motion picture. They created a world in which whole nations and continents could share almost simultaneously in distant events. Lindbergh's flight was "covered" intensely by the press, which transmitted its stories over telegraph and telephone lines. Lindbergh was also photographed mercilessly. His activities were recorded both in newspaper photographs and in the newsreels that accompanied the early silent motion pictures. Hour-by-hour reports of his famous flight were transmitted on the radio—an invention that had come into use only a few years before. As soon as Lindbergh landed in Paris, the news was flashed back to the United States by transatlantic telegraph cable.

In many ways Lindbergh the hero was the creation of mass communications. He was the first celebrity to have the full advantage of every modern form of communication except television. (Television did not come into wide use until after World War II.)

The Communications Revolution The revolution in communications began with the telegraph, which linked California and New York more than half a century before Lindbergh's flight. During the same period, newspapers began to attract a

With the broadcast of the Harding-Cox election returns in November 1920, station KDKA in Pittsburgh gave birth to commercial radio. The broadcast opened a new era in communications.

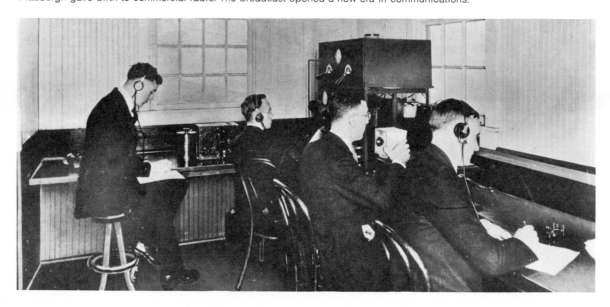

mass audience. The telephone, too, contributed to the rapid and widespread circulation of information. In the first part of the twentieth century the number of telephones in use skyrocketed, from a little over 1 million in 1900 to more than 10 million in 1915. By the time Lindbergh took off for Paris, practically every middle-class American home had its own telephone.

But the communications revolution did not gather full speed until the invention of the radio. The principle of wireless transmission of sound was almost as old as the telephone. In 1887 a German scientist proved the existence of electrical waves in space. He speculated that they might be turned into signals. An Italian inventor, Guglielmo Marconi, applied the theory to wireless transmission of telegraph signals in 1896. From then on it was only a matter of assembling the appropriate tubes, transmitters, and receivers.

In 1920 Americans heard their first commercial radio broadcast. The station was KDKA in Pittsburgh, and the program was a news report on the 1920 presidential election. Soon after that, the winner of the election, Warren G. Harding, installed a radio set in the White House. Gradually Marconi's invention was transformed from a toy into a commercial reality. By the time Lindbergh made his flight to Paris, an estimated 10 million sets were in use in the United States, almost one for every telephone.

Two other inventions, the phonograph and the camera, furthered the revolution in mass communications. Thomas A. Edison found a way of capturing and recreating sound that was to make music available to millions at an instant. George Eastman's perfection of the camera made it possible for newspapers to include pictures on their pages.

All these changes allowed millions of people to participate indirectly in events they were not able to witness in person. In other words, these developing communications facilities had created a potential public that could take part in any happening, frown at any villain, worship any hero.

A Middle-class "Public" The new public that celebrated Lindbergh's flight with such enthusiasm should not be confused with the whole nation. Lindbergh's fame was primarily a middle-class phenomenon. He was, in some ways, a media creation; and the media that made him catered primarily to white, well-to-do citizens. Even newspapers catered mainly to a middle-class audience. Radios and telephones were still the property of the middle class almost exclusively. In 1927, the phonograph and the camera were still alien novelties to many millions of poor Americans. Whole great subpopulations—blacks, many poor white farmers, millions of immigrants in the cities—were practically excluded from the new "public" that the mass media helped create.

Eventually, of course, the new inventions (and the television sets that completed the communications revolution) would become the common property of almost every American, rich or poor. But in the 1920s, and for some time after, they were still middle-class conveniences. If Lindbergh was a symbol of popular values, they were not necessarily values that belonged to all of America. They were the beliefs and hopes of white, middle-class citizens. At the time, it was easy and tempting for the members of this restricted "public" to believe that they *were* America. Most of them would have agreed quickly with the American ambassador to France, who said that Lindbergh represented "the spirit of our people." Similarly, the *New Republic*, a magazine with a small, highly educated audience, could say confidently that Lindbergh "is US personified." But the ambassador and the *New Republic* spoke carelessly. The "people" and the "US" they referred to were in fact only the public defined by the media.

As for the others, the majority—the poor, the blacks, the immigrants—there is no way to know what (if anything) they thought about Lindbergh. In all likelihood, if they noticed Lindbergh at all, it was only for a moment, and with no special sense of identification with him or his feat. Like most of the cultural content of the "Roaring Twenties," the Lindbergh phenomenon occurred mainly within the very class from which he had come. In fact, one of the deepest needs he may have served was the need of this class to believe that it really did possess "the spirit" of the whole nation.

THE MACHINE AND THE MAVERICK IN A TECHNOLOGICAL SOCIETY

Americans were fond of calling the period after World War I the New Era. Much of what they meant by the phrase was summed up symbolically in Lindbergh's airplane. The New Era was above all a machine age, a triumph of advanced technology. Compared with a modern jet or a moon rocket, the *Spirit of St. Louis* was a very primitive machine. But to millions of Americans of the 1920s it was the final and glistening outcome of the industrial and technological revolution that had begun in the preceding century. It symbolized what they believed was happening in the United States: the creation of a new kind of civilization, a miracle of progress in which every barrier to human comfort and achivement would be broken by industry and invention.

The United States of the mid-1920s was much more thoroughly industrialized than it had been at the turn of the century. Total steel production, for example, quadrupled during the period between the death of McKinley and Lindbergh's flight to Paris. The total value of all manufactured goods increased almost eight times in the same period. The number of people engaged in agriculture declined to about one-fourth of the total population. American cities grew at an astounding pace. By 1930, three years after Lindbergh's flight, 40 percent of the total population of the United States lived in twenty-five large metropolitan centers. In short, Lindbergh appealed to a society that was overwhelmingly industrial and urban, and fundamentally dependent on machines and factories.

Electric Power and Assembly Lines In some ways the New Era was an extension of the revolution in industry that had occurred after the Civil War (see Chapter 30). The factory system had continued to expand. New and more complex forms of machinery had been developed to produce more and more goods. But if the basic trends were the same, there were some new elements too. The New Era, to a far greater extent than the old, was powered by electricity and organized around assembly lines.

In 1870, when the industrial revolution was making its first powerful impact, steam and water were used equally to drive industry. Steam continued to be the main form of motor energy in industry until about 1917. But steam had its drawbacks, and the introduction of electricity made possible extraordinary advances in industry.

Again, the basic inventions belonged to the nineteenth century. Within the ten-year period from 1877 to 1887 the dynamo for generating electricity and the motor for converting it into motion were both perfected. This was largely the work of Thomas Edison. During these same years, Edison's incandescent light was introduced into homes and streets. In 1882 the first commerical electric power station, the Edison Illuminating Company, was built in New York.

While electric lighting brightened life in offices, houses, and streets, the electric motor helped transform industrial production. In 1900 electric motors provided only one-twentieth of the power used in American industrial plants. By World War I this figure had increased to about one-third. When Lindbergh flew to France, just ten years later, electricity provided almost two-thirds of the total industrial power in American factories and mills. Between 1870 and 1920 the amount of raw energy used by American industry, measured in horsepower, increased by well over 1,000 percent!

The development of the moving-belt assembly line also had far-reaching effects on industrial production. Assembly lines were first introduced on a large scale by Henry Ford at his automobile plant in Michigan in 1913. The principle was a simple one. Workers were placed in a row in the order of sequence of their jobs. As the product (in this case the automobile) moved past him, each man performed his assigned task. The idea might be simple, but the savings in time and motion were dramatic. Each worker, using a specialized tool to perform a small task, could now produce much more in a given day. Ford's assembly line was copied by dozens of other industries. By the middle of the 1920s it was a standard technique.

DEVELOPMENTS IN TECHNOLOGY, 1865–1930
(DATES REFER TO PATENT OR FIRST SUCCESSFUL USE)

YEAR	INVENTOR	CONTRIBUTION	IMPORTANCE/DESCRIPTION
1869	George Westinghouse	AIR BRAKE	Provided smoother and quicker braking action for railroad cars.
1874	Joseph Glidden	BARBED WIRE MANUFACTURE	Speeded the end of open grazing of cattle.
1876	Alexander Graham Bell	TELEPHONE	Made out of a cigar box, wire, and two toy magnets; revolutionized communication.
1877	Thomas Alva Edison	PHONOGRAPH	Extended availability of music to millions.
1879	Thomas Alva Edison	INCANDESCENT BULB	Made possible electric lighting.
1880	W. E. Sawyer	PRINCIPLE OF SCANNING	Established the possibility of using only a single wire or channel for transmission of a picture, thereby making television possible.
1888	George Eastman	HAND CAMERA	Revolutionized newspaper journalism.
1888	Nikola Tesla	FIRST MOTOR TO BE RUN BY ALTERNATING CURRENT	Made the transmission of electrical power over long distances possible.
1892	John Froelich	MOTORIZED TRACTOR	Powered by a 20-hp., single-cylinder gasoline engine; greatly increased agricultural efficiency.
1895	George B. Selden	INTERNAL COMBUSTION AUTOMOBILE ENGINE	Initiated a new mode of transportation.
1896	Guglielmo Marconi	WIRELESS TELEGRAPH	Formed the basis for radio transmissions.
1903	Orville & Wilbur Wright	FIRST FLIGHT OF A HEAVIER-THAN-AIR CRAFT	Marked the beginning of the air age.
1904	Thomas Alva Edison	SOUND MOTION PICTURE	Inaugurated a new entertainment/information medium.
1913	William M. Burton	CRACKING OIL-REFINING PROCESS	Made possible production of gasoline from kerosene.
1917	Ernst F. W. Alexanderson	HIGH-FREQUENCY ALTERNATOR	Made worldwide wireless transmission possible.
1918	Peter C. Hewitt F. B. Crocker	HELICOPTER	First helicopter to rise successfully from the ground.
1922	Herbert T. Kalmus	TECHNICOLOR PROCESS	Made possible color film.
1926	Robert Hutchings Goddard	ROCKET	First liquid-propellant rocket.

This photograph of a day's production of car chassis at a Detroit Ford plant vividly illustrates the increase in output made possible by the use of the assembly line. Mass-production methods cut assembly time from 12½ to 1½ hours.

Effects of Mechanization The industrial revolution continued. The changes brought about by the electric motor and the assembly line made the lives of most Americans in 1927 very different from their lives a generation or two earlier. More and more, the ways in which people lived and worked were determined by machines and technological innovations. More and more, mechanical devices replaced human energy and skill.

This process of mechanization had two deep effects on American society. First, it made modern Americans more conscious of the efficient use of time and effort than any other people in the history of the world. Second, it threatened to standardize life by reducing the area of imagination and individuality in peoples' daily working environment. The celebration of Lindbergh was connected to both these consequences.

In planning his flight, Lindbergh was almost ruthlessly efficient. The *Spirit of St. Louis* was a nearly perfect machine. It was designed to perform one simple task in the most effective way, with a minimum of wasted energy. Like a machine in a modern factory, the plane represented the harnessing of energy to a carefully designed instrument for the performance of a rigidly defined task. Much of what Americans admired in Lindbergh was precisely what they admired in their own society—his technological achievement.

But there was another side to Lindbergh. He was a maverick. Some of the pet names the newspapers gave him, like "The Flyin' Fool" and "Lucky," made his daring seem more important than his technical skill. Lindbergh seemed to go against the trend toward standardization of life in the New Era. He represented individual imagination, as well as engineering and piloting skill. A large part of Lindbergh's fame probably rested on this contradiction. His flight was both a triumph of technology and a victory for individual daring.

WHEELS AND WINGS: THE MOTOR AGE

The development of electricity had a powerful effect not only on industry but also on American home life. New inventions like the electric washing machine and refrigerator (which utilized small, inexpensive motors) changed the working and eating habits of American families. And a dozen other smaller electric appliances—from toasters to thermostats for home furnaces—helped usher in the American consumer's vision of a New Era.

Perfecting the Automobile The largest change in American social life was brought about by the gasoline engine. The basic principle of the internal combustion engine was understood by the middle of the nineteenth century. The principle was simple. Instead of burning fuel externally to convert water into steam, the internal combustion engine burned fuel in an explosive way inside a chamber. The force of the explosion was then used to drive a piston or a rotor. The first internal combustion engine was built and operated in the 1860s in France. Power for the new engine was available in

HENRY FORD

As much as any other single factor, automobiles caused the dramatic change in American life in the twentieth century. Yet the man who did the most to put the nation on wheels, Henry Ford, disliked the change. The older he grew, the more fondly he looked back on the America of his youth. He valued its rural base, Puritan work ethic, and simple pleasures.

Life began for Henry Ford on a farm near Dearborn, Michigan, on July 30, 1863. Early in his life two traits became apparent: he loved machinery, and he hated farming. He was a born tinkerer. By the time he was thirteen, he could disassemble and reconstruct a watch. He was forever fixing his father's farm machinery and his mother's household appliances. When he ran out of things to repair at home, he repaired the watches, clocks, and machinery of neighbors.

As soon as he could, he left the farm for Detroit to become a machinist. He quickly learned his trade and was soon a well-paid, highly skilled workman. In his spare time he worked on a gasoline buggy in an old brick shed behind his home. By 1896 he was able to drive it through the hole he had knocked out of the shed wall. Mounted on four bicycle wheels was a two-cylinder, four-horsepower engine. Mounted on that was a buggy seat. To steer it he used a curved stick like the tiller on a boat.

From his awkward beginning Ford built a billion-dollar industry over the next fifty years. But as he grew from home-shop tinkerer to industrial tycoon, he never really changed his boyhood attitudes. They remained those of an agrarian Populist of the 1880s and 1890s.

As a result, Henry Ford was a mass of contradictions. While he professed a firm belief in the value of the individual workman and of hard and useful work, he developed an assembly-line process that was truly dehumanizing. He broke down each of the jobs involved in making a car into its tiniest steps. Consequently, a workman did only one thing —like tightening a single bolt—all day long. Ford was even proud of the fact that 43 percent of the jobs in his factories could be mastered in no more than one day.

While he was an expert businessman, as shown by his development of an enormous personal fortune and a vastly profitable corporation, Ford disliked many aspects of capitalism. He had an abiding mistrust of bankers and moneymen.

And while he continued to turn out millions of cars, making Americans a highly mobile and rootless society, he romanticized the stable, well-rooted small-town life. He so loved nineteenth-century rural America that he spent twenty years constructing a reproduction of the community he grew up in— Greenfield Village. There, skilled artisans worked at jobs that had long since been taken over by assembly lines.

Henry Ford died an old man of eighty-four, puzzled and unhappy with the people and the world he had done so much to transform.

the form of gasoline, a "waste" product in the making of kerosene, the basic fuel oil of the nineteenth century.

It was only a matter of time, then, until someone perfected the engine, mounted it on a "horseless carriage," and so created the automobile. No one, however, could have begun to guess at the end of the nineteenth century just how rapid the development of the automobile would be. Nor could they foresee the range of consequences it would have on the ways Americans lived.

The first man in the United States to build a workable automobile powered by a gasoline engine was probably Ransom E. Olds. (His rickety machine was the forerunner of the present-day Oldsmobile.) Five years later, in 1895, Henry Ford put together his first car. The new machine was noisy, unreliable, and expensive. Still, a few Americans were willing to pay the price and stop their ears against the noise. By 1900 there were about 8,000 of the curious new machines operating in the country.

But Ford was not so much an inventor of the automobile as the inventor of a style and a method of production. In the early years of the century Ford began simplifying the automobile. He cut away every fancy decoration and convenience that had been adapted from the luxurious carriages of the day. Moreover, he reduced costs by turning out standardized, mass-produced machines. The results were astonishing. In 1907 the average price of an automobile was over $2,000. The next year Ford introduced a model selling at only $850. By 1914 he was able to cut the price to a little over $500. By the mid-1920s Ford was selling his assembly-line Model T for less than $300. The car was similar in many ways to the *Spirit of St. Louis.* It was the simplest machine possible, designed to do a plain task in the most efficient way.

Other automobile makers began to imitate and compete with Ford. The result was an exploding new industry. By the 1920s the manufacture of automobiles was by far the largest consumer products industry in the United States. It employed tens of thousands of workers at large and growing factories centered in Detroit. The automobile had a remarkable impact on other industries, especially steel and rubber, which provided the raw prod-

ucts for the assembly lines. The oil industry also underwent a major expansion. The automobile turned gasoline into the main stock-in-trade of the petroleum companies.

Life in the Motor Age   The most obvious impact of the automobile was not on industry but on American social life. By 1927 Ford had made 15 million cars. About 20 million American families owned an automobile. The immediate result was that horses and other draft animals disappeared from the landscape and the streets.

But the automobile had other, less obvious and predictable effects. First, the automobile encouraged Americans to move farther and farther out of the cities, into the suburbs. From about the time of Lindbergh's trip to Paris, the "lure of the suburbs" attracted more and more middle-class Americans. Second, cars and buses transformed American education, especially in small towns and farm areas. The school bus made it possible to consolidate school districts into larger units. Gradually the simple one-room schoolhouse, with one or two teachers for all the grades, disappeared.

Finally, the automobile, the truck, and the bus began a process that would take another thirty years to complete: the near destruction of the railroads—the principal technological innovation of the nineteenth century. At first, in the 1920s and 1930s, the car and the bus cut mainly into the railroads' local traffic. But as roads and engines improved, the competition became more and more severe. As for freight, the trucking industry began to compete for what had been almost a railroad monopoly. The train, with its mighty steam engine, had been the great symbol of the industrial revolution up to the 1920s. By the middle of the twentieth century, much of the railroad industry was ailing and unprofitable, no longer able to survive as a private enterprise.

In the long run, the automobile proved to have unwanted as well as unpredicted consequences. Among these the modern decay of central cities was the most serious. Gradually, large sections of cities like New York, Boston, and Chicago became the slums of the poor, who could not afford suburban homes. Also, although no one in Lindbergh's day could have predicted it, the auto-

The automobile soon became a symbol of "the good life." Here a family enjoys a picnic on the grass with their Model T Ford parked behind them.

The prosperity in the 1920s that enabled millions of Americans to purchase automobiles gave rise to that most modern phenomenon—the traffic jam.

mobile caused a major problem of air pollution. Smog resulted from the exhausts of millions of cars and trucks burning hundreds of millions of gallons of gasoline every year.

To most Americans, though, the automobile was an unquestioned miracle. To those who could afford it, it meant freedom to move at will through the city or the countryside. It also provided status, as manufacturers introduced more elaborate models, some costing ten times as much as Ford's Model T. And the automobile meant adventure. Middle-class Americans could get behind the wheel of a powerful, complicated piece of machinery—just as Lindbergh climbed into the cockpit of his machine—and be off on an exciting journey of motion and speed every day. Like Lindbergh, too, Americans went beyond a concern with efficiency and practicality to a romantic affection for their machines. They polished them, paraded them, and gave them pet names like the "old bus," the "flivver," the "tin Lizzie," and the "merry Oldsmobile." Despite its defects, Americans loved the car.

Development of Air Transportation For the first quarter of the twentieth century the automobile had the greatest social and economic impact on America. The development of the aircraft industry and airline passenger service did not become truly important until years after Lindbergh's flight. But the airplane was in many ways more thrilling than the automobile. (This was why Lindbergh and other pilots could make a living in the 1920s barnstorming across America in their aerial circuses.) Like the automobile, the airplane depended on the small, powerful, and efficient gasoline engine.

The first men to fly a real airplane were Orville and Wilbur Wright. In 1903, they camped at Kitty Hawk, North Carolina (a location they chose because it had strong and steady winds, plus a great expanse of beach), with a primitive biplane. It had a tiny gasoline engine, which turned two push-type propellers. The first successful test flight came in December, after a series of dangerous and frustrating failures. This first flight lasted a little less than a minute, and covered only about 800 feet. But the Wright brothers were soon experimenting with larger

planes and engines. In 1909, after six years of work, they sold the first plane to the United States Army.

World War I brought about a dramatic spurt in design sophistication, not only in the United States, but in Europe. The new planes had larger and better engines, and a much more rigid construction than the Wrights' original. The war also romanticized flight and created a new type of military hero, the "aviator." Lindbergh, then, was able to capitalize not only on advances in technology but on a new image of the heroic and daring "ace."

The main civilian use of the airplane was shipping mail. The government began service in 1918. Later, private companies (like the one Lindbergh worked for in St. Louis) took over the service. The operation was dangerous. A majority of the pilots were killed in crashes during the early years. But by the mid-1920s there was regular, all-weather airmail service between most major cities in America.

Lindbergh's flight, combined with the introduction of larger airplanes like Byrd's *America*, did more than any other single event to encourage the growth of air transportation. Lindbergh had faith in the future of aviation. Soon after his return to America in 1927, he began a flying tour of the country to promote airmail and air transportation. By 1930, just three years after his solo transatlantic flight, there were 43 domestic airline companies, operating over 30,000 miles of flying routes.

NEW MANNERS AND MORALS

All these changes—the development of mass communications, the expansion of industry, the introduction of a new technology—brought about another revolution. This revolution marked a dramatic difference in the manners and morals of the American people. Americans of the 1920s knew they were living in a time when the world was undergoing rapid change. They coined new words and phrases—like the "Roaring Twenties," the "lost generation," and "flaming youth"—to describe what was happening to them. Americans were adopting habits and moral standards that their parents found shocking and offensive.

A Revolution for Women At the center of the revolution in manners were women. The revolution that would change women's lives did not begin in the 1920s. During the first two decades of the twentieth century, many middle- and upper-class women had adopted new patterns of behavior (including divorce) that broke with the traditions of nineteenth-century Victorian America. But because of the impact of World War I and the influence of books, radio, and advertising, the trend started at the turn of the century began to affect ever-widening circles of women. By the 1920s the revolution was in full bloom.

Politically, women were new creatures. After decades of agitation, they finally won the right to vote, with passage of the Nineteenth Amendment in 1920. But this new political role was only a small part of the emancipation of women. The new woman of the 1920s wanted to do everything. "Everything" included more opportunities than her mother had had.

She was much more likely than her mother to attend college. She might go to work, too. By

The flapper symbolized the new woman's daring—her flouting of traditional social and moral restraints. Short, bobbed hairdos, knee-length skirts, and sheer silk stockings identify these four women as flappers, as do their nightclub surroundings.

1930, 10 million women were employed in the American labor force. This new experience of education and work increased the number of women who were likely to remain single, or, if they did marry, to get divorced. The divorce rate in 1930 was twice what it had been before the war. This did not mean that marriages were more unhappy. It meant, instead, that women were less likely to put up with a bad marital situation. They would demand their freedom instead.

There was an even more obvious revolution in the way women dressed. The ideal that gradually emerged in the decade of Lindbergh's flight was that of the "flapper." She wore her dress short—above the knees rather than at the ankle. And the dress was not only shorter, it was made of thin material, designed to move with her body as she walked or danced—designed, too, to give an occasional glimpse of thigh above the hemline. The flapper discarded the corsets that her mother had worn, and dispensed with the bustle, too. She put on much more make-up and perfume, and jangled with much more jewelry at her neck and wrists. In advertisements and in movies, and in real life, too, she was likely to pose with a cocktail in one hand and a cigarette in a long holder in the other—the essence of a new "sophistication."

Like Lindbergh, though, the flapper and the "liberation" she symbolized was a middle-class phenomenon primarily. College, careers, divorce, and emancipated dress still touched only a minority of American women. Even though the suffrage now belonged to every woman, in practice, voting was primarily confined to middle-class women. For the rest, life continued to be quite confining. And when women did leave the home to take jobs, they still suffered from a systematic discrimination in wages and opportunities. In the final analysis, the flapper, like Lindbergh, had a significance that was more symbolic than real.

The Jazz Age The new woman was part of a changing culture. A freedom of action and belief unheard of before seemed to go hand in hand with the triumph of industrial technology, with its prosperity and sense of unlimited possibilities for life. Both men and women listened to new music—jazz—and danced new steps. Instead of formal

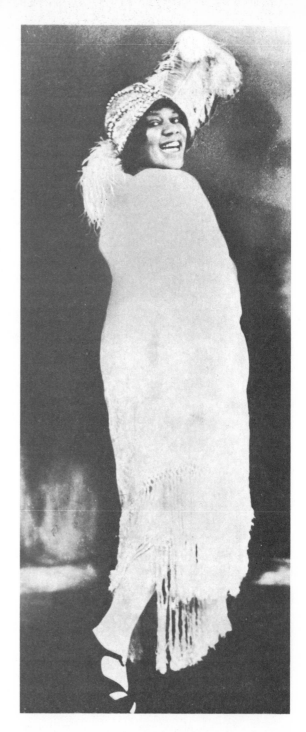

The "Jazz Age" gave birth to the blues, an especially plaintive, bittersweet music of black American origin. Bessie Smith, one of the best American jazz artists, made the singing of the blues uniquely her own.

The Maturing of American Culture

Generations of foreigners, while admiring American achievements in other fields, criticized the nation's artistic backwardness. Even Americans who patronized the arts— like this eager visitor in Frank Waller's 1881 painting of the Metropolitan Museum—were said to appreciate money more than merit. Such views were exaggerated, yet held some truth. Until the late nineteenth century, a distinctive American culture was slow to emerge. But the situation changed in the next few decades. By the 1920s foreigners were admiring American literature, painting, architecture, and music. The United States had found a cultural voice of its own.

[For further information on the foreign observers quoted in this essay, see "Notes on Sources."]

PICTORIAL ESSAY 7

American art is still in a stage of evolution; the painters of today are the precursors of those who shall adorn the Golden Age which is to come. Though there have been, and are, individual artists of distinguished merit and ability, art itself is not yet fully developed nor understood. The nation has had hitherto neither time, opportunity, nor inclination to interest itself intelligently in the fine arts.

[COUNT VAY DE VAYA UND LUSKOD, 1908]

Behold! Mark Twain had curled himself up in the big armchair, and I was smoking reverently, as befits one in the presence of his superior. The thing that struck me first was that he was an elderly man; yet, after a minute's thought, I perceived that it was otherwise, and in five minutes, the eyes looking at me, I saw that the gray hair was an accident of the most trivial. He was quite young. I was shaking his hand, I was smoking his cigar, and I was hearing him talk—this man I had learned to love and admire fourteen thousand miles away.

[RUDYARD KIPLING, 1889]

Mark Twain in 1907. By this time the writer had gained world-wide acclaim for such books as *The Adventures of Tom Sawyer* (1876), *Life on the Mississippi* (1883), and *The Adventures of Huckleberry Finn* (1885).

American paintings are no longer strange to Europe. In the art division of the last Paris Exposition, Americans took their share of the honors, and they are highly appreciated at most of the Berlin and Munich picture shows. Sargent and Whistler are the best known. Sargent, as the painter of elegant ladies, prosperous men, and interesting children, has undoubtedly the surest and most refined gift with his brush of any son of the New World. Whistler is doubtless the greater, the real sovereign. He fathoms each human riddle, and expresses it intangibly, mysteriously. Everything is mood and suggestion, the dull and heavy is lightened, the whole is rendered in rich twilight zones.

[HUGO MÜNSTERBERG, 1904]

The Last of Old Westminster, painted by James Abbott McNeill Whistler in 1862. The scene is London, where Whistler lived for much of his life. This work was followed by a number of outstanding portraits, including the famous one of his mother (which he actually titled *An Arrangement in Grey and Black*).

Miss Cassatt is a true phenomenon. In more than one of her canvases she is on the verge of becoming a notable artist with unparalleled natural feeling, penetrating observation, and a welcome subjection before the model which is the accomplishment of peerless artists.

[ALBERT WOLFF, 1881]

The Bath, by Mary Cassatt, dates from about 1891. The artist—who lived most of her adult life in Paris—liked to paint mothers and children. She communicated feelings of warmth and tenderness without sentimentality.

The taste for plastic art [in the United States] has slowly worked upward. Recent movements have left many beautiful examples of sculpture. Cities are jealously watchful now that only real works of art shall be erected, and that monuments which are to be seen by millions of people shall be really characteristic examples of good art. More than anything else, sculpture has at length come into a closer sympathy with architecture than perhaps it has in any other country. Such a work as Saint-Gaudens' Shaw Memorial in Boston is among the most beautiful examples of modern sculpture. Vigorous and mature is the American, in plastic art as well as in poetry.

[HUGO MÜNSTERBERG, 1904]

This work, showing Augustus Saint-Gaudens in his studio, was painted by Kenyon Cox in 1908. The sculptor was known for his public statuary, including Lincoln, in Lincoln Park, Chicago; General Sherman, near Central Park in New York City; and the Shaw Memorial on Boston Common.

Mr. and Mrs. Isaac Newton Phelps Stokes, portrayed by John Singer Sargent in 1897. These prominent New Yorkers, though pictured in informal dress, epitomize the wealth and refinement typical of Sargent's subjects.

People are inclined to smile at me when I suggest that you in America are at the commencement of a period of fine and vigorous art. The signs, they say, are all the other way. Of course you ought to know best. All the same, I stick to my opinion with British obstinacy, and believe I shall see it justified.

[JOHN GALSWORTHY, 1919]

Willa Cather builds her imagined world almost as solidly as our five senses build the universe around us. She has within herself a sensitivity that constantly presents her with a body of material which would overwhelm most of us. She has also a quality of mountain-pony sturdiness that makes her push on unfatigued under her load and give an accurate account of every part of it.

[REBECCA WEST, 1927]

On the threshold of her career, in 1902, Willa Cather had yet to gain a name for herself. She became noted for such novels as *O Pioneers!* (1913) and *My Antonia* (1918).

Sloan's canvas of girls under the elevated has more of New York in it than anything else I know.

[DIEGO RIVERA, 1942]

Six O'Clock was painted by John Sloan in 1912. He was one of a group called The Eight. They were known more familiarly as the Ashcan School because they depicted scenes of everyday city life rather than the more formal and traditional subjects favored by academic artists.

Characteristic of Frank Lloyd Wright's so-called "prairie houses" is this home in River Forest, Illinois. It was built in 1908. Wright's later works, noted for their daring innovation, included the Imperial Hotel in Tokyo, the Johnson administration building in Racine, Wisconsin, and the Guggenheim Museum in New York City.

Most of Wright's country houses, fitted into the oceanlike endlessness of the prairie, are very low, joined with, indeed pressed down toward, the earth. As a consequence the interior rooms spread out horizontally from one another. Therefore these houses do not seem like some grotesque thing which has grown out of the earth; they appear native to the soil and fitted to it, like the farmhouse.

[LUDWIG HILBERSHEIMER AND UDO RUKSER, 1920]

The chances are that Robert Frost will become a national figure, a sage, a Yankee sage. He has personal thought; he has wisdom; he has a basic conception from which he can speak. He likes the nation, every nation, and he dislikes the state, every state. He is a puritan, but he goes by the dictates of the heart.

[PADRAIC COLUM, 1936]

Robert Frost, as seen by artist James Chapin in 1929. The New England writer had by this time published some of his best-known poems, among them "Mending Wall," "Birches," and "Stopping by Woods on a Snowy Evening."

The mission which this land has, like all others, is to discover it s own being, to fulfill it s task of representing itself. And if one puts his ear to the ground, then one hears millions of forces at work to forge and shape this individual being.

[ANTON ERKELENZ, 1927]

Eugene O'Neill is one of the really great figures in modern drama. O'Neill is an example of what I mean when I say America is producing, and will produce in ever greater quantities, an art I feel is indigenous; it belongs to the American soil. No European dramatist could possibly have written those plays. The drama, under him, has found a new type of artistic expression.

[GERHART HAUPTMANN, 1932]

Eugene O'Neill in 1921, at the start of his career. His greatest plays came later: *Desire Under the Elms* (1924), *Mourning Becomes Electra* (1931), and *The Iceman Cometh* (1946). In 1936 he became the first American playwright to win the Nobel prize.

A scene from *Beyond the Horizon*, by O'Neill. Produced in 1920, it was the first full-length play by the dramatist to be acted.

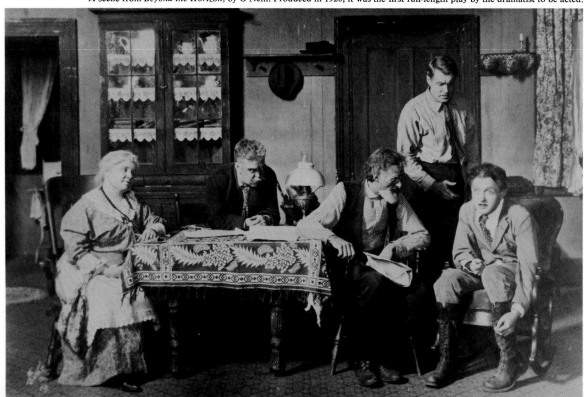

What she gives us is a sort of sculpture in transition. Imagine a dozen statues expressive, say, of the cardinal phases of despair—the poses and gestures and facial expressions of the moment in which each of these phases reaches its maximum of intensity. Then imagine some hundreds of statues that represent, in faultless beauty, every one of the moments of slow transition between these cardinal phases, and you get the art of Isadora Duncan.

[ERNEST NEWMAN, 1921]

The great American photographer Edward Steichen captured some of the magic of dancer Isadora Duncan in this 1921 photo, taken at the Parthenon. Her flowing Grecian costumes and striking interpretive power transformed modern dance.

Gershwin's Rhapsody [in Blue] is by far the most interesting thing of its kind I have yet met with. It really has ideas and they work themselves out in a way that interests the musical hearer. Perhaps it is better not to prophesy. What is at present certain is that Gershwin has written something for a jazz orchestra that is really music, not a mechanical box of tricks.

[ERNEST NEWMAN, 1924]

Mexican artist David Siqueiros painted this *Portrait in a Concert Hall* (George Gershwin) in 1936. The composer, who died the following year, had followed his *Rhapsody in Blue* (1923) with *An American in Paris* (1928) and *Porgy and Bess* (1935).

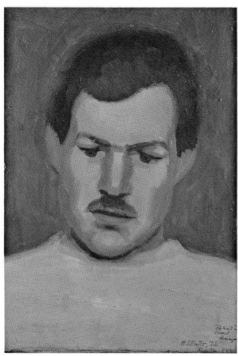

The outstanding achievement of American literature is the swiftness with which it strode from provincialism to half-acknowledged universality. Before 1800 there is nothing, save in the field of politics, which could command, or even deserve to command, a European audience; by 1900 it is true to say that there were few forms of creative effort in which Americans had not done work of the highest quality. America had moved to the very front of the cosmic stage. Henceforth it might be disliked; it could not be neglected.

[HAROLD LASKI, 1948]

It is hardly an exaggeration to say that Ernest Hemingway, more than any of his American colleagues, makes us feel we are confronted by a still young nation which seeks and finds its exact form of expression.

[NOBEL PRIZE CITATION, 1954]

The young Ernest Hemingway was painted by Henry Strater in 1922. His best work, yet to come, included *The Sun Also Rises* (1926), *A Farewell to Arms* (1929), and *For Whom the Bell Tolls* (1940).

Lunched with Sinclair Lewis. He is full of imagination. He tells me he wrote four or five novels before he wrote Main Street, *but they were not successes. I asked him why that had not discouraged him. He laughed, he said it was no use being discouraged, that writing novels was all he could do, he might starve at it, but he was incapable of any other form of work. (Truly an artist!)*

[CLARE SHERIDAN, 1921]

Sinclair Lewis, photographed with his wife in 1916. A year after his meeting with Clare Sheridan, he published one of his best-known novels, *Babbitt*. In 1930 he became the first American to win the Nobel prize for literature.

waltzes and other Victorian dances, they moved to the fast Charleston and the Black Bottom. They also danced close together in the slow fox trot. Many older Americans were shocked by these changes. But these dances became part of the new culture, sweeping their way through high-school gymnasiums and college campuses across the country.

The sexual ideas of Americans were changing, too. The ideas of the Austrian psychologist Sigmund Freud on sex began to be discussed at the dinner table and in the polite magazines of the middle class. Words like "bitch" appeared in novels published by respectable publishers and read by respectable people. "Petting" and "necking" became part of the everyday vocabulary of magazine readers and even ministers. In the movies, sex became a major box-office attraction. Stars like Theda Bara and Clara Bow appeared on the screen in thin clothing, locked in long, passionate embraces with their leading men. When Clara Bow was advertised as the "It" girl, hardly anyone needed to ask what "It" meant.

Americans drank more too. Despite prohibition (see page 694) liquor was easy to obtain. And since liquor was illegal, millions of Americans became technically criminals on an almost daily basis. Probably half of the respectable, middle-class families in the nation had their regular bootlegger. Terms like "bathtub gin" and "speakeasy" became part of the national language. Especially in colleges, drinking became a regular pastime of the "flaming youth" of the decade.

The Search for Innocence As their own lives became more and more confused, Americans began to celebrate innocence. In their movies and sports they created simple, naive heroes who were guided by straightforward codes of justice and virtue. The most popular type of movie hero of the decade was the cowboy, a symbol of innocent, preindustrial man. And the most popular movie star of the period, Rudolph Valentino, played roles that put him on horseback in a country far removed from Fords and factories and modernity. It was no accident, too, that the greatest sports hero of the decade, George Herman Ruth, was nicknamed "Babe."

Lindbergh stirred the deep urge of people to believe in innocence. His youth, honesty, and simple determination made him seem much purer than the public that worshipped him. Lindbergh did not smoke or drink. He displayed no interest in women, at least at the time of his flight. And his boyish face looked out at the world through clear blue eyes. They seemed to say that everything was still the same, that the world had not lost its innocence after all.

Illusions of Disillusionment In the midst of all this change and confusion, intellectuals offered very little help. Beginning in the 1890s, intellectuals in America had produced a remarkable body of literature on the workings of society. In the 1920s, a new generation of intellectuals began to turn out a profusion of superb novels, plays, and essays — as rich a cultural flowering as the country had ever produced. But their work embodied a marked shift away from a concern with social and political problems. With a few exceptions, the new writers either ignored society altogether or viewed it as the enemy, to be mocked or damned.

All in all, the viewpoint of the writers of the 1920s fits Malcolm Cowley's description quite well: "Society was something quite alien . . . a sort of parlor car in which we rode, over smooth tracks, toward a destination we should never have chosen for ourselves." This self-conscious sense of alienation from social structures and purposes governed the literary culture of the decade. It was what prompted the idea that the writers of the period belonged to a "lost generation." The result was a rush of great art that pointed in no particular social direction whatever.

The dominant theme of the writers of the 1920s was disillusionment. Their heroes and heroines usually entered their novels, plays, and stories caught up in some sort of innocent faith — in religion, civilization, progress, freedom, or the like. But, typically, this faith was broken by experience, and the outcome was a ripping away of old illusions. In the typical novel of the decade, the illusions were not replaced by any working new beliefs, but instead by a brooding sense of mistrust and disappointment, and a curious kind of boredom with the world.

The first great subject for disillusionment was the war and the mistaken peace that followed. Several of the best young writers cut their teeth on the war experience—William Faulkner, Ernest Hemingway, John Dos Passos—and for most of them, the conclusion was simple: the war had proved the bankruptcy of what people called "civilization." Hemingway summed up the experience in a story called "Soldier's Home," about the shattered illusions of a veteran named Krebs: "Krebs acquired the nausea in regard to experience that is the result of untruth or exaggeration." The same logic governed Maxwell Anderson's popular *What Price Glory*, E. E. Cummings's *The Enormous Room*—a hilarious book on his arrest and imprisonment in France—and the two war novels of Dos Passos, *One Man's Initiation* and *Three Soldiers*. The only way to escape the "nausea" brought on by the war was to make what Hemingway called "a separate peace."

Actually, when they are looked at carefully, the American war novels were not so much about the war at all, but about what the writers thought lay behind the war: technology, bureaucracy, and propaganda. For people like Faulkner or Dos Passos, the war was not so much a subject as a dramatic metaphor. In many of Hemingway's books and stories of the 1920s—*A Farewell to Arms* (1925) and *The Sun Also Rises* (1926) among them—the war was only the most violent phase of modern civilization. It merely brought into sharper focus the cruelty and inhumanity that were an inherent feature of contemporary social life.

When the writers looked at peacetime subjects, the result was much the same. Sinclair Lewis's riotous parody of the consciousness of a midwestern businessman, in his novel *Babbit*, was just as "disillusioned" as any war novel. In *Winesburg, Ohio*, Sherwood Anderson looked behind the drawn blinds of a small town with exactly the same sense of alienation and distaste. Dos Passos's voluminous novel, *1919*, made little or no distinction between war and peace. All in all, the writers of the decade agreed with the judgment of the poet Ezra Pound that Western civilization was "an old bitch gone in the teeth." Another poet, T. S. Eliot, summed up the attitude in the title of

his most popular work of the period, *The Waste Land.*

For many the only solution seemed to be expatriation. In *The Sun Also Rises*, Hemingway portrayed the aimless confusion of American and British intellectuals in Paris. And for those who did not actually leave the country, there were other forms of withdrawal. William Faulkner—probably the best writer of the period—technically, stayed stubbornly in Mississippi. From that vantage point, he wrote social novels, but they were novels about a rural society whose problems were hardly those of an industrial and urban society. In novels like *The Sound and the Fury* (1929), Faulkner resorted to disarmingly traditional and innocent solutions to human problems—honesty, decency, and even simple modesty. At times, he even seemed to propose religious faith as the only authentic alternative to meaninglessness in modern life.

The writer who best caught the spirit of the "Jazz Age"—as he called it—was F. Scott Fitzgerald. *This Side of Paradise* (1920) rocketed him to a precocious fame. But his reputation was quickly confirmed by *The Great Gatsby* (1925). Fitzgerald's characters inhabited a world of money and sophistication. They were literate and articulate, young and dashing. They drank and smoked and danced their way toward disaster. They were a curious mixture of innocence and disillusionment.

Jay Gatsby, easily Fitzgerald's most characteristic hero, was in some ways a cynical man. He was a criminal who had become extraordinarily wealthy and had invented a false and cultured identity for himself, complete with a great mansion on Long Island. But there was another side to Gatsby, very like Lindbergh. He was a boy from the Midwest who had read Benjamin Franklin, worked hard for "success," and dreamed an innocent dream—that he might find and marry the girl he had loved as a youth. It was this dream, this "romantic readiness," that made Gatsby "great." And if the naive dream led only to corruption and murder, that seemed to Fitzgerald to capture the inner meaning of his generation's experience.

In a sense, Gatsby and Lindbergh were opposite manifestations of the same heroic figure.

Both were simple in the midst of complexity, daring in a world that had become increasingly routine and bureaucratic. Both were driven by a private conviction that had little or no social significance. The difference was that Fitzgerald's hero ended in failure and death; Lindbergh won success and fame and married the daughter of a wealthy financier.

SUGGESTED READINGS– CHAPTERS 37-38

Lindbergh

Charles A. Lindbergh, *The Spirit of Saint Louis* (1953); Kenneth S. Davis, *The Hero: Charles A. Lindbergh* (1959); Walter S. Ross, *The Last Hero: Charles A. Lindbergh* (1968).

General

John D. Hicks, *The Republican Ascendancy, 1921–1933* (1960); David A. Shannon, *Between the Wars, 1919–1941* (1965); John Braeman, R. H. Bremner, David Brody, eds., *Change and Continuity in America: The 1920s* (1968); William E. Leuchtenburg, *The Perils of Prosperity, 1914–1932* (1958).

Communications

Ronald Gellatt, *The Fabulous Phonograph* (1965); Beaumont Newhall, *The History of Photography* (1964); Erik Bernouw, *A Tower in Babel: A History of Broadcasting in the United States to 1933* (1966); F. L. Mott, *American Journalism* (1962).

Technology

Sigfried Giedion, *Mechanization Takes Command* (1948); Henry Ford, *My Life and Work* (1922); Allan Nevins and Frank E. Hill, *Ford* (3 vols., 1954–1962); F. C. Kelly, *The Wright Brothers: Fathers of Flight* (1943); Wilbur and Orville Wright, *Papers* (1953).

Popular Culture

J. W. Krutch, *The Modern Temper* (1929); F. L. Allen, *Only Yesterday* (1931); R. S. and H. N. Lynd, *Middletown* (1929); Arthur Knight, *The Liveliest Art* (1957); Andrew Sinclair, *The Other Half: The Emancipation of the American Woman* (1962); Harold Seymour, *Baseball* (2 vols., 1960–1971); Marshall and Jean Sterns, *Jazz Dance* (1968); Edward Wagenknecht, *Movies in the Age of Innocence* (1962).

Intellectuals

Malcolm Cowley, *Exile's Return* (1934); Edmund Wilson, *Axle's Castle* (1931); Alfred Kazin, *On Native Grounds* (1942); W. B. Rideout, *The Radical Novel in the United States, 1900–1954* (1956); Frederick Hoffmann, *The Twenties* (1955).

39
DEFEAT OF THE
BONUS MARCHERS

R. J. W.

The witness shifted nervously but stood his ground. Having waited a long time to testify, he was not going to be put off. Without formally addressing the committee or saying so much as a polite "Gentlemen," he began: "My comrade and I hiked here from nine o'clock Sunday morning, when we left Camden. I done it all by my feet—shoe leather. I come to show you people that we need our bonus. We wouldn't want it if we didn't need it."

The witness was Joseph T. Angelo, veteran of World War I. He was addressing a committee of the House of Representatives of the United States Congress in 1931. The committee was hearing witnesses testify about a controversial matter: the immediate payment of a "bonus" to all the veterans of the war. The country was in the third year of a depression, and the bonus would pay about $1,000 each to over 3 million veterans and their families.[1] It would, in fact, be the greatest program of direct relief for the poor ever undertaken by the federal government.

For six days officials of the Republican administration testified. President Herbert Hoover was opposed to the bonus. The testimony of government officials reflected this opposition. A few congressmen and one or two officials of veterans' organizations spoke out for the bonus. But they were outnumbered by a long string of bank vice presidents, insurance executives, and other businessmen. The testimony was dull. It was full of statistics designed to prove that the bonus would bankrupt the federal treasury and bring about a dangerous inflation.

But now for the first time an ordinary veteran, with no job, a hungry family, and a plain man's English, was testifying. Before Angelo fin-

---

[1]Congress had set up the bonus (a combination of life insurance and a pension) in 1924. It was not due to be paid until 1945, except to the heirs of veterans who died earlier.

Disciplined regiments of World War I veterans marched silently and gravely to the Capitol in June 1932. This was a veterans' parade with a difference—the men did not want the people's gratitude now, but a bonus that would help them through hard times.

ished, the committee and the audience were stirred to a mixture of laughter, admiration, and stunned confusion.

> I have got a little home back there [in Camden, New Jersey] that I built with my own hands after I came home from France. Now, I expect to lose that little place. Last week I went to our town committee and they gave me $4 for rations. That is to keep my wife and child and myself and clothe us; and also I cannot put no coal in my cellar.

Here, in the poor grammar and tired face of the witness, was the whole meaning of the depression that had begun in 1929. Angelo said he spoke for hundreds like himself in New Jersey. But he spoke, too, for millions all over the country who had not worked for a long time, who stood in bread lines, and who built the shacks in the shabby little towns they wryly called Hoovervilles.

But Angelo was also a veteran. So he spoke from his experience of the two most important events in his time—the war that people still called the Great War and the depression they were beginning to call the Great Depression. There was no economic theory or political philosophy in his testimony. He was just a hungry man who had fought in France.

> All I ask of you, brothers, is to help us. We helped you, now you help us. My partner here has a wife and five children, and he is just the same as I am. He hiked down here at the same time with me, and our feet are blistered. That is all I have to say. And I hope you folks can help us and that we can go through with the bonus.

We don't want charity; we don't need it. All we ask for is what belongs to us, and that is all we want.

Some of the congressmen were confused. Others were curious. Following the custom of congressional committees, they began to question the witness:

MR. FREAR: What is your business?
MR. ANGELO: Nothing. I am nothing but a bum.
MR. FREAR: You say you have not worked for two years?
MR. ANGELO: I have not worked for a year and a half. But there is no work in my home town.
MR. RAINEY: You are wearing some medal. What is it?
MR. ANGELO: I carry the highest medal in America for enlisted men, the Distinguished Service Cross.
MR. RAINEY: You have a Distinguished Service Cross? What is that for?
MR. ANGELO: That is for saving Colonel Patton.

George S. Patton was already a well-known army officer. (In World War II he would become one of the most famous and controversial of America's generals.) Congressman Rainey continued the questioning and pressed Angelo for details. Angelo responded with a startling tale. He had been part of a 305-man unit attacked by German machine guns in the Argonne Forest in 1918. When the battle was over, he said, most of the men were dead. Colonel Patton was wounded, and only he—Angelo—was left standing. Then Angelo showed the committee a tiepin made from a bullet he said was taken from Patton's leg in France. Neither the watch nor the medal had ever gone to "Uncle," Angelo's pet name for the pawnshop that had swallowed up most of his other possessions.

The afternoon was wearing on, but Angelo had roused the attention of the committee members and the audience as none of the other witnesses had. So the congressmen began to ask about his life. As Angelo answered, the audience sometimes laughed, sometimes applauded. He told them of working in a DuPont plant, making munitions for the British before the United States entered the war. When Congress declared war in 1917, he enlisted at once. But he was almost rejected because he weighed a mere 107 pounds. Only after ten doctors had examined him and a general had watched him do a handspring and jump a table was he accepted.

Then, obviously agitated, Angelo wound up with another statement:

I can make money. I can make lots of money. Now, I could go bootlegging. It is just the same way I could have went to France and I could have run out on my outfit. Which is the best, to be a live coward or a dead hero?

When this was put on me, brothers, I wasn't worried when I went through. I don't have nothing to worry about. I wasn't married, and I got a wonderful sendoff when I went to France. My father throwed me out. [Laughter.] And when I came back, I went home to my father. I saw a big, fat woman sitting in the seat. I knowed her from next door. I said, "She is the last woman you want on earth. Pop, what is she doing here?" He says, "That is my wife." I says, "Oh, My God!" She says, "Get out of here," and that was my welcome home, and I got out. [Laughter.]

So, folks, I tell you all I will say to you is, help us through with the bonus. That is the best answer for you folks to give to the fellow at home. Don't forget me for a job. [Applause.]

Joe Angelo was three things: a veteran, a bum, and a victim of the most serious economic depression in American history. In each of these roles he was not just an individual grappling with purely personal problems. He represented over 4½ million soldiers (about half of whom had actually been sent to Europe) suddenly discharged into civilian life in 1918 and 1919. These veterans organized—like other veterans in America's previous wars. More than a million joined the new American Legion and the Veterans of Foreign Wars. They thought of themselves as a special type of citizen, with a special claim on their country's gratitude.

As a bum, Angelo also spoke for countless people, many of them veterans, who had worked unsuccessfully at one job or another but mostly drifted through the 1920s. Naturally, the depression added millions of new "bums." Angelo, who had not been able to find work for a year and a half, was only one of a great, restless mass of unemployed. When he appeared before the congressional committee, at least 5 million men and women were classed as unemployed. Probably another 5 million were able to find only part-time work. Almost every other worker in America had his wages cut after the stock market crash of 1929. Few people could

A group of New York veterans gathered in the yards of the Baltimore and Ohio Railroad at Jersey City, New Jersey, on June 4, 1932. These angry, frustrated men were hoping to seize a train and head for Washington where they would demand payment of their bonus.

doubt in 1931 that unemployment was one of the most serious problems the United States had ever faced.

Joe Angelo's instinct was to turn to Washington for help. On his walk from Camden he had met other small groups of veterans with the same idea. The unemployed, the veterans, and the bums (often one man, like Angelo, was all three) were looking more and more to the federal government for relief. They had one fairly good chance of getting help from a reluctant Congress and a stubborn President—payment of the bonus. This, in Angelo's words, was "the best answer for you folks to give."

Angelo wanted $1,000 immediately, instead of waiting until 1945 to collect a larger amount. This was the heart of an issue that was about to create the most dramatic crisis of the depression—the massing in Washington of a "Bonus Army." Behind the crisis lay the old task of writing a final chapter to the World War and the new, complicated task of dealing with the depression. But for the marchers in the Bonus Army, the problem was quite simple: When and how would they be able to collect their bonus in full?

Veterans could already borrow money against the promise of the government to pay. Over 2 million had taken out loans that averaged $100 each—just enough to pay a back grocery bill, buy some coal for winter, or meet a medical emergency. But veterans everywhere were beginning to ask for ten times more, the payment of the entire bonus. And they found some sympathetic ears in Congress. Representative Wright Patman of Texas introduced a bill to authorize printing almost $2½ billion in new paper money to pay the bonus. As time passed there was more and more talk of the bonus, not only in Washington but wherever knots of hungry veterans gathered.

In November 1931 a group of veterans left Seattle to ride freights to the capital. All over the country others were doing likewise. A movement began that would shake the Hoover administration.

For two years the President had been telling the nation that the depression was not so serious and would soon end. Administration officials had always played down unemployment statistics. They portrayed the crisis as a temporary economic slump that would cure itself. Meanwhile, Hoover kept to his principle that the federal government should not provide direct relief to poor individuals. The veterans who were hitchhiking and jumping freight trains headed toward the capital were not so sure of their principles. Certainly they lacked the President's political experience and skills. But they knew that they needed the bonus.

By May 1932, 300 men from Portland, Oregon, left for Washington in a group. They called themselves the Bonus Expeditionary Force—a play on the name of the American army in France, the American Expeditionary Force. They elected a leader, Walter F. Waters, once an army sergeant, then foreman in a fruit cannery, now unemployed. They rode freight cars east and, by late May, reached East St. Louis, Illinois. There they tried to hop new trains going farther east. When railroad police told them to leave, they began to break up trains by uncoupling cars. They also soaped the rails in some places, making it impossible for engines to move.

The state called for its national guard to drive the veterans away. A scuffle occurred, but no one was hurt badly. The marchers were soon on their way again—in national guard trucks that Illinois had provided in return for their promise to leave the state peacefully. But, most important, for the first time, the Bonus Army won the attention of the newspapers and the public. Other veterans soon followed suit.

The scene was repeated everywhere. Merchants and mayors, railroad officials and governors, found it easier to supply trucks or boxcars than to stop the veterans. Thus a steady stream of Bonus Marchers was pouring into Washington. Each group had a leader or two, and their purpose was the same. They were in Washington to demand their bonus, even if they had to wait there until 1945 to get it.

One man deeply interested in the veterans' cause was Pelham D. Glassford, a West Point graduate and the youngest American in the World War to become a brigadier general. In 1931 Hoover appointed Glassford superintendent of Washington's police force. So he would have to deal with the Bonus Expeditionary Force in the capital.

Glassford hoped that the Bonus Army either would not come or would go home quickly. But, when the marchers arrived, he became sympathetic and helpful. He regarded them as "his boys." He assigned them quarters in abandoned buildings on Pennsylvania Avenue. The location was at the heart of official Washington, between the White House and the Capitol.

At Glassford's suggestion, also, the marchers made a "muster," or list of their groups, to make it easier to track down criminals and keep out the "Reds" and radicals. Gradually the marchers formed companies and then regiments. They elected Walter Waters, leader of the Portland group, as commander of the Bonus Expeditionary Force. He appointed junior officers and divided the men into companies named after states. Soon, the Bonus Army had a structure of command like the regular army.

Glassford's original decision to let the marchers camp along Pennsylvania Avenue was based on his hope that few would come. Soon it was obvious that the Bonus Army was much too large and dangerous (and embarrassing to the administration) to be in the center of things. Glassford sent most of the marchers to a new campsite a few miles southeast of Capitol Hill. The place was Anacostia Flats, a muddy landfill near the forks of the Potomac and Anacostia rivers. There, about 6,000 veterans built a shabby but orderly camp, with shacks and tents arranged in winding rows.

At Anacostia Flats the veterans tried to recreate their old army life. They woke to bugles, conducted roll calls, and had inspections. A company of men was assigned every day to "KP." Waters exercised strict discipline.

Other aspects of camp life were more relaxed. Some men had

General Pelham D. Glassford here watches some men at Anacostia Flats prepare a stew for their dinner. Although as chief of police he was responsible for dealing with the alarming number of veterans arriving in the capital, Glassford was sympathetic to the Bonus Marchers' cause.

brought their wives and children. The Salvation Army set up a post office, a library, and a recreation room. Glassford managed to borrow some field kitchens and other equipment. He supervised the distribution of food donated by Washington citizens, American Legion posts, and others. At one point Glassford gave several hundred dollars of his own money to buy food. There was even a newspaper to keep the veterans informed about the progress of bonus legislation in Congress.

By June 6, 1932, the veterans were ready for their first direct action. About 7,000 left their separate camps around the city and lined up neatly in six "regiments" to parade through Washington. The men felt fairly hopeful as they moved along. The Patman bill, which was in the House, seemed as if it would pass soon. The rumors that they were controlled by communists, spread by some politicians to smear the Bonus Army, were not given much credit. Best of all, their parade had drawn a crowd of about 100,000; mostly Washington clerical workers. Every time another company with its American flag passed, the crowd applauded.

Shortly after dark the long line of march reached a monument circle near the Capitol. (They were forbidden to pass the White House or go to the Capitol itself.) Orders were given to fall out, and the marchers broke ranks to walk quietly back to Anacostia. They had heard that in less than a week the House would vote on the bonus bill. If it passed both the House and Senate and was signed by Hoover, most of the veterans could collect the thousand dollars needed to get their hungry families through another depression year.

The parade was simply a beginning. Veterans kept coming to Washington—the police estimated a hundred every hour. On June 15, when the House passed the bill, there were probably 15,000 veterans, plus some of their wives and children, scattered around Washington. Anacostia Flats was crowded, but new shacks kept going up. By now the ex-soldiers had stripped half the city of every stray board or door, every spare piece of tin or canvas. One man moved a burial vault onto the flats and took up residence in it. The camp was about level with the river, and had to be protected by a levee. When it rained, mud was a foot deep. But the Bonus Army kept building.

Obviously some kind of crisis might soon develop. Health officials predicted a typhoid epidemic. Waters predicted victory when 100,000 more veterans arrived. Hoover's advisers predicted that communists would take over the Bonus Force.

The Bonus Army and the administration were both waiting for the Senate to vote on the Patman bill. Hoover was sure he would win. The House elected in 1930 was Democratic. Since it was the first body of politicians to graduate from the depression, it was full of representatives who had recently promised their constituents direct action. But only a third of the Senate had been elected in 1930. The majority were still firmly Republican and loyal to the President. Both houses were striving for a July adjournment. (It was an election year, and everyone wanted to get home to campaign.) The administration hoped that the Bonus Army would simply disappear after the Senate voted and Congress adjourned.

On June 17 the Senate would debate and vote on the bonus. Waters commanded his marchers to go to the Capitol and fill the galleries, steps, and grounds. By noon, there were 10,000 marchers in and around the Capitol.

Inside, the Senate debated. Men would leave the galleries every few minutes to report to the marchers out on the steps. Opponents of the bill argued Hoover's position on what should be done about the depression: the government ought to cut spending, not spend more. Direct relief to individuals was not a federal responsibility. Recovery would come as large banks, businesses, and railroads regained their health. Then jobs would become available, and the economy would escape from radical tinkering.

Many senators supporting the bill argued that since the veterans were hungry and would be able to collect the bonus in thirteen years anyway, they should have it now. But one or two senators gave a more complicated justification for the bonus. In a depression, they insisted, the government should spend money, not save it. If the government printed 2 ½ billion new dollars for the bonus, the money would swiftly circulate. The veterans would be only the first to gain. The stores where they spent their payments would get the money. These stores, in turn, would order more goods from wholesalers and manufacturers. So every bonus dollar would become a dollar in motion, moving through the economy and stimulating all business. Naturally, when the depression was cured, the government would stop deficit spending—that is, spending more than it raised in taxes. The economy would return to normal. The government would only "prime the pump" with its paper dollars. The happy results would then be automatic.

Though the argument went on, it soon became clear that only a political miracle could save the bonus. The Senate was much too conservative to experiment with such legislation. Even some of the liberal sen-

Thousands of veterans waited tensely on the steps of the Capitol, as the Senate debated the fate of their bonus. The eventual defeat of the Patman bill that would have made their dream a reality nearly triggered a violent confrontation between them and the marines.

ators who usually opposed Hoover questioned the bill. What was need-ed, they said, was a general bill for relief of all the unemployed. Veterans should receive no special favors.

Finally, after eight o'clock, someone came from the galleries and whispered to Waters. The bill had lost decisively, 62 to 18. Waters climbed the steps and turned to face the largest body ever gathered in Washington to demonstrate for a cause. The marchers had been waiting for hours, and for a moment it seemed as if they might riot. Marines were stationed nearby, just in case. Members of the administration wanted to ready machine guns, but Glassford persuaded them not to. Waters shout-ed: "Comrades![2] I have bad news. Let us show them we can take it on the chin. Let us show them we are patriotic Americans." There was a muttering from the crowd. Then a gigantic roar came from 10,000 throats. Waters pleaded for calm:

> We are not telling you to go home. Go back to your camps. We are going to stay in Washington until we get the bonus, no matter how long it takes. And we are one hundred times as good Americans as those men in there who voted against it. But there is nothing more to be done tonight.

The situation was tenser than any in the capital since the Civil War. Ten thousand disappointed people, who had kept good discipline for weeks, were ready to break and mob the Senate. Waters played a final card to keep order: "I call on you to sing 'America,'" he shouted. After a few false starts, the men obeyed. Gradually, the song gathered strength.

The emergency was over, at least for the moment. The singing died out, and bugles sounded assembly. The men milled about, looking for their outfits for the march back to camp. It was dark now, and the ner-vous men waiting in the White House and the Capitol could take a deep breath. The bonus was dead, at least until Congress reconvened in De-cember, after the presidential elections.

But the Bonus Army did not disappear. The government issued reports that the men were leaving. The Bonus Force and the police re-ported, however, that new recruits were arriving about as fast as old ones left. Estimates of the size of the force issued by the government, the po-lice, the newspapers, and the Bonus Army itself varied widely. At its largest, the Bonus Army probably numbered just under 20,000 men. Membership shifted constantly; perhaps as many as 50,000 veterans were in Washington at one time or another during June and July of 1932.

The government offered to lend the marchers train fare or gas money to leave town, plus seventy-five cents a day for other expenses. Many veterans simply took the money and stayed in town. Others used it to recruit new members. Thus, a month after the Senate had defeated the Patman bill, there were about as many marchers as ever. The police

---

[2]This was an old term from the war, not a communist greeting.

Veterans inhabited eyesores such as these, located on government property close to the Capitol. In an election year, the government felt especially threatened by their well-publicized presence.

estimated 15,000 people, two-thirds of them now crowded into Anacostia Flats.

By July, with no hope of a bonus from Congress, the veterans' mood soured. Their newspaper published more militant calls for action. Waters began to allow the small group of about 150 communists to eat occasionally at the Anacostia mess. (He had always thrown them out before.) He even began to talk about a permanent organization of veterans in politics, which he would call "Khaki Shirts," in imitation of the "Brown Shirts" that Adolf Hitler had organized.

In the White House, too, opinions were getting stronger. After the Senate defeated the bonus, the President decided the marchers had no business squatting on government land. He also decided they were not truly patriotic veterans asking for relief. Instead he believed they had been:

> organized and promoted by the communists, and included a large number of hoodlums and ex-convicts determined to raise a public disturbance. They were frequently addressed by Democratic congressmen, seeking to inflame them against me.

The differences grew sharper, the summer hotter, and tempers shorter. On July 16 the most serious incident so far broke out at the Capitol. Congress was about to adjourn. Waters ordered his men to make one last symbolic demonstration. By midday nearly 7,000 Bonus Marchers were at the Capitol. Their mood was much uglier than a month before. Senators and congressmen crowded near every window to watch. Even Glassford lost his nerve.

Glassford ordered Waters taken into custody and moved to the basement of the Capitol. When the veterans saw what was happening, they stopped cheering Glassford and began to boo and jeer. "Waters! Waters!" they shouted. Glassford was forced to bring the Bonus Army's commander onto the platform. After a short, harsh exchange with Glassford, Waters tried to calm his people. Then he ordered them to move to the middle: "Use the center steps. But I want you to keep a lane open for the white-collared birds, so they won't rub into us lousy rats. We're going to stay here until I see Hoover!"

The demonstration was clearly dangerous. Several congressmen came out of the Capitol to speak to the demonstrators, trying to cool them off. Finally the Speaker of the House, John Nance Garner, agreed to meet with Waters and a committee of his aides inside the building. Garner handled the situation well. He made a few empty promises of help and was photographed with Waters. When the conference was over, Waters went back outside and ordered his followers to their camps. For a second time an extremely touchy and potentially violent situation had been controlled.

In the White House, however, tempers were also growing shorter. Hoover had just been renominated by the Republicans to run for a second term. The Democrats would meet soon to nominate Franklin D. Roosevelt, then governor of New York. Hoover knew the campaign would be rough. But he knew he would win if he could overcome the widespread idea that he was responsible for the depression.

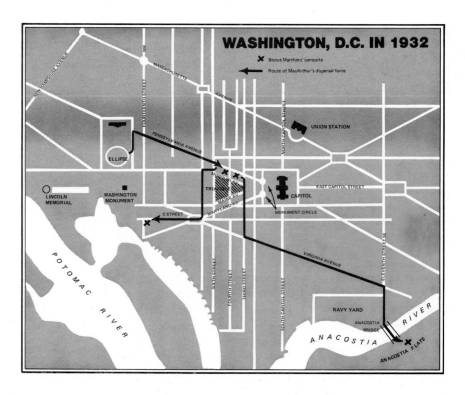

A favorite tactic of Hoover's closest associates was to picture him as the firm opponent of all kinds of radicalism. Unfortunately, the Bonus Army was the most visible kind of radicalism. Hoover had always opposed the bonus. Now he and his advisers decided to move firmly against the veterans. Some even hoped for an incident. Then it would appear that the government had to defend its very life against a radical insurrection.

A few days after Congress adjourned, the administration decided to move. The tensest point in Washington was the two square blocks on the south side of Pennsylvania Avenue, just a block from the Capitol and a mile from the White House. The buildings here were part of a triangle of structures that had been condemned to make way for a government building program. All over the triangle, veterans had camped in and around vacant and half-demolished structures, eyesores that embarrassed the administration. On July 21, on instructions from the Treasury Department, the commissioners who governed the District of Columbia (and were directly responsible to the administration) ordered the veterans to evacuate the two blocks. For various reasons the order was not carried out at once. But Waters told his people to be ready to leave. Glassford was locating another site farther away, where they could take their few possessions and settle again.

Finally, at about 10 A.M. on July 28, Treasury officials accompanied by Glassford and his police entered the area. The veterans began to evacuate the buildings and their makeshift shanties, leaving behind everything that they could not carry or push along in small carts or baby carriages. Everything went peacefully, though a few veterans had to be taken out under arrest. Before noon the first building was empty. In the meantime, a large crowd of Washington citizens had gathered to watch. Their sympathies were divided between the police and the veterans.

Then, a little past noon, veterans from other camps filtered into the area, mixing with the crowd. One group came to stage a formal demonstration. Paul Anderson, a journalist, described what happened next:

> At noon, three bonus men, one carrying a large American flag, started across the block, followed by several hundred. When the leaders encountered a policeman, he grabbed the flag. There was a scuffle, and one of the marchers was hit on the head with a night stick. He wrested it from the officer and struck the cop, and there was a shower of bricks from the buddies in the rear. It looked like an ugly mess, but the cops kept their heads, and no shots were fired.
>
> Glassford dashed into the heart of the melee, smiled when a brickbat hit him on the chest, and stopped the fighting. Within two minutes, the veterans were cheering Glassford.

For another half hour the police continued their work. The veterans were leaving the buildings, but they stood around outside, many on big piles of bricks. No one is certain what happened next. Some witnesses said a policeman tried to clear veterans out of a building that had not even been ordered vacated. They resisted. Another observer said that a policeman started climbing some makeshift stairs, lost his balance, and fell. In a panic he pulled his revolver and began to fire wildly into a crowd near him. General Glassford gave what may be the most accurate account:

> I was about twenty yards away from the building when I heard a commotion. I went to the second floor. One officer had started up the steps, and near the rear, I heard some say, "Let's get him!"
>
> As he started up the steps, bricks started falling on him [Glassford was not certain whether the bricks were being thrown or were just falling], and as I leaned over the railing above, I saw him fall and draw his gun, firing two shots.

Other policemen also started shooting. Then veterans began to throw bricks at every policeman in sight. Again Glassford acted quickly to prevent a vicious riot. He ran outside, shouting, "Stop that shooting!" The firing ended, and the bricks stopped flying. Ambulances rushed to take away the injured. One policeman was hurt seriously by a brick. One Bonus Marcher was dead; another died later of gunshot wounds.

The battle of the Bonus Army might have ended here. Glassford had the situation in hand. The veterans were moving out of the buildings as they had been ordered. On the whole they were reluctant but still willing to cooperate. Waters had supported Glassford every step of the way. Within another hour or two the evacuation of the two blocks would have been complete. But the administration also had decided to act. Hoover had ordered the Chief of Staff of the Army, General MacArthur, to bring troops into the city to restore civil peace.

When the Bonus Marchers were ordered to clear the federal property on which they had been squatting, fights broke out between them and the police that led to a larger battle.

The troops—about 500 at first, then later over 1,000—formed up behind the White House. They came armed with bayoneted rifles and heavy blue canisters of tear gas. There were cavalry with sabers, a machine-gun squadron, several infantry companies, and even a half-dozen tanks. MacArthur put the troops under the command of General Perry L. Miles. But he later wrote, "In accordance with the President's request, I accompanied General Miles." With MacArthur was his aide, Major Dwight David Eisenhower. And in the cavalry was George S. Patton (who had no way of knowing that Joe Angelo had come back to Washington and was out in the troubled city with about 12,000 of his buddies, waiting).

At about four o'clock the cavalry led the way, the iron shoes of their horses clattering on the asphalt of Pennsylvania Avenue. Then came tanks, more cavalry, the infantry, and the mounted machine gunners. They rode, walked, and rumbled up to the triangle, pushing the crowds back and surrounding the buildings. Without any conference or hesitation the troops (who wore gas masks and carried fixed bayonets) began to throw tear-gas bombs into the buildings. They were going to clear the entire area.

The veterans did not resist. A few hung back, and had to be jabbed at with bayonets. Mostly they stumbled out of the area and toward Anacostia. MacArthur, who also had tears streaming down his face from the tear gas, ordered most of his men to herd the veterans south. Another detachment moved west, to attack the small, separate camp of the communist group.[3] Suddenly, it became clear that the general intended to clear the entire District. In the triangle, smoke began to rise. There, the troops had set fire to the shacks, tents, and scattered belongings of the Bonus Army.

MacArthur's forces kept pushing the straggling veterans before them with bayonets and sabers. The sun was going down behind them. Ahead lay the drawbridge to Anacostia. The Bonus Army's rear guard hurried across the bridge at about sunset. Waters had already given the order to evacuate Anacostia and had sent word to MacArthur asking for time to move women and children out of the camp. On the flats about 7,000 men were scurrying around, trying to keep order in a forced retreat.

From the time the troops first appeared, the Bonus Marchers gave no resistance. They booed, they swore—but they moved. MacArthur left his tanks north of the river and paused before Anacostia Flats for an hour before sending the infantry. But when they went onto the flats, the soldiers threw tear gas everywhere. Stragglers were treated very roughly. The soldiers then set fire to the camp. (Many of the veterans had already put matches to their borrowed army tents.) Next they moved out of the camp to the nearby area where many of the veterans still stood watching

General Douglas MacArthur with his aide, Dwight David Eisenhower, led the forces that finally cleared Washington of Bonus Marchers. MacArthur later claimed that if the situation had continued, the institutions of government would have been threatened.

---

[3]Communists in this camp included James Ford, their candidate for Vice President. On July 31 the New York *Times* ran a front-page article quoting the communists. "We agitated for the bonus and led the demonstration of the veterans in Washington." However, the communists were never the Bonus Force's prime movers.

Troopers used tear gas in a final effort to clear the Bonus Marchers out of Washington. The veterans were forced to retreat and in the main did not resist.

their shacks burn. As the troops rushed up the hill, which was not federal property, they continued to throw tear gas. One woman, whose baby had actually been born since the Bonus Army's arrival, told this story:

> The troops came up the hill, driving the people ahead of them. As they passed by the house [where the woman was staying], one of them threw a tear-gas bomb over the fence into the front yard. The house was filled with gas, and we all began to cry. We got wet towels and put them over the faces of the children. About a half an hour later, my baby began to vomit. I took her outside in the air and she vomited again. Next day, she began to turn black and blue.

A few days later the baby died—the third and last fatality of the battle of the Bonus Army.

The day after the action was a time for summing up. The White House and other administration officials issued statements. MacArthur gave his version in a press conference:

> That mob was a bad-looking mob. It was animated by the essence of revolution. They had come to the conclusion, beyond the shadow of a doubt, that they were about to take over either the direct control of the government, or else to control it by indirect methods. It is my belief that had the President not acted today, he would have been faced with a grave situation. Had he let it go on another week, I believe that the institutions of our government would have been severely threatened.

To this version of the threat posed by the Bonus Force, MacArthur added a simple lie—that it was the veterans who had burned their shacks in the triangle.

On July 29, 1932, in a blazing finale that brought the battle of the Bonus Army to an end, the camps at Anacostia Flats went up in flames.

Another kind of summing up came from Joe Angelo, who told a newspaper reporter his story. He was at Anacostia Flats, watching a group of infantrymen in gas masks overrun the shack he had been living in. They were urged on by a tough, confident cavalry officer. Angelo blinked the burning tear gas out of his eyes and recognized George S. Patton. Then like the rest of the Bonus Army, he ran. Soon he was back home in Camden, from where he had started his long hike to Washington a year and a half before.

40
PROSPERITY AND DEPRESSION
R. J. W.

Most of the Bonus March veterans who went to Washington were as politically innocent as Joe Angelo. Some of their leaders had a little political knowledge—and the tiny fraction who were communists thought they understood the basic problems of American society and sought a revolutionary solution. But the great rank and file of the marchers were simply caught in a web of circumstances they did not understand or want.

The marchers' experience was defined by the two great events they had participated in, the Great War and the Great Depression. Between lay the decade of the 1920s, the "Jazz Age." But most of the marchers had experienced only a little jazz. Like most Americans, they had passed through a curiously contradictory decade. On the one hand, American society of the 1920s was characterized by tremendous innovations—some technological, other social. But, alongside all the newness and experimentation, the 1920s had been a decade of profound, sometimes violent conservatism. Both in formal politics, centered in Washington, and in informal politics of organized movements, the keynote had not been innovation but restoration.

Conservatism in politics received a kind of endorsement from the economy. The 1920s was a period of apparent prosperity. In some sectors, in fact, the economy virtually underwent a "boom." And this prosperity made it appear to many Americans that the country had returned from the distortions of progressive reform and war to "normalcy." It took the Depression to show that normalcy was an illusion, and that the 1920s had contained profound distortions of its own.

A TIDE OF REACTION

For millions of Americans, the uncertainties of modernity, the wave of progressive reforms, and the moral crusade of the war were all extremely unsettling. Even before the war was over, millions of people had already decided that change had gone too far, that the republic was in desperate danger of losing its stability and virtue. For some, the threat was simple: the country was being overrun by foreigners and by "foreign" political ideas. For others, the problem was alcohol, and the loose life associated with it. Still others viewed blacks as the principal threat. For many, the danger lay in the growing number and power of Jews and Catholics. Some complained about the inroads new scientific ideas were making on "traditional" values and beliefs.

Not every American participated, by any means, but a large and very active segment of society—especially in the South and the Midwest—joined in a series of movements and organizations to save their country from what were seen by them as the perils of change. Sometimes, the results were merely quaint—as when the sale of alcohol was forbidden by an amendment to the Constitution. Or when schoolteachers were prosecuted for explaining Charles Darwin's theory of evolution in their classrooms. At other times, however, the results were more serious, even tragic, as when dozens of blacks were lynched by mobs, or hundreds of immigrant "radicals" were hounded in court and even sentenced to die for their supposed crimes. This was part of the character of "normalcy," the opposite and darker face of the "Jazz Age."

The Red Scare The conservative reaction focused sharply on radicalism. The Russian Revolution, which had brought the communist government of the Bolsheviks to power, was followed by communist uprisings in Germany and Hungary. These developments created an atmosphere of fear in the United States. Many people, including a number of powerful leaders in federal and state governments, believed that a communist conspiracy was at work among them, ready to "radicalize" the country.

In 1919 a series of spectacular strikes and the outbreak of political sabotage fed the fear. In the spring of that year, two small groups of anarchists attempted to bomb the homes and offices of a number of government officials and businessmen. The bombs, most of which were sent through the mails, were probably the work of mentally unstable persons. Certainly they had nothing to do with the tiny organized Socialist and Communist parties of the country.

In fact, the bombers were incompetent. Most of the bombs were never delivered because they did not have enough postage. Another bomb only damaged the house of its intended victim, but it blew the bomber himself—an Italian anarchist—to bits. Another, addressed to a Georgia politician, was opened by his maid (a black worker, not a capitalist). She lost her hands as a result. But the bombings did convince many people that revolution was at hand.

One of the people who was most convinced was Woodrow Wilson's attorney general, A. Mitchell Palmer. Like Wilson, Palmer was a liberal and a strong antiradical. The attorney general also had his eye on the Democratic nomination of 1920. So he used the "red scare" to make his department the center of the action. He obtained a special appropriation for hunting down radicals. With the money he formed a new antisubversive division of the Justice Department, headed by J. Edgar Hoover.

Beginning in November of 1919 the Justice Department conducted a series of raids against radical groups, seeking out suspected communists at union meetings, at Communist party headquarters, and in their homes. The most spectacular of the raids, which came on New Year's Day 1920, resulted in the arrest of 6,000 people. In the end the Palmer raids led to the conviction of only a handful of citizens, most of them for minor crimes. Immigrant aliens, who were Palmer's main target, suffered more; about 600 were eventually deported, mostly to the Soviet Union.

Palmer's campaign created an atmosphere of near hysteria among many Americans. It led to one tragedy that did more than any other single event of the 1920s to divide Americans of different political beliefs. In 1920 two Italian anarchists were arrested in Boston on a charge of robbing a shoe company and murdering two of its employees. Their trial soon became a political event, a test of the established authority against political radicalism. The trial was unfair. Even the judge privately referred to the defendants, Nicola Sacco and Bartolomeo Vanzetti, as anarchists.

But in the political climate of the red scare, Sacco and Vanzetti were convicted and sentenced to death. The process of appeals was long and unsuccessful. Finally, in 1927, the year of Lindbergh's flight, both men were executed in the electric chair. To the small number of American liberals and radicals of the 1920s, Sacco and Vanzetti were the century's greatest martyrs. They were modern counterparts of the victims of the Salem witch trials and the Haymarket Affair. But to most Americans, they were just Italian radicals who had been properly punished.

The Bonus Marchers of 1932 had to contend with the lingering effects of the red scare. They were accused of being communists, and of serving as tools in a foreign conspiracy. When Douglas MacArthur marched on their camp at Anacostia, he did so in the belief that he was protecting the country from a powerful revolutionary movement. The irony was, however, that the marchers themselves accepted much of the ideology of "Americanism" that underlay the red scare. Their response to the charge that they were communists was to insist on their own patriotism, and to point proudly to their record of military service. Most of the marchers were probably just as devoutly anticommunist, just as insistent on their own "100 percent Americanism" as their critics.

The red scare also made it possible for those Americans who feared immigrants and their ethnic and religious differences to restrict immigration. In February 1921 (over the veto of President Wilson) Congress passed a law that limited immigration, especially from countries in South-

Nicola Sacco and Bartolomeo Vanzetti entered a courthouse to make their final appeal in 1927. They were convicted essentially because they were Italians at a time when hatred of aliens ran high, and because they were anarchists in a politically conservative era.

ern and Eastern Europe. According to the law, the number of immigrants from a country in any given year could not exceed 3 percent of the number of people of that nationality who were already in the United States in 1910. In 1924 the law was made even more restrictive. Quotas would now be based on resident population in 1890, immigration limited to 150,000 a year after 1927, and Asians totally excluded. The effect of the laws was to end, almost at once, the flow of immigration.

Prohibition and Reaction   Like the red scare and the movement for immigration restriction, the prohibition of alcohol in the 1920s had its roots in the progressive period. In 1919 the states had passed the Eighteenth Amendment, which empowered Congress to prohibit the sale of alcoholic beverages. The amendment marked the victory of a long campaign of temperance. It provided anoth-

er rallying point for conservative, small-town Americans. They divided society into the "drys" and the "wets" and opposed any politician who did not favor prohibition.

The prohibition movement failed to stop Americans from drinking. In most cities people continued to drink whiskey in speakeasies. The sale of bootleg whiskey was controlled largely by organized gangs of criminals. Gangs like the one led by Al Capone in Chicago bribed public officials and policemen to cover up their operations. But for most conservative Americans prohibition was above all a moral crusade. It was an issue they could use to split their countrymen into two camps: one composed of decent people, the other of riffraff.

Another conservative campaign of the 1920s was the attempt of many Protestant Americans — again, especially in the South and the Midwest—to prevent schools from teaching dangerous or "un-American" ideas. In several Southern states this crusade was aimed mainly at the idea of evolution. The notion of biological evolution was an old one. It became scientifically respected in the nineteenth century through the work of Charles Darwin. By the 1920s practically every scientist in the world believed that animals, including man, had evolved over a long period of time. But this seemed to many people to go against the fundamentals of their religion. They saw it as a challenge to the biblical story of creation.

Several state legislatures forbade their schools to teach the doctrine of evolution. In 1925 John Scopes, a schoolteacher in Dayton, Tennessee, decided to challenge the law. He was arrested, and his trial became almost as much a spectacle as the trial of Sacco and Vanzetti.

Scopes was defended by the most famous criminal lawyer in the United States, Clarence Darrow of Chicago. William Jennings Bryan led the prosecution. Bryan, an aging but still powerful leader of millions of fundamentalists, stood ready to smite the forces of modernism. He was humiliated on the witness stand by Darrow. Reporters from every major American newspaper—and several European papers—covered the trial.

Scopes lost the case and was fined $100. The Tennessee law stayed on the books. But after the Scopes trial the direction of education in the South and elsewhere shifted away from Bryan's intellectual conservatism toward the acceptance of modern science. Bryan's crusade, like many other conservative movements of the 1920s, was only a temporary victory over twentieth-century ideas and social habits.

The Ku Klux Klan The most spectacular conservative movement of the 1920s was the Ku Klux Klan. The Klan, which had all but disappeared after Reconstruction, was reorganized in 1915 in Georgia. Its membership grew slowly until the war was over. Then, taking many of its cues from the red scare, the Klan began to gain support. Much of its strength still lay in the rural South and Southwest. But there was a new element in this second growth: now, millions in the Northern

states, many of them city dwellers, joined this bizarre organization. At one time or another, about five million Americans took up membership and donned the white sheets that were the uniform of the Klan. The strongest Klan state was not in the South at all, but in Indiana, where the organization appeared for a time to control even the state government.

The Ku Klux Klan was a marginal, fringe organization. It attracted only the most conservative citizens. The white robes and hoods, the secrecy and the rituals, the burning of crosses in the night, demanded considerable dedication from its members. They had to be able to stomach a good deal of violence and torture. And they had to be able to tolerate a large element of the ridiculous—as in the titles of Klan officers, like Dragon, Kleagal, or Kludd. Nevertheless, the Klan was still able to elect one of its Dragons governor of Indiana, able to march openly in Washington in 1925, and able to control the Democratic presidential nomination in 1924.

In the long run, the Klan—like the prohibitionist movement and the fundamentalist attempt to prevent the teaching of evolution—was destined to lose. Blacks would not be lynched in great numbers forever, the freedom to drink alcohol would return, new scientific theories would get taught, eventually. But in the political atmosphere of the 1920s, it was possible for millions of Klansmen, and millions of other conservatives who did not join the organization, to convince themselves that their victory was close at hand, that the country would be saved, after all.

THE POLITICS OF CONSERVATISM

The political instrument of salvation, restoration, and "normalcy" was to be the Republican Party. As the war ended, the Republicans could see as plainly as anyone else that there was a change in the atmosphere. The policies of reform and military crusade, on which Woodrow Wilson and the Democrats had built their success in national poli-

The lunatic fringe of the 1920s had considerable strength, as this parade of Klansmen in the nation's capital in 1925 indicates. Terror was the Klan's chief method of warding off members' own fears of a rapidly changing America.

tics, were clearly going to fall into disrepute. The Republicans met at Chicago in their national convention of 1920 full of hope. They were still the majority party, they knew. And no Democrat on the horizon represented a real threat to the election of a Republican President. Wilson's illness, the failure of the League of Nations, the doings of A. Mitchell Palmer—all had helped to disorganize the Democrats.

The only question seemed to be whether the Republicans could unite on a candidate. The convention deadlocked for six ballots. Then, a few party leaders huddled in one of the most famous "smoke-filled rooms" in American history and chose a surprise candidate—Warren Gamaliel Harding, senator from Ohio.

Harding Harding was a small-town newspaper publisher and politician, reminiscent of the Republican style of the late nineteenth century. He had risen carefully through the party system in Ohio to become a senator. His political virtues were, primarily, loyalty to the organization and a discreet silence on most issues. A handsome but simple man, he was puzzled by complicated issues like taxation, the tariff, and foreign affairs. He was "one of the boys," who enjoyed a night of whiskey and poker with his cronies. He had never proposed an important law or policy, nor made an important speech, in his whole career. But he had a face that voters wanted to trust. And the people who ran the party knew they could trust him, too. He was a party regular. He would not have any strange ideas about regulating business or supporting labor unions; nor would he propose any odd reforms. He was, in a word, conservative.

Warren Harding, who won the presidency by being "one of the boys," was aware of his limitations. About his search for a capable economic adviser he said: "I don't know where to find him and haven't the sense to trust him when I find him." His candor was winning but, unfortunately, prophetic.

For Vice President, the Republicans nominated Calvin Coolidge, another small-town politician. Coolidge had first won a national reputation as a tough antilabor man during the strikes of 1919. When Boston's police organized as an AFL local, and went out on strike, Coolidge was governor of Massachusetts. Without attempting to settle the strike peacefully, he sent armed troops into Boston. The protest of Samuel Gompers, the AFL president, was met with one of Collidge's most famous quasi-grammatical retorts: "There is no right to strike against the public safety, anywhere, anytime."

Coolidge was less a party regular than Harding, but he was even more conservative in matters of policy. Except for his odd flair for terse statements, he was a lackluster man with a crabbed countenance, a striking contrast to Harding's open handsomeness. In any case, no one at the Republican convention thought that they were choosing anything but a Vice President.

The Democrats nominated a lackluster candidate of their own, James M. Cox. However, they tried to spice up the ticket with a dashing young New Yorker, Franklin D. Roosevelt. Roosevelt had served as assistant secretary of the navy under Wilson. The convention hoped the Roosevelt name would attract voters who remembered his cousin Theodore. But probably no Democratic ticket could have won in 1920. The voters wanted a change. Sixty percent of them voted for Harding. They also sent large Republican majorities to both the House and Senate, making it one of the most complete victories in the history of American national politics. Harding carried every state outside the Democrats' solid South and cracked even that by winning Tennessee. The repudiation of Wilson's New Freedom seemed complete.

Return to Normalcy Harding took office with a slogan that coined a new word. He said the country needed a "return to normalcy." No dictionary defined "normalcy," but almost every American probably knew what the President meant. Harding believed that there had been too much experimentation, too many attempts to regulate the economy and the working lives of Americans, too much speculation about new diplomatic arrangements such as the League of Nations. Normalcy meant letting things take their natural course — not interfering in the decisions of businessmen or in the complex affairs of other nations. Normalcy meant, in short, a return to simpler times and uncomplicated politics.

Harding's relaxed conservatism was not a well-defined policy. Rather, it was a wish for fewer policies and less activity by the government. For his cabinet, the President chose people sympathetic to the practices of industrial and business leaders. His most important appointment, in fact, was Secretary of the Treasury Andrew Mellon, a Pennsylvania industrialist who owned the only important company then making aluminum in the United States.

W.E.B. DU BOIS

William Edward Burghardt Du Bois had one of the most extraordinary and creative careers of any modern American writer or intellectual. It spanned from his birth just two years after the assassination of Lincoln to his death just a year before the assassination of Martin Luther King.

During those ninety-six years, Du Bois was a black student at Harvard, a poet, a novelist, a journalist, a reformer, a New York intellectual, a founder of the Pan-African movement, and, at the end, a communist and an expatriate citizen of Ghana.

Du Bois began his life in Massachusetts. Intellectually talented, he made his way through Harvard and did some graduate work in Germany to earn a prestigious Harvard Ph.D. His initial career choice was to be an academic. He taught at Wilberforce College in Ohio, at the University of Pennsylvania, and then at Atlanta University.

But his writing and his move to the South drew him gradually away from academic life and into the politics of race. His first book, *The Philadelphia Negro* (1899), was not only a superb exercise in academic sociology, but a passionate recognition that the "Negro problem" could be solved only when blacks chose no longer to merely imitate whites, but instead to cultivate a new attitude of respect for what they were as blacks.

In *The Souls of Black Folk* (1903), Du Bois pressed the point further. The prevailing program of reform among blacks had been devised by Booker T. Washington. But Washington's plan, as Du Bois saw it, proposed only that blacks should accept white society as they found it and seek gradually to work their way into it, from the bottom up. Du Bois believed this plan would not work partly because of white resistance, which he viewed as determined and even violent. Washington's program was flawed in other ways also. It did not recognize that blacks were different, that many of the black "souls" of which he wrote were kindly, gentle, submissive, and generous, and that it would be fatal merely to toss such souls into the white world of competition, materialism, and greed.

These ideas, combined with an increasing number of violent riots against blacks in all parts of the United States, eventually led Du Bois away from teaching and into political activism. He was one of the founders of an organization called the Niagara Movement, dedicated to a more militant defense of black rights. Du Bois wrote a series of resolutions that voiced the sense of crisis that gave form to the movement, a sense of no "progress" being made. "Stripped of verbose subterfuge and in its naked nastiness, the new American creed says: fear to let black men even try to rise lest they become the equals of the white. And that in the land that professes to follow Jesus Christ. The blasphemy of such a course is only matched by its cowardice."

In 1910, in league with a large number of white reformers and intellectuals, Du Bois formed the Niagara Movement into a new organization, the National Association for the Advancement of Colored People. He was for many years the editor of the Association's magazine, The Crisis. But Du Bois had been losing faith in the capacity of white society ever to accept blacks as blacks. He left teaching and moved into Harlem. He helped found the Pan-African Congress during the peace talks in Paris in 1918. And eventually, at the age of 96, he renounced his United States citizenship, announced his membership in the Communist Party, and moved to the new African state of Ghana, where he died.

Mellon helped to shape the small amount of legislation that the Harding administration presented to Congress. His pet bill was one cutting the maximum income tax on the wealthy from 65 percent to 25 percent. (Congress at first reduced the limit to only 50 percent, but Mellon later got most of what he wanted.) He also proposed, and got from Congress, much higher tariffs on imports, a policy that benefited American business and industry by limiting foreign competition.

The Ohio Gang Specific legislation was less important in Harding's conservative administration than its general relaxation of federal controls over business. Harding did not try to tear down the established regulatory agencies, like the Interstate Commerce Commission or the Federal Reserve Board. Instead, he merely appointed persons to these agencies who were so friendly toward corporations that they administered the law gently or not at all. And Harding named as his Secretary of Commerce Herbert Hoover, who had made a fortune as a mining engineer and investor.

Hoover was clearly the most distinguished of Harding's appointments. He had made an enormous reputation during the war as head of the federal Food Administration. Unlike most of his colleagues in the Harding administration, Hoover was a thoughtful man, with a fairly clear-cut ideological position. He was a promoter of what he called "individualism." His central faith was that private enterprise, left to its own devices, could end poverty and usher in a "new era" of prosperity and progress.

To Hoover, the modern corporation was, ultimately, an instrument of social justice. Capitalism had, he believed, emerged from its nineteenth-century youth into a mature period of development. In this new maturity, corporations would be less concerned with sheer competition for profits and more determined to produce goods efficiently. In the process, the corporations would also contribute a great deal of what Hoover called "service" to society—technological innovation, education, the redistribution of income, and so on, until ignorance, poverty, and disease were banished.

The role of government, Hoover believed, should be to help this process along by providing information and assistance to businesses, not to hinder them through wasteful and inefficient regulation. This was the logic that Hoover applied as secretary of commerce. And this was the logic he would later bring to the White House.

Unfortunately, Harding also brought to Washington a group of friends who soon became known as the Ohio Gang. Some held seemingly harmless positions, like Old Doc Sawyer, a doctor in less than good standing with the medical profession. Old Doc became the White House physician, with the rank of army brigadier general. Other Ohio Gang members were given more important positions, such as attorney general and secretary of the interior.

After two years in office, Harding, who was personally honest about money, begain to realize that his appointees were stealing and peddling influence. In the spring and summer of 1923 two administration officials committed suicide while being investigated. In June, Harding began a

When the Teapot Dome scandal, involving the bribing of Republican officials, broke, a Memphis newspaper published this cartoon entitled, "Assuming Definite Shape."

long vacation in the West. As he left, he complained to a journalist, "My God, this is a hell of a job. I have no trouble with my enemies. But my friends! They're the ones that keep me walking the floor nights!"

Two months later, in California after a trip to Alaska, Harding suffered what Old Doc Sawyer called food poisoning. Harding now had to pay in person for this political appointment, for Sawyer was wrong. The President had suffered a heart attack instead; on August 2 he died. In a way, Harding was lucky. He was mourned by his countrymen almost as much as Lincoln had been. He was spared the knowledge of a new scandal that would later become almost synonymous with his name.

Albert Fall, Harding's secretary of the interior, had finagled Interior Department control of oil reserves set aside for the navy. There were two large reserves, at Elk Hill in California and at Teapot Dome in Wyoming. Private oil interests were willing to pay almost any price to drill the land. And they did.

Two oil company executives, Edward L. Doheny and Harry F. Sinclair, gave and "lent" Fall almost a half million dollars in return for secret leases allowing them to drill on the reserves. The secret leaked out faster than the oil. The government managed to cancel the leases, but Fall went to prison for a year. He was the first cabinet officer in American history to be put behind bars.

COOLIDGE AND BUSINESS

When Harding died, Vice President Calvin Coolidge became President. Though privately a talkative man, "Silent Cal" as Coolidge was called, spoke very little in public. He kept most of Harding's appointees and basically followed his predecessor's policies for the rest of the term. As the 1924 election approached, there was little doubt about what the Republicans would do. Their convention enthusiastically nominated Coolidge.

The Democrats experienced a struggle between two wings of their party. One represented the rural South and West, the old Bryan supporters. They were at least as conservative as the Republicans. The other wing was newer and based in the Northern cities. It was made up mostly of "wets" (opponents of prohibition) and depended heavily on the support of immigrants (many of them Catholics or Jews). After 103 ballots the convention settled on a compromise candidate, John W. Davis.

Coolidge was conservative. But so was Davis, who was associated with the firm of J. P. Morgan. Once more the time seemed right, as in 1912, to try a third party. The Progressive candidate was Robert La Follette, now nearly seventy but still a fiery opponent of business interests. He did well. Although Coolidge won the election easily with 15 million votes, La Follette managed to get almost 5 million votes, and he carried Wisconsin's electoral vote. Davis and his badly split party could muster only 8½ million votes, less than a third of the total.

Coolidge's second term in office was a continuation of the conservative policies of the earlier years, but without the scandals of 1921-1923. Mellon and Hoover still exercised great influence. The new administration went on supporting high tariffs, low taxes on corporations and the wealthy, and a hands-off policy on trusts. It had an essentially do-nothing approach to farm problems and a negative attitude toward labor as well. The entire conservative politics of the 1920s was summed up in Coolidge's most famous sentence: "The business of America is business."

Still, the President was popular, and doubtless he could have been nominated for a second full term and won. But his second most famous sentence was: "I do not choose to run." Coolidge may have meant simply that he would accept a draft. Still, for once, "Silent Cal" had spoken too soon and said too much. The Republicans took him literally and turned to Herbert Hoover, the most prestigious official in the administration.

The Democratic Challenge of 1928 The Democrats partially healed their old split, hoping for victory. Governor Alfred E. Smith of New York won the nomination easily. Smith and Hoover were almost perfect contrasts. Hoover was conservative, even gloomy. He dressed in neat blue suits and was the perfect representative of stability and efficiency. Above all he opposed any extension of federal power over private enterprise (unless, as with tariffs, federal power could be used to help business).

Smith, on the other hand, was a happy, talkative, cigar-chomping Irish American politician. He wore a brown derby and checked suits and talked with an urban twang. During the campaign, Hoover accused Smith of socialism because the New Yorker favored federal ownership of electric power generating facilities.

However different their personalities and political backgrounds may have been, Smith and Hoover actually ran on very similar platforms. To head his campaign, Smith chose a Republican executive from General Motors, a man who had in fact voted for Coolidge in 1924. And, in a variety of other ways, the Democrats strained to capture the political center by hewing to a very conservative policy line. On the surface, at least, the election was a contest between personal styles and religious convictions.

Smith's Catholicism got most of the publicity. Some of the charges were merely nasty, as when the Methodist bishop of Virginia referred to Smith as "this wet Roman Catholic chamberlain of the Pope of Rome." But even literate, liberal Protestant newspapers and magazines were concerned. The *Christian Century,* one of the most popular Protestant journals, said that Smith's victory would be the victory "of an alien culture, of a mediaeval Latin mentality, of an undemocratic hierarchy and of a foreign potentate."

Smith's stand on prohibition also alarmed many voters. Hoover called prohibition a "noble experiment," and it may have been this stand, not Smith's religion, that won Hoover powerful support in the South and Southwest. Smith, on the other hand, was a publicly announced "wet," who believed that prohibition was not only a failure, but an act that unfairly deprived urban workers of their modest pleasures.

In the end, Hoover won what appeared to be a landslide. With 58 percent of the popular vote, he almost equaled Harding's record. In fact, because the turnout was unusually heavy, Hoover amassed 21 million votes—more than the combined votes of Coolidge and La Follette in 1924. In the process, Hoover cut deeply into the traditionally Democratic South, where he carried Virginia, Tennessee, North Carolina, Florida, and Texas.

But there was another side to the election, an aspect that was almost lost in the apparent landslide. Smith had made some gains, too. Although he had won fewer electoral votes than any Democrat since 1872, Smith had succeeded in taking two Eastern states, Massachusetts and Rhode Island. This was an indication of a powerful new source of support that the Democrats might be able to capitalize on later—support from immigrants and the children of immigrants in Eastern cities. In 1924, Coolidge had swept all twelve of the largest cities in the nation, and by a large margin. In 1928, Smith won more urban votes than Hoover.

Despite this straw in the wind, however, the Republican ascendancy was still in full swing. Hoover could look toward the inauguration and the future with confidence. The powerful and profitable industrial system, watched over at a discreet distance by a sympathetic government, did seem to be ushering in an era of unprecedented prosperity for millions. So it looked in the winter of 1928–1929.

BOOM AND BUST

On the surface, at least, the 1920s was a decade of great prosperity. Progress seemed inevitable as more and more cars, radios, washing machines, and other goods poured off assembly lines. More workers were producing more goods than ever before. The United States seemed to have created an economic miracle.

American buyers and investors were confident. The New York Stock Exchange, where the economy's pulse seemed most vital, enjoyed an amazing boom period after 1923. Sales on the Exchange quadrupled between 1923 and 1930. As sales increased, so did the prices of stocks. Americans were on an investment binge. The total amount of money kept in stocks and bonds increased faster than any other economic factor during the period (much faster, for example, than the actual production or sale of goods).

Much of the new investment was made on credit. According to the rules of the New York Stock Exchange, investors could buy stock by putting some money down and owing the rest to their brokers. These "brokers' loans" showed how little of the investment rush was real money and how much was pure speculation. By 1927 almost $4 billion was still owed on such loans. The whole structure of the stock market was rickety.

Such investment was really a form of gambling. If a stock cost $10 a share and an investor expected it to go up, he could buy a share and wait for the price to rise. In fact, for his $10 he could buy ten shares, one for cash and the other nine on loan. When the stock went up, he could sell his shares at the new price, pay off his broker, and pocket the difference in cash. There would be a problem though if the stock went down. Then, when the broker's loan was due, the investor might have to sell not only his ten shares of stock but other assets as well. If the stock market fell too low, he could be ruined.

Year after year, the gambles paid off. More and more ordinary people, with only small amounts of money to invest, began to play the market. The prospering economy appeared to justify their confidence.

A Warped Economy But this prosperity was very unevenly distributed through the population. There were large pockets of people throughout the country who did not share it at all. Blacks in both the South and the North did not benefit much. Nor did most farmers, whose lives had long been difficult.

The problems of farmers were especially difficult. In the second half of the nineteenth century, an agricultural revolution had provided the foundation for industrial expansion. Then, during the war, farmers had prospered because of high demand and government supports. The end of the war brought a sharp drop in the demand for exports, and an end to federal aid. At the same time, something odd happened in the domestic market. Improvements in diet slightly increased the demand for vegetables and fruit. But, at the same time, the demand for cereal grains dropped, partly because men released from heavy labor by ma-

One of every four farms was sold for debt or taxes from 1920 to 1932. Farm machinery proved costly not only in its purchase price but in the overproduction and falling prices it caused. Dust storms on the plains in the thirties proved the final blow to many more farms, like the one pictured here.

chines needed fewer calories. In addition, the prevailing Victorian ideal of a sturdy, almost fat figure for men and women had given way to a new slender image of the ideal American male and female.

At the same time, farmers were trapped by the high-volume, technologically sophisticated agriculture that had made many of them successful during the preceding two generations. In wartime, especially, the invested heavily in expensive machines, and they continued to do so even after the demand for their crops had fallen off. In the 1920s, in fact, the number of working tractors on American farms quadrupled.

The effect of these changes was to cause farm prices to drop and production to increase. In 1920, the income of farmers represented about 15 percent of the total national income. By 1929, this proportion had fallen to only about 9 percent. Several million farmers were driven off the land. They drifted to the cities or joined the ranks of the bums who made up a portion of the Bonus Army. Those who stayed in farming very often lost ownership of their land and had to become either tenant farmers or hired hands.

One solution to the problem was government intervention. Grain farmers, especially, supported a scheme that would guarantee farmers a "fair" price for their crop. The scheme involved two things. First, a tariff on imported foodstuffs was needed to prevent foreign producers from taking advantage of an "artificially" high price on the American market. Second, the domestic price of grain needed to be set at a level that was the average for the ten years preceding 1914. The result would be "parity," or a kind of rough equality of agricultural prices and other prices. Under the sponsorship of a senator from Oregon, Charles McNary, and a congressman from Iowa, Gilbert Haugen, a bill providing for parity for grain crops was introduced in the 1924 Congress, but it was defeated in the House.

Two years later, in a bid for Southern support, the NcNary-Haugen bill was broadened to include cotton, tobacco, and rice. In 1927, it passed both houses of Congress but was turned back by a Coolidge veto that could not be overridden. The next year, 1928, Congress again passed

the act, but President Coolidge once more exercised his veto power. The principle of parity would have to wait until well after the crash of 1929.

For industrial workers, the situation was a little better. Real wages—the actual purchasing power of earned dollars—rose during the decade by over 20 percent. And some corporations began to behave a little like Herbert Hoover's model, with programs of "enlightened" capitalism. Sanitary and safety conditions were improved in some of the more modern factories. Some companies started pension funds that gave workers a tiny share in the stock of the corporations that employed them. But the major purpose behind these "progressive" practices was to undercut the growth of industrial unionism. The AFL, meantime, pursued a very cautious policy throughout the decade. The failure of strikes in 1919 and several succeeding years made many workers hesitate to join even a conservative union like the AFL. The outcome was a decline of about 15 percent in union membership, despite an increase in the total number of factory workers.

Those at the outer edges of the industrial system—blacks, most women, the many underemployed recent immigrants in the cities—simply did not participate in the prosperity of the decade. Such "soft" spots in the economy led to a very serious distortion. Technological innovation increased productivity rapidly. The question was, simply, how would the increased production be absorbed? Who would buy the washing machines, the cars, the clothes, all the products of a sophisticated industrial system? The total quantity of goods for sale was increasing much faster than the population. Either wages would have to rise dramatically, so that workers would have more money to spend on all the things being made, or prices would have to fall, so that everyone could afford more. Otherwise, the gap between production and sales would grow until inventories were clogged with unsalable surpluses of consumer goods.

But businessmen generally raised wages less than they should have. They also kept prices high. In the short run, their measures meant higher profits—and higher profits for corporations meant the price of their stock rose. They could either invest the profits in still larger factories and produce still more goods. Or they could invest them in stock and heat up the stock market even more. Many corporations did both.

The result was a warped economy. The amount of goods being produced ran far ahead of the people's power to purchase them. Sooner or later an adjustment had to be made. Otherwise, factories would have to close until the surplus cars, clothes, tools, and other items could be bought. For a time the problem could be avoided in two ways. The surplus products could be sold, on credit, to people who could not really afford them. A family could pay for a car, for example, over two or three years. Or, the surplus could be exported to foreign countries. But both credit and exporting could help a distorted economic system only briefly.

The Stock Market Crash These facts were difficult to see. On the surface, the economy had never looked better, and Americans continued to bet on the future by speculating in stocks. In 1928 the average price of industrial stocks increased by about 25 percent. An investor who bought, say, $1,000 worth of stock in January could sell it in December for $1,250. He could then pocket the $250 profit or invest it in some new gamble. Most speculators did the latter.

Then, after a few rumblings and warnings, the bubble burst. The stock market was not a sure indicator of the country's economic health or disease. In 1929 reality finally caught up with it.

In September the most popular index of stock prices stood at 452. Two months later it was 234. What this meant, in plain terms, was that the market value of stocks on the Exchange had been halved. Most of the holders of the $4 billion in brokers' loans were ruined. So were many of the brokers. On the worst day of all, "Black Tuesday," October 29, the market index fell 43 points. Other days were almost as bleak and ruinous. Stock prices continued to slide. They reached bottom in 1932. Then most stocks were worth little more than a tenth of their cost in September 1929. The Great Depression had begun.

It was difficult then, and still is, for people to understand why the panic on Wall Street should have had any effect on the real economy. The factories were still there, ready to roll out goods. The farms were still there, ready to produce food. All the hands willing to work before Black Tuesday were still there, still willing to work.

But, month by month, the entire economic machine ground down. The stock market crash was the crucial link in the chain of events leading to this breakdown. It caused people to make the grim decision not to buy or invest. So storekeepers sold less. And factories produced less or closed down altogether. Many foreclosed on loans made to others because they needed money to pay off their own loans.

Farmers behind on their payments lost their farms as banks desperately tried to collect hard cash. The banks needed cash because millions of people with savings accounts, frightened now, lined up at tellers' windows to withdraw their money. The banks often could not produce the cash because they had invested or lent it. So even the banks began to fail.

Builders of houses and offices stopped construction because they could not borrow money to continue. Down at the bottom of this tangle were plain workers who, by the millions, received notices that they need not come to work anymore. Their jobs disappeared. Since they could not work, they could not buy; since they could not buy, others could not sell or make goods.

The jobless were not just the old-line poor. Many had been solid, middle-class citizens, such as bank tellers or factory foremen. Others were farmers, who had barely managed to survive throughout the decade. Now they had lost their farms forever. They moved to the cities, looking for food and work, or they began to drift, looking for migrant workers' jobs. People combed garbage heaps for food for their families. They made soup from dandelions. Mostly, however, they waited in a cold, gloomy fog of despair for something to happen.

Hoover's Optimism The question posed by the Depression and symbolized by the Bonus March was simple. Could the federal government be used as a tool for dealing with economic disaster? In the past the answer had been no. Other depres-

Amid the bright lights of Times Square hundreds of New York's hungry formed bread lines in 1932. Ironically, scarcity was not the problem. As Socialist Norman Thomas remarked: "It remained for us to invent bread lines knee-deep in wheat."

sions had been allowed to run their course without any federal attempt to bring early recovery or relieve human suffering. But the Great Depression was by far the worst ever. Now the industrial economy was so large and complicated that its collapse affected far more people. Countless millions were jobless; banks were failing by the thousands; tens of thousands needed food. Something had to be done.

At first the Hoover administration was optimistic. The stock market crash was called a needed adjustment. The economy, Hoover announced, was fundamentally sound. Recovery would be natural and would come soon. Meanwhile, no federal action of any kind was needed.

Surprisingly, most Democrats agreed. In the congressional elections of 1930, the Democrats made prohibition as big an issue as the de-

pression. Nor did the voters heavily punish the administration for its failure to bring about recovery. The Democrats won the House but the Senate stayed Republican. Hoover was still predicting that a return to prosperity was just around the corner.

But things kept getting worse. In 1929, over 600 banks shut down; in 1930, over 1,000; in 1931, 2,000. For farmers there seemed to be no bottom. Wheat in 1931 sold for $.36 a bushel, compared to $1.03 in 1929. No one even knew how many people were unemployed by 1932, but guesses ran as high as 15 million. For those who still had jobs, pay envelopes grew smaller. By 1932 wages in industry were less than half what they had been in 1928.

As he faced all these facts—or, sometimes, tried not to face them—the President grew gloomy and confused. He tried to stay optimistic in public, believing business confidence was crucial to recovery. In private, however, he was trapped between two different beliefs. A humane man, he did not like to see people suffer. But he still thought that government should not interefere in the economy. Free enterprise would bring the nation back to its feet.

Most important, Hoover believed that the federal government must never give direct relief to the poor, unemployed, and hungry. Direct federal welfare, he thought, would destroy people's moral character. It would make them dependent instead of healthy, strong personalities. This set of attitudes, which he referred to as individualism, made Hoover seem insensitive and cruel. He became the target of bitter jokes. People named their shantytowns Hoovervilles and called an empty pocket, turned inside out, a Hoover flag. Reluctantly, Hoover decided that the government must act.

New Federal Powers Early in 1932 Hoover signed a law creating a new federal agency, the Reconstruction Finance Corporation (RFC). It could lend up to $2 billion to banks, insurance companies, and railroads. These loans, the administration believed, would be used especially by the banks to make other loans to businesses. Businesses would in turn use the money for new construction or to reopen factories. Their moves would create new jobs and save old ones. Thus, eventually RFC loans would end up in the pockets of workers, who would then spend the money and create new demand, resulting in more new production, and so on, in a circle of recovery.

The President also went against his own beliefs by signing another law empowering the RFC to lend relief money to state governments. But the amount of the loans was too small to help much. Pennsylvania, for example, could borrow only enough to provide three cents a day to its unemployed workers. Also, the RFC loans to business were far too small to aid the economy effectively. Compared to previous government activity, Hoover's actions were bold experiments in the use of federal power. But, measured against what was actually needed, they were too little too late, as the Bonus Marchers recognized.

SUGGESTED READINGS— CHAPTERS 39-40

The Bonus March

Donald J. Lisio, *The President and Protest: Hoover, Conspiracy, and the Bonus Riot* (1974); Douglas MacArthur, *Reminiscences* (1964).

The Conservative Reaction

R. K. Murray, *The Red Scare* (1955); W. Preston, Jr., *Aliens and Dissenters: Federal Suppression of Radicals, 1903–1933* (1963); David Chalmers, *Hooded Americanism* (1965); K. T. Jackson, *The Ku Klux Klan in the City* (1967); A. S. Rice, *The Ku Klux Klan in American Politics* (1961); G. L. Jouglhin, *The Legacy of Sacco-Vanzetti* (1948); Francis Russell, *Tragedy in Dedham* (1962); N. F. Furniss, *The Fundamentalist Controversy* (1954); Ray Ginger, *Six Days or Forever* (1958); Herbert Asbury, *The Great Illusion* (1950); Andrew Sinclair, *Era of Excess: A Social History of the Prohibition Movement* (1962).

The Politics of the 1920s

William E. Leuchtenburg, *The Perils of Prosperity, 1914–1932* (1958); Arthur Schlesinger, Jr., *The Crisis of the Old Order* (1957); John D. Hicks, *The Republican Ascendancy* (1960); David Burner, *The Politics of Provincialism: The Democratic Party in Transition, 1918–1932* (1968); Andrew Sinclair, *The Available Man:*

Warren Gamaliel Harding (1965); D. R. McCoy, *Calvin Coolidge, The Quiet President* (1967); Oscar Handlin, *Al Smith and His America* (1958); A. U. Romasco, *The Poverty of Abundance: Hoover, the Nation and the Depression* (1965).

The Economy

George Soule, *Prosperity Decade: From War to Depression, 1917–1929* (1947); Alfred D. Chandler, *Strategy and Structure: Chapters in the History of American Industrial Enterprise* (1962); Allan Nevins and Frank Hill, *Ford: Expansion and Challenge, 1915–1932* (1957); James W. Prothro, *Dollar Decade: Business Ideas in the 1920s* (1954); John K. Galbraith, *The Great Crash, 1929* (1955); H. G. Warren, *Herbert Hoover and the Great Depression.* (1959).

UNIT SEVEN

MODERN AMERICA

Fifteen million Americans were unemployed on March 4, 1933, when the new President, Franklin Delano Roosevelt, was inaugurated. Roosevelt stirred his audience when he told his stricken countrymen: "Let me assert my firm belief that the only thing we have to fear is fear itself." A despairing nation responded eagerly to Roosevelt's determination to act quickly and boldly in confronting the emergency.

Twenty-eight years later another new President, John Fitzgerald Kennedy, also used his inaugural speech to proclaim new energy in national affairs. "Let the word go out," Kennedy intoned, "that the torch has been passed to a new generation of Americans [willing] to pay any price, bear any burden, to assure the survival and the success of liberty."

Roosevelt's address rallied Americans to begin the process of economic recovery. Kennedy's speech summoned Americans to leadership of the Western world. The three decades between these two orations saw the United States emerge from economic catastrophe to become the strongest and most prosperous country in world history. The following chapters trace the steps in this evolution.

The career of Eleanor Roosevelt, narrated in Chapter 41, portrays, through the experiences of America's most famous and influential twentieth-century woman, the country's transition from the relatively affluent Twenties into the era of the Great Depression (and beyond). The accompanying chapter on the New Deal years discusses both the social and economic impact of the Depression on the American people and the political world of

Franklin Roosevelt's pathbreaking Administration. Together, the two chapters offer an avenue into comprehending the formative years of our modern national experience.

The attack on Pearl Harbor, dramatized in Chapter 43, highlights the beginning of a shift in national attention from domestic to foreign concerns. Roosevelt and his successors, determined to avoid future "Pearl Harbors," led the country in a search for collective security through treaty alliances. The wartime "Grand Alliance" of the United States, Great Britain, and the Soviet Union rapidly deteriorated after World War II. A new era of Cold War between the Western allies and the Soviet communist camp began. Pearl Harbor thus vaulted the United States into a position of world leadership. Chapter 44 traces the development of that role from the 1930s to the Kennedy Administration.

Running parallel to Cold War developments in foreign affairs were anticommunist rumblings at home. The Alger Hiss case figured prominently in this. Hiss was a former high government official who was convicted in 1950 of having lied about involvement with Russian agents. His case came to symbolize for many the threat of communism to American society. The Red Scare that the incident helped trigger was central to many political, social, and economic developments that the next chapter discusses. Among those developments are the nation's return to affluence, the rise of a "military-industrial complex," and the evolution of social problems that would haunt the next decade.

41
ELEANOR ROOSEVELT: AN AMERICAN LIFE

A. W.

The coal miners were evidently a good distance beneath the surface. Only the lamps in their helmets illuminated the scene, and revealed the surprise on their faces. "For Gosh Sakes!" one exclaimed to the other, "It's Mrs. Roosevelt!"

Eleanor Roosevelt may never have actually gone down a coal mine, but the most famous cartoon of the 1930s showed that people found the idea plausible. During the worst of the Great Depression, Mrs. Roosevelt went to many places no First Lady had visited before, and she did things that the wife of no previous President had thought worth doing. She went to Appalachia, to the Gulf states' Black Belt, to Puerto Rico, and to just about everywhere else to see firsthand the worst poverty in a depression-stricken country. She explored the slums and alleys of the District of Columbia, which most politicians never saw during a lifetime in Washington. Driving with a friend, she visited one New Deal project after another, trying to see if they really helped the unemployed.

She also met people who had never before talked with a First Lady. Through the Women's Trade Union League she maintained ties with working women and their leaders. She considered herself a personal friend of the activists in the American Youth Congress, even after Communists surfaced in the organization. Mrs. Roosevelt provided the New Deal's most open ear to the problems of blacks and worked ceaselessly to protect their rights in government programs. Walter White, head of the National Association for the Advancement of Colored People (NAACP), remarked once that only the thought of Mrs. Roosevelt kept him from hating all white people.

Mrs. Roosevelt tried to keep her husband available to new ideas and often drove the points home herself. "No one," recalled one New

Dealer, "who ever saw Eleanor Roosevelt sit down facing her husband, and holding his eye firmly, say to him, 'Franklin, I think you should . . . .' or 'Franklin, surely you will not . . . .' will ever forget the experience." From her large correspondence she selected letters from people with ideas and from people needing help and laid them on his desk with the scrawled injunction, "F—read."

But, as First Lady, Eleanor Roosevelt was an individual personality, and not merely the wife of the President. She wrote a daily newspaper column, went on lecture tours, and spoke frequently on the radio. She held her own press conferences, the first President's wife to do so. She constantly tried to increase the role of women in the Democratic party and in government, and told a friend she considered that objective more important than any specific political issue.

Next to her husband, Mrs. Roosevelt was probably the best-known person in the country. Conservatives told each other "Eleanor stories," imitating her high-pitched voice and mocking her ungainly features. Friends remarked that her photographs did not do her justice. "My dear," she told one, "if you haven't any chin and your front teeth stick out, it's going to show on a camera plate."

People all over the United States knew Eleanor Roosevelt, and millions adored her. But her public life did not reflect her personal one. She agonized over a troubled marriage and suffered disappointing relationships with her children. Her private difficulties may have instilled in her the strength to sustain her public role; but they may also have caused her to seek among the poor and the disadvantaged the approval she could not find in her own family.

"My mother was one of the most beautiful women I have ever seen," runs the first sentence of Eleanor Roosevelt's autobiography. That beauty made a particular impression on her because she did not inherit it. Her mother and father were one of the most glamorous couples in New York society. In contrast, Eleanor remembered, "I was a solemn child, without beauty and painfully shy, and I seemed like a little old woman." Her exasperated mother called her "Granny."

Her early life did not tend to build either joy or self-confidence. The homely little Eleanor wore a back brace for two years to correct a curvature of the spine. She felt excluded from her mother's affections after the birth of her healthy, attractive, baby brother. Her father, Elliott (Theodore Roosevelt's younger brother), had begun the slow and painful process of drinking himself to death. He was away from home on one more effort to "dry out" when her mother died. Eleanor was eight years old when her mother's family decided that, because of her father's alcoholism, she and her brother should go to live with her maternal grandmother, a gloomy old lady in a gloomy old house in New York City, who hired governesses to deal with her unwelcome guests. The lonely Eleanor spent much time writing loving letters to her adored father. "He dominated my life for as long as he lived," she recalled, "and was the love of my life for many years after he died." Her father rarely answered

Eleanor, at age six, a shy, pensive child whom her mother addressed as "Granny."

her letters and more rarely saw her. He died two years after her mother. All her life Eleanor would be badly hurt when someone she loved disappointed her.

Eleanor was a good student, but—shy and awkward, dressed by her grandmother in children's clothes until she was fifteen—she made few friends when she was sent to school. And the few she made could not be invited to her house, because her maternal uncles were so often drunk. Her grandmother also severely limited Eleanor's visits to her uncle, Theodore Roosevelt, and his family. Theodore, then a rising young politician, had loved his brother and felt keenly for his daughter. On her rare visits to his house, he embraced Eleanor warmly and tried hard to include her in the rough activities of his own brood. "Poor little soul, she is very plain," noted Theodore's wife Edith. "Her mouth and teeth seem to have no future. But perhaps the ugly duckling will turn out to be a swan."

This situation, Eleanor remembered, "began to develop in me an almost exaggerated idea of the necessity of keeping all of one's desires under complete subjugation." It also taught her something about people, and their need to feel wanted. When she briefly visited a friend in the country, her hostess was surprised to find her writing to her young brother two days in a row. "I write him every day," Eleanor explained. "I want him to feel he belongs to somebody."

Her life improved dramatically when, at fifteen, she was sent to boarding school in England. The headmistress took an interest in the uneasy, gawky, but highly intelligent girl, and Eleanor, hungry for affection, responded happily to the attention. When she returned home, she had acquired enough self-confidence to enter New York society, although convinced that her appearance would keep her from achieving any great success. She soon limited her socializing and began teaching in a settlement house on the Lower East Side.

Yet Eleanor did not lack men who showed interest in her. She was soon seeing a good deal of her distant cousin, Franklin Delano Roosevelt. Their closest common ancestor had died in the seventeenth century. But the two Roosevelt families had always been friendly, although Theodore's Oyster Bay Roosevelts were Republicans and Franklin's Hyde Park Roosevelts were Democrats, Eleanor's father, Elliott Roosevelt, had been Franklin's godfather, and she had seen Franklin occasionally while she was growing up.

Franklin Roosevelt was then a popular and amiable Harvard student. He wrote editorials on school spirit for the *Harvard Crimson*, and was good-looking enough to make people wonder what he saw in the ungainly, strait-laced Eleanor. His father, much older than Franklin's mother, had died when his son was at prep school, and Franklin's mother, Sara, now centered her life around her only child. For two winters she had taken a house in Boston to be near him at college. She bent every effort to break up his relationship with Eleanor, a romance she considered both premature and unsuitable. Nevertheless, they became engaged.

A tall, stately, and elegant bride, Eleanor was married to Franklin on March 17, 1905, in a society wedding at a New York townhouse. Wearing the long satin gown covered with brussels lace in which her mother had been married, Eleanor, at twenty, appeared beautiful. She was given away by her uncle, Theodore Roosevelt, who had just been inaugurated as President, and whose daughter, cousin Alice, was one of the bridesmaids.

Uncle Theodore, now President of the United States, offered use of the White House for the marriage. But Eleanor chose her grandmother's house, selecting a day when the President would be in New York for the St. Patrick's Day parade. It was the outgoing TR—who, in the words of his acid-tongued daughter Alice, "wanted to be the bride at every wedding and the corpse at every funeral"—who stole the show, although, in her wedding gown, Eleanor for once looked almost beautiful.

The couple returned to New York from a European honeymoon to find that Sara had rented them a house three blocks from her own. They spent weekends at Sara's country house at Hyde Park, a hundred miles up the Hudson River, and summers at Sara's house on Campobello Island off the coast of Maine. While Franklin began his law career, Eleanor settled down to bearing children, and Sara to telling her how. Sara had no qualms about being an interfering mother-in-law, and Eleanor lacked the self-confidence to decline her advice. "Franklin's children," she said later, "were much more my mother-in-law's than they were mine."

Sara used her money to control her son and daughter-in-law's lives, doling it out according to her own interests and whims. In 1908, she built a new house for Eleanor and Franklin, at 49 East 65th Street. She also built herself a new house—at 47 East 65th Street. Eleanor normally bore up well under the strain, but Franklin came home once to find her in tears. She had no feeling for her house, she sobbed; her mother-in-law had bought the land, selected the architect, and decorated the rooms. Franklin succeeded in calming her, but he did not really understand.

Soon, other interests provided some diversion for them. Legal business bored Franklin; in 1910 he received the Democratic nomination for state senator from the Hyde Park district. Aided by a national Democratic landslide and a good deal of Sara's money, he won the election. Eleanor had encouraged him to enter politics, but the prospect of meeting new people terrified her, and she found their two years in Albany painfully difficult.

Franklin's political career prospered swiftly. He became an early and active backer of the presidential hopes of Woodrow Wilson, then governor of neighboring New Jersey. When Wilson won in 1912, Franklin snared the job of assistant secretary of the Navy, the same position that had propelled Theodore Roosevelt to national prominence.

Washington seemed no warmer to Eleanor than Albany had, but she doggedly made the effort to fit in. To help with her social obligations, she hired a secretary who knew Washington, Lucy Mercer. Lucy, the twenty-two-year-old daughter of impoverished Maryland aristocracy, had all the social graces that Eleanor lacked. She also had a pretty face, a dazzling figure, and a velvety voice. When Eleanor and the children went to Campobello for summers, Lucy remained in Washington to look after the house and Franklin.

Franklin's association with Lucy soon turned into a love affair that was common knowledge among Washingtonians. The two often appeared together when Eleanor was away, and Lucy became a secretary in the Navy Department. Eleanor's cousin, TR's daughter Alice Roosevelt Longworth, assisted the lovers, inviting them both to her house. "Franklin deserved a good time," explained Mrs. Longworth. "He was married to Eleanor." Not surprisingly, Eleanor did not take this tolerant view when she came across revealing letters from Lucy. Furious, she offered her husband a choice: He must never see Lucy again, or Eleanor would sue for divorce.

The situation really offered Franklin no choice at all. He and Eleanor had five children whom he loved and enjoyed. And a divorce would destroy his political aspirations. For once his mother took Eleanor's side, threatening to cut him off financially. Franklin gave up his mistress. From that point on, however, his wife's bedroom door was closed to him. "I have the memory of an elephant," Eleanor quietly told a friend years later. "I can forgive but I cannot forget."

The episode had a profound effect on Eleanor's attitudes about life. "The bottom dropped out of my own particular world," she remembered later, "and I faced myself, my surroundings, my world honestly for the first time. I really grew up that year." Her attempt to build a life around husband and children had failed. As her children grew, she sought more and more to create a satisfying existence for herself outside her home.

In 1920 the Democratic party, seeking to capitalize on the Roosevelt name, nominated Franklin for Vice President. "I am sure that I was glad for my husband," Eleanor wrote later, "but it never occurred to me to be much excited." Nevertheless, she dutifully went on the campaign trail. At first she hated it, writing home: "I really don't see that I'm of the least use on this trip." But she soon became friendly with the reporters and drew close to Louis Howe, the wizened, coughing little man who managed her husband's political fortunes. Harding's landslide victory buried the Democratic ticket, but Eleanor emerged with an interest in politics. After the election, she joined the board of the New York State League of Women Voters.

Eleanor's long career as a politician's wife exposed her to the demands of public life and to the public eye. During the campaign of 1920, when Franklin ran for Vice President, Eleanor joined Mrs. James Cox, wife of the Democratic Presidential nominee, on a reviewing stand in Ohio to watch a parade in honor of the candidates. On this occasion, the candidates were to be officially informed of their nomination, since it was not the custom at that time for them to appear in person at the national conventions.

The summer after Franklin's defeat the family went to Campobello as usual. He felt particularly tired one afternoon and went for a swim in the icy bay. When that did nothing to revive him, he went to bed early. He awoke the next morning to find both his legs paralyzed. Weeks later, the Roosevelts received a definite diagnosis: At thirty-nine, Franklin had contracted polio.

For two weeks, Eleanor nursed Franklin constantly, sleeping on a couch in his room. "You will surely break down if you do not have immediate relief," the doctor warned. But she and Franklin managed to present to the world an image of cheerfulness, of confidence that he would recover and resume his political career. In the months of agony that followed, the world saw Franklin's courage; only Eleanor saw his desperation.

Eleanor now needed all of her own stamina in a struggle with her mother-in-law. Sara had never liked the strange people with whom her son had to associate in politics, and she felt that he should now retire to Hyde Park and become a gentleman farmer. Eleanor, equally determined, insisted that her husband should continue to lead an active life and not die slowly among his trees. She refused to allow people to treat him as an invalid, and she found a tireless ally in campaign manager Louis Howe, who now moved into the Sixty-fifth Street house.

With Franklin largely confined indoors, Howe trained Eleanor to keep her husband's name before the public. He attended meetings at which she spoke and by pointed criticism managed to eliminate her nervous giggle. She chaired the Finance Committee of the Women's Division of the Democratic State Committee and joined the Women's Trade Union League. With growing confidence, she accepted invitations to speak on the radio and to write for magazines. She was becoming, to her own amazement, a prominent public figure.

Together, she and Louis Howe salvaged Franklin's career. But they did no less for Eleanor. Not only did she know that Franklin needed her; she was also creating a role for herself. When their youngest child went off to prep school, she broadened her activities to include full-time teaching at a New York private school. "I suppose," she once told an interviewer, "that if I were asked what is the best thing one can expect in life, I would say—the privilege of being useful."

But despite Eleanor's success and newly gained confidence, she could not withstand Sara's guerilla warfare on the home front. With Franklin often away in the South, where the good weather and warm water assisted his therapy, Sara and Eleanor shared the responsibility of the children. With Sara's encouragement they soon learned to compare their busy mother, who had never been close to them and who now tried to teach them discipline and self-control, with their generous, available grandmother.

The political careers of the two Roosevelts meshed perfectly in 1928, when Governor Al Smith of New York won the Democratic presidential nomination. At the 1924 national convention, Franklin, in a stirring demonstration of his triumph over polio, had risen from his wheelchair and walked without assistance to the podium, where he gave the speech placing Smith's name in nomination. Four years later, Smith asked Franklin to nominate him again. The candidate also asked Eleanor, whose effectiveness in the New York party he had noted, to run national women's activities in his campaign.

Smith soon requested even more. A New York City Catholic himself, he wanted Franklin, as a well-known upstate Protestant, to run for governor. Roosevelt was reluctant—he had just invested most of his capital in a resort in Warm Springs, Georgia, where he thought the waters would help his legs. Eleanor refused to advise Franklin either way, and Smith wore him down. To critics who questioned Roosevelt's physical ability, Smith snapped, "The Governor of New York does not have to be an acrobat!"

Eleanor exerted herself more actively in Smith's presidential

While FDR was Governor of New York, the Roosevelt family gathered for a portrait, with Franklin's mother, the imposing Mrs. James Roosevelt, seated at the far right. Eleanor and her daughter Anna, then married to stockbroker Curtis Dall, held the grandchildren. During these Albany years, Eleanor was commuting by train to New York every week to teach at the Todhunter School, where she served as vice-principal.

campaign than in her husband's. When the final returns buried Smith in defeat but gave Franklin a narrow win, she seemed more disappointed than elated. Nevertheless, she made preparations to assume new duties in Albany. "When I found I had something to do," she told a reporter once, "I just did it."

But things had changed in eight years. Eleanor would not—and indeed could not—again be merely a supportive wife. She spent only four days a week in the state capital; Monday through Wednesday she was in New York City to teach her classes. Her work for the Democratic State Committee also continued, although she removed her name from the organization's stationery. Even when present in the governor's mansion, Mrs. Roosevelt's approach to her role differed greatly from that of her predecessors.

Women's groups, which previously had met with hostility from the state government, now found an unaccustomed welcome in Albany, where Eleanor tried to advance their social programs with Franklin and the legislature. She also helped her husband by making unannounced inspection tours of state institutions and reporting directly to him. During train rides between New York and Albany she handled an enormous load of letters from people who had problems with the state government. She also managed to keep the mansion going. Although the wall between Franklin and Eleanor had not come down, they functioned as a team. "We are really very dependent on each other," she once wrote him wistfully, "though we do see so little of each other."

Eleanor had adjusted to being the governor's wife, but she did not look forward to the next step. Franklin now led the field of Democratic candidates for President, and the Great Depression made his election a strong probability. But he had acquired a new group of advisers, who found Eleanor too idealistic for serious politics. Their first job, one of them told a new recruit, was "to get the pants off Eleanor and on to Frank." But Eleanor still tried to keep her influence with her husband; when, for political reasons, he came out against the United States joining the League of Nations, she refused to speak to him for three days.

When it became clear, by 23 million Democratic votes to 15 million Republican, that the Roosevelts were going to Washington, Eleanor made plans to keep herself busy. Just before the inauguration, she published a book entitled *It's Up to the Women*, and accepted an offer to edit a magazine called *Babies—Just Babies*. She intended to continue her New York interests and remain active in women's causes. Riding to the inaugural ceremony with Mrs. Hoover, Eleanor asked her what she would miss most about the White House. Being taken care of, the outgoing First Lady answered; not having to worry about anything. Eleanor silently promised herself that she would never adopt that attitude.

She was now confident enough to lend a little self-assurance to the wife of Roosevelt's Vice President. Despite her husband's long career in the House of Representatives, Mrs. John Nance Garner of Uvalde, Texas, feared the publicity of her new role and stood somewhat in awe of the famous personage who was now First Lady. "If you see me making any mistakes, Mrs. Roosevelt," she asked uncertainly, "will you please tell me?" "Of course," Eleanor replied. "If you see *me* making any mistakes, will you please tell *me*?"

The country began to learn more about Eleanor when she beame the first President's wife to hold her own press conferences—which were for women only. The male White House correspondents scorned the idea at first; as the conferences began to produce news, however, they too wanted to attend. But Eleanor refused, wanting to help the newspaperwomen, who were then barred from membership in the National Press Club. "So few women writers," she once complained, "many of whom are just as capable of handling the big stories as the men, get a chance to be front-page writers."

Eleanor followed this policy in other ways as well. The Gridiron Club of Washington correspondents traditionally gave an all-male dinner, inviting most of official Washington and visiting politicos. Eleanor began holding a Gridiron Widows Dinner the same night, inviting woman reporters, cabinet wives, and women bureaucrats. She took a

In the early decades of the twentieth century, Eleanor strongly opposed woman suffrage, but once women had won the vote, she joined the Board of the League of Women Voters and began an intensive apprenticeship in public affairs. In her subsequent career, she became a staunch supporter of women's causes, a leader of women in the Democratic Party, and the most prominent woman in American political life. Eleanor is shown here at the 1952 New York Historical Society exhibit, sponsored by the League of Women Voters, that traced the campaign for woman suffrage.

special interest in increasing the role of women in government and in the Democratic party, frequently inviting the handful of female office-holders to the White House. As a result of her efforts, she had the satisfaction of seeing, for the first time ever, women alternates chosen for the (all male) members of the Resolutions Committee at the 1936 Democratic convention.

Two months after Roosevelt's inauguration in March 1933, a new Bonus Army besieged Washington. Eleanor drove down to the campgrounds with Louis Howe. What should they do? "Well," answered Howe, "you're going out there and I'm going to take a nap." Eleanor walked alone into the tent city and talked to the men, telling them of her own volunteer work during World War I and promising to do what she could to help them. The unemployed veterans cheered as she left. Said one, in words that became famous, "Hoover sent the Army. Roosevelt sent his wife."

The President "sent his wife" to many other strange places. She continued the inspection tours she had started in New York, often arriving unannounced and virtually alone. (She flatly refused to have the Secret Service follow her around, although they finally forced her to carry a pistol in the glove compartment of her car.) She visited the poorest parts of the country and ate a five-cent meal with welfare mothers. She tried to get something done about the slums of Washington and once took two carloads of cabinet wives down into the tenements, trying to awaken their interest in the city. They thanked her, but explained that their husbands took up most of their time.

As First Lady, and as a First Lady known to care about people, Mrs. Roosevelt received a flood of mail. The first year, 300,000 letters addressed to her poured into the White House. Eleanor, her secretary, and her staff read them all. If the problem lay with a federal agency, she got in touch with the agency head; if the problem was personal, she tried to counsel the writer or obtain assistance, using her friends in the Women's Trade Union League to check out the story.

Americans wanted to know more about this Mrs. Roosevelt, already known as the Conscience of the New Deal. She went on two lecture tours a year. Often, she surprised her audience: speaking to the conservative Daughters of the American Revolution (DAR), she called on a new idea of patriotism, one "that will mean living for the interests of everyone in our country, and the world at large, rather than simply preparing to die for our country." She spoke often on the radio, and in 1935 earned fees totaling $72,000. She gave the money earned directly to the American Friends Service Committee (AFSC), until a Republican congressman charged her with tax evasion. She then began accepting the money, paying the tax on it, and giving the rest to the AFSC.

In 1936, Eleanor Roosevelt took the unprecedented step of agreeing to write a daily syndicated newspaper column. "My Day," largely a diary of happenings in her life and her thoughts on them, became widely read. Columns that might be controversial she cleared with her husband, who sometimes used them to test public reaction. Her topics were wide-ranging: in one column she might disagree with the idea that women could not be great playwrights; in another discuss her opposition to war toys; in yet a third express her sympathy for children of both sides in the Spanish Civil War. After speaking at an exclusive prep school, she wrote, "Several of the boys asked me about the unemployed as though the unemployed were some strange species of animal. . . . We should realize that the unemployed are individuals, human beings with all the tastes, likes, dislikes, and passions we have ourselves."

The column gave Eleanor, a long-time supporter of organized labor, the chance to join a union herself. She became a loyal and working member of the Newspaper Guild, although she declined an offer to become its president. Eleanor had usually backed unions. Her interest in the Women's Trade Union League provided preparation for the White House years, during which she clearly stood on the side of workers against management. She tried to proceed as unabrasively as possible, but her bias in favor of such unions as the New York–based Ladies' Garment Workers Union was clear. Sometimes, it must be said, she acted in a labor dispute, writing letters pleading the workers' case or expressing her views in print, without full knowledge of the facts. Eleanor would not cross a picket line, even for a polio benefit meeting; she once canceled an appointment with a dressmaker at a fashionable Fifth Avenue store whose employees were on strike. "I will have to wait before coming to see you again," she explained to the store owner, "until you have some agreement with your people which is satisfactory to both sides." Such New Deal measures as emergency relief, the prolabor section of the National Industrial Recovery Act, social security, and the Wagner labor relations law received Mrs. Roosevelt's enthusiastic support.

Nor did she neglect the even more thorny problem of farm labor. She fostered New Deal agencies to deal with displaced farm laborers and to help those trying to continue in their farm work, and she became involved in a crisis in Arkansas over efforts by sharecroppers to join the Southern Tenant Farmers Union. Attempts to have evicted sharecroppers resettled by the federal government ran into stiff opposition from Arkansas growers and their political allies. Hoping to benefit from a personal acquaintance with Arkansas Senator Joseph Robinson, Eleanor told him the story as she understood it. Robinson remained unconvinced, blaming all the trouble on a "group of agitators." In the face of such stonewalling, Eleanor dropped the correspondence and worked behind the scenes to get immediate relief payments to the evicted sharecroppers.

The White House had brought Eleanor the feeling she most treasured—that of being useful. But although she clearly represented a major political asset to her husband, relations between them did not improve. Even apart from past hurts, their personalities differed too radically. Franklin found it essential to forget all his problems from time to time (exchanging banter with reporters or puttering with his stamp collection). But it seemed that Eleanor never could relax. Asked what she wanted for Christmas, she would answer, towels, sheets, pillowcases; at an election night celebration, she "worried about whether anybody was being neglected and whether there was enough food." These very different traits, which enabled them to complement each other as a political team, kept them from taking any real joy in each other's company. Eleanor saw Franklin filling his need for feminine companionship with his daughter, his daughters-in-law, and his long-time secretary, Missy LeHand. "Missy was young and pretty and loved a good time," wrote Eleanor in her autobiography; and "occasionally her social contacts got mixed with her work and made it difficult for herself and others." (Eleanor did not know that Franklin also looked elsewhere for companionship, to an attractive woman in her forties who was now Lucy Mercer Rutherford. The presidential train frequently stopped for two or three day in South Carolina near the Rutherford plantation on its way to Warm Springs. Lucy also had a house in Washington, and during Eleanor's frequent trips out of town Lucy often dined at the White. House.)

Neither could Eleanor find much comfort in her children, whose marriages collapsed one after another. With the example of her mother-in-law always before her, Eleanor tried not to interfere: "I was almost obsessed with the idea that once the children were grown, they should not be subjected to the same kind of control that held such sway over me." But she could not create close relationships with them, although she tried. "We all turned out to have long memories," one of her sons wrote in 1973. "It was impossible to discount the coldness with which Mother treated us when we were young." Nor did her children inherit Eleanor's social conscience. "Mother!" cried her daughter once when she pressed Franklin on a reform issue at dinner, "Can't you see you are giving Father indigestion?"

The fact that she remained an outsider in her own family was perhaps what gave Eleanor such a strong interest in others who were outsiders—in the unemployed, in women, and, to a degree unique for an American national figure at the time, in blacks.

The latter interest created problems, since racial discrimination was everywhere around her, so ingrained as to seem beyond all remedy. Still, Mrs. Roosevelt labored. It was no surprise that blacks were being shortchanged in the distribution of New Deal aid, North and South. From the very start of the Roosevelt programs, Eleanor insisted on reminding the administrators of the National Recovery Administration (NRA) and of emergency relief that wage and benefit payment scales that set lower rates for Negroes should not be permitted. Harry Hopkins, Roosevelt's "Minister of Relief," responded sympathetically, but, all too often, edicts from the top proved no match for low-level bureaucracy and deeply ingrained prejudices.

Eleanor could only hope that New Deal programs would "spill over" and that blacks would get some appreciable share of the benefits. Certainly her husband had no intention of mounting a presidential crusade specifically in favor of blacks and their rights. FDR counted too much on the votes of Southern Democrats in Congress for that. Even

A pioneer in civil rights activism, Eleanor was well known for her public support of black interests. In addition to backing black appointments to federal civil service jobs and New Deal posts, the First Lady maintained contact with the NAACP, invited black organizations to visit the White House, appeared often as a speaker at Negro colleges, and consistently used her influence to combat bigotry. Here, during the War, she greeted black soldiers at a New York fund-raising event to establish recreation facilities for Negro troops; the U.S. Army and its facilities were not integrated until 1948.

though Roosevelt all but monopolized the Negro vote by 1940, no amount of prodding from his wife could induce the President to support an antilynching bill in Congress.

Eleanor battled on against the prevailing currents. Why should the U.S. Navy, she asked Secretary Swanson, enlist Negroes only as messmen—only as kitchen help? Swanson, who probably found the inquiry distasteful in itself (but, after all, it did come from the First Lady), responded firmly that during most of the 1920s blacks had not been allowed to enlist in the Navy at all. Their relegation to service in ship galleys was necessary, he argued, because otherwise they might rise to be petty officers and be placed in authority over whites; that "would create dissatisfaction, and would seriously handicap ship efficiency." The notion of black naval *officers* was not even broached. All Eleanor could do was to counsel, if not console, a Negro correspondent: "These things come slowly and patience is required in all great changes."

Not only did Eleanor try to get government assistance for blacks, she publicly identified herself with their cause. She urged the appointment of blacks to many New Deal agencies, and, for the first time since the days of Woodrow Wilson's "cleaning out of the Negroes" in the federal civil service, a small but noticeable number of blacks obtained middle-level government jobs. Eleanor refused to succumb to despair on the issue. She had frequent discussions with the head of the NAACP, Walter White, and even "forced" a meeting between White and FDR over the antilynching bill. She spoke at commencements and other ceremonies at black colleges. She praised and aided Richard Wright, the young novelist, as well as other Negro intellectuals. She received black sharecroppers at the White House and visited them in the fields.

In November 1938 Mrs. Roosevelt attended the first Southern Conference for Human Welfare, an interracial meeting of educators and social workers. Birmingham, Alabama, the site of the conference, strictly enforced its segregation ordinance, forcing whites to sit on one side of the aisle, blacks on the other. Eleanor entered the room with Mrs. Mary McLeod Bethune, a prominent civil rights advocate, and, chatting animatedly, sat down with her in the black section of the front row. Immediately a policeman appeared next to Eleanor and loudly cleared his throat. Although he was not about to arrest the First Lady, neither would he let her flout the law of the state of Alabama. Without looking up, Eleanor adjusted her chair slightly, so that she sat neither in the black nor in the white section. The policeman turned red, but left. "At a later meeting," Eleanor wrote, "word came to us that all the audience was to be arrested and taken to jail for breaking one of Birmingham's strongest laws against mixed audiences," but no police wagon appeared.

Early in 1939, Mrs. Roosevelt again had the chance to put preaching into practice. The DAR had barred the use of Washington's Constitution Hall to Marian Anderson, a black singer of international repute. Eleanor, herself a member of the DAR, decided to break with precedent. She had never thought much of resignation as a means of protest, considering it preferable to work for change within an organization But the DAR's refusal to budge on the issue caused her to resign and to express her reasons publicly. In April, Miss Anderson gave a triumphant open-air concert on federal property near the Lincoln Memorial, and a few months later, Mrs. Roosevelt presented her with the Spingarn Medal, the NAACP's award for achievement. "It is the little things that the Roosevelts do," observed a Negro newspaper, "which make them great and increases in the mind of the thinking Negro respect for the New Deal and most of what it represents."

Eleanor also had a particular interest in another powerless group. She was instrumental in starting the National Youth Administration, to aid the great numbers of young people made jobless by the Depression. She worked closely with leaders of the American Youth Congress (AYC), a left-wing organization demanding massive federal expenditures to provide employment for youth. In 1939, when the House Un-American Activities Committee subpoenaed the leaders of the AYC, Eleanor attended the hearings, sitting in the front row and knitting placidly like a benign Madame LaFarge. She had learned not to be frightened of names, perhaps because she had been called so many. (A friend once confessed to her of having voted in 1932 for the Socialist candidate for President. "So would I," Eleanor confided, "if I had not been married to Franklin.") After the student leaders had testified, she brought them back to the White House for dinner. In her column, she warned that if such witch-hunting continued, "It is really going to take quite a strong-minded person with a great indifference to what may be said about him to join an organization, even one with whose principles he is in agreement."

Even after Communist control of the AYC became clear, Eleanor spoke at their national convention, asking amidst angry heckling why they condemned Nazi aggression in Spain but not Soviet aggression against Finland. When her son commented that the AYC people obviously had bad manners she turned on him angrily. "And who are you to talk about their bad manners?" she blazed. "You were brought up in plenty, trained to good manners. You never had to worry about getting a job. Who are you to talk about the manners of young people who had to fight for everything they got, and didn't get much?"

The outburst showed both Eleanor's great empathy for those in need and her difficulties with her own family. Possibly her problems at home strengthened her interest in, and her commitment to, the outside world. For whatever reason, out of an unhappy childhood, a shattering disappointment in marriage, and her husband's paralysis, Eleanor forged a career that affected the history of her country and permanently changed the role of the American woman in public life.

Eleanor Roosevelt, from her particularly privileged vantage point, had done much to become a significant figure on the New Deal scene. With the outbreak of World War II in 1939, she adjusted to new conditions as the United States edged toward involvement in that struggle. The success of fascist totalitarian regimes in Europe caused her to drop her former pacifism in favor of a more "realistic" attitude of moral and material aid to the Western democracies. On that point, she and Franklin saw eye to eye. Eleanor became a leader in the Office of Civil Defense (OCD) during 1940 and 1941, working closely with a talented and flamboyant New Dealer, New York City's Mayor Fiorello La Guardia.

But when Japan attacked the United States in December 1941, Eleanor's course was set for wider horizons than those provided by OCD. She made a well-publicized trip to Britain in 1942 to visit Allied troops. The American buildup of armed forces overseas was proceeding at an astonishing pace, and even Eleanor's fabled stores of energy were hard pressed to keep up with all the war fronts. As a representative of the Red Cross and of the United Services Organization (USO), she became the First Gray Lady, earning the nickname the GI's Friend. A wartime tour of the South Pacific left Admiral William "Bull" Halsey decidedly impressed. During one twelve-hour stretch in New Caledonia, Mrs. Roosevelt inspected almost everything, including the many military hospitals. "When I say that she inspected those hospitals," Halsey reported, "I don't mean that she shook hands with the chief medical officer, glanced into a sun parlor, and left. I mean that she went into every ward, stopped at every bed, and spoke to every patient. . . . I marveled at her hardihood, both physical and mental, she walked for miles, and she saw patients who were grievously and gruesomely wounded. But I marveled most at their expressions as she leaned over them. It was a sight I will never forget."

The pace that both Roosevelts, Eleanor and Franklin, set for themselves during World War II was indeed killing. The President won his fourth presidential election in 1944, and was preparing for a summit meeting of Allied leaders at Yalta in Russia, but it was obvious by that time that his physical condition had deteriorated badly. He no longer wished to drive his car, and he had even surrendered his beloved ritual of cocktail mixing to others. After Yalta, Franklin went down to Warm Springs for rest and recuperation. Eleanor, still in Washington, seemed to convince herself that her husband would be all right. But on April 12, 1945, she learned that the President had died of a massive stroke. It was Eleanor who informed Harry Truman that he was the new President.

In Georgia, Eleanor had to bear the additional grief of learning that Lucy Mercer Rutherford had come to Warm Springs on April 9 and was with Franklin when he died three days later. Reflecting on her relationship with her husband as the funeral train moved toward Washington, Eleanor mused that Franklin "might have been happier with a wife who was completely uncritical. That I was never able to be, and he had

During World War II, Mrs. Roosevelt toured army bases and military hospitals wherever allied troops were stationed, from England to the South Pacific. Riding in jeeps, eating in mess halls, and visiting the wards, the President's wife displayed an energy and compassion that inspired the nation—and kept her in the news. "FIRST LADY DINES WITH DOUGHBOYS" cabled the United Press in 1943, as khaki-clad Eleanor appeared for lunch at an army camp in Australia.

The founding of the United Nations in 1945, after FDR's death, provided an appropriate opportunity for Eleanor to utilize her political and diplomatic talents and to remain active in public life. During her challenging years as United States delegate to the General Assembly, Eleanor served as Chairman of the Commission on Human Rights and was active in UNESCO. Here, she addresses the General Assembly on a human rights issue.

to find it in some other people. Nevertheless, I think I sometimes acted as a spur. . . .

Franklin was gone, but Eleanor never abandoned the conviction that one had to be *useful*. Too many things remained undone; too many desperate people around the world needed help. After the war, Mrs. Roosevelt went on to represent and to voice the best of the American humanitarian impulse. She served as a U.S. delegate to the United Nations from 1945 to 1953, earning worldwide respect and love. For another nine years she fought her version of the good fight as a lecturer and "spur" in support of causes she considered just. Her optimism, if not infectious, was certainly constant. She was, as her friend Adlai Stevenson expressed it following her death in 1962, a person who "would rather light a candle than curse the darkness."

Back in the early 1930s, when Soviet diplomat Maxim Litvinov made his first trip to the United States, President Roosevelt remarked that he regretted Madame Litvinov had not come with him. "Oh well, you know," answered the Russian, "very active woman, career of her own, constantly traveling, making speeches. Impossible to interrupt what she was doing. Came alone because she is individual in politics, just as I am."

Said Franklin Roosevelt, "I think I understand."

42
THE NEW DEAL ERA

A. W.

Eleanor Roosevelt assisted the New Deal in what was possibly its most important function—restoring the confidence of the American people in their government. Her husband, perhaps the country's master politician of the century, made the renewal of confidence a major objective, and in large measure he succeeded in achieving that goal. But Franklin Roosevelt also had to devise concrete policies, in legislation and in executive action, to deal with the crisis.

The Administration's responses followed no set pattern and derived from no single philosophical base. The New Deal was, instead, an extended improvisation in public policy—trying first one program to deal with a problem, then another if the first one failed, and sometimes returning to the original idea. Over six years, in this zigzag pattern, Roosevelt and the New Dealers profoundly changed the face of American government and what the American people expected from it.

The New Deal did not end the Great Depression. It was World War II, with its massive government spending, that finally brought a full revival of production and an end to mass unemployment. By 1939, when foreign policy began to dominate his thinking, Roosevelt had shepherded the country from a crushing depression to a severe recession. Yet he could claim, for better or worse, to have preserved the American political and economic systems through a time when many expected that both would collapse.

ROOSEVELT

"The only thing we have to fear," declared the new President to a numbed nation, "is fear itself." Although the American people could search through the rest of his inaugural address without finding any reason not to be afraid and without learning what Roosevelt planned to do to ease their fears, they seemed to be comforted by his words as they had never been by Herbert Hoover's pronouncement of similar platitudes. Roosevelt's faculty for inspiring confidence by simple force of personality became one of his strongest weapons in the fight against chaos—as important as any bill he ever pushed through Congress.

Franklin Roosevelt was forty-seven when the stock market collapsed in 1929, fifty-one when he became President in 1933. His ideas about the world had already formed. There is no evidence that the Depression changed those ideas significantly. He was in many ways a traditionalist. He was, as we have seen, a wealthy aristocrat: educated in exclusive private schools, a graduate of Harvard, and owner of a country estate where he liked to play at being a gentleman farmer. FDR was a suave, smiling, confident man, who seemed to take the institutions and beliefs of his country very much for granted. A more unlikely candidate for leadership in a revolution is hard to imagine. Roosevelt, wrote a bemused columnist during the 1932 campaign, was a pleasant man, with no particular qualifications, who would like very much to be President.

On the other hand, Roosevelt's confidence opened his mind to experimentation. Because he had no serious doubts about American values and institutions, he could accept almost any specific suggestion for reform. Above all, he often said, the country demanded action. As long as the action was limited in its scope and possible consequences, he was willing to try almost anything.

Roosevelt appreciated fully the seriousness of the Depression. But he was nevertheless sure that, sooner or later, limited reforms would revive the economy. Then, all that would be needed would be a gentle system of laws and regulations to prevent a repetition of the worst mistakes of the 1920s.

SAVING THE BANKS

Yet, as Roosevelt took the oath of office, it appeared doubtful that he would get the chance to try his reforms. Since the fall of 1932, banks had been closing their doors, unable to pay depositors their money. In February, the governor of Michigan closed the state's banks for eight days to prevent collapse; state after state followed suit. By inauguration day on March 4, 1933, thirty-eight states had closed their banks; and before the sun rose on March 5, New York and Illinois had also closed theirs. The New York Stock Exchange and the Chicago Board of Trade shut down. "We are at the end of our rope," said Hoover in despair.

The day after inauguration, Roosevelt (with questionable legality) declared a national bank holiday. Four days later, he sent a mild banking reform and regulation bill to a special session of Congress. It went through both Houses in a day, although few congressmen knew what they were voting for. "The house is burning down," declared a Republican congressional leader, "and the President of the United States says this is the way to put out the fire." Roosevelt then spoke over the radio, in his first "fireside chat," assuring the nation that banks were now safe. When they reopened, bankers were astounded to find that deposits exceeded withdrawals.

Roosevelt's response to the situation clearly demonstrated his attitudes — and disappointed many radicals. A frightened Congress would have passed almost anything Roosevelt had asked for, up to and possibly including a bill nationalizing the banks. But the President clearly intended to preserve capitalism as well as to stimulate recovery. It would, on the other hand, be a controlled capitalism. Two months later Roosevelt signed the Glass-Steagall Act, which strengthened federal controls over banks and set up the Federal Deposit Insurance Corporation (FDIC) to guarantee bank deposits up to $10,000 (now up to $40,000).

The Emergency Banking Act of 1933, accompanied by a confident "Fireside Chat," began the legislative barrage of the First Hundred Days. With thousands of banks out of business and most of the remainder closed by the states, President Roosevelt proclaimed a bank holiday and proposed legislation to bolster the stronger banks with RFC loans and other assistance. When the banks opened their doors four days later, the nation responded by depositing billions in hoarded currency and gold. Above, FDR signs the Emergency Banking Act, and gold is returned to the vaults.

Bank failures ceased immediately. Roosevelt had bought some time.

THE HUNDRED DAYS

Congress and the people now awaited, with both eagerness and anxiety, a legislative program that Roosevelt had not quite worked out. During the campaign, he and other Democrats had called for a cut in spending and a balanced budget, and the Administration took a few halting steps in that

MAJOR NEW DEAL DOMESTIC LEGISLATION

YEAR	ACT/ADMINISTRATION	PURPOSE
REGULATION OF INDUSTRY AND AGRICULTURE		
1933	AGRICULTURAL ADJUSTMENT ACT	Set up the Agricultural Adjustment Administration to encourage stability in agriculture by attempting to control agricultural production.
	NATIONAL INDUSTRIAL RECOVERY ACT	Set up the National Recovery Administration to encourage corporations to create associations for planning production and controlling prices; created a blanket code of minimum wages and maximum hours.
1935	CONNALLY ACT	To prevent overproduction of oil.
	GUFFEY ACT	To control the coal industry.
	NATIONAL LABOR RELATIONS ACT (WAGNER ACT)	To give federal protection to the labor movement by making it illegal for an employer to refuse to recognize a labor union.
	PUBLIC UTILITIES HOLDING COMPANY ACT	To limit the development of holding companies and discourage financial concentration in public utilities.
1936	ROBINSON-PATMAN ACT	To prohibit wholesalers or manufacturers from giving preferential discounts or rebates to large buyers.
	WALSH-HEALY ACT	To set minimum wages and maximum hours for work done on federal contracts (enacted after NRA declared unconstitutional).
1938	AGRICULTURAL ADJUSTMENT ACT	To cut back farm production through marketing quotas, soil conservation payments, export subsidies, and crop loans. It began storage of surpluses.
	FAIR LABOR STANDARDS ACT	To establish minimum wages and maximum hours; forbade child labor.
REFORM		
1933	TENNESSEE VALLEY AUTHORITY	Set up the Tennessee Valley Authority to develop the nation's water resources and, therefore, provide cheap electric power.
1935	SOCIAL SECURITY ACT	To create a system of old-age insurance for Americans.
	WEALTH TAX ACT	To make the federal income tax more equitable.
MISCELLANEOUS		
1934	RECIPROCAL TRADE AGREEMENTS ACT	To lower tariff barriers in order to improve foreign trade.
1939	HATCH ACT	To remedy corrupt campaign practices by prohibiting active political campaigning and soliciting by federal officials.
	REORGANIZATION ACT	To reorganize the executive branch for greater efficiency.

MAJOR NEW DEAL DOMESTIC LEGISLATION

YEAR	ACT/ADMINSTRATION	PURPOSE
BANKING CURRENCY SECURITIES		
1933	EMERGENCY BANKING RELIEF ACT	To save failing banks by providing them with cash to pay their depositors.
	GLASS–STEAGALL ACT	To curb speculation by banks; set up the Federal Deposit Insurance Corporation to "insure" savings deposits up to $10,000.
	"TRUTH IN SECURITIES" ACT	To require corporations floating new securities to register them with the Federal Trade Commission.
1934	GOLD RESERVE ACT	To enable the President to fix the gold content of the dollar.
	SECURITIES EXCHANGE ACT	Set up the Securities and Exchange Commission to regulate the Stock Market.
1935	BANKING ACT	To reform and strengthen the Federal Reserve System by directing interest rates.
DIRECT RELIEF		
1933	FARM CREDIT ADMINISTRATION	To provide emergency relief to farmers in the form of mortgages.
	FEDERAL EMERGENCY RELIEF ACT	Set up the Federal Emergency Relief Administration to provide grants in aid to the states; also set up the Civil Works Administration to relieve unemployment by a temporary work relief program.
	FRAZIER–LEMKE FARM BANKRUPTCY ACT	To enable some farmers to regain their farms even after the foreclosure of mortgages.
	HOME OWNERS REFINANCING ACT	Set up the Home Owners' Loan Corporation to provide emergency relief to home owners in the form of government financed mortgage loans.
	NATIONAL INDUSTRIAL RECOVERY ACT	Set up the Public Works Administration to contract for heavy construction projects in order to increase employment.
	UNEMPLOYMENT RELIEF ACT	Set up the Civilian Conservation Corps to provide jobs for the unemployed on conservation projects.
1934	NATIONAL HOUSING ACT	Set up the Federal Housing Administration to insure mortgages for new construction and home repairs.
1935	WORKS PROGRESS ADMINISTRATION	To relieve unemployment by light public works projects.
1937	FARM SECURITY ADMINISTRATION	To make short–term loans for rehabilitation of farms, and long–term loans for purchase of farms.

direction. Awaiting the repeal of the prohibition amendment, it persuaded Congress to legalize beer, possibly to take people's minds off the Depression. Finally, the Administration produced comprehensive farm and industrial recovery bills.

Both the National Industrial Recovery Act (NIRA) and the Agricultural Adjustment Act (AAA) sought to regulate the economy without changing its private enterprise character. The NIRA also reflected Roosevelt's desire to maintain the broad support he had enjoyed when he assumed office—to move against the Depression at the head of a coalition of government, business, and labor. (His approach in some ways resembled Wilson's approach to fighting World War I—the last period in which Democrats had controlled the federal government.)

The National Industrial Recovery Act was, in essence, a repeal of parts of the old Sherman Anti-Trust Act (see page 730). Under a federal agency known as the National Recovery Administration (NRA), corporations were encouraged to create associations to plan production and control prices. Such a step meant the end of effective competition, but the Administration was prepared during the Depression to sacrifice competition to stability and recovery.

For workers, the act also proposed that employers agree on uniform standards for labor practices, wages, and hours. When some companies were slow to cooperate, the NRA created a blanket code of minimum wages and maximum hours. Companies that cooperated were awarded a flag with the NRA symbol—a blue eagle—to fly as evidence of their public spirit. Up to a point, it worked. Some workers—those who had jobs to begin with—began to work shorter days and take home fatter pay envelopes.

The Agricultural Adjustment Act was a similar but more radical attempt to alter prevailing economics. It recognized that the farmer had a peculiar problem. Manufacturers, when prices fell, could cut back production. The reduction in supply would, sooner or later, raise prices. But farmers had always met falling prices by trying to produce more, not less.

The law created an Agricultural Adjustment Administration (AAA) with the power to pay farm-

ers cash subsidies *not* to plant or harvest crops. The agency could also buy up agricultural products, such as cotton or wheat, and store them. This scheme would reduce supply and raise prices. In other words, a government body, with the cooperation of farmers, would try to control agricultural production. The goal was to enable farmers to earn as much (in real dollars, or purchasing power) as they had earned during the prosperous years from 1909 to 1914—a standard known as parity.

The AAA worked better than the NRA. Using its new powers, the agency in 1933 paid out $160 million to farmers who plowed under about 10 million acres of crops. That same year, farmers also withheld about 6 million pigs in return for $30 million in government money)—a controversial act, when millions of people did not have enough to eat. But these drastic measures worked—reinforced by drought in 1933 and 1934 that destroyed much of the wheat and corn crops. In 1933, farm prices were at 55 percent of parity; by 1936, at 90 percent. The act also had the indirect effect of forcing millions of tenant farmers and sharecroppers off the land, adding them to the unemployment rolls of the country's cities (and beginning a mass migration off the land that accelerated after World War II). Liberal New Dealers, including Mrs. Roosevelt, protested AAA contracts that allowed the eviction of farm tenants. But the group of liberal and radical lawyers that had fought the policy was "purged" from the agency by Secretary of Agriculture Wallace in 1935.

Wide ranging as they were, the NIRA and AAA were only a part of the legislative program achieved by FDR during the first months of his administration—the Hundred Days. He also demanded and received from Congress the Glass-Steagall Act, also known as the "Truth in Securities" Act, to regulate the stock market; and bills to provide emergency relief to farmers and homeowners in danger of losing their property. His advisers also persuaded Roosevelt to abandon his scruples over a balanced budget and set up the Federal Emergency Relief Agency to distribute half a billion welfare dollars to the states. Roosevelt, reversing the previous vetoes of two Republican Presidents, signed a bill creating the Tennessee Valley Authority (TVA), a massive government hydroelectric power development in the Upper South.

Nowhere was the Depression more severe than in the 40,000 square miles of territory spanning seven states known as the Tennessee River Valley. Each year the river swelled to flood stage with an average 52 inches of rain that washed out the area's meager crops. There was little industry and no hope of more, income being not even half the national average. The Tennessee Valley Authority was easily the most creative and far-reaching experiment in regional planning undertaken in American history. The TVA built a series of dams for flood control, thus making successful farming possible in the region and providing an abundance of hydroelectric power. It also made the rivers navigable. Cheap power and easy water transport, in turn, made the area appealing to industry. Schools, improved health facilities, recreational opportunities, reforestation, and other social benefits also flowed from the TVA, which, as the decade wore on, became a successful—if controversial—model for subsequent regional planning efforts in the United States. It marked the first time that government had attempted to mobilize the natural, economic, and human resources of a region to effect a rapid change in the overall conditions of life for most citizens of the area.

RESPONSE

Long before the success of Roosevelt's program could be gauged, it became clear that he had captured the American imagination. The President's picture appeared in homes across the country; journalists estimated his popularity at up to 90 percent. "How do you account for him?" asked William Allen White, a progressive Republican. "Was I just fooled in him before the election, or has he developed?" People now felt the country had begun to move again. "President Roosevelt has done his part, now you do something," read a sign posted in a factory. "Buy something—buy anything, anywhere; paint your kitchen, send a telegram, give a party, get a car, pay a bill, rent a

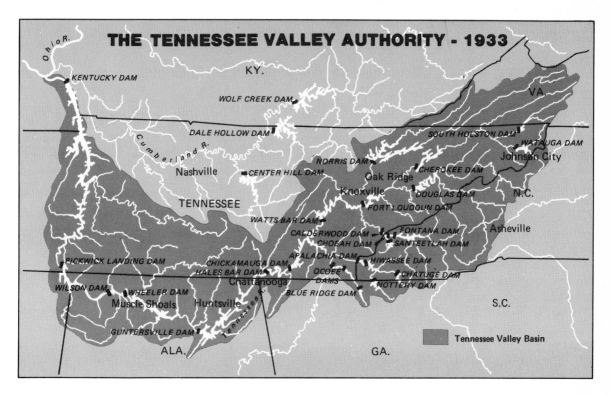

THE TENNESSEE VALLEY AUTHORITY - 1933

Ohio R.

KY.

KENTUCKY DAM

WOLF CREEK DAM

VA.

Cumberland R.

DALE HOLLOW DAM

SOUTH HOLSTON DAM

WATAUGA DAM

Johnson City

NORRIS DAM

CHEROKEE DAM

Nashville   CENTER HILL DAM   Oak Ridge

Knoxville   DOUGLAS DAM   N.C.

TENNESSEE   FORT LOUDOUN DAM

WATTS BAR DAM

CALDERWOOD DAM   FONTANA DAM   Asheville

CHOFAH DAM   SANTEETLAH DAM

APALACHIA DAM

PICKWICK LANDING DAM   CHICKAMAUGA DAM   HIWASSEE DAM

HALES BAR DAM   OCOEE   CHATUGE DAM

Chattanooga   DAMS   NOTTERY DAM

WILSON DAM   BLUE RIDGE DAM   S.C.

WHEELER DAM

Muscle Shoals   Huntsville

GUNTERSVILLE DAM   Tennessee R.   Tennessee Valley Basin

ALA.   GA.

flat, fix your roof, get a haircut, see a show, build a house, take a trip, sing a song, get married."

Although Roosevelt's effect on music and marriage remains unclear, the economy did seem to respond to New Deal efforts. By spring of 1934, the crisis had eased. Unemployment dropped, and business indicators picked up a bit. But that was as far as it went. The NRA's program of voluntary regulation of everything, from the steel industry to show business, apparently could do no more.

Despite Roosevelt's personal popularity, his programs were beginning to draw criticism from both the left and the right. At the low point of the Depression, during Hoover's last two years, Americans had been too demoralized even for radicalism. With millions of people living in shantytowns, the Socialist party ran a disappointing race in 1932, winning less than 900,000 votes, while the Communists polled only 100,000 votes. Now, as vitality seemed to return to the country, the left began to stir as well. Strikes erupted throughout the country in 1934, including a general strike in San Francisco. The greatest radical challenge, however, came not from Marxian philosophers but from uniquely American demagogues—notably, Senator Huey Long of Louisiana (see page 435), who insisted that the New Deal had not been sufficiently reformist.

Wealthy businessmen argued, conversely, that Roosevelt had gone too far. In August 1934, the American Liberty League was organized. Originally financed by the Dupont family, the League soon gained enthusiastic support from leaders of such corporations as General Motors, Montgomery Ward, and General Foods. Calling itself nonpartisan, it could boast endorsement by the Democratic presidential candidates of 1924 and 1928—the conservative John W. Davis and the embittered progressive Al Smith. Smith felt that Roosevelt had cheated him out of the nomination and the presidency in 1932, and in his frustration he joined a group having little to do with his personal background or his political principles. "There can be only one capital," he warned appreciative Liberty Leaguers, "Washington or Moscow."

With such strident criticism apparently on the increase, New Dealers waited anxiously for the elections of 1934, hoping to hold their losses to under forty seats in Congress. The morning after election day, they were stunned and delighted to find Democratic gains in both houses, giving them the tightest control over Congress ever held by a party.

ENTER THE SUPREME COURT

With his massive electoral victories, Roosevelt controlled two of the three branches of government. Conservatives looked hopefully to the third, and the makeup of the Supreme Court seemed to justify their confidence. It would be almost two years before the legislation of the Hundred Days reached the Court, but when it did, it would find a Court roster that was unchanged, and probably unfriendly.

Of the nine men on the Court, seven had been named by conservative Republican Presidents. Although court decisions did not exactly follow a conservative pattern (two of the three liberal justices had been named by Republicans, while Justice McReynolds, possibly the most reactionary, had been nominated by Wilson, a Democrat), the Court did seem to bring the political and constitutional outlook of Calvin Coolidge to the judging of the New Deal. From early decisions, the Administration learned to count four justices as against the New Deal, three as tending to sustain it, and two, including Chief Justice Charles Evans Hughes, as holding the balance of power. For Roosevelt, a bad situation was compounded by simple bad luck; throughout his first term, he did not have a single Court vacancy to fill.

The Court's first decisions only prolonged the suspense. It threw out a section of the NIRA; but it upheld Roosevelt's financial policies by a series of 5 to 4 votes. Then, in May 1935, the Court unanimously ruled the National Recovery Administration unconstitutional. "Extraordinary conditions do not create or enlarge constitutional power," admonished Chief Justice Hughes, as he read the judicial obituary for NRA.

In a way, the Court had done Roosevelt a favor. The NRA, however useful it had been dur-

HUEY P. LONG

Because of an assassin's bullet, Americans will never know just how serious a threat Huey P. Long posed to their political institutions. Unquestioned master of his own state of Louisiana, the most potent demagogue of the Depression, Long attracted national support with a hazy program of redistributing wealth, and the seductive slogan "Every man a king." He was preparing to run for President when he was murdered, but probably not even so gifted a politician as Long could have outmaneuvered Franklin Roosevelt. Still, Long did make Roosevelt—and a great many other people—extremely uncomfortable.

Long grew up in a middle-class but radical-populist family in northern Louisiana. After a brief spell as a traveling salesman, he used his savings and a small loan to put himself through a three-year law course in eight months. But Long did not prosper in private practice and was more interested in finding a way into politics. In 1918, at age twenty-five, he won election to the State Railroad Commission. After six years of denouncing corporations (especially the oil interests), he ran for governor, but lost. The day after his loss in 1924, he declared himself a candidate for 1928, and campaigned hard for the next four years. That second time, he won.

As governor, Long pushed through a reform program that included free textbooks, a large state university, an expanded road system, and a tax on oil production. He also worked unceasingly to extend his own power, firing people throughout the state government and replacing them with his own henchmen. When one of his bills came up in the legislature, Long would go down to the floor of each house and bellow orders at the legislators he controlled.

During his second year as governor, Long tried to pass a bill taxing the refining of oil as well. Aghast, the legislature killed the measure, and impeached Long in a broad indictment covering virtually all impeachable offenses. Long barely managed to persuade, bribe, and threaten enough state senators to enable him to stay in office.

Tightening his control over the state, he began to develop a folksy image, calling himself "Kingfish" after a character in the radio program "Amos 'n Andy." The new nickname covered many activities; a U.S. Treasury agent reported to his superiors that "Long and his gang are stealing everything in the state." In 1930 he defeated an incumbent U.S. Senator and in 1932 played a large role in nominating Franklin D. Roosevelt for President. The Kingfish remained as governor for a year to ensure his control of the state before taking his seat in the Senate.

When he reached Washington, Long found the Democratic leadership too conservative for him, and within a year found he had problems working under President Roosevelt. Partly, the new President moved too slowly for Long; partly, Long was not born to follow.

From the second-best stage in the country (the U.S. Senate), the master showman began to assemble his own movement. He attacked the New Deal and offered his own program of Share Our Wealth. By 1935, he was receiving speaking invitations from all over the country and published a book modestly titled, *My First Years in the White House*. Roosevelt's advisers estimated he might poll several million votes as a third party candidate. Roosevelt showed his concern: he cut off federal patronage to the Long forces in Louisiana, and a small army of U.S. Treasury agents entered the state to examine Long's income tax returns.

In September 1935, the son-in-law of a Long opponent shot the Kingfish down in the lobby of the state capital. According to legend, Long's last words were "God, don't let me die. I have so much to do."

ing the crisis of 1933–1934, was collapsing, and many were charging, with some justice, that its industrial codes benefited big business at the expense of small producers. Clearly, the Administration would need to try a new approach, and the Court had saved FDR from having to admit failure. Nevertheless, the President denounced the justices for adhering to a "horse-and-buggy" definition of interstate commerce. For the next two years, the Administration would pass its bills looking uncomfortably over its shoulder at the Supreme Court.

THE SECOND NEW DEAL

Even before Black Monday, as the day of NRA's death came to be known for a while, Roosevelt had asked the new Congress to take bolder measures to deal with the Depression. The enactments of Roosevelt's second Congress differed greatly in philosophy from those of the first Hundred Days. Motivated by a combination of continuing economic hardship and the counsel of more liberal advisers (including Eleanor, who played a critical role at this time), and reacting to attacks from business and the Supreme Court, Roosevelt abandoned his earlier policy of stabilization and cooperation. He began to frame strategies for reforming the economic system that could bolster the poor and powerless and curb the power of business. The American Liberty League had not known when it was well off.

Faced by a stubborn persistence in the high rate of unemployment, Roosevelt shrugged off his hopes for a balanced budget and asked Congress for five billion dollars for work relief. To administer the agency charged with spending this money, Roosevelt selected a controversial former social worker named Harry Hopkins, the man who would eventually become the second most powerful figure in the Administration. Thin and pale, apparently existing on cigarettes and black coffee, Hopkins seemed perpetually on the point of death from tuberculosis. But he possessed an incredible

The WPA's immediate goal was to provide relief for the unemployed. But in its six-year life span it compiled a remarkable record of public construction, including more than 600,000 miles of road, like this one in Tennessee.

appetite for work and a keen social conscience. To those who suggested the economy would right itself in the long run without expensive government programs, he responded tartly, "People don't eat in the long run. They eat every day."

Hopkins' agency, the Works Progress Administration (WPA), soon employed three million people, paying a wage somewhere between relief and union wages. Careful not to take jobs away from workers already employed, WPA people worked on a wide range of projects, building or extending hospitals, schools, and playgrounds. The Federal Theater Project, Federal Writers' Project, and Federal Art Project subsidized unemployed hopefuls of varying talent and brought drama and art to many isolated communities. The National Youth Administration tried to deal with the enormous number of needy young people, giving part-time employment to help many stay in school, providing training to many who had left school.

Between 1935 and 1941, more than eight million Americans were employed by the WPA. It spent over $11 billion on 250,000 projects. Another $4 billion was spent by a similar agency, the Public Works Administration (PWA), which built large-scale public projects and employed union labor. Critics charged that the programs were involved in useless "make-work" tasks, that WPA stood for "We piddle around," and that the whole organization was a taxpayer-supported boondoggle and patronage plum to get Roosevelt and other Democrats elected. Others pointed out that WPA took care of only about one-third of the unemployed, and that most of the others had to rely on the states or private charity for subsistence.

Shortly after Black Monday, the President demanded immediate passage of five major Administration bills, terming them "must" legislative items. Included in the crash program were the two bills that became the New Deal's most significant legislative accomplishments. Despite the New Deal's reputation for innovation, however, neither of the two was really an Administration idea.

Older people had suffered more in the Depression than any other group. Since 1933, an elderly physician from Long Beach, California, Dr. Francis Townsend, had been promoting a plan to give everybody over sixty years of age a federal pension of two hundred dollars a month. The

During the depths of the depression, the 1934 street scene above was repeated in every city in the nation. The efforts of voluntary agencies and local governments were not enough to help the vast numbers of elderly and unemployed who, depleted of savings and broken in spirit, were reduced to destitution and hand-outs. The Social Security Act of 1935 not only provided immediate relief for the old and disabled, but also prospective annuities for those still at work — its most innovative feature.

movement spread swiftly, and the impoverished elderly at last saw a chance for some dignity at the end of their lives. Several congressmen from both parties were elected with Townsendite backing in 1934, and although the House killed a Townsendite bill (avoiding a roll call, so that those against it would not be identified by name), both Houses saw the political necessity of doing something for the aged. By June, the Congress had passed Roosevelt's Social Security bill.

The bill provided that workers and their employers would contribute a small part of each year's earnings to a common fund. When a person reached retirement age (or could no longer work because of illness), he or she would receive a small pension from the fund. If a worker died, the survivors would receive benefits.

The Social Security Act of 1935 could in no way be considered radical. The pensions were much smaller than those suggested by Townsend, and payments would not start until 1942. Many who needed coverage most, including farm workers and domestics, did not come under its provisions. Finally, while most industrialized countries had instituted old-age pension systems decades earlier, none had tried to pay for them out of workers' current earnings. (Roosevelt himself maintained that workers were assessed for policy reasons: "With those taxes in there, no damn politician can ever scrap my social security program.") Social Security, however modestly begun, represented the longest step yet taken by the federal government toward becoming what Roosevelt's critics called a "welfare state," a government that involved itself directly in the financial security of its citizens.

Angered by the Court decision on NRA, convinced by business attacks on the Administration that his dream of cooperation had died, Roosevelt now insisted on passage of the bill that would have the New Deal's greatest effect on the American power structure. He declared himself a strong supporter of the National Labor Relations Act (or Wagner Act), a bill he had previously all but ignored.

The Wagner Act, the most significant piece of pro-labor legislation ever signed by an American President, became law at a time when organized labor had almost given up on Roosevelt. The act made it illegal for an employer to refuse to recognize a labor union favored by a majority of workers as their bargaining agent. The law also contained a list of "unfair labor practices"—an attempt to curb the power of employers in labor-management relations. And it set up the National Labor Relations Board (NLRB) to hear complaints and to supervise elections by workers who wished to unionize.

As a result of the act, labor unions tripled their membership, from a low of 3 million members in the early 1930s to about 9.5 million in 1941. Although this growth was marked by division between the craft unions of the American Federation of Labor (AFL) and a coalition of industrial unions formed in 1935 by the United Mine Workers' John L. Lewis, the Congress of Industrial Organizations (CIO), it raised organized labor to a new position of power. Unions could now tell prospective members, with some exaggeration, "The President wants you to join," and call in the NLRB to hold elections by secret ballot among workers to choose a union. Possibly exceeding Roosevelt's own desires, the Wagner Act would eventually make Big Labor a political and economic force capable of challenging Big Business.

Of Roosevelt's other legislative demands, for which he kept a reluctant Congress in session through the hot Washington summer, the most dramatic was the Wealth Tax. Throughout the 1920s, Secretary of the Treasury Andrew Mellon had steadily reduced taxes on the rich. Roosevelt now sought to reverse the trend, asking for higher tax rates on large personal incomes, a graduated corporate income tax, and federal inheritance taxes. Congress eliminated inheritance taxes but did institute the highest rates ever for the upper tax brackets: a 75 percent income tax, a 70 percent estate tax, and a 15 percent corporate income tax.

The Wealth Tax, a modest measure that Congress made even more modest, was as far as Roosevelt cared to go in the redistribution of America's wealth. Probably he only went that far under pressure from Senate liberals and a political need to ease criticism from the left. The bill had little real effect; by the end of the 1930s, the top one percent even held a slightly larger percentage of the diminished national wealth than it had before.

But more than any other New Deal measure, except perhaps the Wagner Act, the Wealth Tax infuriated business. A Chamber of Commerce poll in September 1935 revealed that member organizations opposed the New Deal thirty-five to one. Many businessmen could not bring themselves to speak Roosevelt's name, referring to him bitterly as "that man in the White House." They looked forward with eagerness to the election of 1936, when the country could be redeemed from bureaucracy and Bolshevism.

TRIUMPH OF THE NEW DEAL

Having finally abandoned his hopes for a cooperative policy, Roosevelt welcomed the opportunity to confront the rich. In his State of the Union message, he boasted of having "earned the hatred of entrenched greed." He drew a parallel between himself and Andrew Jackson, pointing out that in Jackson's fight with the Bank of the United States he had been opposed by the wealthy and most of the newspapers, and supported only by the people. "History," mused Roosevelt, "so often repeats itself."

Besides calling the New Deal socialistic and un-American, Roosevelt's opponents waged a whispering campaign against the President himself. His polio, they assured one another, had destroyed his mind; late at night, maniacal laughter was rumored to come from the Oval Office. The President was forcing on America a "Jew Deal"; his real name was Franklin Rosenfeld. A wealthy man, whose family money came from stocks, Roosevelt was "a traitor to his class."

To rid the country of this demon, Republicans selected as their candidate the mild-mannered governor of Kansas, Alfred M. Landon. Landon had a double claim to Republican admiration: he was the only Republican governor to win reelection in 1934, and he had balanced his state's budget. (Democrats pointed out that the state of

Father Charles Coughlin, whose national radio broadcasts combined support for the nationalization of banks, utilities, and natural resources with a persistent antisemitism, drew his support from the right.

Kansas had a budget roughly the size of New York City's Department of Sanitation.) Yet Landon was a weak choice to rally the fervid anti-New Dealers. He was a dull speaker, and he did not oppose all of the New Deal. His most forceful claim was that Republicans could provide a cheaper and more efficient federal government.

Riding the crest of an improved economy, Roosevelt compared business to the elderly gentleman who, having been saved from drowning, turns angrily on his rescuer because he has not also saved his top hat. He ignored Landon and focused his attack on the plutocrats of the Liberty League. His campaign staff set up separate organizations, so that Republican progressives and pro-laborites could support Roosevelt without having to align themselves with the Democratic party.

Just before the election, a newspaper wire service asked William Allen White for a story to run in case Landon won. "You have a quaint sense of humor," White wired back. James Farley, the professional politician who ran the Democratic party and dispensed federal patronage for Roosevelt, predicted that the President would win every state but Maine and Vermont. Not even Roosevelt believed him.

But Farley was right. Carrying forty-six of the forty-eight states, Roosevelt beat Landon by twenty-seven million to sixteen million votes. He increased the already whopping Democratic majority in Congress, reducing the Republicans to

Republican candidate Alf Landon, former progressive Governor of Kansas, is shown here campaigning for the presidency in Ohio in October 1936. Despite Landon's promise to continue New Deal programs without running a deficit, FDR won an overwhelming victory, losing only two states to the Republicans. This impressive popular endorsement included a marked shift of black votes to the Democratic party.

sixteen votes in the Senate and less than a hundred in the House. The nation had overwhelmingly ratified the New Deal. "This," mourned the publisher of the Republican *New York Herald Tribune*, "is a great national disaster."

Roosevelt had done more than win an election and further depress the hearts of businessmen. He had redrawn the boundaries of American politics. From 1894 to 1930, Republicans had controlled every Congress except four during the Progressive Era. Roosevelt had changed the Democrats from the minority to the majority party in America.

Besides the Democratic South, the Roosevelt coalition found core support among the Catholic and immigrant voters in the large cities. Although many of these groups had previously voted Democratic, Roosevelt gave them, for the first time, heavy representation in top-level government positions. Of the 214 federal judges appointed by the three preceding Presidents, for example, only eight were Catholics. Roosevelt, on the other hand, named 51 Catholics among the 196 federal judges appointed during the New Deal era. The roll call of New Deal officials and advisers—including such names as Corcoran and Cohen, Frankfurter and Farley, Pecora and Bunche—symbolized this change for ethnic Americans. Big-city mayors, like La Guardia in New York and Curley in Boston, emphasized the point.

The third major factor in the coalition was organized labor, supporting Roosevelt in gratitude for the Wagner Act. Although labor had not yet gained the power and influence it was later to have in the Democratic party, it could supply a significant number of campaign workers. Furthermore, it could supply money, badly needed by a party that received few donations from business in 1936. The United Mine Workers became the largest single contributor to the Democratic war chest, giving $469,000.

Finally, for the first time ever, Roosevelt had drawn black voters into the Democratic party. In 1932, during the worst of a Depression that hurt blacks more than any other group, most black voters had clung to the GOP, the party of Lincoln. But in 1936 Roosevelt won most of the black vote. Remarkably, he effected this revolution while passing no civil rights legislation, while making no major black appointments, and while many New Deal programs existed in the South that were openly discriminatory. Yet relief, at least in the North and West, kept millions of blacks as well as other poor people alive; Roosevelt did appoint black advisers to many departments and agencies; and blacks deeply appreciated Eleanor Roosevelt's frequently expressed concern for their plight. "My friends, go turn Lincoln's picture to the wall," advised one publisher. "That debt has been paid in full."

ELECTION OF 1936

None of these groups had particularly strong feelings for the Democratic party. Their ties were to Roosevelt—and to Eleanor. Many of them idolized the couple. Yet they voted for Democratic governors, congressmen, and state legislators. Four times Roosevelt ran for President, and four times he was elected. By the time he died, the country had acquired the habit of voting Democratic.

THE COURT FIGHT

Roosevelt, with his massive congressional majorities, now contemplated a new round of reform. But all his plans might be frustrated by the Supreme Court. During 1936, the Court had killed the AAA, an Administration act to regulate the coal industry, and a state minimum wage bill. Soon the Wagner Act and the Social Security Act would be coming up before the tribunal.

Roosevelt felt he had to act quickly. He dismissed the notion of a constitutional amendment; the negative vote of only thirteen state legislatures was need to block passage, and he feared that the conservatives could "buy" those negative votes. He also declined to consider a simple bill to expand the size of the Court, something Congress had done before. FDR finally came up with a tricky plan based on the false premise that the Court could not keep up with its work. It would allow him to make a new appointment for every justice over seventy who did not retire, and it would extend this principle throughout the federal court system.

The members of Congress, including many dedicated New Dealers, were stunned by Roosevelt's scheme. The Democratic chairman of the

When FDR proposed his controversial Court Reform Bill in 1937, contending that the Justices were unable to cope with their workload, the *New Masses* supported his views by depicting the "Nine Old Men" dozing off on the bench. Although the size of the Supreme Court had been altered before, constitutionally, many felt that the President's "Court-Packing" bill was political trickery rather than legitimate reform. After Congress rejected the bill, a wave of retirements on the court enabled the President to make his own appointments.

House Judiciary Committee announced, "Boys, here's where I cash in my chips." Republicans hung back, allowing the many irate Democrats to take the lead in fighting against the bill.

Worse for Roosevelt, the same electorate that had ringingly endorsed him was plainly disturbed over the bill. Many asked themselves if Republican charges that Roosevelt dreamed of becoming a dictator had some truth in them. With the rise to supreme power of Hitler and Mussolini in Europe, Americans clung closer to the institutions that they saw as the protectors of their own freedoms, and the Supreme Court stood high on that list of respected institutions. Nevertheless, Roosevelt pushed hard for the plan.

The Court itself, in a variety of ways, actually killed the court-packing proposal. "If they want me to preside over a convention, I can do it," quipped Hughes publicly; but the chief justice, a skilled politician, led efforts by Court members to assure Congress that it could handle its work load. Louis Brandeis, at eighty the oldest and the most liberal man on the Court, lobbied personally against the bill.

Moreover, whether or not influenced by Roosevelt's attack, the Court seemed ready to take a friendlier view toward New Deal legislation. Within two months, it upheld both the Wagner Act and the Social Security Act by 5-to-4 decisions, and Roosevelt's supporters began to lose stomach for a fight. "Why run for a train after you've caught it?" asked one. Roosevelt's case seemed even less pressing when one of the conservative justices resigned.

But despite adverse public reaction and strong negative advice from congressional leaders, Roosevelt pressed for the bill even after it was obviously dead. One hundred sixty-eight days after the fight had begun, the bill was sent quietly back to committee. "Glory be to God!" proclaimed a senator who usually supported Roosevelt. The New Deal had sustained its first major legislative defeat.

A STRAIN ON THE NEW DEAL

Roosevelt's massive coalition of 1936, like any alliance of disparate groups, could not be maintained intact indefinitely. Its various elements had too many conflicting interests. The alliance began to break up shortly after the election. Industrial unionists of the CIO, newly armed with the Wagner Act, renounced the conservative leadership of the AFL and mounted a frontal attack on the most formidable anti-union forces—the steel and automobile industries. The nature of the campaign alarmed many people who had considered themselves liberals.

A half-century earlier, the McCormack Reaper Works in Chicago had been the site of the strike that spawned the Haymarket Riot of 1886. But in 1937, the strike scene at McCormick reflected the new activism of labor and the tripling of union membership that occurred during the New Deal. The Wagner Act of 1935, which insured union recognition by management and enumerated unfair labor practices, contributed greatly to union growth and also won labor support for FDR in the next three elections.

General Motors, as part of its campaign against the unions, paid out almost a million dollars to union-breaking private detectives between 1934 and 1936. Against such company spies and comparable tactics by management, normal union organization could hardly be expected to succeed. Early in 1937, workers occupied seventeen General Motors plants, refusing to come out until GM accepted the union. Thus began the "sit-downs." Strikers defied court orders; with wrenches and other makeshift weapons they turned back company attempts to oust them. They received support and reinforcements from other unionists. In February, the country's largest corporation surrendered.

Despite an early and surprising capitulation by U.S. Steel, the battles in the rest of the steel industry were even worse. Police killed ten strikers on Memorial Day, 1937, at the Republic Steel plant in South Chicago. (A Senate committee later discovered that the company was the largest private purchaser of tear gas in the country.) The unions lost their battle with steel in 1937, yet within a few years the steel industry and other holdouts had to give in, worn down by a combination of skillful union organizers (many radicals among them) and New Deal support for the new unions through the NLRB.

The strikes terrified millions of middle-class Americans, who were alarmed by the violence and by what they considered a threat to private property. Neither were they pleased with Roosevelt's response to the situation: Although he publicly denounced the sit-down strikes, he did not send troops to break them, as most of his predecessors would have done. Millions of Roosevelt voters began drifting back to the Republican party.

They received an even stronger impetus to do so when the fragile economic recovery collapsed in the fall. Although there were still eight million unemployed in 1937, other economic indicators had almost reached their pre-Depression level. Encouraged by those signs, Roosevelt, who had not accepted the idea of a permanent government role in the economy, tried to cut back and balance the budget. He sharply reduced expenditures in both the WPA and the PWA, bringing government "pump-priming" of the economy to a virtual halt. With startling suddenness, the bottom dropped out of the recovery. The Dow-Jones averages fell from 190 to 117 in two months. An additional four million people were thrown out of work. Republicans—and others—began to speak sarcastically of the "Roosevelt recession."

THE LAST NEW DEAL CONGRESS

Hurriedly, Roosevelt recalled the Congress. But he was still reluctant to resume heavy spending. "Everything will work out all right if we just sit tight and keep quiet," he explained, sounding a lot like the man he had replaced five years earlier.

As on so many other issues, New Dealers warred for influence over the President. His secretary of the Treasury, Henry Morgenthau, argued that the government could not support the economy forever; having done all it could, the government must now pull back and let the economy right itself. But Harry Hopkins and the liberal wing called for a final acceptance of the policies of John Maynard Keynes, a British economist who argued that only the government, by pumping money into the economy through deficit spending, could cure a recession. In April 1938, as the recession worsened and congressional elections approached, Roosevelt regretfully abandoned for the last time his hope of a balanced budget. When Congress voted him four billion dollars, he revitalized WPA and PWA, and slowly things began to improve.

Although the new Congress had the greatest Democratic majorities in history, Roosevelt could get little new legislation passed. He had weakened himself greatly in the Court fight, and conservative Southern Democrats, many of whom were alarmed by his popularity among blacks, now joined with Republicans to oppose his measures. Many anti-Roosevelt Southerners held positions of power in Congress, such as committee chairmanships won through seniority of congressional service. They could hurt the Administration badly. This conservative coalition, formed to frustrate Roosevelt, would continue to dominate Congress for years after his departure.

Roosevelt, after a fight lasting more than a year, did manage to get one more reform bill out of Congress. The Fair Labor Standards Act, although seriously weakened by congressional conservatives, established a national minimum wage of twenty-five cents an hour (to rise over eight years to forty cents) and a work week of forty-four hours (to drop to forty). It also prohibited child labor, something Wilson had tried to do twenty years earlier. Southerners, whose region paid the lowest wages in the country, fought hard against the bill. "Cotton Ed" Smith maintained that a man could live in his state of South Carolina for fifty cents a day and called the bill a measure to destroy the South. The opposition succeeded in attaching many exemptions to the bill. Still, it was a beginning.

Roosevelt's other innovation required no congressional endorsement. In previous years he had winked at evidence of business collusion and combination, feeling that such activities stabilized the economy. Now, half-convinced that business had conspired to prevent recovery in order to destroy him, he appointed a vigorous new assistant attorney general in charge of "trust busting," Thurman Arnold. Arnold more than quadrupled the size of the antitrust division of the Justice Department, raising its staff to 190 lawyers, and filed suits against such giant corporations as General Electric and Aluminum Company of America. Within five years, Arnold had filed almost half of the antitrust suits brought by the government since passage of the Sherman Act in 1890.

THE END OF THE NEW DEAL

In November 1938, Roosevelt reaped the fruits of middle-class alarm over sit-down strikes, court-packing bills, and the Roosevelt recession. The Republicans gained eighty-one seats in the House of Representatives, nearly doubling their numbers there. Although Democrats still had a large majority in both Houses, the Republican-Southern Democratic alliance now virtually controlled Congress.

Roosevelt probably had little new legislation to suggest anyway, having gone about as far as he wanted to go. He seems to have entertained no further plans to strengthen government control over business or to deal with the problems of poverty and chronic high-level unemployment.

Moreover, foreign affairs were claiming an increasing part of his time. Roosevelt early saw the threat to the United States posed by European fascist dictators, and he wanted to strengthen the country and take a more active role in foreign policy. Southern congressional leaders were willing to support him on this—if he would soft-pedal domestic reform plans.

From 1933 to 1939, Roosevelt tried to find cures for the Depression within the capitalist system. He never found a complete answer, and in the Roosevelt recession it became clear that he neither understood nor controlled the economy as much as he himself had thought. Certainly, little change in the functioning or power distribution of the economy occurred. The New Deal had not been a coherent body of reform thinking that the nation could adopt; it was mostly a strong belief in Roosevelt. People continued to cherish their old ideas about initiative and free enterprise.

But while Roosevelt may not have wrought deep changes in the American system, he had brought important changes to the American people. Workers saw their position in life anchored by strong unions. The elderly and the unemployed gained some hope. Blacks received some recognition from the national government. Farmers saw their position greatly strengthened. Moreover, if Roosevelt's achievements sometimes appear small next to the magnitude of the crisis, they clearly loom large next to the efforts of previous administrations.

Finally, Roosevelt could at least claim that through his efforts the country had survived a difficult and dangerous period. Millions of Americans had been saved from starvation, and American institutions had come through largely intact. His greatest achievement may have been the appearance of stability and peacefulness in American government and society in 1939, when contrasted with the deprivations and uncertainties so painfully evident in the winter of 1932–1933.

SUGGESTED READINGS— CHAPTERS 41-42

Eleanor Roosevelt

Tamara K. Hareven, *Eleanor Roosevelt: An American Conscience* (1968); James R. Kearney, *Anna Eleanor Roosevelt: The Evolution of a Reformer* (1968); Joseph P. Lash, *Eleanor and Franklin: The Story of Their Relationship Based on Eleanor Roosevelt's Private Papers* (1971) and *Eleanor: The Years Alone* (1972).

Franklin Delano Roosevelt

James M. Burns, *Roosevelt* (2 vols. 1956 and 1970); Frank Freidel, *Franklin D. Roosevelt* (4 vols. to date, 1952–1975); Alfred B. Rollins, *Roosevelt and Howe* (1962); Rexford G. Tugwell, *In Search of Roosevelt* (1972).

The New Deal

William E. Luchtenberg, *Franklin D. Roosevelt and the New Deal* (1963); Arthur M. Schlesinger, Jr., *The Age of Roosevelt* (3 vols. to date, 1957–1960); Daniel Fusfeld, *The Economic Thought of Franklin D. Roosevelt* (1955); Paul K. Conkin, *The New Deal* (rev. ed. 1975); Bernard Sternsher, *Rexford Tugwell and the New Deal* (1964); Sidney Fine, *Automobile Under the Blue Eagle: Labor Management, and the Automobile Manufacturing Code* (1963); Michael E. Parrish, *Securities Regulation and the New Deal* (1970); Charles F. Searle, *Minister of Relief: Harry Hopkins* (1963); Thomas K. McCraw, *TVA and the Power Fight* (1971); Roy Lubove, *The Struggle for Social Security* (1968); J. Joseph Huthmacher, *Senator Robert F. Wagner and the Rise of Urban Liberalism* (1968); Otis L. Graham, Jr., *Encore for Reform: The Old Progressives and the New Deal* (1967); Leonard Baker, *Back to Back: The Duel Between FDR and the Supreme Court* (1967); C. Herman Pritchett, *The Roosevelt Court* (1948); Ellis Hawley, *The New Deal and the Problem of Monopoly* (1966); James T. Patterson, *Congressional Conservatism and the New Deal: The Growth of the Conservative Coalition in Congress, 1933–1939* (1967); and *New Deal and the States: Federalism in Transition* (1969); Mario Eunaudi, *The Roosevelt Revolution* (1959); Jane D. Matthews, *The Federal Theater* (1967); Paul A. Kurzman, *Harry Hopkins* (1974); Bruce M. Stave, *The New Deal and the Last Hurrah: Pittsburgh Machine Politics* (1970); David E. Conrad, *Forgotten Farmers: Sharecroppers in the New Deal* (1965); Barry D. Karl, *Executive Reorganization and Reform in the New Deal* (1963); Richard Polenberg, *Reorganizing Roosevelt's Government: The Controversy Over Executive Reorganization, 1936–1939* (1966); Richard S. Kirkendall, *Social Scientists and Farm Policies in the Age of Roosevelt* (1966); John Braeman, *et al, The New Deal, I: The National Level* (1975) and *The New Deal, II: The State and Local Levels* (1975).

America In the Great Depression

Broadus Mitchell, *Depression Decade* (1947); Studs Terkel, *Hard Times: An Oral History of the Great Depression* (1970); Van L. Perkins, *Crisis In Agriculture* (1969); Charles Trout, *Boston, the Great Depression, and the New Deal* (1977); T. Harry Williams, *Huey Long* (1969); Charles J. Tull, *Father Coughlin and the New Deal* (1965); Abraham Holtzman, *The Townsend Movement* (1963); George Wolfskill, *The Revolt of the Conservatives* (1974); Irving Bernstein, *Turbulent Years: A History of the American Worker, 1933–1941* (1970); Walter Galenson, *The CIO Challenge to the AFL* (1960); Sidney Fine, *Sit-down: The General Motors Strike of 1936–1937* (1969); Lyle W. Dorsett, *The Pendergast Machine* (1968); David H. Bennett, *Demagogues in the Depression* (1969); Arthur Mann, *LaGuardia Comes to Power: 1933* (1965); Richard H. Pells, *Radical Visions and American Dreams: Culture and Social Thought in the Depression Years* (1973); William Stott, *Documentary Expression and Thirties America* (1973).

43
"REMEMBER PEARL HARBOR"

A.W.

On December 7, 1941, while negotiations to avoid war between the United States and Japan were proceeding in Washington, 353 Japanese planes attacked Pearl Harbor. This massive, audacious, and extremely successful attack on the Americans' principal—and supposedly impregnable—naval base in Hawaii came before Japan had even declared war. Grim-faced and resolved, President Roosevelt went before Congress to call it "unprovoked and dastardly" and "a day which will live in infamy."

Until this assault, Congress, like the country as a whole, had been sharply split between interventionists and isolationists. Now Congress and most Americans were furious at this shrewdly planned, superbly executed, and deadly raid. It dealt a staggering blow to American power in the Pacific. Congress swiftly and overwhelmingly voted to enter World War II. During the rest of the long, terrible conflict the single slogan that most readily aroused Americans to action was: "Remember Pearl Harbor!"

The attack on Pearl, referred to as Operation Z by the Japanese, had a history. A key figure in planning the attack was Admiral Isoruko Yamamoto, head of the Japanese Imperial Navy. If Japan's national interest called for war with the United States, the admiral reasoned, why not strike directly at the enemy fleet's Pacific home base? No mere "battleship admiral," the air-minded Yamamoto knew the possibilities of carrier-based warfare.

Yamamoto was neither a visionary nor overly optimistic. He was quite dubious about defeating the United States in war. He knew the country, having studied at Harvard and worked at the Japanese embassy in Washington during the 1920s. He had returned to Japan sobered by

Battleship Row, Pearl Harbor, is seen here from a Japanese bomber during the surprise attack. The Japanese commander of the air strike said of the sight: "Below me lay the U.S. Pacific Fleet in a formation which I would never have dared to imagine. A fleet should always be on alert since surprise attacks can never be discounted."

American industrial might. He harbored no illusions about *conquering* the United States. An invasion of the continental United States never figured seriously in Japanese war plans; Japan clearly lacked the resources for such a long-range, massive effort. "If I am told to fight regardless of the consequences," Yamamoto told the Japanese premier in 1940, "I shall run wild for the first six months, but I have utterly no confidence for the second or third years."

Others in the Japanese military shared Yamamoto's fears over the probable consequences of war with the United States. Then why venture such a dangerous policy, such a desperate gamble? By 1940 Japan was an authoritarian society ruled by a civilian-military government. Its leaders agreed on the country's basic needs. Most important was access to the raw materials vital for a modern industrial nation. Without them, heavily populated Japan would become a third- or fourth-rate power. Without expansion the Japanese would be forced to tighten their belts even to stay alive.

So Japan decided to expand. In 1931 it took Manchuria from a helpless China. American and Western Europe objected strongly but ineffectively. In 1937 Japan launched a full-scale invasion of the rest of China. Despite Western protests the Japanese captured the coastal portions and overran much of the Chinese interior. By mid-1940 Japan's ally, Hitler, had conquered France, the Netherlands, and much of the rest of Europe, isolating Great Britain. Therefore, Tokyo reasoned that it could now expand Japanese control into Southeast Asia. It planned to establish a massive sphere of influence, "the Greater East Asia Co-Prosperity Sphere."

Thus, by early 1941, Admiral Yamamoto was contemplating his strategy. Success hinged on two factors: the attackers must achieve total surprise; and the bulk of the American fleet, especially the capital ships (battleships and carriers), would have to be at their moorings the day of attack.

Isoroku Yamamoto, commander in chief of the Japanese Imperial Fleet, was a strong advocate of the navy's use of air power. Responsible for planning naval operations, he was the mastermind of the audacious attack on Pearl Harbor.

While Japanese and American diplomats in Washington were negotiating, naval aviators began months of intensive practice. When Yamamoto got wind of grumbling and possible footdragging, he threatened to resign if the plan was scrapped. Objections ceased. Yamamoto became for the moment the symbol of the Japanese navy. Under no condition would his fellow officers accept his resignation. Operation Z (named for the signal flag that Admiral Togo hoisted before trouncing the Russians) became a reality. If diplomacy failed, only the date of the attack on America remained to be fixed.

Meanwhile, political developments ominously paralleled the course of these military preparations. After France had fallen to Germany, Japan grabbed the northern half of French Indochina. It held back from the southern half—as well as from British Malaya and the Dutch East Indies (present-day Indonesia)—after the United States warned that action in these areas would have grave consequences. Roosevelt banned shipments of aviation gasoline and scrap metal to Japan, and increased American support to China. The American ambassador to Japan, Joseph C. Grew, noted: "We are getting ready, steadily, for the ultimate showdown."

By summer 1941 matters were even more tense. Hitler had invaded Russia; Japan could now pursue its Asian policy without fear of Stalin. Japan advanced, occupying southern Indochina in late July. The Americans, British, and Dutch responded by seizing all Japanese financial assets in their areas of jurisdiction. They also ended Japan's access to their raw materials. The United States gave an official warning that, if Japan took any further steps "by force or threat of force," the Americans would defend their "legitimate rights and interests."

In diplomacy's stilted language, these were strong words. The Japanese premier suggested that he and President Roosevelt hold a summit meeting, possibly in Hawaii. This could not be arranged. On October 16 a new premier, General Hideki Tojo, came to power. He was an all-out militarist.

Yet the national interests of both countries favored more negotiations. Further talks would hide Japanese war preparations—especially Operation Z, now in high gear. Washington would also benefit. It could use the extra time to reinforce its Pacific bases, particularly in the Philippines. In November 1941 Japan sent a veteran diplomat, Saburo Kurusu, to Washington to head a negotiating team. Diplomatic exchanges would obviously continue for at least a few more weeks.

At the same time, table-top maneuvers at the Japanese Naval War College demonstrated the most effective route for the Pearl Harbor attack force. The fleet would sail in a wide arc across the nearly deserted waters of the North Central Pacific. Then it would turn sharply south on reaching a point 500 miles north of Hawaii. Yamamoto thought that this route would give the best chance for surprise.

On November 5, while the Japanese and Americans negotiated in Washington, Yamamoto issued a secret order outlining the first phase of the Japanese offensive against Hawaii. The twenty-three attack ships included six carriers and two battleships under Admiral Chuichi Nagumo. He disliked the plan and still hoped the madcap attack would somehow be canceled.

The Japanese strike force sailed on November 26. The attack date had been set for December 7 (Sunday morning) in Hawaii. The American navy — even though on military alert because of the dangerous diplomatic situation — had weekends off. So its ships usually anchored in the harbor on Friday and stayed there until Monday. Nagumo's orders did contain one escape clause. If the Washington negotiations succeeded, the attack was off. The fleet would then wait in the North Pacific for new orders.

Yet, any chance that diplomacy could ease the crisis was now vanishing. On November 20 the negotiator Kurusu made Tokyo's final offer: Japan would leave southern Indochina but remain in the northern part, as well as in China. The United States must not only lift its ban on oil to Japan but also cut off aid to China. Secretary of State Cordell Hull immediately rejected these terms. Fearful of being called appeasers, Roosevelt and Hull would make no concessions. The American note of November 26 — the very day the strike force set sail — stated that America's embargo would continue until Japan withdrew from both Indochina and China.

Roosevelt and Hull, along with their top civilian and military colleagues, had good reason to distrust the sincerity of Japanese negotiations. Operation Magic of American naval intelligence had cracked Japan's diplomatic codes. On November 22 — two days after Kurusu's final offer and four days before the formal American reply to it — a cable intercepted from Tokyo read: "THIS TIME WE MEAN IT, THAT THE DEADLINE [November 29] CANNOT BE CHANGED! AFTER THAT THINGS ARE AUTOMATICALLY GOING TO HAPPEN."

What things? Most likely, reasoned the leaders in Washington, the Japanese planned to attack the Philippines and British and Dutch holdings in Asia. Hawaii seemed beyond the range of effective Japanese assault. So American short-sightedness was beginning to aid the future success of Operation Z. Knowledge of Magic was restricted to Washington's inner circle, to keep Tokyo from realizing its code had been broken. Thus American brass in Hawaii had no notion of Magic.

All the Pacific military commanders received some warning on November 27 to expect a hostile move by Japan. But Washington took no action during the next ten days. Only four Magic decoding machines existed then: two in Washington, one in the Philippines, and another in London. There were none in Hawaii. The commanders there, Admiral Husband E. Kimmel and General Walter C. Short, were not even told about Magic.

Admiral Kimmel had seriously considered, but then rejected, the idea of taking his fleet out of Pearl Harbor. In open water, he felt, the ships would be too vulnerable. His four carriers were not then available to provide air cover. (Three were bringing warplanes to American-held Pacific islands; the fourth was in San Diego for repairs.) Besides, moored safely in Pearl, his ships could be protected by the several hundred army planes stationed at Hawaiian bases. Still, Kimmel might well have sent most of the battleships out with the carriers to the other Pacific islands.

General Short reacted to the war warning by increasing the army's antisabotage defenses. Sabotage, he apparently thought, might come from Hawaii's large Japanese-American community. Instead of widely spacing his aircraft or protecting them in concrete shelters already constructed on the major fields, Short ordered the planes bunched together, wing tip to wing tip, so that fewer soldiers could then protect them against saboteurs. But Japanese Americans in Hawaii never aided Japan, although some Japanese diplomats were spies.

In short, Magic had been botched. Hawaiian commanders never received copies of important decoded messages. These messages piled up at the few overworked decoding centers. As far back as September, and with increasing frequency thereafter, Tokyo asked the Japanese consulate in Honolulu for details on the location of American warships in the harbor. By November such naval maps were being transmitted to Tokyo twice a week. Some of these Magic intercepts were not deciphered and translated for many days after reception. Especially revealing Japanese messages of November 29, for example, waited until December 5 to be deciphered. Even then, they received little attention.

Even key Washington officials, including Roosevelt and Hull, apparently did not take the Magic decodings very seriously.[1] But in Tokyo the die had been cast. Hull's note of November 26 refusing to lift the American embargo infuriated Premier Tojo. He thought it proved beyond all doubt American insincerity in the negotiations. Tojo persuaded Emperor Hirohito to let Operation Z proceed. A palace meeting ratified the decision for war. Hirohito did not attempt to intervene. He believed, as he later told an aide, that the United States was looking for nothing less than Japan's humiliation.

Should Kurusu continue negotiating or at least pretend to? Of course he should, Tojo decided; it would facilitate operations. In Wash-

If Admiral Kimmel had initiated adequate air reconnaissance of the seas around Pearl Harbor, Operation Z might have been discovered and foiled. But neither he nor anyone else in authority expected Japanese hostilities to begin there.

---

[1]There were, however, several notable exceptions. On November 25 Roosevelt told Secretary of War Henry L. Stimson of his fears that Japan would strike on December 1 without declaring war, "for the Japanese are notorious for making an attack without warning." Stimson wanted to bomb Japanese convoys if they moved farther south. Roosevelt rejected the notion because "we are a democracy."

Premier Tojo is shown in a respectful posture before Emperor Hirohito at a ceremony celebrating the Japanese Empire's 2,600th anniversary. Tojo's rise to power helped determine Japan's course toward war. Hirohito's role was largely symbolic, but he supported Tojo's militarism and anti-Americanism.

ington Kurusu asked a Japanese newspaperman rhetorically, "Am I being used as a smoke screen?" Indeed he was.

Kurusu had to help screen the task force then steaming across the North Pacific. After leaving port on November 26, the fleet enjoyed seven days of uneventful sailing. The weather cooperated. Light winds made refueling at sea relatively easy. Overcast conditions and generally poor visibility decreased chances of detection. Security precautions were rigidly enforced. No radio contact was made except within the fleet. At night a blackout was enforced. Most ships communicated by signal flags and blinkers. They did not even discard garbage, to avoid leaving a trail.

The fleet's passage north of the American base at Midway provided cause for some real concern. No American planes or ships spotted them, however. On December 6 there was the final fueling. Japanese intelligence from Hawaii reported the presence of many American warships there but no carriers or heavy cruisers. It was decided that the force would strike and destroy whatever was at hand.

A little past noon on December 6 all hands were summoned on deck. Their officers read them the emperor's war message. Yamamoto had also sent a statement: "The moment has arrived. The rise or fall of our empire is at stake." Then Admiral Togo's flag, the signal flag that gave its name to Operation Z, went up above the attack fleet's flagship. The crews shouted *"Banzai!"*—their battle cry—and turned the ships south toward Hawaii. All was ready for the great moment.

The launch itself was almost perfect. Pilots and flight crewmen were aroused at 3:30 A.M. The news that the Americans apparently had not adequately protected their ships encouraged the Japanese airmen. At zero hour (6 A.M.) the carriers were 200 miles from Oahu. As the ships rolled and pitched, the lead pilots waited eagerly for the order to take off. When it came, the first wave of 183 planes left the 6 carriers in 15 minutes, bettering their fastest practice runs. With Commander Mitsuo Fuchida in command, flying one of the high-level bombers, the air fleet headed for its target.

Overconfidence and negligence had made Americans complacent. Many viewed the Japanese as a society adept in imitating Western ways but with little creativity. Informed Americans knew that the Japanese had a history of attacking first and declaring war later. But most thought they would not dare attack the United States. In 1932 the American navy itself had successfully "attacked" the harbor during a mock raid. The event was quickly forgotten. The Navy Department filed the report in its archives as just another war-games exploit.

There were certainly some warnings during 1941. In January a Peruvian diplomat in Tokyo reported that a drunken Japanese official had boasted about Japan's plan to sink the American fleet and knock out Pearl Harbor. Ambassador Grew passed the "fantastic" rumor along to Washington. A few months later Grew noted that Japan was "capable of sudden and surprise action" with "a determination to risk all." In August, the chiefs of American naval and army aviation in Hawaii sent a gloomy memo noting Hawaii's vulnerability to air attack. They correctly predicted the use of six carriers in a dawn assault from the north.

The shortcomings of American defensive reactions were considerable, in view of what was known about Japanese intentions and how much could have been learned if the data from Magic had been properly exploited. One man who worried a great deal was Admiral Kimmel. After November 27—the day Kimmel received the war warning from Washington—naval intelligence lost track of the Japanese fleet. Kimmel asked the head of his intelligence section at Pearl where the fleet was. The officer admitted he did not know. Not entirely in jest, Kimmel asked: "You mean to say that it could appear rounding Diamond Head [a famous high point close to Pearl Harbor] without our knowing it?" The intelligence officer answered: "I hope that it would be spotted before that."

Yamamoto had no intention of parading his ships past Diamond Head, impressive though the sight would have been. Instead, his planes crossed over Oahu's northern coast. At 7:49 A.M. Fuchida broke radio silence to signal Nagumo (and Yamamoto also, since Tokyo picked up the message). Attack by the first wave had begun, blessed with the key element of surprise. Fuchida's first signal was *To-To-To*," repeating the opening syllable of the Japanese word for "charge." Soon he sent an even more welcome message: *"Tora* [Tiger], *Tora, Tora,"* which meant that the Americans were almost completely unprepared.

They were unprepared. Yet that same morning warnings had come. Five full hours before the attack began, Magic in Washington had decoded the final Japanese message breaking off negotiations. The officer in charge took the intercept straight to Admiral Harold R. Stark, chief of naval operations. Though impressed, Stark did not phone Admiral Kimmel.

Yet another chance to prepare for the attack was missed. This occurred on Oahu's north coast, precisely where Fuchida's squadrons would penetrate American air space. The Army Signal Corps had installed a movable radar station there. At 6:45 Private George Elliott, the enlisted man on duty at the station, noted the presence of a single plane on the radar screen.

But at 7:06 Elliott noted much larger blips on the screen, again moving toward Oahu from the north, and rapidly growing larger. He asked the advice of another soldier. They decided to call signal headquarters at Fort Shafter. But the only officer on duty there, a pilot, told

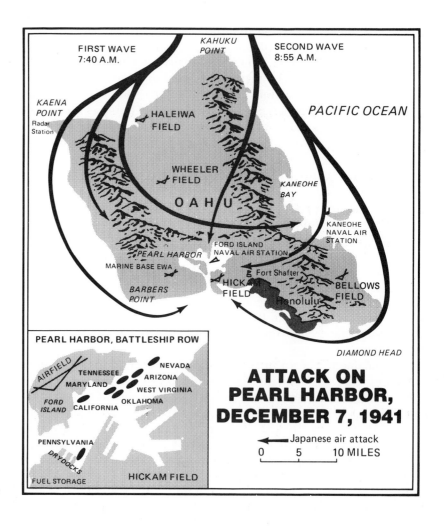

ATTACK ON PEARL HARBOR, DECEMBER 7, 1941

them to forget about it. He knew that a dozen American planes were scheduled to arrive from California that morning. Again the Japanese had benefited from a stroke of luck. Fuchida's first wave was confused with reinforcements from the States.

After sending the signal *"Tora, Tora, Tora,"* Fuchida fired a blue flare from his bomber. It informed pilots in planes without radios that surprise had been achieved. It would produce a prearranged pattern of attack, with the slow-flying but deadly torpedo bombers going in first. But apparently one group of pilots, their vision obscured by the cloud cover, had not seen the luminous signal. At least they did not wiggle their planes' wings in response. Fuchida then committed one of the few Japanese mistakes of the day. He fired a second flare.

This changed the flight plan. Two flares meant that dive bombers would attack first. Fighters and some dive bombers were to concentrate on American airfields and antiaircraft installations, rather than on the fleet. Happily for the Japanese, the commander of the torpedo bomber wing ignored the second flare. His forty heavy but superbly piloted aircraft peeled off and glided down to the prescribed low altitudes, heading straight for their principal targets, the battleships.

Meanwhile, in answer to the second signal, the faster planes went hunting for American aircraft at Wheeler, Hickam, Haleiwa, Bellows, and other fields. Wheeler housed most of the American fighter planes. These planes, already tested in combat, could hold their own against the more maneuverable Japanese fighters. But, owing to General Short's fear of ground sabotage, Wheeler's planes had been crowded together like sheep in a pen. The attackers quickly destroyed a third of the planes and damaged many more. Fires broke out in the hangars and storage buildings. One of them contained ammunition, which exploded, causing additional losses.

American military aviation tried to respond but it was useless. At Wheeler, for instance, most of the pilots were still sleeping. But Lieuten-

A special Japanese invention, the midget submarine operated by a crew of two, was used in the advance attack upon American battleships. The submarines failed in their mission that day and were not widely used in the war.

The devastation on the ground after the attack was extensive. By 10 A.M. Hickam Naval Air Station was in chaos and a smoking ruin.

ants George Welch and Ken Taylor, who were breakfasting at the officers' club, saw the dive bombers swoop. They rushed for a car and sped at a hundred miles an hour to an auxiliary airstrip unknown to the Japanese. There they took off, headed for a Japanese squadron, and shot down three planes before landing to refuel. During the dogfight one of the three machine guns in Welch's plane jammed. Taylor was wounded twice.

At Kaneohe Naval Air Station the commanding officer was drinking his morning coffee. When he heard planes, he glanced up. To his anger several V-formations of planes — all flying lower than regulations allowed — were turning toward the right into the bay where most of his thirty-three new flying boats were at anchor. He leaped to his feet shouting, "Those fools know there is a strict rule against making a right turn!" His young son, who was with him, exclaimed, "Look, red circles on the wings!" Realizing it was the Japanese rising-sun symbol, the commander rushed to his headquarters and set up a fierce antiaircraft fire against the invaders.

At the moment of attack only a fourth of the antiaircraft guns on the ships moored in the harbor were manned. Land-based antiaircraft guns could not respond immediately because ammunition had been stored to prevent deterioration. Their effectiveness increased as the morning wore on, however. Unluckily, the B-17s arrived from California about then. Weary after fourteen hours in the air, the American bomber pilots and crews thought they had flown into a nightmare. Columns of smoke rose from the ground. Airfields were ablaze, including the one the B-17s were supposed to use on Ford Island. Incredibly, not one Flying Fortress was shot out of the air. All landed at various fields, though some were shot at and destroyed after landing.

Ironically, Admiral Kimmel and General Short had arranged to play golf together that morning. Kimmel rose early. At about 7:30 he received a phone call from a staff officer. The destroyer *Ward* had sighted a submerged submarine and dropped depth charges. Kimmel headed for his office. Just as he was leaving, he received a second call adding some details about the *Ward* incident. Suddenly, the officer at the other end shouted that Japanese planes were attacking. Kimmel ran out to his garden, which overlooked the harbor. What he saw froze him. The carnage was under way. The sky over the bay seemed alive with attack planes. Kimmel knew his ships were doomed.

Kimmel got to his headquarters at 8:10, during the height of the first-wave attack. There was nothing he could do but stand at the window and watch his fleet and men under attack. A spent Japanese bullet crashed through the window and bounced off Kimmel's chest. He felt that "it would have been merciful had it killed me."

Fuchida's pilots wanted to destroy the American fleet. Disappointed over not finding carriers in port, they concentrated on the battleships. Seven of the eight were lined up on Battleship Row in the harbor. Five were moored to the docks, and two were on an "outside" parallel column. Thus the two inside battleships could not be attacked by torpedoes. The dive bombers went after them. Soon every battleship had been hit.

On the *Nevada*, at one end of the row, Bandmaster Oden McMillan stood with his musicians, ready to play morning colors at 8 A.M. As they began "The Star-Spangled Banner," a Japanese plane dropped its deadly burden on the nearby *Arizona*, then peeled off just feet above the band. The *Nevada's* deck officer, Ensign Joe Taussig, shouted over the public-address system: "All hands, general quarters. Air raid!" The *Nevada*, though damaged, tried to steam out to sea. The Japanese bore in, hoping to sink her at Pearl Harbor's mouth and thus close the port indefinitely. The *Nevada* took six bomb hits but made it to the other side of the bay, keeping the channel clear.

The *Oklahoma* took four torpedoes within one minute and began to capsize. The *California* sustained hits that caused her to settle slowly and finally sink. And so on down the row: *Tennessee, West Virginia, Maryland, Pennsylvania*. Fuchida, who was supervising the attack in his bomber overhead, frowned in disapproval as his pilots raced in. They were bunched up in their assault, instead of diving in stages as prearranged. But their formation no longer really mattered—every enemy ship was a sitting duck.

The worst blow for the Americans came when the *Arizona* blew apart and sank, trapping more than a thousand men inside. Later, it was claimed that a bomb had gone straight down her stack. But the probable cause of the disaster was the detonation of the ship's ammunition store. Whatever the cause, a gigantic pillar of fire and smoke rose 500 feet. The shock was so tremendous that, far above, Fuchida could feel his bomber tremble. Miraculously, many American seamen survived this searing blast. Some of these survivors tried to swim to shore and safety, but burning oil engulfed most of them.

The second wave, 170 additional planes, came in at 8:55. Fuchida and his pilots had taken more time than planned because of additional bomb runs. The fresh attackers went to work shortly after the first wave pulled out. They encountered considerably more opposition from heavy antiaircraft fire, and lost twenty-one planes. Towering columns of smoke cut visibility. Still, the second wave of bombers did considerable damage in its one-hour attack, knocking out some ships not previously hit. They withdrew at 9:45 to return to their carriers.

On Battleship Row the rescue effort began at once. Most of the giant ships were ablaze. One had overturned, while another had settled straight down into the mud. In the plotting room of the heavily damaged *West Virginia* Ensign Victor Delano watched smoke and oily water seep in. He and several others headed forward to another compartment. Just before closing a watertight door, they heard frantic calls from seamen, blown from the deck above them by the explosions, but had to go on. Delano then returned to the plotting room, risking his life to help a wounded sailor. Neither he nor his companion could get his footing on the oil-slick deck. The ship's angle compounded the problem.

The Japanese victory would have been more complete and would have had more serious consequences for the United States if American aircraft carriers had been in port. As it was, the Japanese had to be satisfied with destroying American battleships.

Luckily, one compartment wall was a switchboard. By grabbing its knobs, they were at last able to reach the door. As the men moved forward, they could hear the shouts and pleas of others, sealed off by the watertight doors in compartments that were rapidly filling with water. The damage-control officer had ordered the doors closed. He knew that this order condemned many men to death. But opening the doors would merely cause the ship to sink quickly and doubtless drown even more men. Many of the men did manage to make their way to the upper decks; others were able to swim to the surface by escaping through portholes. The harbor was filled with boats and launches rescuing the survivors.

The overturned *Oklahoma* posed special problems. Dozens of men, perhaps hundreds, were still alive in a crazy house where floors had become ceilings. Partial flooding meant that air pockets existed in most compartments. There, survivors could exist for awhile, if they treaded water or grasped whatever protruded from walls. About thirty men trapped in the dispensary waited an hour. Noting with alarm the decreasing amount of oxygen in the air, they decided to move. But where?

Diving into the water that covered most of the dispensary, they found a porthole. Though no one knew where it led, staying in the dispensary meant sure death. Those who were thin enough to squeeze through the porthole swam clear of the ship and were rescued. Others tried but could not squeeze through the porthole. They died in the dispensary.

Another group of sailors trapped near the *Oklahoma's* center seemed doomed beyond any hope. Amazingly, one of them dived downward through a funnel. He emerged directly under the capsized ship, reached topside, then swam clear of the wreckage and reached the surface. He led rescuers to his mates.

The rescue crews relied on this kind of information. Without it, they had no way of locating the living. Rescuers banged on ship hulls, and survivors lost no time in signaling back. Yet the sounds seemed to come from everywhere and nowhere. Several times crews laboriously cut holes in a hull, then found nobody.

Sometimes they unwittingly added to the tragedy. Acetylene torches consumed the oxygen in the air pockets once the hull had been punctured. Slower working pneumatic drills allowed precious air to escape as the water continued to rise in the compartments. Despite these dangers, inaction spelled sure doom for the trapped. So people worked through the night. They had surprisingly good results in the number of men saved.

The Japanese had fashioned a striking yet limited victory at Pearl Harbor. The casualty figures were all in their favor.[2] But, in the long run, Operation Z failed to cripple American power. First, no American carrier was in port; the war that followed showed conclusively that carriers were more vital than battleships. Second, American plane losses would soon be dwarfed by the huge air armadas that were already beginning to roll out of American factories. Third, the naval base itself had not suffered severe damage. Fouth, and possibly most significant, the Japanese—concentrating on ships and planes—had ignored the oil storage tanks. If Hawaii's fuel supply had been destroyed (as it easily could have been), Japan might have: (1) forced the carriers and other ships still functioning back to California for oil; (2) made Pearl useless as a base for several months and perhaps a year; and (3) thus given Japan freedom to expand in the Pacific without worrying about counterattacks. Instead, Pearl began to function right after December 7 as the staging area for a massive American build-up of military power.

By bombing the harbor, Japan gained some time—but little more. Even some of the sunken battleships came back to haunt their attackers. All but two were put back in service. But these consequences lay in the

---

[2]All 8 battleships in Pearl on December 7 were either sunk, capsized, or badly damaged. Ten other ships, including 3 cruisers and 3 destroyers, were also casualties. In military aviation 188 American planes were destroyed, and nearly all the others were damaged. About 100 civilians and 2,403 men in uniform died. Japan lost only 29 planes, 5 two-man submarines, and a total of 54 lives.

Secretary of State Cordell Hull and Japanese negotiators met several times to prevent a direct confrontation. But both sides took hard-line stands, so that the course of events was determined weeks before the final meeting at 2:00 P.M. on December 7.

future. December 7 was Japan's day. The assault on Hawaii was only part of a mighty Japanese drive. Simultaneous attacks took place on the Philippines and on British and Dutch colonies.

Some diplomatic strings remained to be tied. The final Japanese note to Secretary Hull was supposed to be delivered at 1 P.M.. But delay in decoding and typing the long document kept the Japanese diplomats from arriving at Hull's office until 2 P.M. In the meantime, Hull had read the Magic intercept of the note. Roosevelt got the news of the attack at 1:47 from Secretary of the Navy Knox.

Roosevelt called Hull at 2:05. The Japanese diplomats had just arrived and were in the waiting room. Roosevelt instructed Hull to receive them but say nothing about the attack. The Japanese ambassador, by way of apology, said he had been told by his government to hand over the note at 1 P.M. Hull pretended to read it (he knew its contents already) and handed it back saying it was "crowded with infamous falsehoods and distortions." With a disgusted shrug Hull dismissed the envoys.

In Tokyo, Ambassador Grew still hoped to achieve something positive. The day before the attack, Roosevelt had sent a personal appeal for peace to Emperor Hirohito. Grew asked for an audience with the emperor. At 7 A.M. Grew was awakened and told that the foreign minister wished to see him. Hoping to see Hirohito, Grew rushed to the ministry, only to be handed the note breaking off negotiations. Two hours later he heard that Japan had declared war on the United States and its European allies.

Japan greeted the news of war and victory at Pearl Harbor jubilantly. Newspaper extras appeared on the streets, and the radio alternated between martial music and patriotic slogans. At the end of December the fleet returned to Japan, and the government and people welcomed the heroes of Operation Z with celebrations and medals. Hirohito granted an audience to Nagumo and to Fuchida and several other task force leaders. The rising sun reached its zenith. But Yamamoto, clearheaded as usual, warned that "this war will give us many headaches in the future."

Roosevelt and most Americans never doubted this. On December 8, when the President asked Congress to declare war on Japan, he assured his listeners that, whatever the cost, Japan would be vanquished.

44 THE UNITED STATES AS A SUPERPOWER

A. W.

After Pearl Harbor anything seemed possible for the Japanese. Their plan for domination of Asia (the Greater East Asia Co-Prosperity Sphere) became a reality, at least temporarily. Japan had signed a mutual security treaty with Nazi Germany, and Hitler hastily declared war on the United States just after Pearl Harbor.

Only twenty-three years had elapsed since the end of World War I. Now another generation of American youth would have to fight overseas. Ironically, America's entry into the war came after a decade of intense isolationist feeling.

A profound disillusionment with World War I had spread throughout the United States. It no longer seemed a clean-cut crusade to "make the world safe for democracy." Instead, some regarded it as a capitalist war that the United States had fought to protect loans made to European Allies by American bankers. This in turn had benefited the arms manufacturers, the "merchants of death." Republican Senator Gerald P. Nye of North Dakota developed these themes in sensational congressional hearings during the mid-1930s. Nye's claims helped pressure Americans into favoring isolationism as a foreign policy.

THE NEUTRALITY ACTS

The Neutrality Act of 1935 limited Roosevelt's ability to respond effectively to overseas aggression, even if American interests were endangered.

This law attempted to close the gap between a President's control of foreign relations and Congress's right to declare war. Henceforth, if war broke out anywhere, the President had to issue a proclamation of neutrality. More important, the law forbade shipping arms to any nation at war, whether victim or aggressor. Roosevelt sought power to ban or "embargo" shipments to unfriendly or aggressor nations while permitting arms to go to the victims of aggression. Congress refused this request.

Yet isolationist hopes proved no match for events in the later 1930s. Italy invaded Ethiopia in October 1935. Roosevelt invoked the Neutrality Act, this time willingly, since an arms embargo would hinder Italy more than Ethiopia. He also asked American oil producers for a "moral embargo" on shipments to Italy, limiting amounts to prewar levels. Ethiopia fell to the Italian invaders.

Charles A. Lindbergh and Senator Gerald P. Nye stirred popular sentiment for isolationism. Americans had viewed World War I as a noble crusade. But Nye's munitions industry investigations uncovered less noble reasons for this country's entrance into the war, which led Lindbergh to campaign for nonintervention in future world power struggles.

Italy then quit the League of Nations, following the example of Japan and Germany. The foundations for the Axis alliance had been laid.

Further Triumphs for the Dictators The menace to the Western democracies increased in 1936. Hitler armed the Rhineland, which had been demilitarized after World War I. General Francisco Franco, leader of Spain's fascists, led a revolt—which was ultimately successful—against the Spanish government. Congress reacted by passing a second Neutrality Act, tightening the isolationist provisions of the first law.

So the first series of fascist moves, instead of weakening isolationism, strengthened it. Believing the Atlantic and Pacific oceans gave the United States ample security, isolationists argued that America should be a fortress prepared for any outside attack. But the United States should not meddle in foreign politics or wars. Yet isolationists were not pacifists. They favored American rearmament, particularly a larger, two-ocean navy.

Rise of the Interventionists In October 1937 Roosevelt sent up an anti-isolationist trial balloon, only to see it shot down quickly. In his "Quarantine Speech" he noted that an "epidemic of world lawlessness is spreading." Thus it was foolish to assume "that America will escape, that America may expect mercy, that this Western Hemisphere will not be attacked." To counter the threat, Roosevelt called for a quarantine of aggressor nations. Though some Americans agreed, the massive and negative outcry afterward caused Roosevelt to abandon his proposal.

A small but growing number of interventionists insisted, however, that the fascist Axis powers, if left unchecked, would eventually attack America. Like the isolationists, interventionists saw a world moving toward war. But, they also foresaw United States involvement—sooner or later. Better sooner, they thought, while Americans still had some overseas friends.

Events in 1938 and 1939 emphasized the failure of appeasement—the policy of buying off dictators with compromises. Compromises only brought new demands. France and Britain sold out part of Czechoslovakia to Germany at Munich

in September 1938. Not satisfied yet, Hitler merely kept on expanding. Having already absorbed Austria as part of the German Third Reich, in March 1939 he occupied all of Czechoslovakia. Then he threatened Poland.

Hitler took advantage of Russian weakness (and Stalin, in turn, of the apparent German willingness to turn elsewhere for immediate conquest) and the two totalitarian dictatorships negotiated a nonaggression pact in August 1939. The Nazi-Soviet Pact allowed Hitler to turn his undivided attention to the conquest of Poland without fearing Russian retaliation. (As it turned out, Stalin's armies helped Hitler to dismember and then divide Poland the following month.)

Roosevelt had approved of appeasement at Munich, but by 1939 he realized his mistake. He began a long campaign to repeal, or at least soften, the neutrality laws. He spoke of "many methods short of war" that might discourage aggression. But Congress would have to allow some presidential flexibility. Congress did not budge. No one can say to what extent American inertia and isolationism helped Hitler decide on war. Nevertheless, the American attitude surely encouraged him. On September 1, 1939, Germany invaded Poland. Britain and France declared war on Germany two days later, and World War II was under way.

GLOBAL CONFLICT

The start of World War II put American views on neutrality to a real test. Hitler quickly conquered Poland and divided it with Russia. Roosevelt was legally bound to issue a proclamation of neutrality. He was far from neutral, however. Nor did he try to hide his pro-Allied sentiments.

For Roosevelt, defeat of the Axis was basic. If American isolation meant defeat for Britain and France, American security would be disastrously, perhaps fatally, damaged. Thus, Roosevelt would go to war before letting the other Western democracies perish.

Since 1900, American foreign policy had increasingly involved British-American cooperation. Roosevelt developed a close friendship with Winston Churchill, Britain's prime minister.[1] Still, neither sentiment nor deep concern for the fate of democracy elsewhere in the world provided Roosevelt's chief motivation. He saw the savagery of dictators, especially Hitler. He concluded that, once Europe and Asia had been overrun by these "New Barbarians," America's turn would come.

Although Roosevelt accepted the risk of war, Congress would probably never have declared war prior to Pearl Harbor. Thus, Roosevelt's carefully worded pro-Allied efforts had to be made bit by bit. First, he asked Congress to repeal the arms embargo so that the United States might sell war goods to other Western powers. This passed with surprising ease. Now Britain and France might buy American arms but only on a "cash-and-carry" basis. Many Americans still hoped Hitler would be defeated without the necessity of making war loans to the Allies or placing American ships in Atlantic war zones.

These unreal hopes evaporated in the spring of 1940. Hitler launched a series of spectacular and successful campaigns that conquered much of Continental Europe. By May, five countries had been overrun—Denmark, Norway, Luxembourg, the Netherlands, and Belgium. In June the "impossible" happened: France collapsed before the Nazi onslaught and agreed to German occupation of half its territory, including Paris. This left Britain the only effective Axis opponent.

Steps toward Intervention These events profoundly disturbed Americans and shifted the isolationist-interventionist balance. Americans were shocked by the well-publicized picture of Hitler inspecting his new toy—the city of Paris—and dancing a little victory jig. What would come next? Americans might accept Allied defeats in limited wars, but this war seemed to have no limit.

Interventionists, who wanted massive aid for the battered Allies, grew bolder and better organized. Heroic British resistance to a German air assault on their homeland armed these interventionists with plenty of effective propaganda. The Committee to Defend America First, however, fought against any American involvement in the war. The America Firsters, like Charles Lindbergh, hero of the 1920s, argued that the war was simply none of our business. Many felt that a seemingly invincible Germany should not be stirred up unnecessarily.

Roosevelt moved shrewdly (1) to rearm America and (2) to aid Britain to the extent legally permissible and politically possible. Since 1940 was also a presidential election year, he had to be cautious. Meanwhile, Roosevelt broke the traditional ban on third-term Presidents by running again. Significantly, Republican isolationists could not nominate their man, Senator Robert A. Taft of Ohio. An internationalist named Wendell Willkie, a utilities executive with little political experience, won the nomination.

In the midst of the campaign Roosevelt made a daringly unneutral move. He transferred fifty World War I destroyers to the British navy. In exchange the United States received a dozen British air and naval bases in the Western Hemisphere. Churchill said of this: "It marked the passage of the United States from being neutral to being nonbelligerent [but involved]." Roosevelt won the election by a narrower margin than in 1936. Republican gains meant that Roosevelt had to take the views of the opposition party into greater account in facing the world crisis.

Every President who wins reelection regards it as a mandate for his policies. Now Roosevelt went even further than the destroyers-for-bases swap. He asked Congress for a Lend-Lease program. Under this law, passed in March 1941, the President could "lend" war material to countries whose security was deemed vital to American interests. The United States would become the "arsenal of democracy." By the end of World War II over $50 billion in Lend-Lease equipment and supplies had been distributed to America's allies.

Undeclared Naval Hostilities Further support for Britain soon materialized. The American navy patrolled the western half of the North Atlantic, freeing British ships for duty nearer Europe. American ships and planes fed data on Nazi sub-

---

[1]The Roosevelt-Churchill correspondence consisted chiefly of long, candid cables between the two men. Roosevelt ended one such message: "It is fun to be in the same decade as you."

marines to the Royal Navy. British ships used American ports freely, while this country kept sixty-five Axis ships tied up in its harbors. Some Americans joined the British or Canadian air forces, and British pilots trained at American airfields. The situation, as Germany knew, was not at all neutral. But Hitler was not yet ready to declare war on America; in the summer of 1941 he attacked Russia instead.

But American "nonbelligerence" soon provoked German countermeasures. When American warships began escorting Allied shipping halfway across the Atlantic, German submarines (or U-boats) responded. Several American destroyers were fired on; several merchant ships went down. In October a German submarine sank an American destroyer near Iceland. Congress then removed the last restriction of the neutrality laws: armed American ships could now take war supplies directly to Britain. An undeclared naval war raged in the Atlantic.

Some members of the Roosevelt cabinet wanted an immediate declaration of war against Germany. But Roosevelt preferred to continue active nonbelligerence. He would arm those fighting the Axis (including Soviet Russia). He would cement relations with Britain, as in the meeting with Churchill that produced the Atlantic Charter.[2] And he would let the Axis powers decide when to declare war.

THE UNITED STATES AT WAR

Japan, not Germany, made the decisive move. The assault on Pearl Harbor and other bases in the Pacific on December 7, 1941, ended the isolationist-interventionist debate. It also united the nation. Roosevelt's critics, including Lindbergh of America First, now pledged their hearty support for the war. One major isolationist, Michigan's Republican Senator Arthur H. Vandenberg, conceded that

Pearl Harbor had opened his eyes: "That day ended isolationism for any realist."

Could the war with Japan have been avoided? Not unless one of the two nations, Japan or the United States, had been willing to change its basic policy. Japan was determined to expand in China and Southeast Asia. The United States was determined never to recognize Japan's partial conquest of China; it was equally opposed to any Japanese moves against Allied colonies like British Malaya or the Dutch East Indies. Neither side would budge. Japan's decision to expand by force made conflict with America almost inevitable.

Americans had a long job ahead. It was made even longer when Germany and Italy honored their Axis commitments by declaring war on the United States just after Pearl Harbor. In one way, however, this step simplified matters. American leaders believed that Hitler, the greatest threat to democracy, should be defeated first. Japan could not be ignored—Americans would indeed "Remember Pearl Harbor"—but the war in Europe against Germany, Italy, and their Axis allies received top priority. Hitler, then at the height of his power, relished the idea of smashing Franklin "Rosenfeld." (Hitler had the strange notion that Roosevelt, an Episcopalian since birth, was Jewish.)

Whatever his motives, Hitler's actions caused the creation of the Grand Alliance, a coalition of all nations fighting the Axis. America, Britain, and Russia were senior partners. Starting with a declaration by "United Nations," signed in January 1942 by twenty-six countries, the alliance grew to forty-seven members by 1945. This provided the basis for the United Nations (UN). Technically, all were equal. But in reality the great powers ran the war largely to suit themselves.

Joining the Allies was a new step for the United States. Even in World War I, America was only an "associated power" rather than an "ally." The difference went beyond hairsplitting over the meaning of words. World War II was unique; Americans felt their own security threatened. The world had indeed changed.

Big Three Relations Within the Grand Alliance, or United Nations, the closest cooperation existed

[2]The Atlantic Charter stated common British and American beliefs: The right of people to choose their own form of government and the need for worldwide economic cooperation and an international security system to prevent future wars.

between Britain and the United States. Churchill and Roosevelt met almost a dozen times to develop the partnership and sometimes to prepare a united strategy against Russia, the other major ally. It was not that the Soviet Union was an uncooperative ally. After withstanding the first German offensive of 1941 (a surprise attack by a supposed ally), the Russians fought the Germans tenaciously. The Nazi army was spending itself in Russia, winning many battles but nothing decisive. Churchill and Roosevelt hastened to assure Stalin, the Soviet dictator, of their esteem. They promised military aid as soon as possible.

But Stalin wanted immediate action by his allies in the West. Specifically, he called for an Anglo-American invasion of Western Europe launched across the English Channel in 1942. But instead of a dangerous, and probably disastrous, cross-channel invasion of occupied France that year, Western leaders settled for landings in North Africa. This move took little pressure off Russia. Stalin angrily rejected suggestions that this weak move represented a so-called second front against Germany.

Further friction developed during preliminary discussions of the postwar political settlements. Stalin, like Roosevelt and Churchill, never doubted his side would win. He wanted a hand in carving national boundaries after the war. Roosevelt conceded this point, but Churchill usually tried to pacify but contain Stalin. Roosevelt often urged the postponement of political decisions until later in the war.

Events in Asia and the Pacific The war was fought on many fronts. After the Japanese struck Pearl Harbor, they took over most of Southeast Asia. First they conquered the rest of French Indochina (Vietnam, Laos, and Cambodia). Then Malaya, Singapore, and Burma—all British colonies—fell. The Dutch East Indies were next. Australia was so sure its turn had come that it almost withdrew its troops from North Africa for a last-ditch homeland defense.

Meanwhile, the Japanese occupied most of America's colony, the Philippines. General Douglas MacArthur, the commander there when the Philippines were attacked (on the same day as Pearl Harbor), was ordered to Australia. What remained of the American army—including Filipino units—held out bravely for several months on the Bataan peninsula near Manila until overwhelmed by superior force. Most Filipinos opposed the Japanese invasion. The islands had been promised independence; the war upset this timetable, forcing a postponement until 1946.

The Japanese drive of 1941–1942 was soon halted. Though a naval battle in the Coral Sea in May 1942 brought neither side victory, it removed the threat of a Japanese invasion of Australia. In June a key naval battle took place near Midway. Japanese strategy called for the capture of Midway, then a move against Hawaii. Japan probably should have made these two attacks right after Pearl Harbor. By mid-1942 things had changed. American aircraft carrier strength, though limited, was undamaged. Also, because Magic had broken the Japanese code, the American navy knew where to concentrate its forces.

Midway signaled the end of traditional naval warfare. Planes replaced guns and torpedoes as the most important offensive weapons. Enemy aircraft carriers were therefore the main target. Four Japanese carriers were sunk but only one American flat-top.[3] This gave the United States naval supremacy in the central Pacific, a factor of incalculable importance for the remainder of the Pacific war. Moreover, the troop transports had turned back toward Japan after the Coral Sea action. The Japanese never again made a serious thrust in the mid-Pacific.

Coral Sea and Midway set the stage for Allied offensive operations. In August 1942 Americans landed on Guadalcanal in the Solomon Islands. The battle there was long and fierce—a warning of what lay ahead. This "island hopping" followed a long and bloody course from Guadal-

---

[3]All four of the carriers Japan lost at Midway had been used to attack Pearl Harbor. Likewise lost at Midway—or during the harsh fighting that followed in the Solomon Islands—were nearly all the daring Japanese pilots of December 7. Neither the flat-tops nor the aviators were ever properly replaced. Admiral Nagumo, who had led the victory at Pearl and the defeat at Midway, survived until 1944. Then he died, evidently by suicide, during the American capture of Saipan.

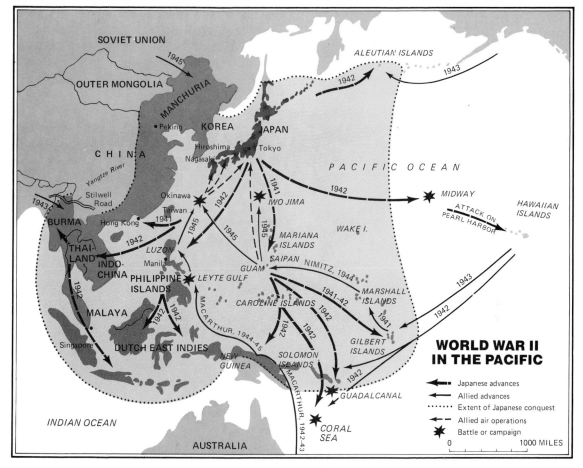

WORLD WAR II IN THE PACIFIC

Japanese advances
Allied advances
Extent of Japanese conquest
Allied air operations
Battle or campaign

0   1000 MILES

The day after the Japanese surprise attack on Pearl Harbor on December 7, 1941, the United States declared war on Japan. On that same day, the Japanese invaded Thailand and Malaya. By late December they had captured Guam, Hong Kong, and Wake Island. The Japanese invasion of the Philippines began December 10; they took Manila on January 2, 1942. General Douglas MacArthur retreated to Australia.

In February 1942 the Japanese took Singapore and, by early March, most of the Dutch East Indies. In June they seized two of the Aleutian Islands. The Battle of the Coral Sea was fought between Japanese and Allied forces of May 7–8, which stopped Japan's advance on Australia. The air and naval battle of Midway (June 3–6) was a turning point in the Pacific war, and within two months the United States was for the first time on the offensive.

The first major Allied offensive, beginning in August 1942, was fought at Guadalcanal. The Japanese were driven from it in February 1943. During March–August the Japanese were driven from the Aleutians. In the second half of 1943 the South Pacific offensive took place. It gave the Allies control of the waters adjacent to the Solomon Islands. A Central Pacific offensive was launched in November under Admiral Chester Nimitz, during which

the Allies took the Solomons, Gilberts, Marshalls, and Marianas. In December General Joseph W. Stilwell began a campaign in Burma; Burma was not completely retaken, however, until May 1945.

In June 1944 air attacks were opened against cities on the Japanese home islands. The Philippines campaign of June–December saw General MacArthur's return there. The naval Battle of Leyte Gulf (October 23–25), was a decisive defeat for Japan. It destroyed most of its remaining sea power. The Philippines campaign ended after the taking of Manila.

After heavy fighting, United States Marines took Iwo Jima in March 1945 and conquered Okinawa by late June. In May–August the greatest air offensive in the Pacific was launched against the Japanese home islands, culminating in the dropping of atomic bombs on Hiroshima (August 6) and Nagasaki (August 9). On August 8, the Soviet Union declared war on Japan and invaded Manchuria.

Japan surrendered and sued for peace on August 10. President Harry Truman announced August 14 as V-J Day. Japan's formal surrender took place September 2 in Tokyo Bay aboard the United States battleship *Missouri*.

The war in the Pacific was fought by island-hopping—retaking island by island territory captured by the Japanese. This marine landing in the Solomons in 1943 helped push Japanese forces back to the home islands.

canal in 1942 to Okinawa in 1945. In a series of landings on the various islands in between, United States troops fought for every bit of territory, notably the first few yards of each beachhead. Japanese resistance never let up. Even losing battle after battle did not diminish the enemy's will to fight.

After Midway, the Americans had sea and air superiority. The American fleet, especially the number of carriers, grew enormously. Even when the Japanese navy and air force came out in full strength (as when the United States recaptured the Philippines in 1944), Japan suffered staggering losses. On one day American pilots shot down nearly 500 Japanese planes. At Leyte Gulf, much of Japan's navy was destroyed.

American submarines (though less publicized than German U-boats) sank hundreds of Japanese ships. Many of them were carrying raw materials from Southeast Asia to Japan's factories. By early 1945 Japan had no hope for victory. The war in China ground on inconclusively. The Pacific, which three years before had seemed to belong to Japan, was now an American lake. The only way left to preserve Japanese martial honor or punish the American invaders was suicide assaults by *Kamikaze* pilots.[4]

Events in Europe and the Mediterranean The Allies mounted an equally relentless (and equally successful) effort in Europe and the Mediterranean. American and British forces overran North Africa and routed German General Erwin Rommel's *Afrika Korps*. In 1943 the Allies invaded Sicily and then mainland Italy. Meanwhile, massive preparations for invading France went on, with Britain as the staging area.

On another front the Russians took terrible losses. Yet they stopped the farthest German penetration at the Volga River in the Battle of Stalingrad. For the next two years the "Eastern Front" repeatedly saw Russian advances and German retreats.

The invasion of France on June 6, 1944, put Hitler's neck in the noose. Despite strong resis-

---

[4]*Kamikaze* pilots crashed their planes, loaded with bombs, into American ships.

Pleasures and Pastimes in a Mass Society

''The Americans are a queer people: they can't play. Americans rush to work as soon as they get up. They can't play. They try to, but they can't.'' Canadian humorist Stephen Leacock indulged in some poetic license when he described his neighbors to the south. Americans do play, of course. They enjoy light entertainment. They love competitive sports. And they find pleasure in the simple satisfactions of everyday life. (A happy man indeed is greeting *The New Television Set* in Norman Rockwell's 1949 painting.)

Foreign observers sometimes complain about the ''canned'' amusements of a mass society, but even French critic André Maurois commented favorably on them. He wrote, ''Americans who never meet each other and who live under different skies come to have innumerable common memories and brotherly thoughts.''

For further information on the foreign observers quoted in this essay, see ''Notes on Sources.'']

Stronger than in various other countries, and perhaps also than in Turkey, seems to be the predilection in America for the lighter types of musical and theatrical entertainment—for jazz and operettas, or for comedies and thrillers rather than plays that have a pessimistic note or are centered around philosophical and social themes.

[ÖMER CELÂL SARC, 1959]

Broadcasting a radio drama, 1934

Scene from *Oklahoma!* (original production, 1943)

I could not agree that the creation of films is not an art at all, only an industry. It is actually a curiously mixed activity, coming into a new category, needing all the resources and organization of a large industry, but by no means devoid of genuine artistic impulses. The public looked to films for general entertainment, on a scale hitherto unknown, and accepted the moving pictures as a substitute for theaters, books, gossip, and dreams.

[J. B. PRIESTLEY, 1935-36]

A scene from *Gold Diggers of 1933*

Let's listen to Louis Armstrong on Broadway, the black Titan of the cry, of the apostrophe, of the burst of laughter, of thunder. An imperial figure, Armstrong makes his entrance. His voice is as deep as an abyss, it is a black cave. He bursts out laughing, he roars and puts the trumpet to his mouth. With it he is in turn demoniac, playful, and massive, from one second to another, in accordance with an astounding fantasy. The man is extravagantly skillful; he is a king.

[LE CORBUSIER, 1947]

Louis Armstrong

Elvis Presley and fans

Female teenagers are in the habit of greeting their heroes, the young crooners —the one best known being Elvis Presley, of the writhing hips and thighs—with a shrill yell that seems to issue from a single throat. The picture of young and well-dressed girls comporting themselves in this fashion is enough to send cold shivers down an adult's spine. Significantly, however, it has been observed that only the girls in the rows lit up by the stage lights break out in this yell; that is, only those who can be seen by the others. Moreover, they are looking not so much at the singer as at the other members of their own group.

[HERBERT VON BORCH, 1962]

/ PE 8–3

Miami defeats Holy Cross at the Orange Bowl, 1946

Willie Mays at second base, 1957

I do not pretend to understand even the coarser of the finer points of American college football, which must have been originally devised during an early revolutionary phase of American life, for like a revolution it is an odd mixture of secret plotting, with so many heads motionless and close together, and sudden violent action. When either side pressed towards goal, we all stood up. The danger over or the prize lost, we sat down again. The enormous clock ran off the seconds when the ball was actually in play. It stopped when the game stopped. And the game was always stopping.

[J. B. PRIESTLEY AND JACQUETTA HAWKES, 1954]

I have studied hundreds of photos of Louis in his big fights, of Louis preparing for his big fights, of Louis just after his big fights. His face almost never changes. The man is dignified, in the toughest sport in the world, whether he's giving a licking or taking one. You cannot get away from this impression of the man being so superbly equipped to fight that he didn't need the window-dressing of a big grin of confidence, or glib phrases by the publicity boys. Louis wasn't just a great fighter. He was an admirable man.

[HARRY CARPENTER, 1964]

The Brown Bomber, Louis and Schmeling Fight, by Robert Riggs

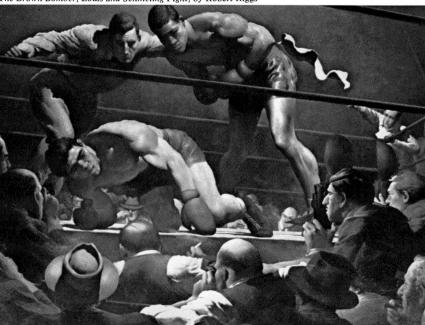

Robinson's character was the key. A fierce competitor, Jackie had in the early days to curb his angry pride. He ignored insults, and won recognition as a baseball player, on equal terms with others, whether white or black. Today ability is the key, not pigmentation. Some day Jackie's greatest honor will come when he is simply a name in a record book, when, because there was a Jackie Robinson and others like him, future generations have forgotten there was ever a need for a Jackie Robinson.

[CANADIAN SPORTSWRITER]

Cheerleaders at a high-school basketball game

To observe the North American in a large crowd within the United States—at a World Series game or a popular football game—is one of the most cheering spectacles in the world. Here we have an enormous mass of people, well balanced, attractive, determined to enjoy to the utmost an afternoon of relaxation, applauding their favorite team but wihout ill will or malevolence toward the adversary, on the contrary always disposed to recognize and applaud the courage and skill of the opposition.

[DANIEL COSÍO VILLEGAS, 1959]

We went into a bowling alley. It is the old game of skittles which the dwarfs of Rip Van Winkle played, but it has been brought up to date. Instead of a wild gully, I found a bar with tables and chairs: the bowling alleys, set side by side, are of varnished wood, and when the bowling ball has knocked over the ninepins, it falls through a trap door and is returned by an automatic device to the player. The game is so popular that the alleys are booked for days in advance. It is monotonous to watch.

[SIMONE DE BEAUVOIR, 1947]

Bowling at a fifty-six-lane alley, California

Woman playing bingo in Muncie, Indiana

Father and son tossing a football, Newton, Iowa

America is a modern land where technical ingenuity is apparent at every point, in the equipment of a kitchen as well as of a car, but at the same time a land of gardens, of flowers, of home activities, where a man, away from his office or his work-place, enjoys tinkering at his bench, making a piece of furniture, repainting his house, repairing a fence, or mowing his lawn. A land of luxury but also of simple pleasures. There is an America that strolls in the parks in its suburban Sunday clothes, or cavorts on the beaches, and plays base-ball everywhere.

[JACQUES FREYMOND, 1959]

Teenagers at a "sock hop," Carlsbad, New Mexico

Wisconsin Farm Auction, by Joan Arend Kickbush

Girls jumping rope, Cleveland

The American smile, which has been so ridiculed by those who believe the intelligent thing is to know everything already—without, of course, knowing much of anything at all—seems to me to be the expression of love for one's fellow man, of the basic fact that in the United States it is firmly believed that living together is a blessing. This is derived, in my opinion, from the historical makeup of the United States and from the American spirit, from its loneliness and the fact that for so long the presence of other men was an occasion for joy.

[JULIAN MARIAS, 1959]

Children playing at an open water hydrant, New York City

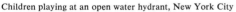

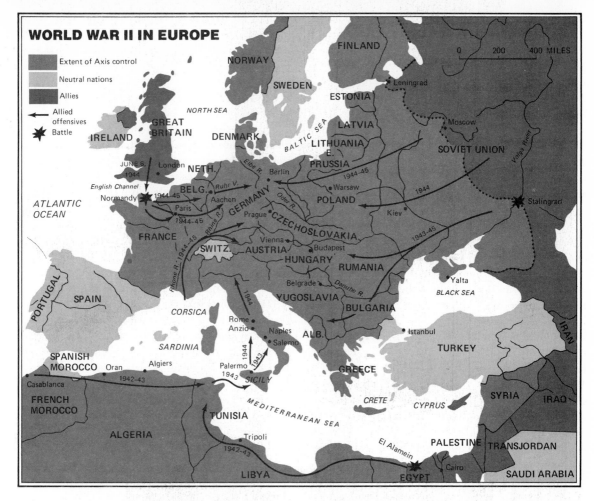

WORLD WAR II IN EUROPE

Extent of Axis control

Neutral nations

Allies

Allied offensives

Battle

When Germany was at the height of its power, its armies had overrun much of European Russia, defeated France, occupied Norway and Denmark, and held much of North Africa. In December 1941 England and the Soviet Union were the only allies in Europe still undefeated by Germany.

The first United States troops for the European theater of the war arrived in northern Ireland in January 1942. Six months later in North Africa, the British checked the Axis advance at El Alamein. In November General Eisenhower's Allied forces landed in North Africa. By May 1943 the Germans had been defeated there. In Europe the Russians defeated the German armies, attacking Stalingrad in December 1942 after a four-month siege—a major turning point. Thereafter the Russians began to take the offensive.

The Allied invasion of Italy began in July 1943. Italy's unconditional surrender to the Allies in September was followed by stiff German resistance in northern Italy. The Germans were not finally defeated there until 1945.

The air offensive against Germany began in January 1944 in preparation for an Allied invasion. On June 6, D-Day,

Allied armies invaded Normandy in northern France in a surprise attack. By August 10 this offensive was concluded and a second front in southern France was opened that began a drive up the Rhone Valley. All of France, Belgium, and Luxembourg was liberated by September. By this time the Russians had driven the Germans out of the Soviet Union and into Eastern Europe.

The battle for Germany began in September 1944. The first large German city to fall, Aachen, was taken in October. Within five months Belgrade, Budapest, and Warsaw had fallen.

A German counteroffensive in the west was launched in December 1944. The Germans almost succeeded in breaking through the American line in the Battle of the Bulge, but they were repulsed. Then a British offensive was launched in the Netherlands. By March United States troops had penetrated the Ruhr Valley and crossed the Rhine; a month later, they reached the Elbe. The Russians entered Berlin late in April. Berlin fell on May 2. The formal end of the war in Europe occurred on May 8. Germany surrendered unconditionally to the Allies.

tance, Allied invaders stormed the Normandy beaches. Happily, Hitler insisted that the Normandy invasion was unimportant. He refused to concentrate his available forces there. After several nerve-racking weeks American tank columns led by General George S. Patton pushed beyond Normandy and raced across France.

But the Nazi army could not be crushed in 1944. It withdrew toward the Rhine. Germany, as helpless now as Japan, was the target of massive air attacks. (Over 1,000 Allied planes participated in a single raid on Berlin.) Hitler still dreamed of victory, though he mistakenly believed his own people were betraying him. He forbade his generals to retreat. He hastened the murder of millions in concentration camps. Yet neither demoniac raving nor barbarous cruelty could produce military victories. Early in 1945 the Allies pushed ahead on all fronts.

The Big Three leaders—Roosevelt, Stalin, and Churchill—had long been preparing for victory. Stalin and Churchill met in Moscow in October 1944. There they began carving out spheres of influence. Roosevelt wanted to end the war first and then make such decisions. The Axis must accept defeat and unconditional surrender; the Allies should not squabble until they had won. Thus the 1943 Big Three meeting at Teheran, Iran, had dealt mainly with wartime strategy.

By early 1945 territorial questions could not be further postponed. Germany would surely surrender that year; Japan was next in line. Russian participation in the invasion of Japan could mean a shorter campaign, with fewer Western casualties. What price would Stalin demand, though, to bring Russia into the Pacific war? The answer emerged at the Yalta Conference of February 1945, a Big Three meeting at a Russian resort in the Crimea.

Stalin set a high though not outlandish price. He wanted Russian power in the Far East to equal its extent in 1904, before his country lost the Russo-Japanese War. Russia was to receive the northernmost islands of the Japanese chain, plus territorial and commercial rights in Manchuria and northern China. In return, Stalin would declare war against Japan within three months of the end of the war in Europe.

The Yalta discussions produced agreement on another subject, which later became a matter of grave contention between the Soviet Union and the Western powers: the fate of Poland. At Yalta, Roosevelt and Churchill agreed to allow the Soviet Union to annex large areas of Eastern Poland, presumably as a buffer region against any future German attack. Stalin, in turn, agreed to allow "free elections" to be held after the war, although the commitment was a meaningless one given his views on the "necessity" for a "friendly" (i.e., a Communist) regime in that country.

Polish-Americans and other opponents of the Yalta agreements would later denounce FDR for having "sold out" Poland and other Eastern European countries. Roosevelt, however, felt that he had exacted about as much as he could from Stalin on the question, given three elemental facts of international life: (1) the Russian armies would be controlling the country (as would American armies in Italy and a British one in Greece, countries where pro-Western governments were established); (2) Poland was clearly a security problem for the Soviet Union and not for the West; and (3) the issue was not of overriding importance to the United States compared to the future of Germany or securing Soviet entrance into the war with Japan.

Roosevelt's military advisers had warned that invading Japan without Russia might cost the United States a million casualties. The President had no wish for this. Nor could he count on the still untested atom bomb to end the war. Stalin's offer seemed the only reasonable choice.

The Yalta agreements included provisions for the dismemberment of Germany. The Allied powers (the Big Three and France) would each occupy a section. Germany must also pay reparations for the wartime destruction it had caused. Stalin wanted to weaken Germany so that the Germans might never again attack Russia. Reparations would keep Germany feeble. Moreover, splitting Germany into occupation zones assured Stalin that the eastern zone would remain firmly under Soviet control.

Within a half year of Yalta, the Axis was subdued. In April 1945 Hitler committed suicide in Berlin as the Allies overran Germany. Four

The strain of war was visible on FDR's face as he met with his allies, Churchill and Stalin, for the last time at Yalta. The concessions made to Stalin there to secure Russia's entrance into the Pacific war were denounced by some postwar critics as "appeasement."

months later the Pacific war ended spectacularly and ominously. In the meantime, Roosevelt had died and been succeeded as President by Vice President Harry S. Truman.

The Atomic Bomb Two American B-29s approached the southwestern tip of Japan on the morning of August 6, 1945. One of them was the *Enola Gay.* Its mission was to drop the first atomic bomb in the history of mankind. The target was the Japanese city of Hiroshima. At about 31,000 feet the doors of the bomb bay opened, and the bombardier released "Little Boy," a weapon that had twenty times the power of a ton of TNT. At 2,000 feet the bomb detonated.

A young Hiroshima girl who was riding a trolley gave this account.

At that moment my eyes were suddenly blinded by a flash of piercing light and the neighborhood was enveloped in dense smoke of a yellow color like poison gas. Instantly everything became pitch dark and you couldn't see an inch ahead. Then a heavy and tremendously loud roar. The inside of my mouth was gritty as though I had eaten sand, and my throat hurt. I looked toward the east, and I saw an enormous black pillar of cloud billowing upward. "It's all over now," I thought.

As the plane made a sharp turn to avoid the blast, the tail gunner looked down at the falling bomb. Within seconds he was looking directly into the center of the atomic detonation. He watched the shock wave approach the plane like a shimmering heat wave. The mushroom cloud started forming immediately. He described it as "a bubbling mass of purple-gray smoke, and you could see it had a red core to it and everything was burning inside."

Within an instant 70,000 people died. Another 30,000 would later die of radiation burns and

A mushroom-like cloud rose over Hiroshima—the first city ever to suffer the devastation of an atomic bomb.

History's greatest war ended with unconditional surrender by the Axis. Yet victory found the Grand Alliance anything but united. Differences over postwar policy produced visible strains, with the possibility of a new and dangerous confrontation. The United States and Russia were now superpowers. Their growing disagreements would soon be called a Cold War.

Soviet-American cooperation broke down completely after World War II. Eastern and central Europe came under Russian domination. The Baltic countries of Latvia, Lithuania, and Estonia ceased to be independent nations. Finland avoided the same fate by curbing its foreign policy in a treaty with Russia. The countries between Western-occupied Germany and the Soviet Union, plus the Balkan nations, became Soviet satellites. (Yugoslavia would later break away.) A Soviet empire emerged. Countries on its borders (Greece, Turkey, and Iran, for example) all felt the pressure of the new superpower.

The United States had hoped for cooperation, not conflict, among the major powers after the war. A return to the status quo and the isolationism of earlier periods was out of the question. Americans could not pull back as in 1919 and expect to maintain their interests in a vacuum. World War II had exhausted Britain and France. If North Atlantic leadership of the world were to continue, the United States had to step in. Thus Washington pushed for a new world organization, despite the League of Nations' failure and America's own sorry role in that failure.

Roosevelt had wanted a league. Unlike Wilson, though, he had made sure that Republicans participated in the sessions that preceded the founding of the United Nations in 1945 (soon after Roosevelt's death). The UN differed from the League in various ways. It was located in New York, not Geneva. More important, the great powers established a Security Council whose permanent members (the United States, Britain, France, Russia, and China) could defeat any pro-

a strange new disease, radiation sickness. Approximately 75 percent of the buildings in Hiroshima were destroyed. As another eyewitness said of those first few seconds. "Everything had crumbled away in that one moment and changed into streets of rubble, street after street of ruins."

What caused the decision to use this devastating weapon? President Truman had been told that if the Japanese fought to the end in defense of their own islands, as they vowed, the war would last more than another year, and an additional half million American lives would be lost. He thought a quick one-two punch—one atomic bomb dropped, followed swiftly by a second on another target—would force Japan to surrender.

Historians have conjectured that there may also have been other reasons. Soviet-American relations were strained. Truman may have wanted to show the Russians that American strength was superior. Or he may have wanted to end the war before the Soviet Union could occupy Asia as it had eastern Europe.

The atomic bomb did end the war. Three days after Hiroshima was bombed, Nagasaki suffered the same fate. The next day the Japanese asked for peace terms, though many Japanese still wished to fight to the death.

posal with a single negative vote. This big-power veto, a recognition of both national sovereignty and great-power interests, gravely limited UN effectiveness in crisis situations. Yet the veto was desired by all the large powers.

Containment in the Mediterranean American hopes for postwar stability suffered as a result of Roosevelt's death. The late President had not mapped a precise blueprint for peacetime policy; he had become increasingly disillusioned over Russian behavior. But he did possess enormous prestige. This was not true of President Truman, a man without experience in either high-level administration or foreign policy. Truman's baptism of fire in summit diplomacy—direct meetings by heads of government—came in July 1945, when he, Stalin, and Britain's new prime minister, Clement Attlee, met at Potsdam, Germany. Full agreement proved impossible. With Japan still undefeated, Truman accepted postponement of various pending issues.

Russia's expansionism and the weakness of America's allies soon ruled out further delay. By 1947 Western Europe seemed ready to collapse. Britain, France, Italy, and West Germany (not yet a separate country) were sliding downward, perhaps toward a chaos that could only benefit Russia. Britain had to give up its empire. The British move that most affected the United States was its decision to end aid to Greece and Turkey, Britain's anticommunist Mediterranean allies. The Russians and Turks had been at odds for centuries. The post-World War II period proved no exception. The Soviets tried to gain parts of eastern Turkey and establish bases at the Dardanelles—Turkey's (and Russia's) gateway to the Mediterranean.

The Greeks (unfriendly toward the Turks but now allied with them as another target of Russian expansionism) also needed help. A communist guerrilla movement was fighting the Greek government. Only active American intervention could keep Greece and Turkey out of the Soviet sphere. In March 1947 the President enunciated the Truman Doctrine "to help free peoples to maintain their free institutions" against the threat of "subjugation by armed minorities or by outside pressures." Congress appropriated $400 million to aid Greece and Turkey.

The congressional action and Truman's strong words were highly significant. They proved the Cold War had truly begun. The United States would, by threat of a third world war, contain Russia within the areas the Soviets had occupied or dominated in 1947. The support Truman received from Republicans in Congress signaled that the policy of containment had bipartisan support.

Containment in Western Europe After containing the Russian advance in the eastern Mediterranean, the United States turned to Western Europe. Secretary of State George C. Marshall announced in mid-1947 American willingness to contribute huge sums toward European reconstruction. All Europe was included; even Russia sent envoys to a preliminary conference. But the Russians quickly withdrew and kept their satellites from joining the European Recovery Program (ERP), better known as the Marshall Plan.

Congress moved more cautiously than on Greece and Turkey. But a communist takeover of Czechoslovakia in 1948 spurred it on. Billions of dollars flooded into Western Europe, stimulating the area's economic recovery. This also ended any early possibility that Communist parties there would reach power through elections.

The Western allies took an added step in containing communist advances in Europe by creating a formal military alliance in 1949. The North Atlantic Treaty Organization (NATO) included a dozen North Atlantic nations. They pledged to take any action necessary "including the use of armed force, to restore and maintain the security of the North Atlantic area." To implement the promise to defend any NATO country attacked by an outside power, large numbers of United States troops were sent to Germany. The American navy took over from Britain in the Mediterranean.

Through NATO the United States in effect became the policeman for the Western world, a break with American tradition. Not since the French alliance of 1778 had the United States linked itself formally in a military alliance with another power. NATO made the containment policy a firm one. Though the Soviets exploded their first nuclear weapon in 1949, they knew that further expansion to the west was unthinkable. NATO was soon functioning, with General Dwight D. Eisenhower (Supreme Allied Commander in Europe during World War II) heading NATO's forces. Obviously Washington would not allow a Russian "iron curtain" to fall over Western Europe.

The Struggle for Mainland China Unsettling events in Asia contrasted sharply with the success of containment in Europe. Events in postwar China were particularly disappointing for Americans. Civil war broke out there between the communists under Mao Tse-tung and the Nationalists under Chiang Kai-shek. Mao had fought for control of China long before the Japanese invasion. War with Japan temporarily united the two sides, but afterward, they returned to civil war.

By 1948 it became clear the Nationalists would lose. The next year Chiang fled to the island of Taiwan, while on the mainland Mao proclaimed his communist government, the People's Republic of China (often referred to as Red China). Massive American military intervention might

have prevented the communist takeover some American leaders thought, though few recommended it. And the history of later large-scale American involvement in Vietnam casts grave doubt on the wisdom of that course. In any case, two things were certain: by 1949 Red China possessed considerable power, and this power would increase.

The Korean Conflict The United States refused diplomatic recognition to Red China. Yet soon after the Chinese civil war ended, Americans were forced to recognize the Red Chinese army in combat. The scene was Korea, which had regained independence from Japan in 1945. But now Korea had been divided into communist-occupied North Korea and American-occupied South Korea. The communist North invaded the South in June 1950, perhaps because Washington had declared Korea outside the zone of American vital interest. (U.S. troops had been pulled back to Japan.)

When South Korea asked for American help, Truman quickly provided it. Available combat forces (two American divisions stationed in Japan) were sent at once to Korea. Also, a Soviet

Warfare in Korea was conventional in employing large numbers of men with standard weaponry in set battles. But since it was fought for limited aims —containing rather than destroying the enemy—it foreshadowed later combat in Vietnam.

mistake let Truman make the American response a United Nations venture. In June 1950 Russia was boycotting all UN meetings. The Security Council promptly branded North Korea an aggressor and authorized a UN military force to repel the attack. General Douglas MacArthur, leader of the occupation forces in Japan, also headed the UN army (mostly American soldiers) in Korea.

The Korean conflict was both a success and a failure for the United States. Two Koreas still exist. Thus the 1950–1953 military effort there did prevent a communist takeover. But this venture became a political liability for Democrats and a lasting frustration for all Americans. After a year of seesaw campaigns up and down the Korean peninsula, fighting ended close to the original dividing line.

Total victory was unattainable because the war had limited aims. And Washington permitted only limited means to achieve them. MacArthur, a great soldier and a great egotist, was especially frustrated. He had sent his troops to within sight of China's border in 1950, provoking full-scale Chinese intervention in Korea and an American retreat. Despite this—and the risk of bringing Russia into combat also—MacArthur wanted to bomb China and fight the war more vigorously. Truman refused. When MacArthur aired his contrary views in public, Truman fired him.

REPUBLICANS BACK IN POWER

Truman fought the war his way; he and his party then paid the political price. When the Republicans regained the presidency in 1952, after twenty years, they promised changes in foreign policy. Dwight Eisenhower and his party came into power in part due to charges that the Democrats had not resisted communism as strongly as they could and should have. Containment, declared the Republican campaign platform, was "negative, futile, and immoral." Once in power, the Republicans assured the country, not only would they stop losing countries to communism, but, they hinted, countries already communist would be redeemed.

Eisenhower selected perhaps the ideal secretary of state to implement this policy. John Fos-

Secretary of State John Foster Dulles reporting on one of his many trips around the globe to President Eisenhower on May 17, 1955. Dulles had just returned from Europe where he signed a treaty restoring sovereignty to Austria and participated in the admission of West Germany to NATO. On several occasions, such as the one shown here, he briefed the President in informal public addresses that were broadcast to the nation from the White House.

GEORGE C. MARSHALL

One of George C. Marshall's biographers has described him as "the least typical of generals." He notes that what is remarkable in him is a "beautifully balanced mind thinking in terms of the dignity and integrity of the country which gave him birth."

Marshall was a soldier-statesman in the tradition of George Washington and Andrew Jackson. He was a military genius who turned diplomat, secretary of state, and secretary of defense after the close of his career as a professional soldier. His actions in war caused President Harry Truman to state in 1945: "In a war unparalleled in magnitude and horror, millions of Americans gave their country outstanding service. General of the Army George C. Marshall gave it victory." His actions in peace won him the Nobel Peace Prize in 1953. He was the first soldier ever to receive it.

Marshall was an absolute master of organization and military strategy. But he sometimes considered this talent a liability, for although his army career involved two world wars, he was never to lead troops in battle. He was considered too valuable a planner to be risked in field command.

In the 1930s Marshall had a tedious job as an instructor in the Illinois National Guard. But by 1936 his star began to rise. He was promoted to Chief of Staff of the Army on September 1, 1939, the opening day of World War II in Europe. Between that day and the end of the war Marshall built up the army and air corps from fewer than 200,000 men to over 8 million. Without his planning it has been estimated that the invasion of Europe would have come a full year later than it did in 1944.

At war's end Marshall wished to retire. But President Truman asked him to undertake a diplomatic mission to China to try to bring the warring Nationalist and communist forces together in a coalition government. The soldier hero's second career as a controversial statesman began.

After China Marshall was named secretary of state. He found himself in a new war—the Cold War with the Soviet Union. He helped to hammer out the Truman Doctrine and, of course, the Marshall Plan. Then he tried to retire again. This time, however, Truman wanted him to become secretary of defense.

In 1951 Senator Joseph McCarthy, whose crusade against communism became a witch hunt, lashed out at Marshall. He published a speech attacking Marshall's wartime strategy, his mission to China, and his actions as secretary of state. McCarthy accused this public servant of being "a man steeped in falsehood," who was guilty of "invariably serving the world policy of the Kremlin."

Marshall resigned soon after this vicious attack, because his effectiveness in office had been greatly reduced. It was a melancholy ending to a frequently brilliant and selfless career in the service of the nation. He was remembered by one of his colleagues in the State Department as "the image of the American gentleman at his best—honorable, courteous, devoid of arrogance, exacting of others, but even more of himself, intolerant only of cowardice, deviousness, and cynicism."

ter Dulles, a sixty-four-year-old Wall Street corporation lawyer, had long been one of the leading foreign policy spokesmen of the Republican party. Dulles's strong belief in the righteousness of the American system and the iniquity of communism appeared to have a great deal to do with the Christianity of the one and the atheism of the other.

Guided by this Manichaean view of the world, Dulles managed American foreign policy for six years, from 1953 to 1959. While retaining the final power of decision, Eisenhower believed strongly in delegating authority to cabinet members, and he reposed special trust in Dulles. Dulles became the most influential secretary of state of the postwar era, at least until the coming of Henry Kissinger. The secretary made diplomacy a personal affair, visiting forty-seven countries and flying half a million miles during his tenure.

Liberation The new Republican leaders proposed to differentiate themselves most dramatically from Truman with regard to the "captive nations" of Eastern Europe. The United States, said Dulles, should "make it publicly known that it wants and expects liberation to occur." During the election campaign, the policy had won the Republicans millions of votes from Americans of Polish, Hungarian, and other East European descent. Dulles quickly explained, once in office, that he meant that America should frequently restate its position that Eastern Europe should be free; he did not mean military action. Constant moral pressure, maintained Dulles, would lead to liberation.

Brinkmanship and Massive Retaliation Dulles labored hard and often to inform the world that the United States was not "scared to go to the brink," that it would not regard all-out war as unthinkable if its vital interests were threatened. As part of this strategy, Dulles purposely left unclear what situations would push the United States over the brink. Such a policy may have frightened America's enemies; it also discomfited America's allies.

Massive retaliation became a crucial corollary to brinkmanship. But it was partially forced on Dulles by the rest of the Eisenhower administration. As a result of the Korean War, defense spending had more than tripled, from $14 billion

in 1950 to $49 billion in 1953. The cabinet's fiscal conservatives hoped to reduce expenditures and balance the budget. To curb military expenses, they imposed on the armed forces a policy called the New Look.

The New Look became more popularly known as the policy of "more bang for a buck." Atomic weapons, its proponents argued, could most economically defend the country, far more so than large naval and land forces. By concentrating on American nuclear strength, especially the deterrent of the Strategic Air Command, the administration could prune the army and navy and cut the defense budget by 10 percent. Thus, when Dulles approached the brink, he threatened opponents with massive retaliation with nuclear weapons. The logic of the administration's fiscal policies dictated the all-or-nothing approach.

Ending the Korean War Eisenhower had pledged during his campaign, "I will go to Korea," to inspect battle lines and examine possibilities for peace. His visit, in December 1952, left him more than ever convinced of what he had believed from the start—Americans should not be fighting a land war in Asia.

The new President and his secretary of state rapidly began to test out their brinkmanship ideas. If the war did not end soon, Eisenhower proclaimed, the United States would take action "under circumstances of our own choosing." Chiang Kai-shek, driven by the Chinese communists to the island of Formosa, began bombing raids against the Chinese coast. Finally, Dulles sent a message to the Chinese through the government of India: If a Korean agreement was not reached soon, the United States would seriously consider using nuclear weapons. Within two weeks, the communists agreed to a settlement.

In its first innings, brinkmanship appeared to have scored a success. But some maintained that the war had ended largely because of stalemate on the battlefront and the death of Stalin two months earlier. In the next two years, Stalin's successors in Moscow appeared to be pursuing a more conciliatory role on several fronts, abandoning some territorial claims and improving relations with several countries. Eventually, the Soviets agreed to withdraw from their occupation zone in Austria, on condition that the reunited country follow a neutral foreign policy. The Soviets also indicated that they would be willing to solve the problem of German reunification the same way.

Dulles responded to all Soviet actions with deep suspicion. After the settlement of the Korean War, he explained, "This is the time to crowd the enemy—and maybe finish him, once and for all." Soviet overtures, he felt, reflected Soviet weakness, which the United States should exploit.

Problems in the Far East If Dulles distrusted Soviet policies and aims, part of his attitude stemmed from communist actions in the Far East, actions that the secretary interpreted as the direct work of the Kremlin. Since 1945, a dedicated Vietnamese nationalist and communist named Ho Chi Minh had been at the head of a rebellion to drive the French out of Indochina. France appealed for American aid against communism, and this valued ally received millions of American dollars to finance its colonial war. But by April 1954 France was through in that area. French troops had entrenched and trapped themselves in a fortress near Hanoi called Dien Bien Phu. In May, the Dien Bien Phu garrison surrendered.

Meanwhile, the communist insurgents and the French had begun negotiating in Geneva. After the fall of Dien Bien Phu they agreed to divide Vietnam temporarily, with Ho Chi Minh taking over the north and the French remaining in the south. Internationally supervised elections, aimed at reuniting the country, were supposed to be held by 1956. The elections never took place. In South Vietnam, an American-backed regime, headed by a Vietnamese Catholic named Diem, established a separate government in Saigon. The United States poured in support, and elections, which everyone knew Ho Chi Minh would win, were postponed. Dulles, who attended the Geneva sessions as an unhappy "observer" (the United States did not sign the final accords), had salvaged something: a noncommunist South Vietnam. On the list of American Pyrrhic victories, the 1956 Geneva Conference ranks at the top.

Dulles had been frustrated in Indochina by a lack of support from America's allies. He now

John Foster Dulles is the protective nurse guarding the "children" of Asia from the lure of the "Red Piper of Peking" by herding them around the SEATO carriage.

attempted to head off such embarrassments in the future by organizing the Southeast Asia Treaty Organization (SEATO) (ostensibly an Eastern NATO), comprising the United States, Britain, France, Australia, New Zealand, Thailand, Pakistan, and the Philippines. But many noncommunist states of Asia (India, Indonesia, Burma) refused to join or to align themselves with the United States. Nonetheless, Dulles believed he now had the means to repel future communist advances in the region.

Toward a European Settlement Neither Russians nor Americans expected substantive results from the Geneva conference of 1955. Neither side brought any new proposals to deal with the major East-West problem, the reunification of Germany. West Germany was being rearmed and had joined NATO, and the Soviet Union had organized its Iron Curtain satellites into the Warsaw Pact, which East Germany would join a few months later. Germany, like Europe, would remain divided for the forseeable future. The only positive result of the meeting was an intangible, rapidly dissolving "spirit of Geneva," which implied that the two countries would not seek to settle their differences by war.

This easing of tensions did not sit well with Dulles. It looked too much like American acceptance of the status quo, including permanent Soviet control of Eastern Europe. Accordingly, the United States continued to issue statements about "liberation" remaining a high-priority item in American foreign policy. Especially during the presidential election year of 1956, the administration would not forgo restating the crucial policy that differentiated it from the Truman administration.

But events soon demonstrated tragically the emptiness of these promises of liberation. In October 1956, discontent in Eastern Europe exploded in the streets of Hungary and forced changes in the government. Flushed with their success, Hungarians demanded the withdrawal of the Rus-

sian Army, which began evacuating the country, or at least pulled out of Budapest. Eisenhower had been careful not to urge on the "rebels," but CIA-sponsored Radio Free Europe offered encouragement, and Dulles mentioned the possibility of American economic aid.

Hungary maintained its independence for several days. But when the new premier announced that Hungary would withdraw from the Warsaw Pact, the Russians sent in their tanks. Hungarians resisted, pleading all the while for help from the West.

Given the realities of nuclear stalemate, Eisenhower never considered sending in Ameri-

Hungarian patriots hold an anti-Soviet demonstration on a torn-up Budapest street on October 24, 1956. In the week of bloody rebellion that followed, Soviet troops and tanks crushed the Hungarians' attempt to establish their own government. Although the United States joined in a U. N. resolution censuring the Soviets, and was to admit thousands of Hungarian refugees in the wake of the revolution, it did not intervene in Hungary.

can troops to Hungary. The Soviets would have construed such an action as an attack on them and would have responded, possibly with nuclear weapons. Despite the rhetoric of liberation, Eisenhower and Dulles had always known this. Now the East Europeans knew it too.

The Middle East Dulles's problems were just beginning. At the time of the Hungarian revolution, the secretary's ability to influence world events suffered another dramatic blow, as a crisis erupted in the Middle East involving America's closest allies. Without consulting the United States, Britain and France took military action against Egypt. Their joint expedition produced only frustration for both European nations, and further frayed the bonds of the Atlantic alliance.

The crisis arose, in part, from Dulles's own bumbling. He had attempted to improve America's standing with the Arab nations by agreeing to aid in building the Aswan Dam on Egypt's Nile River. But by 1956 the young nationalist Egyptian leader, Gamal Abdel Nasser, had moved to establish ties with communist countries as well. As a result, Dulles abruptly informed the Egyptians that the United States would not finance the dam (the Russians eventually did). Nasser, angered and humiliated, bolstered his prestige by nationalizing the Suez Canal.

This action infuriated the British and French, who considered control of the canal vital to their interests. When negotiations did not produce satisfaction, they allied with Israel in a combined attack on Egypt. (This development undoubtedly helped assure the Russians that they could move into Hungary without fear of Western reprisal.)

The United States reacted angrily, both at the invasion and at not having been consulted. Eisenhower immediately demanded that the British and French forces withdraw, before they had even reached the canal. Khrushchev, bidding for support among the Arabs, threatened Western Europe with nuclear weapons. Under pressure from both the Russians and the Americans, the British and French had no choice but to withdraw.

Dulles had ended the invasion, but he seemed to have accomplished little else. The af-

fair injured NATO prestige and allowed the Russians to ingratiate themselves with Nasser, gaining a base on the Mediterranean. To maintain the American position, the United States, in early 1957, proclaimed the Eisenhower Doctrine, affirming its intent to support established Arab governments against subversion. By the end of that year, Eisenhower had strengthened American ties with Jordan and Saudi Arabia. A year later, he committed American troops for the only time in his presidency, ordering a landing by United States Marines in Lebanon as a show of American strength. As on previous occasions, Eisenhower moved in a far more limited fashion than his military advisers or his secretary of state had wanted.

Problems with the Third World Eisenhower and Dulles presided over American foreign policy at a time when nationalism was rising throughout Asia, Africa, and Latin America. As shown by their difficulties in handling Egypt's Nasser, American policymakers had recurrent problems dealing with the new phenomenon. Although strongly opposed to old-style European colonialism, Americans did not know exactly what they wanted in its place.

Their major aim, to prevent the spread of communism, often lapsed into a policy of support for established regimes and opposition to virtually any insurgent movement, whether communist-led or not. While this did not restructure American policy, the Eisenhower-Dulles world view often clashed with the plans of emerging Third World countries to quicken their own development. The United States sought to strengthen existing governments, assist development, and turn the new nations from communism with offers of military and economic aid. By 1961, Eisenhower was asking $4.2 billion from Congress for such aid.

The United States faced a particular problem in Latin America, where it tried to maintain traditional hemispheric influence and safeguard nearly $10 billion of American investment. Strains developed in an area that many Americans regarded as their backyard. In 1954, after the Central American republic of Guatemala took a turn toward the left, Dulles denounced the existing government. But more than words were involved. The CIA helped finance Guatemalan groups opposed to the left-leaning government in a successful seizure of power. Dulles had seemed to pay little attention to Latin America. But when rock-throwing crowds later attacked Vice President Nixon in Venezuela, Washington began to worry about its position. For at least one country, Cuba, when Fidel Castro's guerillas overthrew a pro-American regime in 1958, this concern came too late.

Sputnik and U-2 In August 1957 the Soviet Union startled the United States, and the world, by orbiting its first space vehicle, Sputnik. Whatever the implications for interplanetary travel, Sputnik symbolized rapid advances by the Soviets in rocketry and atomic warhead delivery systems. The United States had also advanced in these directions, and had made great strides in developing nuclear submarines. More and more, international relations reflected a "balance of terror," with traditional considerations becoming less and less important.

Both sides now sought another summit conference to ease tensions and deal with international problems. But events seemed stalemated until Eisenhower decided to follow a more conciliatory policy. Dulles, terminally ill with cancer, had to retire in 1959. Ike invited Khrushchev to the United States, with an Eisenhower visit to Russia to follow. Khrushchev's visit passed pleasantly, including extensive conferences with the President at Camp David, the presidential retreat in Maryland. The two leaders agreed to hold a summit conference in Paris, in May 1960.

But, before the conference could take place, the Russians shot down an American U-2 spy plane over Sverdlovsk, deep in Soviet territory. (This was the same type of spy plane later used over Cuba.) The United States denied that the plane had been on a spy mission until the Russians produced the pilot, who had survived and confessed. Eisenhower then took personal responsibility for the flights, which had started in 1956, stating that he was obligated to keep a close watch on Russia for the sake of American security.

Khrushchev, possibly because of pressure from Kremlin hard-liners and from the Chinese,

The Khrushchev-Eisenhower meeting at Camp David, Maryland, in 1959 produced a temporary thaw in the Cold War. Khrushchev's new policy of peaceful coexistence with the West provided economic competition as an alternative to direct military confrontation in the world.

used the U-2 incident to torpedo the summit conference. He delivered a long anti-American tirade at a news conference and demanded an apology from Eisenhower. The President refused, the proposed meeting evaporated, and Khrushchev canceled Eisenhower's invitation to visit Russia.

Eisenhower thus concluded his foreign policy stewardship on an embarrassing note, although his popularity at home soared after the summit debacle. During Ike's eight years in office, no one had been liberated from the communist yoke—unless one can describe the creation of anticommunist dictatorships in South Vietnam and Guatemala as "liberation." Still, he had preserved peace and put some limits on defense spending. If he had not offered a daring or imaginative approach to the Third World, the Russians and later the Chinese would also learn the difficulty of maintaining relations between the "have" and the "have-not" nations.

Although Eisenhower was not active in the presidential campaign of 1960, his foreign policy came under attack. During his final presidential term, the United States had frequently seemed to be not acting but reacting, often too late, to Soviet initiatives. Democratic candidate John F. Kennedy made shrewd use of this issue in his campaign against Republican Vice President Richard M. Nixon. Kennedy's promise to get the country "moving again" won him a narrow election victory. Americans looked forward to the 1960s, keenly anticipating his fulfillment of that pledge. But when the turbulent sixties had become history, many looked back with nostalgia to the eight relatively quiet years of the Eisenhower era.

SUGGESTED READINGS— CHAPTERS 43–44

Pearl Harbor

Adolph A. Hoehling, *The Week Before Pearl Harbor* (1963); Walter Lord, *Day of Infamy* (1957); Roberta Wohlstetter, *Pearl Harbor: Warning and Decision* (1962).

Interventionists Versus Isolationists

Selig Adler, *The Isolationist Impulse* (1957); James M. Burns, *Roosevelt: The Soldier of Freedom* (1970); Mark Chadwin, *Hawks of World War II* (1968); Wayne S. Cole, *America First: The Battle Against Intervention, 1940–1941* (1953); Robert A. Divine, *The Reluctant Belligerent* (1965); Saul Friedlander, *Prelude to Downfall: Hitler and the United States, 1939–1941* (1967); Townsend Hoopes, *The Devil and John Foster Dulles* (1973); Manfred Jonas, *Isolationism in America, 1935–1941* (1966); Robert E. Osgood, *NATO, the Entangling Alliance* (1962); Martin J. Sherwin, *A World Destroyed: The Atomic Bomb and the Grand Alliance* (1975).

Depression Diplomacy

Dorothy Borg and Shupei Okamoto (eds.), *Pearl Harbor as History: Japanese-American Relations, 1931–1941* (1973); L. Ethan Ellis, *Republican Foreign Policy, 1921–1933* (1968); Lloyd C. Gardner, *Economic Aspects of New Deal Diplomacy* (1964) and *Architects of Illusion: Men and Ideas in American Foreign Policy, 1941–1949* (1970); David Green, *The Containment of Latin America* (1970); William L. Langer and S. Everett Gleason, *The World Crisis and American Foreign Policy* (2 vols., 1952–1953); Bryce Wood, *The Making of the Good Neighbor Policy* (1967); Allen Guttmann, *The Wound in the Heart: America and the Spanish Civil War* (1962); John E. Wiltz, *From Isolation to War, 1931–1941* (1968).

The Cold War

Selig Adler, *The Uncertain Giant: American Foreign Policy Between the Wars* (1965); Gar Alperovitz, *Atomic Diplomacy* (1965); Lynn E. Davis, *The Cold War Begins* (1973); John L. Gaddis, *The United States and the Origins of the Cold War* (1972); Akira Iriye, *The Cold War in Asia* (1974); Walter LaFeber, *America, Russia, and the Cold War* (1967); Joyce and Gabriel Kolko, *The Limits of Power: The World and United States Foreign Policy, 1945–1954* (1972); Gabriel Kolko, *The Politics of War* (1969); Robert J. Maddox, *The New Left and the Origins of the Cold War* (1974); Adam B. Ulam, *The Rivals: America and Russia Since World War II* (1972); Richard Walton, *Henry Wallace, Harry Truman and the Cold War* (1976); Daniel Yergin, *The Shattered Peace* (1977).

The Near East and the Far East

Dorothy Borg, *The United States and the Far Eastern Crisis of 1933–1938* (1964); Herman Finer, *Dulles Over Suez* (1964); Robert L. Neumann, *America Encounters Japan* (1963); John W. Spanier, *The Truman-MacArthur Controversy* (1965); Tang Tsou, *America's Failure in China, 1941–1950* (2 vols., 1963).

Wartime Diplomacy

A. Russell Buchanan, *The United States and World War II* (2 vols., 1964); Diane S. Clemens, *Yalta* (1971); Robert A. Divine, *Roosevelt and World War II* (1969); Herbert Feis, *Churchill, Roosevelt, Stalin,* 2nd edition (1967); Gaddis Smith, *American Diplomacy During the Second World War, 1941–1945* (1965).

45
THE ALGER HISS CASE

A.W.

Whittaker Chambers, star witness in the Hiss case, reflected on the importance of the case some years later and wrote to his children:

> Beloved Children,
>
> I am sitting in the kitchen of [our Maryland farm] writing a book. In it I am speaking to you. But I am also speaking to the world. To both I owe an accounting.
>
> It is a terrible book—terrible in what it tells about men, more terrible in what it tells about the world in which you live. It is about what the world calls the Hiss-Chambers case, or even more simply, the Hiss case. It is about a spy case. All the props of an espionage case are there—foreign agents, household traitors, stolen documents, microfilm, furtive meetings, secret hideaways, phony names, an informer, investigations, trials, official justice.
>
> But if the Hiss case were only this, it would not be worth my writing about or your reading about. It would not be what, at the very beginning, I was moved to call it: "a tragedy of history."
>
> For it was more than human tragedy. Much more than Alger Hiss or Whittaker Chambers was on trial in the trials of Alger Hiss. Two faiths were on trial. Human societies, like human beings, live by faith and die when faith dies. At heart, the Great Case was this critical conflict of faiths; that is why it was a great case. On a scale personal enough to be felt by all, but big enough to be symbolic, the two irreconcilable faiths of our time—communism and freedom—came to grips in the persons of two conscious and resolute men. Both had been schooled in the same view of history (the Marxist view). Both were trained by the same party in the same selfless, semisoldierly discipline. Neither would nor could yield without betraying, not himself, but his faith [and] both knew, almost from the beginning, that the Great Case could end only in the destruction of one or both of the contending figures.
>
> My children, as long as you live, the shadow of the Hiss case will brush you. In time you will ask yourselves the question: What was my father?
>
> I will give you an answer: I was a witness. A witness, in the sense that I am using the word, is a man whose life and faith are so completely one that when the challenge comes to step out and testify for his faith, he does so, disregarding all risks, accepting all consequences.

Alger Hiss, chief among those high government officials accused of communist connections, related the circumstances surrounding his involvement in the investigation:

In August 1948 I was living in New York City. For the preceding year and a half I had been president of the Carnegie Endowment for International Peace. To accept that position I had resigned from the State Department, where I was director of the office responsible for proposing and carrying out our policies in the United Nations.

My new work was closely related to what I had been doing in Washington, for the Endowment had decided to concentrate its activities on support of the United Nations as the appropriate means of furthering Andrew Carnegie's aim "to hasten the abolition of international war, the foulest blot upon our civilization."

On Monday, August 2, 1948 a reporter reached me by telephone at my apartment. He told me that, according to information coming from the Committee on Un-American Activities of the House of Representatives, a man named Chambers was going to appear before the committee the next morning and call me a communist. The reporter asked whether I had any comment.

I did not. The untruthful charge of communism had been the lot of many who had been New Deal officials in the Washington of the 1930s and the early 1940s. I had not taken such charges seriously when made against others, and I saw no reason why I or anyone else should pay much attention to a similar fanciful charge that might now be made against me.

The next morning a witness named Whittaker Chambers appeared before the committee and said that years before he had been "attached" to "an underground organization of the United States Communist party" in Washington. He said that I had been a member of that group.

As I knew no one named Whittaker Chambers I chose to make my denials not only to the newspapers but in the same setting where the charges had been made. Therefore, I sent a telegram to the committee that same afternoon saying that I wanted to appear to deny Chambers's charges under oath.

Richard Nixon, then an obscure congressman from California, considered the case the first major crisis he would face while in public life:

My name, my reputation, and my career were ever to be linked with the decisions I made and the actions I took in that case, as a thirty-five-year-old freshman congressman in 1948. Yet, when I was telling my fifteen-year-old daughter, Tricia, one day about the [subject], she interrupted me to ask, "What was the Hiss case?"

I realized for the first time that a whole new generation of Americans was now growing up who had not even heard of the Hiss case. And now, in retrospect, I wonder how many of my own generation really knew the facts and implications of that emotional controversy that rocked the nation. I experienced [the case] not only as an acute personal crisis but as a vivid case study of the continuing crisis of our times, a crisis with which we shall be confronted as long as aggressive international communism is on the loose in the world.

The Hiss case began for me personally when David Whittaker Chambers appeared before the House Committee on Un-American Activities to testify on communist infiltration into the federal government. Never in the stormy history of the committee was a more sensational investigation started by a less impressive witness.

Chambers did not ask to come before the committee so that he could single out and attack Alger Hiss. The committee had subpoenaed him. Both in appearance and in what he had to say, he made very little impression on me or the other committee members. None of us thought his testimony was going to be especially important.

August 3, 1948. Six congressmen took their seats in a nearly empty House committee hearing room: Karl E. Mundt (South Dakota), John McDowell (New Jersey), John E. Rankin (Mississippi), J. Hardin Peterson (Florida), F. Edward Hébert (Louisiana), and Richard M. Nixon (California). Robert E. Stripling, chief investigator of the House Un-American Activities Committee (HUAC), called the sole witness waiting to testify—Whittaker Chambers. Chambers, not an impressive-looking witness, nevertheless had quite good credentials. He had combined two public careers over the previous twenty years, as a journalist and a gifted translator. Educated at Columbia College, he was fluent in several languages and had translated from German into English such popular works as the children's book *Bambi.*

Chambers had been subpoenaed the previous day. In answer to Stripling's questions Chambers said that in the 1920s and 1930s he had been a Communist party member "and a paid functionary of the party." He added:

> In 1937 I repudiated Marx's doctrines and Lenin's tactics. For a number of years I had served in the underground, chiefly in Washington, D.C. The underground group [included] Alger Hiss. The purpose of this group at that time was not primarily espionage. Its original purpose was the communist infiltration of the American government. But espionage was one of its eventual objectives.

The committee members questioned Chambers at length about his charges. He pointed out that on several previous occasions in the past decade, he had given similar testimony to high State Department officials and to the FBI. No action, however, had ever been taken against any officials he had named as communists. The witness went on to suggest that he and Hiss had been particularly close:

On his role as star witness in the case against Alger Hiss, Chambers said, "I have testified against him with remorse and pity, but in the moment of history in which this nation now stands, so help me God, I could not do otherwise."

> MR. STRIPLING: When you left the Communist party in 1937, did you approach any of these seven [alleged underground members] to break with you?
> MR. CHAMBERS: No. The only one of those people whom I approached was Alger Hiss. I went to the Hiss home one evening at what I considered considerable risk to myself and found Mrs. Hiss at home. Mrs. Hiss is also a member of the Communist party. Mr. Hiss came in shortly afterward, and we talked and I tried to break him away from the party. As a matter of fact, he cried when we separated; but when I left him, he absolutely refused to break. I was very fond of Mr. Hiss.

Despite repeated questions by committee members, Chambers stood by his charges and pointedly denied that the alleged communist underground group within the New Deal had ever committed espionage:

> These people were specifically not wanted to act as sources of information. These people were an elite group, which it was believed would rise to positions—as, indeed, some of them did—notably Mr. Hiss—in the government. Their position in the government would be of much more service to the Communist party.

Newsmen present promptly reported the hottest news item in the morning's testimony: a senior editor of *Time* magazine had accused the president of the Carnegie Endowment of being a secret Soviet agent!

August 5, 1948. It was now Alger Hiss's turn to appear before the committee. He offered a striking contrast to his stout and untidy accuser. His handsome face seemed cool and relaxed. His tall, lean body was fitted with elegant, carefully pressed clothes. Furthermore, he displayed none of Chambers's evident nervousness under questioning. Hiss began his testimony with a prepared statement.

> I am not and never have been a member of the Communist party. I do not and never have adhered to the tenets of the Communist party. I am not and never have been a member of any communist-front organization. I have never followed the Communist party line, directly or indirectly. To the best of my knowledge, none of my friends is a communist. To the best of my knowledge I never heard of Whittaker Chambers until 1947, when two representatives of the Federal Bureau of Investigation asked me if I knew him and various other people. I said I did not know Chambers. So far as I know, I have never laid eyes on him, and the statements made about me by Mr. Chambers are complete fabrications. I think my record in the government service speaks for itself.

Committee members questioned Hiss at length about his impressive government career. It included being secretary to the great Chief Justice Oliver Wendell Holmes and assistant counsel to the Senate's Nye Committee (see Chapter 44). He had also served with the solicitor general of the United States and then held high posts in the State Department until he left in 1947 to head the Carnegie Endowment.

Then HUAC members and Stripling questioned Hiss about Chambers's accusations:

> MR. MUNDT: I wonder what possible motive a man who edits *Time* magazine would have for mentioning Alger Hiss in connection with [communist involvement].
>
> MR. HISS: So do I, Mr. Chairman. I have no possible understanding of what could have motivated him.

The committee members recognized by this time that, in Stripling's words, there was "very sharp contradiction" between Hiss and Chambers. One of the two men was a monumental liar. Yet according to Mundt, both men were "witnesses whom normally one would assume to be perfectly reliable. They have high positions in American business or organizational work. They both appear to be honest. They both testify under oath [yet their] stories fail to jibe."

At this point Congressman Nixon suggested that Hiss and Chambers "be allowed to confront each other so that any possibility of a mistake in identity may be cleared up." The other HUAC members ignored Nixon's suggestion, and the questioning continued. After Hiss had concluded his testimony, a large crowd of spectators and reporters rushed up to congratulate him. Nixon later expressed the feelings of most of them—and of most members of HUAC—when he said that a terrible mistake had been made. The committee, he thought, should not have allowed Chambers to testify without first checking into the possibility of such a mistake.

A journalist confirmed this reaction when he asked Hiss: "How is the committee going to dig itself out of this hole?" HUAC was already being criticized widely for its careless handling of hearings. There was even a strong possibility that President Truman, if he won the upcoming 1948 election, would ask Congress to disband the committee. That same morning, while Hiss was denying Chambers's charges before the committee, Truman denounced HUAC's current spy investigation. He called it a red herring organized by the Republican-dominated committee to distract the public from the party's failure to pass an effective domestic economic program.

Thus, from the beginning, the Hiss-Chambers testimony was an issue in national politics, threatening Republican chances in the fall elections. "This case is going to kill the committee," one reporter told Nixon after the morning session had ended, "unless you can prove Chambers's story." The reporter did not know that this was exactly what Nixon intended to do.

Richard Milhous Nixon was then a freshman representative from Southern California. His family, like millions of others, had suffered during the depression. He had worked hard from his earliest years. After largely supporting himself through college and law school, Nixon worked briefly in Washington and then served as a naval officer during World War II. Returning to California, he ran for Congress. In his campaign he charged his Democratic opponent with being a radical and pro-communist. The tactic was successful, and he won the election. During his first year and a half in Congress, he had not acquired any wide reputation beyond his home district. Soon this would change.

Nixon later wrote that when HUAC met privately after Hiss testified, "it was in a virtual state of shock." For his part Nixon argued:

> While it would be virtually impossible to prove that Hiss was or was not a communist—for that would simply be his word against Chambers'—we should be able to establish whether or not the two men knew each other. If Hiss were lying about not knowing Chambers, then he might also be lying about whether or not he was a communist.

Nixon managed to persuade the acting committee chairman, Karl Mundt, to appoint him head of a subcommittee to question Chambers again. This time the session was to be private, with no spectators or press present.

August 7, 1948. The HUAC subcommittee headed by Nixon questioned Chambers secretly in New York City. Nixon asked in what period Chambers had known Hiss as a communist. The witness answered "roughly, between the years 1935 and 1937." Chambers said Hiss knew him not by his real name but "by the party name of Carl." He also asserted that he collected Communist party membership dues from Mr. and Mrs. Hiss. According to Chambers, therefore, Hiss was a member of the communist underground infiltrating the government. Moreover, he was also a dues-paying member of the party itself. At this point Nixon

Alger and Priscilla Hiss at first denied any knowledge of Chambers, then conceded that they knew him under another name when he exposed numerous details of their personal lives to the committee.

plunged into a detailed, rapid-fire series of questions testing whether Hiss had known Chambers. Specifically, Nixon noted, he wanted to know "What should one man know about another if he knew him as well as Chambers claimed to know Hiss?"

Chambers apparently remembered a great deal about Hisses, although as Nixon later admitted: "All of this information might have been obtained by studying Hiss's life without actually knowing him. But some of the answers had a personal ring of truth about them beyond the bare facts themselves." Chambers claimed he had seen the Hisses on numerous occasions. He had been a guest at their home several times. He also seemed to recall a great many details about the Hisses' private lives: nicknames for one another, eating and drinking habits, pets, personal mannerisms, relatives, the exteriors and furniture of their various homes.

Perhaps the most damaging details that Chambers provided about Hiss during the questioning concerned two episodes. One was the transfer of a car Hiss owned to another communist with Chambers or an associate acting as intermediary. The other impressed Nixon because it had a "personal ring of truth." It concerned a hobby the Hisses and Chambers had in common. Both were amateur ornithologists, bird watchers. Chambers testified, "I recall once they saw, to their great excitement, a prothonotary warbler." At this point Congressman McDowell, also a bird lover, interrupted to ask, "A very rare specimen?" Chambers replied. "I never saw one. I am also fond of birds."

The mass of detail concerning the Hisses' lives—birds, cars, homes, nicknames, and the like—restored a faith in Chambers's honesty among committee members.

Alger Hiss lived in this apartment house in Washington, D.C., during the period 1934–1935. He admitted that he let Chambers sublet his apartment for a time in 1935.

August 16, 1948. At this closed session of HUAC Hiss seemed under severe strain. The cool composure of his earlier appearance before the committee had given way to a mixture of nervousness and anger. Nixon showed Hiss two pictures of Chambers and asked again whether he knew the man "either as Whittaker Chambers or as Carl or as any other individual." Hiss began to waver, admitting the "the face has a certain familiarity." Chief counsel Stripling and the committee members confronted Hiss with Chambers's detailed claims concerning their friendship. They probed for evidence confirming the *Time* editor's account.

Hiss repeatedly protested the committee's refusal to provide him with a transcript of Chambers's earlier testimony. He became increasingly hostile. He was angry that the committee found it difficult to decide whether truth was on the side of Chambers—"a confessed former communist" and "self-confessed traitor"—or himself, a highly respected man. Stripling, in turn, snapped back sharply that Chambers had "sat there and testified for hours. He said he spent a week in your house, and he just rattled off details like that. He has either made a study of your life in great detail or he knows you."

Moments after this exchange Hiss announced: "I have written a name on this pad in front of me of a person whom I knew in 1933 and 1934 who not only spent some time in my house but sublet my apartment." Hiss was not sure this person—a free-lance writer named George Crosley—was Chambers. He insisted that he had not seen Crosley since 1934. Hiss gave a detailed account of this relationship, claiming to have met Crosley while he was legal counsel to the Nye Committee in 1933.

Crosley, he said, wished to write several magazine articles about the Nye Committee's munitions-industry investigation. Hiss added that he took a liking to the young journalist. When moving his family to a new apartment, Hiss briefly sublet his old apartment to Crosley and his family. At the same time he gave the journalist "an old Ford we had kept for sentimental reasons." Crosley never paid the rent money, according to Hiss. As for the car, "I threw it in along with the rent" because of a desire to "get rid of it." Deciding that he "had been a sucker and [Crosley] was a sort of deadbeat using me for a soft touch," Hiss said he never saw the man again after 1935. (He later changed the date to mid-1936.)

Hiss also remembered taking several drives with Crosley and giving him "loans [he] never paid back." Once Crosley gave him "a rug he said some wealthy patron gave him. I have still got the damned thing." At one point Nixon asked Hiss about his hobbies. When the witness mentioned bird watching, Congressman McDowell asked: "Did you ever see a prothonotary warbler?" "I have right here on the Potomac," Hiss replied, unaware of Chambers's earlier testimony.

Several members of HUAC remarked during Hiss's testimony that either he or Chambers was obviously committing perjury. "Whichever one of you is lying is the greatest actor that America has ever produced," exclaimed Congressman Hébert. Before adjourning the bitterly tense executive session, the committee decided to have Chambers and Hiss

Alger Hiss and Whittaker Chambers silently confront each other before the House Un-American Activities Committee in August 1948. The case helped trigger a Red scare that was to have widespread effects in the fifties.

testify publicly, together, nine days later on August 25. Actually, the pair confronted one another the following day at a hurriedly arranged HUAC meeting in New York City.

August 17, 1948. The session was moved up, according to Nixon, to prevent Hiss from gaining "nine more days to make his story fit the facts." In fact there may have been another motive. The committee was uneasy over the death of Harry Dexter White, a former high Treasury Department official. He had died of a heart attack. White had appeared before a HUAC public hearing a few days earlier to deny charges leveled by Chambers that he had been either a party member or procommunist. He had asked for a postponement because of his bad heart but was refused. White had proved a good witness in his own defense despite the committee's attempt to browbeat him. Nixon and the other HUAC subcommittee members may have hoped to divert public outrage over White's untimely death following this grueling interrogation. They would shift attention to the still active Hiss-Chambers investigation.

Throughout the session, Hiss was extremely irritable, angry, and defensive. He observed that Harry Dexter White's death had upset him greatly, so that testifying would be difficult. He also protested that the committee (despite promises to the contrary) had leaked portions of his previous day's testimony to the press. (Both Nixon and Stripling denied this charge.) Finally Chambers, who had been waiting in an adjoining room, was brought in.

> MR. NIXON: Sit over here, Mr. Chambers. Mr. Chambers, will you please stand? And will you please stand, Mr. Hiss? Mr. Hiss, the man standing here is Mr. Whittaker Chambers. I ask you now if you have ever known that man before.
> MR. HISS: May I ask him to speak? Will you ask him to say something?
> MR. NIXON: Yes. Mr. Chambers, will you tell us your name and your business?
> MR. CHAMBERS: My name is Whittaker Chambers. [At this point, Hiss walked toward Chambers.] I am senior editor of *Time* magazine.
> MR. HISS: Are you George Crosley?
> MR. CHAMBERS: Not to my knowledge. You are Alger Hiss, I believe.
> MR. HISS: I certainly am.
> MR. CHAMBERS: That was my recollection. [Chambers read from a magazine so that Hiss could test his voice pattern.]

Hiss then announced that Chambers was probably the man he knew as Crosley. Nixon and Stripling began a lengthy series of questions comparing Hiss's version of the relationship with Crosley—apartment rental, car transfer, gift of a rug, and other details—with the facts previously supplied by Chambers. Hiss of course denied that Crosley had been more than a casual acquaintance, saying, "He meant nothing to me." Chambers again stressed their common bond, stating, "I was a communist, and you were a communist." At last Hiss acknowledged, "I am perfectly prepared to identify this man as George Crosley." But he denied knowing whether "Crosley" had ever been a communist and pointed out that "it was a quite different atmosphere in Washington then than today." He insisted he had known Crosley only as a journalist.

August 25, 1948. The hearing room was jammed with reporters and spectators. The hearing lasted nine hours. (Hiss testified for six, Chambers for three.) Not only Hiss but all seven other alleged members of the communist cell whom Chambers had named had meanwhile testified before HUAC. Except for Hiss's brother, Donald, who joined Alger in specifically denying any communist associations, the others refused to say whether they had been communists. In their refusals all invoked the Fifth Amendment, which provides protection from possible self-incrimination.

From the start Hiss, accompanied by his lawyer, treated the occasion as a kind of trial. He was convinced that HUAC believed Chambers and wished mainly to prepare evidence for a perjury charge against him. Therefore, Hiss was extremely guarded in responding. He qualified his answers with phrases such as "to the best of my recollection" more than 200 times. On several occasions he accused HUAC of believing Chambers largely for political reasons. The Republican-controlled committee, he claimed, wanted to expose a top civil servant closely identified with

Democratic-sponsored programs like the New Deal, the Yalta agreements, and the United Nations.

The day went badly for Hiss. At the start both Hiss and Chambers were directed to stand. Hiss again identified the *Time* editor as Crosley. Chambers again claimed to have known Hiss in the communist underground. Some of the most damaging passages for Hiss involved the Ford car. He had previously testified turning it over to Crosley along with his apartment.

> MR. NIXON: Did you give Crosley a car?
>
> MR. HISS: I gave Crosley, according to my best recollection . . .
>
> MR. NIXON: You certainly can testify yes or no as to whether you gave Crosley a car. How many cars have you given away in your life, Mr. Hiss?
>
> MR. HISS: I have had only one old car of a financial value of $25 in my life. That is the car I let Crosley use.
>
> MR. NIXON: My point now is, is your present testimony that you did or did not give Crosley a car?
>
> MR. HISS: Whether I transferred title to him in a legal, formal sense; whether I gave him the car outright; whether the car came back — I don't know.

Unfortunately for Hiss, a title search by HUAC agents produced evidence that Hiss had transferred the car on July 23, 1936, to William Rosen, the alleged communist about whom Chambers had testified earlier. The Hiss signature on the document had been notarized by W. Marvin Smith. He was a lawyer with the Justice Department. Smith told HUAC that he knew Hiss and that Hiss had personally signed the transfer in his presence. (Strangely, Smith fell or jumped to his death soon after he testified.)

Hiss now counterattacked. He denounced HUAC's investigation as a political attack on liberal Democrats. He reviewed his fifteen years of impressive public service and named as references for his achievements, personal character, and loyalty thirty-four prominent public figures. Nixon termed this an effort by Hiss to prove his "innocence by association," an ironic reference considering HUAC's past reputation for trying to show a witness' guilt by association.

During this day's testimony the two major witnesses reversed their previous roles completely. Chambers was now a cool, placid witness, calmly answering every question put to him. Hiss testified nervously and emotionally. But Hiss emphasized that some of Chambers's most obvious statements about him were incorrect. Thus the Hisses were not teetotalers and Hiss did attend church. Hiss's stepson was not a "puny little boy." Despite these and other errors about the Hisses, Chambers still displayed remarkable familiarity with their private life.

Hiss offered some explanation for this apparent familiarity. He claimed that Chambers, with access to *Time*'s excellent research records, could have discovered most of the personal material on Hiss in such publications as *Who's Who*. Congressman Hébert retorted: "Nobody could have read in *Who's Who* that you found a rare bird [the prothonotary warbler]." Hiss responded that he had "told many, many people." But this did not persuade the committee.

For his part, Chambers denied that he harbored any secret reason for wishing to ruin Hiss, as the latter charged. He went so far as to call Alger Hiss "the closest friend I ever had in the Communist party." Fighting back tears, he said softly:

> I am [not] working out some old grudge, or motives of revenge or hatred. I do not hate Mr. Hiss. We were close friends, but we are caught in a tragedy of history. Mr. Hiss represents the concealed enemy against which we are all fighting, and I am fighting.

By the time HUAC finally adjourned its August 25th session at 8 P.M., Alger Hiss had been placed on the defensive. Three days later HUAC issued an interim report. It called Hiss's testimony "vague and evasive," Chambers's "forthright and emphatic." In the committee's opinion "the verifiable portions of Chambers's testimony have stood up strongly; the verifiable portions of Hiss's testimony have been badly shaken."

The next act in this "tragedy of history" took place on a national radio show, *Meet the Press*. There, Chambers charged that "Alger Hiss was a communist and may be now." Several weeks passed without Hiss responding. His supporters grew impatient. "Mr. Hiss has created a situation," complained the liberal Washington *Post,* "in which he is obliged to put up or shut up." Finally, on September 27, Hiss brought suit against Chambers for slander. By then the election campaign was in full swing. HUAC members (including Nixon) had returned to their various states. An exciting four-way battle for the presidency crowded "the Hiss-Chambers case" off the front pages.

Nixon himself faced no reelection problem. He had won his district's Democratic *and* Republican nominations, then possible under California's cross-filing system that allowed candidates to enter both primaries. He did campaign for other Republicans, however, regaling crowds with a dramatic account of the Hiss investigation.

In the presidential election Truman ran against Governor Thomas E. Dewey of New York, who avoided the anticommunist issue because he believed no case could be made against Truman as "soft" on communism. After a hard-fought campaign Truman won a startling reelection victory. The Democrats, moreover, regained control of Congress.

Prospects for continuing the Hiss-Chambers inquiry looked bleak, since Truman still considered it a political red herring directed against his administration. After the election, many in Washington thought the President would try to abolish HUAC. The Hiss case itself dropped from public attention and went into its legal phase—a slander suit.

Deeply depressed by Truman's victory, Chambers even contemplated suicide (an action he considered at other critical points in the case). He also fretted at the possibility that a Justice Department controlled by Democrats might indict him, not Hiss, for perjury. Pressed for written proof of his charges and under severe emotional strain, Chambers (according to his own account) took a mid-November trip to Brook-

A smiling Alger Hiss shakes hands with President Truman at a conference to establish the United Nations. Because Hiss was a New Deal liberal, his fall from grace carried the implication that the government was permeated with communists.

lyn. There he visited a nephew with whom, he claimed, he had left a package ten years earlier. The nephew drew from a disused dumbwaiter shaft the "proof" Chambers needed—a dusty envelope containing papers and microfilms that (Chambers later insisted) he had forgotten about until the libel suit jogged his memory.

The papers were dated from early 1937 through April 1938. If genuine, they indicated that Hiss had lied in claiming not to have seen "Crosley" or Chambers after mid-1936. Furthermore, the papers had apparently been typed on an old Woodstock typewriter that belonged to the Hisses until 1937 or 1938. (The exact date that the Hisses got rid of the machine would later become a major point at issue.) Chambers hurried back to his farm with this evidence and hid the microfilms. On November 17, he submitted some of the material to Hiss's attorneys at a

Under pressure to provide HUAC with all the evidence against Hiss in his possession, Chambers led two HUAC investigators to the pumpkin patch on his farm (an arrow identifies the patch) and retrieved the microfilms from a hollowed-out pumpkin where he had hidden them earlier that day.

pretrial hearing—sixty-five pages of copied State Department documents, four memos in Alger Hiss's handwriting, and the envelope in which they had been hidden for a decade.

Chambers now claimed that he had tried until then to "shield" Alger and Priscilla Hiss from exposure as Soviet spies. But because of the pressures imposed by Hiss's libel suit, he had to reveal "that Alger Hiss had also committed espionage." Chambers then testified to Hiss's attorneys about a new claim. He alleged that he was a courier for Hiss while the latter stole secret State Department documents. Some of these Mrs. Hiss had retyped. The *Time* editor now asserted that he had actually left the party in April 1938 rather than in 1937, since some of the stolen documents dated from the later period. Hiss vigorously denied this new charge. His lawyers grilled both Chambers and his wife about the numerous contradictions between his previous and his new testimony.

The typed documents were explosive evidence. The Hiss and Chambers lawyers immediately turned them over to Alex Campbell, head of the Justice Department's Criminal Division. Campbell warned both parties to the slander suit not to discuss the envelope's contents (neither Campbell nor Hiss then knew of the microfilms) until the material had been investigated. But then a story in the pro-Hiss Washington

Post indicating that the Justice Department might drop its investigation of Hiss spurred Nixon into action. Before leaving for a Caribbean vacation, Nixon signed a subpoena ordering Chambers to provide HUAC with any further evidence he had relating to his charges against Hiss.

On December 2 HUAC staff members served the subpoena. A few days earlier, because of rumors that Hiss investigators were prowling around his farm, Chambers had taken the microfilms from his bedroom and hidden them in his pumpkin patch. Now he went to the hollowed-out pumpkin, removed the microfilms, and handed them to the HUAC representatives. "I think this is what you are looking for," he said. Within hours the press began headlining Chambers's mysterious "pumpkin papers" (actually not papers but microfilms). That same day Hiss confirmed that Chambers had turned over the typed stolen documents on November 17.

The Justice Department finally swung into action. Both Chambers and Hiss were called several times, beginning on December 6, to testify before a New York federal grand jury. After a hurried and well-publicized return from his Caribbean vacation, Nixon led HUAC in a new series of hearings. At one of these new sessions Assistant Secretary of State John Peurifoy (in charge of security matters) testified. He declared that the Soviet Union or any other foreign country possessing these microfilmed documents would have been able to break all the secret State Department codes then in use.

Clearly, the Republican-controlled HUAC, which had no legal authority to put Hiss on trial, was competing with the Democratic-controlled Justice Department for jurisdiction in what was now a criminal case. Nixon frankly stated that his committee "did not trust the Justice Department to prosecute the case with the vigor it deserved." On December 9 Truman again labeled the case a red herring. On December 10 Chambers resigned from *Time*.

On December 13 the FBI produced for the grand jury several old letters typed by Priscilla Hiss on the same machine that had typed the State Department documents. That day, Alger Hiss left the Carnegie Endowment on a three-month paid leave of absence. He never returned. The New York grand jury indicted Hiss on two counts of perjury on December 15. The first was for claiming he had not stolen State Department records and given them to Chambers. The second was for swearing he had not seen Chambers after January 1, 1937. Only the statute of limitations and the absence of witnesses who could back up the charge kept the grand jury from charging Hiss with espionage.

The former State Department official underwent two trials. The first ended on July 8, 1949, with a deadlocked jury that had voted 8 to 4 to convict Hiss. The prosecutor at both trials, Thomas Murphy, presented several types of evidence to prove the government's perjury charges. These included evidence that the two men knew one another more intimately (after 1936) than Hiss admitted, that Hiss had been a communist, and that Hiss had stolen the State Department documents. The weakest link in the government's case concerned Hiss's alleged communism. Only one witness, an ex-communist named Hede Massing, confirmed Chambers's claim that Hiss had been a party member. Her testimony was challenged, however, by a defense witness who swore that Mrs. Massing had been confused about the question of Hiss's involvement when discussing it at a party.

At both trials Chambers repeated the story he first told to Hiss's attorneys in November 1948 during pretrial hearings involving the libel suit. According to this story, Hiss had been recruited for espionage by Chambers's communist superior during the fall of 1936. Chambers said he served as Hiss's courier until April 1938. Then he broke from the party. (He previously testified to leaving the party months earlier.) At this point he turned the final batch of stolen documents over to his nephew in Brooklyn for safekeeping.

The microfilms and retyped State Department messages were at the heart of the case against Hiss. Prosecutor Murphy called them "immutable" witnesses, therefore presumably reliable ones. At neither trial did Hiss's attorneys challenge the testimony of an FBI expert who testified that a comparison of typing on the documents with letters written by Mrs. Hiss on the same machine established her as the typist. Nor did they challenge the argument that the documents had been typed on a Woodstock machine belonging to Hiss. Hiss did claim he had given the machine away sometime before the material was typed. But this claim was never proved conclusively in court, one way or the other. (Moreover, three defense experts confirmed that the stolen documents had been typed on the Hiss Woodstock.)

The jury at the second trial convicted Hiss of perjury on both counts. After that, Hiss's lawyers began arguing that the typewriter itself was a false piece of evidence constructed by either Chambers or the FBI. They also argued that the typed documents had been prepared only to implicate Hiss. (This argument, of course, did not affect the microfilmed documents or the handwritten Hiss memos.) Since the defense had actually located the typewriter in question prior to the first trial, Hiss's supporters began arguing that the FBI had somehow gained possession of the machine earlier, then "planted" it on the defense. This remains unproven even today, though those who argue that Alger Hiss was innocent tend to assume some degree of FBI involvement. The FBI files on the case, recently opened to researchers, failed to bear out this charge. They show that the FBI conducted a widespread, but unsuccessful, hunt for the Woodstock and that it was seriously embarrassed when the defense turned up the machine.

At the Hiss trials themselves, the defense paraded a distinguished group of Americans before the jury to testify to Hiss's outstanding career and good character. At the same time, they tried to throw doubt on Chambers's reliability. They placed a psychiatrist on the stand who labeled Chambers "a psychopathic personality" with irrational hostilities.

Richard Nixon and chief investigator Robert Stripling are shown examining microfilms of secret State Department documents, the most damaging evidence against Hiss.

Prosecutor Murphy ridiculed these defense efforts at both trials. He pointed repeatedly to the evidence that Hiss's lawyers could never adequately explain—the stolen government documents. The twelve jurors at the second trial, overlooking Chambers's minor inconsistencies, all believed Murphy. On January 21, 1950, they found Hiss guilty. Later appeals to overturn the verdict were rejected, and Hiss served forty-four months in prison. He emerged in November 1954, still proclaiming his innocence.

Hiss, now a convicted perjurer, did not return to the Carnegie Endowment, of course. He has had a series of obscure and ill-paying business jobs. He has written his version of the episode and worked continuously to revive public interest in the case. (The Watergate crisis revived attention in the episode because of its link to Richard Nixon.)

A withdrawn and beaten Alger Hiss sits on a New York subway trying to ignore headlines telling of his indictment the day before on perjury charges. He was eventually convicted.

Chambers returned to his Maryland farm, did special assignments as a journalist, and wrote his memoirs. In 1961 he died from a heart attack.

Nixon won a Senate seat in 1950, largely because of his efforts in the Hiss case. He went on to become Vice President in 1953. The House Committee on Un-American Activities temporarily regained its public prestige as a result of Hiss's conviction. Truman abandoned his effort to abolish it.

Less than three weeks after Hiss's conviction, a then obscure Wisconsin senator announced: "I have here in my hand a list of 205 known to be members of the Communist party and who, nevertheless are still working and shaping the policy of the State Department." With Joseph R. McCarthy's speech a new era of anticommunist politics in the United States acquired its leader—and its name.

46
AFFLUENCE AND ANTICOMMUNISM

A.W.

The depression ended — with a bang, not a whimper — when Japan attacked Pearl Harbor. The war years changed the lives of the people who were later to become key figures in the Hiss case very little. Alger Hiss remained a top official of the State Department, while Whittaker Chambers rose in importance on *Time* magazine. But Richard Nixon saw his life altered dramatically. Although reared as a Quaker, Nixon yearned for some role in the war effort. He first joined a new government agency, the Office of Price Administration (OPA), created to regulate wartime price levels. Then the young lawyer joined the navy and served on various Pacific islands, handling duties as a supply officer.

Nixon returned to a restless year of private practice in California before winning his first race for Congress in 1946. The war had clearly opened up significant career possibilities for Nixon, as it did for millions of his contemporaries. A nation still climbing uncertainly out of the depression in 1941 had regained, by war's end, most of its pre-1930 affluence and self-confidence.

THE WORLD WAR II HOME FRONT

Almost 4 million Americans were still unemployed on the eve of Pearl Harbor. Other millions still labored at government-sponsored jobs for such agencies as the WPA. Some 40 percent of America's families lived below the $1,500 annual minimum income needed for a family of four. (This amounted to only $30 a week to cover food, housing, clothing, and everything else!) Over 7½ million workers earned salaries below the legal minimum wage of 40 cents an hour.

Still, there were many signs of change by 1941. The economy, thanks largely to $8 billion spent on defense production, was now strong, almost booming. Of the country's 134 million people, one-third held civilian jobs while one-tenth worked on defense contracts at top wages. Farm prices had reached a new high in 1940, as had average hourly wages in the two dozen major defense-oriented industries.

Moreover, on the eve of war, most Americans supported the pro-Allied policies of the Roosevelt administration. But they did not expect a war to improve their condition much. Twelve years of depression had left the country somewhat doubtful of future prospects and skeptical of idealistic visions.

Bolstering Morale The government went to great lengths to counteract pessimism and ensure the cooperative involvement of most Americans in the war effort. The Office of Civilian Defense (OCD) sponsored various programs to stimulate patriotism. These included "town meetings" throughout the country. Their basic objective was "that of awakening all the elements of the community to their responsibilities for total participation for victory." Patriotic sentiments were also aroused by stage, screen, and radio productions, all of which tried to bolster national morale, particularly in the first year, when news from the fronts was often grim.

Usually such entertainment aimed at stirring up hatred toward the enemy, Germans and Japanese. Seldom did it assert any positive American war goals. Movie heroes such as John Wayne and radio idols like Jack Armstrong ("the all-American boy") battled tirelessly against Nazi saboteurs and Japan's "fanatical yellow hordes." American advertising encouraged sales of government war bonds or warned defense workers and soldiers to beware of possible spies in their midst. ("Loose lips sink ships!") Such efforts were remarkably successful in boosting home-front efforts.

Politically, the job of defending the country against attack had turned bipartisan even before the war began. A number of leading Republicans accepted Roosevelt's invitation in 1940 to help meet the impending emergency.

Mobilizing the Economy Conversion to military preparedness had preceded Pearl Harbor. Total mobilization of both the American people and their economy, however, advanced swiftly after December 1941. An army of 1,600,000 existed then. By war's end the number of troops who had served or were serving in the army, navy, marines, air corps (then still part of the army), and coast guard exceeded 15 million—including 200,000 women.

The home front resembled one vast factory. A few statistics tell much of the story. Many Americans felt that Roosevelt was being unrealistic when in 1942 he called for an output of 60,000 planes, 45,000 tanks, and 8 million tons of shipping. Yet in 1944 the nation's factory workers—keeping plants open 24 hours daily on continuous shifts—produced over 96,000 planes. By 1945 the country's naval yards had turned out over 55 million tons of merchant shipping and 71,000 warships. Federal purchases grew from $6 billion in 1940 to $89 billion by 1944. During the first six months of the war alone, the government placed over $100 billion worth of war contracts with private industry.

Total federal spending during the three and a half years of war amounted to over $320 billion, an amount twice as large as the total of all previous spending from 1789 to 1941! The government financed this vast increase through higher taxes on both corporations and individuals. Even after taxes, though, corporate profits doubled between

Significant numbers of women belonged to the labor force that produced the winning margin in World War II, a continuous flow of planes from American factories.

1939 and 1944 (reaching $10 billion that year). War production clearly finished the job that the New Deal had begun of ending the country's economic depression. Much of the government's revenues came from taxes or public borrowing through war bonds. A still higher percentage came from running huge budget deficits throughout the war. The American national debt grew to $247 billion by 1945, nearly six times that of 1941.

Meanwhile, prosperity returned to the United States and unemployment vanished. Many women took full-time factory jobs to meet the shortage of labor created by the armed forces' need for men. Public confidence in the business community increased, replacing the widespread hostility apparent during the depression decade.

Rationing and Inflation   Full employment during the war gave millions of Americans bigger bank accounts. It put more money in their pockets, though they had less to spend it on. "Disposable income" (income after taxes) increased from $67 billion in 1939 to $140 billion by 1945. Consumer spending alone rose from $62 billion in 1939 to $106 billion by 1945. Wartime rationing and shortages of consumer goods, as well as higher wages and profits, led to higher inflationary prices for those goods and services that were available.

The government tried to control inflation and regulate prices—which rose an average of 2 percent monthly during the war—by establishing official wage and price levels. It set ceilings on legal prices through OPA. Richard Nixon remembered his experiences in this agency as a time when he "became more conservative [and] greatly disillusioned about bureaucracy." Yet OPA did succeed in holding down runaway inflation throughout the war years, despite an enormous increase in the disposable income of most Americans.

On the nation's farms, conditions improved at this time, too. Farm income doubled during the war because of the insatiable demand for agricultural products by the armed forces and civilians alike. Despite a decline in the number of farm laborers, increased mechanization helped double farm output during the war years, 1941 to 1945. Legislation by powerful farm-bloc Democrats

brought farmers' incomes to an all-time high.

Average weekly earnings among industrial workers also increased by 100 percent during the war years. Both the AFL and the CIO made "no-strike" pledges. But the number of strikes increased as prices and profits continued rising at a level greater than wage increases. Union membership increased from 10 to 15 million. The demand for factory workers led to a reduction of total unemployment from 5.6 percent of the work force in 1941 to 1 percent by war's end. More important, the war guaranteed the future of industrial unionism, which had grown with New Deal encouragement during the depression.

The wartime domestic economy lay in the hands of a triple alliance of big government, big business, and big labor. The three differed on specific policies. But each accepted the need for negotiated settlements with the other two. Wartime cooperation among union leaders, government officials, and corporation heads—all eager to maximize production for the war effort—shaped a new industrial state in America.

The Atomic Bomb   The period's single most significant scientific and military achievement, which would notably affect postwar American policy, was the development of the atomic bomb. Wartime scientific research was placed in the hands of an Office of Scientific Research and Development (OSRD), headed by Vannevar Bush and James Conant. The United States benefited greatly from the work of refugee scientists, many of them Jews who had fled Nazi Germany or fascist Italy. Albert Einstein, Leo Szilard, and Enrico Fermi led this intellectual migration. It affected not only science but many other aspects of American life and culture.

At a cost of billions, a massively organized project was undertaken to develop an atomic bomb before the Germans, who were working on a similar project. The secret program, known as the Manhattan Project, involved scientists, technicians, and industrial workers. It included design laboratories at Columbia University, the University of Chicago, the University of California at Berkeley, and—most important—at a central headquarters near Los Alamos, New Mexico. There, under the leadership of physicist J. Robert Oppenheimer, the first atomic device was assembled. It was detonated on July 16, 1945, at Alamorgordo, New Mexico.

The bombs dropped subsequently at Hiroshima and Nagasaki led directly to Japan's defeat in August 1945. By then the United States had sent over $350 billion to achieve victory in World War II—apart from the tremendous cost in American casualties.

The Relocation Policy   The country paid not only a high cost in human life but also a certain moral cost for its victory. For the Japanese attack on Pearl Harbor led to what the American Civil Liberties Union called "the worst single invasion of citizens' liberties" during the war. This was the confining in relocation centers of 112,000 Japanese Americans (more than half of them born in the United States). After Pearl Harbor, white residents of west coast states feared an internal threat from the Japanese Americans. They appealed to President Roosevelt to remove the entire community from the west coast.

Actually, there was no evidence whatsoever of sabotage. But officials such as California's attor-

Japanese American children are shown saluting the flag in their San Francisco elementary school two days before their relocation to internment camps.

ney general Earl Warren (later a great civil libertarian as chief justice of the United States) urged their evacuation to protect the region's civil defense. Bowing to these pressures, President Roosevelt signed an executive order in February 1942 authorizing the relocation of Japanese Americans to nine inland centers. Driven from their homes into what were virtually an American version of concentration camps, these loyal Japanese Americans needlessly suffered loss of their freedom, homes, land, and dignity. This unfair treatment did not deter over 33,000 Japanese Americans from enlisting and fighting bravely for the United States. Although the Supreme Court upheld the relocation policy, the government later paid compensation to the displaced for their property losses.

THE TRUMAN YEARS

Franklin D. Roosevelt, reelected for an unprecedented fourth term in 1944, died in April 1945. He left to Vice President Harry S. Truman the responsibility for governing the world's most militarily powerful and economically prosperous nation. On learning of Roosevelt's death, Truman quite understandably felt "as though the moon and all the stars and all the planets have fallen on me."

Harry Truman was an accidental President. Roosevelt had chosen him for the vice-presidential nomination in 1944 almost as an afterthought. Truman had little formal preparation for holding the office. While Vice President, for example, he was not even told about the atomic bomb. Less than four months after taking office, he had to make the fateful decision whether to drop it on Japan.

A Missouri farm boy who served in World War I, Truman entered politics as a member of the notorious Pendergast machine that ran Kansas City politics. Although personally honest, he served this corrupt political machine loyally. Truman rose through its ranks and was first elected to the Senate in 1934.

Several factors helped Truman obtain the vice presidency in 1944. Hard-working and extremely liberal (by Missouri's border-state standards), he had fought the Ku Klux Klan in his home state, battled loyally for New Deal programs, and served with distinction as chairman of a Senate committee that investigated national defense spending.

Many of Truman's most pressing concerns during his first months in office were vitally important decisions on war policy and postwar settlements (see Chapter 44). Of immediate concern to the new President, once Japan surrendered, was the fact that the men overseas wanted to come home quickly. ("No Boats, No Votes," was the gist of GI mail.) Congress and President Truman responded by rapidly demobilizing (releasing from duty) the great bulk of American armed forces. By mid-1946 an army and air force that had numbered over 8 million troops the previous year was reduced to less than 2 million. A navy of almost 4 million was cut back to less than 1 million. Total military strength fell to 1½ million by mid-1947, and Congress had ordered even this number reduced to under 1 million by January 1948.

Postwar Economic Policy Congress allowed the 1940 draft to expire in mid-1947. Cold War military planning focused more and more on the defense shield provided by America's monopoly of nuclear weapons. Furthermore, the discharged servicemen found that Congress had provided more generously for them than for the Bonus Marchers. Under the Servicemen's Readjustment Act (which most people called the GI Bill of Rights), more than $13.5 billion was spent on veterans over the next decade. This money went not only for college educations and vocational training but also for special unemployment insurance (for a year) to smooth the return to civilian life. Funds were spent as well to provide medical services at veterans' hospitals and rehabilitation programs for the wounded. Finally, low-interest loans were made available to veterans to start businesses and to buy or build homes. This was particularly helpful because of the housing shortage at war's end.

There was widespread fear among the public, and many economists too, that without war spending the country would suffer a major postwar recession. A Council of Economic Advisers, created by Truman's Maximum Employment Act, committed Washington for the first time to using the nation's resources to ensure "maximum employment, production, and purchasing power." By mid-1946 Congress had also ended most wartime price and wage controls, cut taxes over $6 billion, and begun to tackle the massive problems of reconversion to a peacetime economy. These efforts were hindered by a wave of strikes and runaway inflation.

Auto workers struck for 113 days beginning in November 1945, and miners for a shorter period in mid-1946. Truman's decision to have the soft coal mines run by the government (control that continued until June 1947) lost him much support from businessmen. A railroad strike was settled the same month the mines were seized (May 1946) only when Truman threatened to take over the railroads, too. More strikes occurred in 1946 than in any other single year in American history. Over 4,750,000 workers were involved.

Truman faced a hostile congressional coalition of Republicans and antiadministration Southern Democrats in every area of his domestic program after Republicans won control of both Houses in the 1946 congressional election. This coalition responded to the strikes and general unrest among American unions with a tough law (passed over Truman's veto) regulating the labor movement. The Taft-Hartley Act of 1947 limited the President to seeking an eighty-day injunction to stop any strike that endangered "national health or safety" (rather than taking an extreme step like running an industry under government supervision). The new law also (1) required unions to accept a sixty-day "cooling-off" period before striking, (2) outlawed the closed shop, (3) restricted union involvement in political campaigns, and (4) required that union officials (but not company officers) take an oath that they were not communists.

Congress also passed the Twenty-second Amendment to the Constitution limiting future Presidents (although not Truman) to two full terms. This was a direct slap at FDR's four-term success. In various ways the Eightieth Congress prevented Truman from getting his own legislative program.

The Fair Deal   The President called his program the Fair Deal. He viewed it essentially as an effort to continue the social welfare policies of Roosevelt's New Deal. Thus, soon after he took office, Truman had proposed to Congress legislation that would guarantee full employment, vastly expand public housing, and raise farm price supports. Other proposals were to continue a permanent Fair Employment Practices Committee (FEPC) to block discrimination against blacks and other minorities, nationalize atomic energy, and increase the minimum wage. A few parts of the program passed quickly. Congress approved a civilian Atomic Energy Commission in mid-1946 that took control of peaceful uses of atomic energy. Most of the program, however, was blocked by the same Republican–Southern Democratic coalition that opposed Truman on so many issues.

Truman went on the offensive in 1948. He proposed not only the enactment of his entire Fair Deal program but also a set of civil rights proposals to guarantee first-class citizenship for black Americans. These proposals included a perma-nent FEPC, measures against lynching and the poll tax, plus other laws that would ensure blacks full federal protection of their civil and political rights. After his renomination by a divided Democratic convention in 1948, Truman called Congress into special session to dramatize its opposition to his programs. He requested repeal of the Taft-Hartley Act and passage of civil rights, housing, health, and Social Security programs. Congress rejected it all.

This rejection allowed Truman to conduct his successful "whistle-stop" campaign (see Chapter 45) against what he called the "do-nothing Eightieth Congress." The public liked Truman's new stance as an aggressive, "give-em-hell" fighter. The Man from Independence scored the most smashing upset in American presidential history. The Democrats also recaptured both houses of Congress.

Still dominated in large measure by the Republican–Southern Democratic coalition, the new Eighty-first Congress blocked Truman's farm program and his request for a permanent FEPC.

The culmination of Harry Truman's 1948 whistle-stop campaign was this triumphant pose before a crowd at St. Louis's Union Station. He called the headline "one for the books."

But it did pass a major low-income housing and urban-renewal program, raised the minimum wage, abolished segregation in the armed forces, and enlarged existing conservation programs. All in all, it enacted more liberal legislation than any Congress since that of 1937–1938.

The onset of the Korean War in June 1950, however, diverted the primary attention of Congress and the administration from home-front reforms to foreign policy. Little important domestic legislation passed in Truman's final two years in office. His energy between 1950 and 1952 was spent primarily fighting the Korean War and improving American security against communism abroad. Ironically, he also had to defend his administration against allegations of "softness" toward communism at home.

McCARTHYISM: "THE SECOND RED SCARE"

Truman reacted angrily whenever Republicans charged that his and Roosevelt's administration had "sold out" Eastern Europe and China to communist control. To Republican cries of "Twenty Years of Treason," Truman replied that he had welded the free nations of Western Europe into military and political alliances against the Soviet Union's expansionism. The Truman Doctrine, the Marshall Plan, and NATO had largely restored European stability. China had been lost—not for lack of American help—but through Chiang Kai-shek's political and military weakness.

Elsewhere, American troops (along with UN forces) defended South Korea against communist attack. Further, the Seventh Fleet prevented communist invasion of the Chinese Nationalists' last stronghold, the island of Taiwan. To achieve this global strategy of containment, the Truman administration had increased defense expenditures from $13 billion in 1949 to $22.5 billion the next year and $44 billion by 1951. Military expenses absorbed two-thirds of the federal budget in 1952, up from only one-third in 1950. In the process of increasing defense spending so swiftly and enormously, the country's gross national product rose from $264 billion in 1950 to $339 billion by 1952. A continued high level of economic prosperity was almost assured.

None of these facts, however, silenced Republican critics. They continued to attack Truman and Secretary of State Dean Acheson. Nor were Republican anticommunist investigators like those on HUAC happy with Truman's efforts to rid the federal government of suspected subversives. The President, despite assurances from the FBI that the problem was under adequate control, had issued an executive order in May 1947 setting up a Loyalty Review Board. Its purpose was to check every federal employee and dismiss any found questionable "on reasonable grounds for belief in disloyalty." Over the next five years, such loyalty boards investigated over 6½ million government employees and their families. Of this number only 490 were dismissed on loyalty grounds. The boards uncovered no cases of espionage, but the investigations wrecked the careers of many loyal government officials accused without proof.

Prosecution of Leading Communists Under mounting pressure from Congress after Alger Hiss's indictment, Truman prosecuted the eleven leaders of the American Communist party under the 1940 Smith Act. They were indicted for organizing a group advocating the overthrow of the American government by force. The Communist party leaders were convicted in 1949, and other prosecutions of communists began, despite the fact that prosecutors never claimed they had uncovered an *actual* conspiracy to overthrow the government. The Supreme Court upheld the convictions in 1951. Through such actions Truman contributed to a growing climate of American fear over communism.

No single episode did more to spread this Red scare than the indictment and eventual conviction of Alger Hiss. The fact that Dean Acheson and other high administration officials testified on behalf of Hiss lent a touch of credibility to charges that the Democrats, under Roosevelt and Truman, were soft on left-wingers.

At this point Senator Joseph McCarthy began a series of speeches. It mattered little that McCarthy's figures for "known communists" in

To Senator Joseph McCarthy communism was a nationwide threat. He accused the Democrats of communist sympathies and also charged that the Protestant clergy had been infiltrated.

the State Department varied from speech to speech. Britain had just arrested communist Klaus Fuchs for atomic espionage; the new communist government had full control of the Chinese mainland; and Americans were jittery over possible new Russian moves against Berlin. Accordingly, many people were prepared to believe that something dire was about to befall the United States. McCarthy himself never actually located a single "known communist."

McCarthy's charges offended several Republicans in Congress, including Senators Margaret Chase Smith of Maine and Ralph Flanders of Vermont, who both denounced him publicly. Yet he was extremely useful to his party, despite his wild charges of disloyalty and communist activity in government. A significant number of Americans approved of McCarthy's relentless attacks. McCarthy's method, like that of most successful demagogues, was simple. He used "the multiple untruth," statements so complex and many-sided that they were extremely difficult to deny intelligently.

Flow of Political Melodrama Among those McCarthy tried to smear were George Marshall (author of the Marshall Plan), Philip Jessup (later chief UN delegate under President Nixon), Secretary of State Dean Acheson, and even President Truman himself. In short, McCarthy turned this tactic of "red-baiting" against the Democrats. For a time, he had remarkable success. Little about his methods was new. He used the tactics of HUAC and even borrowed Nixon's files on the subject. From these he wrung a constant flow of political melodrama out of the noisy pursuit of "secret conspirators" and (occasionally) admitted communists. There were, after all, some American communists, even a few who had reached middle-level posts in the Roosevelt years.

The onset of the Korean War in June 1950 gave McCarthy and other Republican opponents of Truman additional ammunition. If communists were killing our soldiers in Korea, many Americans reasoned, why give possible reds the benefit of any doubt in this country? Loyalty oaths and security investigations soon involved millions of people in industries and labor unions, public schools and universities, as well as in government jobs at every level.

There is much irony in the fact that Truman spent his last two years in office using American and UN forces against communist aggression in Korea while trying to prove that he was not a dupe or agent of communism at home. Truman's attorney general carried on a vigorous prosecution of alleged communist agents. In April 1951 Julius and Ethel Rosenberg were convicted of having directed a spy ring that transmitted to the Russians diagrams and other data on the firing mechanism and internal structure of the atomic bomb. According to the Rosenbergs' accusers, this information had speeded up by years completion of the Soviet atomic bomb, first exploded in 1949. The Rosenbergs received the death sentence, while their accomplices were sentenced to long prison terms.

Such episodes persuaded Congress that tighter laws were needed to protect the country against domestic communists. So it passed the McCarran Internal Security Act in 1950. This law established a Subversive Activities Control Board to keep track of communist activities in America. The act made membership in the Communist party illegal and also ordered communist organizations to register with the attorney general. Other provisions barred former members of totalitarian groups from the United States and forbade communists to hold federal office or receive passports. Many of these provisions have since been declared unconstitutional by the Supreme Court. But the act passed by a two-thirds majority over Truman's veto, which showed how politically potent the anticommunist issue had become.

"Korea, Communism, and Corruption" The Democratic administration was very unpopular by 1952. Many voters accepted McCarthy's reckless charges against Truman and his associates, despite the Democrats' strong commitment to Cold War foreign policies. Truman's decision to seize the steel industry to prevent a nationwide strike in April 1952 (declared unconstitutional by the courts two months later) reminded Americans of his earlier troubles with labor and management. Several scandals involving big businessmen and some of Truman's associates had also come to light. So Republicans raised the issue of widespread government corruption. The Korean War dragged on, with American casualties mounting in a war that was increasingly unpopular.

The issues of "Korea, communism, and corruption" that Republicans stressed in 1952 would probably have brought about the election of any candidate after twenty years of Democratic rule. Still, the out-of-power party took no chances. At their 1952 convention the Republicans rejected the candidacy of the able conservative Senator Robert A. Taft of Ohio because they were not sure he could win. They nominated General Dwight David Eisenhower—World War II hero, university president, commander of American NATO forces, and easily the most popular public figure in the country. The party then reaffirmed its concern for the anticommunist issue by nominating Richard Nixon as Vice President.

The Democrats drafted Governor Adlai Stevenson of Illinois, a man who, though able, was assailed by Republicans as an "egghead" because of the intellectual quality of his campaigning. Stevenson's efforts to defend Democratic achievements and promise a continuation of Fair Deal reforms fell flat. Many voters were tired after two decades of depression, reform, world war, and Cold War. The public voted to make its grandfatherly first citizen, Dwight Eisenhower, President by an overwhelming 33 to 27 million popular vote margin and a 442 to 89 electoral majority. After two decades in the political wilderness the Republican party returned to full national power, winning not only the White House but also Congress.

THE EISENHOWER YEARS

With Eisenhower's inauguration in 1953, control of the federal government returned essentially—

JONAS SALK

Polio is a disease of civilization. It strikes hardest where sanitation is highest. It is also a disease that most frequently strikes children. It can keep a victim bedridden for weeks in intense pain; but, much worse, it can cause severe, life-long paralysis or even death. Since 1894, when the first cases of polio appeared in the Green Mountains of Vermont, epidemics of the disease had been a common and dreaded occurrence. And nothing could be done to prevent them until in 1953 a young researcher, Dr. Jonas Salk, announced the development of polio vaccine.

Dr. Salk's discovery was not one of medicine's happy accidents but rather the result of years of intensive research. Salk himself is said to have worked sixteen hours a day, six days a week over a long period of time before succeeding. His background had prepared him for such a test of endurance. Born in New York City on October 28, 1914, the son of an immigrant garment worker, he put himself through school largely by part-time jobs and scholarships. He entered New York University Medical School in 1934. There he met Thomas Francis, Jr., who was conducting a study on methods of killing influenza virus. In 1943, the two men field-tested a vaccine effective against both influenza A and influenza B.

In 1947, Salk joined the University of Pittsburgh School of Medicine as head of the Virus Research Laboratory. The polio vaccine that Salk finally developed was made by growing a representative strain of each of the three types of virus in a broth made with monkey kidney. The viruses were then killed with formaldehyde, which rendered them incapable of causing the disease. However, they did not lose the power to stimulate the human body to produce antibodies. These antibodies would give a person at least limited immunity to polio.

Salk, his wife, and their three sons were among the first to receive his vaccine. Then in the fall of 1954 a massive twelve-state test, sponsored by the National Foundation for Infantile Paralysis, was held. Almost one million school children in the primary grades participated. Half the children received the vaccine; the other half did not. The results were conclusive: in April 1955 the vaccine was pronounced safe and effective in preventing polio.

By the summer of 1961, there was a reduction by approximately 96 percent in the amount of polio in the United States as a whole compared to the five-year period before the introduction of vaccination, even though only 50 percent of the population had been vaccinated. Contributing to the eradication of polio, an oral vaccine was being developed and tested by another American researcher, Albert Sabin. In 1959 Sabin's oral vaccine had been accepted for use by the Soviet Union and in August of 1961 it was approved for use in the United States. One year later manufacture started, and the oral polio vaccine was licensed for general distribution.

Salk's discovery catapulted this shy, retiring man to instant and unwanted fame. He became a public figure deluged with offers to lecture and even to make his life into a movie. He was awarded a congressional gold medal for "great achievement in the field of medicine," and the people of San Diego voted to donate a tract of land on a bluff overlooking the Pacific on which to build an institute in his honor. The research center was dedicated in 1963. Under Dr. Salk's direction, it is now a leading center of research in immunology and cellular and molecular biology.

for the first time since Herbert Hoover—to businessmen. The new President's cabinet officers were either corporation executives or closely allied to the business community. Eisenhower was determined to run a less active presidency than either Truman or Roosevelt and was suspicious of the federal bureaucracy and New Deal–Fair Deal social welfare programs. He set himself the task of keeping the nation calm.

Eisenhower interfered less often than Roosevelt or Truman with his various department heads. Instead, he allowed each to make his own decisions with minimal overall supervision. Frequently, for example, Secretary of State John Foster Dulles and not Eisenhower made essential foreign policy decisions. Similarly Treasury Secretary George Humphrey slashed departmental budgets throughout the government—except for the military. Here the Joint Chiefs of Staff got many of the programs they wanted, especially those proposed by the air force and navy. The chain of command under Eisenhower thus often resembled that of a loosely organized corporation.

The Republican party's right-wingers became a real problem for Eisenhower. McCarthy, by his actions as head of the Senate's Government Operations Committee, posed a serious threat to Eisenhower's ability to rule. He publicly led the strong opposition to Eisenhower's nomination of career diplomat Charles E. Bohlen as ambassador to Russia because Bohlen had been Roosevelt's interpreter at Yalta! (However, Bohlen was eventually confirmed by the Senate.)

McCarthy's Fall Until 1954 the administration tried to compromise with the senator. In that year, however, McCarthy opened an investigation of subversion in an army base at Fort Monmouth, New Jersey. This attack on the military and on Eisenhower's army secretary, Robert Stevens, for "coddling" communists proved to be the last straw. It forced a reluctant Eisenhower to take a public stand against McCarthy and his tactics.

Senate hearings considered McCarthy's charges against the army. They reviewed the army's counter charges that the senator had sought special favors for an aide, David Schine, drafted into the Army. The hearings were watched on television by over 20 million Americans. McCarthy proved an adept television performer. But even more adept was the Army's counsel, Joseph N. Welch. He baited McCarthy into losing his temper, thus widely exposing the browbeating tactics that McCarthy had used so effectively against unfriendly witnesses before his committee in the past. McCarthy's influence began to decline.

In December 1954 the Senate (supported by the Eisenhower administration) "condemned" Senator McCarthy for "conduct unbecoming a member." After this censure he lost his remaining political influence. He died in May 1957. But "McCarthyism" lingered on.

The reckless hunt for possible communist subversives in American society, without proof of guilt or adequate safeguards for defense, continued to be a problem during the 1950s. Many thousands of Americans lost their jobs, suffered ruined careers because of blacklisting in their professions, and went to jail or even into exile because of it. The list of victims is long. It includes industrial workers and labor union officials, as well as prominent editors, broadcasters, and others in the arts.

"Peace, Progress, and Prosperity" The Eisenhower years signified far more than simply the tail end of McCarthyism. Eisenhower avoided tampering with New Deal–Fair Deal programs, even presiding over some extensions for them. He created the Department of Health, Education, and Welfare, approved a measure that added 7 million people to the Social Security rolls, signed another that raised the minimum wage, and supported a housing act that greatly increased urban-renewal projects. The decline of such public facilities as schools, hospitals, and public transport systems also received little attention in the 1950s.

Eisenhower avoided the type of scandal that had rocked Truman's second administration. His relations with the Democratic leaders who ran Congress were generally amicable, unlike Truman's with congressional Republicans. Eisenhower regularly consulted House Majority Leader Sam Rayburn and Senate Majority Leader Lyndon Johnson, the two Texans who dominated Congress during the 1950s.

Adlai Stevenson, twice the Democratic nominee for President, was an eloquent and witty campaigner. But Eisenhower's image as a war hero and elder statesman proved unbeatable.

When the President decided to run for reelection in 1956, despite a serious heart attack in 1955, there were no issues that the Democrats could exploit. Eisenhower had negotiated peace in Korea, run a basically budget-conscious and honest administration, and toned down McCarthyism. Also, he had flown to Geneva in 1955 for a summit meeting on peaceful coexistence with Russia's post-Stalin leaders (the first such meeting since Potsdam). He kept the country out of major foreign involvements in the Indochina crisis of 1954 and the Hungarian and Suez crises of 1956. Not surprisingly, Eisenhower again whipped Adlai Stevenson, winning a landslide 58 percent of the popular vote.

There seemed little public interest during the 1950s in rocking a very prosperous national boat. Eisenhower provided an image of safe, solid leadership that appealed even to many Democrats.

Farm income in the 1950s netted more for farmers than even the thriving war years. Moreover, the much larger pie had to be divided among a smaller farm population. Median family income rose from $4,293 in 1950 to $5,904 in 1960. By 1956 white-collar workers outnumbered those in blue-collar jobs. Even for those in the latter group (particularly those unionized) real spendable income increased by 60 percent between 1940 and 1960. Much of this prosperity came in new industries—dealing with military weapons systems and space technology. These greatly expanded after the Russians sent the world's first missile, Sputnik I, into space in 1957. Suddenly, Americans found they had a lot of catching up to do if they were to equal the Russians in scientific pursuits. Many people realized that education had been lacking, and government funds were quickly demanded to inject the schools and universities with new monies for the expansion and updating of their facilities.

While *Brown* v. *Board of Education of Topeka* (1954) outlawed segregated education, the Supreme Court's Implementation Ruling of 1955, which called for "all deliberate speed" in school desegregation, actually paved the way for dilatory tactics, if not resistance. In some cases, federal intervention was eventually necessary to insure black children's rights to integrated education.

UNSETTLED PROBLEMS

Yet various social and economic problems of enormous scope remained during the Eisenhower era. These would haunt Americans in the 1960s. For one thing, the affluent society remained a myth in 1960 for the 42 million people (almost a third of America's families) with annual family income levels of less than $4,000. The "invisible poor," as Michael Harrington described them, were not "invisible" by their own choice. They were not so much unseen as ignored by those who had made dramatic economic gains.

"Making it" often involved drawing firm barriers between oneself and those left behind. Groups heavily represented among the poor were the elderly, unskilled or nonunion workers, migrant farm laborers, blacks, and Spanish Americans. The average black family income in 1960, for example, was $3,838 compared with $6,508 for white families.

The wartime FEPC had opened thousands of jobs in Northern industries to blacks. President Truman's 1950 executive order desegregated the armed forces and barred discrimination in federal employment. The next great civil rights advance for blacks came in 1954. The Supreme Court, in the famous case of *Brown* v. *Board of Education of Topeka, Kansas,* ruled unanimously that segregation in public school education was illegal.

The case, *Brown* v. *Topeka Board of Education,* came before the Court on December 9, 1952.

It continued for over a year. The decision the Court handed down on May 17, 1954, presents the question the justices faced: "Does segregation of children in public schools solely on the basis of race, even though the physical facilities and other 'tangible' factors may be equal, deprive children of the minority group of equal educational opportunities?"

The Court answered this question with an affirmative: "We conclude that in the field of public education the doctrine of 'separate but equal' has no place. Separate educational facilities are inherently unequal." Later, the Supreme Court instructed schools to move "with all deliberate speed" to desegregate their facilities.

Although 792 of 2,985 biracial school districts had been integrated by 1959, none were in the Deep South or Virginia. There, massive resistance from leading politicians and local white citizens councils raised the level of racial tension to dangerous heights. In 1956 a hundred Southern congressmen promised to overturn the *Brown* decision by "all lawful means." Then in 1957 at

Little Rock, Arkansas—with white parents threatening violence against court-ordered desegregation—Governor Orval Faubus called out the National Guard to bar nine black students from a high school. After a court order removed the guard, a riot broke out. Eisenhower, himself a moderate on the segregation issue, sent federal paratroopers to help escort the nine children into the school. Elsewhere, one Virginia county even closed its public schools to avoid integration. The University of Alabama, after a riot on the campus, expelled a black student admitted under Supreme Court order.

Meanwhile, blacks in Montgomery, Alabama, led by an eloquent young minister, the Reverend Martin Luther King, Jr., organized a boycott against segregation on local buses in December 1955. Segregation on interstate buses had been banned the previous month. King's "direct action" tactics spread to other Southern cities. Soon he and other Southern black ministers formed the Southern Christian Leadership Conference (SCLC) to fight discrimination and all forms of bigotry.

In February 1960 a student wing of the SCLC held the first sit-in at a Greensboro, North Carolina, lunch counter to protest segregation in public eating places. Two mild civil rights acts in 1957 and 1960 somewhat strengthened federal authority against efforts to keep blacks from voting or exercising other rights. But as the sixties began, Americans knew that the major battles to secure full equality for blacks were still ahead.

Other critical problems faced the nation as Eisenhower's second term ended. He himself emphasized a major one in a January 17, 1961, farewell speech.

The conjunction of an immense military establishment and a permanent armaments industry of vast proportions is new in the American experience. The total influence—economic, political, even spiritual—is felt in every city, every state house, every office of the federal government. We must guard against the acquisition of unwarranted in-

In his inaugural address John Kennedy challenged a complacent citizenry with the words: "Ask not what your country can do for you; ask what you can do for your country."

fluence, whether sought or unsought, by the military-industrial complex. We must never let the weight of this combination endanger our liberties or democratic processes.

A fair warning, but Eisenhower himself had speeded the growth of the "military-industrial complex." Militarists and industrialists became more powerful during the ten years following. Still, the checks of the American system have kept them from getting complete control of the nation's political or economic structure.

Return of the Democrats America faced still other unsolved problems, but it entered the 1960s in a confident mood, sure of its purposes and powers. Though this confidence would not long remain, both 1960 presidential candidates reflected this basic assurance about the American future.

Richard Nixon, while defending the Eisenhower record, promised progressive and dynamic new policies. John Kennedy urged Democrats to rally behind him for vigorous leadership. Little separated the two candidates in terms of issues, domestic or foreign, except that Kennedy attacked a presumed decline of American prestige abroad under Eisenhower and an alleged missile gap that threatened to make the Soviet Union dominant.

Kennedy benefited from a united party. His Texas Protestant running mate, Lyndon Johnson, helped keep much of the South Democratic for the Catholic Kennedy. He also profited from television debates with Nixon, which helped undercut the Republican charge of inexperience and youth. (Kennedy was forty-three, the youngest man ever elected President.) Most of all, his election resulted from the strong support he received among Catholics and blacks—who gave him over 70 percent of their votes. Nixon received only mild backing from Eisenhower. Nixon's earlier career as a "red hunter" haunted him and hurt him severely among Democratic and independent voters in 1960. Still, Kennedy won by only a tiny popular margin—113,000 votes out of 68,800,000 cast.

In his inaugural address Kennedy promised to lead the United States toward a New Frontier headed by young people: "The torch has been passed to a new generation of Americans, born in this century, tempered by war, [and] disciplined by a hard and bitter peace." The sense of promise and hope was strong among Americans that day, as the youthful new Chief Executive issued "a call to bear the burden of a long twilight struggle, year in and year out against the common enemies of man: tyranny, poverty, disease, and war itself." Few Americans doubted in 1961 that the country felt itself adequate to these great tasks.

SUGGESTED READINGS— CHAPTERS 45-46

Alger Hiss

Alistair Cooke, *A Generation on Trial: U.S.A. v. Alger Hiss* (1950); Meyer A. Zeligs, *Friendship and Fratricide: An Analysis of Whittaker Chambers and Alger Hiss* (1967); Allen Weinstein, *Perjury: The Hiss-Chambers Case* (1978).

The Truman Administration

William C. Berman, *The Politics of Civil Rights in the Truman Administration* (1970); Barton J.

Bernstein (ed.), *Politics and Policies of the Truman Administration* (1970); Richard M. Freeland, *The Truman Doctrine and the Origins of McCarthyism* (1972); Alonzo L. Hamby, *Beyond the New Deal: Harry S. Truman and American Liberalism* (1970); Earl Latham, *The Communist Controversy in Washington* (1966); Merle Miller, *Plain Speaking: An Oral Biography of Harry S. Truman* (1974); Cabell Phillips, *The Truman Presidency* (1966); Allen Yarnell, *Democrats and Progressives* (1974).

The Eisenhower Administration

Charles C. Alexander, *Holding the Line: The Eisenhower Era, 1952–1961* (1974); Richard Dalfiume, *Desegregation of the United States Armed Forces* (1969); Peter Lyon, *Eisenhower: Portrait of a Hero* (1974); Herbert S. Parmet, *Eisenhower and the American Crusades* (1975); James T. Patterson, *Mr. Republican* (1972); John B. Martin, *Adlai Stevenson of Illinois* (1976).

Communism and Anticommunism

William F. Buckley and L. Brent Bozell, *McCarthy and His Enemies* (1954); Richard Fried, *Men Against McCarthy* (1976); Walter Goodman, *The Committee* (1968); Robert Griffith, *The Politics of Fear* (1970); Robert Griffith and Athan Theoharis, *The Spectre* (1974); Alan D. Harper, *The Politics of Loyalty: The White House and the Communist Issue, 1946–1952* (1969); Louis Nizer, *The Implosion Conspiracy* (1975); Gary W. Reichard, *The Reaffirmation of Republicanism* (1975); Michael Paul Rogin, *McCarthy and the Intellectuals* (1967); Karl M. Schmidt, *Henry A. Wallace: Quixotic Crusader, 1948* (1960); Walter and Miriam Schneir, *Invitation to an Inquest* (1965); David A. Shannon, *The Decline of American Communism* (1959); Athan Theoharis, *Seeds of Repression* (1971).

Affluence

John K. Galbraith, *The Affluent Society* (1958); David M. Potter, *People of Plenty* (1954); Herbert Stein, *The Fiscal Revolution in America* (1969); Harold G. Vatter, *The United States Economy in the 1950's* (1963).

General Overview

Jacobus Broek, et al., *Prejudice, War and the Constitution* (1954); John M. Blum, *V Was for Victory: Politics and American Culture During World War II* (1976); Eric F. Goldman, *The Crucial Decade and After: America 1945–1960* (1960); Robert A. Garson, *The Democratic Party and the Politics of Sectionalism, 1941–1948* (1974); Douglas Miller and Marion Nowak, *The Fifties: The Way We Really Were* (1977); Richard Polenberg, *War and Society: The United States 1941–1945* (1972).

UNIT EIGHT

CONTEMPORARY AMERICA

The burst of optimism about the American future that marked the early 1960s barely survived the assassination of John Fitzgerald Kennedy in 1963. By mid-decade, the United States had been shaken by a series of domestic upheavals ranging from the Black Power protests to campus demonstrations and the beginnings of antiwar agitation. As the United States became more deeply involved in the Vietnamese War under Presidents Johnson and Nixon, national self-confidence disappeared—a casualty of bitter social unrest at home and battlefield stalemate abroad.

Older allies and enemies began to challenge their earlier acceptance of American dominance in the world, while a confused and divided American people reassessed their national values, grievances, problems, weaknesses, and strengths. The three pairs of chapters in Unit Eight describe milestones in the United States' fateful encounter with the vicissitudes of historical tragedy and loss during the past generation.

Chapter 47 portrays the 1962 drama of the Cuban missile crisis—the Soviet-American

confrontation that nearly unleashed World War III. The accompanying chapter, 48, charts the complex "decline of *Pax Americana*"—the erosion of the United States' domination of international affairs under the impact of the Vietnamese War and other problems. Martin Luther King's stirring leadership of the black struggle for equality in the U.S. and his violent death form the subject of Chapter 49, while Chapter 50 sketches out the contours of political stalemate and social crises in the 1960s. Finally, the Watergate ordeal—the gravest political and constitutional crisis in American life since the Civil War—emerges in Chapter 51, accompanied by an analysis of American politics and society in the mid-1970s in Chapter 52. All six chapters relate part of the overall story of the United States in what may prove to be the formative years of a new society: more sober and restrained in the exercise of its global influence, more committed and fair-minded than ever to correcting the inequities of its own socio-economic order, and more faithful than in some earlier epochs to its noble, if imperfect, heritage of freedom and justice.

47 THE CUBAN MISSILE CRISIS

A. W.

For a week in October 1962 the United States and the Soviet Union, the two nuclear giants, stood facing each other in combat readiness. With the relatively "primitive" military weaponry of that time, probably no more than half a billion people were in actual danger. The year before, the Department of Defense had estimated a total of 120 million American casualties should crisis deepen from confrontation into all-out war. A like number of Soviets would probably die, along with most of the populations of Europe and Canada. If the war spread to China, of course, the final toll would run incalculably higher.

The crisis of 1962 began with strange markings on photographs taken from a U-2 spy plane flying ten miles above the island of Cuba. No one disputed the CIA's interpretation of the pictures: on an island ninety miles from Florida, the Soviet Union was installing medium-range guided missiles, capable of carrying nuclear bombs to the United States.

The United States had had many problems with Cuba since 1959, when Fidel Castro led his rebels out of the mountains and toppled the existing American-supported Batista dictatorship. The U.S. government was wary of Castro; the CIA had noted the presence of many Cuban communists in his government. When he began nationalizing extensive American holdings on Cuba, Washington refused his requests for loans. Just before leaving office in January 1961, Eisenhower decided to break diplomatic relations with Havana. Meanwhile, Castro was steadily strengthening his ties with the Soviets.

On October 14, 1962, two United States Air Force pilots, flying specially equipped U-2 planes borrowed from the CIA, revealed how close those ties had become. When the U-2 photographs reached Washington, analysts from the Defense Intelligence Agency agreed that the Cuban sites closely resembled missile bases in Russia. The head of the

DIA sent two officers to show the pictures to his superior, Roswell Gilpatric, the second-ranking civilian at the Pentagon, who relayed the news on to the President's special assistant for national security affairs, McGeorge Bundy.

In his twenty-one months as President, John F. Kennedy had dealt often with "the Cuban question." Campaigning in 1960 as a dynamic alternative to the bland do-nothingism of the Eisenhower years, Kennedy charged that Republican policies had created a communist state in Cuba. Once in office, Kennedy discovered that the Eisenhower Administration had been fostering a CIA-sponsored invasion of Cuba by anti-Castro Cubans living in the United States. Kennedy agreed to back the plan, which suffered a humiliating defeat in April 1961, when Castro's troops routed the invaders at the Bay of Pigs on Cuba's south shore.

Early on the morning of Tuesday, October 16, 1962, Kennedy learned about the missile site photos. The President immediately called a meeting for 11:45 that morning, summoning a group that would soon become known as ExComm, short for Executive Committee. Summonses went to Vice President Lyndon Johnson, Secretary of State Dean Rusk, Secretary of Defense Robert McNamara, Bundy, Gilpatric, Taylor, and a few other close advisors, notably the President's brother, Attorney General Robert Kennedy. "The President did not specify the problem over the telephone," recalled Robert Kennedy. "He said only that we were facing great trouble."

The news stunned the nation's highest councillors. Despite evidence of great Soviet shipping activity to Cuba, they had never concluded that the Russians were putting missiles there. Unlike the United States, which had established missile bases in Turkey, Italy, and Britain, the Soviets had never before placed missiles outside their own borders. According to one explanation, they distrusted the Poles, the East Germans, and other satellite allies. Moreover, Khrushchev and his envoys had gone out of their way in recent months to assure the American government that no major moves would be taken by Moscow before the U.S. election in November. In light of the new evidence, it was clear they had been trying to buy time until the missiles became operational.

Every one of the dozen men assembled in the Cabinet Room that morning agreed that the missiles must be sent back to Russia with haste. A missile base in Cuba would greatly improve the Russians' nuclear capability and would subvert the U.S. warning system. It could threaten Latin America, vastly increasing the Soviets' prestige and diminishing U.S. power in the area. On the basis of his new strength, Khrushchev might demand American concessions in other parts of the world, such as the withdrawal of troops from West Berlin.

ExComm deliberated all day, moving briefly to the State Department in the afternoon and returning to the White House that evening. Rather than planning specific responses, they spent the first day discussing the overall situation, evaluating the effect of the missiles, and speculating on why Khrushchev had tried this awesome gamble. That night they had reached only one conclusion: something had to be done.

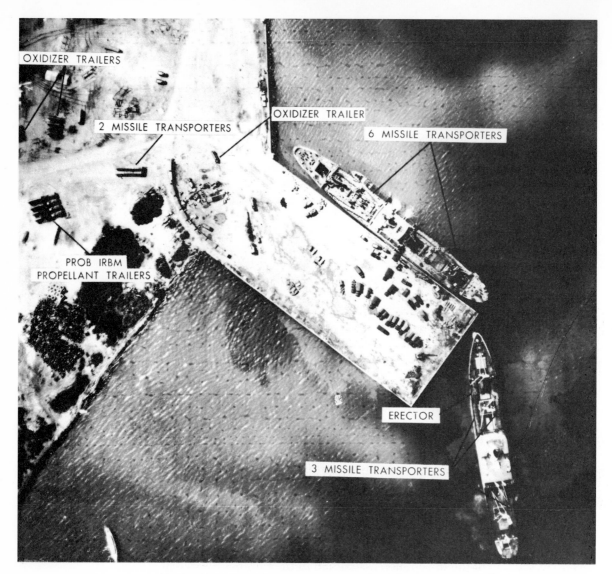

OXIDIZER TRAILERS

2 MISSILE TRANSPORTERS

OXIDIZER TRAILER

6 MISSILE TRANSPORTERS

PROB IRBM
PROPELLANT TRAILERS

ERECTOR

3 MISSILE TRANSPORTERS

An American reconnaissance plane photographed Soviet freighters, loaded with intermediate-range ballistic missile parts, in a Cuban port.

On Wednesday, October 17, ExComm met throughout the day in the State Department conference room to discuss policy options. No immediate consensus emerged; although these twelve men, scuttling in and out of the meeting from their other official duties, all served the same administration, they regarded the problem from a dozen different perspectives.

The group considered diplomatic options first: either to make a private demand to the Russians that they get the missiles out or to take the case to the United Nations. But swiftly, ExComm decided that diplomacy alone could not work. The Soviets would only stall for time while construction of the sites continued. Finally, the Soviets would demand a world conference on the missiles, further delaying any decisive decision.

The military men on ExComm proposed a straightforward response: send in B-52 bombers to blast the bases. According to evidence from stepped-up U–2 flights, between sixteen and thirty-two missiles would be ready for firing in a week. Bombing was the only strategy sure to eliminate the missiles before that point. This approach became known as "the fast track."

The most impassioned opposition to a military solution came from Robert Kennedy, the President's closest advisor, who rapidly emerged as a leading voice in the discussions. His intimate relationship with his brother added weight to his comments, and other cabinet officers tended to defer to RFK.

A surprise attack, argued Robert Kennedy, was not in the tradition of the United States. It would hurt the country in the eyes of the world and affront its conscience at home. The country that had been attacked without warning at Pearl Harbor would now seem to be following the Japanese example. "My brother," he warned the group, "is not going to be the Tojo of the 1960s." Furthermore, he doubted whether an air attack, even one referred to by the military as a "surgical strike," could be relied on to take out all the missiles. Very possibly, the United States would have to follow it up with an invasion, and would have to accept a heavy toll in Cuban and American lives.

The "slow track," advocated by most nonmilitary advisors, included a naval blockade of Cuba. This would prevent the Russians from sending more missiles in and could be maintained until they removed the weapons already there. With the United States Navy's total control of the Caribbean and the eastern Atlantic, the blockade could be made to work. But, according to international law, a blockade is an act of war.

Although the slow and fast tracks emerged as the major alternatives, the lines in the room did not harden during the Wednesday session. Most participants changed sides at least once. ExComm argued the alternatives throughout Thursday and Friday. McGeorge Bundy, who had originally stood with Stevenson for a diplomatic approach, now led the "surgical" air-strike faction. Llewellen Thompson, former Ambassador to the Soviet Union and the group's Kremlinologist, warned that bombing the missile bases was the worst course; Soviets would be killed, and Khrushchev's response to that could not be safely predicted. The Joint Chiefs unanimously argued for bombing; General Taylor suggested giving twenty-four hours' warning to minimize loss of life. McNamara argued that if the proposed blockade failed, the United States could then try bombing; but after bombing, the President could not go back to the blockade.

The discussions gave two new words to the American language — terms that would later be applied to hard-liners and soft-liners on Vietnam. Those favoring the air strike became known as "hawks," while supporters of the blockade were identified as "doves."

Slowly, a majority began to develop in favor of blockade. Treasury Secretary Douglas Dillon abandoned his support of the air strike, announcing himself convinced by the arguments of Robert Kennedy and McNamara. Former Secretary of State Dean Acheson, unable to support the blockade, left in a huff, "resigning" from the group.

On Saturday, ExComm made its report to the President. John Kennedy had campaigned in Chicago the day before but had cancelled Saturday's appearances because he had "a cold." He now sat at the cabinet table in a chair designed to ease the pain in his back and listened to the final recommendations of each side. Neither faction could maintain that their policy would be safe or easy.

The President came down on the side of the blockade. He did not wish to put Khrushchev totally into a corner. Although he wanted to speak again with tactical bombing specialists, he doubted that bombing could guarantee destruction of all the missiles. Aware of the possible consequences, Kennedy nevertheless ordered the blockade, instructing McNamara to ready all U.S. forces for the confrontation. "I guess," he had told Acheson the day before, "this is the week I earn my salary."

Fifty-one hours later, Kennedy planned to announce the blockade on television. He directed his top speechwriter, Theodore Sorenson, to prepare the address, and Sorenson retired to his office with copies of the speeches of Woodrow Wilson and Franklin Roosevelt in which they asked Congress to declare war.

The American military began moving well in advance of public announcements. Transport planes flew a thousand marines from Camp Pendleton, California, to reinforce the U.S. base at Guantánamo Bay, Cuba. The First Armored Division was loaded aboard special trains from Texas to Fort Stewart, Georgia, preparing its artillery for immediate use. One hundred eighty naval ships steamed toward blockade stations in the Atlantic, although their captains did not yet know their assignments.

The military was preparing for the possibility that the crisis would outgrow Cuba. Strategic Air Command planes began leaving their bases for civilian airports all over the country to guard against a sneak attack. B-52s loaded with atomic bombs were kept in the air at all times; as one landed, another would replace it in the sky. Crews tending ICBMs went on maximum alert. Warnings of an impending crisis went out to American military commanders all over the world.

Early Sunday morning, before going to church, President Kennedy reconfirmed his decision on the blockade by speaking to General Walter C. Sweeney, commander of the Tactical Air Force. Sweeney could pledge only 90 percent destruction of the missiles with an air strike. A few missiles would probably survive—and possibly be fired immediately at the United States. His mind now definitely made up, the President met with ExComm in the Oval Office at ten o'clock.

The Sunday morning session served to solidify the previous decisions and plans of operation. At the suggestion of Robert Kennedy, each participant brought his own ideas in writing. Assistant Secretary of Defense Paul Nitze's pocket contained a chilling but possible scenario: construction work on the missiles would continue, forcing a U.S. air strike; the remaining missiles would be fired at the United States, which would have to invade Cuba and launch a "purely compensatory" attack on the Soviet Union. Nitze's scenario did not say what would happen next.

As Sunday afternoon passed into Monday evening, the government prepared itself. Sorenson's draft of the President's speech was edited, rewritten, and edited again. American women and children were evacuated from Guantánamo Bay. Spanish-language stations in Florida were checked to make sure that Monday night's speech could be heard in Cuba. General Thomas S. Power, commander of the Strategic Air Command, issued his final orders from underground headquarters near Omaha.

One substantive alteration was made in the speech. Abram Chayes, the State Department's Legal Advisor, and his assistant Leonard Meeker, persuaded the President not to use the word "blockade," widely considered to be an act of war. Instead, they suggested that Kennedy announce that he was placing a "quarantine" around Cuba. The semantic change in no way altered the plan.

Kennedy had one more task before he made his public announcement. The presidential jet had hopped around the country Monday, rounding up nineteen Congressional leaders, most of whom were in their home states campaigning. They came to the White House at five o'clock Monday afternoon, to be briefed by Rusk, McNamara, and John McCone of the CIA, and then to meet with the President.

Their reaction stunned and angered Kennedy. He had expected Republicans to question his approach and oppose his policies, but two Democratic leaders, Chairmen Richard Russell of the Senate Armed Services Committee and William Fulbright of the Senate Foreign Relations Committee, dismissed a blockade as ineffective and insisted on an immediate invasion. For an hour, Kennedy angrily repeated all the arguments from the meetings of ExComm. The Congressmen were not convinced, so the President stormed out of the room to make final preparations for his speech.

Beginning with the traditional "My fellow citizens," Kennedy rapidly outlined the evidence of Soviet military activity on Cuba. The installation of missiles, he said flatly, "is a deliberately provocative and unjustified change in the status quo which cannot be accepted by this country."

To deal with the problem, Kennedy explained, a defensive quarantine would begin. "All ships of any kind bound for Cuba from whatever nation or port will, if found to contain cargoes of offensive weapons, be turned back." Later that evening, McNamara publicly confirmed what Kennedy had merely implied: ships that did not turn back would be seized or sunk.

The United States, Kennedy continued, wanted immediate emer-

When the Soviet Union began supplying Cuba with missiles, the Cold War reached crisis proportions. As the nation watched, President Kennedy announced a counteraction that brought the world perilously close to nuclear confrontation.

gency sessions of the U.N. Security Council and the OAS. But although he talked of negotiations, the President issued a warning: any missile launched from Cuba would be considered as coming from Russia "requiring a full retaliatory attack upon the Soviet Union."

A half hour after the President had begun speaking, the United States was in the middle of its most serious crisis since World War II.

"We have won a considerable victory," Dean Rusk told his undersecretary of state the next morning, waking him from his sleep on the couch in Rusk's office. "You and I are still alive." The absolute worst possibility—that Khrushchev would be so enraged he would immediately launch an attack on the United States, on Berlin, on the Turkish missile bases—had not occurred. But the next move still belonged to the Soviets; it would come when an American ship tried to stop one of their vessels heading for Cuba.

That morning, Tuesday, October 23, the OAS met to vote on the blockade issue. The United States needed fourteen votes, a two-thirds majority, and the assistant secretary of state for Inter-American Affairs estimated one chance in four of getting that many. Latin-American delegates listened to Rusk's speech and desperately called home for instructions. When a vote was taken, one by one the Latins rose and endorsed the position of the United States. The final vote was 19–0, with only Uruguay abstaining. The next day, when instructions came through from Uruguay, the vote became unanimous.

At the White House, the day passed in working out plans for the blockade to go into effect Wednesday morning at ten o'clock. If a vessel bound for Cuba refused to stop, the navy would attempt to cripple it by firing at the rudders and propellors—not to sink it. And rather than board the vessel by force, the Navy would attempt to tow it into Jacksonville or Charleston.

Cuban refugees gather in a Manhattan hotel to watch President Kennedy's televised address to the nation on October 22, 1962. In the Monday-night speech, the President outlined a 7-point program of American response to the missile crisis, including a limited "quarantine" of Cuba—in effect, a blockade. Calling the Soviet actions provocative, Kennedy threatened U.S. retaliation were any of the Cuban missiles to be launched at any nation in the Western Hemisphere.

ExComm worked out another contingency plan that day. To protect the missiles, the Russians had also installed SAMs (surface-to-air missiles) in Cuba. Since Tuesday, three U-2s a day had flown over Cuba. If a SAM destroyed a U-2, Kennedy and McNamara agreed that such an attack would require American bombers to destroy a SAM site, but that no action would be taken without the President's approval.

Still, the day brought no inkling of what the Russians might do. On the President's urging, his brother went to meet with Soviet Ambassador Anatoly Dobrynin, with whom he had developed a rapport. The meeting produced nothing, since Dobrynin denied that the missile bases even existed. Afterwards, the Ambassador attended a reception at his embassy for Lieutenant General Vladimir A. Dubovik. "We Russians are ready to defend ourselves against any acts of aggression, against ourselves or any of our allies," boasted the General. "Our ships will sail through."

The blockade would go into effect Wednesday morning, and Soviet ships were still steaming toward Cuba. Tuesday night, American intelligence picked up coded messages to the ships, but they were undecipherable.

Wednesday's regularly scheduled ten o'clock meeting of ExComm would coincide with the arrival of the first Russian ships at the blockade line. The President, sitting with his brother before the meeting, found some comfort in the thought that, had he not acted, he "would have been impeached." As the other members of ExComm gathered, the group quietly listened and waited. Some pored gloomily over the more recent U-2 photos, which showed that work on the missile sites was proceeding and that Soviet bombers were being uncrated and assembled. McNamara informed everyone that two merchant ships, the *Gagarin* and the *Komiles,* would reach the blockade line within minutes.

The next report ExComm received was not encouraging: a Russian submarine had joined the two ships. The group sat in frozen apprehension. The President held his hand over his mouth, but his eyes showed the strain. "We must expect that they will close down Berlin," he said, thinking ahead to the next step; "we must make the final preparations for that."

At 10:25, a CIA courier appeared at John McCone's elbow with a note. McCone read it rapidly and announced, "Mr. President, we have a preliminary report which seems to indicate that some of the Russian ships have stopped dead in the water."

Now information began to come in rapidly, confirming early reports. Twenty Russian ships near the line had indeed halted, and some had turned around and headed back across the Atlantic. "If the ships have orders to turn around," directed the President, eagerly grasping at the reprieve, "we want to give them every opportunity to do so."

A great burden seemed to have been lifted from the participants. Dean Rusk remarked bouncily: "We're eyeball to eyeball and I think the other fellow just blinked." In a more sober vein, Robert Kennedy reflected: "For a moment the world stood still, and now it was going around again."

The Soviets had not responded militarily, but the United States still did not know exactly what their next step would be. As ExComm had predicted, Khrushchev called for an international conference to discuss the problem. But his statement also struck a menacing note: "If the United States government carries out its program of piratical actions," he warned, "we shall have to resort to means of defense against the aggressor to protect our rights."

At 2:00 P.M. Wednesday, Acting U.N. Secretary-General U Thant of Burma, pressured by alarmed Asian and African nations, asked for an end to both the American quarantine and the Soviet weapons shipments. He urged a two-week cessation of both, during which the parties could

Opposing groups of pickets outside the White House at the end of October 1962 supported divergent strategies of retaliation against Soviet establishment of nuclear missile bases in Cuba, only 90 miles from the Florida coast. The "Hawks" wanted the U.S. to bomb the missile sites in Cuba before they could be completed. The "Doves" supported a naval blockade of Cuba that would continue until the missile bases were dismantled, a position endorsed by Attorney General Robert Kennedy and Secretary of Defense McNamara.

meet to resolve their differences. Khrushchev accepted the offer, but the United States did not. Time, ExComm felt, was essential; in two or three weeks, the missiles and bombers would be firmly established on Cuba. Before that happened, Khrushchev must be made to see the danger of keeping them there.

The Navy was letting ships with nonmilitary cargoes through the blockade. Among Soviet ships, these were mostly tankers, which clearly did not carry missiles. Yet a faction on ExComm strongly urged stopping and searching one of the tankers, to demonstrate American seriousness. After consideration, Kennedy rejected the idea as needlessly provocative.

Thursday, October 25, the United States presented its case to the U.N. Security Council. This day belonged to Adlai Stevenson, who had originally questioned the blockade and who was considered by some on ExComm to be too much of a dove. The Security Council meeting provided the most dramatic public moment of the crisis. Stevenson demanded of Soviet delegate Valerian Zorin whether the Russians had put missiles on Cuba.

> STEVENSON: Do you, Ambassador Zorin, deny that the USSR has placed and is placing medium- and intermediate-range missiles and sites in Cuba? Don't wait for the translation, answer yes or no.
> ZORIN: I am not in an American courtroom . . . . In due course, Sir, you will have your answer. . . .
> STEVENSON: I am prepared to wait for my answer until hell freezes over, if that's your decision. And I am also prepared to present the evidence in this room.

Stevenson then revealed blown-up photographs of the Cuban missile sites. Zorin refused to make any further statement, and the Security Council adjourned. The crisis was not resolved, but the exchange had focused world-wide attention on the photographic evidence.

Early Friday morning, October 26, the United States decided it was necessary to stop and search a ship. President Kennedy had personally selected the vessel, with great care. Although the *Marucla* was indeed sailing from Russia to Cuba, it was not a Soviet ship, but Panamanian-owned, registered in Lebanon, and chartered by the Soviets. Without incident, U.S. Navy men boarded the ship, inspected one of the holds, and then let it pass.

Still, depression and doubt reigned in ExComm on Friday as new evidence suggested that the Russians were speeding up construction. Even doves were coming to the conclusion that the United States would have to take more decisive action — an air strike against the missile sites, perhaps followed by an invasion.

McNamara warned that an invasion might entail forty to fifty thousand casualties. "They have a hell of a lot of equipment," CIA chief McCone warned. "And it will be damn tough to shoot them out of those hills." Nevertheless, the President ordered the State Department to prepare a program for civil government in Cuba after an invasion. That afternoon, ExComm developed plans for an air strike on the missiles.

THE RANGE OF CUBAN–BASED SOVIET MISSILES

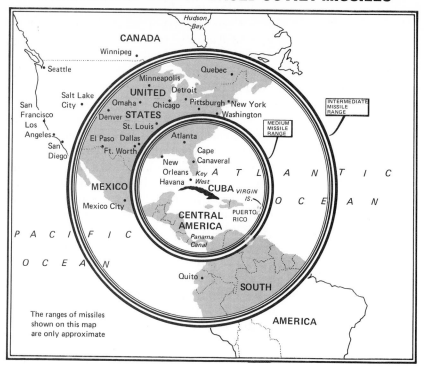

The ranges of missiles shown on this map are only approximate

The administration strove to make the urgency of the situation clear to the Soviets. Officials and congressmen now talked publicly of American readiness. Robert Kennedy warned Dobrynin that there were at most two days left. Now ExComm could only wait to hear from Khrushchev.

The first intimations of a response came in a roundabout, totally unexpected fashion. John Scali, diplomatic correspondent from ABC-TV, received an unusual phone call early Friday afternoon. It came from Alexander Fomin, an official at the Soviet Embassy, who was rumored to be a colonel in the Soviet secret police. Could Scali meet him for lunch in ten minutes? To Scali's comment that he was busy, Fomin replied forcefully that it was urgent. Scali agreed to go.

Immediately after ordering his lunch, Fomin asked if the State Department would be interested in a three-part settlement: the missiles would return to the Soviet Union; the Russians would put no offensive weapons in Cuba in the future; and the United States would pledge not to invade Cuba. Scali said that he thought such a proposal showed promise. Upon the urging of Fomin, Scali went immediately to the State Department.

The Department's intelligence chief took Scali to seek Rusk. The Secretary, after consulting with the White House, sent Scali back with positive words of interest and a warning against delay. Scali and Fomin met again at 7:35 that evening in a coffee shop around the corner from the Soviet Embassy. After assuring himself that the statement came from the "highest circles," Fomin left to inform his superiors.

By that time, the White House teletype had already clacked out a strange letter from the American Embassy in Moscow. It was relaying a personal communication from Nikita Khrushchev to John Kennedy—a long, rambling letter, indicating a fear of war and a desperate search for a way out. Khrushchev wrote that he had seen war, and he detailed his experiences during two German invasions of his country. There were, he admitted, Soviet missiles in Cuba. But they were defensive, not offensive, weapons. (Khrushchev appeared to be playing the same semantic game with the word "defensive" that Kennedy had played in describing the "quarantine.") The missiles were there, Khrushchev said, because the United States had sponsored an invasion of Cuba, and Castro feared there might be another. The crisis must end before it spun out of control. If the United States would lift the quarantine and pledge not to invade Cuba, a solution might be possible. The Soviet Union would then have no further need to keep nuclear weapons in Cuba.

"Mr. President, you and we ought not now to pull on the ends of the rope in which you have tied the knot of war, because the more we pull, the tighter the knot will be tied," warned the Russian leader. "And a moment may come when the knot will be tied so tight that even he who tied it will not have the strength to untie it, and then it will be necessary to cut that knot . . . ."

ExComm went over the letter word-by-word, looking for traps and hoping not to find any. The group was not totally relieved: Khrushchev said nothing specific about withdrawing the missiles. But ExComm decided to treat Khrushchev's letter and Fomin's proposal as one single offer, an offer that the United States could accept.

Khrushchev's eagerness to extricate himself from the situation did not explain why the Soviets had put missiles in Cuba in the first place. Apparently, they wanted, first, to score a political victory and, second, to improve their country's military position. Khrushchev needed both in 1962. After four years of running his government's policy with a combination of probing, accommodation, and bluster, he had failed to gain ground. West Berlin remained in "enemy" hands, and the Soviets now faced opposition from the Chinese, who were beginning to chart a separate course from Moscow, one that threatened to flare into open hostility. In the end, Khrushchev suffered greatly from the crisis. The Chinese denounced him for adventurism in putting the missiles in—and for cowardice in taking them out. Within two years, he like Admiral Anderson, would be out of office.

Saturday, October 27, destroyed the fragile optimism of the night before. A new letter had arrived from the Kremlin, stripped of the rambling emotionalism of the first. The Soviet Union, Khrushchev wrote, would remove its missiles from Cuba when the United States removed *its* missiles from Turkey. Both major countries would pledge not to interfere in the affairs of their neighbors. Kennedy was not the only head of state who could issue an ultimatum.

ExComm studied the new note with perplexity. Had there been a *coup d'etat* in the Soviet Union? Did Khrushchev no longer control the government? Thompson, the Kremlinologist, had his doubts. He speculated that Khrushchev's new communiqué was in response to the feeling of the Soviet military and his other advisers that he was losing face in the way he was dealing with the crisis. For the first time, awareness of a Soviet ExComm pervaded the group.

The new offer contained a curious irony. The Turkish missiles were hardly essential to American defense and were, in any case, obsolete. Months before, Kennedy had given orders that they be removed. But the Turks, eager to retain the economic benefits of the bases, opposed removal, and the President's order had not been implemented. Now the President faced an unpleasant choice: risking a war over bases he no longer wanted, or giving European allies the impression that the United States would "sell them out" if its own security appeared in danger.

Other developments heightened the fragility of the situation. FBI Director J. Edgar Hoover notified Robert Kennedy that Soviet officials in New York were burning confidential documents, as though in preparation for war. McCone reported that construction of the bases on Cuba continued at a rapid pace. And the worst news was that Soviet missiles had downed an American U-2 in flight over Cuba. "There was the feeling," wrote Robert Kennedy, "that the noose was tightening on all of us, on Americans, on mankind, and that the bridges to escape were crumbling."

A decision to knock out the SAM bases could not be postponed much longer. Work continued on the bases, and they might be ready in a matter of hours. "It was generally agreed," remembered one member of ExComm, "that we couldn't go beyond Sunday without a further decision. At the very least . . . that would have been a decision to take out the missile sites by air attack." Invasion of Cuba would inevitably follow. McNamara stated that an air attack could be readied in forty-eight hours, but he would rather broaden the blockade to include petroleum.

Meanwhile, Khrushchev's letters remained unanswered. All Saturday afternoon, ExComm unsuccessfully tried to block out a way to remove the missiles from Turkey without giving the appearance of bowing to Soviet pressure. Rather, it drafted a series of responses refusing the terms offered by Khrushchev. Robert Kennedy found all of the drafts to be inadequate; they did not, in his opinion, sufficiently acknowledge the strong desire Khrushchev had shown for peace.

RFK then cut the knot brilliantly by suggesting that ExComm simply ignore Khrushchev's second letter and respond to the first—the one that offered withdrawal of Russian missiles but that did not mention the Turkish bases. He retired with Ted Sorenson to produce a draft. With some revisions, Robert Kennedy's letter went off to Khrushchev.

The same night, the Attorney General met with Dobrynin and told him of the letter going to Moscow. Regarding the problem of the Turkish missiles, he told the Ambassador that the United States could not re-

On October 31, 1962, President Kennedy met in his office with the U.S. Army Chief of Staff General Earle Wheeler, seated next to him, and two other key military officers to discuss American military preparedness. Fortunately for Kennedy, the Cuban Missile Crisis had ended three days earlier when Kruschev agreed to remove the missiles if the U.S. would end its naval "quarantine" and promise not to invade Cuba.

move them under threat. But Kennedy also told Dobrynin: "It was our judgment that, within a short time after this crisis was over, those missiles would be gone."

Dobrynin, however, was not optimistic, and neither were the Americans. ExComm met again at nine o'clock that evening to begin preparations for an attack not later than Tuesday. At 9:20 P.M., McNamara called twenty-four squadrons of the Air Force Reserve to active duty. Sixty thousand Army and Marine troops, the forces for the invasion, were ready in Florida and the Panama Canal Zone. "Now," said the President, utterly drained, "it can go either way."

Sunday morning, October 28, Kennedy was to meet at nine with McNamara and the generals to check details on the air strike. A few minutes before the meeting, Radio Moscow announced that at 9:00 A.M. (5:00 P.M. Moscow time) it would broadcast an important message. As the men in the White House listened, a Russian announcer read in English the Kremlin's response to the letter of the previous night. Khrushchev had agreed at last to dismantle and withdraw the missiles. The United States, in turn, would end the island's quarantine and pledge not to support any future invasion of Cuba. The crisis was over.

48

PAX AMERICANA IN DECLINE: THE KENNEDY-JOHNSON YEARS

A. W.

The Cuban missile crisis provides a convenient dividing line for American foreign policy in the postwar era. It ended one period of U.S.-Soviet relations and inaugurated another. Since the start of the Cold War, American diplomacy had consisted largely of responding to Soviet challenges (some real, some imaginary) with a counter-policy that in Eisenhower's time was called "brinkmanship." But in October 1962, the leaders of both superpowers peered into the abyss of thermonuclear war. What they saw frightened them as badly as many of their policies had frightened the world in the past.

The foreign policy pursued by Eisenhower in the 1950s, and continued by Kennedy in the early 1960s, perceived a world dominated mainly by the United States and the Soviet Union, in that order, and relied heavily on the threatened use of American atomic power to settle or deflect disputes between them. Although the two countries had never before come so close to an atomic exchange as during the Cuban missile crisis, public proclamations of their immediate readiness for mutual disaster, and the swollen size of nuclear

stockpiles, was, for both, evidence enough of such intention beyond reasonable doubt.

The United States and the Soviet Union did not resolve their differences after the Cuban missile crisis; they still pursued widely differing objectives in the world. But both countries, as if sobered by the experience, began to take steps to guard against a repetition of the terrifying days of October by improving communication and deemphasizing "nuclear diplomacy." Not since 1962 have the populations of the two superpowers waited desperately to hear whether they would live out the week.

THE "NEW FRONTIER" IN FOREIGN AFFAIRS

As Democrats before him had done throughout the Eisenhower years, the campaigning Senator John F. Kennedy claimed in 1960 that the President had not used the country's full power to maintain its position and prestige. He charged that Ike's cuts in the military budget had limited America's power to act, had narrowed its options, and had caused the United States to lose its status of world leadership. Kennedy singled out Cuba as one example of the Republicans' misdirected foreign policy, and he accused Eisenhower of not doing enough to topple Castro.

As President, Kennedy did not allow any one advisor to exercise the amount of power wielded by John Foster Dulles under Eisenhower; he made his own foreign policies. But in other areas he made a strong effort to attract capable and perceptive individuals, such as McNamara from Ford Motor Company and Bundy from Harvard University. Less than two years after his inauguration, Kennedy's "team" was to become ExComm during the missile crisis.

Kennedy also tried to bring new ideas to international policy. Regarding the Third World, he expressed greater willingness to work with nationalist leaders. He initiated the Peace Corps, sending thousands of young Americans overseas to teach and work in underdeveloped countries.

A Peace Corps volunteer from Baltimore conducts a gym class at a girls' secondary school in Chepkurio, Kenya. Established by President Kennedy in 1961, the Peace Corps trained thousands of volunteer workers, many of them young, and stationed them abroad, for two-year terms, in underdeveloped areas of the world.

But, like Truman and Eisenhower, Kennedy intended to prevent the spread of Communism, and to hold the line in Europe.

The sharpest break with Eisenhower's policies came in the area of defense. Kennedy downplayed "massive retaliation" in favor of a new policy called "flexible response," giving him more options in an emergency. One of Kennedy's favorite programs, the Army's Green Berets (specially trained counterinsurgency fighters), reflected both his wish to bolster military capability and his desire for a more imaginative approach to the problems of Communist power and the Third World.

THE BAY OF PIGS

Regardless of Kennedy's new ideas and his new advisors, within months he sustained one of America's most humiliating foreign policy defeats. Cuba proved to be as painful a problem for him as it had been for President Eisenhower, and the new President sought a way to deal with Castro on American terms. "Communist domination in this hemisphere," declared Kennedy, "can never be negotiated."

Once in office, Kennedy learned that the CIA, under Eisenhower's orders, was training anti-Castro Cuban exiles for an invasion of Cuba. Kennedy seemed to have advocated just this kind of action while a candidate, and he ordered the program continued. American planners calculated that when the exiles landed in Cuba, one-third of Castro's army would join them, another third would desert, and the rest would not be able to withstand the invaders. Hoping to achieve this aim, but with as little direct U.S. commitment as possible, Kennedy cancelled CIA air cover for the landing.

The invasion, in April 1961, failed miserably. Castro's forces remained loyal, fought well, and routed the invaders in two days. Moreover, the role of the United States in the fiasco could not be concealed. America had been caught intervening in the domestic affairs of another country—and in a clumsy and ineffectual fashion. Kennedy regained some prestige in the United States by taking on himself all responsibility for the action, but the American position in the world had suffered a serious setback.

VIENNA AND BERLIN

Two months after the Bay of Pigs, Kennedy met for the first time with Khrushchev in Vienna.

Skeptical of the new President's strength, Khrushchev apparently tried to bully him, demanding "adjustment" of the situation in West Berlin and Taiwan; neither of the two areas, he warned, could stay as they were indefinitely. Kennedy replied with a defense of existing conditions and warned that the United States could not watch more territory go Communist without taking action. Khrushchev answered that revolution was sweeping the world; the Soviet Union, he said, would assist the process. Kennedy left the meeting angry and shaken.

Khrushchev seemed most perturbed over the status of Berlin. The four wartime allied powers still governed the city, deep in the center of Communist East Germany. West Berlin—consisting of the British, French, and American sectors of the divided city—stood as an island of prosperity and democracy in the midst of the then drab Russian satellite. The contrast itself galled Khrushchev enough, but West Berlin's position as an escape hatch for fleeing East Germans presented a more tangible problem. Three million East Germans, mostly the young and educated, had escaped to the West since the war, and by the early 1960s they were leaving the German Democratic Republic at a rate of 300,000 a year.

Khrushchev continued to demand changes in the situation; Kennedy continued to decline to make any concessions. Tension increased, and the United States began to build strength for a confrontation. Kennedy tripled the draft call, called up 150,000 reserves, and sent another 40,000 troops to Europe. The president of East Germany threatened to cut West Berlin off from the rest of West Germany—to reinstitute the Berlin Blockade. "I hear it said that West Berlin is militarily untenable," Kennedy told Americans in a TV address. "Any dangerous spot is tenable if men—brave men—will make it so."

On August 13, 1960, Khrushchev and the East Germans responded to the crisis by building a barrier around West Berlin, (first barbed wire, later a brick wall), effectively cutting off further emigration. Although such an action violated the Four-Power treaty on Berlin, the United States took no action. The Russians had not touched West Berlin, and the United States would not go to war over a wall.

CONFLICTS WITH EUROPEAN ALLIES

From the start of Kennedy's term, American policymakers worried about a problem that the Cuban missile crisis—their greatest triumph—would only aggravate. The United States' relations with Western European nations, its closest world allies,

The foreign and economic ministers of Western Europe are shown conferring at a Common Market meeting in 1961. Since then, with its growing economic power, that bloc of nations has become an influential third force in world politics.

ROBERT F. KENNEDY

The life of Robert Kennedy, more so than most Americans of the 1960s, was profoundly shaken by the events of November 22, 1963. Before that day, he had operated as a satellite of his brother John, as his closest adviser, his campaign manager, and his attorney general. He had acquired a reputation for ruthlessness in pursuit of his brother's interests, often acting as "hatchet man" for JFK. After the day President Kennedy was shot down in Dallas, Robert Kennedy had almost to reassemble himself, to draw new strength from new people and things.

In 1960, Robert Kennedy would tell local Democratic leaders that he did not care what they thought of him, that he did not care what happened to him, that he wanted only to get his brother elected President. After John became the first President to name a brother to the cabinet, Robert still seemed to be characterized mostly by a driving intensity. As attorney general, he devoted a large part of his own and the Justice Department's time to putting Jimmy Hoffa of the Teamsters, a labor leader he considered corrupt, in prison. Realizing, once assuming office, the desperate situation of Southern blacks, he assisted them to an extent no previous attorney general had considered. Kennedy's response to situations tended to be visceral rather than intellectual, but he could also be the poised and effective advisor at the time of the Cuban missile crisis.

After the death of his brother, a friend described Robert Kennedy as "a kind of bruised animal." He wanted to be Lyndon Johnson's running mate in 1964, but the two men had long hated each other, and their respective positions now infused a strong element of mutual resentment. Since his brother Edward was already senator from Massachusetts, Robert Kennedy (RFK) ran for the Senate from New York. He won, with the help of the growing legend of his brother, family, wealth, and, ironically, a Lyndon Johnson landslide in the state.

Kennedy disliked both the routine of the Senate and the details of party leadership in New York. Although he made efforts to work in both directions, his real interest was developing and expanding his national constituency—Kennedy loyalists, minorities, liberals—for his eventual attempt to reclaim his brother's office.

After publicly attacking Johnson's Vietnam War policy, he faced demands that he run for President in 1968. Certain that it was not politically wise, he refused, and Senator Eugene McCarthy of Minnesota first carried the antiwar standard. Only when McCarthy ran strong in the New Hampshire primary did Kennedy announce he would run. The first month of the campaign held one more surprise; Johnson withdrew from the race.

Old New Frontiersmen hurried to the support of the second (but perhaps not the last), Kennedy to run for President. McCarthy now refused to withdraw, and Vice President Hubert Humphrey declined to challenge Kennedy in the primaries. Observers watched with awe—and foreboding—the intense emotion Kennedy evoked among widely differing groups. He won several primaries; but even after his June victory in the California primary, he faced a long and highly uncertain road to nomination at the convention. As he was leaving his victory party at a Los Angeles hotel, a young Palestinian-American named Sirhan Sirhan, shot and killed Robert Kennedy.

seemed to be fraying. Although Kennedy felt the United States had convincingly demonstrated its commitment to defend Western Europe in the Berlin crisis, many Western Europeans continued to express dissatisfaction with their role in the Atlantic Alliance and NATO.

Under Kennedy, the United States developed a two-part policy toward Europe. As an ultimate goal it urged a plan called the Grand Design, a united Western Europe (based on an expanded version of the European Common Market, the extremely successful economic alliance of France, West Germany, Italy, Belgium, Holland, and Luxemburg), which would share burdens and decisions with the United States. Until then, it urged Western Europeans to strengthen their conventional defenses while the United States controlled nuclear weapons.

Across both these plans fell the long shadow of France's President Charles de Gaulle. General de Gaulle wished to see France neither swallowed up in a greater Europe nor dependent upon the United States for its ultimate defense. He greatly distrusted both the Americans and the British, feeling that "the Anglo-Saxons" wished to control and divide the western world between them. Despite American objections, he decided that France, like Britain, must have its own nuclear weapons.

The Cuban missile crisis, with its proof that the United States would engage in nuclear diplomacy without consulting its allies, intensified de Gaulle's determination. In January 1963, he vetoed British entry into the Common Market, thus frustrating a long-time American policy aim. He also loosened France's ties with NATO, formed a close relationship with West Germany, and began to make his own overtures to Eastern Europe.

The United States tried to discourage France, and other European nations, from building their own bombs with a plan called the Multi-Lateral Force. This project called for ships carrying nuclear weapons to be manned by mixed crews representing all the NATO powers, but it stirred no interest outside Washington. Although Britain ultimately joined the Common Market, France continued to pursue a course independent of the United States, and eventually pulled out of NATO.

THE BEGINNINGS OF DETENTE

But if the Cuban missile crisis damaged America's relationship with its allies, it greatly improved relations with "the other side." Following the confrontation, both the United States and the Soviet Union looked for ways to lessen the probability of nuclear holocaust—intentional or accidental. Soon after the days of October, they cooperatively set up a two-way "hot-line" linking the White House and the Kremlin with a separate teletype system. The ability to communicate quickly would, they hoped, greatly lessen chances of nuclear war arising from misunderstandings.

The thaw in the Cold War yielded even more specific results in August 1963, when the two superpowers signed a treaty banning nuclear tests in the earth's atmosphere. The agreement reflected in part the fears of both nations about their allies—fears that proved well-founded when France, Communist China, and Cuba refused to ratify the document.

Further, both powers seemed more inclined to recognize the problems of the other, and to see the necessity of getting along. In June 1963, Kennedy expressed this growing tolerance in one of the best speeches of his career, declaring: "In the final analysis, our most basic common link is the fact that we all inherit this planet. We all breathe the same air. We all cherish our children's future. And we are all mortal."

ENTERING VIETNAM

Even with the nuclear pressures eased, major troubles loomed for the United States in a "fringe area." After the cancellation of the elections intended to unite Vietnam, America had supported Ngo Dinh Diem's government in South Vietnam.

Diem, a Catholic in a predominantly Buddhist country, had been having increasing problems with Communist Viet Cong guerrillas, and Kennedy chose to help him defeat the rebels. Much military and economic aid had already been sent to South Vietnam. And starting in 1961, Kennedy sent several thousand military personnel, including Green Berets, to aid Diem. Kennedy wanted to create a strong, pro-Western government in South Vietnam and to show that such a force, with American help, could defeat a Communist insurrection.

During 1961, Kennedy also dispatched both his Vice President, Lyndon Johnson, and General Maxwell Taylor of the Joint Chiefs of Staff to Vietnam to consult with Diem and examine the situation at first hand. Their reports to him, and his own reading of Mao Tse-tung and Che Guevara on guerrilla warfare, led Kennedy to increase the number of American soldiers and airmen in Vietnam. By November 1963, the U.S. presence had grown from a few hundred to 16,000, some of them combat troops. The South Vietnamese government, however, did not seem to be doing its part in holding off the rebellion.

Mounting discontent with Diem's government partly explained the ineffectiveness of the South Vietnamese effort. Buddhist leaders and others complained, justifiably, that the Saigon government was corrupt. Government officials gave favored treatment to their relatives, and they persecuted dissenters. Demonstrators demanded Diem's ouster, and several Buddhist monks gained international attention for their cause by publicly burning themselves to death. In Saigon, crisis piled upon crisis as Diem retreated to the temporary security and isolation of his palace. Then, probably with the covert support, and certainly with the knowledge of the American government, the South Vietnamese military took over the country on November 1, 1963. Diem and his

brother were executed. What Kennedy might have done next is speculation; he outlived Diem by only three weeks.

LYNDON JOHNSON's POLICY

In foreign affairs, as with domestic questions, Johnson was determined to continue Kennedy's example. This determination, plus his own reading of international conditions, made victory in Vietnam a priority issue for him. Retaining Kennedy's foreign-policy advisors, including Rusk, McNamara, and Bundy, Johnson hoped to win the war without greatly increasing American involvement.

In the election of 1964, Barry Goldwater, the Republican candidate, severely criticized Johnson's policy, charging that the United States was taking a "no-win" approach. He even talked vaguely about bringing nuclear weapons into

Senator Barry Goldwater of Arizona, Presidential hopeful and popular conservative, waves to supporters as he arrives in San Francisco for the Republican National Convention in July, 1964. In control of the convention throughout, Goldwater forces produced a conservative platform and jeered Nelson Rockefeller of New York, when the liberal Republican Governor proposed a strong Civil Rights plank.

President Johnson, amidst supporters, arrives in Chicago in April, 1964, to address a Democratic fund-raising dinner. During the campaign for the presidency that fall, Republican nominee Goldwater criticized Johnson for not winning the war in Vietnam, while the incumbent President opposed enlarging the conflict or increasing American involvement. As the "peace" candidate, Johnson not only won the election handily but also received more votes, and a larger plurality, than any other presidential contender in American history.

play. Against such an attack, Johnson campaigned as an opponent of a wider war. "We don't want our American boys to do the fighting for Asian boys," he declared frequently.

But Johson also cultivated the image of toughness. In August 1964, American destroyers clashed with North Vietnamese torpedo boats in international waters. (Later, it was revealed that the American ships were convoying South Vietnamese raiders.) Denouncing the North Vietnamese action as piracy, Johnson ordered air strikes against their naval bases.

Shrewdly seizing the opportunity to enlarge the mandate for his Vietnam policy, he went to Congress for authority to "take all necessary measures to repel any armed attack against the forces of the United States, and to repel any further aggression." Johnson had apparently been waiting for a chance to present to Congress such a resolution, similar to Eisenhower's Formosa resolution. In the years that followed, the Johnson Administration would refer often to this Tonkin Gulf Resolution as the authority for all subsequent military actions. It passed unanimously in the House; and only two senators voted against it, warning that it probably would lead the nation into a wider war. Johnson, the peace candidate in 1964, easily won the election.

ESCALATION

Shortly after Johnson's inauguration in 1965, the Viet Cong attacked an American base in Vietnam. The President then ordered sustained bombing of North Vietnam, allegedly to bring the Hanoi communists to the peace table and force them to stop supplying the Viet Cong guerrillas in the South. But heavy American bombing produced the opposite result, steadily drawing the North Vietnamese deeper into the war and increasing the amount of supplies that came in from other communist powers. During this period, the U.S. government apparently rebuffed various North Vietnamese "peace feelers," fearing that the South Vietnamese government was too weak even to negotiate, since the removal of Diem had not brought stability to Saigon.

The weaknesses of successive South Vietnamese governments further complicated the American effort. For four years after the fall of Diem, governments came and went in Saigon. One of them lasted only eight days. No leader emerged strong enough to unite the non-communist elements in the country, to control corruption

When the Vietnamese War "escalated" under President Johnson in 1965, the U.S. intensified bombing raids on North Vietnam and increased by eight times, the number of American troops stationed in Vietnam. Here, soldiers from the U.S. 173rd Airborne brigade, who have just received supplies by helicopter, continue a "search and destroy" patrol through the jungle in Phuoc Tuy Province, in June 1966. This landing zone is guarded by an armored personnel carrier, in the rear.

in the South Vietnamese army, or to win the loyalty of the peasants. When a relatively stable government finally emerged, under two generals, it proved repressive and ineffectual, a creature spawned by U.S. aid and kept alive by the ever-increasing U.S. military commitment.

The worse the war went for Saigon, the deeper the United States became involved. Bombing raids intensified in the north and against communist positions in the south until American planes ultimately dropped more bombs on Vietnam than had been used during all of World War II. In 1965 American troop strength in Vietnam increased from 23,000 to 180,000. By the end of 1967 there were nearly half a million American soldiers in the country.

The failure of the American expedition in Vietnam and Washington's determination to seek military victory worried and alienated many American allies. The United States tried desperately to attract support for the war, to make Vietnam appear a joint action similar to the UN Command in Korea. A few Asian countries—Korea, the Philippines, and Australia—made token commitments. But no NATO ally would join the United States in Vietnam, and France (the previous West-

ern colonial power there) publicly derided American policy. The nature of the Vietnam war, the absence of a clearly defined front line, the inability to tell Vietnamese friend from foe—all these factors frustrated the U.S. effort. Indiscriminate use by American forces of napalm fire bombs and defoliant chemicals also weakened the moral position of the United States throughout the world.

Escalation of the war cost thousands of American lives and billions of dollars in equipment, divided public opinion at home, and strained foreign relations. Still, it did not lead to confrontation with the Soviets, who seemed content to let the United States sink deeper and deeper into the never-ending and costly Vietnam adventure. Soviet-American relations continued on fairly friendly terms during the period, although Russia supplied much of the arms used by the communist Vietnamese. In 1968, the United States, the Soviet Union, and sixty-six other nations signed a nuclear nonproliferation treaty, pledging not to assist additional countries in obtaining or developing nuclear weapons. President Johnson and Premier Kosygin met briefly, but amicably, during one trip by the Soviet leader to the United Nations headquarters in New York.

With the defeat of the French at Dienbienphu in 1954, Vietnam was, in effect, divided into two countries: North Vietnam with its capital at Hanoi, and South Vietnam with its capital at Saigon. Soon Communists and nationalists began guerrilla and terrorist activity against the Saigon government, which received support and increasing amounts of military aid from the United States. These guerrilla forces, formally titled the National Liberation Army, came to be known as the Viet Cong.

In August 1964 North Vietnamese torpedo boats reportedly fired on United States ships in the Gulf of Tonkin. President Johnson ordered the bombing of North Vietnamese naval bases in retaliation. The United States was soon bombing North Vietnam regularly and also areas in South Vietnam held by the Viet Cong. In turn, United States naval bases, such as the one at Danang, were attacked. American bombers then attacked eastern Laos in an attempt to stop the flow of men and supplies from North Vietnam over the Ho Chi Minh trails. United States military involvement increased until nearly 540,000 American troops were in Vietnam.

In early 1968 the Vietcong launched their Tet Offensive—simultaneous attacks on the major cities of South Vietnam. During an American counterattack, a massacre of Vietnamese civilians by American soldiers occurred at My Lai. In the same year President Johnson called a limited halt to the bombing of North Vietnam on March 31 and a full bombing halt on November 1. In 1970 occasional air attacks were resumed.

United States and South Vietnamese forces drove deep into Cambodia in April 1970 in an effort to locate and destroy Vietcong bases there. In February 1971 South Vietnamese troops, with United States air support, crossed the border into Laos in an unsuccessful attempt to cut the Ho Chi Minh trails.

In March of 1972 the Vietcong and North Vietnam launched a massive offensive, capturing the provincial capital of Quang Tri and scoring other successes; in May the United States began systematic bombing of all North Vietnam and mined North Vietnamese rivers, canals, and ports—including Haiphong Harbor.

Under President Nixon the number of American troops in Vietnam was drastically reduced—down to 65,000 in May 1972—and combat duties were transferred to South Vietnamese forces under a policy of "Vietnamization." In 1973 a cease-fire was concluded in Vietnam.

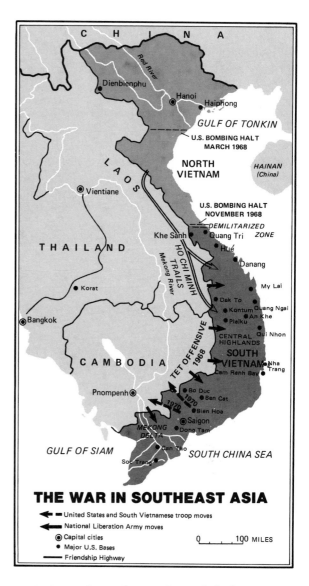

THE WAR IN SOUTHEAST ASIA

◀ ▬ United States and South Vietnamese troop moves
◀ National Liberation Army moves
◉ Capital cities
● Major U.S. Bases
▬ Friendship Highway

0 _____ 100 MILES

SANTO DOMINGO

Early in his administration, Johnson became engaged in a policy that, although as unpopular internationally as Vietnam, appeared more successful. Since the violent death of its dictator, Rafael Trujillo, in 1961, the Dominican Republic had undergone several changes in government, and in 1965 a military dictatorship ruled the country. That year, a group of low-level officers and political radicals mounted what looked like a successful coup against the generals. The ruling junta appealed to the United States for help.

Johnson, acting on unconfirmed reports of communist and Castroite participation in the revolution, sent in 30,000 Marines. He announced, however, that he was acting to safeguard the lives of Americans in the country. But when all American civilians had been evacuated, American troops remained, and Johnson then warned of communist domination of the revolutionary forces.

Despite the resultant Latin American hostility, the Dominican intervention succeeded on one level. The left-wing revolution had been stopped, peace-keeping forces from the Organization of American States reinforced the Americans, and an election held in 1966 resulted in a pro-American president. But Johnson's action, like Kennedy's during the missile crisis, appeared to reconfirm in the minds of American leaders the effectiveness of armed intervention. Virtually all the members of ExComm were still holding top government posts during the Dominican intervention, and many remained to carry out further escalation in Vietnam.

JOHNSON STEPS DOWN

By early 1968, opposition to the Vietnam war echoed across the country. College students, in danger of being drafted and sent to fight in a war that was going nowhere, protested loudly. Some burned their draft cards or fled into exile. John-son's Vietnam schemes had all gone awry. Even Robert McNamara, a key architect in formulating war plans, the "Whiz Kid" of the Pentagon, became dove-ish and began questioning the military effort. He dropped out as secretary of defense. An antiwar candidate, Senator Eugene McCarthy of Minnesota, began to challenge Johnson in the Democratic primaries. Johnson rebuffed all his critics, declaring, "I'm the only President you've got." He would try to tough it out.

In January, battle reports from Vietnam shattered the President's apparent composure. During Tet, the lunar new year, the communists mounted their largest offensive of the war. They briefly captured Hué, South Vietnam's second-largest city, as well as parts of Saigon, besieging the American embassy for six hours. American forces counterattacked and recaptured the cities, but casualties were heavy on both sides. The Viet Cong and North Vietnamese seemed as strong as ever, despite a half million American troops and a steady barrage of optimistic public statements from the White House and the Pentagon. The Tet offensive revealed the obvious: the United States had failed to win the war in Vietnam.

Aided by the shockwaves from the Tet offensive, McCarthy nearly defeated President Johnson in the New Hampshire primary. This

Throughout the late 1960s, nationwide opposition mounted to U.S. involvement in Vietnam. On April 15, 1967, thousands of anti-war demonstrators attended a protest in New York's Central Park to demand an end to the fighting in Vietnam. Here, a twenty-three-year-old demonstrator in Green Beret Uniform, Gary Rader, burned his draft card in a ceremony at the start of the rally.

First Lieutenant William Calley, Jr., second from left, arriving at Fort McPherson, Georgia to take the stand as the first defense witness in the court-martial of Army Captain Ernest Medina in September 1971. Medina was being tried by the Army for his role in the My Lai Massacre of March 16, 1968, when South Vietnamese civilians were shot to death by American soldiers who occupied their village. Calley himself was convicted of unpremeditated murder during the massacre and was imprisoned.

By early 1968, opposition to the war in Vietnam and the popularity of anti-war candidates both altered President Johnson's policy and squelched his hopes for re-election. In a broadcast to the nation from the White House on March 31, 1968, Johnson dramatically announced that he would not be a candidate. In the same address, he revealed that he was halting the air attacks on North Vietnam.

strong antiwar showing led Robert Kennedy to enter the race as well. To add to Johnson's woes, his close friend Clark Clifford, the man who replaced McNamara, had also grown skeptical about the war. He began mobilizing sympathizers and amassing evidence in an effort to get the President and America off the Vietnam treadmill.

On March 31, Johnson announced an unconditional stop to the bombing of North Vietnam. This met North Vietnam's first-step requirement for negotiations. Johnson then added that to keep his action from being interpreted as a political gesture, he would not run for reelection. The Vietnam war had claimed yet another American casualty.

SUGGESTED READINGS– CHAPTERS 47–48

The Missile Crisis

Elie Abel, *The Missile Crisis* (1966); Graham T. Allison, *Essence of Decision: Explaining the Cuban Missile Crisis* (1971); Haynes B. Johnson, *The Bay of Pigs* (1964); Robert F. Kennedy, *Thirteen Days* (1969).

The Kennedy Years

Richard R. Fagen, *Cubans in Exile: Dissatisfaction and the Revolution* (1968); Maurice Halperin, *The Rise and Decline of Fidel Castro* (1972); John F. Heath, *John F. Kennedy and the Business Community* (1969); William Manchester, *The Death of a President* (1967); Lewis J. Paper, *The Promise and the Performance: The Leadership of John F. Kennedy* (1975); Jack M. Schick, *The Berlin Crisis, 1951–1952* (1971); Arthur M. Schlesinger, Jr., *A Thousand Days* (1965); Hugh Sidey, *John F. Kennedy, President* (1964); Theodore C. Sorenson, *Kennedy* (1965); Theodore H. White, *The Making of the President, 1960* (1961); David Halberstam, *The Best and the Brightest* (1972); Bruce Miroff, *Pragmatic Illusions: The Presidential Politics of John F. Kennedy* (1976).

The Johnson Years

Edward J. Epstein, *Inquest: The Warren Commission* (1966); Philip L. Geyelin, *Lyndon B. Johnson and the World* (1966); Herbert Y. Schandler, *The Unmaking of a President: Lyndon Johnson and Vietnam* (1977). (Additional biographies and studies of Johnson are cited in the "Suggested Readings to Chapters 49–50.)

The Cold War

Jerome Levinson and Juan de Onis, *The Alliance That Lost Its Way* (1970); James L. Sundquist, *Politics and Policy: The Eisenhower, Kennedy, and Johnson Years* (1968); Richard J. Walton, *Cold War and Counterrevolution* (1972).

Vietnam

John B. Martin, *Overtaken by Events* (1966); George M. Kahin and John W. Lewis, *The United States in Vietnam* (1967); Robert Shaplen, *The Lost Revolution: The U.S. in Vietnam* (1966); Theodore Draper, *Abuse of Power* (1967); Henry Brandon, *Anatomy of Error* (1969); Seymour M. Hersh, *My Lai 4* (1970); Bernard B. Fall, *Vietnam Witness, 1953–1966.*

49
MARTIN LUTHER KING: THE MAN AND THE DREAM

A.W.

The day had been long and hot. The interracial crowd of 250,000 that started August 28, 1963, in a jubilant, festive mood at the base of the Washington Monument and marched triumphantly to the steps of Lincoln Memorial had grown tired and restless in the heat of the late afternoon. They listened to freedom songs by Joan Baez, Bob Dylan, and Peter, Paul, and Mary. They heard demands for greater strides toward black equality from numerous civil rights leaders and celebrities. Exhausted marchers on the fringes of the crowd began to amble back toward the buses that had brought them. But Mahalia Jackson rose to the platform and sang most of the weary protestors back to life with her, "I Been 'Buked and I Been Scorned." Now came the last speaker of the day — Martin Luther King.

The band played "The Battle Hymn of the Republic" as King approached the microphone to give a speech that would become memorable in the annals of the struggle for black freedom. Combining Baptist oratory with civil rights rhetoric, Martin Luther King preached to the marchers and to America about his vision:

> I have a dream today.
>> I have a dream that one day [in] the state of Alabama . . . little black boys and black girls will be able to join hands with little white boys and white girls and walk together as sisters and brothers.
>> I have a dream today.
>> I have a dream that one day every valley shall be exalted, every hill and mountain shall be made low, the rough places will be made plain, and the crooked

places will be made straight, and the glory of the Lord shall be revealed, and all flesh shall see it together.

This is our hope. This is the faith with which I return to the South. With this faith we will be able to hew out of the mountain of despair a stone of hope. With this faith we will be able to transform the jangling discords of our nation into a beautiful symphony of brotherhood. With this faith we will be able to work together, to pray together, to struggle together, to go to jail together, to stand up for freedom together, knowing that we will be free one day. . . .

And if America is to be a great nation, this must become true. So let freedom ring from the prodigious hilltops of New Hampshire! Let freedom ring from the mountains of New York! Let freedom ring from the heightening Alleghenies of Pennsylvania!

But not only that; let freedom ring from Stone Mountain of Georgia!

Let freedom ring from every hill and mole hill of Mississippi. From every mountainside, let freedom ring.

When we let freedom ring, when we let it ring from every village and every hamlet, from every state and every city, we will be able to speed up that day when all of God's children, black men and white men, Jews and Gentiles, Protestants and Catholics, will be able to join hands and sing, in the words of that old Negro spiritual, "Free at last! Free at last! Thank God Almighty, we are free at last!"

The response was deafening. People wept and cheered. Martin Luther King had put into words the great emotional cry of blacks who had been oppressed and ignored for three hundred years. The speech filled them with optimism: his dream would one day become a reality.

King triumphed that day. The minister himself probably believed that such dramatic changes were at hand; and there were reasons for his optimism. What had started eight years before in Montgomery, Alabama, as a campaign for desegregating a city bus line had grown into a national civil rights movement; and King, who had started his career as a minister in a small southern Baptist church, had become the nationally recognized leader of American Negroes.

Martin Luther King, Jr., was born in Atlanta, Georgia, on January 15, 1929, product of a complex inheritance. His maternal grandfather had founded the Ebenezer Baptist Church, and his father had nurtured it into one of the largest and most successful churches in the city. Martin inherited not only his father's name; it was also understood that he would be the next minister of the Ebenezer Church.

But King entered Morehouse College, an all-black male college in Atlanta, at the age of fifteen, still undecided about his future career. Despite his inheritance, he was then trying to choose between law and medicine. The ministry appeared to him as intellectually crude; he was too familiar with the image of the black pastor working his congregation into an evangelical fever. But by the end of his junior year, Martin announced his commitment to the church.

During his years at Morehouse, King began to develop the philosophical basis for his later stance on nonviolent protest against discrimination. Henry David Thoreau's justification for "Civil Disobedience" especially impressed the young man. "One has a moral responsibility to disobey unjust laws. . . . An unjust law is a code that is out of harmony with the moral law," wrote King later, much in the spirit of Thoreau.

Two hundred thousand people, black and white, filled the Washington Memorial mall in August 1963 to give a visible form to Martin Luther King's dream of racial harmony.

Martin Luther King, Jr., was the most eloquent spokesman for racial justice in the 1960s. For many, his passionate plea for nonviolence was undercut by his own violent death at the hands of an assassin.

King graduated from Morehouse at the age of nineteen. He could have moved directly into the ministry, as the assistant pastor of his father's church, but he chose instead to continue his education by attending, first, Crozer Theological Seminary in Chester, Pennsylvania, and later, Boston University. It was at Crozer that King first became acquainted with the writings of Mahatma Gandhi and became strongly attracted to the Indian leader's philosophy of pacifism.

While King pursued his graduate studies at Boston University, he was introduced to Coretta Scott, a graduate of Antioch College, whom he later married. The Kings stayed in Boston while Martin completed his dissertation and received his doctorate.

In May 1954, King accepted the pastorate of the Dexter Avenue Baptist Church in Montgomery, Alabama. That same month, the United States Supreme Court decided *Brown* v. *Board of Education of Topeka.* The unanimous Court opinion declared racially separate school systems unconstitutional. Neither the court nor the twenty-five-year-old minister realized it, but a revolution was about to begin.

It started without fanfare, and, as it turned out, had nothing to do with the schools. On Thursday, December 1, 1955, Rosa Parks entered her usual crowded bus and took a seat behind the vehicle's white section. Farther down the line more whites boarded, and Mrs. Parks was ordered by the driver to give up her seat to a white man. She refused. The bus driver called the police and she was arrested for violating the city's segregation code. Four similar episodes had occurred in Montgomery the previous year, but this time the black community responded.

The groundwork had been laid for concerted black action. Negro leaders had been active in NAACP (National Association for the Advancement of Colored People) programs, and many black women of the community had been working for equality of public facilities through their Women's Political Council. Jo Ann Robinson, head of the women's organization, had already formulated plans for a bus boycott by blacks; she had only been waiting for a defendant like Rosa Parks, a determined and respected member of the black community. When news of the arrest reached Mrs. Robinson, she approached various leaders to seek support for her plan. She first called Ed Nixon, an NAACP official who, in turn, telephoned the Reverend Ralph Abernathy and Martin Luther King, Jr. After King conferred with Abernathy, he decided to give the boycott his full support.

On Friday evening, December 2, black community leaders met at King's church and called a boycott for the following Monday, December 5. They spent the weekend getting news of the boycott to the rest of the black community. On Monday morning the bus boycott proved a total success. Blacks walked to work or used taxis driven by other blacks who had agreed to charge bus rates. Late that afternoon, the leaders met again. They decided, on the basis of this initial success, that the boycott would continue, and they founded the Montgomery Improvement Association (MIA) to superintend it. Martin Luther King, Jr., was elected President of the MIA, and blacks and whites alike recognized him as leader of the boycott. That evening, at a seven o'clock rally, King both challenged and inspired his audience with a call for community protest against the years of racial oppression. As the boycott continued throughout the next year, King was to find that not only were Montgomery blacks ready for protest but the nation itself was prepared to listen.

King and the MIA spent most of December attempting to negotiate with the city government. The city's lawyer warned that recognition of MIA's demands would destroy the social fabric of the South; the negotiations were doomed. By January 1956, the white establishment, frightened by the overwhelming success of the black boycott, began to fight back, legally and extralegally. Police harassment of private car pools among blacks became commonplace. On January 30 King was arrested for speeding. His short imprisonment added impetus to the black movement, and a crowd gathered at the jail to demand his release.

While in jail, King learned that his home had been dynamited. For a man less committed to nonviolence, this would have become a time to seek revenge. Instead, King pleaded for restraint. From the steps of his demolished porch, he spoke of love, not hate. "We want to love our enemies. We must love our white brothers no matter what they do to us." For the moment, violence was averted, and the crowd dispersed.

In February the city indicted the leaders of MIA for conspiring to interfere with normal business. By this time, the Montgomery bus boycott had become an issue of wider scope. King was fast becoming the national symbol of civil rights; his arrest and trial in March received national press coverage, and the majority reaction nationwide was overwhelmingly sympathetic. The local judge found the MIA leaders guilty. At a subsequent appeal, a higher court ruled the bus ordinance unconstitutional. The city appealed the ruling, and the case began a long journey through normal appelate channels that led eventually to the United States Supreme Court. King used the next three months to carry his message across the country, speaking at rallies from coast to coast.

The first of ninety defendants to go on trial for illegal conspiracy in the Montgomery bus boycott, King left the Montgomery courthouse with his wife, Coretta, on March 19, 1956. Although found guilty, along with other MIA leaders, the defendants won the case on appeal, when the Montgomery bus ordinance was found unconstitutional.

Eleven months after the boycott began, MIA faced another crisis. In November the city issued an injunction against the carpool. Without the pool, the boycott would fail. On the morning of November 13, 1956, King and the other MIA leaders entered the Montgomery court in a gloomy frame of mind. And as their trial wore on, it gave them little cause for hope. Suddenly, during a recess, there was a news bulletin that the Supreme Court had reached its decision: segregated buses were indeed unconstitutional. Triumphantly, on the morning of December 21, 1956, King entered a bus and took a seat in one of the first ten rows. His success was marred, however, by the violence that followed. For a month, Montgomery experienced dynamitings and individual assaults, but eventually the city moved to establish peace. Seven white men were arrested and tried for participating in the violence, but they were acquitted.

King and his supporters felt, however, that their legal campaign in Montgomery had succeeded. They had won their court battle, and could now count the federal judiciary as an ally. More important, Montgomery had awakened the nation to the issue of civil rights for blacks in a specific, admirable, and dignified way.

In the years that followed, King devoted his energies to mobilizing his following and organizing his ideas. Meetings in early 1957 led to the formation of the Southern Christian Leadership Conference (SCLC), with King as its president. Originally, SCLC was intended to supplement the efforts of existing civil rights organizations such as the NAACP and the Urban League. But the leaders of these older, established groups opposed King's primary strategy of passive resistance. The NAACP felt that the best way to achieve racial equality was through the courts; Urban League leaders believed that black economic gains would provide the answer.

Not all of King's activities during these years were directed toward civil rights organizing. In February 1959, he and his family visited India, where he was received enthusiastically. King returned to America with an even deeper commitment to Gandhi's principles of nonviolence.

When King returned to America, his father offered him, for a second time, the co-pastorate of his Ebenezer Baptist Church in Atlanta. This time King accepted, for reasons that went beyond simply pleasing his father. By this time the SCLC had grown into a full-fledged organization, with headquarters in Atlanta. King believed that to put Gandhian principles into action, he would have to devote more time to the civil rights crusade. In January 1960 he moved his family to Atlanta and prepared to escalate his campaign with an antisegregation movement centered in that city.

Like the campaign in Montgomery, the Atlanta movement started quietly and simply. On February 1, 1960, in Greensboro, North Carolina, two black university students refused to leave a Woolworth's lunch counter when they were denied service. Within a week, their simple demonstration had sparked similar "sit-ins" in other major Southern cities. By March, the sit-in movement had reached Atlanta, where Atlanta

The lunchcounter sit-ins, started in 1960 in Greensboro, North Carolina, proved an effective technique of protest against racial discrimination in public places. The proliferation of sit-ins in the early 1960s, and the attention they drew, contributed to the passage of the 1964 Civil Rights Act.

University students issued a manifesto demanding an end to racial discrimination in education, housing, jobs, voting, law enforcement, hospitals, and entertainment facilities.

The Atlanta campaign operated under the careful guidance of King and the SCLC. In April, King called a civil rights student conference, advocating the establishment of a permanent student organization (later to become known as SNCC—Student Nonviolent Coordinating Committee), a campaign of selective economic boycott, and the establishment of a volunteer army of student demonstrators. King was facing pressure from both sides of the black community. The student movement's potential for violence had to be controlled, while the older civil rights groups—the NAACP and the Urban League, which opposed the new civil disobedience techniques—had to be won over. King moved quickly to maintain the momentum of protest and to retain control of the unfolding situation.

On October 19, he and thirty-six other demonstrators were arrested and charged with trespassing when they would not leave the lunch counter of Rich's department store after being denied service. King and the others refused to post bond. The judge proposed a two-month truce. Arrangements between the prisoners and the city government were being negotiated when an unexpected move by the DeKalb County authorities pushed King's case into headlines all over the nation. Six months earlier, the minister had been arrested in DeKalb County, Georgia, for driving with an invalid out-of-state license, and had been placed on probation for twelve months. The DeKalb authorities maintained that

King's October arrest violated his probation. The prisoner was transferred to DeKalb County and given a sentence of four months hard labor at Reidsville State Prison.

The imprisonment created national outrage, and demands poured into the White House for King's release. President Eisenhower declined to intervene in matters of local concern, however, and Vice-President Nixon, then embroiled in his presidential campaign against John F. Kennedy, refused to comment. But Kennedy showed no reluctance. After telephoning Mrs. King, the Democratic presidential nominee instructed his brother, Robert, to help get King out of jail. King himself was not especially impressed by Kennedy's move, which he saw as one primarily of political expedience, designed to win Kennedy black support at the polls in November.

In March 1961 the combined organizations of three civil rights groups—CORE (Congress of Racial Equality), SNCC, and King's SCLC—initiated a new program: the Freedom Rides. King was appointed chairman of the Freedom Rides Coordinating Committee. The rides were designed to "mobilize" the sit-in; the riders travelled from Washington, D.C., through the South to Montgomery, Alabama. Participants tested the segregation codes of each city enroute by staging sit-ins in public facilities such as bus station waiting rooms and lunch counters.

The results were damaging to King personally and to his philosophy of nonviolence. The first riders met with disaster in Anniston, Alabama, where one of the buses was attacked and set on fire. The second bus made it safely as far as Birmingham. There, the riders were brutally beaten by a mob of whites while police looked on. The riders continued to Montgomery, but many demonstrators were left bruised and bloodied on the highway. King and 700 special marshals appointed by Attorney General Robert Kennedy rushed to Montgomery, but the damage was irreparable.

King then decided to compromise: in May, SCLC suggested a "temporary lull" in the Freedom Rides. This suggestion was totally ignored by SNCC, and during the summer of 1961 more rides and more violence occurred throughout the South. King had been labelled a moderate, and he had lost much of his support among black youth. But there was more to come.

Albany, Georgia, typified many Southern black belt towns. The subordination of the black race was accepted and recognized as the socially correct way of life. The unwritten code provided that blacks were mildly tolerated as long as they kept to themselves. For the black community, Albany was not particularly better or worse than other Southern hamlets. But the events in Montgomery and other civil rights confrontation sites eventually had their impact on Albany.

SNCC decided to test the September 1961 Interstate Commerce Commission ruling that outlawed segregation in bus station waiting rooms. In October, nine students entered the white section of the Trailways bus depot in Albany and were arrested. When the ICC took no immediate action, black leaders decided to mobilize. The Albany Movement was born. Trial for the original "offenders" was set for December 11. That same day, five black and four white Freedom Riders arrived in Albany. They left their bus, entered the white waiting room of the station, and were arrested.

Their arrests touched off protest marches and more demonstrations. By December 15, many people were in jail. That day, King arrived in Albany to lead the campaign. The SNCC leaders reacted angrily to what they saw as a usurpation of their control. Their jealousy would seriously hamper the campaign's effectiveness.

Pitched battles between civil rights groups and city authorities continued. King and his followers staged sit-ins and marches. King was jailed twice, and the city refused to honor its December truce agreement, issuing injunctions against demonstrations of any kind. In July, news of an assault on a pregnant black woman touched off a battle involving several thousand blacks and the police. This appalled King, and he called for a one-day moratorium on demonstrations, which served to alienate further the SNCC. Moreover, black leaders of the conservative NAACP and Urban League continued to hold King's methods ultimately responsible for the outbreaks of violence.

The struggle continued throughout August. King attacked the Kennedy administration for its failure to act. The Albany city officials refused to yield to any of the Albany Movement's demands, and the white community stiffened its determination to retain supremacy. September was a month of white retaliation. Within one week, the Ku Klux Klan bombed four black churches.

King, meanwhile, had returned to Atlanta, where he turned his energies toward another and larger-scale campaign—this time in Birmingham, Alabama. Albany had taught him that future campaigns must be better organized and must be directed toward an assault on specific issues rather than an attack on racial discrimination in general.

The industrial metropolis of Birmingham, Alabama, was especially tough on blacks. Its police commissioner, Eugene "Bull" Connor, was an outspoken racist, and King was anxious to challenge its overbearing, white-dominated control. King had no major worries about divided leadership here; Fred Shuttlesworth, leader of the black Birmingham community, was a long-time personal friend.

Neither did the Birmingham venture suffer from lack of organization. Many meetings and much paramilitary planning went into the formulation of "Project C" (C for confrontation). On April 3, 1963, the campaign opened with the declaration of "B Day" (B for Birmingham). For two days, blacks staged sit-ins and picketed in front of white businesses. On April 6 the second stage of Project C began. Shuttlesworth led forty-five people on a march to city hall. Connor had them arrested and jailed. The next day, Palm Sunday, another group of marchers set out for city hall to join those in jail. Three days later city officials obtained an injunction against the black leaders.

Again King had decided to defy the court order. On the morning of Good Friday, he and Abernathy led fifty hymn-singing marchers toward city hall as black spectators lined the streets shouting encouragement. Soon after they had begun, Connor ordered their arrest. King was placed in solitary confinement. Disturbed by her inability to find out what might have happened to her husband, Coretta King phoned President Kennedy for help. On Monday the President returned the call, giving Mrs. King personal assurances concerning her husband's safety.

While King and Abernathy remained in jail, matters worsened in the city. King's brother was imprisoned for demonstrating without a permit, and his arrest touched off further street disturbances. Governor George Wallace, who had personally defied court orders to desegregate the University of Alabama, was meanwhile encouraging counterdemonstrations by whites. King and Abernathy were released on bail on April 20. The relatively mild sentences meted out to them six days later indicated that the white power structure feared the consequences of imprisoning King, and thus creating a black martyr.

Early May saw more marches and more violence. On May 2nd, 6,000 children marched and 959 were arrested. For the next four days, the nation watched with horror as police swung their clubs and unleashed their dogs. By May 7, open rioting flared in the streets. Kennedy could no longer remain inactive. The next day King was rearrested and Kennedy made his move.[1]

Behind the scenes, the President had already put pressure on Birmingham businessmen to negotiate, and a truce was beginning to take shape. When King was returned to jail, Robert Kennedy immediately called Birmingham city officials to warn them of imminent federal intervention unless the city agreed to black demands that public facilities be desegregated. That evening King was released; the next morning, white officials agreed to meet with black leaders.

The outcome of those meetings in Birmingham were disappointing. The pact between the civil rights leaders and the city was informal, and in the following months the city reneged on much of it. Certainly the pact had not put an end to white violence. In the week after the compromise, King's brother's home was bombed, and more violence ensued. But on the national scale, Birmingham seemed a "success." King's personal prestige soared, and blacks in Birmingham took pride in what they considered a tactical victory. On May 20 the United States Supreme Court upheld the constitutionality of sit-ins. King had succeeded in arousing the country to the issue of civil rights. In June, after several years of directly confronting the issue, Kennedy called for a comprehensive civil rights bill.

---

[1]Both President Kennedy and his successor, Lyndon Johnson, authorized FBI investigations into King's personal life. FBI Director Hoover, who was trying to find evidence that King's SCLC was "Communist-infiltrated," supervised an extensive probe of the black leader that included wiretaps and close surveillance of his activities. At one point, the FBI sent a note to King that threatened that if he did not commit suicide, compromising tape recordings of his personal life would be publicly released. The entire FBI probe continued right up to King's death; it never produced an iota of evidence that sustained the attacks on King's loyalty as an American. The entire episode—only recently revealed—was one of the most shameful abuses of governmental authority in recent American history.

After Birmingham, civil rights and Martin Luther King became truly national concerns. During 1963 and 1964, King received immense personal recognition; but he also suffered severe moral defeats, as the country rocked with violence. On June 12, 1963, Medgar Evers, the NAACP field secretary, was murdered in Jackson, Mississippi. The militancy of black youth, which had surfaced briefly in the Albany and Birmingham campaigns, was on the rise. King found it increasingly difficult to keep the black movement identified with nonviolence.

Throughout June 1963, King toured the nation giving speeches and leading marches in the major cities. But the teachings of the Muslim separatist Malcolm X and other black leaders were also being heard. King's national fame was now drawing criticism from persons who equated his efforts with publicity-seeking. He was seen as a creation of the media, as a peacefully protesting black man—an image more or less acceptable to the country's white majority. King had little control over his image, although he did try to reshape his program.

To gain more national support, King and the SCLC planned a March on Washington, to be held in August 1963. Though originally conceived in 1962, the plan took on special significance as the civil rights bill before Congress faced defeat by a Southern filibuster. In July, leaders from five civil rights organizations and representatives of many national organizations sympathetic to the movement met in New York to plan the march. Black militants censured the meeting, charging that a white conspiracy was seeking to moderate black demands by limiting the demonstration's objectives. Despite this internal discord, the march went on, and King's emotional speech moved the world.

In the South, in Birmingham and Atlanta and elsewhere, violence continued. On September 22, 1963, yet another church was dynamited, this time in Birmingham. Four little black girls were killed and in the ensuing confusion Birmingham police shot and killed two black youths near the scene. In Atlanta, where past demonstrations had been generally peaceful, violent battles raged between blacks and policemen. But neither King nor the nation was prepared for the events of November 22, 1963. John Kennedy's assassination threatened not only King's dream— it threatened the American dream as well. To King, Kennedy's murder reaffirmed the malignant role of violence in the American way of life: "We mourned a man who had become the pride of the nation, but we grieved as well for ourselves, because we knew we were sick."

The events of 1964, in both the North and the South, further dramatized the extent of the illness. A drive to desegregate beaches and other public facilities in St. Augustine, Florida, proved both bloody and frustrating. Promises extracted from the city were quickly retracted, and racial polarization bred more violence. The Mississippi Freedom Summer is remembered more for the brutal slaying of three young civil rights workers—one black, two white—than for the significant gains in registering black voters. In the North, the cities of Rochester, Detroit, and Philadelphia were rocked by racial rioting. These disturbances foreshadowed the even greater violence in Los Angeles, Chicago, Detroit, and Newark

CIVIL RIGHTS GROUPS

Year Founded	Group Name	Purpose
1909	National Association for the Advancement of Colored People (NAACP)	An association that aims to achieve equal citizenship rights for all American citizens, through peaceful and lawful means, by eliminating segregation and discrimination in housing, employment, voting, schools, the courts, transportation, and recreation.
1910	National Urban League	A community service agency that aims to eliminate racial segregation and discrimination in the United States and to help black citizens and other economically and socially disadvantaged groups to share equally in every aspect of American life.
1918	Southern Regional Council	A research and information center that seeks the improvement of economic, civic, and racial conditions in the South by providing community relations consultation and field services when requested by official and private agencies; distributing pamphlets that deal with desegregation of various public facilities, and fostering elimination of barriers to black voting registration.
1935	National Council of Negro Women	A coalition of twenty-five national organizations and concerned individuals that seeks to stimulate the development and utilization of the leadership of women in community, national, and international life.
1939	NAACP Legal Defense and Educational Fund	The legal arm of the civil rights movement that represents civil rights groups as well as individual citizens who have bona fide civil rights claims.
1942	Congress of Racial Equality (CORE)	A black nationalist organization that seeks the right of black people to govern themselves in those areas that are demographically and geographically defined as theirs.
1957	Southern Christian Leadership Conference	A coordinating and service agency for local organizations that aims to improve civic, religious, economic, and cultural conditions through nonviolent resistance to all forms of racial injustice,

in the summer of 1965. "Black Power," a slogan symbolizing violent retaliation to white oppression, became an increasingly popular rallying cry for militant black youth.

King feared that Johnson, Kennedy's successor, would oppose civil rights legislation. But his optimism was renewed in the early days of the new administration, as he and the President worked together amicably. On July 2, 1964, Johnson signed a new, tough Civil Rights Bill into law. During this period, King's emphasis shifted from desegregation to an attack on poverty and economic discrimination. Johnson's antipoverty program, launched in August 1964, complemented King's moves, and prospects for continued support from the White House looked good.

CIVIL RIGHTS GROUPS

Year Founded	Group Name	Purpose
1960	Student Nonviolent Coordinating Committee (SNCC)	including state and local laws and practices. Formerly: Student Nonviolent Coordinating Committee. A committee that sought to help poor people, eliminate slums, and reduce long working hours (now moribund).
1960	National Catholic Conference for Interracial Justice	A religious organization that initiates programs within and without the Catholic Church to end discrimination in community development, education, employment, health care, and housing.
1962	Scholarship, Education and Defense Fund for Racial Equality	An organization that creates programs to provide services in community development, including Eleanor Roosevelt scholarships for students who have demonstrated leadership in civil rights, leadership training programs, and technical assistance for newly elected black officials.
1962	Voter Education Project	A project created as part of the Southern Regional Council to investigate the causes and remedies of low political participation by southern blacks.
1963	Commission for Racial Justice	Commission's purpose is to make racial justice a reality in our national life.
1963	Law Students Civil Rights Research Council	An independent, civil rights legal organization that recruits, trains, and places law students in legal clerkship positions and aims to influence the attitudes of future lawyers about law and social change.
1964	A. Philip Randolph Institute	A nonmembership institution established to serve civil rights activists and promote cooperation between labor and the black community.
1964	Student Afro-American Society	A society that seeks to combat apathy toward the civil rights movement among black college students.
1970	Southern Poverty Law Center	An organization that seeks, through legal precedents it helps to establish via court decisions, to protect and guarantee the legal and civil rights of poor people of all races throughout the nation.

Adapted from *Gales Encyclopedia of Associations*

The results of the 1964 voter registration drive in Alabama were impressive. The number of registered blacks rose from 6,000 in 1947 to 110,000. But at the start of 1965, King returned to the South with plans for a new registration campaign. He singled out Selma, Alabama, as the campaign's focal point. On February 1, King, Abernathy, and 770 demonstrators marched on the courthouse and were promptly arrested. After being jailed for four days, and feeling the momentum dying, King organized a march from Selma to Montgomery to confront Governor Wallace. The marchers, however, threatened with violence, dispersed before reaching Montgomery. But in Selma, three white ministers sympathetic to the black movement were beaten, one of them fatally.

At this point, President Johnson made a historic move. Addressing Congress on March 15, he introduced a voting rights bill designed to guarantee black voting in the South. Johnson also called for a national drive to end racial discrimination. Thus he identified himself with the aspirations of blacks more strongly than had any other President: "Their cause is our cause, too. Because it is not just Negroes, but really all of us who must overcome the crippling legacy of bigotry and injustice. And we shall overcome." Two days later the Selma-to-Montgomery march received federal protection. On March 21 King and his supporters set out, triumphantly entering Montgomery four days later. Clearly, King had succeeded in rallying national support behind a voting rights bill.

And King's dream grew. Encouraged by his recent success, he decided the time had come to broaden his crusade: he began to express his opposition to the Vietnam war. In October 1964 he had won the Nobel Peace Prize. In keeping with his status as an international advocate of peace, he attacked the United States for waging war and for wasting federal funds sorely needed for domestic programs. This new stand cost him considerable support among many conservative black leaders. And it ended his chances of future support from President Johnson, whose administration had widened America's involvement in the war.

The King family moved North to Chicago in June 1966. There, King began a program of organizing black tenants to force their landlords to improve housing in the slums. The opposition to King's first assault on Northern abuses of the Negro was both sophisticated and well organized. Chicago's Mayor Richard Daley commanded one of the best-run municipal political machines in the history of American politics; also, the city's black leaders were disorganized and their political leader, Congressman William Dawson, owed his primary allegiance to Daley. Moreover, the problems of poverty and racism in an urban metropolis

A revolutionary manifestation of black militance, "black power," and separatism, the Black Panthers presented a threatening counterpoint to the nonviolent, integrationist spirit that had dominated the Civil Rights movement in the early 1960s. The Panthers' influence was eclipsed at the end of the decade by the murder of several of their leaders in Chicago.

were unfamiliar to the Southern minister. In the final analysis, they would prove to be more than he could control.

King's announcement of a June march drew only criticism from black militants. Black Power advocates Stokely Carmichael and Adam Clayton Powell both called for excluding whites from the black movement. The June rioting in Chicago's black ghetto postponed the march until July 10, and the turnout was disappointingly small. The aftermath was even worse. Three more terrible days of rioting followed, and King found himself and the SCLC on the defensive.

Faced with the indifference of Mayor Daley and President Johnson, as well as an injunction that limited the size of any further demonstrations, King played his full hand—by this time a weak one. He called for a march on Cicero, a Chicago suburb and the center of white resistance to black demands. Two days before the march was scheduled, black leaders and city officials announced a compromise, but its terms brought no real victory for King and his program. He had obviously ended his Chicago campaign without making clear gains for the city's black poor.

Reverend Martin Luther King, Sr., on June 12, 1977, at a press conference held before he spoke at a Baptist Church in Knoxville, Tennessee.

Although King failed in Chicago, he did not desert his aim of economic racial equality. Rather, in the months following that drive, he devoted even more energy to economic issues. But the rumblings of discord that had started in Albany and had increased over the years had by this time escalated into public attacks on King and the SCLC. Militant blacks characterized King's position as "tokenism"; conservative blacks condemned his anti-Vietnam pronouncements and held him personally responsible for black violence.

Although King continued to urge nonviolent resistance as the most effective way to minimize racial conflict, by 1967 he began to devote far more time and energy to the peace movement than to civil rights. In March and April he headed peace marches and spoke out against the war. Civil rights issues had become overshadowed by the growing national opposition to the war in Vietnam.

In April 1968 King began to plan a Poor People's March on Washington, D.C.—a two-barreled protest against poverty and military involvement overseas. While details were being worked out by the SCLC staff, he received word that his help was needed by black organizers in Memphis, Tennessee. After conferring with his staff, King agreed to go.

A strike of Memphis garbage workers, mostly blacks, had become the focal point for organizing black protest. The effort appealed to King. He believed that a victory in Memphis would provide badly needed momentum for the supporters of nonviolent protest elsewhere in the country. Therefore, he announced plans for a peaceful march to support the garbage workers. But March 28, 1968, the day of the demonstration, was anything but peaceful.

Shortly after the march began, a group of young blacks began breaking windows. The confusion that followed quickly escalated into a riot. Fifty persons were injured, and more than twice that number were arrested. The march was a personal defeat for King. His inability to control his own followers triggered vicious attacks from all sides, and the

Dr. King's funeral, on April 9, 1968, was attended by 150,000 persons, who marched through the streets of Atlanta, after final ceremonies at the Ebenezer Baptist Church. King's murder, five days earlier, had been followed by riots in sixty-three cities across the nation. The riots, according to Dr. King's widow, were "an ironic tribute to the apostle of non-violence."

city obtained an injunction against further demonstrations. Once again, King announced his decision to defy the court order and to lead another march. That evening, King delivered one of his most fiery sermons to a group of followers in a Memphis church, pleading with them to remain nonviolent toward their enemies. "I have been to the mountain," he intoned, reminding his supporters that he had witnessed the triumphs and tragedies of their movement for over a decade.

King did not march again. The next day, Thursday, April 4, 1968, King was shot in the head as he leaned over the balcony railing of his Memphis motel room. He died before reaching the hospital.[2]

World leaders and thousands of Americans gathered in Atlanta to attend his funeral. Although many speakers eloquently lauded his contributions to racial justice, a simple inscription was carved on the slain minister's monument: "Free at Last, Free at Last, Thank God Almighty, I'm Free at Last."

_____

[2]Several months later, an escaped convict, James Earl Ray, was arrested, and confessed the crime. Ray later recanted his confession, but still serves a life sentence for the crime.

50
AMERICA IN THE 1960s: CRISIS AND CHANGE

A. W.

On January 20, 1961, John F. Kennedy became the thirty-fifth President of the United States. Though he won narrowly over Richard M. Nixon, for many Americans of all races Kennedy symbolized the same hope for a better future that Martin Luther King symbolized for blacks. But, in the decade of the sixties, there were over 100,000 American casualties in the Vietnam war. At home, great masses of antiwar protestors spoke out. Black people vented their anger in the March on Washington and in violent riots in the ghettos. University students demonstrated their outrage at government defense research being conducted on their campuses. The voices of women loudly protested sexual inequality. The 1960s, in short, were characterized by an enormous release of energy both within the government and among groups seeking change within the society. What emerged was a mixture of achievement and anguish, confrontation and crisis, impressive social changes and the most depressing of national tragedies.

THE KENNEDY ANSWER: THE NEW FRONTIER

In his acceptance speech at the Democratic Convention in 1960, Kennedy summarized what *he*
hoped to do for his country under the banner of the New Frontier. His domestic program was designed to benefit everyone. He promised to strengthen the economy by reducing inflation and unemployment. To improve the lot of the poor, he intended to provide medical care and increased social security benefits. Blacks were assured that their civil rights would be federally protected. Education was to receive additional federal funding. And all Americans would see the age of consumerism replaced by the virtues of commitment.

Kennedy's Cold War program involved "out-gunning" the Russians. Using the "missile gap" argument in 1960 (the claim that Russia had a greater nuclear striking capacity than the United States), Kennedy supported defense spending designed to ensure that the existence of American arms superiority would deter Russia from initiating nuclear war. This type of thinking ignited a nuclear arms race with Russia in the early sixties, with ramifications evident at home. In 1961 and 1962, hundreds of Americans built nuclear fall-out shelters near or under their homes; millions of school children were drilled on where to go in case of an atomic war; a federal and civil defense bureaucracy plastered shelter signs and stored dehydrated emergency food rations in public buildings all over the country.

The shelters were not used, and the American people breathed sighs of proud relief after the Berlin and Cuban crises. But an important lesson had been learned. Although the Red Scare atmosphere of the fifties had not vanished completely, the outcome of the Cuban and Berlin crises definitely lessened perceived threats of Russian aggression. The Cold War produced a confusing set of circumstances. On the one hand, Americans were led to believe that nuclear war and Communist domination of the world were constant threats. On the other hand, when "eyeball-to-eyeball" crises occurred, the Russians backed down. Was Russia really an aggressive and powerful adversary?

Kennedy's domestic programs met with less success. The civil rights issue exploded in 1961 and 1962, and all Kennedy could do was to ask for a cooling-off period. Kennedy's social reform plans faced stiff resistance from Congress. He failed to win approval for his education, tax revision, and Medicare programs. But he did win moderate increases in federal spending, expanded trade, and stabilized interest rates, which brought the economy out of the recession of the Eisenhower years. These gains, however, did not decrease the 5.5 percent unemployment rate. Kennedy's biggest domestic triumph was the space program, but even that achievement had its drawbacks.

The space program was partially, if not entirely, initiated as another race with the Russians. Distressed that Russia got into space first in the 1950s with Sputnik, Kennedy decided that Ameri-

Neil Armstrong took this photograph of Edward Aldrin preparing a scientific experiment on the surface of the moon. Their successful lunar landing fulfilled John Kennedy's promise of 1961 to put Americans on the moon before 1970.

cans would be the first to land a man on the moon. On May 6, 1961, Alan Sheppard made the first American suborbital flight. Less than a year later, John Glenn circled the earth. Both flights were part of phase one, the Mercury project. Phase two, Gemini, involved two-man space trips. Apollo, the third phase, took men to the moon. This feat was first accomplished on July 20, 1969, when Neil Armstrong took his "giant step for mankind" on the moon.

Although few failed to be impressed by this major technological achievement, some wondered whether it was worth the cost. When three astronauts died on the launch pad in 1967, some scientists blamed their deaths on America's obsession to get to the moon first. Moreover, second to the defense budget, the moon shot proved to be the most expensive of Kennedy's programs. Many critics challenged this expenditure in light of other pressing domestic programs that were seeing their funding reduced or held to inadequate levels.

Despite the complaints and setbacks, Kennedy remained optimistic in 1963, and with some reason. The civil rights movement was gaining momentum. Kennedy's foreign policies won America prestige abroad and fostered American pride at home. In the summer of 1963, the Soviet Union and the United States agreed to ban above-ground nuclear testing. Although this agreement did not end the arms race, Kennedy reassured Americans that their air would no longer be polluted by radioactive materials. Kennedy's popularity began to soar. In the fall of 1963, the President planned a political tour to drum up support for his programs and for the Democratic party. The last stop planned was in Dallas. For Kennedy, it proved the final stop of his career. On November 22, 1963, Lee Harvey Oswald shot and killed the President. The assassin was himself gunned down the next day in the basement of the Dallas police headquarters. For the next week, the American people sat stunned while the events of Kennedy's life, death, and funeral filled the media. Few will forget the blood-stained clothes of Jacqueline Kennedy, or the traditional riderless horse of the funeral procession. John Kennedy passed from the presidency into mythology. His actual achievements and failures became blurred and the prom-

President Kennedy's funeral procession, with its riderless horse, is shown here at the Capitol. At the time he was assassinated, November 22, 1963, Kennedy had been visiting Dallas in quest of Southern support for the 1964 Presidential election. His successor, Lyndon Johnson, soon after being sworn into office, told Congress that he intended to memorialize Kennedy by enacting the legislative program of the New Frontier.

ise he symbolized took hold of the public imagination. His life became an emblem of honesty and peace; his death, in turn, symbolized the corruption and violence in American life.

A presidential commission, headed by Chief Justice Earl Warren, investigated the assassination but did little to alleviate American bitterness. Warren and his colleagues concluded that Oswald had acted alone. But since many questions remained unanswered, the Commission report only heightened public frustration and doubt. The understaffed Commission passed over conflicting data, which led many to believe that the whole truth had not been told. Conspiracy theories mushroomed, some more plausible than others, but distrust of the official explanation continues to disturb the American consciousness.

THE JOHNSON ANSWER: THE GREAT SOCIETY

If Kennedy symbolized a new breed of politicans, the man who inherited Kennedy's challenge stood for the old. Though Lyndon Johnson was only nine years older than Kennedy when he was sworn into office aboard Air Force 1, his style was quite different. Johnson's terms in Congress, including several years as Democratic leader of the Senate, had taught him the intricacies of power politics. Though this kind of political strength helped push his domestic programs through Congress, many Americans, especially younger ones, came to view this power as a corrupting force. And the formation of a "credibility gap" pointed up the distrust enveloping the nation.

In the first months after Kennedy's death, Johnson used his political might—and support from black leaders such as King—to ram through Congress a comprehensive Civil Rights Bill and to launch his antipoverty program. Other Kennedy bills that had bogged down also slid through Congress during Johnson's first year in office. Congress authorized federal funding for higher education, made appropriations for mass transit, and approved a tax cut. In May 1964, Johnson announced that this "drive" was part of his new program—the Great Society, "a place where men are more concerned with the quality of their goals than the quantity of their goods."

Johnson continued to press his domestic programs. In the fall of 1965, Congress passed an impressive number of domestic bills, many originating in or supported by the White House. Health care for the aged and indigent became law under Medicare and Medicaid. The Elementary and Secondary Education Act called for billions of dollars of assistance to low-income children, and private schools received federal assistance for the first time. A new Cabinet post, the Department of Housing and Urban Development (HUD) came into existence. And numerous other bills to combat disease, clean up the environment, make highways safer, equalize immigration quotas, and provide more money for the war on poverty passed easily. Johnson's accomplishments in domestic areas drew applause and even astonishment. Apparently he could do no wrong — until his magical political fingers were burned to a crisp on Vietnam.

The "credibility gap" in foreign affairs grew out of the 1964 election. Like Wilson, who in 1916 campaigned as the man who kept the United States out of war, Johnson promised in 1964 that American boys would not do the job of Asian boys in Vietnam. Johnson fashioned his image as a dove using fabricated cabinet and Pentagon reports on conditions in Vietnam. The South Vietnamese, Americans were told, had the war all but won; United States intervention would be discontinued. Voters believed the Democrats and returned Johnson to office in a landslide victory.

On February 7, 1965, Johnson approved air strikes on North Vietnam, and his image as a peacemaker was soon discarded. Explanations for the bombings did little to restore faith. Americans were told that in order for the war to be ended, it would have to be escalated. Debates on escalation raged across the country, but the Johnson administration wanted victory in Vietnam.

From then on, Johnson's main concern would be the war. Billions of dollars and thousands of lives were committed to the effort. Every night, Americans witnessed the atrocities of war on television screens and wondered which of their husbands, fathers, sons, or friends would die next. No other war in history was so graphically brought home to the nation. The impact of the media coverage of Vietnam, generally, was disastrous to Johnson. The administration's contention that the South Vietnamese supported the American-supported Saigon government was hard to reconcile with televised coverage of Buddhist riots and self-immolations.

But even harder to understand or believe was the notion that United States involvement truly aided the Vietnamese people. Night after night, Americans viewed the charred bodies of Vietnamese and their demolished villages — the aftermath of American air raids. And even if, somehow, Americans got used to hearing reports of napalm air strikes to burn out the Viet Cong, they were not ready to digest the slaughter of 347 Vietnamese men, women, and children by an American unit on a "search and destroy" mission at My Lai on March 19, 1968.

THE SUPREME COURT ANSWER: CIVIL LIBERTIES

The years of Vietnam involvement — and Vietnam disaster — were also years during which legislation broadening personal freedom was being passed at an intense rate. This expansion for civil liberties received support from the decisions of the Warren Court (named for Chief Justice Earl Warren, who presided over the court from 1953 to 1969). The majority of justices who served on the Supreme Court during these years believed strongly that individual freedoms must be preserved; they maintained that an active judiciary should protect these rights against local, state, and federal infringement. The impact of this judicial philosophy was felt in decisions on a wide range of cases, from the issue of civil rights to that of prayer in public schools.

The Warren Court dropped a major bombshell opinion in May 1954. In *Brown* v. *Board of Education of Topeka, Kansas,* Chief Justice Warren and all his colleagues maintained that separate education based on race, regardless of the "equality" of facilities offered to those separated, was inherently unequal. Segregation violated the equal protection clause of the Fourteenth Amendment.

The South, angered by the *Brown* decision, fought the ruling. In Arkansas, conflict over desegregation of a high school in Little Rock erupted into a confrontation between states' rights and federal power. The Arkansas governor attempted first to delay school integration and later to close the high school, but the federal courts were determined to fight school segregation. Ultimately, President Eisenhower had to send United States Army troops to Little Rock to enforce the court order. In subsequent cases involving school segregation, the Supreme Court has upheld the *Brown* ruling.

The Land Americans Have Shaped

How to describe the United States of today? Travelers use words like "size," "diversity," "achievement," "efficiency," "wealth." All are valid. But all seem somewhat abstract without a sense of the people who have worked to make America what it is. Their monuments may be as modest as a tiny New England village—this one in Vermont—or as vast as Boulder Dam. Clearly, they have transformed the land first explored by Europeans over 450 years ago. Wrote Mohamed Mehdevi of Iran: "My imagination could not keep pace with the trials and labors that must have gone into this spanning and building of a continent, an achievement of man. And it had been done not by heroes and great warriors, but everyone."

[For further information on the foreign observers quoted in this essay, see "Notes on Sources."]

PICTORIAL ESSAY 9

Skyscrapers, New York City

New York is a vertical city. It is a catastrophe with which a too hasty destiny has overwhelmed courageous and confident people, though a beautiful and worthy catastrophe. Nothing is lost. Faced with difficulties, New York falters. Still streaming with sweat from its exertions, wiping off its forehead, it sees what it has done and suddenly realizes: "Well, we didn't get it done properly. Let's start over again!" New York has such courage and enthusiasm that everything can be begun again, sent back to the building yard and made into something still greater, something mastered!

[LE CORBUSIER, 1947]

Levittown, Pennsylvania

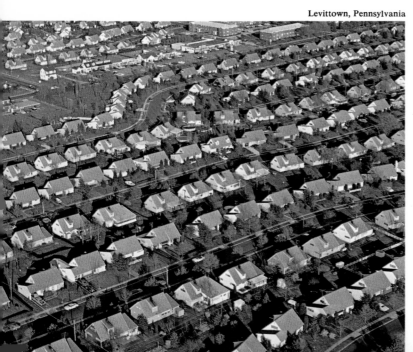

Already, three out of every five American families own homes. The horizontal trend which has replaced the vertical trend of the skyscrapers is covering the great green spaces around the cities with the individual houses of suburbia. Suburbia is a way of life. In the family-centered society which America has become in recent years, suburbia is regarded as the ideal place to rear children. In this world of carefully mowed lawns there already lives one-third of the nation.

[HERBERT VON BORCH, 1962]

On the banks of the Mississippi stands a stately home with pillared porch, dappled oak alley and a spacious lawn, on which magnolias shed their heavy-lidded blossoms. The home is open to visitors on Sundays, though a family is in residence. There is a guide in the shape of an overpowering lady who waits until the number of visitors meets her approval. The lady praises the past in a voice that echoes in the marble halls.

[JAN DE HARTOG, 1961]

South Carolina plantation

The Americans are proud of their Lincoln and Jefferson Memorials, and they enjoy showing visitors their National Art Gallery, a splendid white Tennessee marble building which looks pink after a rain. Next we visited the Library of Congress. As we walked around the city this evening in the warm moist air filled with swirling leaves, we saw the dome of the Capitol illuminated against the dark sky. Washington is not a provincial city but a melting pot for people from every state who come to do business, petition, or simply visit.

[NIKOLAI MIKHAILOV AND ZINAIDA KOSSENKO, 1960]

Joint session of Congress

The Capitol, Washington, D.C.

Assembly line workers, Detroit

Steel works, Gary, Indiana

I became aware of the pace of work in North America, a pace that was not the international one but that of Uncle Sam. During the eight-hour day people really attended to their job, and it was taken for granted that the chiefs would set an example of punctuality and dedication. Among us Chileans, and I believe also in all the Latin countries, the boss enjoys the privilege of arriving late at the office and staying away whenever he feels like it, and the employees, by the same token, can refrain from showing too much devotion to their work. Compared with us, the North Americans strike me as a much more powerful and better run machine.

[AMANDA LABARCA H., 1959]

American architecture has beauty, audacity, and a superb sense of scale, absorbing what is best in modern architecture in Western Europe, adapting itself to American needs, scenery, and wide horizons, and yet presenting what is exciting, new, and vital. The architect works in freedom and according to the needs he must satisfy and the function his building must perform.

[MORRIS BROUGHTON, 1959]

University of Chicago Law Library, designed by Eero Saarinen

Then there are the cities, and especially those small towns that hold the secret of the United States—with their frame houses, their adjoining gardens always open to the view, their grass of a succulent and hospitable green, their tall, powerful trees, their modest and silent intimacy, softened in the whiteness of the snow or expressed passionately in the floral effusion of the springtime; their hospitable and secluded churches, their bustling schools, their solitary streets along which there shine at night, among the trees, the lights of so many open windows; and the business streets with the bank, the gasoline station, the tempting and ingeniously arranged shop windows.

[JULIAN MARIAS, 1959]

Parade at Taylor, Wisconsin

Wheat farm on the Great Plains

If you come from the Eastern states, or farther east still, from Europe, going west is a continuous journey of suspense, from the moment you are over the Appalachians and know that the Atlantic has gone for good. In the Midwest, the sky is a little wider, and the prairie is a kind of sea all its own; so much so that in the wheat-lands of Kansas you get the illusion of great heaving yellow swells, and the silos float by like battleships on the horizon.

[ALISTAIR COOKE, 1968]

Taos Pueblo, New Mexico

Taos is the most characteristic of all the reservations. We were struck at once by its beauty. On two sides of an open space, traversed by a stream, are enormous blocks of buildings, as high as they are long, in which adobe houses are encrusted and super-imposed one above the other. The dominant color is a dull yellow, but red and violet cloths, hung up to dry on the flat roofs and fluttering in the breeze, light up the sombre background.

[SIMONE DE BEAUVOIR, 1947]

Hoover Dam (Boulder Dam), on the Arizona-Nevada border

Boulder Dam is something more than a vast utilitarian device, a super-gadget. Enchanted by its clean functional lines and at the same time awed by its colossal size, you might be tempted to call it a work of art; as if something that began with utility and civil engineering ended somewhere in the neighborhood of Beethoven's Ninth Symphony.

[J. B. PRIESTLEY, 1935-36]

Street signs, Las Vegas

Harbor Freeway, Los Angeles

A feature of Las Vegas hotels is that there are no windows or clocks. Gamblers must not be reminded to go to bed. The less expensive gambling avenue caters for a poorer class of tourist and is known as Glitter Gulch. Its electric signs made it as bright as day. It is ridiculous to sneer at the lighted advertisements of the U.S. Romantic historians are always saying how wonderful Elizabethan London must have been "with all those painted inn signs swinging in the wind." Well, here you have it still alive. Why sneer? It is living, it is folk art, it is exquisite from an aircraft, and I personally like *to be saluted by an electric cowboy a hundred feet high who waves his arm in a gesture of Hi!*

[T. H. WHITE, 1964]

Just leaving my hotel [in Los Angeles] I feel lost —the distance to the nearest drugstore is the same as between two villages in France. One's helplessness in such vastness is paralyzing. In a car with a girl I said: "Let's go somewhere out of town. . . ." "But where?" she asked. "Oh, no matter where . . .," I smiled, ". . . where the city ends." "Los Angeles never ends," she said firmly.

[LEOPOLD TYRMAND, 1966]

San Francisco at night

We sped toward the Mark Hopkins [and went to] the top floor. The walls were of glass, and we walked slowly around the room, looking at the myriad lights below; it was far more beautiful than Los Angeles at night, than even New York itself, because of the bay traced out in shining lines against a background of dark water and also those fiery ladders rising from the sea. We looked for a long time. There are, in such travels, moments which are promises and others which are only memories: this one was complete in itself.

[SIMONE DE BEAUVOIR, 1947]

There is enough wilderness in the world to increase very greatly the number of national parks and to see to it that some of them are preserved in their original condition with access kept so strenuous that the solitary walker is most unlikely to be crowded out.

And this perhaps is the ultimate meaning of the wilderness and its preservation—to remind an increasingly urbanized humanity of the delicacy and vulnerability of all the living species—of tree and plant, of animal and insect —with which man has to share his shrinking planet. As he learns to observe their interdependence and their fragility, their variety and their complexity, he may remember that he, too, is a part of this single web and that if he breaks down too thoroughly the biological rhythms and needs of the natural universe, he may find he has destroyed the ultimate source of his own being. If somewhere in his community he leaves a place for silence, he may find the wilderness a great teacher of the kind of planetary modesty man most needs if his human order is to survive.

[BARBARA WARD AND RENÉ DUBOS, 1972]

Beach and cliffs, Kauai Island, Hawaii

Glacier Peak Wilderness, Washington

EARL WARREN

Of the three men generally considered great Chief Justices of the U.S. Supreme Court, Earl Warren served only about half as long as John Marshall or Roger Taney. He was over sixty when named to the Court and had never served as a judge before. Yet from 1953 to 1969, Chief Justice Warren stirred up as much controversy—and helped write as much new law—as most men do in life-long judicial careers. While millions of Americans hailed the bold initiatives of the Warren Court, others bought billboard space and bumper stickers demanding, "IMPEACH EARL WARREN."

The son of a Norwegian immigrant, Warren had slowly and painstakingly worked his way up in California politics, from Alameda County district attorney, to attorney general, to governor. Although a very private man, not given to backslapping, he rapidly became the most popular politician in the state, establishing a strong record as a liberal, effective administrator. Taking advantage of California's unique election laws of that era (laws that allowed "cross-filing"), he won both the Republican and Democratic nominations in 1946, and overwhelmingly won a third term in 1950.

Defeated as the Republican candidate for Vice President in 1948, Warren hoped for the presidential nomination in 1952. But instead, he helped Dwight Eisenhower win the prize. Shortly after the election, President Eisenhower, although himself a conservative, named his useful supporter chief justice. Ike—stung by Warren's liberal activism—later regretted the act, calling it the biggest mistake he had made during his presidency.

Less than a year after his appointment, on May 17, 1954, Warren spoke for a unanimous court in *Brown* v. *Board of Education*, declaring racial segregation in public schools to be unconstitutional. At least one Justice had been dubious about the ruling; the chief justice persuaded him that a decision of such importance had to be unanimous. *Brown* was the first of many decisions in which the Warren Court upheld the rights of minorities.

Not all of Warren's major decisions, however, received unanimous consent from Court members. In a long series of rulings on the rights of criminal suspects, the Chief Justice and four colleagues comprised the bare majority. In *Gideon,* they ruled that the state must provide a lawyer for any defendant unable to afford one; in *Escobedo*, that a suspect can have a lawyer present during questioning; in *Miranda,* that a suspect has the right to remain silent and refuse to answer questions.

In perhaps its most far-reaching decisions, the Warren Court ruled that legislative districts had to be drawn on the basis of population, rather than of county or township borders. These became known as the "one-man-one-vote" rulings, because they voided long-standing practices that gave rural voters greater political power than underrepresented city dwellers.

If such rulings caused right-wingers to hang Warren in effigy, he also earned the distrust of the left while presiding over the Warren Commission, which investigated the assassination of President Kennedy. Warren issued a controversial report which asserted that Lee Harvey Oswald had been the lone gunman. By the time Warren retired in 1969, at age seventy-eight, some but not all of the bitterness directed against him and his Court by extremists had died down.

Still the evasions continued. One technique to evade the ruling was to close public schools and subsidize all-white private schools with county funds. In *Griffin* v. *County Board of Prince Edward County* (1964), the Supreme Court ruled that this practice "denied petitioners the equal protection of the laws." The next assault on the *Brown* decision came through "freedom of choice" plans adopted by many Southern states. Under these, parents could choose the student's school, and local custom insured that black children attended black schools. The Supreme Court overturned this practice in subsequent rulings, which also held that the *Brown* decision required desegregation be accomplished as quickly as possible. These decisions did not achieve immediate desegregation, but more than simply deny the constitutionality of segregation, they required that measures be taken to ensure desegregation.

In a number of other cases involving racial discrimination heard from 1955 through 1966, the Warren Court invalidated segregation of public facilities and laws prohibiting racial intermarriages. It also confronted the legality of convictions growing out of "sit-ins." From 1961 through 1963, the Supreme Court concluded in several cases that demonstrators had lawfully exercised the right of free speech and that arrests had been based on illegal segregation codes. In cases involving housing, the Court ruled that discriminatory practices in sales and rentals were unconstitutional.

The judicial attack on discriminatory voter registration practices had ample precedent. As early as 1927, the Court invalidated Texas's "white primary" law. In 1949, an Alabama law requiring that voters understand and explain any articles of the state constitution was ruled "patently unconstitutional" under the Fifteenth Amendment. After passage of the Twenty-Fourth Amendment prohibiting poll taxes as a voting requirement, and the Voting Rights Act of 1965, the Supreme Court continued to rule against laws designed to deny blacks the right to vote. In a series of cases it upheld federal power to prohibit poll taxes, discrimination tests, and literacy tests as voting requirements.

While defending the rights of black people to equal protection of the law, the Warren Court also enunciated new procedures for guaranteeing the rights of political dissenters and accused criminals. With its attack on various acts designed to suppress political dissent, the Court undermined much of the legality of the McCarthy era assault on Communists, subversives, and political dissenters. In *Yates* v. *United States* (1957), the Warren Court held that, to be prosecuted under the Smith Act, it must be proven that an individual engaged in specific acts advocating revolution. Subsequent cases involving state prosecution of subversives resulted in Court declarations that states could not outlaw mere advocacy of the use of force, because to do so would deny freedom of speech. The requirement that government employees sign loyalty oaths was attacked by the Court in a number of cases from 1962 to 1967. In 1967, the Court held that the requirement of loyalty oaths "threatened the cherished freedom of association protected by the First Amendment." The right of persons to plead the Fifth Amendment to avoid self-incrimination was also reinforced by Warren Court rulings.

Perhaps the most revolutionary aspect of this civil liberties revolution came in cases involving the rights of suspected or accused criminals. In *Mapp* v. *Ohio* (1961), the Court applied an earlier ruling to invalidate the use in court of illegally obtained evidence. *Gideon* v. *Wainwright* (1963) obliged states to provide counsel for defendants who could not pay for their own attorneys. Confessions obtained under duress were declared a violation of due process. In *Escobedo* v. *Illinois* (1964) and *Miranda* v. *Arizona* (1966), the Court ruled out confessions obtained before defendants had been advised of the right to consult an attorney or the right to refuse to answer police questions. The right of the defendant to a jury trial was extended to include state criminal procedures in 1968.

Freedom of the press, protected under the First Amendment, posed difficulties for the Supreme Court in the 1960s. At issue was the constitutionality of censoring obscene or pornographic literature. As one writer expressed the problem, "obscenity, at bottom, is not crime; obscenity is sin." But the Warren Court tried to define obsceni-

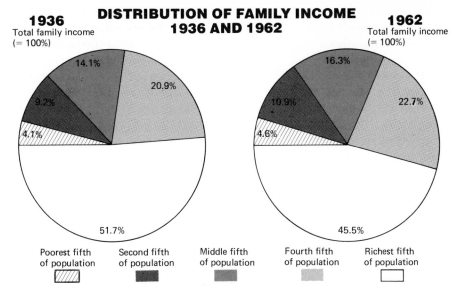

DISTRIBUTION OF FAMILY INCOME 1936 AND 1962

1936
Total family income
(= 100%)

14.1%
20.9%
9.2%
4.1%
51.7%

1962
Total family income
(= 100%)

16.3%
22.7%
10.9%
4.6%
45.5%

Poorest fifth of population

Second fifth of population

Middle fifth of population

Fourth fifth of population

Richest fifth of population

In this chart, the first "pie" shows the percentages of the total income for 1936 received by the poorest fifth of the people, the richest fifth, and the three fifths in between. The second pie reflects the same data for 1962.

ty constitutionally. The Court tended to vacillate between declaring some censorship invalid as a violation of the First Amendment and, at the same time, upholding censorship as the prerogative of the local community. As a result, the issue became more confused than before.

The Court also threatened many established patterns in American politics by a revolutionary decision, neatly summed up as "one man, one vote." This ruling (*Baker* v. *Carr*, 1962) declared that electoral districts for Congress and state legislatures had to be drawn so that they contained almost equal numbers of people. For generations, cities had been underrepresented in both state and national legislatures. In contrast, rural areas had enjoyed disproportionately higher political representation. The Court ruling threatened this practice and shifted the balance of political power toward the cities.

But the Court provoked the most controversy in the 1960s by deciding against public school prayers. In 1962 the Court declared that the daily recitation of a nonsectarian prayer in New York schools violated the First Amendment injunction that "Congress shall make no law respecting an establishment of religion." One year later it de-

clared unconstitutional a Pennsylvania statute requiring the daily reading of ten Bible verses. These decisions elicited vehement criticism from congressmen and the public. Some irate Court critics wanted to impeach Earl Warren. Attempts were made to pass a "prayer amendment" to the Constitution to overrule the Court's decision, but the measure stalled in the Senate.

By the end of the 1960s the Supreme Court had established an unprecedented record for defending civil liberties in a wide variety of areas. But in the final years of the decade, it became increasingly apparent that this trend toward judicial libertarianism would slow down. The Nixon appointees to the Supreme Court, like Warren Burger, the man who replaced Earl Warren, began to shift the Court's balance toward a more conservative stand.

THE BLACK ANSWER: EQUALITY FOR ALL

The start of Martin Luther King's crusade in the late 1950s took most white Americans by surprise.

Many believed that blacks held inferior positions in society because they *were* inferior. They gave credence to the American work ethic—those who work hard get ahead, and those who fall behind have no one to blame but themselves—to rationalize the oppression of blacks. And King's new tactical program of civil disobedience, although the backbone of the Founding Fathers' opposition to George III, seemed decidedly alien. Still, King's actions forced thoughtful people to admit that perhaps racism *was* part of the American system. This proposition once accepted, King's nonviolent tactics could then be applauded. King merely asked for a fair share of the American dream; other militants who followed attacked the dream itself.

Although King's demonstrations were often accompanied by violence, it appeared that he was succeeding and improving American society's ability to cure its own ills. By 1965, several important federal measures put the seal of governmental approval on King's campaign. The Civil Rights Bill of 1964 outlawed racial discrimination in pub-

lic facilities. The ratification of the Twenty-third Amendment in 1964 ended poll taxes in federal elections. In August 1965, Johnson signed the Voting Rights Act, ending literacy tests and authorizing voter registration by federal examiners.

But some blacks remained angry over what remained undone. Since Birmingham, a feeling of frustration had been mounting. In 1965, the first of four successive summers of racial rioting erupted in the ghettos of Watts, Detroit, and Newark. Black militancy was superceding civil disobedience. During a march to Jackson, Mississippi, Stokely Carmichael of SNCC heralded the new black image—Black Power. Many black leaders tried to tone down the implications of Carmichael's approach, but the primary message came through. "Black and white together" (a stanza from "We Shall Overcome") was no longer viable. Black Power meant white exclusion from the movement. Black Power also meant that black people would not wait for justice to be dispensed like welfare payments. The new organization that

Among those influenced by King's advocacy of nonviolent tactics was Cesar Chavez, leader of the Mexican American farm workers. Here he ends a twenty-three day fast in support of striking grape growers by breaking bread with Robert Kennedy.

promoted these ideals most truculently was the Black Panthers.

Even before this, another black, and much more radical than King, Malcolm Little (or Malcolm X as he was known after he joined the militant, but separatist, Black Muslims) had already presented a serious challenge to King's moderate leadership in New York and other Northern cities. Malcolm X himself was killed at a New York rally in 1965. His death—combined with King's and the killing of several Black Panther party leaders in Chicago in 1970—opened the way for a more and more splintered contest for public leadership of black Americans.

By the time Martin Luther King was assassinated in 1968, the crusade for black equality had been transformed into black separatism. Even followers of King's nonviolent philosophy began to question whether blacks would ever be integrated into American society on an equal basis; the Black Panthers and other black nationalist groups had already decided that they would not—nor did they want to be. Although the Panthers were not the only black nationalists, they did receive the most publicity, thus providing Americans with a fractured picture of what black nationalism meant. In the end, some Panthers were killed in police raids. Others were arrested on a variety of charges. Still others shifted to electoral politics and community action to achieve their goals.

During 1968 and 1969, the years of "nonnegotiable" demands, black militants confronted college and university administrations. They called for more black admissions, black faculty, and black studies programs. At many schools, the administration moved quickly to satisfy the blacks. At others, black students took over buildings and conducted teach-ins to apply pressure on

The nonviolent spirit of protest that characterized the early Civil Rights movement, as seen in the peaceful demonstration on the left, during the 1965 march from Selma to Montgomery, gave way within the decade, to a mood of strident militance. The shift in attitude reflected increasing internal division within the Civil Rights movement, the growth in influence of separatist and nationalist leaders, and a mounting sense of frustration, most manifest in the ghetto riots of the later 1960s.

the administration. The long-range effects are hard to assess. Colleges and universities did admit more black students and hire more black faculty, but the gap in educational equality is not so easily closed.

The black response to the 1960s had more to it than black nationalist separatism. All black groups, from the NAACP to the Black Panthers, shared at least a common opposition to racial oppression. What they achieved through their varied approaches and policies still cannot be accurately measured, but by the end of the sixties, the slogan, "I'm Black and I'm Proud" had become a "non-negotiable" reality.

THE STUDENT ANSWER: FREEDOM NOW

College life in the 1950s evokes images of football games, sorority and fraternity parties, and political apathy. But in the 1960s, a number of university students caught the public eye through political demonstrations, takeovers of school administration buildings, and antiwar protests. A variety of explanations have been offered for the new activism. Some maintain that it was the effect of keeping young people bottled up in institutions for the first two decades of their lives. Others contend that by the 1960s, universities had become so bureaucratic that students felt lost and alienated. Still others argue that the consumer culture of the 1950s provided no ideological goals for its youth. Whatever the explanation, students in the sixties demonstrated that they wanted their country to honor its commitments to free speech, equality of opportunity, world peace, and individual freedom. More often than not, the means they adopted to reach these goals defeated their purposes.

Many college and university students were introduced to the tactics of political activism in 1964, during the Freedom Summer and the Berkeley Free Speech Movement. Hundreds of students spent their summer vacation canvassing the back country of Alabama and Mississippi trying to get potential black voters registered. Others parti-cipated in the Freedom Rides. Many activist groups, such as the SDS (Students for a Democratic Society), became increasingly vocal in their opposition to the Vietnam War and to the anonymity of the university complex.

The first student movement to receive intensive national attention was the 1964 Free Speech Movement (FSM) at the University of California, Berkeley. Students and administrators disagreed over the use of a campus sidewalk for distributing student activist literature. When the university ordered the students' tables evacuated, they refused to leave. The confrontation escalated into an attack on the bureaucratic nature of the university itself. A student strike proved 50 percent effective. The next day, the faculty met and voted to remove all restrictions on speech. The FSM had won. Students learned that they had some power to change university policy.

The campus protests quickly spread. From 1965 through 1970, student disturbances rocked universities throughout the country. Many of these disturbances resulted in greater student participation in a university's management. But a backlash by conservatives, appalled at student militancy, was also taking hold. In California, these sentiments helped elect Ronald Reagan governor. Reagan appealed to the disaffected public with promises to discipline students and professors involved in the FSM.

This polarization increased when college campuses became the centers for antiwar demonstrations. Most of the participants and organizations in the antiwar movement had university or college connections. In 1965 numerous campus teach-ins took place; faculty and students discussed and debated American involvement in Vietnam, and most condemned the action. In September the SDS launched a campaign against the draft, declaring October 16–21 "Stop the Draft Week." Students responded with protest meetings and draft card burnings. Not all of the demonstrations were peaceful. A protest march from the University of Wisconsin on Dow Chemical Company (Dow had been selected because it manufactured napalm) ended in battles between the students and police. The week climaxed with a march on the Pentagon building itself. American

Antiwar demonstrators at Stanford University in May 1969, were rousted out of Encina Hall, a University administration building, after voicing their objections to U.S. policy in Vietnam. The array of protagonists typifies social protest confrontations of the 1960s: on one side, the helmeted forces of "law and order," and on the other, a taunting remnant of the counterculture, young and defiant.

TV viewers witnessed the spectacle of armed policemen beating off the protesters.

Organized student opposition grew, and so did violence. Another march on the Pentagon took place in October 1967. And again America witnessed bayoneted rifles confronting militant students.

Antiwar sentiment had been gathering momentum in other strata of society as well. Congress began expressing doubts about the war by the mid-1960s. In January 1966, Senators Mansfield and Fulbright began to hold committee hearings on the conduct of the war. In February, Mansfield announced that Americanization of the war had gained nothing. The Senate Foreign Relations Committee headed by Fulbright brought the congressional debate into American homes with televised hearing on American involvement. While these hearings did not appear to sway President Johnson, they gave some legitimacy to the antiwar movement.

The student movements in the 1960s left their mark, especially in attacking the university's paternalistic tradition. Administrators and regents had to pay more attention to student needs, and students gained a larger voice in shaping policy. Still, the impact of student representation on policy formulation remained minimal.

The antiwar movement was more than somewhat successful in demonstrating the need to reevaluate American foreign policy, but much public hostility toward students surfaced in response to splinter extremist groups that preached revolution. Organizations like the Black Panthers and the Weathermen, although small in numbers, alienated a significant portion of the adult population. To many Americans, the student movement of the 1960s seemed but one part of a widespread and threatening counter-culture.

THE COUNTER-CULTURE

The term "counter-culture" is a handy label for describing the social phenomenon of the 1960s. In simplest terms, the counter-culture represented an unorganized and varied attack by young people on the "Establishment." Student protest and antiwar activity were not the only elements of the movement. Nor were campuses the only settings for expressing counter-culture ideology or attitudes. The counter-culture "mind-set" defies succinct description. But in practice, the idea of a counter-culture implied a rejection of traditional cultural values.

American attitudes toward sexual experience underwent the greatest change. Sexual freedom became a national preoccupation — traditional sex roles were denounced. Young men rejected the time-honored outward manifestations of manhood by letting their hair grow long and adorning themselves with jewelry. Women rejected lace and frills, choosing blue jeans and workshirts instead. Young people of both sexes openly rejected the taboos against premarital sex. College dorms went coed, and the practice of living together replaced or preceded marriage for many couples.

The entertainment world responded to the new sense of personal liberation by exploiting and promoting it. Rock musicians sang about sexual openness. Theater groups produced plays like "Hair" and "Oh! Calcutta," displaying nudity and simulated sex acts. Movies became progressively more sexually explicit. Certainly the easy availability of contraceptives (especially birth control pills) contributed to this revolution and its underlying philosophy: that all middle-class inhibitions on sexual freedom must be repudiated.

In some cases, the general attack on sexual attitudes took organized forms. Many women began to denounce the repressiveness of sexual roles. A growing movement designed to eradicate male domination in American society, Women's Liberation, arose in the late 1960s. Schooled in the tactics of activism by earlier involvement in the black and antiwar movements, many women began to see their most pressing social problems in terms of gender, not class or race. "Male chauvinism" was added to "racism" and "imperialism" in describing American "repression."

Like other movements in the decade, Women's Liberation adopted varied means for ending male dominance. Some organizations like NOW (National Organization of Women) advocated political techniques. Hiring policies in businesses and college and university campuses were attacked for practicing sexual discrimination. Women demanded stronger penalties for rape. A number of women supported legalized abortion. The Women's groups lobbied for the passage of an Equal Rights Amendment, which they hoped would provide the same constitutional basis for

The movement for black civil rights inspired other movements like Women's Liberation. These demonstrators use the foremost symbol of freedom as the backdrop for their demands for political and economic equality.

woman's rights as the Fourteenth Amendment had for blacks, although a number of women fought the amendment as destructive of woman's special rights within American society.

Not all women involved in Women's Liberation saw politics as the correct or only path. Other women's organizations worked on issues closer to home. Female collectives and female consciousness-raising groups formed in most parts of the country. Other feminist groups rejected marriage, the traditional role of the mother as the primary parent, and the concept that the women's place was in the home. Some women extremists advocated an abandonment of heterosexuality. Many American women remained sympathetic to the movement's more immediate and practical demands for full equality in employment opportunities and pay scale, liberalized abortion laws, and expansion of day-care centers. Certainly the Women's Movement of the late 1960s and 1970s eroded the image that most women were content homemakers alone.

Another institution that found itself under attack by the counter-culture was the family. The Women's Movement gave strength to this assault by questioning traditional sex roles within the family, but other counter-culture groups posed more serious threats. One such group was the Gay Liberation League. During the sixties, homosexuals denounced society's legal and moral sanctions against them. They demanded an end to job discrimination and to legal prosecution of their members.

Another challenge to established definitions of family came from the commune movement. Some young people in the sixties started living together in groups, reviving a tradition of utopian communal living with roots that went back to the 1840s. Some of the communes survived, although many were plagued by economic pressures and internal conflicts.

Other counter-culturists challenged basic American traditions and values, questioning the work ethic and the idea that American technological growth guaranteed progress. Some young Americans declared that technology degraded and corrupted life. They decided to return to the rural environment. Organic farming—agriculture without chemical fertilizers or pesticides—became a popular symbol of their philosophy. Others found the answer in Timothy Leary, and the drug culture. Marijuana use skyrocketed in America. This, and other psychedelic drugs, became an integral part of the counter-culture.

The counter-culture thrived in the 1960s and the early 1970s. Though American traditions had been attacked, they were not toppled. Yet a new level of tolerance for alternative life styles

was achieved. Nonconformity was tolerated to a far greater degree by the end of the 1960s than ever before.

THE MAJORITY ANSWER: A CONSERVATIVE PRESIDENT

Nineteen sixty-eight was a bad year for many Americans, and an especially bad one for Democrats. On January 31, the Viet Cong launched its Tet offensive in South Vietnam, illustrating a determination and ability to continue the war. The attack spelled disaster for President Johnson. After having assured the American people for more than four years that the United States was winning the war, he was forced to concede his overconfidence. In March, Johnson announced deescalation of the war and a drive for a negotiated peace. The second part of this televised message, however, stunned his audience. "I have concluded that I

Lyndon Johnson's legislative experience helped him get an impressive domestic program through Congress during his presidency. This same activism in foreign affairs, however, proved to be his downfall.

With the Democrats about to nominate Hubert Humphrey inside, the passions of demonstrators outside intensified—but so did the reaction of the police. Here police are shown dispersing demonstrators outside convention headquarters.

should not permit the presidency to become involved in the partisan divisions that are developing in this political year. Accordingly, I shall not seek, and I will not accept the nomination of my party for another term as your President." Johnson, the shoo-in victor of 1964, had dropped out.

Johnson's dramatic withdrawal came in part because he could not hold the Democratic party together. Senator Eugene McCarthy had already effectively demonstrated that fact by nearly beating Johnson in the New Hampshire primary. McCarthy's promise to end the war in Vietnam had won him the support of the student activists. His campaign in New Hampshire succeeded largely because of their volunteer efforts. After Johnson's withdrawal, Robert Kennedy, then holding a New York Senate seat, entered the presidential race. Vice President Hubert Humphrey appeared on a few primary ballots as a pro-administration surrogate candidate. But McCarthy won

some primaries and Kennedy others. Gradually, attention focused on the last primary, California. There, Kennedy won by a narrow margin. There, too, leaving a victory celebration in a Los Angeles hotel, Robert Kennedy was murdered by a young Palestinian immigrant, Sirhan Sirhan.

This assassination—Kennedy's removal from the political scene—turned the Democratic convention into a struggle between a liberal wing, led but not controlled by Eugene McCarthy, and the party regulars, who rallied behind Hubert Humphrey. The regulars held a sufficient number of delegate votes to nominate Humphrey. But while the party regulars were winning inside the convention hall, the actions of demonstrators in the streets outside were losing them votes in the election. Thousands of people, most of them young, had come to Chicago not to attend the convention but to protest the Johnson administration's domestic and foreign policy.

President Nixon and former President Johnson at the Nixon inauguration in January 1969, with Chief Justice Earl Warren, at the left. Nixon, who had refused to debate his opponent, Vice President Humphrey, during the campaign, had won the presidency by a narrow popular margin of about five hundred thousand votes out of seventy-three million. Neither he nor Humphrey had aroused overwhelming enthusiasm among the electorate, nor had the campaign reflected the vital issue of the day—U.S. policy in Vietnam.

On millions of television sets around the country, Americans watched the two simultaneous events: the convention went on with the cumbersome and traditional speeches and roll calls, while outside, the police broke discipline and began to attack the demonstrators. Some protestors fought back with rocks, bottles, fists, and feet. But the main battle ended quickly. The police assumed control, and the crowd scattered to other parts of the city.

The federal government eventually indicted eight protest march leaders on conspiracy charges. But a spectacular trial produced no convictions. And little or no disciplinary action was taken against the Chicago police.

The convention itself was bitterly split between anti-Johnson forces and Administration stalwarts. In that sense the battle almost assured the defeat of Hubert Humphrey, the presidential nominee and Johnson's Vice President, and the election of a Republican President that November. Richard Nixon easily won the Republican nomination at a much more peaceful convention in Miami, although the election itself proved close.

Nixon won a marginal victory. He received fewer votes than in 1960 and won by only seven-tenths of one percent of the popular vote. Both

Nixon and Humphrey represented the old guard of politicians, the latter more liberal in his policies, but both urged on immediate end to street protests and a return to "law and order."

When Nixon took office, he promised to bring Americans into an era of retrenchment and tranquility. To accomplish this, he sought to buy off the right while undercutting the left. But this center-of-the-road plan often ran into difficulties. The first three years of the Nixon administration ran a decidedly zig-zag course. To appease moderate liberals, he advocated a sweeping reform of the welfare system that would set up a guaranteed minimum income for every family; but he ignored the issues of urban development and civil rights. In foreign policy, Nixon promised to end the Vietnam war, but to end it "with honor." His plan for accomplishing this surfaced slowly [see Chapter 52].

The economy presented even stickier problems. Nixon vowed allegiance to big business and big labor, whose support had been instrumental in getting him the presidency. In 1969 he promised no government interference and ridiculed the idea of economic controls. But rapid inflation and growing unemployment cut into his popularity. In August 1971 the President announced a three-month freeze on prices, wages, and rents, and after that he placed a ceiling on price and wage in-

U.S. GROWTH OF POPULATION, 1920–1970

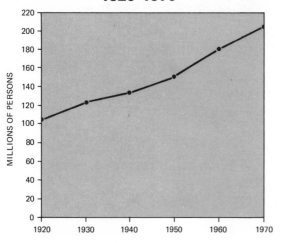

creases. Neither big business nor the unemployed were pleased, but Nixon had demonstrated a surprising flexibility.

If the silent majority was happy with Nixon, a vocal minority was not. The war in Vietnam continued; and despite United States troop withdrawals, the end did not seem near. In April 1970 Nixon announced that American troops had entered Cambodia. The promise of peace had been betrayed. Within days, protests erupted on campuses across the country. Four days after Nixon's announcement, students at Ohio's Kent State University were battling police and National Guardsmen. This now-familiar scene escalated to an unfamiliar and tragic climax. In the middle of a May 4 demonstration, National Guardsmen, without warning, opened fire on the students. Four students were killed, eleven wounded. Some of the dead were bystanders. During the rest of the month, buildings were burned and more battles took place on major college campuses. By the end of the month, hundreds of universities and colleges had been shut down, either by student strikes or by administrators fearful of violence. The President's Committee on Campus Unrest reported that, although the use of live ammunition was unwarranted, the Kent State students shared the responsibility for the events of May 4, 1970. The Cambodia spring of 1970 provoked the last of the large campus demonstrations, but never before had student anger and frustration been displayed on such a massive scale.

SUGGESTED READINGS– CHAPTERS 49-50

Martin Luther King

Coretta Scott King, *My Life with Martin Luther King, Jr.* (1969); Martin Luther King, Jr., *Why We Can't Wait* (1964); David L. Lewis, *King: A Critical Biography* (1970); Lerone Bennett, *What Manner of Man* (1968).

Civil Rights and Civil Disorders

Richard Bardolph, *The Negro Vanguard* (1959); Numan V. Bartley, *The Rise of Massive Resistance* (1969); Harold Cruse, *The Crisis of the Negro Intellectual* (1967); James Forman, *The Making of Black Revolutionaries* (1972); Charles V. Hamilton and Stokely Carmichael, *Black Power* (1967); Marshall McLuhan, *Understanding Media* (1964); August Meier and Elliott Rudwick, *CORE* (1973); *The Autobiography of Malcolm X* (1965); Howard Zinn, *SNCC: The New Abolitionists* (1964).

The Supreme Court

Alexander M. Bickel *The Supreme Court and the Idea of Progress* (1970); Albert P. Blaustein and

Clarence P. Ferguson, Jr., *Desegregation and the Law* (rev. ed., 1962); Richard M. Dalfiume, *Desegregation of the U.S. Armed Forces, 1939–1953* (1969); Samuel Krislow, *The Negro in Federal Employment* (1967); Philip B. Kurland, *Politics, the Constitution, and the Warren Court* (1970); Clifford M. Lytle, *The Warren Court and Its Critics* (1968); Loren Miller, *The Petitioners . . . the Supreme Court . . . and the Negro* (1966).

J.F.K. and L.B.J.

Carl M. Brauer, *John F. Kennedy and the Second Reconstruction* (1977); Eric Goldman, *The Tragedy of Lyndon Johnson* (1969); Theodore H. White, *The Making of the President, 1964* (1965); Tom Wicker, *JFK and LBJ* (1968); Rowland Evans and Robert Novak, *Lyndon B. Johnson* (1966).

Protests of the 1960s

William Henry Chafe, *The American Woman* (1968); Robert M. Fogelson, *Violence as Protest* (1971); Betty Friedan, *The Feminine Mystique* (1963); Robin Morgan, ed., *Sisterhood is Powerful* (1970); Kate Millett, *Sexual Politics* (1970); William L. O'Neill, *Coming Apart* (1971); Theodore Roszak, *The Making of a Counter-Culture* (1969); Kirkpatrick Sale, *SDS* (1973); Doris Kearns, *Lyndon Johnson and the American Dream* (1976).

Prosperity and Poverty

Edward C. Banfield, *The Unheavenly City* (1970); Erik Barnouw, *The Image Empire: From 1950* (1970); Scott Donaldson, *The Suburban Myth* (1969); Jane Jacobs, *The Death and Life of Great American Cities* (1961); Charles E. Silberman, *Crisis In Black and White* (1964); Sam B. Warner, Jr., *The Urban Wilderness* (1972).

(For books on the United States in Vietnam, see the Suggested Readings for Chapters 47–48.)

51
WATERGATE

A. W.

The young man on the witness stand was in trouble. Federal prosecutors had enough evidence to put him away for a long time. He had obstructed justice, failed to report a crime, and helped destroy evidence. Like many other people in similar situations, he was trying to soften the coming blows by testifying against his associates. But John Wesley Dean III, former White House counsel, differed from most informers. He was testifying during the last week of June 1973, not in court, but before a U.S. Senate committee probing illegal presidential campaign activities, as millions of Americans watched on television. Under penalty of perjury, John Dean was calling the President of the United States a criminal.

Tensely awaiting Dean's disclosures, the White House was prepared to fight the accusations—the President's lawyer had already given the committee fifty questions designed to discredit Dean. Furthermore, the White House now claimed that Dean himself and former Attorney General John Mitchell had masterminded both the illegal activities and the attempt to cover them up.

Disowned by the White House and hopelessly ensnared by federal prosecutors, John Dean told his story for five suspense-filled days. Senators and committee lawyers questioned him closely, and journalists examined his account for contradictions. All the while the White House offered opposing evidence. Everyone, especially the large television audience, searched Dean's face for clues as to his truthfulness. But at the end of his testimony, the committee and the public knew only what they had known before—either John Dean or Richard Nixon was lying. If Dean was lying, the country had just witnessed a dramatically effective performance. If President Nixon was lying, he would have to pay for it with his office.

The Watergate hearings reached a dramatic climax with the testimony of John Dean, here being sworn in before the Senate investigating committee by its chairman, Sam Ervin. To test the truthfulness of Dean's testimony, Senate investigators subpeonaed presidential tapes, and a confrontation with the executive branch resulted.

On May 4, 1972, speaking at the funeral of J. Edgar Hoover, President Nixon said, "The American people are tired of disorder, disruption, and disrespect for law. America wants to come back to the law as a way of life."

One month and thirteen days later, a night watchman at Washington's fashionable Watergate office/apartment complex noticed a door handle taped so that it would not lock. Frank Wills removed the tape, but on his next rounds he found the door taped again. At 2:30 A.M., convinced of the presence of intruders, Wills called the police. Within minutes of Wills's call police cars arrived. On the sixth floor, in the offices of the Democratic National Committee (DNC) the police found five men and a large amount of electronic equipment. They appeared to be attaching wiretaps to the DNC telephones. The police took them all downtown in handcuffs.

That afternoon the five appeared at a preliminary hearing to set bail. The government prosecutor stated that the burglars were carrying $2,300, mostly in consecutively numbered hundred-dollar bills, plus elaborate and expensive electronic equipment. He asked the judge not to grant bail. When asked to state their occupations, one of the burglars (one of four Cuban-Americans in the group) answered "anticommu-

Former Attorney General John Mitchell went on trial in New York on February 19, 1974. The ex-cabinet officer was indicted for an attempt to get favorable treatment for millionaire Robert Vesco at the S.E.C. in exchange for a secret cash contribution to the Nixon reelection campaign in 1972.

G. Gordon Liddy, former counsel to the Committee for Re-election of the President, at court on January 30, 1973 for a session in the Watergate bugging trial. The enigmatic Liddy, who refused to testify, was found guilty.

nist." Their leader, James McCord, said that he was a security consultant recently retired from the Central Intelligence Agency.

The CIA connection and the presence of a reporter in the courtroom put the story on the front page of the next day's Washington *Post*. Then the Associated Press discovered for whom McCord worked as a security consultant—the Committee to Reelect the President (CRP), an independent group set up to run Richard Nixon's campaign and bypass the Republican National Committee. Contacted for a comment, John Mitchell, former attorney general, close friend of the President, and current director of CRP (popularly pronounced "CREEP"), said, "There is no place in our campaign or in the electoral process for this type of activity, and we will not permit or condone it."

Bob Woodward, the reporter who had happened to drop in on the hearing, found another lead. The *Post*'s police reporter had learned that one of the burglars carried an address book that included an entry: "E. Howard Hunt—W. House." Woodward called the White House and was given another number to call. When Woodward explained why he was calling, Hunt blurted, "Good God!" and then refused further comment. Although presidential press secretary Ron Ziegler dismissed the affair as "a third-rate burglary," the grand jury on September 15 brought in indictments against the five burglars as well as E. Howard Hunt and G. Gordon Liddy—McCord's boss at CRP. The prosecution indicated it would argue that these seven had planned and executed the Watergate break-in.

Despite its scoop, the Washington *Post* seemed to lose interest shortly after the arrests. Woodward and the other Watergate reporter, Carl Bernstein, were reassigned. The paper regained interest only in late July when the New York *Times*—the *Post*'s archrival—revealed that, before the break-in, fifteen phone calls had been made from the Miami home of one of the burglars to CRP. The *Post* now sent Bernstein to Miami. There, at the district attorney's office Bernstein found the bank records of the burglar, showing deposits of $114,000. Most of the checks came from Mexico.

Other evidence began to appear. The General Accounting Office found a large "slush fund of cash" kept at CRP. On a second trip to Miami, Bernstein learned of a practice called laundering—money was sent through a bank in Mexico so it could not be traced. The Mafia did it all the time, an aide to the Miami district attorney told him, and CRP had done it with $750,000 collected just before April 7 to beat the deadline established by a new law prohibiting secret political contributions. Bernstein also learned that Bernard Barker, one of the Watergate burglars, had told a friend, "I'm not worrying. They're paying for my attorney." Woodward and Bernstein now began digging in Washington, piecing bits of data together. The FBI was not pressing very hard on the case, they learned. Several people were known to have lied to investigators. Money was still going through the slush fund. Woodward also developed his own source—a high-ranking official whom he identified as "Deep Throat." Another source was Hugh Sloan, a young Republican who had

Investigative reporters Carl Bernstein (left) and Bob Woodward, (right) astounded the nation with their dogged inquiry into the Watergate burglary and their exposé of its ramifications in the Washington *Post*. Although their investigation drew intensive pressure from the White House, Woodward and Bernstein persisted with their phone calls, interviews, and diligent pursuit of all leads.

resigned as treasurer of CRP. Sloan would not talk for publication, on the advice of his attorneys. But he did confirm stories Woodward and Bernstein uncovered elsewhere.

Sloan's confirmation proved crucial for their next big story, the revelation that Mitchell, while still attorney general in 1971, had approved payments from the secret fund. The two reporters, armed also with confirmation from sources in the Justice Department, told the story to Benjamin Bradlee, Washington *Post* editor. Bradlee examined the evidence and, after considering the interests of the paper and of Katherine Graham, its publisher, decided to let them go ahead with the story.

Bernstein called Mitchell, who had since resigned from CRP, asking him to comment on the story so far. "Jeeesus!" said Mitchell, stunned. Then "All that crap, you're putting it in the paper? It's all been denied. Katie Graham's going to get her tit caught in a big fat wringer if that's published." The *Post* printed Mitchell's comments, and Mrs. Graham asked Bernstein if he had any further messages for her.

By October other newsmen—from *Time, Newsweek,* the Los Angeles *Times*—had picked up the story. On October 5 the Los Angeles *Times* printed a long interview with Alfred Baldwin, who on the night of the Watergate breakin had been in a nearby motel, linked to the burglars by walkie-talkie. Baldwin said he had delivered logs of wiretapped DNC conversations to somebody at the Committee to Reelect the President. Each new discovery spurred Woodward and Bernstein to dig deeper. Encouraged by Bradlee the two reporters now pushed to keep their advantage, but they could find only scattered fragments of evidence. Unwisely and illegally they tried to get to a member of the grand jury to find out what evidence the government was presenting. The grand juror reported it, and the judge issued a warning—but without naming the culprits.

As November and December passed, the *Post* faced worse problems than judicial disapproval or professional rivalry. "Deep Throat" had warned that the White House was about to move against the *Post.* Under administration pressure to remain silent, the *Post*'s information sources dried up. Bradlee warned Woodward and Bernstein to do nothing they did not want known, to be careful on the telephone, and to have a lawyer handle all their personal tax matters. The White House began to exclude *Post* reporters from social occasions and, more significantly, to give news leads to its competitor, the Washington *Star.* People (known to be friends of the President) challenged the broadcasting licenses of the *Post*'s two Florida television stations. "As soon as the election is over," proclaimed Charles Colson, a White House aide with a reputation for ruthlessness, "we're going to really shove it to the *Post.*"

The White House gave another sign of what Nixon's second term would be like. A few days after his easy reelection the President gathered his cabinet, thanked them for their efforts, and announced that he planned major changes. He then turned the meeting over to H. R. Haldeman, his chief of staff, who liked to describe himself as "the President's son-of-a-bitch." "I'm not entirely sure you people understood what the President said," explained Haldeman to the secretaries of State, Defense, and the nine other departments. "When he said he wanted your resignations, *he meant he wanted your resignations.*"

H. R. "Bob" Haldeman, former top White House aide, during a pause in his testimony at the Senate Watergate Committee Hearings, on July 30, 1973. Throughout his testimony, Haldeman denied John Dean's allegations that he had been involved in the Watergate cover-up.

Richard Nixon had often complained about lenient judges contributing to the breakdown of law and order in America. By anybody's standards John J. Sirica was a tough judge. The son of an Italian immigrant, he had worked his way through law school as a boxing coach, and his stern philosophy on sentencing earned him the nickname "Maximum John." Even before the trial began, he had jailed one reporter for refusing to give tapes of an interview to the court. In the pretrial hearing, Sirica made his intentions clear. "The jury is going to want to know: What did these men go into that headquarters for? Who hired them? Who started this?"

All seven defendants had entered preliminary pleas of not guilty. But, just before the trial opened in January, Hunt, who knew the four Cubans from his stint in the CIA, apparently persuaded them to plead guilty, as Hunt himself would. He promised that their families would be taken care of while they were in jail and that after a few months they would receive executive clemency. When the trial opened, all five pleaded guilty.

"Don't pull any punches—you give me straight answers," warned Sirica when the four burglars appeared before him to change their pleas. Who gave them their orders? Liddy, they answered, who was acting on his own. Had anyone mentioned executive clemency? No. Where had the $114,000 in the bank come from—the "hundred dollar bills floating around like coupons"? They didn't know—the money had arrived one day in the mail. "I'm sorry," said Sirica, "but I don't believe you."

The trial of Liddy and McCord lasted only two weeks. The prosecution argued that Liddy had received the money for legitimate security but had decided to use it for the break-in. Liddy refused to say anything; McCord insisted that he had bugged the Democrats to uncover plans for radical violence against the Republicans. Liddy was determined to keep his secret even in the face of repeated interrogation and a possibly long jail sentence. (He had earlier suggested to CRP a surefire way to guarantee his permanent silence—he would go to a specific place, and CRP could send somebody to shoot him.)

Day by day Judge Sirica grew angrier. As Theodore White wrote later, "Sirica's intelligence and dignity had been insulted by the testimony before him." Because he regarded the prosecution's questioning as inadequate, Sirica at one point dismissed the jury and asked one CRP witness forty-one questions of his own.

The jury took an hour and a half to find both Liddy and McCord guilty on all counts. After the verdict Sirica stated, "I have not been satisfied, and I am still not satisfied that all the pertinent facts have been produced before an American jury." And, he complained, "I don't think we should sit up here like nincompoops." He told all seven defendants that final sentencing would be based on their cooperation with investigators, including the Senate select committee that was then being formed to probe Watergate. Sirica put off sentencing until March 23. This would give the seven almost two months to ponder how much time they might spend in prison.

When John Sirica adjourned the trial on February 2, 1973, Watergate suspicions remained several steps away from the President. Little hard evidence implicated either the highest men at CRP or those closest to the President in the White House. In the next three months, one by one, the men between the scandal and the President went down.

On February 17, Nixon named L. Patrick Gray to head the FBI. As acting director, Gray had directed the bureau's investigation of Watergate, maintaining that the White House had not interfered. Although the President had so far refused to say whether administration officials would testify before the committee, Gray had no choice. Requiring confirmation by the Senate for his FBI appointment, he had to face the Judiciary Committee. On the first day of his confirmation hearings, Gray made a damaging admission without even being asked: While conducting the Watergate probe, he had met often with John Dean, counsel to the President, and shown all the evidence to him. But Gray denied that such action implied White House interference and offered to show the investigating files to the senators. Nevertheless, committee members were startled and disturbed by this admission.

Immediately the committee subpoenaed Dean. But the White House announced that Dean would not appear, citing "executive privilege" for the first though not the last time. Nixon also ordered Gray to keep his files confidential. That order came too late. On March 6 Gray released the FBI files, including one headed "Interview with Herbert Kalmbach" (the President's personal attorney). In the interview Kalmbach admitted that he had routed money for undercover political activities. The White House had been caught in an open lie, and now the scandal had reached a presidential aide. On the last day of Gray's doomed confirmation hearings he revealed that Dean had "probably" lied to agents during the investigation.

Thirty-four year old attorney John W. Dean III, former White House Counsel, was President Nixon's chief accuser at the nationally televised Senate Watergate hearings in June 1973.

John D. Ehrlichman, formerly the key White House aide in charge of domestic affairs, appeared before the Senate Watergate Committee on July 30, 1973, for his fifth day of testimony. Ehrlichman attempted to discredit John Dean's testimony, as well as to defend his own role in the break-in of the office of Daniel Ellsberg's psychiatrist.

Almost before the White House could absorb the impact of that assertion, John Sirica walked out of his chambers to find James McCord holding a letter for him. Three days later, on March 23, Sirica read the letter in open court. "Several members of my family have expressed fear for my life if I disclose knowledge of the facts in this matter," wrote the convicted burglar. But he wanted to talk. He said the defendants had been pressured to "plead guilty and remain silent"; also, that "others involved in the Watergate operation were not identified during the trial." Sirica postponed the sentencing of McCord. Hunt and the others who had pleaded guilty received "provisional" sentences of between thirty-five and forty years. Sirica told them that their final sentences would "depend primarily on whether or not you cooperate with the United States Senate."

Within days Washington knew that McCord, talking to Senate investigators, had blown the case wide open. McCord swore that Dean and Jeb Magruder, assistant director of CRP, had known beforehand of the break-in plan. He later added John Mitchell's name to the list. Hunt now testified before the grand jury. On April 2 Dean's lawyers told U.S. attorneys that he was willing to talk. Ten days later Magruder confessed having committed perjury in the Watergate trial.

It seemed that many in the administration were racing to reach the federal prosecutors first, to plead guilty and perhaps lighten their sentences. The prosecutors, of course, encouraged the panic atmosphere, telling Watergate figures that only early confession would count, that the government had virtually completed its cases. The confessional wave uncovered new issues. Why had the FBI not discovered the involvement of all these people earlier? Had there been, as McCord had indicated, a strong effort by the top government men to suppress the truth? Anyone involved in such efforts had committed a crime, obstruction of justice. Slowly interest shifted from the break-in to its aftermath—the coverup.

Dean held the key, since he had met regularly with the President and his closest aides, Haldeman and John D. Ehrlichman. Haldeman warned Dean in early April, "Once the toothpaste is out of the tube, it's going to be very difficult to get it back in." But Dean had no intention of imitating Liddy by going stoically and silently to jail. He announced publicly on April 19 that he would not be made a "scapegoat." He had already turned over to the prosecutors documents implicating Haldeman, Ehrlichman, and Mitchell.

Richard Nixon now saw only one choice. On April 30 he announced the resignation of Haldeman and Ehrlichman, "two of the finest public servants it has been my privilege to know." Speaking on television, flanked by a picture of his family and a bust of Abraham Lincoln, Nixon finished, "I must now turn my full attention to the large duties of this office. I owe it to this great office that I hold, and I owe it to you—to our country." Nixon also chose a new attorney general, Elliot Richardson, a man of unquestioned honesty, and Richardson in turn named a special Watergate prosecutor—Archibald Cox, a Harvard Law School professor and former U.S. solicitor general.

Less than three weeks later, the Senate hearings opened in Washington. Senator Sam Ervin of North Carolina, chairman of the Watergate committee, rejected the idea of calling in the higher-ups first. Instead the hearings started with the lesser fry, who confirmed what the committee already knew: authority for the break-in had come from the top echelons of the CRP, and the defendants had been paid off during the trial. As the hearings gained momentum, the committee members rapidly became a focus of public attention. But Sam Ervin, the seventy-six-year-old chairman, stole the show. A constitutional conservative and anti-civil rights senator in the 1950s, by the late 1960s Ervin showed increasing concern for civil liberties and the boundaries of presidential power. He quickly captivated the nation with his drawling rebukes to witnesses — when his jowls would bounce and his eyebrows waggle with indignation. Responding to a complaint that he was badgering a witness, he responded, "I'm just a country lawyer from North Carolina. I just have to do it my way." Then, Samuel J. Ervin, scholar and Harvard Law School graduate, would lean back and smile not-so-innocently.

Important new revelations came out of the dramatic hearings. Magruder implicated a dozen White House and/or CRP people in the break-in and coverup, including Haldeman, Ehrlichman, and Mitchell. Originally Liddy had suggested a program costing $1 million, involving electronic surveillance, kidnapping radical leaders and holding them in Mexico until after the Republican convention, and anchoring a yacht off the Miami coast during the Democratic convention that would be supplied with prostitutes and wired for sound and photographs. Magruder testified that when Liddy offered his plan in January 1972, Attorney General Mitchell balked — but mostly at the cost. Mitchell, however, later approved a cheaper plan to bug the DNC.

Magruder had named everyone but the President. John Dean completed the list. He had met with Nixon four times to discuss the coverup, Dean stated — once in September 1972 and three times in the spring of 1973. He had told the President details of the coverup and had conveyed the demands of the Watergate burglars of up to a million dollars in aid. The President had told Dean it could be raised. In their final meeting, which Dean suspected was being taped, Nixon had said his earlier statement had been a joke. Dean's account stood up under a full week of cross-examination.

So far no one had explained what had motivated the Watergate conspiracy. Dean said that the activities had arisen from an "insatiable appetite for all political intelligence, all coupled with a do-it-yourself White House staff, regardless of the law." Dean cited examples of White House paranoia, including the "enemies list" — a secret list of political opponents singled out to be given trouble by the Internal Revenue Service (IRS) and other arms of the government. This list included Democratic politicians, reporters, and liberal show business people, such as Paul Newman, as well as various figures whose presence was difficult to explain, such as Joe Namath, quarterback of the New York Jets. Many of those listed proclaimed their delight at being considered a Nixon enemy.

Over the next four weeks the committee heard from all but one of the men accused. Mitchell continued to deny that he had ordered the break-in or conspired with anyone in the coverup. He admitted only that he had kept information from the President in order to ensure Nixon's reelection. Mitchell proved himself a recalcitrant witness; at the end of his second day of testimony before the increasingly skeptical committee, he muttered sarcastically, "It's a great trial being conducted up here, isn't it?" Haldeman and Ehrlichman testified that John Dean had been the mastermind behind the coverup and had misled them. The President's men were stonewalling — not without success from their point of view.

Soon another astounding development overshadowed their testimony. A committee investigator, talking to former White House aide Alexander Butterfield, discovered almost accidentally that the President had been taping conversations in the Oval Office since 1971. Three days later Butterfield told his story publicly, saying that only Nixon, Haldeman, and he had known of the White House tapes. It was no longer John Dean's word against Richard Nixon's.

On August 1 at a state dinner for Japanese Prime Minister Kakuei Tanaka, President Nixon said, "Let others spend their time dealing with the murky, small, unimportant, vicious little things. We will spend our time building a better world."

Outside, bumper stickers read: "Honk if you think he's guilty."

On October 10, NBC News interrupted a baseball game to broadcast a bulletin. Vice President Spiro Agnew had resigned. While serving as Vice President, and earlier, as governor of Maryland, he had accepted cash bribes.

Over the summer of 1973, U.S. attorneys in Maryland had built a tight case against Agnew, but the evidence was not made public until August. Attorney General Elliot Richardson had watched the evidence accumulate since July and was now convinced that the Justice Department had a solid case against the Vice President. In September, before he was brought to trial, Agnew appealed to the House of Representatives, arguing that according to the Constitution a President or Vice President could not be indicted. However, the Democratic majority in the House showed little interest in helping Agnew out of his dilemma. Because Nixon too had maintained that the President was not subject to court action, he had a personal stake in the constitutional issues that would have to be decided if Agnew went to court. Richardson and the White House finally struck a compromise — over the protests of the Maryland prosecutors, who wanted to indict and convict Agnew.

The compromise was simple. Agnew resigned and pleaded no contest to one charge of income tax evasion. For this he received three years probation and a fine of $10,000. The judge announced that he would have sent Agnew to jail, given the evidence mounted against him.

After pleading no contest to a tax evasion charge at a Baltimore federal court, Vice President Spiro Agnew resigned his office. He claimed that he acted to avoid a divisive struggle in the courts.

But Richardson in making the compromise had reasoned that it was of prime importance to have Agnew removed, since he was first in line as presidential successor. After all, Watergate might topple Nixon, or Nixon's health might break down. A long bribery trial would leave the problem of presidential succession dangerously in suspense.

Even after the Justice Department had released the evidence against him, Agnew was not contrite. Five days after resigning, the former Vice President addressed the nation on television, complaining that he was merely the victim of "the new post-Watergate political morality."

On October 6 the Providence *Journal* revealed that President Nixon on a salary of $200,000 had paid income tax of only $792.81 for 1970 and $873.03 for 1971.

Once the existence of the tapes became known, Archibald Cox wanted them. Two days after Butterfield's testimony, Cox requested nine crucial tapes. When the White House refused to deliver, claiming the tapes were covered by executive privilege, Cox went to court, asking Judge Sirica to order the President to give him the tapes. Earlier, Sirica had ruled that the tapes should be delivered to him personally so that he could determine their relevance. The judge rejected the White House argument that the President had "absolute power" to withhold the tapes, and he denied that the constitutional doctrine of separation of powers protected the Executive Branch from court orders. Throughout September these issues were argued before the district court of appeals, with the White House, Cox, and Sirica himself submitting briefs.

On Friday, October 12, the court of appeals ruled 5 to 2 that Nixon had to deliver the tapes to the Senate. But it gave the President one week to work out an alternative arrangement with Cox. On the last day of the week Nixon announced a unilateral solution. He would make summaries of the tapes available to the court, and Senator John Stennis, a pro-Nixon Democrat from Mississippi, would verify the accuracy of the summaries. The President ordered Cox to cease court efforts to obtain the full tapes—or he would be fired.

The next day Cox held his own press conference. Almost apologetically, Cox said that the proposed arrangement ran counter to the pledges made when he became special prosecutor, and he would not stop seeking the tapes. He also stated that the President could not fire him—only the attorney general could.

At 8:31 that night the White House acted. Richardson had refused to fire Cox when ordered to do so and had resigned. William Ruckelshaus, deputy attorney general, had refused to fire Cox and had himself been fired. Solicitor General Robert Bork, convinced that someone had to carry out the President's orders, became acting attorney general and fired Cox. Reporters referred to the removals and resignations as the "Saturday Night Massacre."

Immediately after the announcement, callers jammed Western Union switchboards. In thirty-six hours 70,000 telegrams reached Washington, in four days 220,000, in ten days 450,000. Almost unanimously they denounced the President's action. Many newspapers called for Nixon's resignation. *Time* magazine, in its first editorial ever, asked that he quit. Nixon had badly misjudged the temper of the American people.

The White House held out for three days, then capitulated. On Wednesday Nixon's lawyer stood before Sirica to announce that the President would yield the tapes. "This President," he explained, "does not defy the law." Within two weeks the President named a new special prosecutor, Leon Jaworski of Texas, promising not to fire him without consulting congressional leaders.

But it all came too late. Congress had ample opportunity to gauge the widespread anger rising all across the country against Richard Nixon. Slowly the House leaders began moving toward impeachment. During the next eight months, while the House Judiciary Committee put its case together, the President's situation grew more and more desperate.

On November 17 Nixon spoke to a convention of newspaper editors at Disney World in Florida. He assured them, "I am not a crook."

On November 19 the President promised a group of Republican governors that there would be no more "bombshells" coming out of Watergate. The next day the White House told Sirica that one of the tapes—a conversation Nixon had with Haldeman three days after the break-in—had an eighteen-minute "gap" in it.

On December 20, Peter Rodino as chairman of the House Judiciary Committee named John Doar special counsel for the impeachment hearings. Doar was a Republican who had served in the civil rights division of the Justice Department. Congress rented space in a local hotel for Doar to carry out his work—he eventually filled it with a staff of 106 people. Soon the first partisan consequences of Watergate were being felt outside of Washington. After Congressman Gerald Ford had been appointed to succeed Agnew as Vice President, a Democrat won the special election to fill Ford's seat in the House—the first Democrat to be elected by the district in sixty-four years.

But the scandal had not played itself out yet. On March 1, 1974, the Watergate grand jury indicted seven people in the Watergate cover-up, including Haldeman, Ehrlichman, and Mitchell. The Washington *Post* calculated that twenty-eight persons formerly associated with the White House or CRP had been indicted. On April 3 the Congressional Joint Committee on Internal Revenue Taxation, to whom the President had given all of his tax materials, ruled that he owed $432,787.13 in back taxes. The President said he would pay it.

Finally, on April 29, Nixon made a stark attempt to quiet the scandal. He released to the public twelve hundred pages of transcripts from the tapes. In a television address he argued that he had had little control of the 1972 campaign, for he had spent the year pursuing peace in Moscow and Peking. Incredibly, the President's transcripts were the most damning evidence yet. When Dean said that the defendants might want a million dollars, the President replied, "I know where it could be gotten. It is not easy, but it could be done." The tapes revealed an almost total concentration on political expediency, as well as appalling indecision. And they were studded with the phrase "expletive deleted"— meaning that a profanity had been edited out. This made what was already bad seem even worse. Thus when Dean told the President that Hunt wanted $120,000 immediately, Nixon answered, "(Expletive deleted), get it." Instead of calming the storm, Nixon's release of the tapes touched off a new wave of demands for his resignation and seriously weakened his position as the Judiciary Committee hearings opened.

Unassuming Congressman Peter Rodino of Newark, New Jersey, would never be the folksy, Bible-quoting television star Sam Ervin had been. But in a methodical, cautious fashion, Rodino and Doar began organizing evidence, taking time to assemble every shred. In March, Rodino killed a move by committee liberals to subpoena Nixon. Instead Doar politely requested more tapes. In the spirit of fairness, Rodino's committee allowed the President's lawyer to participate in the hearings. Nevertheless, the White House attacked the committee's motivation and delayed in supplying material.

When Doar began presenting evidence to the committee in May, many politicians complained about his and Rodino's slow, careful style. Some Democrats on the committee were ready to vote right away, and some Republicans charged that the Democrats were prolonging the agony. By the end of June, as Doar continued to present evidence with no vote in sight, Majority Leader O'Neill exerted pressure. But Rodino refused to be hurried. His committee included three conservative Southern Democrats, and Rodino wanted to hold all of them; it had seventeen Republicans, and Rodino wanted at least five of their votes. He did not want his committee to recommend impeachment on a narrow or party-line vote.

Finally in July the situation began to crystallize. Dean and other witnesses appeared before the committee. Doar made his final argument, summarizing the evidence for impeachment. Rejecting the administration argument—that impeachment required proof of a criminal act—he urged the committee to look at the pattern of all the President's acts, which added up to "the terrible deed of subverting the Constitution." He recommended four articles of impeachment: the Watergate coverup; abuse of power, including using the CIA and IRS for political ends; failure to respond to committee subpoenas for the tapes; and the President's tax case.

At last the time had come for the committee members to make a decision. The thirty-eight members of Congress, barely known outside their own districts, had been readying themselves. The Southern Democrats had consulted with one another, as well as with Rodino and Doar. The half-dozen undecided Republicans had consulted with one another and with the Southern Democrats.

Meanwhile Leon Jaworski had been pressing for access to the tapes that had cost Cox his job—and the issue had reached the highest court in America. On the morning of July 24 the Supreme Court ruled that Richard Nixon must release the tapes. Speaking for a unanimous Court, Chief Justice Warren Burger, a Nixon appointee, declared that the courts, not the President, would decide what evidence was required by the courts: Nixon must hand over the tapes.

The President had run out of options. Defiance of the Supreme Court would precipitate impeachment by the committee and catapult the issue into the House and Senate. To avoid this, Nixon announced from San Clemente that he would surrender the tapes, although preparing them might take a little time. That same night the Judiciary Committee began its televised hearings. Each member opened with a fifteen-minute statement, which proved to be a fascinating preview of the issues

The House Judiciary Committee, headed by New Jersey Congressman Peter Rodino, opened debate on July 24, 1974 on whether to recommend impeachment of President Nixon. After months of inquiry, as well as several subpoenas of the damaging White House tapes, the politically divided committee assessed the evidence they had amassed. At the conclusion of their session, the House Committee voted to recommend three articles of impeachment.

at stake. "This is no ordinary set of speeches," wrote one reporter. "It is the most extraordinary political debate I have ever heard—perhaps the most extraordinary since the Constitutional Convention."

On the third day the committee began considering the first impeachment article—charging that the President and his agents had acted "to delay, impede, and obstruct the investigation" and listing the means used. The last sentence stunned the room, although everyone had known it was coming: "Wherefore, Richard M. Nixon, by such conduct, warrants impeachment and trial, and removal from office."

Charles Sandman, Republican of New Jersey, opened the attack on the article, demanding "specificity"—hard facts. Proponents of the article, stung by the challenge, prepared to present justification for each clause. If Sandman and others wanted specificity, specificity they would get. For two days Democrats and Republicans rehashed the entire story: the payments to Hunt and the burglars, proven on the tapes; Dean's monitoring of the FBI investigation; the President's lack of interest in finding out the facts about the break-in; his discussing the case with Haldeman and Ehrlichman when he knew both were under suspicion; his knowledge of perjury all around him; his refusal to supply the tapes; his firing of Cox. The pro-Nixon Republicans listened to the exposition bitterly, noting only that no one had yet produced the "smoking gun" that would indisputably establish Nixon's guilt.

On the night of July 27, 1974, the Judiciary Committee passed the first article, recommending that the House impeach the President. The roll call ran down twenty Democrats, all voting aye in soft voices. The first four Republicans voted no; then one voted aye, and another, until six Republicans of the seventeen had voted to remove the President, head of their own party. Rodino, casting the last vote, made the total 27 to 11 for impeachment.

Many of the congressmen tried to compose themselves as they left the committee room to talk to reporters. Several, including Rodino, could not—they went into the antechamber and wept. The margin was big enough to counter the charge of partisanship. During the next week the committee passed two additional articles and defeated two more.

Although John Doar had not been able to present it, the "smoking gun" did exist. The President's lawyer, James St. Clair, had found it while listening to the tapes about to be turned over to Judge Sirica. He showed the transcript to Alexander Haig, a general serving as the President's chief of staff. Haig, who had assumed almost the duties of "acting President" while Nixon concentrated on his impeachment troubles, showed it to a Nixon loyalist in the Senate. The senator told Haig that the Senate would convict Nixon with this information. On the afternoon of August 2 Haig called Nixon defender Congressman Charles Wiggins, who was busy organizing the President's defense on the House floor, to the White House and showed him the key transcript. Wiggins went back to the Capitol and tore up his defense notes.

Haig and Republican leaders now sought a quick resignation. They tried to nudge the President toward that decision. On the afternoon of August 5 the President—at Haig's insistence—released three of the tapes to the public, acknowledging that they "may further damage my case." The tapes he stated "are at variance with certain of my previous statements." Nevertheless, he did not believe that the new evidence justified impeachment.

Later that night the incriminating transcript reached the press. It was taken from the tapes for June 23, 1972—six days after the Watergate break-in. In it Haldeman informed Nixon that the FBI was pushing the investigation hard and would soon trace the burglars' cash back through Mexico to the CRP. The only way to avoid this, he told Nixon, was to direct the CIA to tell the FBI to back off for "national security" reasons. Nixon ordered Haldeman to do just that.

The next day, all ten Republicans who had supported the President on the Judiciary Committee announced that they would vote for impeachment. So did John Rhodes, the House minority leader. Senator Barry Goldwater, one of the Republican party's most respected politicians, told a group of senators, "You can only be lied to so often." Washington by now was discussing an Agnew-like deal: Nixon's resignation in exchange for immunity from prosecution. On Wednesday, August 7, Goldwater, Rhodes, and Senate Republican Leader Scott went to the White House. Impeachment by the House and conviction by the Senate would come, they told the President. Even they might have to vote to impeach on at least one article.

On Thursday evening Nixon became the first President of the United States to step down from office. His resignation took effect at noon of the next day, by which time Richard M. Nixon was already in an air force plane flying home to California.

Surrounded by his family, President Nixon gave a resignation speech to his staff in the East room of the White House, before a tearful departure for San Clemente. After a year of trials and convictions, hearings and debates, subpoenas and revelations, impeachment by the House and conviction by the Senate now seemed inevitable.

52
AMERICA IN THE 1970s
A.W.

Many Americans considered Watergate as much a symptom as a cause of this country's troubles during the first half of the 1970s. The nation endured its final humiliation in Southeast Asia—the Communist takeover of all of Vietnam—and Americans began to question some of their longest-held assumptions about foreign policy. The racial violence of the sixties, while largely abated, had left a large residue of resentment on both sides, one that flared up hotly as school integration struggles moved North.

In the midst of these sobering realities, the country suffered its worst economic crisis since the Great Depression. Unemployment rose steadily, while at the same time—and in defiance of conventional theory—inflation also became a major problem. By the middle of the decade the rate of inflation had eased slightly; but prices continued upward, and government anti-inflationary monetary policies did little to curb the rise in unemployment.

Following on the heels of these social and economic crises, the forced resignations of the President and Vice President of the United States left the country stunned. Polls showed that Americans felt less confidence in politicians than in any other group or profession. The country tried to extract some comfort from the performance of other public institutions during Watergate—Congress, the courts, the press. Although Americans as they prepared for the bicentennial cele-

bration had by no means given up on their system, attitudes toward government contrasted disturbingly with the bouncing optimism that is supposed to animate such affairs.

THE NIXON ERA

Nixon Takes Over the War When Richard Nixon entered the White House in 1969, his most urgent problem was the war in Vietnam. The issue had done much to destroy the previous administration and to get him elected. During the campaign he had announced—but refused to reveal details of— a plan to get the United States honorably out of Vietnam. As the futility of the Paris peace negotiations became apparent, Nixon's strategy assumed an even greater importance.

Gradually the President unveiled a policy of slow withdrawal of American troops with continued or increasing military and economic aid to the South Vietnamese government. This approach gained the name of "Vietnamization." Nixon broadened the idea to include future problems in Asia by proclaiming a "Nixon Doctrine"—that America would aid anticommunist governments in Asia but would avoid further land wars on that continent.

Although Nixon would not accept outright defeat in Vietnam, neither would he let the war interfere with his broader aims in foreign policy. He had a particular interest in foreign affairs and often remarked that the country could almost run itself domestically. For advice and assistance, Nixon bypassed the State Department and relied on his special assistant for national security, a Harvard professor named Henry Kissinger.

The Nixon Administration and Dissent The upheaval following the Cambodian invasion, while it did little to alter his foreign policy, deeply impressed Nixon. It appeared, as Jeb Magruder later told the Watergate Committee, that radicals and dissenters were tearing the country apart. The government launched strong public and covert efforts to stop them, by devising a broad plan calling for a council of all American intelligence organizations, including the CIA and the FBI. This group would be authorized to open mail, tap telephones, and conduct illegal break-ins. Files of the Internal Revenue Service were considered especially valuable for use against critics. In July 1970, President Nixon approved this plan. But steady opposition by FBI chief J. Edgar Hoover, who wanted no reorganization that affected his bureau, prevented its implementation.

Nixon then carried his attack on dissenters into the political arena. During the congressional elections of 1970, Vice President Spiro Agnew, whose attacks on the media had already gained him a wide following, proclaimed that the President would not be intimidated by "a disruptive, radical, and militant minority—the pampered prodigies of the radical liberals in the United States Senate." Nixon himself campaigned actively, claiming that "creeping permissiveness" allowed violent dissenters to "increasingly terrorize decent citizens." But the 1970 election results proved disappointing. Republicans gained only two seats in the Senate while losing nine seats in the House and seven governorships.

Nixon also had problems with the courts. Attorney General John Mitchell had obtained a lower court injunction to prevent the *New York*

Times from publishing the "Pentagon Papers," but by a 6-to-3 vote the Supreme Court ruled that the newspaper had acted within its First Amendment rights. A year later, on June 19, 1972, a unanimous Court that included three Nixon appointees rejected Mitchell's contention that the President possessed inherent power to wiretap without a court order. The decision came two days after the Watergate burglars' arrest.

Nixon and the Economy Nixon had originally intended to reduce federal spending and work toward a balanced budget—an aim piously invoked by many Presidents (including FDR) but seldom pursued. Nixon followed such a belt-tightening policy during his first year in power. By mid-1970 the country had entered a serious recession, and at the end of that year unemployment stood at 6.2 percent—almost twice the level under Johnson.

At the same time prices rose steadily. This unaccustomed combination of high unemployment, inflation, and limited economic growth soon acquired the name, "stagflation," although Democrats preferred the political label, "Nixonomics." Actually, the inflation was hardly Nixon's fault. It resulted largely from heavy spending for the Viet-

When the dollar was devalued in February 1973, brokers in international currency were deluged with calls. The dollar's weakness was a sign of the economy's illness.

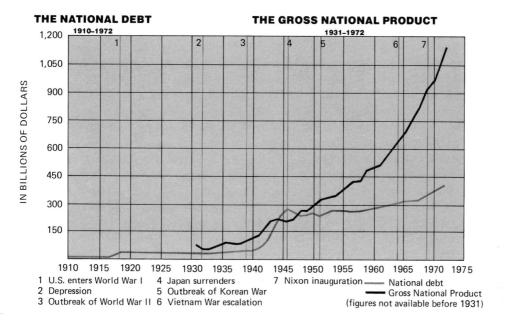

THE NATIONAL DEBT 1910–1972 **THE GROSS NATIONAL PRODUCT** 1931–1972

IN BILLIONS OF DOLLARS

1,200
1,050
900
750
600
450
300
150

1910 1915 1920 1925 1930 1935 1940 1945 1950 1955 1960 1965 1970 1975

1 U.S. enters World War I 4 Japan surrenders 7 Nixon inauguration ===== National debt
2 Depression 5 Outbreak of Korean War ——— Gross National Product
3 Outbreak of World War II 6 Vietnam War escalation (figures not available before 1931)

It seems less disturbing in comparison with the even more rapid growth of the economy, as measured by the increase in the Gross National Product. The GNP for a given year represents the total value, at current prices, of all goods and services produced in the country during that year. The growth of the GNP reflects a rising price level as well as an increasing output of goods and services. The actual increase in output has been much less, therefore, than the graph seems to indicate.

nam War and expanded social programs, combined with Johnson's refusal, for political reasons, to raise taxes. By 1971 the state of the economy posed a potent threat to Nixon's reelection, causing him to make a turnaround on spending and taxes. By election time he had managed to force down the unemployment rate.

In August of 1971 Nixon made an even more startling turnaround. Throughout his career he had opposed government controls on wages and prices. But with little more than a year to go before the election, the President imposed a ninety-day freeze on wages and prices, which he labeled Phase I of a new economic plan. In the fall the economy entered Phase II, with limits on wage and price increases. Both phases worked fairly well, controlling inflation throughout 1972.

After the election Nixon began cutting back on government programs, especially social welfare programs. He inaugurated Phase III, a system of largely voluntary limits on increases. The removal of mandatory controls, combined with the

additional money the administration had pumped into the economy, produced the sharpest burst of inflation since World War II.

Détente with Russia and China Phase I was not the only shock Nixon produced in the summer of 1971. The President, who had been perhaps the country's leading anticommunist for twenty years, announced that he would visit China—not what he used to call "Red China," the international outlaw, but the People's Republic of China. Henry Kissinger had already secretly visited Peking and made arrangements for Nixon's trip.

Only a politician like Nixon, possessing impeccable credentials as an anticommunist, could have altered American policy toward China. The President's visit early in 1972 provided a startling experience for Americans still thinking in Cold War stereotypes. There was Dick Nixon, the man who had talked down Nikita Khrushchev, cozying up to Mao Tse-tung and Chou En-lai while admiring the Great Wall as if viewing Hoover Dam on a campaign tour. By the time of Nixon's visit the United States had acquiesced in the admission of mainland China to the United Nations. Shortly after the President's visit, China and the United States established offices in each other's capitals, although continued American support for the Nationalist Chinese on Formosa ruled out full diplomatic relations.

Three months later, Nixon was traveling again, this time to the Soviet Union. Nixon and Kissinger were determined to build on the easing of Soviet-American relations (détente) that had begun during the Kennedy and Johnson years. Since 1969 the two superpowers had been engaged in the SALT (Stategic Arms Limitation Talks) negotiations, and Nixon and Soviet leader Brezhnev now signed SALT I, a temporary and limited agreement to cut back on some new weapons. The leaders also agreed to expand trade, beginning with a large Russian purchase of Ameri-

During President Nixon's visit to China in February 1972, he and Premier Chou En-lai reviewed the Chinese Red Guard. Televised scenes like this startled the American public, long accustomed to thinking in Cold War terms.

can wheat. The total sale amounted to a quarter of the American crop for 1972, at a price well below that of the American market. For Americans the first concrete result of détente was a sharp increase in the price of bread.

Nixon did not intend, however, that more relaxed relations should include an American defeat in Vietnam. Indeed, his dealings with two communist powers, Russia and China, who feared one another at least as much as each feared the United States, apparently enabled him to take bolder steps in Indochina. In March 1972, responding to expanded North Vietnamese activities in the south, Nixon first unleashed heavy American bombing on Hanoi and Haiphong (the largest cities of North Vietnam) and then mined the harbor of Haiphong, closing it to all ships. Despite rumblings from Moscow and Peking, as well as protests from many Americans, neither the communist superpowers nor the American people reacted strongly to Nixon's new military offensive. The U.S. effort in Vietnam had become an enormously expensive and costly bore — costly in human as well as in dollar terms.

The Election of 1972 Nixon had greatly strengthened his political position with his trips to China and Russia as well as some easing of the recession. He also gained strength from political floundering on the Democratic side. Originally, Senator Edmund Muskie of Maine seemed to have a good chance to unite the Democrats, still divided by the passions and violence of 1968. But Muskie's campaign fizzled. Senator Hubert Humphrey of Minnesota cut deeply into Muskie's support among moderates. George Wallace, former governor of Alabama, returning to the Democratic party after an independent race in 1968, ran strongly in many primaries, including a surprising victory in Michigan. Senator George McGovern of South Dakota led the forces of antiwar activists and students that had been symbolized by Eugene McCarthy and Robert Kennedy in 1968.

Benefiting from divided opposition and recent party reforms, McGovern won Democratic convention delegates faster than any other candidate. Finally he defeated Humphrey in a close California primary. To most of the Democratic

Governor George Wallace's third-party candidacy in 1968 siphoned off nearly ten million votes, making that election one of the closest in recent history.

political pros and to labor leaders allied with the party McGovern seemed too extreme. But he had enough delegates, barely enough, to win nomination, and he named Senator Thomas Eagleton of Missouri as his running mate.

McGovern's nomination did not heal the party division. Many Democratic politicians refused to rally behind him. He represented something novel on the American political scene. The "new politics" centered on youth, the rights of ethnic minorities, and the aspirations of women. McGovern proposed several controversial schemes—for example, that every family whose income fell below $10,000 should receive a yearly cash grant of $1,000. Ideas such as these, as well as the overall "too liberal" impression he and his campaigners created, alienated many normally reliable sources of Democratic political power.

McGovern's slim chances faded when reports began to circulate that Eagleton had been treated for psychiatric disorders. That posed a problem which McGovern's maladroit response turned into a crisis. McGovern at first announced that he supported Eagleton "one thousand percent." But soon he asked for the vice-presidential

candidate's resignation, an act interpreted by many as both vacillating and ruthless. After four Democrats had publicly rejected McGovern's offer, Sargent Shriver, a brother-in-law of John and Robert Kennedy, became Eagleton's replacement.

Nixon, meanwhile, campaigned by seeming to be above politics. He stayed in the White House while presidential surrogates took on McGovern. To separate himself from the Republican party organization, he set up CRP (Committee to Reelect the President), and he put an emphasis on "Democrats for Nixon," a group of Democrats alienated by McGovern. Aiming for the largest victory possible, he refused to associate his campaign with those of Republican congressional candidates.

Nixon's personal victory, or at least McGovern's defeat, was enormous. The President carried forty-nine states, losing only Massachusetts and the District of Columbia. But, while the President claimed a broad mandate, he had brought in only thirteen Republican congressmen, and his party had actually lost two seats in the

George McGovern, in attempting to open the Democratic party to groups shut out of the 1968 convention, alienated the traditional base of Democratic support—blue-collar workers. Richard Nixon capitalized on this to win in a landslide.

Senate. The "deadlock of democracy" (GOP control of the White House and Democratic control of Congress) would continue.

PREPARING FOR THE SECOND TERM

Shortly after the election Haldeman's demand for the resignation of cabinet members was echoed throughout the executive branch, and many high-level appointees were replaced by Nixon loyalists. Jeb Magruder, for example, became undersecretary of commerce. The actions reflected a long-standing Nixon desire to centralize control of the executive branch by the White House.

The President also tightened control over the cabinet. Congress had earlier rejected a reorganization plan, but Nixon now named Kissinger, Secretary of the Treasury George Schultz, and Roy Ash, director of the Nixon-created Office of Management and Budget, as a "supercabinet," to whom other cabinet members would report. The supercabinet, in turn, would report to Haldeman and Ehrlichman. With such a structure, Nixon made himself the most isolated President of modern times.

The President also claimed ever-widening powers for his office. He issued a broad definition of "executive privilege," limiting the information Congress could require the executive branch to supply. He also announced that he would impound funds appropriated by Congress that he felt should not be spent, refusing to release $6 billion appropriated by Congress for environmental programs. In March, vetoing a number of spending bills, the President announced that even if Congress overrode his vetoes he would impound the money.

Nixon also celebrated his reelection with a treaty in Vietnam. Kissinger had announced a few days before the election that "peace is at hand." But snags developed, and Nixon responded with the heaviest bombing of the war in December—a saturation "carpet bombing" of parts of Hanoi. Shortly after Nixon's inauguration, the two sides signed a treaty calling for a permanent cease-fire and removal of American troops. But despite American troop withdrawal, the war continued among the Vietnamese, and U.S. B-52 bombers continued to pound communist forces in Cambodia.

Government During Watergate Despite his ambitious plans, Watergate quickly closed in on Nixon. After McCord, Magruder, and Dean began talking, the President lost standing in the country, and what little influence he had retained over Congress evaporated. In August 1973 Congress forced Nixon to end the bombing in Cambodia. Shortly thereafter Congress passed the War Powers Act, stating that unless Congress approved an American military intervention within sixty days the President must withdraw troops. Nixon vetoed the bill, but both houses overrode his veto.

By then, Nixon's ability to govern was shaken. After the forced resignation of Agnew, Nixon hosted a White House extravaganza to announce his selection of House Minority Leader Gerald Ford as Vice President, the first exercise of a new presidential power under the 25th Amendment. A cabinet member remarked to House Majority Leader O'Neill that they might not see something like it again for a long time. "No," answered O'Neill, "not for about eight months."

Within certain limits, however, Nixon could still act decisively. In October, Egypt, Syria, and Iraq, with heavy Soviet arms support, attacked Israel. Nixon, in the midst of the Agnew and Watergate crises, launched a huge American airlift to the Israelis, possibly preventing a disastrous defeat for the Jewish state. America's European allies, heavily dependent on Arab oil, refused to assist and publicly expressed their anger.

Despite the strain on the NATO alliance, Nixon and Kissinger could claim success in preventing Israel's extinction and, later, in negotiating a Middle East cease-fire. But when Nixon, warning of the danger of Russian intervention in the area, put all American forces on a worldwide military alert, the effects of Watergate-inspired skepticism became obvious. Americans openly speculated on how much Nixon's political difficulties had influenced him in calling the alert.

Daniel Ellsberg, with his wife Pat, talks to reporters before testifying for the second day at the "Pentagon Papers" trial in April 1973. Ellsberg had been responsible for leaking the secret Defense Department study of the Vietnam War. The court case was dismissed, however, after Nixon had Ehrlichman offer the Judge a position as Director of the FBI.

Even the President's success brought problems, as the Arab countries cut off petroleum exports to the United States. Long before the embargo, the country had faced the prospect of shortages. Fuel consumption had been increasing far more rapidly than domestic fuel production. Moreover, the country's output of polluting fuels such as coal was being cut back for environmental reasons.

The Arab embargo intensified the country's problems, with immediate and unpleasant results. The price of heating oil tripled, and gas prices doubled—when gas was available. Long lines of cars formed outside and around gas stations, which stayed open for limited hours each day.

What angered Americans most, however, were skyrocketing profits for oil companies.

The President refused to enforce controls on oil prices or profits, preferring to try to ease demand. A national speed limit of fifty-five miles an hour was adopted, Sunday gasoline sales were banned, and Nixon asked Americans to turn down their thermostats. With voluntary restrictions, and an unusually mild winter, the country came through the boycott.

During the winter, Kissinger, now secretary of state, made numerous trips to the Middle East, testing his hand at shuttle diplomacy. Since the Arabs refused to talk directly with the Israelis, he had to fly between the hostile capitals and suc-

The Arab Oil Embargo of 1973 intensified an energy crisis that had just begun to be felt in the United States. Although the Arabs ended their boycott after a month, the impact of the crisis, the prospect of winter fuel shortages, and the endless lines of cars waiting for service at gas stations, made it clear that an energy policy was needed at home.

ceeded in working out a disengagement of opposing troops. By March the Arabs ended the oil boycott, and the situation ended. But the U.S. government had failed to establish a long-term answer to the problem of diminishing energy resources.

Henry Kissinger's accomplishments in the Middle East provided the one and only consola-

tion for Richard Nixon's administration in its last days. Through mid-1974, as Nixon approached his final reckoning, the White House became increasingly paralyzed. By the summer of that year, as the Judiciary Committee began its hearings, the President was almost entirely preoccupied with the unsuccessful efforts to clear his name and to remain in office.

Criss-crossing the globe for negotiations, Secretary of State Kissinger confers with Morocco's King Hassan II at Rabat in November 1973, while en route to China. Kissinger joined Nixon's staff as a special assistant for national security and became Secretary of State at the outset of Nixon's second term. Kissinger not only replaced "Containment" with "Detente," but also introduced his own brand of "shuttle diplomacy"—a one man patrol of the world's trouble spots.

THE FORD ADMINISTRATION

Gerald Ford's electorate had never been larger than the voters of Grand Rapids, Michigan. Still, President Ford received strong support when he assumed the office. His openness seemed a welcome change after Nixon's secretiveness; Americans relaxed when he announced, "Our long national nightmare is over." The comic strip *Doonesbury* showed a brick wall around the White House being demolished. A television crew went into the White House to show the new President making his own breakfast.

Some of the beatific aura faded, however, a month after the inauguration—when Ford pardoned Nixon for any criminal actions committed during his presidency. Ford had said during his confirmation hearings that he did not expect to take such an action, and his new press secretary resigned in protest. At a time when most of Nixon's White House associates faced prosecution and possible jail terms, many Americans objected to Ford's action as charity misplaced and presidential power misused.

The pardon played a large role in the congressional campaign of November 1974. Republicans had originally thought that Ford, by replacing Nixon, would save the party from heavy

The first man to reach the White House without ever winning a national election, Gerald R. Ford, shown here with his wife Betty, had entered the House of Representatives in 1948 as Congressman from Grand Rapids, Michigan. After twenty-five years in the House, ten of them as Minority Leader, Ford was appointed to the Vice Presidency when Spiro Agnew resigned in August 1973. He became President on August 9, 1974, upon Nixon's resignation.

congressional losses. Ford campaigned strenuously and tried to rally support for his policies with the slogan "WIN—Whip inflation now." But Democrats increased their already large majorities in both houses of Congress.

Ford and the New Congress With top-heavy majorities and in the new post-Watergate atmosphere, Democrats in Congress now sought to take policy initiative away from the White House.

Many journalists and political scientists had warned, after Vietnam and Watergate, that the presidency had become too powerful.

Congress and the President faced off over two major issues during the balance of Ford's term—the economy and the energy crisis. By early 1975 the economy appeared to be approaching disaster. Unemployment was running at levels near 10 percent, especially among auto workers and in the construction and aerospace industries.

Demonstrators at the Capitol protest both the upswing in military expenditures in Vietnam and the spectre of rising unemployment at home. The advent of "stagflation," with its combination of rising prices, low economic growth, and consequent shortage of jobs, forced the Nixon Administration to confront an economy in which both unemployment and inflation were getting out of hand. A sequence of controls and decontrol, plus the dismantling of Johnson era social welfare programs, did little to lessen the rising tide of unemployment.

Although inflation had been brought under some control and the rate of price increases had slackened, economic growth had also declined.

Energy seemed to be at least as great a problem. The Arab nations and other Third World oil producers had formed a cartel—OPEC (Organization of Petroleum Exporting Countries)—and quadrupled oil prices within a short period. The United States' own supplies of oil could not last much longer, and intensive efforts to find and develop more, such as on the north slope of Alaska and off the Atlantic and Pacific coastlines, raised environmental questions and political controversy. The same problems applied to the development of America's huge supplies of coal; and widespread use of alternative fuel sources, such as solar and atomic energy, were decades and billions of dollars away.

Congressional militancy proved no match for problems of such magnitude. Democrats struggled in vain to produce an energy bill acceptable to one another, let alone strong enough to override a presidential veto. Congress did manage to produce a number of bills intended to boost the economy, but only one major bill—a compromise tax cut in the spring of 1975—became law. Most of the others were vetoed by Ford, and Democrats rarely managed to muster the two-thirds majority needed to override. Although the new Congress had restated some congressional prerogatives, it had again been shown that effective national government depended on strong presidential leadership.

RALPH NADER

Ralph Nader became America's best-known and most influential critic of corporate practices through the direct assistance of America's largest corporation, General Motors, in 1965. Nader was an obscure thirty-one-year-old graduate of Harvard Law School, researching the issue of automobile safety, and barely supporting himself with articles and lectures on the subject. That year, he had published a book called *Unsafe at Any Speed*, examining in particular the performance of the Corvair, a product of GM's Chevrolet Division. The Corvair, Nader charged, had a tendency to roll over even when driven carefully, and the car had been involved in a startlingly high number of serious accidents.

In 1966, at a Senate hearing on auto safety, General Motors admitted that its response to Nader's charges had been to send out private detectives to find some "dirt" on Nader. They had been instructed to keep Nader under surveillance, to investigate his drinking and sex habits (especially why he had never married), and to check whether Nader, the son of Lebanese immigrants, might be anti-Semitic. All "leads" checked out negative. Nader got wind of the snooping, and filed a $26 million lawsuit. GM's president tried to get off with a private apology to Nader. Four years later, Nader settled out of court for $425,000, declaring he would use the money to monitor General Motor's future business practices.

But by then Nader had already become a virtual legend. GM's action had made him famous, and focused attention on his investigations, which rapidly broadened to include new subjects. Young lawyers and researchers flocked to work for his Center for the Study of Responsive Law, and later his Corporate Accountability Research Group—groups known more popularly as "Nader's Raiders." They have issued critical reports on the workings of federal regulatory commissions, the criminal justice system, various corporate practices, and Congress itself. In a style somewhere between scholarship and journalism, the reports have helped pass legislation in several areas (motor vehicle safety, meat inspection, and safety in mining, for example), although the results have rarely been strong enough to satisfy Nader.

Besides running what has been called an investigative conglomerate, Nader is a congressional lobbyist, a publicist for his causes, and an untiring lecturer. He speaks to civic groups, professional bodies, and college students all over the country, demanding that all Americans become involved in local citizens' action groups. "We can't possibly have a democracy," he warns, "with two hundred million Americans and only a handful of citizens."

General Motors' investigators had discovered that Nader worked nonstop and seemed to have no other interests. This life style, widely reported by the media, is now a key aspect of the Nader legend. Nader puts in eighteen to twenty hours a day, sleeping only four to five hours in his $80-a-month room in a Washington boarding house. He expects lawyers working for him to keep up a similar pace, for salaries well below what they might earn elsewhere. He is rarely tolerant of lesser effort. "You go off on a trip for a week with some twenty-five-year-old lawyer," he once complained, "and when you come back *he wants the weekend off!*" But Nader's zeal, his small army of devoted and equally hard working associates, and his political skills have made him the most durable and effective single reformer in contemporary America.

Ford and Foreign Affairs Congress had some success in deflecting Ford's foreign policy proposals. In March 1975, North Vietnamese troops launched a major offensive, and the South Vietnamese retreat quickly turned into a rout. With the Saigon government on the verge of collapse, Ford requested $700 million in emergency aid for South Vietnam and a smaller amount for Cambodia, also threatened by a communist takeover.

At virtually the last moment in the fifteen-year Indochina War, Congress asserted itself and refused the request for aid, which would probably have come too late to change the outcome. By mid-April the communist armies had captured the capital of Cambodia, and by the end of the month Saigon had fallen. The war was over.

But its final scene would remain to haunt Americans. Thousands of Vietnamese who had cooperated with the American forces tried desperately to get aboard departing American helicopters and ships. Many had been promised passage out of the country and had remained at their jobs on the strength of those assurances. Now American marines fought off the thousands of terrified Vietnamese swarming over the walls of the American embassy, begging to be taken along. One American devised a simple, hard rule for the last days: "Don't look in their eyes."

Post-Vietnam Foreign Policy By mid-1975 it was becoming more and more difficult to see American foreign policy as an anticommunist crusade. Ford had retained both Nixon's secretary of state, Henry Kissinger, and his policy of détente with the Russians. America and the Soviet Union reached a new level of agreement in the SALT talks and, along with the European powers, signed a major agreement at Helsinki calling for peace and recognizing territorial changes made at the end of World War II.

But some Americans, including many liberals, upset with Russian policy on the Middle East and treatment of Soviet Jews, began to question the value of détente. They pointed out that parts of the Helsinki Agreement, such as those calling for respect for human rights and free travel from country to country had been ignored by the Soviet Union. Those opposed to détente also cited the large Soviet involvement in Angola, where a withdrawal of Portuguese colonial authority in that African state had led to a civil war between Marxist and pro-Western factions. With hundreds of millions of dollars in Russian military aid, and several thousand Cuban soldiers, the Marxists won easily. But if Angola showed the unchanged nature of Soviet policy, it also illustrated the different attitude of Congress, which refused President Ford's request for aid to the pro-Western Angolans and directed an immediate end to all American involvement.

Aid to Angola and congressional attitudes were also involved in another controversy related to foreign affairs. Congressional committees dug out large amounts of evidence of illegal and disturbing activities by the CIA, including aborted assassination plots against foreign leaders. Ford announced new controls on the agency. But neither Congress nor the public seemed to consider the new directive the final answer, possibly because neither seemed sure what actions would simultaneously serve the interests of American freedom *and* security.

Ford and the Economy By early 1976 the economy seemed to be making some improvement. The President declared the recession over. Unemployment although still high had come down somewhat, and the stock market was running surprisingly high. The White House pointed to the improvement as an argument against further bills passed by Congress to stimulate the economy.

In the midst of the improvement at least one highly disturbing situation boiled over. New York City was rapidly going bankrupt and would soon be unable to cover its debt obligations. Nobody knew exactly how far the effects of a default by the nation's largest city would extend, but many people felt that it would have an appalling effect on the sluggishly improving economy. Others argued that New York had brought the problem on itself through fiscal mismanagement and overgenerous welfare and employee benefits. President Ford, bidding for conservative support, delivered a speech so strong that the pro-Republican *New York Daily News* headlined the story, "FORD TO CITY: DROP DEAD."

Antibusing parents and children demonstrate outside a federal building in downtown Detroit on January 22, 1976, four days before a court-ordered school integration program, affecting 22,000 public school students, was due to begin. By the mid-seventies, two decades after the Supreme Court's historic desegregation decision, the problem of school integration was no longer solely a Southern one. Court-ordered integration plans, requiring busing, now evoked controversy in big Northern cities.

In the end, Ford approved some federal aid to the city. But while New York's problem remained to some extent unique, it gave a foretaste of what might happen to many American cities. Since World War II, the middle and upper-middle classes and many businesses had fled the inner city, while welfare costs and the cities' low-income population stayed behind. New York's plight reminded Americans that the urban crisis, while no longer receiving the attention it had during the 1960s, had not been solved or even eased.

THE BICENTENNIAL ELECTION

When the two major presidential candidates gained their parties' first-ballot nominations at the par-

ty conventions, it would appear that the preconvention presidential battle was a cut-and-dried affair. Although the 1976 campaign produced first-ballot nominations, things were anything but predetermined.

First, Gerald Ford had to fashion for himself a credible image as a presidential candidate, something more than the caretaker role assigned him by the Watergate mess and the Nixon resignation. Second, Ford had to fight off a strong challenger.

To avoid becoming an interim president, an appointed lame duck, Ford announced early that he would run for President. He became less apologetic about his status, acting more like a chief executive and less like a political accident. He even took to the skies, emulating Nixon's eye-opening visits to China and Russia, but not necessarily reaping the same results. Ford also stripped himself of another lame duck, the man he had appointed Vice President, New York's ex-governor Nelson Rockefeller—a person who carried an aura of liberal Republicanism about him. GOP conservatives still viewed Rockefeller with suspicion and wanted his head. They got it.

In the wings (the right wing, to be precise) stood Ronald Reagan, ex-movie star, former two-term governor of California, and still a dashing figure in his mid-sixties. Reagan offered a fundamentalist Republican line, attacking the federal government, the welfare state, and the détente policy of cozying up to the Russians and the Chinese.

At first it appeared that Ford had nothing to worry about. The President scored handily over Reagan in the initial Republican primaries. But in North Carolina Reagan won his first primary. And

during the spring primary season he and the President came closer and closer in delegate strength. At convention time it looked like a toss-up. Then Reagan took a daring, costly gamble. He broke tradition by announcing in advance who his vice-presidential running mate would be. That was novel. But Reagan chose a very liberal Republican senator from Pennsylvania. To GOP conservatives that was shocking. Some, including Barry Goldwater, the party's "conservative conscience," came out in support of Ford. It was no runaway, but the Republican convention nominated Ford on the first ballot.

In the enemy camp, the Democrats began the election year with more generals than buck privates. At least a dozen persons declared for the nomination. One of them, a Georgia politician with a permanent smile and an undistinguished

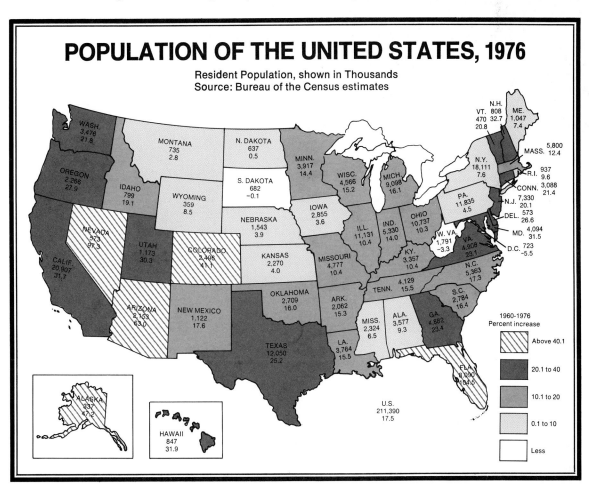

POPULATION OF THE UNITED STATES, 1976

Resident Population, shown in Thousands
Source: Bureau of the Census estimates

record in his state's politics seemed the least likely to succeed.

James Earl Carter, Jr. (he preferred to be called Jimmy) had announced in 1974 that he intended to become President. Those outside of his entourage thought Carter was as likely to walk on the moon. But Carter's persistence slowly changed his candidacy from something almost comic into something substantial. Though he was not taken too seriously before the primaries, Jimmy would not quit—soon enough his considerable political talents began to draw the public's attention.

In January 1976, Carter won Iowa delegates; a month later he repeated with a win in New Hampshire. He was moving away from the pack, a process accelerated greatly in subsequent Southern primaries, which included his rout of Alabama's perennial maverick George Wallace. Democratic leaders such as Senators Henry Jackson and Birch Bayh pulled out of the contest. A few more entered. But it was over by early June, when Carter won the Ohio primary and endorsements from most of the party's establishment poured in. So it was off to New York City for the Democratic convention in mid-July for this self-styled Georgia peanut farmer. (Actually the Carter family's wholesale peanut business and land holdings in Plains, Georgia, kept them moderately wealthy.)

Before the politicos got together, the country had an anniversary to face—July 4, 1976. Presi-

Former Georgia Governor Jimmy Carter, surrounded by his family, at the Democratic National Convention of 1976 in New York City. The front-runner in the primaries, Carter had stressed his role as a non-Washingtonian "outsider," at a time when the memory of Watergate put "insiders" under suspicion.

U. S. Ambassador to the United Nations, Andrew Young, one of the most prominent appointees of the new Carter Administration, visits Israeli Ambassador Chaim Herzog at the Israeli Mission on January 31, 1977. A former Democratic Congressman from Atlanta, the youthful Georgian soon drew world-wide attention by his outspoken comments and candor.

dent Ford spent the preceding days in Pennsylvania—at Valley Forge and then at Independence Hall in Philadelphia, where one million persons celebrated America's two hundredth birthday. Then on to New York. The city and its neighbors spent a festive, frolicsome Sunday on the Glorious Fourth, a day remarkably filled with good cheer. The highlight of this spectacular was the procession of hundreds of ships and boats up the Hudson River, featuring sixteen "tall ships"— beautiful high-masted sailing ships from naval academies around the world. Not since the moon

landing in 1969 had American morale received a greater boost.

New York's Fourth of July euphoria lingered on a bit. Democrats in convention there from July 12 through 15 took advantage of it. Carter knew he had the nomination, and to help re-cement the Democratic coalition he put a Northern, prolabor liberal—Walter Mondale of Minnesota—on the ticket. At that point it looked as if Carter would trounce Ford.

But midyear polls and November election results seldom jibe. The campaign, not nearly so exciting as the primary fights, narrowed the margin established by the pollsters. Carter's religiosity (a "born again" Southern Baptist) was always an issue, but a lessening problem for him as he became better known. Jimmy did gain unfavorable headlines because of an interview he granted *Playboy* magazine, in which he admitted harboring sexual impulses. Ford, meanwhile, had to fire his foot-in-mouth secretary of agriculture, Earl Butz, because of a tasteless and racist remark made by Butz.

Election year 1976 saw the return of direct presidential debates, a device used only once before, in 1960. This time the incumbent President, Ford, decided to gamble by debating with Carter three times. The debates were televised, and Carter later stated that it was his performances in the second and third debates that won him the election.

But in close elections any positive factor can be isolated as decisive. 1976 was close. Electoral vote counts usually show a good spread, but in 1976 it was only Carter 297 to Ford 241. Carter got 50.4% of the popular vote (to Ford's 48.5%), so he could at least claim to be a majority president. But neither he nor Ford had excited the voters—only 53 percent of Americans eligible to vote did so, a drop of 2 percent since 1972, and a considerable drop from the 63 percent of eligibles who had voted in 1960. Many Americans simply did not care. And among the least involved in the electoral process were those in the 18-to-21 age group granted voting rights in 1972. Despite the stay-at-homes, Carter had carried enough of the industrial Northeast, and his own near solid South to win election. It was virtually an East-West split, with

Ford carrying most Western States.

Carter's inaugural day, January 20, 1977, was upbeat and informal. The address contained a characteristic biblical quotation and a plea that "we must again have faith in our country—and in one another." The President also issued an inaugural statement to the world, imprecise but reassuring, indicating that he appreciated both the extent and the limits of American power. Once installed, the President and Mrs. Carter walked from Capitol Hill to the White House, a distance normally traveled by a President in a glass-topped bullet-proof limousine. At night, inaugural parties replaced inaugural balls, and no one seemed to mind the informality.

All new Presidents want to begin afresh. They certainly want to bury old, divisive issues, those that can upset their administrations as badly as they did those of their predecessors. The day after assuming office, Carter pardoned Vietnam era draft evaders. The President wanted to heal that wound left from the past.

Too many pressing elements of the present had to be faced, and some might even have to be solved: the United States had become increasingly dependent on foreign oil in the 1970s, the welfare system had not been reformed, the urban crisis had not eased, environmentalists and those fighting stagflation could not agree, and America's relations with the rest of the world had to be worked out in a post-Vietnam context. So too did individual Americans have to ponder what their country meant to them and where they thought it was headed—no small task in view of the sobering events and many changes of the preceding decade.

SUGGESTED READINGS–CHAPTERS 51-52

Watergate

Carl Bernstein and Bob Woodward, *All the President's Men* (1974) and *The Final Days* (1976); John Dean, *Blind Ambition* (1976); William B. Dickinson, Jr., *Watergate: Chronology of a Crisis* (2 vols., 1974); Leon Jaworski, *The Right and the Power: The Prosecution of Watergate* (1976).

Politics: Nixon and Beyond

Marvin and Bernard Kalb, *Kissinger* (1974); Leonard W. Levy, *Against the Law: The Nixon Court and Criminal Justice* (1974); Earl Mazo and Stephen Hess, *Nixon: A Political Portrait* (1968); Joe McGinnis, *The Selling of the President, 1968* (1969); Arthur M. Schlesinger, Jr., *The Imperial Presidency* (1973); James F. Simon, *In His Own Image: The Supreme Court in Richard Nixon's America* (1973); Theodore H. White, *The Making of the President, 1968* (1969) and *Breach of Faith: The Fall of Richard Nixon* (1975); Gary Wills, *Nixon Agonistes* (1970); George B. Reedy, *The Twilight of the Presidency* (1970); R. Reeves, *A Ford Not A Lincoln* (1974); Samuel Huntington, *The Crisis of Democracy* (1977); Sumner Rosen, ed., *Economic Power Pailure* (1975).

Interpretations of Society

Jonathan Schell, *The Time of Illusion* (1975); Harland B. Moulton, *From Superiority to Parity: The United States and the Strategic Arms Race, 1966–1971* (1973); Otis L. Graham, Jr., *Toward a Planned Society: From Roosevelt to Nixon* (1976); Alexander M. Bickel, *The Supreme Court and the Idea of Progress* (1970); Robert L. Heilbroner, *An Inquiry into the Human Prospect* (1974); Andrew Hacker, *The End of the American Era* (1971); Daniel Bell, *The Coming of Post-Industrial Society* (1976).

THE DECLARATION OF INDEPENDENCE

In Congress, July 4, 1776. *The unanimous Declaration of the thirteen united States of America,*

When in the Course of human events, it becomes necessary for one people to dissolve the political bands which have connected them with another, and to assume among the powers of the earth, the separate and equal station to which the Laws of Nature and of Nature's God entitle them, a decent respect to the opinions of mankind requires that they should declare the causes which impel them to the separation.—

We hold these truths to be self-evident, that all men are created equal, that they are endowed by their Creator with certain unalienable Rights, that among these are Life, Liberty and the pursuit of Happiness.—

That to secure these rights, Governments are instituted among Men, deriving their just powers from the consent of the governed,—

That whenever any Form of Government becomes destructive of these ends, it is the Right of the People to alter or to abolish it, and to institute new Government, laying its foundation on such principles and organizing its powers in such form, as to them shall seem most likely to effect their Safety and Happiness. Prudence, indeed, will dictate that Governments long established should not be changed for light and transient causes; and accordingly all experience hath shown, that mankind are more disposed to suffer, while evils are sufferable, than to right themselves by abolishing the forms to which they are accustomed. But when a long train of abuses and usurpations, pursuing invariably the same Object evinces a design to reduce them under absolute Despotism, it is their right, it is their duty, to throw off such Government, and to provide new Guards for their future security.—

Such has been the patient sufferance of these Colonies; and such is now the necessity which constrains them to alter their former Systems of Government. The history of the present King of Great Britain is a history of repeated injuries and usurpations, all having in direct object the establishment of an absolute Tyranny over these States. To prove this, let Facts be submitted to a candid world.—

He has refused his Assent to Laws, the most wholesome and necessary for the public good.—

He has forbidden his Governors to pass Laws of immediate and pressing importance, unless suspended in their operation till his Assent should be obtained; and when so suspended, he has utterly neglected to attend to them.—

He has refused to pass other Laws for the accommodation of large districts of people, unless those people would relinquish the right of Representation in the Legislature, a right inestimable to them and formidable to tyrants only.—

He has called together legislative bodies at places unusual, uncomfortable, and distant from the depository of their public Records, for the sole purpose of fatiguing them into compliance with his measures.—

He has dissolved Representative Houses repeatedly, for opposing with manly firmness his invasions on the rights of the people.—

He has refused for a long time, after such dissolutions, to cause others to be elected; whereby the Legislative powers, incapable of Annihilation, have returned to the People at large for their exercise; the State remaining in the mean time exposed to all the dangers of invasion from without, and convulsions within.—

He has endeavoured to prevent the population of these States; for that purpose obstructing the Laws for Naturalization of Foreigners; refusing to pass others to encourage their migrations hither, and raising the conditions of new Appropriations of Lands.—

He has obstructed the Administration of Justice, by refusing his Assent to Laws for establishing Judiciary powers.—

He has made Judges dependent on his Will alone, for the tenure of their offices, and the amount and payment of their salaries.—

He has erected a multitude of New Offices, and sent hither swarms of Officers to harrass our people, and eat out their substance.—

He has kept among us in times of peace, Standing Armies without the Consent of our legislatures.—

He has affected to render the Military independent of and superior to the Civil power.—

He has combined with others to subject us to a jurisdiction foreign to our constitution, and unacknowledged by our laws; giving his Assent to their Acts of pretended Legislation:—

For quartering large bodies of armed troops among us:—

For protecting them, by a mock Trial, from punishment for any Murders which they should commit on the Inhabitants of these States:—

For cutting off our Trade with all parts of the world:—

For imposing Taxes on us without our Consent:—

For depriving us in many cases, of the benefits of Trial by Jury:—

For transporting us beyond Seas to be tried for pretended offences:—

For abolishing the free System of English Laws in a neighbouring Province, establishing therein an Arbitrary government, and enlarging its Boundaries so as to render it at once an example and fit instrument for introducing the same absolute rule in these Colonies:—

For taking away our Charters, abolishing our most valuable Laws, and altering fundamentally the Forms of our Governments:—

For suspending our own Legislatures, and declaring themselves invested with power to legislate for us in all cases whatsoever.—

He has abdicated Government here, by declaring us out of his Protection and waging War against us.—

He has plundered our seas, ravaged our Coasts, burnt our towns, and destroyed the lives of our people.—

He is at this time transporting large Armies of foreign Mercenaries to compleat the works of death, desolation and tyranny, already begun with circumstances of Cruelty & perfidy scarcely paralleled in the most barbarous ages, and totally unworthy the Head of a civilized nation.—

He has constrained our fellow Citizens taken Captive on the high Seas to bear Arms against their Country, to become the executioners of their friends and Brethren, or to fall themselves by their Hands.—

He has excited domestic insurrections amongst us, and has endeavoured to bring on the inhabitants of our frontiers, the merciless Indian Savages, whose known rule of warfare, is an undistinguished destruction of all ages, sexes and conditions.—

In every stage of these Oppressions We have Petitioned for Redress in the most humble terms: Our repeated Petitions have been answered only by repeated injury. A Prince, whose character is thus marked by every act which may define a Tyrant, is unfit to be the ruler of a free people.

Nor have We been wanting in attentions to our British brethren. We have warned them from time to time of attempts by their legislature to extend an unwarrantable jurisdiction over us. We have reminded them of the circumstances of our emigration and settlement here. We have appealed to their native justice and magnanimity, and we have conjured them by the ties of our common kindred to disavow these usurpations, which, would inevitably interrupt our connections and correspondence. They too have been deaf to the voice of justice and of consanguinity. We must, therefore, acquiesce in the necessity, which denounces our Separation, and hold them, as we hold the rest of mankind, Enemies in War, in Peace Friends.—

We, therefore, the Representatives of the united States of America, in General Congress, Assembled, appealing to the Supreme Judge of the world for the rectitude of our intentions, do, in the Name, and by Authority of the good People of these Colonies, solemnly publish and declare, That these United Colonies are, and of Right ought to be, Free and Independent States; that they are absolved from all Allegiance to the British Crown, and that all political connection between them and the State of Great Britain, is and ought to be totally dissolved; and that as Free and Independent States they have full Power to levy War, conclude Peace, contract Alliances, establish Commerce, and to do all other Acts and Things which Independent States may of right do.—

And for the support of this Declaration, with a firm reliance on the protection of divine Providence, we mutually pledge to each other our Lives, our Fortunes and our sacred Honor.

John Hancock
(MASSACHUSETTS)

NEW HAMPSHIRE
Josiah Bartlett
William Whipple
Matthew Thornton

MASSACHUSETTS
Samuel Adams
John Adams
Robert Treat Paine
Elbridge Gerry

DELAWARE
Caesar Rodney
George Read
Thomas McKean

NEW YORK
William Floyd
Philip Livingston
Francis Lewis
Lewis Morris

NEW JERSEY
Richard Stockton
John Witherspoon
Francis Hopkinson
John Hart
Abraham Clark

NORTH CAROLINA
William Hooper
Joseph Hewes
John Penn

MARYLAND
Samuel Chase
William Paca
Thomas Stone
Charles Carroll
   of Carrollton

SOUTH CAROLINA
Edward Rutledge
Thomas Heywood, Jr.
Thomas Lynch, Jr.
Arthur Middleton

RHODE ISLAND
Stephen Hopkins
William Ellery

CONNECTICUT
Roger Sherman
Samuel Huntington
William Williams
Oliver Wolcott

PENNSYLVANIA
Robert Morris
Benjamin Rush
Benjamin Franklin
John Morton
George Clymer
James Smith
George Taylor
James Wilson
George Ross

VIRGINIA
George Wythe
Richard Henry Lee
Thomas Jefferson
Benjamin Harrison
Thomas Nelson, Jr.
Francis Lightfoot Lee
Carter Braxton

GEORGIA
Button Gwinnett
Lyman Hall
George Walton

THE CONSTITUTION OF THE UNITED STATES OF AMERICA

We the People of the United States, in Order to form a more perfect Union, establish Justice, insure domestic Tranquility, provide for the common defence, promote the general Welfare, and secure the Blessings of Liberty to ourselves and our Posterity, do ordain and establish this Constitution for the United States of America.

The preamble establishes the principle of government by the people, and lists the six basic purposes of the Constitution.

ARTICLE I • LEGISLATIVE DEPARTMENT

Section 1. All legislative Powers herein granted shall be vested in a Congress of the United States, which shall consist of a Senate and House of Representatives.

Section 2. The House of Representatives shall be composed of Members chosen every second Year by the People of the several States, and the Electors in each State shall have the Qualifications requisite for Electors of the most numerous Branch of the State Legislature.

Representatives serve two-year terms. They are chosen in each state by those electors (that is, voters) who are qualified to vote for members of the lower house of their own state legislature.

No Person shall be a Representative who shall not have attained to the Age of twenty-five Years, and been seven Years a Citizen of the United States, and who shall not, when elected, be an Inhabitant of that State in which he shall be chosen.

Representatives and direct Taxes shall be apportioned among the several States which may be included within this Union, according to their respective Numbers, which shall be determined by adding to the whole Number of free Persons, including those bound to Service for a Term of Years, and excluding Indians not taxed, three-fifths of all other Persons. The actual Enumeration shall be made within three Years after the first Meeting of the Congress of the United States, and within every subsequent Term of ten

The number of representatives allotted to a state is determined by the size of its population. The 14th Amendment has made obsolete the reference to "all other persons"—that is, slaves. A census must be taken every ten years to determine the number of representatives to which each state is entitled. There is now one representative for about every 470,000 persons.

Years, in such Manner as they shall by Law direct. The Number of Representatives shall not exceed one for every thirty Thousand, but each State shall have at Least one Representative; and until such enumeration shall be made, the State of New Hampshire shall be entitled to chuse three, Massachusetts eight, Rhode Island and Providence Plantations one, Connecticut five, New York six, New Jersey four, Pennsylvania eight, Delaware one, Maryland six, Virginia ten, North Carolina five, South Carolina five, and Georgia three.

"Executive authority" refers to the governor of a state.

When vacancies happen in the Representation from any State, the Executive Authority thereof shall issue Writs of Election to fill such Vacancies.

The Speaker, chosen by and from the majority party, presides over the House. Impeachment is the act of bringing formal charges against an official. (See also Section 3.)

The House of Representatives shall chuse their Speaker and other Officers; and shall have the sole Power of Impeachment.

Section 3. The Senate of the United States shall be composed of two Senators from each State, chosen by the Legislature thereof, for six Years; and each Senator shall have one Vote.

The 17th Amendment changed this method to direct election.

Immediately after they shall be assembled in Consequence of the first Election, they shall be divided as equally as may be into three Classes. The Seats of the Senators of the first Class shall be vacated at the Expiration of the second Year, of the second Class at the Expiration of the fourth Year, and of the third Class at the Expiration of the sixth Year, so that one third may be chosen every second Year; and if Vacancies happen by Resignation, or otherwise, during the Recess of the Legislature of any State, the Executive thereof may make temporary Appointments until the next Meeting of the Legislature, which shall then fill such Vacancies.

The 17th Amendment also provides that a state governor shall appoint a successor to fill a vacant Senate seat until a direct election is held.

No Person shall be a Senator who shall not have attained to the Age of thirty Years, and been nine Years a Citizen of the United States, and who shall not, when elected, be an Inhabitant of that State for which he shall be chosen.

The Vice President may cast a vote in the Senate only in order to break a tie.

The Vice President of the United States shall be President of the Senate, but shall have no Vote, unless they be equally divided.

The president *pro tempore* of the Senate is a temporary officer; the Latin words mean "for the time being."

The Senate shall chuse their other Officers, and also a President pro tempore, in the absence of the Vice President, or when he shall exercise the Office of President of the United States.

No President has ever been successfully impeached. In 1868 the Senate fell one vote short of the two-thirds majority needed to convict Andrew Johnson. Twelve other officials —ten federal judges, one senator, and one Secretary of War—have been impeached; four of the judges were convicted.

The Senate shall have the sole Power to try all Impeachments. When sitting for that Purpose, they shall be on Oath or Affirmation. When the President of the United States is tried, the Chief Justice shall preside: And no Person shall be convicted without the Concurrence of two thirds of the Members present.

Judgment in Cases of Impeachment shall not extend further than to removal from Office, and disqualification to hold and enjoy any Office of Honor, Trust or Profit under the United States: but the Party convicted shall nevertheless be liable and subject to Indictment, Trial, Judgment and Punishment, according to Law.

Elections for Congress are held on the first Tuesday after the first Monday in November in even-numbered years.

Section 4. The Times, Places and Manner of holding Elections for Senators and Representatives, shall be prescribed in each State by the Legislature thereof; but the Congress may at any time by Law make or alter such Regulations, except as to the Place of chusing Senators.

The 20th Amendment designates January 3 as the opening of the congressional session.

The Congress shall assemble at least once in every Year, and such Meeting shall be on the first Monday in December, unless they shall by Law appoint a different Day.

Section 5. Each House shall be the Judge of the Elections, Returns and Qualifications of its own Members, and a Majority of each shall constitute a Quorum to do Business; but a smaller number may adjourn from day to day, and may be authorized to compel the Attendance of absent Members, in such Manner, and under such Penalties as each House may provide.

Each House may determine the Rules of its Proceedings, punish its Members for disorderly Behavior, and, with the Concurrence of two thirds, expel a Member.

Each House shall keep a Journal of its Proceedings, and from time to time publish the same, excepting such Parts as may in their Judgment require Secrecy; and the Yeas and Nays of the Members of either House on any question shall, at the Desire of one fifth of those Present, be entered on the Journal.

Neither House, during the Session of Congress, shall, without the Consent of the other, adjourn for more than three days, nor to any other Place than that in which the two Houses shall be sitting.

Each house of Congress decides whether a member has been elected properly and is qualified to be seated. (A quorum is the minimum number of persons required to be present in order to conduct business.) The House once refused admittance to an elected representative who had been guilty of a crime. The Senate did likewise in the case of a candidate whose election campaign lent itself to "fraud and corruption."

Section 6. The Senators and Representatives shall receive a Compensation for their Services, to be ascertained by Law, and paid out of the Treasury of the United States. They shall in all Cases, except Treason, Felony and Breach of the Peace, be privileged from Arrest during their Attendance at the Session of their respective Houses, and in going to and returning from the same; and for any Speech or Debate in either House, they shall not be questioned in any other Place.

No Senator or Representative shall, during the Time for which he was elected, be appointed to any civil Office under the Authority of the United States, which shall have been created, or the Emoluments whereof shall have been encreased during such time; and no Person holding any Office under the United States, shall be a Member of either House during his Continuance in Office.

Congressmen have the power to fix their own salaries. Under the principle of *congressional immunity,* they cannot be sued or arrested for anything they say in a congressional debate. This provision enables them to speak freely.

This clause reinforces the principle of separation of powers by stating that, during his term of office, a member of Congress may not be appointed to a position in another branch of government. Nor may he resign and accept a position created during his term.

Section 7. All Bills for raising Revenue shall originate in the House of Representatives; but the Senate may propose or concur with Amendments as on other Bills.

Every Bill which shall have passed the House of Representatives and the Senate, shall, before it become a Law, be presented to the President of the United States; If he approve he shall sign it, but if not he shall return it, with his Objections to that House in which it shall have originated, who shall enter the Objections at large on their Journal, and proceed to reconsider it. If after such Reconsideration two thirds of that House shall agree to pass the Bill, it shall be sent, together with the Objections, to the other House, by which it shall likewise be reconsidered, and if approved by two thirds of that House, it shall become a Law. But in all such Cases the Votes of both Houses shall be determined by Yeas and Nays, and the Names of the Persons voting for and against the Bill shall be entered on the Journal of each House respectively. If any Bill shall not be returned by the President within ten Days (Sundays excepted) after it shall have been presented to him, the Same shall be a Law, in like Manner as if he had signed it, unless the Congress by their Adjournment prevent its Return, in which Case it shall not be a Law.

Every Order, Resolution, or Vote to which the Concurrence of the Senate and House of Representatives may be necessary (except on a question of Adjournment) shall be presented to the President of the United States; and before the Same shall take Effect, shall be approved by him, or being disapproved by him, shall be repassed by two thirds of the Senate and House of Representatives, according to the Rules and Limitations prescribed in the Case of a Bill.

The House initiates tax bills but the Senate may propose changes in them.

By returning a bill unsigned to the house in which it originated, the President exercises a *veto.* A two-thirds majority in both houses can override the veto. If the President receives a bill within the last ten days of a session and does not sign it, the measure dies by *pocket veto.* Merely by keeping the bill in his pocket, so to speak, the president effects a veto.

The same process of approval or disapproval by the President is applied to resolutions and other matters passed by both houses (except adjournment).

Section 8. The Congress shall have Power to lay and collect Taxes, Duties, Imposts and Excises, to pay the Debts and provide for the common Defence and general Welfare of the United States; but all Duties, Imposts and Excises shall be uniform throughout the United States;

To borrow money on the credit of the United States;

To regulate Commerce with foreign Nations, and among the several States, and with the Indian Tribes;

To establish an uniform Rule of Naturalization, and uniform Laws on the subject of Bankruptcies throughout the United States;

To coin Money, regulate the Value thereof, and of foreign Coin, and fix the Standard of Weights and Measures;

To provide for the Punishment of counterfeiting the Securities and current Coin of the United States;

To establish Post Offices and post Roads;

To promote the Progress of Science and useful Arts, by securing for limited Times to Authors and Inventors the exclusive Right to their respective Writings and Discoveries;

To constitute Tribunals inferior to the supreme Court;

To define and punish Piracies and Felonies committed on the high Seas, and Offenses against the Law of Nations;

To declare War, grant Letters of Marque and Reprisal, and make Rules concerning Captures on Land and Water;

To raise and support Armies, but no Appropriation of Money to that Use shall be for a longer Term than two Years;

To provide and maintain a Navy;

To make Rules for the Government and Regulation of the land and naval Forces;

To provide for calling forth the Militia to execute the Laws of the Union, suppress Insurrections and repel Invasions;

To provide for organizing, arming, and disciplining the Militia, and for governing such Part of them as may be employed in the Service of the United States, reserving to the States respectively, the Appointment of the Officers, and the Authority of training the Militia according to the discipline prescribed by Congress;

To exercise exclusive Legislation in all Cases whatsoever, over such District (not exceeding ten Miles square) as may, by Cession of particular States, and the acceptance of Congress, become the Seat of the Government of the United States, and to exercise like Authority over all Places purchased by the Consent of the Legislature of the State in which the Same shall be, for the Erection of Forts, Magazines, Arsenals, dock-Yards, and other needful Buildings;—And

To make all Laws which shall be necessary and proper for carrying into Execution the foregoing Powers, and all other Powers vested by this Constitution in the Government of the United States, or in any Department or Officer thereof.

Section 9. The Migration or Importation of such Persons as any of the States now existing shall think proper to admit, shall not be prohibited by the Congress prior to the Year one thousand eight hundred and eight, but a tax or duty may be imposed on such Importation, not exceeding ten dollars for each Person.

The privilege of the Writ of Habeas Corpus shall not be suspended unless when in Cases of Rebellion or Invasion the public Safety may require it.

Side notes:

These are the *delegated,* or *enumerated,* powers of Congress.

Duties are taxes on imported goods; *excises* are taxes on goods manufactured, sold, or consumed within the country. *Imposts* is a general term including both duties and excise taxes.

Naturalization is the process by which an alien becomes a citizen.

Government *securities* include savings bonds and other notes.

Authors' and inventors' rights are protected by copyright and patent laws.

Congress may establish lower federal courts.

Only Congress may declare war. *Letters of marque and reprisal* grant merchant ships permission to attack enemy vessels.

Militia refers to national guard units, which may become part of the United States Army during an emergency. Congress aids the states in maintaining their national guard units.

This clause gives Congress the power to govern what became the District of Columbia, as well as other federal sites.

Known as the *elastic clause,* this provision enables Congress to exercise many powers not specifically granted to it by the Constitution.

This clause concerns the slave trade, which Congress did ban in 1808.

The *writ of habeas corpus* permits a prisoner to appear before a judge to inquire into the legality of his or her detention.

No Bill of Attainder or ex post facto Law shall be passed.

No capitation, or other direct, Tax shall be laid, unless in Proportion to the Census or Enumeration herein before directed to be taken.

No Tax or Duty shall be laid on Articles exported from any State.

No Preference shall be given by any Regulation of Commerce or Revenue to the Ports of one State over those of another; nor shall Vessels bound to, or from, one State, be obliged to enter, clear, or pay Duties in another.

No Money shall be drawn from the Treasury, but in Consequence of Appropriations made by Law; and a regular Statement and Account of the Receipts and Expenditures of all public Money shall be published from time to time.

No Title of Nobility shall be granted by the United States: And no Person holding any Office of Profit or Trust under them, shall, without the Consent of the Congress, accept of any present, Emolument, Office, or Title, of any kind whatever, from any King, Prince, or foreign State.

Section 10. No State shall enter into any Treaty, Alliance, or Confederation; grant Letters of Marque and Reprisal; coin Money; emit Bills of Credit; make any Thing but gold and silver Coin a Tender in Payment of Debts; pass any Bill of Attainder, ex post facto Law, or Law impairing the Obligation of Contracts, or grant any Title of Nobility.

No State shall, without the Consent of the Congress, lay any Imposts or Duties on Imports or Exports, except what may be absolutely necessary for executing its inspection Laws: and the net Produce of all Duties and Imposts, laid by any State on Imports or Exports, shall be for the Use of the Treasury of the United States; and all such Laws shall be subject to the Revision and Controul of the Congress.

No State shall, without the Consent of Congress, lay any duty of Tonnage, keep Troops, or Ships of War in time of Peace, enter into any Agreement or Compact with another State, or with a foreign Power, or engage in War, unless actually invaded, or in such imminent Danger as will not admit of delay.

ARTICLE II • EXECUTIVE DEPARTMENT

Section 1. The executive Power shall be vested in a President of the United States of America. He shall hold his Office during the Term of four Years, and, together with the Vice President, chosen for the same Term, be elected, as follows.

Each State shall appoint, in such Manner as the Legislature thereof may direct, a Number of Electors, equal to the whole Number of Senators and Representatives to which the State may be entitled in the Congress: but no Senator or Representative, or Person holding an Office of Trust or Profit under the United States, shall be appointed an Elector.

The Electors shall meet in their respective States, and vote by Ballot for two persons, of whom one at least shall not be an Inhabitant of the same State with themselves. And they shall make a List of all the Persons voted for, and of the Number of Votes for each; which List they shall sign and certify, and transmit sealed to the Seat of the Government of the United States, directed to the President of the Senate. The President of the Senate shall, in the Presence of the Senate and House of Representatives, open all the Certificates, and the Votes shall then be counted. The Person having the greatest Number of Votes shall be the President, if such Number be a Majority of the whole Number of Electors appointed; and if there be more than one who have such Majority, and have an equal

---

A *bill of attainder* is an act of legislation that declares a person guilty of a crime and punishes him or her without a trial. An *ex post facto* law punishes a person for an act that was legal when performed but later declared illegal.

The object of Clause 4 was to bar direct (per person) taxation of slaves for the purpose of abolishing slavery. The 16th Amendment modified this provision by giving Congress the power to tax personal income.

States are hereby forbidden to exercise certain powers. Some of these powers belong to Congress alone; others are considered undemocratic.

States cannot, without congressional authority, tax goods that enter or leave, except for a small inspection fee.

Federal officials are ineligible to serve as presidential electors.

The 12th Amendment superseded this clause. The weakness of the original constitutional provision became apparent in the election of 1800, when Thomas Jefferson and Aaron Burr received the same number of electoral votes. The 12th Amendment avoids this possibility by requiring electors to cast separate ballots for President and Vice President.

Number of Votes, then the House of Representatives shall immediately chuse by Ballot one of them for President; and if no Person have a Majority, then from the five highest on the List the said House shall in like Manner chuse the President. But in chusing the President, the Votes shall be taken by States, the Representation from each State having one Vote; a quorum for this Purpose shall consist of a Member or Members from two thirds of the States, and a Majority of all the States shall be necessary to a Choice. In every Case, after the Choice of the President, the Person having the greatest Number of Votes of the Electors shall be the Vice President. But if there should remain two or more who have equal Votes, the Senate shall chuse from them by Ballot the Vice President.

The Congress may determine the Time of chusing the Electors, and the Day on which they shall give their Votes; which Day shall be the same throughout the United States.

A naturalized citizen may not become President.

No person except a natural born Citizen, or a Citizen of the United States, at the time of the Adoption of this Constitution, shall be eligible to the Office of President; neither shall any Person be eligible to that Office who shall not have attained to the Age of Thirty-five Years, and been fourteen Years a Resident within the United States.

The Vice President is next in line for the presidency. A federal law passed in 1947 determined the order of presidential succession as follows: (1) Speaker of the House; (2) president *pro tempore* of the Senate; and (3) Cabinet officers in the order in which their departments were created. (So far, death has been the only circumstance under which a presidential term has been cut short.) This clause has been amplified by the 25th Amendment.

In Case of the Removal of the President from Office, or of his Death, Resignation, or Inability to discharge the Powers and Duties of the said Office, the same shall devolve on the Vice-President, and the Congress may by Law provide for the Case of Removal, Death, Resignation or Inabiltiy, both of the President and the Vice President, declaring what Officer shall then act as President, and such Officer shall act accordingly, until the Disability be removed, or a President shall be elected.

The President shall, at stated Times, receive for his Services, a Compensation, which shall neither be encreased nor diminished during the Period for which he shall have been elected, and he shall not receive within that Period any other Emolument from the United States, or any of them.

Before he enter on the Execution of his Office, he shall take the following Oath or Affirmation:—"I do solemnly swear (or affirm) that I will faithfully execute the Office of the President of the United States, and will to the best of my Ability, preserve, protect and defend the Constitution of the United States."

This clause suggests written communication between the President and "the principal officer in each of the executive departments." As it developed, these officials comprise the Cabinet—whose members are chosen, and may be replaced, by the President.

Section 2. The President shall be Commander in Chief of the Army and Navy of the United States, and of the Militia of the several States, when called into the actual Service of the United States; he may require the Opinion in writing, of the principal Officer in each of the executive Departments, upon any subject relating to the Duties of their respective Offices, and he shall have Power to Grant Reprieves and Pardons for Offenses against the United States, except in Cases of Impeachment.

Senate approval is required for treaties and presidential appointments.

He shall have Power, by and with the Advice and Consent of the Senate, to make by and with the Advice and Consent of the Senate, shall appoint Ambassadors, other Treaties, provided two thirds of the Senators present concur; and he shall nominate, and public Ministers and Consuls, Judges of the supreme Court, and all other Officers of the United States, whose Appointments are not herein otherwise provided for, and which shall be established by Law: but the Congress may by Law vest the Appointment of such inferior Officers, as they think proper, in the President alone, in the Courts of Law, or in the Heads of Departments.

Without the consent of the Senate, the President may appoint officials only on a temporary basis.

The President shall have Power to fill up all Vacancies that may happen during the Recess of the Senate, by granting Commissions which shall expire at the End of their next Session.

Section 3. He shall from time to time give to the Congress Information of the State of the Union, and recommend to their Consideration such Measures as he shall judge necessary and expedient; he may, on extraordinary Occasions, convene both Houses, or either of them, and in Case of Disagreement between them, with Respect to the Time of Adjournment, he may adjourn them to such Time as he shall think proper; he shall receive Ambassadors and other public Ministers; he shall take Care that the Laws be faithfully executed, and shall Commission all the Officers of the United States.

The President delivers a "State of the Union" message at the opening of each session of Congress. Woodrow Wilson was the first President since John Adams to read his messages in person. Franklin D. Roosevelt and his successors followed Wilson's example.

Section 4. The President, Vice President and all civil Officers of the United States, shall be removed from Office on Impeachment for, and Conviction of, Treason, Bribery, or other high Crimes and Misdemeanors.

ARTICLE III • JUDICIAL DEPARTMENT

Section 1. The judicial Power of the United States, shall be vested in one supreme Court, and in such inferior Courts as the Congress may from time to time ordain and establish. The Judges, both of the supreme and inferior Courts, shall hold their Offices during good Behaviour, and shall, at stated Times, receive for their Services, a Compensation, which shall not be diminished during their Continuance in Office.

Federal judges hold office for life and may not have their salaries lowered while in office. These provisions are intended to keep the federal bench independent of political pressure.

Section 2. The judicial Power shall extend to all Cases, in Law and Equity, arising under this Constitution, the Laws of the United States, and Treaties made, or which shall be made, under their Authority;—to all Cases affecting Ambassadors, other public Ministers and Consuls;—to all Cases of admiralty and maritime Jurisdiction;—to Controversies to which the United States shall be a Party;—to Controversies between two or more States;—between a State and Citizens of another State;—between Citizens of different States;—between Citizens of the same State claiming Lands under Grants of different States, and between a State, or the Citizens thereof, and foreign States, Citizens or Subjects.

This clause describes the types of cases that may be heard in federal courts.

The 11th Amendment prevents a citizen from suing a state in a federal court.

In all Cases affecting Ambassadors, other public Ministers and Consuls, and those in which a State shall be Party, the supreme Court shall have original Jurisdiction. In all the other Cases before mentioned, the supreme Court shall have appellate Jurisdiction, both as to Law and Fact, with such Exceptions, and under such Regulations as the Congress shall make.

The Supreme Court handles certain cases directly. It may also review cases handled by lower courts, but Congress in some cases may withhold the right to appeal to the highest court, or limit appeal by setting various conditions.

The trial of all Crimes, except in Cases of Impeachment, shall be by Jury; and such Trial shall be held in the State where the said Crimes shall have been committed; but when not committed within any State, the Trial shall be at such Place or Places as the Congress may by Law have directed.

The 6th Amendment strengthens this clause on trial procedure.

Section 3. Treason against the United States, shall consist only in levying War against them, or in adhering to their Enemies, giving them Aid and Comfort. No Person shall be convicted of Treason unless on the Testimony of two Witnesses to the same overt Act, or on Confession in open Court.

Treason is rigorously defined. A person can be convicted only if two witnesses testify to the same obvious act, or if he confesses in court.

The Congress shall have Power to declare the Punishment of Treason, but no Attainder of Treason shall work Corruption of Blood, or Forfeiture except during the Life of the Person attainted.

Punishment for treason extends only to the person convicted, not to his or her descendants. ("Corruption of blood" means that the heirs of a convicted person are deprived of certain rights.)

ARTICLE IV • RELATIONS AMONG THE STATES

States must honor each other's laws, court decisions, and records (for example, birth, marriage, and death certificates).

Section 1. Full Faith and Credit shall be given in each State to the public Acts, Records, and judicial Proceedings of every other State. And the Congress may by general Laws prescribe the Manner in which such Acts, Records and Proceedings shall be proved, and the Effect thereof.

Each state must respect the rights of citizens of other states.

The process of returning a person accused of a crime to the governmental authority (in this case a state) from which he or she has fled is called *extradition*.

The 13th Amendment, which abolished slavery, makes this clause obsolete.

Section 2. The Citizens of each State shall be entitled to all Privileges and Immunities of Citizens in the several States.

A Person charged in any State with Treason, Felony, or other Crime, who shall flee from Justice, and be found in another State, shall on demand of the executive Authority of the State from which he fled, be delivered up, to be removed to the State having Jurisdiction of the Crime.

No Person held in Service or Labour in one State, under the Laws thereof, escaping into another, shall, in Consequence of any Law or Regulation therein, be discharged from such Service or Labour, but shall be delivered up on Claim of the Party to whom such Service or Labour may be due.

A new state may not be created by dividing or joining existing states unless approved by the legislatures of the states affected and by Congress. An exception to the provision forbidding the division of a state occurred during the Civil War. In 1863 West Virginia was formed out of the western region of Virginia.

Section 3. New States may be admitted by the Congress into this Union; but no new State shall be formed or erected within the Jurisdiction of any other State; nor any State be formed by the Junction of two or more States, or parts of States, without the Consent of the Legislatures of the States concerned as well as of the Congress.

The Congress shall have Power to dispose of and make all needful Rules and Regulations respecting the Territory or other Property belonging to the United States; and nothing in this Constitution shall be so construed as to Prejudice any Claims of the United States, or of any particular State.

A *republican* form of government is one in which citizens choose representatives to govern them. The federal government must protect a state against invasion and, if state authorities request it, against violence within a state.

Section 4. The United States shall guarantee to every State in this Union a Republican Form of Government, and shall protect each of them against Invasion; and on Application of the Legislature, or of the Executive (when the Legislature cannot be convened) against domestic Violence.

ARTICLE V • AMENDING THE CONSTITUTION

An amendment to the Constitution can be proposed (a) by Congress, with a two-thirds vote of both houses, or (b) by a convention called by Congress when two-thirds of the state legislatures request it. An amendment is ratified (a) by three-fourths of the state legislatures, or (b) by conventions in three-fourths of the states. The twofold procedure of proposal and ratification reflects the seriousness with which the framers of the Constitution regarded amendments. Over 6,900 amendments have been proposed; only 26 have been ratified.

The Congress, whenever two thirds of both Houses shall deem it necessary, shall propose Amendments to this Constitution, or, on the Application of the Legislatures of two thirds of the several States, shall call a Convention for proposing Amendments, which, in either Case, shall be valid to all Intents and Purposes, as part of this Constitution, when ratified by the Legislatures of three fourths of the several States, or by Conventions in three fourths thereof, as the one or the other Mode of Ratification may be proposed by the Congress: Provided that no Amendment which may be made prior to the Year One thousand eight hundred and eight shall in any Manner affect the first and fourth Clauses in the Ninth Section of the first Article; and that no State, without its Consent, shall be deprived of its equal Suffrage in the Senate.

ARTICLE VI • GENERAL PROVISIONS

All Debts contracted and Engagements entered into, before the Adoption of this Constitution, shall be as valid against the United States under this Constitution, as under the Confederation.

This Constitution, and the Laws of the United States which shall be made in Pursuance thereof; and all Treaties made, or which shall be made, under the Authority of the United States, shall be the supreme Law of the Land; and the Judges in every State shall be bound thereby, any Thing in the Constitution or Laws of any State to the Contrary notwithstanding.

The supremacy clause means that if a federal and a state law conflict, the federal law prevails.

The Senators and Representatives before mentioned, and the Members of the several State Legislatures, and all executive and judicial Officers, both of the United States and of the several States, shall be bound by Oath or Affirmation, to support this Constitution; but no religious Test shall ever be required as a Qualification to any Office or public Trust under the United States.

Religion may not be a condition for holding public office.

ARTICLE VII • RATIFICATION

The Ratification of the Conventions of nine States shall be sufficient for the Establishment of this Constitution between the States so ratifying the Same.

The Constitution would become the law of the land upon the approval of nine states.

DONE in Convention by the Unanimous Consent of the States present the Seventeenth Day of September in the Year of our Lord one thousand seven hundred and eighty-seven and of the Independence of the United States of America the Twelfth. In Witness whereof We have hereunto subscribed our Names.

Gᵒ WASHINGTON
Presidᵗ and deputy from
VIRGINIA

Attest: *William Jackson,* Secretary

DELAWARE
Geo: Read
Gunning Bedford, jun
John Dickinson
Richard Bassett
Jaco: Broom

MARYLAND
James McHenry
Dan: of St Thos Jenifer
Danl Carroll

VIRGINIA
John Blair
James Madison Jr.

NORTH CAROLINA
Wm Blount
Richd Dobbs Spaight
Hu Williamson

SOUTH CAROLINA
J. Rutledge
Charles Cotesworth
Pinckney
Charles Pinckney
Pierce Butler

GEORGIA
William Few
Abr Baldwin

NEW HAMPSHIRE
John Langdon
Nicholas Gilman

MASSACHUSETTS
Nathaniel Gorham
Rufus King

CONNECTICUT
Wm Saml Johnson
Roger Sherman

NEW YORK
Alexander Hamilton

NEW JERSEY
Wil: Livingston
David Brearley
Wm Paterson
Jona: Dayton

PENNSYLVANIA
B Franklin
Thomas Mifflin
Robt. Morris
Geo. Clymer
Thos. FitzSimons
Jared Ingersoll
James Wilson
Gouv Morris

AMENDMENTS

AMENDMENT I • (1791)

Establishes fredom of religion, speech, and the press; gives citizens the rights of assembly and petition.

Congress shall make no law respecting an establishment of religion, or prohibiting the free exercise thereof: or abridging the freedom of speech, or of the press; or the right of the people peaceably to assemble, and to petition the Government for a redress of grievances.

AMENDMENT II • (1791)

States have the right to maintain a militia.

A well regulated Militia, being necessary to the security of a free State, the right of the people to keep and bear Arms, shall not be infringed.

AMENDMENT III • (1791)

Limits the army's right to quarter soldiers in private homes.

No Soldier shall, in time of peace, be quartered in any house, without the consent of the Owner, nor in time of war, but in a manner to be prescribed by law.

AMENDMENT IV • (1791)

Search warrants are required as a guarantee of a citizen's right to privacy.

The right of the people to be secure in their persons, houses, papers, and effects, against unreasonable searches and seizures, shall not be violated, and no Warrants shall issue, but upon probable cause, supported by Oath or affirmation, and particularly describing the place to be searched, and the persons or things to be seized.

AMENDMENT V • (1791)

To be prosecuted for a serious crime, a person must first be accused (indicted) by a grand jury. No one can be tried twice for the same crime (double jeopardy). Nor can a person be forced into self-incrimination by testifying against himself or herself.

No person shall be held to answer for a capital, or otherwise infamous crime, unless on a presentment or indictment of a Grand Jury, except in cases arising in the land or naval forces, or in the Militia, when in actual service in time of War or public danger; nor shall any person be subject for the same offence to be twice put in jeopardy of life or limb; nor shall be compelled in any criminal case to be a witness against himself, nor be deprived of life, liberty, or property, without due process of law; nor shall private property be taken for public use, without just compensation.

AMENDMENT VI • (1791)

Guarantees a defendant's right to be tried without delay and to face witnesses testifying for the other side.

In all criminal prosecutions, the accused shall enjoy the right to a speedy and public trial, by an impartial jury of the State and district wherein the crime shall have been committed, which district shall have been previously ascertained by law, and to be informed of the nature and cause of the accusation; to be confronted with the witnesses against him; to have compulsory process for obtaining witnesses in his favor, and to have the Assistance of Counsel for his defence.

[*The date following each amendment number is the year of ratification.*]

AMENDMENT VII • (1791)

In suits at common law, where the value in controversy shall exceed twenty dollars, the right of trial by jury shall be preserved, and no fact tried by a jury, shall be otherwise reexamined in any Court of the United States, than according to the rules of the common law.

A jury trial is guaranteed in federal civil suits involving more than twenty dollars.

AMENDMENT VIII • (1791)

Excessive bail shall not be required, nor excessive fines imposed, nor cruel and unusual punishments inflicted.

AMENDMENT IX • (1791)

The enumeration in the Constitution, of certain rights, shall not be construed to deny or disparage others retained by the people.

The listing of specific rights in the Constitution does not mean that others are not protected.

AMENDMENT X • (1791)

The powers not delegated to the United States by the Constitution, nor prohibited by it to the States, are reserved to the States respectively, or to the people.

Limits the federal government to its specific powers. Powers not prohibited the states by the Constitution may be exercised by them.

AMENDMENT XI • (1798)

The Judicial power of the United States shall not be construed to extend to any suit in law or equity, commenced or prosecuted against one of the United States by Citizens of another State, or by Citizens or Subjects of any Foreign State.

A state cannot be sued by a citizen of another state in a federal court. Such a case can be tried only in the courts of the state being sued.

AMENDMENT XII • (1804)

The Electors shall meet in their respective states and vote by ballot for President and Vice-President, one of whom, at least, shall not be an inhabitant of the same state with themselves; they shall name in their ballots the person voted for as President, and in distinct ballots the person voted for as Vice-President, and they shall make distinct lists of all persons voted for as President, and of all persons voted for as Vice-President, and of the number of votes for each, which lists they shall sign and certify, and transmit sealed to the seat of the government of the United States, directed to the President of the Senate; —The President of the Senate shall, in presence of the Senate and House of Representatives, open all the certificates and the votes shall then be counted;—The person having the greatest number of votes for President, shall be the President, if such number be a majority of the whole number of Electors appointed; and if no person have such majority, then from the persons having the highest numbers not exceeding three on the list of those voted for as President, the House of Representatives shall choose immediately, by ballot, the President. But in choosing the President, the votes shall be taken by states, the representation from each state having one vote; a quorum for this purpose shall consist of a member or members from two-thirds of the states, and a majority of all the states shall be necessary to a choice. And if the House of Representatives shall not choose a President whenever the right of choice shall devolve upon them, before the fourth day of March next following, then the Vice-President shall act as President, as in the case of

Revises the process by which the President and Vice President were elected (see Article II, Section 1, Clause 3). The major change requires electors to cast separate ballots for President and Vice President. If none of the presidential candidates obtains a majority vote, the House of Representatives— with each state having one vote—chooses a President from the three candidates having the highest number of votes. If no vice presidential candidate wins a majority, the Senate chooses from the two candidates having the highest number of votes. The portion printed in color was superseded by Section 3 of the 20th Amendment.

the death or other constitutional disability of the President.— The person having the greatest number of votes as Vice-President, shall be the Vice-President, if such number be a majority of the whole number of Electors appointed, and if no person have a majority, then from the two highest numbers on the list, the Senate shall choose the Vice-President; a quorum for the purpose shall consist of two-thirds of the whole number of Senators, and a majority of the whole number shall be necessary to a choice. But no person constitutionally ineligible to the office of President shall be eligible to that of Vice-President of the United States.

AMENDMENT XIII • (1865)

Abolishes slavery.

Section 1. Neither slavery nor involuntary servitude, except as a punishment for crime whereof the party shall have been duly convicted, shall exist within the United States, or any place subject to their jurisdiction.

Section 2. Congress shall have power to enforce this article by appropriate legislation.

AMENDMENT XIV • (1868)

This section confers full civil rights on former slaves. Supreme Court decisions have interpreted the language of Section 1 to mean that the states, as well as the federal government, are bound by the Bill of Rights.

Section 1. All persons born or naturalized in the United States, and subject to the jurisdiction thereof, are citizens of the United States and of the State wherein they reside. No State shall make or enforce any law which shall abridge the privileges or immunities of citizens of the United States; nor shall any State deprive any person of life, liberty, or property, without due process of law; nor deny any person within its jurisdiction the equal protection of the laws.

A penalty of a reduction in congressional representation shall be applied to any state that refuses to give all adult male citizens the right to vote in federal elections. This section has never been applied. The portion printed in color was superseded by Section 1 of the 26th Amendment. (This section has also been amplified by the 19th Amendment.)

Section 2. Representatives shall be apportioned among the several States according to their respective numbers, counting the whole number of persons in each State, excluding Indians not taxed. But when the right to vote at any election for the choice of electors for President and Vice-President of the United States, Representatives in Congress, the Executive and Judicial officers of a State, or the members of the Legislature thereof, is denied to any of the male inhabitants of such State, being twenty-one years of age, and citizens of the United States, or in any way abridged, except for participation in rebellion, or other crime, the basis of representation therein shall be reduced in the proportion which the number of such male citizens shall bear to the whole number of male citizens twenty-one years of age in such State.

Any former federal or state official who served the Confederacy during the Civil War could not become a federal official again unless Congress voted otherwise.

Section 3. No person shall be a Senator or Representative in Congress, or elector of President and Vice-President, or hold any office, civil or military, under the United States, or under any State, who, having previously taken an oath, as a member of Congress, or as an officer of the United States, or as a member of any State legislature, or as an executive or judicial officer of any State, to support the Constitution of the United States, shall have engaged in insurrection or rebellion against the same, or given aid or comfort to the enemies thereof. But Congress may by a vote of two-thirds of each House, remove such disability.

Section 4. The validity of the public debt of the United States, authorized by law, including debts incurred for payment of pensions and bounties for services in suppressing insurrection or rebellion, shall not be questioned. But neither the United States nor any State shall assume or pay any debt or obligation incurred in aid of insurrection or rebellion against the United States, or any claim for the loss or emancipation of any slave; but all such debts, obligations and claims shall be held illegal and void.

Makes legal the federal Civil War debt, but at the same time voids all Confederate debts incurred in the war.

Section 5. The Congress shall have power to enforce, by appropriate legislation, the provisions of this article.

AMENDMENT XV • (1870)

Section 1. The right of citizens of the United States to vote shall not be denied or abridged by the United States or by any State on account of race, color, or previous condition of servitude.

Gives blacks the right to vote.

Section 2. The Congress shall have power to enforce this article by appropriate legislation.

AMENDMENT XVI • (1913)

The Congress shall have power to lay and collect taxes on incomes, from whatever source derived, without apportionment among the several States, and without regard to any census or enumeration.

Allows Congress to levy taxes on incomes.

AMENDMENT XVII • (1913)

The Senate of the United States shall be composed of two Senators from each State, elected by the people thereof, for six years; and each Senator shall have one vote. The electors in each State shall have the qualifications requisite for electors of the most numerous branch of the State legislature.

Provides for election of senators by the people of a state, rather than the state legislature.

When vacancies happen in the representation of any State in the Senate, the executive authority of such State shall issue writs of election to fill such vacancies: *Provided,* That the legislature of any State may empower the executive thereof to make temporary appointments until the people fill the vacancies by election as the legislature may direct.

This amendment shall not be so construed as to affect the election or term of any Senator chosen before it becomes valid as part of the Constitution.

AMENDMENT XVIII • (1919)

Section 1. After one year from the ratification of this article, the manufacture, sale, or transportation of intoxicating liquors within, the importation thereof into, or the exportation thereof from the United States and all territory subject to the jurisdiction thereof for beverage purposes is hereby prohibited.

Legalizes prohibition—*that is, forbidding the making, selling, or transporting of intoxicating beverages. Superseded by the 21st Amendment.*

Section 2. The Congress and the several States shall have concurrent power to enforce this article by appropriate legislation.

Section 3. This article shall be inoperative unless it shall have been ratified as an amendment to the Constitution by the legislatures of the several States, as provided in the Constitution, within seven years from the date of the submission hereof to the States by the Congress.

AMENDMENT XIX • (1920)

Gives women the right to vote.

The right of citizens of the United States to vote shall not be denied or abridged by the United States or by any State on account of sex.

Congress shall have power to enforce this article by appropriate legislation.

AMENDMENT XX • (1933)

The "lame duck" amendment allows the President to take office on January 20, and members of Congress on January 3. The purpose of the amendment is to reduce the term in office of defeated incumbents—known as "lame ducks."

Section 1. The terms of the President and Vice-President shall end at noon on the 20th day of January, and the terms of Senators and Representatives at noon on the 3d day of January, of the years in which such terms would have ended if this article had not been ratified; and the terms of their successors shall then begin.

Section 2. The Congress shall assemble at least once in every year, and such meeting shall begin at noon on the 3d day of January, unless they shall by law appoint a different day.

Section 3. If, at the time fixed for the beginning of the term of the President, the President elect shall have died, the Vice-President elect shall become President. If a President shall not have been chosen before the time fixed for the beginning of his term, or if the President elect shall have failed to qualify, then the Vice-President elect shall act as President until a President shall have qualified; and the Congress may by law provide for the case wherein neither a President elect nor a Vice-President elect shall have qualified, declaring who shall then act as President, or the manner in which one who is to act shall be selected, and such person shall act accordingly until a President or Vice-President shall have qualified.

Section 4. The Congress may by law provide for the case of the death of any of the persons from whom the House of Representatives may choose a President whenever the right of choice shall have devolved upon them, and for the case of the death of any of the persons from whom the Senate may choose a Vice-President whenever the right of choice shall have devolved upon them.

Section 5. Sections 1 and 2 shall take effect on the 15th day of October following the ratification of this article.

Section 6. This article shall be inoperative unless it shall have been ratified as an amendment to the Constitution by the legislatures of three-fourths of the several States within seven years from the date of its submission.

AMENDMENT XXI • (1933)

Section 1. The eighteenth article of amendment to the Constitution of the United States is hereby repealed.

Repeals the 18th Amendment.

Section 2. The transportation or importation into any State, Territory, or possession of the United States for delivery or use therein of intoxicating liquors, in violation of the laws thereof, is hereby prohibited.

States may pass prohibition laws.

Section 3. This article shall be inoperative unless it shall have been ratified as an amendment to the Constitution by conventions in the several States, as provided in the Constitution, within seven years from the date of the submission hereof to the States by the Congress.

AMENDMENT XXII • (1951)

Section 1. No person shall be elected to the office of the President more than twice, and no person who has held the office of President, or acted as President, for more than two years of a term to which some other person was elected President shall be elected to the office of the President more than once. But this Article shall not apply to any person holding the office of President when this Article was proposed by the Congress, and shall not prevent any person who may be holding the office of President, or acting as President, during the term within which this Article becomes operative from holding the office of President or acting as President during the remainder of such term.

Limits a President to only two full terms plus two years of a previous President's term.

Section 2. This article shall be inoperative unless it shall have been ratified as an amendment to the Constitution by the legislatures of three-fourths of the several States within seven years from the date of its submission to the States by the Congress.

AMENDMENT XXIII • (1961)

Section 1. The District constituting the seat of Government of the United States shall appoint in such manner as the Congress may direct:

By giving the District of Columbia three electoral votes, Congress enabled its residents to vote for President and Vice President.

A number of electors of President and Vice-President equal to the whole number of Senators and Representatives in Congress to which the District would be entitled if it were a State, but in no event more than the least populous State; they shall be in addition to those appointed by the States, but they shall be considered, for the purposes of the election of President and Vice-President, to be electors appointed by a State; and they shall meet in the District and perform such duties as provided by the twelfth article of amendment.

Section 2. The Congress shall have power to enforce this article by appropriate legislation.

AMENDMENT XXIV • (1964)

Section 1. The right of citizens of the United States to vote in any primary or other election for President or Vice-President, for electors for President or Vice-President, or for Senator or Representative in Congress, shall not be denied or abridged by the United States or any State by reason of failure to pay any poll tax or other tax.

Forbids the use of a poll tax as a requirement for voting in federal elections.

Section 2. The Congress shall have power to enforce this article by appropriate legislation.

AMENDMENT XXV • (1967)

Outlines the procedure to be followed in case of presidential disability.

Section 1. In case of the removal of the President from office or of his death or resignation, the Vice-President shall become President.

Section 2. Whenever there is a vacancy in the office of the Vice-President, the President shall nominate a Vice-President who shall take office upon confirmation by a majority vote of both Houses of Congress.

Section 3. Whenever the President transmits to the President pro tempore of the Senate and the Speaker of the House of Representatives his written declaration that he is unable to discharge the powers and duties of his office, and until he transmits to them a written declaration to the contrary, such powers and duties shall be discharged by the Vice-President as Acting President.

Section 4. Whenever the Vice-President and a majority of either the principal officers of the executive departments or of such other body as Congress may by law provide, transmit to the President pro tempore of the Senate and the Speaker of the House of Representatives their written declaration that the President is unable to discharge the powers and duties of his office, the Vice-President shall immediately assume the powers and duties of the office as Acting President.

Thereafter, when the President transmits to the President pro tempore of the Senate and the Speaker of the House of Representatives his written declaration that no inability exists, he shall resume the powers and duties of his office unless the Vice-President and a majority of either the principal officers of the executive department or of such other body as Congress may by law provide, transmit within four days to the President pro tempore of the Senate and the Speaker of the House of Representatives their written declaration that the President is unable to discharge the powers and duties of his office. Thereupon Congress shall decide the issue, assembling within forty-eight hours for that purpose if not in session. If the Congress, within twenty-one days after receipt of the latter written declaration, or, if Congress is not in session, within twenty-one days after Congress is required to assemble, determines by two-thirds vote of both Houses that the President is unable to discharge the powers and duties of his office, the Vice-President shall continue to discharge the same as Acting President; otherwise, the President shall resume the powers and duties of his office.

AMENDMENT XXVI • (1971)

Lowers the voting age to eighteen.

Section 1. The right of citizens of the United States, who are eighteen years of age or older, to vote shall not be denied or abridged by the United States or any state on account of age.

Section 2. The Congress shall have the power to enforce this article by appropriate legislation.

ILLUSTRATION CREDITS

The initials **PE** *denote Pictorial Essay.*

CHAPTERS 23 and 24

402, Culver Pictures, Inc.; **403,** Brady Collection, U.S. Signal Corps, National Archives; **404,** N.Y.P.L. Prints Division; **406,** Charles Colcock Jones Papers/Manuscript Dept., Special Collections Division, Tulane University Library; **407,** N.Y.P.L. Prints Division; **409,** Library of Congress; **410,** Library of Congress; **416,** Penn Community Services Cultural Program; **420(top),** Courtesy, Chicago Historical Society; **(bottom),** Brady Collection, U.S. Signal Corps, National Archives; **422,** Valentine Museum, Richmond, Va.; **423,** Brady Collection, U.S. Signal Corps, National Archives; **426,** National Archives; **428(top and bottom),** Library of Congress; **431,** Library of Congress; **432,** Library of Congress; **434,** Culver Pictures, Inc.; **436,** Brown Brothers; **438,** Library of Congress; **439(left and right),** Library of Congress; **443,** Brown Brothers; **445,** Louisiana State Museum; **446,** Brown Brothers; **447,** Culver Pictures, Inc.

UNIT FIVE

Page 451, Culver Pictures, Inc.; **453,** Library of Congress; **455,** Library of Congress; **457,** Culver Pictures, Inc.; **460,** Library of Congress; **461 (top and bottom),** Library of Congress; **462,** Culver Pictures, Inc.; **464,** Culver Pictures, Inc.; **467,** Library of Congress; **468,** Culver Pictures, Inc.; **469,** Culver Pictures, Inc.; **473,** United Press International; **474,** Culver Pictures, Inc.; **475,** Culver Pictures, Inc.; **476,** Culver Pictures, Inc.; **478,** Culver Pictures, Inc.; **481,** Smithsonian Institution/ National Anthropological Archives; **482,** U.S. Signal Corps/National Archives; **487,** Smithsonian Institution/National Anthropological Archives; **488,** Smithsonian Institution/National Anthropological Archives; **489,** Smithsonian Institution/National Anthropological

Archives; **490,** U.S. Signal Corps/ National Archives; **491,** U.S. Signal Corps/National Archives; **497,** Nebraska State Historical Society; **500(top),** Library of Congress; **(bottom),** Minnesota Historical Society; **501,** Permission of Huntington Library, San Marino, Calif.; **502,** Southern Pacific Railroad; **505,** Library of Congress; **507,** Manitoba Archives; **509,** Smithsonian Institution/National Anthropological Archives; **510,** Naval Observatory/National Archives; **513,** Western History Dept., Denver Public Library; **514,** Bureau of Reclamation/National Archives; **517(top and bottom),** International Harvester Company Historical Archives; **518,** International Harvester Company Historical Archives; **524,** Library of Congress; **533,** Library of Congress; **534,** A.T.&T.; **536,** Library of Congress; **541,** International Museum of Photography at George Eastman House; **542,** Photo by Jacob A. Riis—Jacob A. Riis Collection, Museum of the City of New York; **544,** Kansas State Historical Society, Topeka, Kansas; **PE 6-1,** Culver Pictures, Inc.; **PE 6-2(top),** New-York Historical Society; **(bottom),** Metropolitan Museum of Art; **PE 6-3 (top and center),** Bettmann Archive; **(bottom),** N.Y.P.L. Picture Collection; **PE 6-4(top),** Los Angeles County Museum of Art; **(bottom),** Museum of the City of New York; **PE 6-5(top),** Bettmann Archive; **(bottom),** N.Y.P.L. Picture Collection; **PE 6-6(top left),** Wisconsin State Historical Society; **(top right),** Missouri Historical Society; **(bottom),** Chicago Historical Society; **PE 6-7(top),** Illinois Department of Conservation; **(bottom),** Chicago Historical Society; **PE 6-8(top),** Thomas Gilcrease Institute, Tulsa, Okla.; **(bottom),** Franklin D. Roosevelt Library, Hyde Park, N.Y.; **545,** Museum of the City of New York; **550,** Brown Brothers; **551,** Culver Pictures, Inc.; **552,** Culver Pictures, Inc.; **553,** Culver Pictures, Inc.; **554(top),** Culver Pictures, Inc.; **(bottom),** Brown

Brothers; **556,** Culver Pictures, Inc.; **557,** Culver Pictures, Inc.; **558,** United Press International; **565(top),** Culver Pictures, Inc.; **(bottom),** Brown Brothers; **566,** Culver Pictures, Inc.; **568,** Culver Pictures, Inc.; **572,** Culver Pictures, Inc.; **573,** Culver Pictures, Inc.

UNIT SIX

Page 579, Culver Pictures, Inc.; **581,** Brown Brothers; **582,** Brown Brothers; **584,** New-York Historical Society; **587,** Brown Brothers; **589,** Brown Brothers; **591,** Brown Brothers; **592,** Library of Congress; **596,** Brown Brothers; **600(top and center),** Library of Congress; **(bottom),** Culver Pictures, Inc.; **601,** Cleveland Public Library Picture Collection; **602,** Library of Congress; **605,** Library of Congress; **607,** Library of Congress; **610,** Library of Congress; **613,** Bettmann Archive; **614,** Naval Photographic Center; **615,** U.S. Signal Corps/National Archives; **620,** Library of Congress; **622,** Library of Congress; **623,** U.S. Signal Corps/National Archives; **624,** U.S. Signal Corps/National Archives; **625,** Library of Congress; **628,** New-York Historical Society; **631,** Library of Congress; **634,** U.S. Signal Corps/ National Archives; **635,** Library of Congress; **638,** U.S. War Dept. General Staff—National Archives; **642,** U.S. Signal Corps/National Archives; **644,** Culver Pictures, Inc.; **650,** National Air and Space Museum, Smithsonian Institution; **651,** National Air and Space Museum, Smithsonian Institution; **653,** Brown Brothers; **656,** Brown Brothers; **659,** National Air and Space Museum, Smithsonian Institution; **660,** Culver Pictures, Inc.; **662,** Westinghouse Broadcasting Company; **666,** Ford Archives; **667,** Ford Archives; **669(top),** Brown Brothers; **(bottom),** Michigan History Division; **671,** Bettmann Archive; **672,** Bettmann Archive; **PE 7-1,** Painting of the Museum's Interior in 1881 by Frank Waller; Photo by Francis G. Mayer— Metropolitan Museum of Art; **PE 7-2**

(top), Culver Pictures, Inc.; (bottom), Museum of Fine Arts, Boston; **PE 7-3**(top), Art Institute of Chicago; (**bottom left**), Metropolitan Museum of Art; (**bottom right**), Museum of Modern Art—Gift of Friends of the Sculptor in 1908; **PE 7-4** (top), N.Y.P.L. Picture Collection; (bottom), Phillips Gallery; **PE 7-5**(top), Hedrich-Blessing; (bottom), Amherst College Collection; **PE 7-6** (top), Culver Pictures, Inc.; (bottom), Museum of the City of New York; **PE 7-7**(top), Edward Steichen; (bottom), Courtesy of Mr. Ira Gershwin and The Humanities Research Center, University of Texas at Austin; **PE 7-8**(top), Museum of Art at Ogunquit; (bottom), Brown Brothers; **677**, United Press International; **679**, Wide World Photos; **681**, United Press International; **683**, Wide World Photos; **685**, Acme News-Pictures, Inc. (UPI); **688**, Wide World Photos; **689**, United Press International; **690**, Underwood and Underwood; **691**, Wide World Photos; **694**, United Press International; **696**, Wide World Photos; **697**, Wide World Photos; **698**, Courtesy The Moorland-Stingarn Research Center, Howard University; **699**, Cartoon by Alley—*Memphis Commercial Appeal;* **702**, Wide World Photos; **705**, Wide World Photos.

UNIT SEVEN
Page 709, Courtesy, United Nations; **712**, United Press International; **713**, United Press International; **715**, United Press International; **717**, Brown Brothers; **719**, United Press International; **723**, United Press International; **726**, United Press International; **727**, Culver Pictures, Inc.; **729**, United Press International; **735**, United Press International; **736**, Wide World Photos; **737**, United Press International; **739**, Culver Pictures, Inc.; **740**, United Press International; **742**, Brown Brothers; **743**, Brown Brothers; **748**, Navy Dept./National Archives; **749**, Naval Photographic Center; **751**, United Press International; **752**, U.S. Office of War Information/National Archives; **755**(top and bottom), Navy Dept./National Archives; **758**, Navy Dept./National Archives; **760**, United Press International; **762**, Acme Newspictures, Inc. (UPI); **768**, U.S. Information Agency/National Archives; **PE 8-1**, Detail of "The New

Television Set" by Norman Rockwell—Permission, Los Angeles County Museum of Art; **PE 8-2**(top left), Culver Pictures, Inc.; (top right), Eileen Darby/Graphic House; (bottom), Brown Brothers; **PE 8-3** (top), Globe Photos; (bottom), Time-Life Picture Agency; **PE 8-4**(top left), Acme News-Pictures, Inc. (UPI); (top right), Hy Peskin/Time-Life Picture Agency; (bottom), Capricorn Art Gallery; **PE 8-5**(top), Francis Miller/Time-Life Picture Agency; (bottom), Ralph Crane/Time-Life Picture Agency; **PE 8-6** (top), Margaret Bourke-White/Time-Life Picture Agency; (bottom), Leonard McCombe/Time-Life Picture Agency; **PE 8-7**(top), Nina Leen/Time-Life Picture Agency; (bottom), University of Wisconsin Dept. of Photocinema; **PE 8-8**(top), Frank Scherschel/Time-Life Picture Agency; (bottom), Peter Stackpole/Life Magazine, © Time, Inc.; **771**, Acme Newspictures, Inc. (UPI); **772**, U.S. Office of War Information/National Archives; **774**, U.S. Information Agency/National Archives; **775**, United Press International; **776**, Wide World Photos; **778**, Estate of David Low; **779**, United Press International; **781**, Wide World Photos; **785**, Wide World Photos; **787**, United Press International; **788**, Wide World Photos; **790**, Wide World Photos; **794**, Wide World Photos; **795**, Wide World Photos; **798**, Wide World Photos; **799**, Wide World Photos; **801**, Wide World Photos; **803**, Dorothea Lange Collection—Oakland Museum; **805**, United Press International; **807**, Wide World Photos; **809**, Wide World Photos; **811**, Wide World Photos; **812**, Wide World Photos; **813**, Wide World Photos.

UNIT EIGHT
Page 817, CBS News Photo from UPI; **820**, United Press International; **823**, United Press International; **824**, United Press International; **827**(top and bottom), Dan Budnik/Woodfin Camp & Assoc.; **832**, United Press International; **834**, Marc & Evelyne Bernheim/Woodfin Camp & Assoc.; **835**, Wide World Photos; **836**, United Press International; **838**, United Press International; **839**, United Press International; **840**, United

Press International; **842**, United Press International; **843**(top and bottom), United Press International; **847**(left and right), Wide World Photos; **849**, United Press International; **851**, United Press International; **859**, Stephen Shames/Magnum; **860**, Burk Uzzle/Magnum; **861**, United Press International; **862**, United Press International; **863**, United Press International; **PE 9-1**, Esther Henderson/Rapho/Photo Researchers; **PE 9-2**(top), Charles Moore/Black Star; (bottom), Van Bucher/Photo Researchers; **PE 9-3** (top), Bruce Roberts/Rapho/Photo Researchers; (**bottom left**), Fred J. Maroon/Photo Researchers; (**bottom right**), Porterfield Chickering/Photo Researchers; **PE 9-4**(top), Ford Motor Company; (**center**), Charles E. Rotkin/Photography for Industry; (bottom), Hedrich-Blessing; **PE 9-5** (top), Lucia Woods/Photo Researchers; (bottom), F. Hulnegle/Monkmeyer; **PE 9-6**(top), Myron Wood/Photo Researchers; (bottom), Ray Manley/Shostal Photos; **PE 9-7** (top), Russ Kinne/Photo Researchers; (**center**), Tom McHugh/Photo Researchers; (bottom), Joe Munroe/Photo Researchers; **PE 9-8** (top), Jack Fields/Photo Researchers; (bottom), Ray Ateson; **865**, United Press International; **868**, United Press International; **869**(left), Dan Budnik/Woodfin Camp & Assoc.; (**right**), United Press International; **871**, United Press International; **872**, United Press International; **873**, Wide World Photos; **874**, Wide World Photos; **875**, Elliott Erwitt/Magnum; **879**, United Press International; **880**(top and bottom), United Press International; **881**, Mark Godfrey/Magnum; **882**, United Press International; **884**(top and bottom), United Press International; **887**, United Press International; **890**, United Press International; **892**, Mark Godfrey/Magnum; **896**, United Press International; **897**(top), United Press International; (bottom), Wide World Photos; **899**, United Press International; **900**, Sepp Seitz/Magnum; **901**, United Press International; **902**, Mark Godfrey/Magnum; **903**, Alex Webb/Magnum; **904**, United Press International; **906**, United Press International; **908**, Elliott Erwitt/Magnum; **910**, United Press International .

blacks (*cont.*)

Reconstruction conditions for, 447; and Garfield, 458; and Populist party, 555, 573, 574; in garment factories, 583; and Theodore Roosevelt, 604; and Wilson administration, 609–10; and Eleanor Roosevelt, 722–24; and 1936 elections, 741; and Truman administration, 805, 806; vs. segregation, 812–13; and Kennedy-Nixon election, 814; and Martin Luther King, 845–61, 867–68; and Warren Court, 864; and Black Power movement, 868–70. *See also* slavery; slaves

Blaine, James G., 452, 457, 468, 471, 472, 629; and foreign commerce, 629

Blanck, Max, 590–91

blockade: in Civil War, 424. *See also* Cuban missile crisis

Bonfield, John, 521, 525–26

bonus marchers, 666–91, *m686*, 693

Booth, John Wilkes, 437

Botkin, Benjamin, 435

Boulder Dam, PE9–6

Boxer Rebellion, 635

Brandeis, Louis, 585, 610–11, 743

Bremer, Fredrika, PE6 to 7

Britain: and Panama Canal, 635–36; and World War I, 639–40; and World War II, 763, 764, 765, 768; and Middle East, 780

Broughton, Morris, PE9–4

Brown, Joseph E., 403

Brown v. Board of Education, 812, 848, 864, 866

Bryan, William Jennings, 637, 368, 640, 695; vs. McKinley, 551–63, 575–76; and Treaty of Paris, 634

Bryce, James, 466

Bulge, Battle of the, *m767*

Bull Head, 491, 492, 493

Bull Moose party, 607–08

Bull Run, battle of, 424, *m424*

Bunau-Varilla, Phillippe, 636

Bundy, McGeorge, 821

Burton, William M., c665

Butterfield Overland Express, 501–02, *m504*

Byrd, Richard E., 647

California (ship), 757

Cambodia, *m841*, 876, 898

Cardozo, Francis L., 443

Carnegie, Andrew, 538

Carpenter, Harry, PE8–4

carpetbaggers, 443–44

Carranza, Venustiano, 638

Carter, James Earl, Jr., 907–09

Carteret, George, 74, 115

Cassatt, Mary, 547, PE7–3

Castro, Fidel, 781, 818

Cather, Willa, PE7–4

Catt, Carrie Chapman, 603

cattle, and western expansion, 503–05, *m504*

Central Pacific Railroad, 502

central powers, 639

Chambers, Whittaker, and Alger Hiss, 783–99

Chancellorsville, Md., 424, *m424*

Chattanooga, Battle of, *m429*

Chesnut, Mary Boykin, 427, 430, 434

Cheyenne Indians, 508

Chiang Kai-shek, 774, 777

Chicago, Ill., 531; labor problems in, 522–30

Chickamauga, Battle of, *m429*

child labor, 593, 602, 610

China, 774; policy toward, 634–35; vs. Japan, 747–48, 768; and Nixon, 895–96

Chippewa Indians, 482

Churchill, Winston, and World War II, 764, 766, 770

CIA, 779, 781, 818

cities, 905–06; corruption in, 472–75; reorganization of, 597, 599; and progressivism, 600; and automobile, 669. *See also* urbanization

civil liberties and rights: during Civil War, 432; and Warren Court, 864–67. *See also* blacks

Civil Rights Act of 1866, 440

Civil Rights Bill of 1964, 857

Civil War, *m424*, *m425*, *m428–29*; and Sherman's March, 401–14; and postwar pardons, 415; characterized, 419–21; mobilization for, 421–22, c421; Southern strategy in, 422–23; Northern strategy in, 423–24; eastern front of, 424–25; western front of, 425–26; and southern home-front, 427, 430; and northern home-front, 430, 432; final campaigns of, 426; cost of, 427; overview of, 426–27. *See also* Sherman's March

Clayton Antitrust Act, 609

Clemenceau, Georges, 643

Clemens, Samuel, 545–46

Cleveland, Grover, elections of, 469–70; and tariffs, 478; and Populists, 571, 573; and depression, 574–75; and foreign commerce, 629; and Cuba, 630

Cleveland, Ohio, 601

Clifford, Clark, 843

codes of personal conduct, for politicians, 468

Cold Harbor, Battle of, *m424*

Cold War: beginning of, 772–73; and Eisenhower-Dulles policies, 774–81

colleges and universities, and antebellum reformers, 296–97

Colorado, settlement of, 499

Colored Farmer's Alliance, 555, 569

Colum, Padraic, PE7–5

Columbia, 636

combine, 532

Committee to Defend America First, 764

Common Market, 837

communication, revolution in, 662–63

communism: and red scare, 692–94; and Hiss-Chambers case, 783–99; and McCarthyism, 806–08, 810

Communist Party, 734

competition, and consolidation, 537–38

Compromise of 1877, 446–47

Comstock Lode, *m504*

Confederacy: formation of, 419. *See also* Civil War

Congress: and slavery, 433; and Freedmen's Bureau Bill, 417; and Reconstruction, 439–42; and Hawaii, 633; and New Deal policies, 728, 744–45; and World War II, 747; and Neutrality Acts, 762–63; and Ford administration, 902–03. *See also* congressional elections; Senate

congressional elections: of 1866, 440; of 1870s–80s, 470–71; of 1894, 559, 574; of 1920, 697; of 1930, 705; of 1934, 734; of 1936, 740–41; of 1938, 745; of 1952, 808; of 1972, 897–98

congressmen, and big business, 476

Congress of Industrial Organizations (CIO), 738, 743–44

Conkling, Roscoe, 461, 471

Connally Act, c731

conscription: in Civil War, 422; and World War I, 641

conservatism: and red scare, 692–94; politics of, 695–701

consolidation and competition, 537–38

Constitution, U.S.: and progressivist reforms, 602–03

Constitution of Confederacy, 419

Cooke, Alistair, PE9–5

Coolidge, Calvin, 697; administration of, 700

Coral Sea, 766, *m767*

corporation, and industrial revolution, 535, 537

Corresca, Rocco, PE6–5

corruption: and Grant administration, 472; in cities, 472–75; and Harding administration, 699–700. *See also* Watergate scandal

and urbanization, 541, 543–44; cultural impact of, 545–47; and mechanization, 664–66
inflation: and Civil War, 430; and McKinley administration, 576; and World War II, 802; post-World War II, 804; and Nixon administration, 875–76, 893, 894–95; and Ford administration, 903
intellectuals, 673
International Harvester Company, 537–38
International Ladies' Garment Workers Union, 580, 585, 595
Interstate Commerce Act, 478
interventionists, and World War II, 762–65
Irish-Americans, PE6–7; riot by, 433; and McCormick Harvester strike, 517–18, 519, c540
isolationism, pre-World War II, 762–65
Israeli-Arab war, 898–900
Italian-Americans: and Jews, 583; in garment industry, 582–83, 584; in Triangle fire, 588–89
Italy, and World War II, 762–63, m769
Iwo Jima, m767

Jackson, T. J. (Stonewall), 423, 424
James, Henry, 545
Japan, and World War II, 747–61, 762, 766–68, 770
Japanese-Americans, 803
Jarlson, Axel, PE6–2
Jaworski, Leon, 888
jazz, 672–73, PE8–3
Jews, 539, 540; in garment industry, 582–83, 584; and Italian-Americans, 583; in Triangle fire, 588–89
Jim Crow laws, 610
jingoism, 630
Johnson, Andrew, general pardon by, 415, 416; and blacks, 415, 417; and Reconstruction, 437–40; impeachment of, 441–42
Johnson, Lyndon B., 873–74; and Vietnam, 838–41, 842–43; and Dominican Republic, 841–42; and civil rights, 857, 858; Great Society of, 863–64
Johnson, Thomas, 601
Jones, Mary, 405–07, 408
Jones, Samuel M., 601

Kalmus, Herbert T., c665
Kamikaze pilots, 768
Kennedy, John F., election of, 781–82; vs. Nixon, 814; and Cuban missile crisis, 818–32; foreign policy of, 833–38, 861; and Martin

Luther King, 852, 854, 857; New Frontier policies of, 861–63; assassination of, 862–63
Kennedy, Robert F., 836; and Cuban missile crisis, 819, 820, 822–23, 825, 826, 829, 831–32; assassination of, 874
Key, Francis Scott, 226
Keynes, John Maynard, 744
Khrushchev, Nikita, 780, 781, 834–35; and Cuban missile crisis, 819, 826, 827, 830
Kicking Bear, 487
Kimmel, Husband E., 751, 753, 756
King, Martin Luther, Jr., 813, 867–68; biography of, 845–61
Kipling, Rudyard, 629, PE7–2
Kissinger, Henry, 893, 894, 899–900, 905
Knights of Labor, 521, 595
Korean Conflict, 774–75, 777–78, 806
Kossenko, Zinaida, PE9–3
Ku Klux Klan, 438, 444, 695, 853
Kurusu, Saburo, 749–50, 751–52

Labarca H., Amanda, PE9–4
labor unions: and McCormick Harvester strike, 516–22; and garment industry, 580–85; rise of, 594–96; pre-Depression, 703; and Eleanor Roosevelt, 721; and NRA, 738; after 1936 elections, 743–44; and World War II, 802. See also strikes; workers
LaFollette, Robert M., 600, 601, 607
LaGuardia, Fiorello, 583, 597, 725, 741, 742
Lambert, John, PE3–4, PE3–8
land, and Indians, 486, 511
Landon, Alfred M., vs. Roosevelt, 739–40
Laos, m841
Laski, Harold, PE7–8
Las Vegas, Nev., PE8–7
Leacock, Stephen, PE8–1
League of Nations, 643–45
Lease, Mary, 558, 570, 573
Lebanon, 780
Le Corbusier (Charles Edward Jeaneret), PE8–3, PE9–2
Lee, Robert E., 420; and Civil War, 425, 426
leisure-time activities, American, Pictorial Essay 8
Lend-Lease Act, 764
Lewis, John L., 738
Lewis, Sinclair, PE7–8
Leyte Gulf, Battle of, m767
Liddy, G. Gordon, 880, 882–83, 885
Lincoln, Abraham: and Civil War, 419, 421, 424, 432; on blacks, 433, 437; and Reconstruction, 435–37; assassination of, 437

Lindbergh, Charles, 666, 764, 765; transatlantic flight of, 648–62
Lindsay, Vachel, 563
Lipschitz, Diana, 586
literature: and industrial revolution, 545–47; and New Era, 673–75; American, Pictorial Essay 7
Lloyd, Henry Demarest, 561, 596, 597
lockouts, 595
Lodge, Henry Cabot, 644
London, Meyer, 583
Long, Huey, 734
Looking Backward (Bellamy), 546, 596
Los Angeles, Cal., PE9–7
Louis, Joe, PE8–4
Louisiana, m441
Low, Seth, 601
Lower Brulé Reservation, m484
Loyalty Review Board, 806
Lusitania (ship), 640
Luzon, 617, 619, 621, 624

MacArthur, Arthur, 621, 624, 625
MacArthur, Douglas, 766, m767, 775; and bonus marchers, 688–90
McCarran Internal Security Act, 808
McCarthy, Eugene, 842, 874
McCarthy, Joseph, 776, 799; anticommunist crusade of, 806–08, 810
McClellan, George, 424, m424, 425
McCormick, Cyrus, II, vs. strikers, 517–22, 530
McCormick, Cyrus Hall, 516
McCormick Harvester Works, strikes at, 516–22
McCormick, Nettie Fowler, 516–17
McGovern, George, 896–97
McKinley, William, 478, 570; vs. Bryan, 552–63, 575–76; and prosperity, 575–76; and Philippines, 617, 618, 619; and Cuba, 630; and Spanish-American War, 632, 633; assassination of, 576
McLaughlin, James, and Sioux, 490, 493, 494
McNamara, Robert, 821, 842
McPadden, Myles, 521
McReynolds, Justice, 734
Maggie: A Girl of the Streets (Crane), 546
Magruder, Jeb, 884, 885
Mahan, Alfred T., 627–28
Maine (ship), 630, 632
Malcolm X, 869
Mallard, Mary Jones, 405–06
Malvar, Miguel, 626
Manchuria, 747
Manhattan Project, 802–03
Manila Bay, Battle of, m619, m632
Mao Tse-tung, 774
Marconi, Guglielmo, 663, c665

Marias, Julian, PE8–8, PE9–5
Marshall, George C., 807
Marshall Plan, 773
Maryland, in Civil War, *m424, m429*
Maryland (ship), 757
mass production, 535, 537
Maurois, André, PE8–1
Mays, Willie, PE8–4
Mead, George, *m424*
meat inspection, 604
Mellon, Andrew, 697, 699, 738
Merrimack (ship), *m424*
Merritt, Wesley, *m632*
Mexican Americans, PE6–8
Mexico, and Wilson administration, 637–38
middle class, 663
Middle East, and Eisenhower-Dulles policies, 780
Midway, 766, *m767*
Mikhailov, Nicolai, PE9–3
military-industrial complex, 813–14
Milledgeville, Ga., and Sherman's March, 405
Mindanao, 625
mining, and frontier settlements, 499–501, *m504*
Miranda v. Arizona, 866
Mississippi, *m425, m441*
Mitchell, John, 878, 880, 881, 884, 885, 886, 889
money. *See* currency
Monitor (ship), *m424*
monopolies, 478–79. *See also* big business; trusts
Montana, 501
Montgomery Improvement Association, 848–50
Morgan, J. Pierpont, 538, 606
Morgenthau, Henry, 744
Mosby, John S., 423
movies, PE9–2
Muskie, Edmund, 896
Myers, Robert, PE6–5
My First Years in the White House (Long), 735
My Lai, *m841,* 864

Nader, Ralph, 904
Nagasaki, *m767,* 772
Nagumo, Chuichi, 750
Nashville, Battle of, *m429*
Nasser, Gamal Abdel, 780
National Association for the Advancement of Colored People (NAACP), formation of, 610
national debt. *See* debt (national)
National Housing Act, *c730*
National Industrial Recovery Act (NIRA), 732
National Labor Relations Act, 738, 742, 743
National Organization of Women (N.O.W.), 872

national parks, 605
National Recovery Administration (NRA), *c731,* 732, 734, 736
National Securities Company, 606
national uprisings, 420
National Youth Administration, 736
Nazi Germany. *See* Hitler, Adolf; World War II
Nazi-Soviet Pact, 763
Neutrality Acts, 762–63, 765
Nevada (ship), 757
New Deal: function of, 728; legislation of, *c730,* 732–33; responses to, 733–34; and Supreme Court, 734, 736; 742–43; after NRA repeal, 736–39; and 1937–38 recession, 744–45; end of, 745
New Era, 664–76
New Frontier, 861–62
New Look, 777
Newman, Ernest, PE7–7
New Orleans, *m425*
New York City, PE9–2, 905–06
New York Stock Exchange, 701–02, 704
Nicaragua, 636, 637
Nimitz, Chester, *m767*
Nineteenth Amendment, 603
Nitze, Paul, 823
Nixon, Richard, 781, 782, 800, 802; and Hiss-Chambers case, 784, 786–96, 799; vs. Kennedy, 814; general policies of, 875–76; economic policies of, 894–95; and Watergate scandal, 878, 882, 884–92, 898; vs. dissenters, 893–94; and détente, 895–96; vs. McGovern, 896–98; and Middle East, 898–900; resignation of, 892; pardon of, 901
Normandy invasion, 768–70, *m769*
North Africa, and World War II, 766, 768
North Atlantic Treaty Organization (NATO), 773–74, 837
North Carolina, in Civil War, *m429;* and Reconstruction, *m441*
Noyes, John Humphrey, 458, 459
Nye, Gerald P., 762

oil, 668; and industrial revolution, 534; and John D. Rockefeller, 538
Okinawa, *m767*
Olds, Ransom E., 668
Olney, Richard, 629
Oneida Community, 459
Open Door policy, 634–35
Operation Magic, 750, 751, 753–54, 766
Oppenheimer, J. Robert, 803
Origin of Species (Darwin), 629
Orlando, Vittorio, 643

Oswald, Lee Harvey, 862, 863
Otis, Elwell S., 618, 619, 623–24

Pacific front, World War II, *m767*
padrones, 543
Paiute Indians, 487
Palmer, A. Mitchell, 693
Palmer, John M., 560
Panama Canal, 635–36
parity, 732
Parker, Theodore, 344, 367, 392
Parsons, Albert R., and Haymarket riot, 525–26
party politics: of 1870s–80s, 469–71; and immigrants, 542–43
pastimes, American, Pictorial Essay 8
Patman, Wright, 680
Patton, George S., 678, 689, 770
Peace Corps, 833
Pearl Harbor attack, *m754;* planning of, 747–48, 749–52; execution, 752–59; effects of, 759–61
Pennsylvania, in Civil War, *m424*
Pennsylvania (ship), 757
Pentagon Papers, 894
Perkins, Frances, 593, 599
Pershing, John J.: and Mexico, 638; and World War I, *m641,* 642
Petersburg, Va., *m429*
Philippines: vs. Spain, 612–13; and Spanish-American War, 613–17, *m619,* 633–34; vs. United States, 618–26; and World War II, 766, *m767*
Pike's Peak, 499
Pinchot, Gifford, 603, 606
Pine Ridge Reservation, *m484*
Pingree, Hazen, 601
Pinkertons, vs. strikers, 519
Pittsburgh, Pa., 534, 601
Platt, Thomas C., 461
Poland, and World War II, 763, 770
politicians of 1870–80s, attitudes and backgrounds of, 466–68
pony express, 502, *m504*
population: in 1920–1970, *m876;* in 1976, *m907, c421, c539*
Populist Party: founding of, 570–71; and elections of 1892, 571, 573–74; in election of 1896, 555–59; decline of, 574
Port Hudson, La., *m425*
Potsdam, 773
Pratt, W. Spencer, 613–14
presidential elections, *m741,* 781–82; Hayes-Tilden (1876), 446–47, 469; Garfield-Hancock-Weaver (1880), 457, 469; Cleveland-Blaine (1884), 468, 469; factors in (1870–80s), 469–71; Cleveland-Harrison (1888), 469–70; Cleveland-Harrison-Weaver (1892), 571, 573–74;

ABOUT THE AUTHORS

Allen Weinstein is a Professor of History at Smith College, where he directed American Studies for six years and teaches U.S. political and social history. Recently, he published *Perjury: The Hiss-Chambers Case*, and he is now writing two additional books on the Cold War Period. He also directs The Twentieth Century Fund's study on the impact of the Freedom of Information Act upon U.S. intelligence agencies. His previous books include *Prelude to Populism* and *American Negro Slavery: A Modern Reader*. Professor Weinstein's articles have appeared in *The Dictionary of American Biography, Esquire, The Journal of American History, The Journal of American Studies* (on whose Editorial Board he serves), *The New York Times, The New York Review of Books*, and in many other journals. He has lectured throughout Europe and Israel, twice served as Fulbright Lecturer in Australia, and has taught at Amherst College, Brown University, Hartford College for Women, Teacher's College (Columbia), and the University of Maryland.

R. Jackson Wilson is a Professor of History at Smith College, where he also teaches American Studies and Philosophy. His special field of interest is cultural history, and he is currently at work on a study of nineteenth-century American writers. His books include *In Quest of Community: Social Philosophy in the United States* and *Darwinism and the American Intellectual*. He has taught at an unusually wide range of institutions, including the University of Wisconsin, the University of Arizona, Columbia University, Yale University, Hartford College for Women, the University of Massachusetts, Amherst College, and Teacher's College (Columbia).